“The Book of Tribulations”

EDINBURGH STUDIES IN ISLAMIC APOCALYPTICISM AND ESCHATOLOGY

This series features studies devoted to end-time expectations in Islam and the intellectual, social and political contexts in which they occur and become virulent, from the beginning of Islam until the twenty-first century. Concerning the apocalyptic aspect, the series is dedicated to investigating apocalypticism in Muslim thought and history: notions of the catalytic events ushering in the end of history, mahdism and other forms of (political and non-political) millenarianism. Eschatologically, studies in this series will examine traditions of imagining and reasoning about the hereafter: judgment, salvation, and reward and punishment in paradise and hell.

Series Editors
Professor David Cook (Rice University) and Professor Christian Lange (Utrecht University)

Editorial Advisory Board
Professor Abbas Amanat, Professor Fred Donner, Professor Jean-Pierre Filiu, Professor Yohanan Friedman, Professor Mercedes García-Arenal, Professor Mohammed Khalil, Professor Daniel De Smet and Professor Roberto Tottoli

Titles in the series

"The Book of Tribulations": The Syrian Muslim Apocalyptic Tradition, An Annotated Translation by Nu`aym b. Ḥammād al-Marwazī's
Edited and translated by David Cook

Eschatology in Classical Islamic Mysticism From the 9th to the 12th Centuries
Michael Ebstein

The World of Image in Islamic Philosophy: Ibn Sina, Suhrawardi, Shahrazuri and Beyond
L. W. C. van Lit

An Apocalyptic History of the Early Fatimid Empire
Jamel A. Velji

edinburghuniversitypress.com/series/esiae

"The Book of Tribulations": The Syrian Muslim Apocalyptic Tradition

An Annotated Translation by Nu`aym b. Ḥammād al-Marwazī

Edited and translated by David Cook

EDINBURGH
University Press

Edinburgh University Press is one of the leading university presses in the UK. We publish academic books and journals in our selected subject areas across the humanities and social sciences, combining cutting-edge scholarship with high editorial and production values to produce academic works of lasting importance. For more information visit our website: edinburghuniversitypress.com

Edinburgh University Press Ltd
The Tun—Holyrood Road
12 (2f) Jackson's Entry
Edinburgh EH8 8PJ

Typeset in Cambria by
Servis Filmsetting Ltd, Stockport, Cheshire

A CIP record for this book is available from the British Library

ISBN 978 1 4744 2410 3 (hardback)
ISBN 978 1 4744 2411 0 (webready PDF)
ISBN 978 1 4744 2412 7 (epub)

Contents

Acknowledgments x
Introduction xii
Abbreviations and key names and terms xxxix
Caliph/Emperor list xlii

Translation of Nu`aym b. Ḥammād al-Marwazī, *Kitāb al-fitan* **1**

What was related by the Messenger of God and his Companions after him concerning the Tribulations to come 1
Naming of the Tribulations which are to come, and their Number from the death of the Messenger of God until the Rising of the Hour 12
The Loss of Intelligence and Absence of People's Dreams during the Tribulations 21
Allowance for People's Desire to Die because of the Prevalence of Trials and Tribulations 26
The Regret of Some of the Prophet's Companions and Others with regard to the Tribulation 30
The Desirability of having Few Possessions and Children during the Tribulations 39

The Number of the Caliphs after the Messenger of God in this Community 40
The Caliphs who were mentioned after the Messenger of God 42
Distinguishing the Caliphs from the Kings 43
Naming those reigning after the Messenger of God 46
The Dominion of the Umayyads and Naming them after `Umar 52
The End of the Umayyads' Dominion 54
Protection from Tribulations and the Desirability of Holding Back and Withdrawing during them, and Undesirability of Looking out over them 61
Those who believed in Withdrawal during Tribulations 92
The Portents of the end of the Umayyads' Dominion 94
Appearance of the `Abbāsids 100
The First Portent of the end of the Period of the `Abbāsids 110
The First of the Portents of the end of their Dominion will be the Appearance of the Turks after a dissension between them 113
Portents in the Heavens concerning the end of `Abbāsids' Dominion 117
Beginnings of the Tribulation in Syria 124
The Triumph of the Lowliest and Weakest of Peoples 128
Refuges from Tribulations 132
The Center of Islam is in Syria 134
The First Portent will be the Portent of the Berbers and the Westerners 138
The Appearance of the Berbers and the Westerners 140
The Corruption and Fighting of the Berbers in Syria and Egypt, and whoever fights them, and the end of their appearance, and the evil conduct that will happen at their hands 142
The Description of the Sufyānī, His Name and Ancestry 150
The Beginning of the Appearance of the Sufyānī 153
The Three Flags 155

The Flags that will disperse in the Lands of Egypt and Syria, and other [countries], and the Sufyānī and his Victory over them 155
The Conflict between the `Abbāsids, and the Easterners, and the Sufyānī and the Marwānids in Syria towards Iraq 161
The Conflict between the People of Syria, the `Abbāsid rulers at al-Raqqa, and what the Sufyānī will do 164
What the Sufyānī will do in the Suburbs of Baghdad and Madīnat al-Zawrā' when his Expedition will reach Iraq, and the Destruction that will happen 171
The Sufyānī and his Army enter al-Kūfa 173
The Mahdi's Black Banners after the `Abbāsids' Banners, and what will happen between the Sufyānī's army and the `Abbāsids 174
The Beginning of the End for the Sufyānī, and the Appearance of the Hāshimī from Khurāsān leading the Black Banners, and the Fighting between them until the Horsemen of the Sufyānī reach the East 178
The Sufyānī will meet the Black Banners in Battle, and there will be an Apocalyptic Battle between them, in which the People will desire the Mahdi and seek him 179
Sending the Troops to Medina and the Killing that will happen in it 181
Swallowing up of the Sufyāni's Troops that he will send to the Mahdi 184
The Signs of the Mahdi in his Appearance 187
Another Sign at the Time of the Mahdi's Appearance 190
The People's Gathering Together at Mecca to swear to the Mahdi in it, and the Confusion, Fighting, Seeking the Mahdi that will happen that year in Mecca after the Battle and their Gathering to him 192
The Mahdi's Departure from Mecca to Jerusalem and Syria, after which they will swear to him, and His Traveling towards the Sufyāni and his Supporters 197

The Conduct and Justice of the Mahdi and the Plenty of his Time 203
The Description of the Mahdi 209
The Name of the Mahdi 210
The Ancestry of the Mahdi 211
The Length of the Mahdi's Reign 214
What will happen after the Mahdi 215
The Raid on India 237
What will happen in Ḥimṣ during the administration of the Qaḥṭānī, and between Quḍā`a and Yaman after the Mahdi 238
Al-Ā`māq and the Conquest of Constantinople 242
The Imam of the Muslims in Jerusalem and his Victory on the Plain of Acre, and the Conquest of Ḥimṣ 280
Concerning the Appearance of the Byzantines in Alexandria, the Edges of Miṣr and its Harbors (*mawāḥīz*) 315
What will happen to People previous to the Appearance of the Antichrist 319
Signs before the Appearance of the Antichrist 322
Where will the Antichrist appear? 327
The Appearance of the Antichrist, his Conduct, and the Corruption at his hands 329
The Length of the Antichrist's Staying 345
Jesus son of Mary will kill the Antichrist at the Gate of Lydda at the distance of sixteen Cubits 346
Refuges from the Antichrist 348
Jesus' Return and his Conduct 350
The Length of Jesus' Staying after his Return 360
The Appearance of Gog and Magog 361
Swallowing up by the Earth, Earthquakes, Tremors, and Metempsychosis 378
Concerning the Fire that will Gather [People] to Syria 388
Among the Portents of the Hour 395
The Portents of the Hour after the Rising of the Sun from the West 397
The Rising of the Sun from the West 406

The Appearance of the Beast (*Dābba*) 409
The Ethiopians 414
The Emergence of the Ethiopians 415
The Turks 419
The Times, Months, and Days that are Dated in the Tribulations 425

Bibliography 447
Index 458

Acknowledgments

I would like to acknowledge the help of a number of friends and colleagues in translating Nu`aym. First and foremost, my best friend, Deborah Tor, without whom I would have never been able to come this far in the study of Islam. She, together with Michael Decker, Matthias Henze, Richard Landes, Christian Lange, Christian Sahner, and Steven Shoemaker read over the manuscript and critiqued it. Devin DeWeese, Clare Fanger, Yohanan Friedmann, Peter Golden, and Scott McGill were gracious in answering queries I had about problematic sections of the text. Thank you, one and all, and of course any errors are my own responsibility.

For my father, Dr. W. Robert (Bob) Cook,
died October 3, 2015
Rom. 11:22–4
Thank you eternally

Introduction

Nu`aym b. Ḥammād al-Marwazī's *Kitāb al-fitan*, dating from approximately 820,[1] is the oldest complete Muslim apocalyptic text that has survived to the present. Its collection was accomplished mostly in Syria, so on this basis, we are justified in seeing it as the Syrian Muslim apocalyptic tradition. This conclusion, of course, does not mean that all of the Syrian Muslim apocalyptic traditions current in the eighth and ninth centuries are attested in it; there is no way to know what was omitted or lost due to marginalization of controversial traditions. We have virtually no Syrian sources with which to compare Nu`aym. Given the relative size of the text, the fact of the numerous unique traditions cited in it, and that the Syrian Muslim heritage overall is known from only a paltry number of sources, translation of this source is worthwhile.

[1] This date is tentative, as Nu`aym died some twenty-four years later, and is based upon the most recent dated tradition in the collection (no. 930 listing the year 204/819–20). Some of the traditions such as those of al-Walīd b. Muslim (see nos. 590, 868, 1008) that are related in the first person may have been collected as early as 790 (as al-Walīd died that year).

Nu`aym and his Times

Comparatively little is known about Nu`aym b. Ḥammād al-Khuza`ī, who was from Marv Rūdh, one of the bases for the `Abbāsid revolution.[2] It seems rather doubtful that Nu`aym was ethnically full-Arab. For someone who so thoroughly presents the Syrian apocalyptic tradition in *The Book of Tribulations*, virtually nothing is known about his time in Syria. While one can extract his sources from the chains of transmitters, none of his experiences there apparently left a mark on his personal biography. Even Ibn `Asākir's *History of the City of Damascus* just gives us a bare list of his Syrian informants, but does not cite apocalyptic traditions from him (except one, concerning moral deterioration at the end of the world).

He is said to have sought traditions assiduously in Iraq, the Hijaz and Yemen (but *not* Syria), and to have settled in Egypt. Virtually the only personal encounter with him is when he meets the great legal scholar al-Shafī`ī, but our record of this meeting is extremely abbreviated.[3] During the period of the *mihna* (inquisition), he was tortured to confess the doctrine of the creation of the Qur'ān, which he refused to acknowledge, was imprisoned at Sāmarrā', and died in prison in 228/843–4 (during the reign of al-Wāthiq). Al-Dhahabī tells us that his body was not washed, wrapped or prayed over after his death, but just thrown into a pit. Although most of *The Book of Tribulations* is well organized, the last ten traditions do not appear to have been

[2] Biographical material from *EI*^{2} s.v. "Nu`aym b. Ḥammād" (Ch. Pellat); Fuat Sezgin, *GAS* (Leiden: E. J. Brill, 1967), i, pp. 104–5; sources are Ibn Sa`d, *Ṭabaqāt* (Beirut: Dār al-Kutub al-`Ilmiyya, 1990), vii, p. 359 (no. 4085); al-Khatib al-Baghdādī, *Tā'rīkh madīnat al-salām* (Beirut: Dār al-Gharb al-Islamī, 2001), xv, pp. 419–30; Ibn `Asākir, *Ta'rīkh madīnat Dimashq* (Beirut: Dār al-Fikr, 1995–8), lxii, pp. 149–71 (no. 7909); Ibn al-Jawzī, *al-Muntaẓam fi al-tā'rīkh* (Beirut: Dār al-Kutub al-`Ilmiyya, 1993), xi, p. 149 (no. 1326); al-Dhahabī, *Siyar a`lām al-nubalā'* (Beirut: Mu'assasat al-Risāla, 1992), x, pp. 595–612 (no. 209); *idem*, *Tadhkirat al-ḥuffāẓ* (Beirut: Dār al-Kutub al-`Ilmiyya, 2012), ii, pp. 6–7 (no. 434); al-Mizzī, *Tahdhīb al-kamāl* (Beirut: Mu'assasat al-Risāla, 1998), vii, pp. 350–3 (no. 7046); and Ibn al-`Imād, *Shajarat al-dhahab* (Damascus: Dār Ibn Kathīr, 1992), iii, pp. 133–4.

[3] Yāqūt, *Mu`jam al-udabā'* (Beirut: Dār al-Gharb al-Islamī, 1993), p. 2404.

placed within their respective categories. This final disorganization suggests that Nu`aym might have been working on the text when he died (or was imprisoned), and was unable to complete it.

Nu`aym was a comparatively minor and forgotten figure within the *ḥadīth* literature overall. He is remembered for having contributed a supplement to `Abdallāh b. al-Mubārak's (d. 181/797) *Kitāb al-zuhd*,[4] but was not considered to have been an especially reliable transmitter, most probably because he involved himself in questionable subjects such as apocalyptic and ascetic traditions.[5] Historians such as al-Balādhurī, al-Tamīmī, al-Ṭabarī, and others[6] cited Nu`aym, but again this fact just serves to highlight his distance from the mainstream of Sunni legal literature. And he is not cited in any of the canonical Six Books of the Sunna, even though he is known to have taught al-Bukhārī.

The Book of Tribulations

Nu`aym's work in apocalypse, however, is almost unique, and its influence upon Islam, especially upon Sunni apocalyptic thinking, is quite inordinately huge. To date Nu`aym was the first to take the vast collection of apocalyptic traditions that had been growing since the period of the conquests, and to organize them into a reasonably coherent order. One cannot say that this order is anywhere near the level of the literary apocalypse as it was known in Judaism and

[4] See Ibn al-Mubārak, *Kitāb al-zuhd wa-l-raqā'iq* (Alexandria: Dār Ibn Khaldūn, n.d.), where pp. 377–468 are listed as *ziyādāt Nu`aym.*

[5] al-Dhahabī, *Siyar*, x, p. 604 gives a list of all the subjects on which it is forbidden to write; apocalypse is not one of them.

[6] E.g., al-Balādhurī, *Futūḥ al-buldān* (Beirut: Mu'assasat al-Ma`ārif, 1987), p. 169; al-Tamīmī, *Kitāb al-miḥan* (Beirut: Dār al-Gharb al-Islamī, 1988), pp. 197, 389, 417, 460; extensively in al-Ṭabarī, *Tā'rīkh al-rusul wa-l-mulūk* (Beirut: Rawā'ī` al-Turāth, n.d.), index; also Abū Zur`a al-Dimashqī, *Tā'rīkh* (Beirut: Dār al-Fikr, 2008), i, p. 484; al-Ṣāliḥī al-Shāmī, *Subul al-hudā wa-l-rashād* (Beirut: Dār al-Kutub al-`Ilmiyya, 2013); al-Musharraf b. al-Murajjā', *Faḍā'il bayt al-maqdis* (Shafar`am: Dār al-Shurūq, 1995), nos. 221, 322–7, 329–30; Ibn Rajab, *Faḍā'il al-Shām* (al-Riyāḍ: Dār al-Waṭan li-l-Nashr, 1999), p. 159 (no. 297); al-Kindī, *Kitāb wulāt Miṣr* (Beirut: Dār Ṣādir, n.d.), p. 57; and Waqī`, *Quḍāt* (Beirut: `Ālam al-Kutub, n.d.), iii, pp. 122–3.

Christianity from Late Antiquity (below), and that sense of disorder increases once one takes into consideration the internal variants inside individual traditions that might contradict the overall order that Nu`aym established. But having said that, previous to him there was nothing like a timeline for the endtimes, and *The Book of Tribulations* establishes one.

Basic to the understanding of the book is the word *fitna*, pl. *fitan*, which I have translated as "tribulations" or in the case of civil war, "dissension."[7] As will be seen within the translation, the word also covers political and religious dissension, and division between Muslims, or even some element which constitutes a temptation to Muslims (cf. Q 8:25, 28–9). The basic meaning of *fitna* is the process by which metal is rid of dross (see no. 1535), which is a common conception in the monotheistic traditions. All of these various meanings are reflected in the subject matter of *The Book of Tribulations*, which takes its reader through the events in roughly the following manner: firstly, definitions and warnings, secondly, signs, thirdly, political events connected to the Umayyads and `Abbasids, fourthly, the appearance of the Sufyānī and his opponent the Mahdi, fifthly, the apocalyptic wars with the Byzantines, sixthly, the appearance of the Dajjāl(Antichrist) and his opponent Jesus, seventhly, the peoples of the apocalypse (Gog and Magog, the Ethiopians, the Turks), and finally, the times of the apocalypse.

From the names and the place names, it is possible to obtain a vision, to some degree, of the world in which Nu`aym's apocalyptic informants lived. They knew Syria intimately, and were able to refer to even small place names with care and accuracy. However, this intimate knowledge is confined to the area around Ḥimṣ, Damascus and the region of the Sea of Galilee in addition to the region of the northern Jordan River valley. Curiously, they show little intimate knowledge of the region of Filasṭīn (Palestine), whose capital, Ramla, is mentioned six times in the text. Jerusalem, also, while mentioned frequently, is never given the intimate descriptions of geography that one finds for

[7] See glossary for a list of definitions.

the more northern locations. The extreme north, around Aleppo, is also not described in detail.

One of the oddities concerning intimate place-descriptions in Nu`aym is in the sequences concerning the Antichrist/Dajjāl. There we would expect to find the common tradition concerning the tribesman Tamīm al-Dārī, who supposedly met the Dajjāl while on an island (in the Mediterranean?), but is entirely absent. This is quite puzzling given the further affinities of the Tamīm al-Dārī tradition,[8] which appears in a number of the major collections, in that Tamim is associated with the tribe of Lakhm, which is featured in Nu`aym, and there are a number of allusions to cryptic events due to occur in the area of Syria prior to the Dajjāl's appearance inside the tradition. In the version cited by Ibn Māja the key questions are:

> He [the Dajjāl] said: "What is the Spring of Zughar doing?" They [Tamīm and his group] said: "Well—their crops and palm-irrigations are watered by it." He said: "And how are the palm trees between `Ammān and Beth-Shean (Baysān)?" They said: "Well—they give their fruit every year." He said: "And what is happening with the Sea of Galilee (*buḥayrat al-Ṭabariyya*)?" They said: "Its sides overflow because of the abundance of water."[9]

These questions strongly suggest a locus for the tradition in the region of the northern Jordan Valley, between Beth-Shean and Tiberias. Indeed, ultimately Tamīm and his family are closely associated with Hebron, which is featured in Nu`aym (nos. 660–2), supposedly deeded to them by Muḥammad. These different connections with the region of Syria make it virtually a certainty that the Tamīm-Dajjāl tradition originated in the region, but there is no mention of it

[8] See my "Tamīm al-Dārī," *Bulletin of the School of Oriental and African Studies* 61 (1998), pp. 20–8; and the summary in *Studies*, pp. 227–30.

[9] Ibn Māja, *Sunan* (Beirut: Dār al-Fikr, n.d.), ii, p. 1355 (no. 4074); Abū Dā'ūd, *Sunan* (Beirut: Dār al-Jīl, 1988), iv, p. 117 (no. 4328); Ḥanbal b. Isḥāq, *al-Fitan* (Beirut: Dār al-Bashā'ir al-Islāmiyya, 1998), p. 89–90 (no. 1); the version in Muslim, *Ṣaḥīḥ* (Beirut: Dār Jīl, n.d.), viii, p. 204 is slightly different; there is even an Iraqi version, Ibn Abī Shayba, *Kitāb al-muṣannaf* (Beirut: Dār al-Kutub al-`Ilmiyya, 1995), vii, pp. 497–8 (no. 37508).

whatsoever in *The Book of Tribulations*. Moreover, the tenor of the questions given the destruction of the earthquake of January 18, 749, strongly suggests that the apocalyptic sign to which they are pointing is this destruction, enabling us to tentatively date the tradition. One could theorize that perhaps the tradition is a southern Palestinian one rather than a northern Ḥimṣī one, but it is still odd that it would not be included within Nu`aym's collection, if the dating above is accurate.

Further afield, the apocalyptic informants had a fairly good knowledge also of the Byzantine Empire and the eastern Mediterranean. It is interesting to realize that Cyprus which can be seen from the coastline of Syria, itself lying just a few miles away from Ḥimṣ, is mentioned but twice (nos. 1382, 1412), and just as a name at that, while Crete is not mentioned at all. In general, the Mediterranean Sea in Nu`aym is seen as a hostile location. Invaders have a fairly free use of the sea, according to the traditions in his collection, and there is not much of a sense that the Muslims are or could be dominant in the Mediterranean basin. This perception is probably linked to the fact that Ḥimṣ was not a port. At a time when the Arabic language was developing a vast nautical vocabulary, there are only four of the most general words for "ship, boat" in Nuaym. Knowledge of North Africa and Spain is quite partial, and there is little reality to the figures emerging from these locations (although the One with the Mane [Dhū al-`Arf] traditions, no. 1300, etc., may reflect the rise of Charlemagne). Egypt and Ethiopia are known, although the latter more as a caricature rather than an actual place. The region around Mecca and Medina is quite well known with specific place names, but Yemen is much more shadowy, with few details of place names.

Iraq, and most especially the region around Baghdad, is well known to the Syrian apocalyptic informants, and is given full details. The Persian north road to Transoxiana through Rayy and Nishapur is the one with which the apocalyptic informants are familiar. But very quickly place names in the east become quite hazy—Kūfa, for example, is frequently named, but absolutely no locations inside of it are detailed, and Baṣra is quite shadowy—and the important Umayyad Iraqi center of al-Wāsiṭ is not mentioned even once in the text. The

Turks are just "out there"—a group whose origins are not clear, who are making and will make regular depredations for no apparent reason into the Muslim world. India is the most distant, where it is even difficult to get a sense of what geographical section of the subcontinent is being referred to by the term *Hind* (see nos. 1196–1201).

All in all, the world of Nu`aym is the world of the Fertile Crescent, with the addition of Byzantium. There are no identifiable place names in Europe beyond Constantinople, other than the city of Rome. One has to say, however, that the level of detail concerning Rome is surprisingly high (nos. 1295, 1308, 1313), and may be the result of trade.[10] The historical memory demonstrated by the informants in *The Book of Tribulations* is more or less consistent with the late Umayyad and early `Abbāsid period, corresponding to the 720s until the early 800s, most especially from the 760s onwards. Mu`āwiya and the period of the early conquests are remembered fondly, sort of as "the good old days" of plenty, but there are virtually no personal recollections from this time.

The personal recollections in Nu`aym are all of the later failures of the Umayyads against the Byzantines from the early eighth century, the worries that the Turks and Ethiopians are going to invade the Umayyad or `Abbāsid Empire, and a very strong fear concerning the Berbers (who revolted 740–3), and most especially the rise of the `Abbāsids. There is some amount of disbelief at the rise of the `Abbāsids, as parvenus, as being from Khurāsān, and a great deal of disgruntlement on the part of Syrian Muslims that their prime position in the empire had been usurped by the Iraqis. All in all, the attitude of the traditions in Nu`aym is that of remembering a lost empire (the Umayyad Empire), and being on the sidelines of a yet greater one (the `Abbasid Empire), hoping that someday primacy would come back to Syria.

It is easy to find parallels to Nu`aym's traditions, even though he is

[10] See Michael McCormick, *Origins of the European Economy: Communications and Commerce AD 300–700* (Cambridge: Cambridge University Press, 2002), pp. 219, 622f.

not personally cited, in the canonical Six Books, especially in Muslim, Abū Dā'ūd and Ibn Māja (with the caveat described in section vii). There is a great deal of parallel material in the non-canonical *ḥadīth* collections, such as Ibn Abī Shayba and `Abd al-Razzāq. But for the most part, the citations of Nu`aym, when they appear, are to be found in other apocalyptic works, in which *The Book of Tribulations* makes a fairly consistent appearance. Only the Shi`ite scholar Ibn Ṭāwūs (d. 664/1265–6), however, reproduced whole sections of his work.[11] Fundamentally, Nu`aym serves as a bridge between the Jewish and Christian apocalypses of Late Antiquity and Islam. Therefore, when we are looking for affinities, it is to the past that we should look.

Comparative Apocalypse and Categorizations

The Book of Tribulations did not appear in a vacuum. From the Hellenistic period in Syria (second century BCE) until the rise of Islam in the early seventh century the genre of apocalypse was a common one. Although the definition of apocalypse is contested somewhat, especially in the transition that occurs between the Judeo-Christian material and the Islamic material, in its most basic form an apocalypse is a revelation from God, usually via an angel, of either future events or cosmological mysteries. Some literary apocalypses are contained within the Bible (the books of Daniel, Revelation), but more commonly the literary apocalypse was not accepted into the canon. Later apocalypses are usually pseudonymous, ascribed to prominent biblical or patristic figures, and most likely their true authors will never be known.

This hesitancy with regard to apocalypse is fairly widespread, existing in all of the mainstream monotheistic religions. Apocalypse represents a dramatic break in the natural order of authority, and along with the dream-revelation, constitutes a possible challenge to

[11] Ibn Ṭāwūs, *al-Malāḥim wa-l-fitan fi ẓuhūr al-ghā'ib al-muntaẓar* (Beirut: Mu'assasat al-Wafā', 1992), pp. 20–102. Note also al-Maqdisī, *al-Bad' wa-l-tā'rīkh* (Beirut: Dār Ṣādir, n.d.), ii, pp. 165, 173; and al-Mutaqqī al-Hindī, *Kanz al-`ummāl* (Beirut: Dār al-Risāla, 1982), xiv, pp. 189–352 (nos. 38,329–38,911) both cite Nu`aym.

ecclesiastical authority on a popular level. This fact is also true of apocalypse in Islam.

Later literary Christian and Jewish literary apocalypses tended to build upon this heritage, but there is a marked change with the rise of Islam in the seventh and eighth centuries among Christian authors. This period was the first one in which significant sections of the Christian world were lost to a non-Christian faith (first to the Sasanian Persians, and then to the Muslim Arabs) that were not recovered. The most dramatic Christian response to this loss is the Apocalypse of Pseudo-Methodius, probably composed in northern Syria-Iraq around the end of the seventh century in Syriac, and quickly translated into Greek and then into Latin.[12] Although this apocalypse is still rooted in the classical narrative of the Book of Revelation and other biblical apocalypses, it is striking that most of the biblical citations are not of an apocalyptic but a theological nature.

At the core of apocalypse stands the ideal of a just society, or at least a fulfillment of the cardinal ordinances of a given religious tradition. Usually the messianic figure, either Jesus or the Mahdi, is designed to create the society that the believers to whom the original apocalypse is addressed can envision but are unable to bring to fruition. The critique of present-day society—and it is possible to use this in a continuous fashion, because the critique is always true—is the moral apocalypse: the litany of the evils of society. This material is very graphic in nature, but is still generic enough that popular preachers can and do use it for the condemnation of social ills (from

[12] Francisco Martinez, *Eastern Christian Apocalyptic Literature* (Unpub. Ph.D. dissertation, Catholic University of America, 1985); trans. Gerrit Reinink, *Die Syrische Apokalypse des Pseudo-Methodius* (Louvain: Peeters, 1993 [CSCO vols 540–1]); trans. Aerts, and Kortekaas, *Die Apokalypse des Pseudo-Methodius: Die ältesten Griechischen und Lateinischen übersetzungen* (Louvain: Peeters, 1998 [CSCO vols. 569–70]); and trans. Benjamin Garstad, *Apocalypse: Pseudo-Methodius* (Cambridge, MA: Harvard University Press, 2012) (Greek and Latin). There are also partial translations in Andrew Palmer, *The Seventh Century in the West-Syrian Chronicles* (Liverpool: Liverpool University Press, 1993), pp. 230–42 (trans. Sebastian Brock); and Michael Philip Penn (trans.), *When Christians first met Muslims: A Sourcebook of the Earliest Syriac Writings on Islam* (Berkeley: University of California Press, 2015), pp. 116–29.

their perspective) as if those are being foretold by an authority. Moral apocalypse is a major theme in Christian and Muslim apocalyptic, but curiously it is lacking in Nu`aym to a large degree. Most apocalypse for him and his informants is political and social.

One should also note that in contradistinction to Jewish and Christian apocalypses, in Islamic apocalyptic traditions the role of angels is comparatively muted. None are used to transfer the secret knowledge of apocalypse, as this function was already performed at the dawn of Islam by the angel Gabriel to Muḥammad. Although angels, such as Gabriel and Michael, appear in Nu`aym, their role is that of conversants with God and of fighters and supporters in the human arena.

Apocalypse also focuses attention upon a pure subset of the larger religious community, sometimes called "the remnant" or the "saved group" (in Arabic, either *al-firqa al-nājiya* or *al-ṭā'ifa al-manṣūra*) that will make it through the tribulations into the just or messianic society. Nu`aym offers two possibilities for being part of that remnant: one is quietistic and involves a radical, almost Gandhian non-violence, where it is preferable to be slaughtered than to take part in the political dissensions of the end (no. 431), while the second involves the salvational struggle (*jihād*), usually against the Byzantines. Fighting the outside non-Muslim enemy can at least preserve the true believer from the inter-Muslim fighting that is likely to corrupt his faith. The historical connections of the fighting against the Byzantines will be examined below.

The traditions in *The Book of Tribulations* give voice to the nexus of a number of divisions, some of them overlapping, between believers and unbelievers, religions, ethnicity, tribes and languages, and these are not easy to categorize or to separate. To explain these divisions, I will prefer to use the language of the text itself, rather than what we "know" about these terms, especially from later texts. In short, in the *Book of Tribulations* we find all the disorganization and messiness in definition that we would expect to find from what would later be called "Islam" in its formative period.

Comparatively the terms believer (*mu'min*) and unbeliever (*kāfir* or *mushrik*) are the easiest, as both polarities have considerable roots in the Qur`ān. Donner has argued for the existence of some type of ecumenical group of "believers" of which the caliph (or commander of the believers) would be the head.[13] There is no evidence for such a community inside *The Book of Tribulations*. However, there is considerable latitude as to what constitutes the "in-community" of believers. For the most part the definitions are ethnic or tribal in nature. The Arabs, who are seen as the "settled" Arabs (as opposed to the desert or "tent-pole" Arabs) are in three basic groupings: the Yemenites, southern Arabs, who are considered to be the Emigrants, and whose tribal chauvinism is frequently expressed in Nu`aym; the Quḍā`a grouping, which is more or less those tribes identified as "southern" that had been settled in Syria and adjoining regions for some time, and who were (because of the Umayyads' efforts) being joined together with the Yemenites; and the northern tribal grouping of Qays (also called Muḍar and Nizār), to whom many of the traditions in Nu`aym are hostile. However, it is worth noting that at several key points unity is urged between the southern and the northern tribes (no. 1281).

These three groupings can be considered to be "proto-Muslims" or even "Muslims" (although what meaning this term had during the Umayyad period is problematic), but there are a number of tribes who were clearly reluctant to be "Muslims." These are called the *musallimat al-`arab* (no. 1216), and from the list given of them, they would appear to have all been those originally Christian tribes long allied with the Byzantines (during the fourth, fifth, and sixth centuries), who are considered by the Emigrants to be likely to desert in the case of any war situation. Since we know from Christian sources that tribes such as Tanūkh were still largely Christian during the early `Abbāsid period[14] it is not surprising that the apocalyptic traditions from this same period would be suspicious of them.

[13] Fred Donner, *Muhammad and the Believers at the Origins of Islam* (Cambridge, MA: Harvard University Press, 2010).

[14] Michael the Great, p. 517 (the time of al-Mahdi).

Far more problematic are the two groups that are also part of the proto-Muslims, but are not ethnically Arab. The first and most loyal of these are the *mawālī* (clients), who were attached to the various tribes. In Nu`aym their loyalty is occasionally doubted, and they are even sometimes invited to join the Byzantines (nos. 1218, 1269, 1310), but they never do and are usually said to be angry at the suggestion. As a matter of fact, consistently the *mawālī* are said to be the "noblest of the Arabs" (nos. 1303, 1372), whatever this means. It is not at all unusual for the *mawālī* to take the initiative and fight the Byzantines, or demonstrate other methods of loyalty to Islam. The other ethnicity is the skin color of *aḥmar/ḥamrā'* ("red", but said to indicate "white"[15]), which here is taken to mean "non-Arab" and includes those who either have converted to proto-Islam but are retaining their local identity, or are fighting for the Muslims (such as the well-known groups *zuṭṭ* and *sayābija* perhaps) without having converted at all. These are also invited to join the Byzantines, but unlike the *mawālī* they occasionally betray the proto-Muslims (e.g., no. 1256).

From the Byzantines' perspective (according to Nu`aym of course—one should not take what the Byzantines are said to be thinking as authoritative), the conflict was ethnic. The Byzantines never refer to their opponents as "Muslims", but always as Arabs, which one should see as equivalent to the term "Saracen" that is commonly employed by the Byzantines in reality.[16] Consistently, while there are religious issues that are in the front, such as the question of who wins victories—the Cross or God (Allah)[17]—when the apocalypse describes how the Byzantines *themselves* describe the conflict, it is never couched in religious terms. After their cross is broken, the Byzantines usually report to their ruler "the Arabs betrayed us" rather than speaking of the religious issues involved.

15 Ibn al-Athīr, *al-Nihāya fi gharīb al-ḥadīth* (Beirut: Dār Iḥya al-Kutub al-`Arabiyya, n.d.), i, pp. 437–8 (Ibn al-Athīr is dubious about the idea that every time Arabs use the term *aḥmar* they mean *abyaḍ*, "white," though).

16 Alexis Savvides, "Some notes on the terms *Agarenoi*, *Ismaelitai* and *Sarakenoi* in Byzantine sources," *Byzantion* 67 (1997), pp. 89–96

17 See nos. 1253, 1256.

When the Byzantines and Muslims fight in Syria, and the Byzantines' objectives are discussed, consistently those are said to be returning territory said to have belonged originally to their ancestors (such as the coastal region of Palestine, no. 1384 or Ḥimṣ, no. 1253), or to have people who the Byzantines consider to be originally theirs returned. Never do they make any claims to Jerusalem (even though according to the accounts below it is briefly recaptured), nor do they make any claims to desire new, not previously held territory. While the apocalyptic texts recognize that the end result of a Byzantine victory would probably be the end of Islam, this is not stated to be one of the Byzantines' goals.

It is interesting that one of the most common Muslim terms, that of *umma* (community) is used quite pejoratively in Nu`aym, other than when it is specifically "my [Muḥammad's] community." The *umam* (peoples) are invariably negative, and in other cases, such as with Gog and Magog (no. 1605) or with the locust being described as an *umma* (no. 627) the attitudes are not positive.

At all times the genre of apocalypse has been used to channel social frustrations from a given population. This is also true of Nu`aym's *Book of Tribulations,* which in general focuses upon Syria—a recently dispossessed population—and most especially upon the town of Ḥimṣ, which also felt a sense of lost grandeur and power. This feeling of loss is palpable throughout the entire book, and stands behind the idea of apocalypse: what was once will be yet again. Glory will be returned at the end of the world, because of divine justice.

Textual Sources and Language

The primary source for *The Book of Tribulations* is a group of informants, who were mostly Syrian, but also including a range of Iraqis, Medinans and Egyptians. Names such as that of al-Walīd b. Muslim, who were close to the later Umayyad regime, continually crop up in Nu`aym. When we look at the initial narrators, which are the ones listed in the translation below, it is easy to see the predominance of Abū Hurayra (104 traditions), Ḥudayfa b. al-Yamān (83 traditions), Ka`b al-Aḥbār[18] (265 traditions), `Abdallāh b. `Amr (114 traditions), `Abdallāh b. `Umar (44 traditions),[19] Abū Sa`īd al-Khudarī (35 traditions), and a few others. Taken together, this group is said to be responsible for 673 out of a total of 1959 traditions (I have not counted duplicates). However, this number obscures the overwhelming role of Ka`b al-Aḥbār, who is the backbone of the book. Ka`b is the only person who is represented throughout the book, and is responsible for many of the longer traditions. Additionally, while others cite on the authority of Muḥammad (for the most part), Ka`b is his own authority. The apocalyptic material, however, at this early stage lacks complete chains of transmission, and there are numerous historical interpolations or comments by onlookers. These asides are some of the most interesting elements of Nu`aym, and should be considered in some cases to be historical.

The role of the Qur'ān in Nu`aym is comparatively minimal. Citations occur inside traditions,[20] and occasionally there is some attempt to comment on the holy text. However, the fact was that the Qur'ānic apocalypse is an immediate one, rather than one in the apocalyptic future (near or far). Therefore, it is not easy to make use of the Qur'ān in these historical apocalyptic traditions. The major exceptions to this rule are the Qur'ānic sequences of Gog and Magog, where there is invariably citation of Q 21:96 (however it is odd that the parallel text of 18:94 is not cited at all), and the sequence of *dābbat al-arḍ* (the Beast from the earth, cf. Q 27:82). By far the most common Qur`ānic citation is 47:4 "when the war shall lay down its burdens,"[21] which parallels the biblical messianic ideal of Is. 2:4. Other Qur`ānic citations, such as 6:65, 158 (each cited seven times) very much

[18] Although in the text of Nu`aym Ka`b receives this appellation only four times (nos. 638, 1203, 1417, 1933).

[19] A further thirty-six traditions are marked "`Abdallāh" so it is impossible to know which `Abdallāh is being cited.

[20] There are eighty-five Qur'ānic citations in the text; there are a further twenty-nine Qur'ānic allusions.

[21] Cited eight times out of the eighty-five total citations.

parallel the use of the Bible in Ps. Meth in that the citations tend to be non-apocalyptic in content.

From a comparative point of view there are several elements in Nu`aym of special interest. The first of these are the numerous foreign words, such as Syriac/Aramaic (nos. 2, 1407, 1551), Farsi (nos. 511, 1260), Hebrew (nos. 8, 42, 1252, 1597, 1845), Ge`ez (possibly no. 1836), Greek (no. 1499), mock Greek (no. 720), Old South Arabian (no. 1217) and mock Old South Arabian (nos. 247, 1117). However, it is striking that for a comprehensive body of apocalyptic materials being produced in Syria not 100 years after Greek was the official language, there are so few traceable Greek words in Nu`aym.

There are also numerous foreign names and place names, the significance of which has been discussed. Some of those names indicate a direct dependency upon foreign, mainly Christian, materials. The major example would be the list of the peoples of Gog and Magog (no. 1605), which although partial in Nu`aym, closely parallels the list found in Pseudo-Methodius, and the sequence of the Dajjāl and Jesus. The latter sequence has direct linguistic and stylistic affinities with extant Christian apocalypses.

An anomalous apocalypse contained within Nu`aym is the Apocalypse of Weeks (no. 1949), which has been discussed previously.[22] This apocalypse is unique because of its comparative length, and because it is associated with an unknown prophet, named Nāth. I have speculated elsewhere that perhaps this is a radical misreading for "Baba" the Harranian, whose ecstatic statements sometimes resemble the Apocalypse of Weeks. There is also the anomalous importance of the city of Harran within the Apocalypse of Weeks that indicates its origin. However, the fact remains that this speculation is unproven, and may be unprovable. It is not clear why Nu`aym, otherwise so steeped in the mainstream of Sunni Islam, would casually accept an otherwise unknown "Nāth" as a prophet, without further explanation. The names in the chain indicate a Christian origin, but

[22] Michael Cook, "A Muslim Apocalyptic Chronicle," *Journal of Near Eastern Studies* 52 (1993), pp. 25–9.

forcing any Christian or biblical prophetic figure into the name "Nāth" is difficult. The first element of the text has a very Daniel-esque aspect to it, with weeks being emphasized (cf. Daniel 9:24).

Of special interest to comparativists is the group of apocalypses associated with Yashū` (nos. 206, 257, 490, 1933), identified as a monk. These have certain common characteristics, such as being a conversation between Yashū` and Ka`b, as well as a heavy focus upon the political future of the Muslim states. These represent transmissions from Christian sources, and are markedly less filled with Muslim themes. Both this family of apocalypses and the Apocalypse of Weeks should be compared to the Christian Apocalypse of Daniel from the same period (translated in the appendix).

Similarly, we can speak about dating the traditions that call Jerusalem *iliyā'* versus those utilizing *bayt al-maqdis*. Most probably these date from different times, with the *iliyā'* traditions being the earlier of the two (note the gloss for the term *iliyā'* to *bayt al-maqdis* in no. 530).[23] It is striking to note the correlations between the use of the terms *mu'min* (believer) in the *iliya'* traditions, as opposed to the use of terms like Muslim or Emigrant in the *bayt al-maqdis* traditions.[24] The most obvious conclusion to be drawn from this terminology is that the *mu'min* traditions are indeed the older ones, and that the section of Valleys (A`maq) traditions (nos. 1212–1415), in which the term *mu'min* is virtually absent, is the later one.

When we turn to the question of political theology, it is clear that Nu`aym in a number of places represents almost the sole remaining example of what Umayyad legitimacy would have looked like. The standard traditions of the "four rightly-guided" caliphs (*rāshidūn*) appear here frequently minus `Alī b. Abī Ṭālib. Although this type of "three caliphs" tradition is not well represented in Sunni materials as they now stand, one cannot doubt that these are in fact the earlier versions. Such a conclusion is proven absolutely by similar rejections of

23 Note the odd term *bayt iliyā'* in no. 1312.

24 There are two traditions (nos. 1562, 1625) in which believer is used in a *bayt al-maqdis* tradition, and one in which *muslim* is used with *iliyā'* (no. 1332).

`Alī in the Christian sources, who had no need to knuckle under to the rehabilitation of `Alī that occurred during the `Abbasid period.[25] The Umayyad political religious legitimacy emphasized the continuity of the caliphate from the time of Abū Bakr through `Umar and `Uthmān to the first Umayyads, and simply ignored `Alī altogether. In *The Book of Tribulations* `Alī is reduced occasionally to begging his own followers not to oppose Mu`āwiya (no. 267), and predicting his own defeat (nos. 262, 347). While one cannot say that the picture of `Alī in Nu`aym is negative, it is far less heroic than what one sees in Shi`ite or Sufi-influenced literature.

A great deal of Nu`aym concerns the killing of the caliph `Uthmān, the first Umayyad to rule. If one were to take literally the copious citations of statements supposedly said on the day of his assassination, then `Uthmān is portrayed in almost a Gandhian manner of passive resistance to mob rule. He stands as the centerpiece for the ideology of *The Book of Tribulations*, which is that during a time of violence one should withdraw, saying "a plague on both your houses." Although `Uthmān is not the absolute best fit for this ideal—he was, after all, the caliph, and did not actually withdraw from the situation—he is the best personality in early Islam to exemplify a passive martyrdom (Shi`ites such as al-Ḥusayn were active in their martyrdoms). And this very passivity was both key to the apocalyptic outlook of passivity, as well as to the Umayyad political legitimacy that fed off of sympathy for `Uthmān.

But because Nu`aym straddles the divide between the Umayyads and the `Abbasids, there is also a great deal of `Abbasid imperial messianic propaganda that is represented here as well. Probably only a collector at the time of Nu`aym could have gathered such a unique selection, since within a couple of generations the Umayyad materials began to die out even in Syria—although some were preserved a bit later in Umayyad Spain—and were replaced with a slightly different conception of Sunni legitimacy. However, the major source of

[25] See Palmer, *The Seventh Century*, pp. 43 (list of caliphs composed after 705), 49 (a list of caliphs trans. from Arabic around 724), 51 (account of 775), etc.

Nu`aym's material appears to have been Syrian-Palestinian Muslims. We should not discount or depreciate the level of imagination and ingenuity on a popular level that is represented by the apocalyptic fragments of Nu`aym. It is easy to see how the fragments jostle with each other, sometimes changing phraseology slightly in order to communicate an idea better, often stitched together into longer pieces, which then become mini-literary apocalypses.

Political, Social and Military History

One of the tangled scholarly debates concerning the genre of apocalypse is the extent to which the material can be relied upon for historical purposes.[26] There can be no doubt that a great deal of the apocalyptic traditions are in fact wild predictions or cryptic allusions that might never be "solved" (see notes). The apocalyptic writer is under no obligation to relay events as they actually occurred; only to place them in such a manner so as to prove that the end of the world is nigh. But many would argue that the role of "salvation history" such as *sīra* (biography of the Prophet Muhammad), and the early conquest materials is hardly much better.

That apocalypse communicated the vast social changes that happened with the rise of Islam cannot be doubted. A tradition appearing in the Syrian collection of al-Ṭabarānī gives us a sense of the change that occurred for the Arabs with the coming of Islam:

> `Abdallāh b. Ḥawwāla[27] said: We were with the Messenger of God, and we complained to him about the poverty, the nakedness and the general lack of things. The Messenger of God said: "Take heart, because I am more worried about the plethora of things for you. This matter [of Islam] will continue until you have conquered the lands of Persia and the Byzantines and Ḥimyar [Yemen]—you will have three army-provinces (*ajnād*): one in Syria, one in Iraq and one in Yemen—and until a man will be given 100 dinars and be

[26] Paul Alexander, "Medieval Apocalypses as Historical sources," *American Historical Review* 73 (1968), pp. 997–1018.

[27] Companion, lived in al-Urdunn, or Damascus, d. 58/677–8.

> insulted by it [because of the general wealth]." Ibn Ḥawwāla said: "O Messenger of God, who could possibly take Syria when the many-horned Byzantines (*al-rūm dhāt al-qurūn*) are in it?" He said: "God will conquer it for you and appoint you as successors in it, until a group of them [the Byzantines] will become white-robed, with shaved necks, standing in service for a little black man (*al-ruwayjil al-usayawid*)—whatever he tells them to do, they do it. [This will happen] even though today there are men in it [Syria] who view you as more contemptible than the lice which inhabit the buttocks of camels (*aḥqar fī a`yūnihim min al-qirḍān fī a`jāz al-ibl*)."[28]

This type of tradition is reflected inside *The Book of Tribulations* (no. 1215), where the Arabs' previously humble status is contrasted with their present exalted one, or where especially the Byzantines are presented as desiring to return the Arabs back to the Arabian Peninsula. Although these fears might not accurately represent what the Byzantines felt, there can be no doubt that such traditions reflected the Arab Muslims' insecurities.

These insecurities are most evident in the Valleys (A`māq) section (nos. 1212–1415), which detail a possible alliance between the Arab Muslims of Syria and the Byzantines, which is projected to break down under strains of religious differences focused upon the Cross (nos. 1216, 1223, 1226). Some fifty plus pages of almost unique traditions (with some cited in the collections of Muslim, Abū Dā'ūd or Ibn Māja) give us a taste of the frontier atmosphere current in Ḥimṣ during the early and middle eighth century, when the wars with the Byzantines were at their peak. Probably the most astonishing revelation to come from this section is the idea that the apocalyptic writers, although extremely hostile at times to the Byzantines, were at other times willing to ally themselves with them under fairly equal terms—to attack their respective enemies. That the Syrian Muslims' "enemy" would actually be the Iraqi Muslims, most especially those of Kūfa, is

[28] Al-Ṭabarānī, *Musnad al-Shāmiyyīn* (Beirut: Mu'assasat al-Risāla, 1996), iii, p. 396 (no. 2540).

not a conclusion that one would naturally draw from the religious and historical sources currently available.

Whether or not this apocalyptic alliance was ever a reality, the other sections of the A`maq that deal with the internal politics and social tensions of Ḥimṣ strike one as being quite believable. For one thing, as previously noted, the apocalyptic materials give us a wealth of geographical and sociopolitical knowledge that is not found in any other source. Only Ibn `Asākir's *History of the City of Damascus* occasionally alludes to such a richness in source material.[29] Monasteries, topographical features, springs, lakes and rivers, and even the location of prominent stones and trees are featured in Nu`aym. Since it seems unlikely that an early city-history of Ḥimṣ will ever emerge, it is possible to see *The Book of Tribulations* in that light.

Historical material concerning Ḥimṣ abounds within *The Book of Tribulations.* An excellent example is in no. 491, which is a detailed description of Marwan II's siege of Ḥimṣ in 746. This is a siege that is mentioned in a number of sources—Balādhurī, Ṭabarī, Michael the Great—and given little prominence in any of them.[30] The description of the siege is not related to any of the apocalypses at all, and inside the text appears to be more illustrative of the sort of sieges that could happen at the end of the world, and could be a unique source for a section of Syrian history that is little documented.

Another example of historical allusions is the section on natural events, most specifically the earthquakes of the 700s (no. 590) and the sightings of comets. The description of the comet (no. 590) could be the earliest documented sighting of Halley's Comet, of 760, in the Arabic sources (although there are some problems with the dating

[29] Some of the other city-histories of Syria, like Ibn al-`Adīm, *Bughyat al-ṭālib fī tā'rīkh Ḥalab,* would perhaps have filled this gap, but only a quarter of Ibn al-`Adīm has survived. Al-Musharraf b. al-Murajjā', *Faḍā'il al-bayt al-maqdis* does fill this gap to some extent.

[30] Al-Balādhurī, *Ansāb al-ashrāf* (Damascus: Dār al-Yaqẓa al-`Arabiyya, 1997), vii, p. 175; al-Ṭabarī, *Tā'rīkh,* vii, pp. 312–13; Michael the Great, *The Syriac Chronicle of Michael Rabo (the Great).* Trans. Matti Moosa (Teaneck, NJ: Beth Antioch Press, 2014), p. 503; Bar Hebraeus, *Chronography,* trans. Budge (Piscataway, NJ: Gorgias Press, 2003) (vol. 1), pp. 111–12.

discussed in the notes). Further semi-historical material would be the detailed fears concerning the Turks, from a period approximately 100 years previous to the large-scale importation of Turkish slave-soldiers under al-Mu`taṣim (833–42). These traditions also no doubt reflect the fears of the population at that time.

There is a great deal of social history to be extracted from *The Book of Tribulations.* It is easy to see the social isolation of the Muslim Arabs and their insecurities with regard to the local Christian population (who are not featured very much, but are in the background). This insecurity is reflected in the fear that the local Christians will betray the Muslims while the latter are out fighting and violate their families inside Ḥimṣ. One surprise is that there is comparatively little mention of the role of plagues and locust in the region of Syria, which from other Syrian-based chronicles are known to have been omnipresent (or even characteristic of Syria). It is curious that not more use is made of these types of disasters in the attempt to build up the suspense. On the positive side, technological developments such as the widespread use of waterwheels (no. 321, 1387) are mentioned, as are the components of basic shipbuilding (no. 1331). But of course the majority of these allusions are in fact symbolic.

Symbols and Visual Imagery

The use of symbols helps us understand a religious system at its basic level of communication. Apocalypse is more than the sum of its parts, but there are continually recurring symbols and imagery that help us locate the apocalyptic informants' world. Since Nu`aym includes so many fragments, we can see in the text how those partial or "failed" apocalypses interact with the more successful longer pieces. Even the materials that ultimately were not accepted by the Muslim community influenced the growth of its traditions.

The world of Nu`aym is an agrarian-nomadic one. Most of the symbols and imagery are taken from the Syrian-Palestinian world of the time. Sheep and goats are easily transportable in difficult times, horses are the symbols of the rider's power and authority, cattle are the symbols of peace and plenty, while dogs bark to annoy passers-by.

Camels are surprisingly almost absent in Nu`aym, and are definitely the feature of the Arabian Peninsula rather than that of Syria-Palestine. There is a contrast agriculturally between the plenty of Syria, exemplified by the saffron (nos. 834 and apocalypse of weeks, 1949) or wheat (no. 1232) as opposed to the waste of Arabia (nos. 1286, 1479). When Constantinople is destroyed, its location will be planted with mallows and the thorny carob (no. 1280). And fighters when they reach Rome, hang their swords on acacia trees (no. 1340), whatever those were in reality.

Both horses and donkeys for riding purposes are highly symbolic. Horses are divided up into the *birdhawn* (nag ponies) and the roan types, which are both associated with Arabs,[31] while regular horses are associated with nomadic peoples like the Turks. The donkey is not associated with any type of power, except that the Dajjāl is always pictured riding upon one.

Women are present in the apocalyptic materials mainly as symbols, although it is worthy of note that a number of women appear in the chains of transmitters, such as `Abda, the daughter of Khālid b. Ma`dān, Asmā' bint Yazīd al-Anṣāriyya. Four of the Prophet's wives, `Ā'isha, Ḥafṣa, Umm Ḥabība, and Zaynab, daughter of Jaḥsh, are cited in the text as authorities. Inside the traditions, there are symbolic descriptions such as that of the Sufyānī's having female captives' bellies split open (no. 519) or the picture of a woman walking the path to the Byzantine Empire in safety (nos. 1222, 1284, 1334), making the pilgrimage safely without male companionship (no. 995), or the woman walking provocatively in the marketplace (nos. 1126, 1152, 1180).[32] However, there are only a few named women who have actual prominence in *The Book of Tribulations*, such as the women of the Prophet's family (nos. 889, 1934), who are often brutalized, or the female witness, Ṭayyiba, who stands against the Dajjāl (no. 1427), and is probably taken from the Christian tradition.

31 See al-Ghassānī, *al-Aqwāl al-kāfiya wa-l-fuḍūl al-shāfiya fī al-khayl* (Beirut: Dār al-Gharb al-Islamī, 1987), pp. 88, 160–1 for the various classifications.

32 It is surprising to find a reference to lesbianism (no. 1760) in such an early text, but comparatively minimal references to male homosexuality.

Symbolism serves to communicate what are perceived to be eternal truths to the audience and enables it to visualize quickly and effectively the world of the end-times. This issue is more critical in Islam than it is in Christianity because of the comparatively minimal artistic role of apocalypse in Islam. While it was possible to communicate themes of peace and verdancy in Islamically acceptable art forms—such as are apparent in the Dome of the Rock, and at Hishām's palace at Khirbet al-Mafjar (Jericho)[33]—depictions of the horrors of the apocalypse are much more difficult. One might speculate, therefore, that this gap is the driving force in the creation of a rich apocalyptic heritage such as Nu`aym. Primarily we can expect that this material would have been communicated orally, embellished and retold, much in the same way as sagas and epics would have been from later, more documented, periods in Islamic history.

One should always remember that the symbolism and imagery of *The Book of Tribulations* is ultimately the result of the frustrations and impotence of the northern Syrian Muslims during the later Umayyad and early `Abbāsid periods. Not only had they failed to conquer the Byzantine Empire during the Umayyad dynasty's rule, but by the time Nu`aym was collecting traditions, political power had long been stripped from them.[34] The Syrian Muslims were reduced to apocalyptic fantasies and memories of bygone glories.

Present-day Relevance of Nu`aym

There have been several points in the recent past when Nu`aym has attracted attention. The first one was during the Gulf War (1990–1) when a number of apocalyptic prophecies, usually those favoring the putative victory of Saddam Hussein (d. 2006) were published. With the rise of the Taliban in Afghanistan in 1994–6 there was frequent mention of the "black banners from the east" family of traditions, heralding the possible re-establishment of the caliphate. Indeed, the

[33] See Hannah Taragan, *Patronut ve-omanut bi-armon ha-Umayyi bi-Yeriho* (Jerusalem: Yad Yitzhak Ben Zvi, 1997), pp. 85f.

[34] Paul Cobb, *White Banners: Contention in `Abbasid Syria, 750–880.* (Albany, NY: SUNY Press, 2001), pp. 58–60, 85.

Taliban leader, Mullah `Umar (d. 2013), did take the caliphal title of *amīr al-mu'minīn* (Commander of the Believers), although it is not clear that he intended by that to make a pan-Islamic claim. The publication history of Nu`aym is reflected in these expectations, as it was edited by Suhayl Zakkar in 1993.

However, with the beginning of the Syrian Civil War (2011–present) significant use of the apocalyptic heritage began to be mainstream.[35] The Islamic State's proclamation of the caliphate on June 29, 2014 and the publication of its online magazine *Dābiq* has fueled massive interest in the apocalypse,[36] especially as so many of the names are taken from the apocalyptic literature.

Probably the most interesting revival is the name of Dābiq itself, which appears just once in the *ḥadīth* literature, in the authoritative collection of Muslim:

> The Hour will not arise until the Byzantines descend upon the A`māq (valleys) or in Dābiq, so an army from Medina will emerge against them, who are the best of the earth's people at that time. When they will line up for battle, the Byzantines will say: "Give way between us and those who were made captive from among us, so we can fight them," but the Muslims will say: "We will never make way between you and our brothers," so they will fight them. One third will retreat, who God will never accept their repentance, one third will be killed, who are the best martyrs (*shuhadā'*) in God's eyes, and one third will conquer, who will never be tempted (*yuftanuna*), then they will conquer Constantinople. While they are dividing the spoils, having hung up their swords on olive trees, Satan will shout among them: "The [false] Messiah is behind you, among your families!"[37]

35 Nu`aym is cited and translated (partially) on a number of websites: http://anderbal.blogspot.com/2012/12/escatologia-Islamīca-otras-guerras-y.html (accessed January 16, 2016); http://www.inter-islam.org/faith/mahdi1.htm (accessed March 8, 2016); and see https://www.youtube.com/watch?v=QDq8SypJEpM.

36 Issues of *Dābiq* are found at http://www.clarionproject.org/news/Islamīc-state-isis-isil-propaganda-magazine-dabiq#.

37 Muslim, *Ṣaḥīḥ*, viii, pp. 175–6. Ironically, Mango and Scott (trans.), *The Chronicle of Theophanes Confessor* (Oxford: Clarendon Press, 1997), p. 624, does mention Dabiq (Dabekon).

The tradition then continues into the saga of the Dajjāl, of which below. Probably the most interesting element of this tradition is that it upends expectations. In Nu`aym we clearly see the process by which canonical traditions were created: there are a massive number of traditions circulating during the seventh and eighth centuries, products of the confusion created by the first conquests, the people movement out of Arabia, and the beginnings of conversion to Islam. During the ninth and tenth centuries these traditions are gradually winnowed out, with the usual paradigm being that whatever is most specific in the earlier traditions is accepted in the canonical versions in the most generic form. Alternatively, if there are names, then they are focused upon the Muslim holy figures and locations, not allowed to be spread out to numerous other people and sites. (An excellent example of this tendency is the comparison of the cities of refuge from the Dajjāl in Nu`aym to those in al-Bukhārī: while Nu`aym mentions numerous locations throughout Syria, Bukhārī only mentions Mecca and Medina.) From Nu`aym, this process is easily seen—the vast number of names and dates are ignored by the canonical collections.

However, here we have a rare example of Nu`aym being the more generic. The name of Dābiq, known from the historical and military literature of the Umayyad period as the staging ground for Muslim Arab armies invading the Byzantine Empire, is not mentioned in Nu`aym, although the alternate location of al-A`māq (the more generic one) is. The Islamic State has latched on to the only occurence of the name in all the tradition literature. Thus it is possible for a highly Salafi and literalist group to focus upon an apocalyptic location that is outside the general "holy sites" of Islam—Mecca, Medina and Jerusalem—in order to complete its fulfillment of the apocalypse.

The texts, the Research and the Translation

There are three published editions of Nu`aym, all of which have their deficiencies. The standard manuscript is BL Or 9449.[38] I have used the

[38] It is mentioned by Ḥajjī Khalīfa, *Kashf al-ẓunūn* (Beirut: Dār Ṣādir, n.d.), v, p. 128 as *Kitāb al-fitan wa-l-malāḥim.*

Suhayl Zakkar edition of 1993 as the basis for the translation below (marked SZ), with corrections from the manuscript (marked BL), and from the two other editions (marked MM and DKI). It seems probable on the basis of the text that we have that Nu`aym was in the process of completing *The Book of Tribulations*, but had not finished it. There are several sections that have minimal traditions, which seem to be waiting to be fleshed out. The final ten traditions of the book are rather a grab bag, and make one wonder whether the original intention was to complete the text with the lengthy "Apocalypse of Weeks."

Jorge Aguadé is the first scholar who made use of Nu`aym,[39] although F. Krenkow was the first who noticed his importance.[40] However, the two most significant scholars who have worked on Nu`aym have been Wilferd Madelung in a series of articles published during the 1980s,[41] and Suliman Bashear, also with a series of articles during the later 1980s and early 1990s.[42] Others since then have made use of Nu`aym, especially my *Studies in Muslim Apocalyptic* (2002), however, the text is rarely cited in the broader historical literature on the critical time-period of the seventh and eighth centuries. It is to publicize it that this translation has been made.

I have not repeated those traditions that are exact duplicates, but marked them **(1)**, **(2)**, which mean double and triple repetition, etc. Some very short traditions have been omitted if they have nothing new in content. Otherwise the translation is of the entire text. The goal of the translation has been to be as literal as possible, and in general to use the same translated words across the translation. However, because of the nuances of the Arabic, that is not always possible.

39 *Messianismus zur Zeit der frühen Abbasiden: das Kitāb al-fitan des Nu'aim ibn Ḥammād* (Unpub. Ph.D. dissertation, University of Tübingen, 1978).

40 F. Krenkow, "The book of strife (i.e., the *Kitāb al-fitan* of Nu`aim b. Ḥammad al-Marwazī)," *Islamic Culture* 3 (1929), pp. 561–8.

41 "Apocalyptic Prophecies in Ḥimṣ during the Umayyad Age." *Journal of Semitic Studies* 41 (1986), pp. 141–85; "The Sufyānī." *Studia Islamīca* 63 (1986), pp. 5–48, among others.

42 "Early Muslim Apocalyptic Materials." *Journal of the Royal Asiatic Society* 1991, pp. 173–207; "Muslim Apocalypses and the Hour: a Case-Study in Traditional Interpretation." *Israel Oriental Studies* 13 (1993), pp. 75–99.

Place names are translated in the following manner: when the name is common, and commonly known in English (e.g., Constantinople, Mecca, Medina), then it is left in the English form throughout. The only exceptions to this rule are when there are sub-names such as Bizantiya (Byzantium) for Constantinople, and the variants on Jerusalem. When a name is reasonably certain, but exists in both an Arabic and a foreign version, then the foreign one is placed first while the Arabic one for a given section is placed in parentheses. When an identification is tenuous or unknown, then either the name or the translation of the name will be in the text, with the Arabic original in the notes for explanation. Most personal names are left in Arabic transliteration. Titles and nicknames are translated so that the reader can understand the nuances.

Probably the most controversial issue of names has to do with the Arabic regions of Syria. I have chosen to translate the name of *al-shām* as "Syria" even though its true translation should be "Greater Syria" (inclusive of the countries of Syria, parts of Turkey, Lebanon, Jordan and Israel, plus the Palestinian Territories). I have left *filasṭīn*, "Palestine," untranslated, as the region in the classical period was the southern half of the British mandate territory of Palestine (today Israel and the Palestinian Authority territories). Similarly, *al-urdunn*, "Jordan," is also untranslated, as the region in the classical period is that of northern Israel and southern Lebanon around the Sea of Galilee. Unfortunately, the fact is that the classical names Filasṭīn and al-Urdunn do not convey any meaning to the contemporary reader that would offset the misapprehensions conveyed by the use of the names Palestine and Jordan.

Abbreviations and key names and terms

Allāhu akbar!—one of the most popular Muslim slogans, "God is greater" (or sometimes "God is greatest!").

Amīr al-Mu'minin—Commander of the Believers (Sunnism and Shi`ism), in Shi`ite contexts, meaning `Alī b. Abī Ṭālib.

Dajjāl—the Antichrist (throughout the text these terms are used interchangeably).

Filasṭīn—Palestine, what is today central Israel and the Palestinian territories, south of the Esdraelon Valley, with its capital of Ramla.

Fitna/fitan "a burning with fire, the melting of gold and silver in order to separate or distinguish the bad from the good, a trial, affliction, distress, a means whereby the condition of a man may be evinced, in respect of good and of evil, punishment, castigation, slaughter, civil war, or conflict occurring among people, sedition, discord, dissension, difference of opinions among the people, seduction, temptation, error, women."[1]

al-Ḥamdu li-llahi—"Praise be to God!"

[1] E. W. Lane, *An Arabic-English Lexicon* (Beirut: Libraire du Liban, 1997 (reprint)), vi, p. 2335 (right col.)

Imam—a prayer leader (Sunnism), a legitimate leader (Sunnism), a descendent of Muhammad through Fāṭima, one of twelve would-be rulers (including `Alī b. Abī Ṭālib, who actually ruled 656–61) (Shi`ism).

Jāhiliyya—the pre-Islamic period, seen in Nu`aym less as the classic Islamic conception of "ignorance, barbarism"[2] than a period of knowledge concerning future events that rivals that of the People of the Book. We could more understand it as being a period of stability as opposed to the tribulations of the Islamic period.

Lā ilaha illā Allāhu—the short form of the *shahada*, testimony of faith, "there is no god but [the] God! [or Allah]" Stating this testimony with intent makes one a Muslim. Later it is elongated to add on "and Muḥammad is His Messenger."

Maghrib—the Islamic west, translated when presented by the text as a directional geographical term, "the westerners" (especially as opposed to "the easterners") but left as is when meant as a location, i.e., in the Maghrib (Morocco).

Mahdi—the "Guided One," a Muslim messianic figure. Also called al-Hāshimī, because of his ancestry.

Manṣūr—the "One made Victorious [by God]", an originally South Arabian messianic figure appropriated by the `Abbasids.

Mawlā/mawālī—clients, freedmen, associated with Arab tribes, usually converted to Islam.

Piebald One—an apocalyptic opponent of the Sufyānī in Syria.

Qaḥṭānī—the South Arabian messianic figure.

Speckled One—an apocalyptic figure associated with Egypt.

Sufyānī—the Syrian messianic figure, descendent of Mu`āwiya b. Abī

[2] I. Goldziher, *Muslim Studies* (trans. S. M. Stern, Chicago: Aldine, 1966–7), i, pp. 201–9.

Sufyān, an opponent of the Mahdi, especially in Shi`ism. Also known as al-Ṣakhrī (because of Abū Sufyān's given name), the ugly one (*al-mushawwah*).

Al-Urdunn—Jordan, what is today the region around the Sea of Galilee, northern Israel and southern Lebanon to the coastlands, with its capital at Tiberias.

Caliph/Emperor list

Muḥammad, 622–32

***Rāshidūn* caliphs**

`Abū Bakr (11–13/632–4)`

`Umar (13–23/634–44)

`Uthmān (23–35/644–56)

`Alī b. Abī Ṭālib (35–40/656–61)[1]

Umayyad caliphs

Mu`āwiya b. Abī Sufyān (36–60/657–80)

Yazīd b. Mu`āwiya (60–4/680–3)

Mu`āwiya b. Yazīd (64/683)

`Abdallāh b. al-Zubayr (anti-caliph, 64–72/683–92)[2]

Marwān b. al-Ḥakam (64–5/683–5)

`Abd al-Malik b. Marwān (65–86/685–705)

Al-Walīd b. `Abd al-Malik (86–96/705–15)

Sulaymān b. `Abd al-Malik (96–9/715–17)

`Umar b. `Abd al-`Azīz (99–101/717–20)

[1] Only in Iraq and the Ḥijāz.

[2] Only in Iraq and the Ḥijāz.

Yazīd b. `Abd al-Malik (101–5/720–4)
Hishām b. `Abd al-Malik (105–25/720–43)
Al-Walīd b. Yazīd (125–6/743–4)
Yazīd b. al-Walīd (126/744)
Ibrāhīm (126/744)
Marwān b. Muḥammad (127–32/744–50)

`Abbāsid caliphs
`Abdallāh b. Muḥammad al-Imām, Abū al-`Abbās al-Saffāḥ (132–6/749–54)
`Abdallāh b. Muḥammad al-Imām, Abū Ja`far al-Manṣūr (136–58/754–75)
Muḥammad b. `Abdallāh, Abū `Abdallāh al-Mahdi (158–69/775–85)
Mūsā b. Muḥammad, Abū Muḥammad al-Hādī (169–70/785–6)
Hārūn b. Muḥammad, Abū Ja`far al-Rashīd (170–93/786–809)
Muḥammad b. Hārūn, Abū Mūsā al-Amīn (193–8/809–13)
`Abdallāh b. Hārūn, Abū Ja`far al-Ma'mūn (198–218/813–33)

Byzantine Emperors
Heraclian dynasty
Heraclius (610–41)
Constantine III (641)
Heraklonas (641)
Constans II (641–68)
Constantine IV (668–85)
Justinian II (685–95, 705–11)
Leontios (695–8)
Tiberius III (698–705)
Philippikos (711–13)
Anastasios (713–15)
Theodosios (715–17)

Isaurian dynasty
Leo III (717–41)
Constantine V (741–75)

Leo IV (775–80)
Constantine VI (780–97)
Irene (797–802)

Nikephorian dynasty

Nikephorus I (802–11)
Michael I Rangabe (811–13)
Leo V (813–20)

Translation of Nu`aym b. Ḥammād al-Marwazī, *Kitāb al-fitan*

What was related by the Messenger of God and his Companions after him concerning the Tribulations to come

1. Abū Sa`īd al-Khudarī:[1] The Messenger of God led us in the afternoon prayer in the day, then spoke to us until the sun went down. He did not leave out anything that was to happen until the Day of Resurrection—whoever remembered it, remembered it, whoever forgot it, forgot it.
2. `Abdallāh b. `Umar[2]: The Messenger of God said: "God raised this world up for me, so that I could gaze upon it, and upon everything that will happen until the Day of Resurrection, just as I can gaze upon my palm—a revelation (*jillyān*)[3] from God, revealed to His Prophet, just as He revealed it to the previous prophets." [14]

[1] Sa`d b. Mālik al-Anṣārī, d. either 64/683–4 or 74/693–4 in Medina.
[2] Son of the second caliph, `Umar, a very respected figure in Sunni Islam, d. 73 or 74/692–3 or 693–4.
[3] Most likely the Syriac *gelyono*, cf. Payne-Smith, *Syriac-English Dictionary*, p. 71 (right col.).

3. Ḥudhayfa b. al-Yamān[4]: I am the most knowledgeable of the people concerning every tribulation that will happen until the Day of Resurrection. It is not that the Messenger of God would confide in me that which he did not tell to others, but the Messenger of God would tell an assembly, teaching them concerning the tribulations which were to come, both small and great, but that group has all departed [died] other than me.
4. Ḥudhayfa b. al-Yamān: The Messenger of God said: "Tribulations will come like the falling of dark-night, each one following the other, coming upon you in a similar fashion, like the faces of cattle, until you do not know which is which."
5. Ḥudhayfa b. al-Yamān: These tribulations have overshadowed [us], like the foreheads of cattle. Most people will perish in them, other than those who know of them from previously.
6. Abū Hurayra[5]: The Messenger of God said: "When the time draws near, the black she-camel (*al-shuruf al-jawn*)[6] will kneel next to you, tribulations like the falling of dark-night."
7. Kurz b. `Alqama al-Khuzā`ī[7]: A man said to the Messenger of God: "Does Islam have an end?" He said: "Yes. Any family from the Arabs or the non-Arabs (*`ajam*) to which God wishes well, He will cause to enter Islam." He said: "Then what?" He said: "Then tribulations like they were clouds." He said: "By no means, if God wills!" He [Muḥammad] said: "Yes, and by the One whom my soul is in His hands, then you will return during them [tribulations] to being snakes (*asāwid*) striking, cutting each other's necks off." Al-Zuhrī[8] said: An *aswad* (sing.

[4] Ḥudhayfa b. al-Yamān al-`Absī, Companion, one of the indigent *ahl al-ṣuffa*, d. 36/656.

[5] There is no agreement concerning his name—`Abd al-Raḥmān or `Abdallāh are the most commonly cited (al-Mizzī, *Tahdhīb*, viii, pp. 447–51 [no. 8276]), d. 57, 58 or 59/677, 678, 679, buried close to Tiberias.

[6] Lane, *Arabic-English Lexicon*, iv, p. 1538 (mid. col.) "trials like portions of the dark night," apparently with an ominous connotation.

[7] Companion, Syrian, was in charge of the war-flags for Mu`āwiya and Marwān I, *fl.* 1st/7th century.

[8] *EI*[2] "al-Zuhrī" (M. Lecker); he was the most important religious figure to associate

of *asāwid*) is a snake which when it bites, it springs forward,[9] lifts its head, and then strikes. **(1)** [15]

8. Abū Mūsā al-Asha`rī[10]: The Messenger of God said: "There will be killing (*haraj*)[11] before the Hour." They said: "What is *haraj*?" He said: "Killing and lying." They said: "O Messenger of God, killing more than the unbelievers who are killed now?" He said: "This will not be your killing the unbelievers, it will be a man killing his neighbor, his brother and his cousin."
9. Usayyid b. al-Mutashammis b. Mu`āwiya[12]: I heard Abū Mūsā say: There will be killing and *haraj* with regard to the people of Islam before the Hour, such that a man will kill his grandfather, his cousin, his father, and his brother. By God, I fear that it will envelope you and me!
10. Abū Mūsā: After you there will be tribulations like the falling of dark-night, in which a man will wake up a believer, but go to bed an unbeliever, or go to bed a believer, and wake up an unbeliever.
11. Mujāhid[13]: The Messenger of God said: Before the Hour there are tribulations like the falling of dark-night, in which a man will go to bed a believer, but wake up an unbeliever, or go to bed a believer and wake up an unbeliever. Some of them will sell their religion for a paltry amount of this world. **(2)**
12. Ibn `Umar: The Messenger of God said: The tribulation is a terrible thing in the land of God, it treads on its halter. It is not permitted for anyone to inflame it—woe to the one who takes up its halter.

themselves with the Umayyads, d. 123, 124 or 125/741, 742 or 743. Often called Ibn Shihāb.

9 Variant, *nadhdhat*, "to exude mucus."

10 `Abdallāh b. Qays al-Asha`rī, d. 49, 50, 51, 52 or 53/669, 670, 671, 672 or 673, either in Mecca or just outside Kūfa.

11 The Hebrew word *hereg*, "killing," although al-Bukhārī, Ṣaḥīḥ, viii, p. 115 (no. 7065) says that it is Ethiopian (*lisān al-ḥabasha*).

12 Usayyid b. al-Mutashammis b. Mu`āwiya al-Tamīmī, Baṣran, participated in the conquest of Iṣfahān, and later as a commander in Khurāsān, *fl.* 1st/7th century.

13 Probably Mujāhid b. Jabr al-Qurashī, *mawlā* to Banū Makhzūm, Meccan, d. 100, 101, 102, 103 or 104/718, 719, 720, 721 or 722.

13. `Abdallāh b. `Amr[14]: You will see nothing in this world but trial and tribulation, and matters will only get worse.
14. Ḥudhayfa: "There is absolutely no stirrer of dissension, whose [group] reaches 300 men, who I could not name by his name and his [16] father's name, and his dwelling until the Day of Resurrection—all of this the Messenger of God taught me." They said: "Exactly?" He said: "Or approximately, so that the jurists would know them." Or he said: "the learned (*`ulama'*). You used to ask the Messenger of God concerning the good, but I would ask him about the evil. You would ask him about what was, I would ask him about what would be."
15. Ḥudhayfa: I heard the Messenger of God say: 300 men will emerge in my community, with them 300 banners, known, and their tribes are known, seeking the face of God, but being killed in [the state of] error.
16. Ḥudhayfa: If I were to tell you of all that I know you would not guard me during the night.
17. `Abdallāh b. `Amr: You will continue in trial and tribulation, and the matter will only get worse. When the ruler does not rule for the sake of God, and the client (*al-mawlā*) does not fulfill his obedience to God, then you are on the verge of God's disapproval—and God's disapproval is worse than the people's disapproval.
18. Abū Idrīs[15]: I was with Abū Ṣāliḥ[16] and Abū Muslim,[17] and one of them said: [32] to his companion, "Do you fear anything?" They said: "We fear pursuit." So I said: "Only the people of the end-times will experience pursuit." They said: "You are right, but there is never theft without there being pursuit. No theft (*nahb*) has happened to people greater than that of

[14] Son of the conqueror of Egypt, where he died in 96/714–15.

[15] Abū Idrīs al-Khawlānī, `Ā'idh Allāh b. `Abdallāh, d. 80/699–700.

[16] Possibly Abū Ṣāliḥ al-Asha`rī, from the people of al-Urdunn, *fl.* 1st/7th century (Ibn `Asākir, lxvi, pp. 295–300).

[17] Abū Muslim al-Khawlānī, `Abdallāh b. Thawb, who was a Yemenite, an ascetic, lived in Syria, d. during the caliphate of Yazīd I (680–3).

Islam,[18] and tribulation pursues it, but this will only happen to the people of the end-times."

19. Qays b. Abī Ḥāzim[19]: The Messenger of God said: Tribulations will be sent upon the earth like rain. **(1)**
20. `Ubaydallāh b. Abī Ja`far[20]: When God told Moses the story of this community [Islam], he wished that he could be one of them. So God said: "O Moses, the end of it [the community] will be struck by trials and hardships," some of them said: "tribulations," so Moses said: "O Lord! Who can bear these?" God said: "I will give them such patience and faith that the trial will be easy for them."
21. `Abdallāh b. `Amr: The Messenger of God said: There will be tribulations in my community, until they will cause separation between a man, his father, and his brother, until a man will be condemned because of his trial, the way that a fornicatress is condemned for her fornication. [17]
22. Usāma b. Zayd[21]: The Prophet looked over a fort, and said: "Do you see what I see? I see the places of tribulations, through your homes, like the rainy places."
23. Ḥudhayfa: There is no more worthy guide for paths than I for every tribulation which will be, each tribal-crier and leader until the Day of Resurrection.
24. Ḥudhayfa: There is no more knowledgeable guide to the villages and townships than I for that which will come other than `Uthmān b. `Affān.

18 Presumably from the perspective of non-Muslims.

19 Ḥuṣayn b. `Awf al-Bajalī, Yemenite, from Kūfa, d. either 84, 97, 98/703, 715, 716 or at the end of the caliphate of Sulaymān (715–17).

20 A jurisprudent, Egyptian, a *mawlā* of Kināna, d. 136/753–4. Al-Mizzī, *Tahdhīb*, v, p. 30 (no. 4214): "We raided Constantinople, but our boat broke up, then a wave threw us on to a stray piece of wood on the sea, while we were five or six. God caused a leaf to grow for each of us, so that we could suck on it, so we were satisfied and filled, and when it was evening God caused another in its place until a boat passed and picked us up."

21 Son of Zayd b. Ḥāritha al-Kalbī, Muḥammad's (formerly) adopted son (cf. Q 33:37), d. during the caliphate of Mu`āwiya (661–80).

25. Abū Sālim al-Jayshānī[22]: I heard `Alī say in Kūfa: "There are no less than 300 men who will appear, if I wished I could name every leader and tribal-crier of them until the Day of Resurrection." [34]
26. Ḥudhayfa: The people would ask the Messenger of God concerning the good, but I would ask him concerning the evil, fearing that it would catch up with me. I said: "O Messenger of God, we were in a *jāhiliyya* and evil, but God brought this good, so is there evil after it?" He said: "Yes." I said: "Is there good after that evil?" He said: "Yes. In it there will be dissension"' I said: "What is the nature of this dissension?" He said: "A group following [something] other than my way (*sunna*), taking incorrect guidance, enjoining [the good] from them, and forbidding [the evil]." I said: "And after this good is there evil?"[23] He said: "Yes. Callers towards the gates of hell, whoever responds to them, they are thrown inside." I said: "Describe them, O Messenger of God!" He said: "They are of our skin, speaking our language." **(3)** [18]
27. Ḥudhayfa: The people would ask the Messenger of God concerning the good, but I would ask him concerning the evil, fearing that it would catch up with me. While I was with the Messenger of God that day, I said: "O Messenger of God, after this good which God has brought us, is there evil, just as there was evil before it?" He said: "Yes." I said: "Then what?" He said: "A truce on the basis of dissension."[24] I said: "And what is after the truce?" He said: "Callers towards error—if you meet a caliph who belongs to God during those days, cling to him."
28. Ḥudhayfa: The Messenger of God said: "My community will never perish until discrimination (*tamāyuz*), variance (*tamāyul*) and confusion (*ma`āmi`*) appear among them." Ḥudhayfa said: "May my father and mother be your redemp-

[22] Sufyan b. Hāni', participated in the conquest of Egypt, d. in Alexandria during the caliphate of `Umar b. `Abd al-Azīz (715–17).
[23] This question seems misplaced, as the situation described previously is evil.
[24] Ibn al-Athīr, *Nihāya*, ii, p. 109, s.v. *d.kh.n* (also meaning "smoke").

tion, O Messenger of God, what is *tamāyuz*?" He said: "Tribal chauvinism (*`aṣabiyya*) which the people will renew in Islam after me." I said: "And what is *tamāyul*?" He said: "When a tribe tends against another tribe, and allows its sanctities to be violated unjustly." I said: "And what is *ma`āmi`*?" He said: "When the garrison cities (*al-amṣār*) march against each other, when their necks are intertwined in war in this way"—and the Messenger of God intertwined his fingers. "When most," meaning the leaders, "are corrupt, a few will be righteous—blessed is the man who God makes his few [people] righteous!"

29. Ibn `Abbās[25]: There is nothing that happened to the Israelites that will not happen to you.
30. Abū al-`Āliya[26]: When Tustar[27] was conquered, we found [19] in the treasury of the Hurmuzān[28] a codex, placed near the head of a dead man on a litter, and he said: "It was Daniel, according to what is reckoned."[29] We took it [the codex] to `Umar [b. al-Khaṭṭāb], so I was the first of the Arabs who read it, then he sent for Ka`b, who copied it into Arabic—it in there was what will happen, meaning tribulations.
31. `Abdallāh b. Mas`ūd[30]: Concerning His Word, mighty and majestic, "You who believe! Look to yourselves. No one who goes astray can harm you, if you are rightly guided."[31] I did not

[25] `Abdallāh b. `Abbās, first cousin of the Prophet, ancestor of the `Abbāsid dynasty, traditional source for interpretation of the Qur'ān, d. 68/687–8.

[26] Rufay` b. Mihran al-Riyyāḥī, a *mawlā* of a woman from Banū Riyyāḥ b. Yarbū`, lived in Baṣra, d. 90, 93, 106 or 111/709, 712, 724–5, 729–30.

[27] Tustar = present-day Shushtar, in Khuzistan; compare version in al-Maqdisi, *al-Bad' wa-l-tā'rīkh*, ii, p. 165.

[28] The commander of the Persian Sasanian armies in 19–21/640–2, eventually converted to Islam, and murdered by `Abdallāh b. `Umar after his father's assassination: Ibn Hajar, *al-Isaba fi tamyiz al-sahaba* (Beirut: Ihya al-Turath al-`Arabi, n.d.), iii, pp. 618–19 (no. 9046).

[29] Note the similar account in the early Khuzistan Chronicle, Michael Penn (trans.), *When Christians first met Muslims* (Berkeley: University of California Press, 2015), pp. 50–1.

[30] One of the early Companions of the Prophet, associated with a (pro-Shi`ite) version of the Qur'ān, d. either 32 or 33/652 or 653–4.

[31] Q 5:105.

find the exegesis of this verse afterwards. `Abdallāh said: God revealed the Qur'ān when He revealed it—some verses, their exegesis is in the past, prior to its revelation, some verses, their exegesis was during the time of the Prophet, while some verses, their exegesis will happen a little after the Prophet, some verses, their exegesis will happen after today, and some verses, their exegesis will happen on the Day of Reckoning. That is the Reckoning, [both] Paradise and Hell which are mentioned.

32. Elders who fought in [the Battle of] Ṣiffīn: We came to Mt. al-Jūdī,[32] and suddenly we ran into Abū Hurayra. We encountered him while he was clasping his hands, each upon the other, behind his back, leaning on the mountainside, remembering God Most High, so we wished him the peace (*salām*) greeting, and he returned it. We said: "Tell us about this tribulation." He said: "You will be victorious over your enemy in it," then he said: "There will be a tribulation where this one will be nothing but water in honey comparatively—it will leave you when you are few, and regretful."
33. Samura b. Jundab[33]: The Hour will not arise until you see terrible things, which you thought that you would never see, and never narrate to yourselves.
34. Salama b. Nufayl[34]: I heard the Messenger of God say: You will stay after me, until you will say: "When?" Companies will come, annihilating each other, and before the Hour there will be a terrible slaughter and after it years of earthquakes. [20]
35. Makḥūl[35]: "You will indeed ride story upon story."[36] He said: "Every twenty years you will be in a situation different from the one in which you are."

[32] The mountain where Noah's Ark landed, Q 11:44.

[33] Samura b. Jundab al-Fazārī, a Companion, lived in Baṣra, d. end of 59, beginning of 60/679–80 in al-Kūfa or Baṣra.

[34] Salama b. Nufayl al-Sakūnī, lived in Ḥimṣ, no death date.

[35] Makḥūl al-Shāmī, lived in Damascus, known as a jurisprudent, d. 112, 113 or 114/730, 731, 732–3.

[36] Q 84:19.

36. Sa`d b. Abī Waqqāṣ[37]: The Messenger of God recited this verse: "Say: He is the One able to raise up punishment against you, from above you or from beneath your feet."[38] The Messenger of God said: "As for that which will happen, its exegesis will not come until after."
37. Mu`ādh b. Jabal[39]: As for you, you will never see anything but trial and tribulation in this world, and it will only get worse. You will never see anything that frightens you or is harsh towards you without what follows causing it to pale by comparison.
38. Zirr b. Ḥubaysh[40] heard `Alī saying: "Ask me! By God, you will never ask me concerning a band that will go out to fight 100, or guide 100 without me telling you of its driver, its leader or its tribal-crier—between now and the rising of the Hour."
39. Mu`āwiya b. Abī Sufyān[41]: The Messenger of God said: "Nothing remains of this world other than trial and tribulation." [40]
40. Anas b. Mālik[42]: No year happens without being worse than the one before. I heard it from your Prophet.
41. Abū al-Jild[43]: Trial will strike the people of Islam, while the people around them are gladdened, until the Muslim will want to go back to being a Jew or a Christian because of the effort.
42. Ḥudhayfa and Abū Mūsā both: The Messenger of God said: "Before the Hour there will be [battle] days, in which ignorance will be revealed, and killing (*haraj*) will increase." They said: "And what is *haraj*, O Messenger of God?" He said: "Killing."
43. Al-A`mash[44]: There will never be any matter about which you

[37] Companion, one of the ten promised paradise, conqueror of Iraq, d. approx. 55/675.
[38] Q 6:65.
[39] Companion, well-known ascetic, lived in Syria, d. of the plague, 18/639.
[40] Zirr b. Ḥubaysh al-Asadī, lived in al-Kūfa, d. either 82 or 83/701 or 702.
[41] Companion, governor of Syria, fifth caliph (661–80).
[42] The Prophet's personal servant, lived in Baṣra, d. 91, 92, or 93/710, 711, or 712.
[43] Probably Abū al-Jild al-Tamīmī, probably a *mawlā* associated with `Abd al-Malik (Ibn `Asākir, lxvi, pp. 118–19).
[44] Sulaymān b. Mihrān al-Asadī, lived in al-Kūfa, *mawlā*, originally from Ṭabarastān, d. 148/765.

will clamor, without it being followed by another that will distract you from the first one. [21]

44. `Abdallāh: "How will it be for you when a tribulation is covering you in which your elderly become decrepit, and your youth grow up, so that the people will take it [the tribulation] as a way (*sunna*)—when people abandon part of it, it will be said: 'You have abandoned the Way (*sunna*)!' It was said: 'O `Abū `Abd al-Raḥmān! When will that be?' He said: 'When your ignorant are many, your learned and knowledgeable ones are few, your readers [of the Qur'ān] and your rulers are many, but your trustworthy ones are few, and when this world is sought at the price of the deeds of the next.'"
45. Ḥudhayfa: There is nothing between you and that evil will be sent upon you for the distance of miles, other than the death of `Umar [b. al-Khaṭṭāb].[45] **(1)**
46. Ḥudhayfa: O `Āmir, do not let that which you see deceive you—those are about to be parted from their religion, just as a woman parts her pudenda (*qubul*).[46]
47. Abū Hurayra: The Messenger of God said: The first people to perish will be Persia, then the `Arabs in their wake.
48. Muḥammad b. `Abd al-Raḥmān b. Abī Dhi'b[47]: I heard Ibn al-Zubayr[48] saying: "I never heard Ka`b[49] say anything that would happen during my rule without seeing it." [22]
49. Ibn `Umar that he saw a building on Mt. Abū Qays,[50] and said: "O Mujāhid! When you see the houses of Mecca appearing on its rugged mountains (*akhāshib*), and the water coming through its lanes, then beware!"

[45] Second caliph, considered by Sunnis to have been one of the best caliphs (634–44).

[46] Ibn Abī Shayba, *Muṣannaf*, p. 450 (no. 37126) adds "not forbidding any who come to her [sexually]."

[47] Listed as Muḥammad b. `Abd al-Raḥmān b. Abī Dhu'ayb (Ibn Sa`d, *Tabaqat*, v, p. 342), Medinan, *fl.* 1st/7th century.

[48] `Abdallāh b. al-Zubayr, anti-caliph, ruled much of Arabia and Iraq (683–92).

[49] Ka`b b. Mati` al-Ḥimyarī, called Ka`b al-Aḥbār, lived in Ḥimṣ, d. 32/652.

[50] Near Mecca.

50. Ḥudhayfa: We were with `Umar, and he said: "Which one of you remembers the words of the Messenger of God about the tribulation?" I said: "I remember them as he said them." He said: "Well, what are you waiting for!" I said: "The tribulation of a man is concerning his wife (*ahl*), his possessions, his children and his neighbors—but his prayer, his charity, and his commanding the good and forbidding the evil will expiate it [the tribulation]." He said: "This is not what I asked you, but about that which crashes like the waves of the ocean." I said: "Do not be afraid, O Commander of the Believers. Between you and it is a locked door." He said: "Could the door be broken and opened?" I said: "Yes, it could be broken." `Umar said: "Then it is not locked for eternity?" I said: "Certainly." We said: "Did `Umar know who was the door?" He said: "Yes, just as there is day on the other side of night, because I told him a narrative in which there were no mistakes." Shaqīq said: "Allow us to ask him who is the door." So we ordered Masrūq, and he asked him, and he said: "`Umar is the door." **(2)**

51. Ka`b: There will come a time for the people in which the believer will be condemned for his faith, just as today the immoral is condemned for his immorality, such that it will be said to a man: You are a believing jurisprudent (*faqīh*).[51]

52. `Urwa b. Qays[52]: A man went to Khālid b. al-Walīd[53] in Syria, while he was preaching, and said: "The tribulations have appeared." Khālid said to him: "When Ibn al-Khaṭṭāb is alive, no—that will only happen when the people are in a state of trial." The man began to describe the earth, there is nothing on it like someplace to flee to it from him [`Umar] so that he cannot find him. Then the tribulations will appear.

[51] There must be a mistake, or perhaps an ironic statement.

[52] Or `Urwa b. Abī Qays (see no. 1330), who may be identical with the `Azra b. Qays al-Aḥmasī al-Bajalī (no. 781), lived in Kūfa, d. during reign of Mu`āwiya (Ibn `Asākir, *Tā'rīkh*, xl, p. 311 notes the confusion with this name).

[53] Companion, conqueror of Syria, exiled by `Umar, d. in Ḥimṣ 31 or 32/651 or 652–3.

53. `Abdallāh: The worst of the nights and days, months and times are those closest to the Hour. [23]
54. Abū Mūsā al-Ash`arī: The Messenger of God said: "Before the Hour there will be killing (*haraj*)." I said: "What is *haraj*?" He said: "Killing." We said: "More than are killed today?" He said: "Including the Muslims yet to be born." [24] He said: "It will not be your killing of unbelievers, but your killing each other, such that a man will kill his brother, his cousin, and his neighbor." The people were speechless, so that not one man showed his teeth in laughter.
55. I [Abū Qubayl][54] heard Maslama b. Mukhallad al-Anṣārī say[55]—he used to send frequent expeditions to sea, and the army hated that—when he was on the pulpit: "O people of Egypt! Take vengeance for me, because by God, I have added to your stores, I have multiplied your stocks, and strengthened you against your enemy. Know that I am better than those who will follow me. The end will be evil."
56. Ḥudhayfa: The Hour will not arise until you kill your imam, draw your swords, and the evilest of you inherit this world. [25]

Naming of the Tribulations which are to come, and their Number from the death of the Messenger of God until the Rising of the Hour

57. `Awf b. Mālik al-Ashja`ī[56]: The Messenger of God said to me: "Count, O `Awf, six before the Hour, the first of which is my

[54] Ḥuyayy b. Hānī' al-Ma`āfirī, lived in Egypt, participated in the raid on Rhodes, known to have been knowledgable concerning tribulations (al-Mizzī, *Tahdhīb*, ii, p. 330 [no. 1570]), d. in al-Burulas (?) 128/745–6.

[55] Governor of Egypt under Mu`āwiya.

[56] Companion, lived in both Ḥimṣ and Damascus, where his house was near the old thread market, d. 73/692–3. One the best-known stories about him: "I was going along in Syria on a camel when I saw a man of the *ahl al-dhimma* leading a woman on a donkey. When they were alone, he poked the donkey and the woman fell to the ground. He left her there. I caught up with my camel and hit him on the head with my whip and bloodied him." (Ibn `Asākir, *Tā'rīkh*, xlvii, pp. 39–40).

death," so I was moved to tears, such that the Messenger of God began to quiet me, then he said: "Say: One, and the second is the conquest of Jerusalem (*bayt al-maqdis*), say: two, and the third will be two deaths among my community like a plague of flocks, say: three, and the fourth will be a tribulation among my community." He [`Awf] said: And he magnified it, "Say: four, and the fifth will be wealth that overflows among such that a man will be given 100 dinars and look upon it with contempt. Say five, and the sixth will be a truce (*hudna*) between you and the Byzantines (Banū al-Aṣfar),[57] then they will come to you to fight you. The Muslims on that day will be in a land called al-Ghūṭa, in a city called Damascus."

58. `Awf b. Mālik: The Messenger of God said: "There are six before the Hour, the first of them is the death of your prophet, say: one, the second is the conquest of Jerusalem, and the third is a death that will happen among you like a plague of flocks, the fourth is a tribulation between you, which will enter every house [26] of the Arabs, the fifth is a truce between you and the Byzantines (Banū al-Aṣfar), then they will gather to you after the duration of a woman's pregnancy, nine months."
59. `Awf b. Mālik: The Messenger of God said: Six are before the Hour: the first of which is the death of your prophet, the conquest of Jerusalem, death like a plague of flocks, a truce that will be between you and the Byzantines (Banū al-Aṣfar), the conquest of the city of unbelief, and a man returning 100 dinars in contempt.[58]
60. `Awf b. Mālik: The Messenger of God said to me: There are six before the Hour, the first of which is my death, then the conquest of Jerusalem, then a settlement which my community will settle in Syria, then a dissension that will happen among

57 The Byzantines, see nos. 87, 1221; and Fierro, "al-Aṣfar," *Studia Islamīca* 77 (1993), pp. 169–81; *idem*, "al-Aṣfar again," *Jerusalem Studies in Arabic and Islam* 22 (1998), pp. 196–213.

58 Because of the abundance of money.

you, which will enter every Arab house, then the Byzantines will make a peace with you.

61. Ḥazn b. `Abd `Amr[59] said: We entered the land of the Byzantines during the raid of al-Ṭawāna,[60] and camped on a field. I took the heads of my companions' riding beasts, and took some time about it. My companions departed, seeking fodder, so while I was in that situation, suddenly I heard: "Peace be upon you and God's mercy!" so I turned, and suddenly there was a man there, wearing white clothing. I said: "Peace be upon you, and God's mercy!" and he said: "Are you from the community of Aḥmad?" I said: "Yes," and he said: "Be patient, for this is a community receiving mercy. God has ordained for you five dissensions (*fitan*), and five prayers." I said: "Name them for me." He said: "Hold on, the first of them is the death of their prophet, and its name in the Book of God is *bughtatan* (suddenly), then the killing of `Uthmān, and its name in the Book of God is *al-ṣammā'* (the deaf), then the tribulation of Ibn al-Zubayr, and its name in the Book of God is *al-`amiyā'* (the blind), then the tribulation of Ibn al-Ash`ath,[61] and its name in the Book of God is *al-batirā'* (the cut-off)." Then he turned, while he was saying: "*al-Ṣaylam* (misfortune) remains, *al-ṣaylam* remains!" but I did not know where he went. [27]

62. `Alī b. Abī Ṭālib[62]: God made five tribulations for this community, a general tribulation, then a specific tribulation, then a general tribulation, then a specific tribulation, then a dark black-night tribulation in which people will become like cattle, then a truce, then callers to error, so if any creation remains for God on that day, cling to Him. In a variant, he said the same,

[59] Unidentified.

[60] Classical Tyana, today Adana, in Cilicia; the raid was probably in 88/707 (see Michael the Great, p. 488, who dates it to 706).

[61] Led a revolt in the east against al-Ḥajjāj b. Yūsuf al-Thaqafī in 81–4/700–3.

[62] Fourth caliph, considered by Shi`ites to have been the legitimate successor to the Prophet, assassinated in Kūfa 41/661 by a Kharijite, and ancestor of the Prophet's blood descendents.

but he said: The blind deaf (*al-`amiyā' al-ṣammā'*) one that covers [everything].

63. Ḥudhayfa: There will be tribulation, then community (*jamā`a*), and repentance, then tribulation, then community and repentance, until he mentioned the fourth, then there will be no further community nor repentance.
64. Ḥudhayfa: In Islam there will be four tribulations, the fourth of which will hand them over to the Dajjāl, *al-raqṭā'* (the speckled), the dark-night, both of those.
65. Ḥudhayfa: The Messenger of God said: There will be a tribulation, and then community, then a tribulation, then community, and then a tribulation in which the minds of men will be crippled.
66. `Abdallāh: The Messenger of God said: Among my community there will be four tribulations; at the fourth there will be annihilation.
67. Some of the elders of the army-province[63]: When Khālid b. Yazīd b. Mu`āwiya was an overseer for Marwān b. al-Ḥakam,[64] while he was staying at the house of `Umar b. Marwān, he had a knife with him, and a scroll. Suddenly he said: "The five and the ten have passed, but the twenty remain, whose evil will be common east and west—none will survive them other than the people of Anṭablus."[65] Shufayy b. `Ubayd said to him: "May God make you righteous, what is this?" He said: "The first tribulation was five, the second was ten years, the tribulation of Ibn al-Zubayr, then the third will be twenty years, whose evil will be common east and west—none will survive them other than the people of Tortosa."
68. Ḥudhayfa: The tribulations [28] that the Messenger of God enumerated until the Hour will arise are four: the first of them

[63] Presumably that of Ḥimṣ.

[64] Caliph in Syria, the first of the Marwanid branch of the Umayyad caliphs.

[65] Close to Barqa, the pre-Islamic region of Cyrenaica (present-day Benghazi in Libya).

is five [years], the second is ten, the third is twenty, and the fourth is the Dajjāl.

69. Yazīd b. Abī Ḥabīb[66]: There will be a tribulation which will encompass all of the people; none but the western army-province will be safe from it.

70. `Imrān b. Ḥaṣīn[67]: The Prophet said: There will be four tribulations: in the first shedding blood will be permitted, in the second blood and wealth will be permitted, in the third, blood, wealth and sexual abuse will be permitted, and the fourth will be the Dajjāl.

71. `Abdallāh b. Mas`ūd: The Messenger of God said to us: "I warn you of seven tribulations that will happen after me—a tribulation that will come from Medina, a tribulation that will come from Mecca, a tribulation that will come from the Yemen, a tribulation that will come from Syria, a tribulation that will come from the east, a tribulation that will come from the west, and a tribulation that will come from within Syria, which is the tribulation of the Sufyānī." Ibn Mas`ūd said: "Some of you will see the first, and from this community some will see the last." Al-Walīd b. `Ayyāsh[68] said: "The tribulation from Medina was that of Ṭalḥa and al-Zubayr,[69] and the tribulation of Mecca was that of Ibn al-Zubayr. The tribulation of the Yemen was that of Najda,[70] while the tribulation of Syria was the Umayyads, and the tribulation of the east was those [the `Abbāsids]."

72. Abū Hurayra: The Messenger of God said: "There will be four tribulations after me. In the first blood will be spilled, in the second, blood and wealth will be permitted, in the third, blood, wealth and sexual abuse, and the fourth, the 'blind deaf one,' in which my community will be scraped like leather."

[66] Suwayd al-Azdī, a *mawlā*, lived in Egypt, d. 128/745–6.

[67] `Imrān b. Ḥasīn al-Khuzā`ī, Companion, lived in Baṣra, was a judge, d. 52/672.

[68] Unidentified, but probably from Kūfa.

[69] Who revolted against `Ali b. Abī Ṭālib, and were both killed in the Battle of the Camel, 36/656.

[70] Identified with the rebellion of al-Najda b. `Āmir al-Ḥarūrī, killed 72/692.

73. Abū Hurayra: The Messenger of God said: Four tribulations will come upon you after me. In the first, blood will be permitted, in the second blood and wealth, in the third, blood, wealth and sexual abuse, while in the fourth, the deaf blind one, overwhelming, tossing like the waves in the sea, until none of the people will find a refuge from it. The [tribulations] will appear in Syria, strike Iraq, trample al-Jazīra with its arm and leg, [29] and because of the trial, the community will be scraped like leather. None of the people will be able to say: "Easy, easy!" They will not be able to lift it from one side without it breaking down on the other.

74. Abū Hurayra: The Messenger of God said concerning His Word, Most High, "or to confuse you (into different) parties,"[71] he said: "Four tribulations will follow. In the first one, blood will be permitted, in the second, blood and wealth will be permitted, in the third, blood, wealth and sexual abuse, but the fourth, the blind dark-night, tossing like the waves in the sea, will spread out until there is no Arab house into which it has not entered."

75. Arṭāt b. al-Mundhir[72]: It has reached me that the Messenger of God said: "There will be four tribulations in my community—at the end, continuous tribulations will strike my community. As for the first, trial will strike them, such that the believer will say: 'This is my destruction!' Then the second will be revealed, such that the believer will say: 'This is my destruction!' Then the third will be revealed—every time it is said that it has finished, it returns. In the fourth tribulation they go towards unbelief, since the community will be with this one for a while, then that one, with an imam but without community (*jamāʿa*). Then the Messiah [Jesus], and then the rising of the sun from the west. Short of the Hour there will be seventy-two

[71] Q 6:65.
[72] Arṭāt b. Mundhir al-Alhānī al-Sakūnī, lived in Ḥimṣ, d. 163/779–80.

deceivers (*dajjāl*); among them there will be those who only one man will follow."

76. Ḥudhayfa: The tribulations are three: the fourth will lead them to the Dajjāl, the [tribulation] which will cast red-hot stones, [the one] which will cast black basalt stones, the black dark-night one, and the one which will toss like the sea.

77. `Umayr b. Hāni'[73]: The Messenger of God said: The tribulation of the mobile [horse-back riders] (*al-aḥlās*): in it there is war and fleeing, the tribulation of the torrent[74] in which its smoke will issue from under the foot of a man {from my Family}, claiming it is from me. None other than my pious friends are from me. Then the people will make peace under [the rule of] a man. At that time there will be the tribulation of darkness—every time people say it is cut off, it is [actually] extended, until there it has entered every Arab house—fighting [30] in it, without anybody knowing whether for right or wrong. They will continue like this until they become two camps: the camp of belief without any hypocrisy, and the camp of hypocrisy without any belief in it. When they have gathered [in this manner], then expect the Dajjāl that day or the next.[75]

78. `Alī: The tribulations are four: a tribulation of happiness and sadness, this-and-that tribulation, then he mentioned a mine of gold. Then a man from the family of the Prophet will appear, who will make everything right.

79. Abū Sa`īd al-Khudarī: The Messenger of God said: "There will be tribulations after me, among them the tribulation of the masses, in which there will be war and fleeing, then after it there will be tribulations worse that that—every time people

[73] `Umayr b. Hāni' al-`Absī, lived in Damascus and Dārayā, killed by al-Saqar b. Ḥabīb al-Murrī 127/744–5.

[74] Ibn al-Athīr, *Nihāya*, ii, p. 361 is unclear as to the meaning of the word *sarrā'* in this context.

[75] Compare the version in Abū Dā'ūd, *Sunan*, iv, p. 92 (no. 4242) (addition is from Abū Dā'ūd).

say it is cut off, it is extended until it has struck every Arab or Muslim house, until a man from my Family will emerge."

80. `Abdallāh b. Hubayra[76]: Three are four tribulations: the first is of perception, the second tribulation is of sectarianism, the third tribulation is blind, the fourth is the Dajjāl.

81. Ka`b: There will be tribulations, three, like your days of past: a tribulation in Syria, then east, the destruction of kings, then the west will follow it, and he mentioned the yellow flags—the western is the blind [tribulation].

82. Ka`b: "The mill of the Arabs will turn twenty-five [years] after the death of your Prophet,[77] then a dissension will develop—there will be killing and fighting in it—then you will return to security and calm until you will be in [a state of] constant stability, meaning Mu`āwiya, then tribulation will develop—there will be killing and fighting in it—I find it in the Book of God to be the dark-night one which bends everyone possessed of pride."

83. Ka`b said, when the mosque of Medina was being built: [31] "By God, I wish that not a tower of it would be built without a tower falling." It was said: "O Abū Isḥāq,[78] did you not say that prayer in it was better than 1000 prayers in any other mosque, other than that of Mecca?" He said: "I did say that, but it is a tribulation come down from the heavens—there is only a span between it happening. If they stopped building this mosque, that would not happen." This was at the killing of this elder, `Uthmān b. `Affān. So somebody said: "Isn't his killer just like the killer of `Umar?" But Ka`b said: "Nay, 100,000 or more [differences], then killing has become permissible between `Adan Abyan[79] and the Byzantine passes/roads. An army will issue from the west, and an army will issue from the east, then they will meet in battle at a place called Ṣiffīn. There

[76] `Abdallāh b. Hubayra al-Ḥaḍramī, lived in Baṣra, d. 126/743–4.

[77] 36/656, the year of `Uthman's assassination.

[78] Ka`b's patronymic.

[79] The southernmost section of Yemen.

will be an apocalyptic battle between them, then they will only be divided by two arbiters . . ." to the end of the tradition.

84. Ka`b came to Ṣiffīn and when he saw the stones on the face of the road, he stood and stared at them, so his companion said to him: "What are you staring at, O Abū Isḥāq?" He said: "I found its description in the books of the Israelites, who fought here nine times until they were annihilated. The Arabs will fight here a tenth time until they are annihilated; they will bombard each other with the same stones that the Israelites used."
85. Abū al-Jild: There will be a tribulation, after it another, the first with regard to the second is like the whip followed by the drawing of the sword, then there will be a tribulation in which the sanctities will be permitted. The community will gather to the best one of it, coming to him humbly, while he is sitting in his house.
86. `Alī: "Did I not tell you of the tribulation of separation?" It was said: "What is the tribulation of separation?" He said: "Even if a man was tied with ten cords among the people of wrong, he would be transferred to the people of right, and even if he was tied with ten cords among the people of right, he would be transferred to the people of wrong."
87. `Awf b. Mālik al-Ashja`ī: The Messenger of God said to me: "Hold on to six before the Hour, the first of which is the death of your Prophet." So I cried, "and the second is the conquest of Jerusalem, the third is a dissension that will enter each house of hair and clay, the fourth is two deaths among the people like a plague of flocks, the fifth is abundance among you so that a man would be given 100 dinars and he would hold it in contempt, and the sixth is a truce between you and the Byzantines (Banū al-Aṣfar)—then they will come to you with eighty flags, under each flag 12,000 [troops]." [32]
88. Ḥudhayfa: A man said to him: "The Dajjāl has emerged," but Ḥudhayfa said: "As long as there are Companions of Muḥammad among you, not, but by God, he will not emerge

until people want him to emerge. He will not appear until his emergence will be more desirable for some people than drinking cold water on a hot day. Verily, there will be for you, O community, four tribulations: the speckled, the dark-night, and such-and-such, and truly the fourth one will hand you over to the Dajjāl. Two bands will surely fight at this lowly area—I do not care which one of them shoots with the arrows of my quiver."

89. Ṭāwūs[80]: A man obstructed Abū Mūsā al-Asha`rī, and said: "Is this the tribulation you used to mention?"—which was when him and `Amr b. al-Āṣ had gone apart to arbitrate[81]—so Abū Mūsā said: "This is nothing but a zig-zag on the road to the tribulations. The overwhelming heaviness still remains, whoever stays aloft, it will keep him aloft. The one who sits in it is better than the one who rises, while the one who rises is better than the one who walks, when the one who walks is better than the one who hurries, and the one who is silent is better than the one who speaks, and the sleeper is better than the one who is awake." [33]

The Loss of Intelligence and Absence of People's Dreams during the Tribulations

90. Ḥudhayfa: The Messenger of God said: "There will be a tribulation in which the intelligence of men will be crippled until you would see an intelligent man" . . . and he mentioned this with regard to the third tribulation.
91. `Umayr b. Hāni': that the Messenger of God said: In the third tribulation, the darkened tribulation, a man will fight without knowing whether he is fighting for right or wrong.

[80] Ṭāwūs b. Kaysān al-Yamānī, a *mawlā* to Hamdān, d. 106 or approx. 110/724–5 or 728–9.

[81] After the inconclusion of the Battle of Ṣiffīn in 37/657 the result was to nominate two arbiters who would decide which of the two contenders, `Ali and Mu`āwiya, should be caliph.

92. Ḥudhayfa: "The tribulations will encircle[82] hearts"—al-Fazārī[83] said: *al-ḥaṣīr* [encircling] is a way—"which means that the heart that rejects [the tribulations] a white dot will be dotted on it, while the heart that drinks [the tribulations] in a black dot will be dotted on it, so that the heart will become two hearts." He took two pebbles, white and black, and said: "Hearts will become two hearts: a white heart like the stone: no tribulation will harm it as long as heavens and earth continue. But the other dust-colored dark [one], like a jug lying on the ground"—he said this while his hand was upside down—"he does not approve of good or reject evil,[84] but whatever his nature drinks in. Outside of that there is a locked door—this door is a man who is about to be killed or die." This is a tradition (*ḥadīth*) which does not have errors. [34]
93. Ḥudhayfa: The tribulation, when it is presented to hearts, whichever heart rejects it the first time, is dotted with a white dot, but whichever heart does not reject it is dotted with a black dot. Then there will be tribulation, which will present itself to the hearts, so that whoever rejects it the first time will get dotted with a white dot. If he does not reject it the first time he will get dotted with a black dot. Then there will be tribulation, which will present itself to the hearts, and whoever rejects it twice, will be dotted with a white dot, and then he continued describing this. No tribulation will ever harm him, but if he did not reject the tribulation the first two times then he will be dotted with a black dot, and his entire heart will be blackened and ash-colored. Then he is turned upside down, since he does not approve of the good, and reject the evil.

[82] Ibn al-Athīr, *Nihāya*, i, p. 395 on this tradition states that it is a band that encircles the body of a quadruped.

[83] Marwān b. Muʿāwiya al-Fazārī, lived in Mecca, then moved to Damascus, d. 193/808–9.

[84] Alluding to the basic doctrine of "commanding the right and forbidding the wrong"; cf. Q 3:110.

94. Abū Hārūn al-Madanī[85]: The Messenger of God said: "How will it be for you when you consider the good to be evil, and the evil to be good?" They said: "Will that happen, O Messenger of God?" He said: "Yes."

95. Abū Tha`laba al-Khushanī[86]: Among the portents of the Hour is that intelligence will decrease, wombs will be stopped up, and anxiety will increase.

96. Ibn `Umar: The Messenger of God said: Tribulations will overcome my community after me, in which the heart of a man will die just like his body.

97. Abū al-Zāhiriyya[87]: When tribulation bombards a group of people, even if there are prophets among them, they will be tempted, the intelligence of every intelligent person is yanked from him, from everyone who has perspicacity and understanding as well. They will continue as long as God wills, so when it seems good to God, He will return their intelligence, perspicacity and understanding to them so that they would be heartbroken about what they had done.

98. Abū Mūsā al-Ash`arī: The Messenger of God mentioned: "There will be killing (*haraj*) before the Hour, such that a man will kill his neighbor, his brother and his paternal cousin." They said: "In full possession of our faculties?" He said: "Most of the people of the time will have their intelligence yanked from them, leaving behind a blindness in the people, so that one will think that he did something, but he did not." **(1)** [35]

99. `Abdallāh b. Mas`ūd: I fear for you tribulations like they were smoke, in which the man's heart will die just as his body.

100. Abū Dharr `Abd al-Raḥmān b. Faḍāla[88]: When Cain killed

85 Mūsā b. Abī `Īsā al-Ḥannāṭ al-Ghifārī, lived in Medina, no death date given.

86 No agreement about his name, a Companion, lived in Dārayā, in the palace (*balāṭ*), d. 75/694–5.

87 Ḥudayr b. Kurayb al-Ḥaḍramī, lived in Ḥimṣ, d. 129/746–7.

88 Lived in Medina, a *mawlā*, d. approximately 165/781–2 (death-date of his brother).

Abel[89] God metamorphosed his intelligence, emptied his heart and he remained bewildered until he died.

101. Ḥudhayfa: It was said to him: "Which of the tribulations is the worst?" He replied: "When both good and evil are presented to your heart, but you do not know upon which of them to embark."
102. Ḥudhayfa: There will come a time upon the people when a man will wake up seeing, but turn in at night not be able to see his eyelashes.
103. Ibn Mas`ūd: These tribulations have overshadowed like the falling of black-night; every time messengers come from it, messengers go, with the heart of the man dying within it just as his body dies.
104. Abū Mūsā: O people, this is a divisive tribulation, in which the clement feels like he was born yesterday—it comes to you from a safe place like a sickness of the belly, without you knowing where it came from.
105. Abū Tha`laba al-Khushani: Rejoice in a wide world, which will consume your faith! Whoever of you is certain with regard to his Lord, a white enduring tribulation will come to him, but whoever is in doubt with regard to his Lord, a black dark-night tribulation will come to him. God does not care which of the valleys/directions he goes.
106. Kathīr b. Murra[90]: The Messenger of God said: Among the signs of the trial and the portents of the Hour are that intelligence will be distance, and dreams will be decreased, but anxiety will increase, and the signs of truth will be lifted, so that injustice appears. [36]
107. `Alī: During the fifth tribulation—the overshadowing blind deaf one—the people will become like cattle. **(1)**
108. Abū Hurayra: The Prophet said: [During] the fourth tribulation my community will be scraped like leather, with the trial

[89] Q 5:27–31.

[90] Kathīr b. Murra al-Ḥaḍramī, lived in Ḥimṣ to the time of `Abd al-Malik (685–705).

harsh upon it until good will not be known, and evil will not be forbidden.

109. Abū Hurayra: The Messenger of God said: Four tribulations will come upon you after me, but the fourth is the overshadowing deaf blind one in which the community will be scraped by the trial like leather, such that the good will be forbidden, but the evil will be approved, with your hearts dying during it just as your bodies die.

110. Ḥudhayfa b. al-Yamān: I wish that I had with me 100 men with hearts of gold, so I could climb a rock to tell them in a narration that the tribulation after it will never harm them, then I would go and never see them again.

111. Ḥudhayfa: Tribulation will be presented to the hearts, so whichever heart drinks of it, a black dot will be dotted on it, but whichever heart rejects it, a white dot will be dotted on it. Whoever would like to know whether the tribulation will strike him or not, let him consider: does he see permitted as forbidden, or forbidden as permitted? Then it has struck him. Ḥudhayfa said: A man will wake seeing but turn in at night not able to see his eyelashes.

112. Ka`b: When it is the year 160 [=776–7] dreams of dreamers and perspicacity will decrease.

113. Ḥudhayfa: In the tribulation, right and wrong will be in doubt, but whoever knows right will not be harmed by the tribulation.

114. Abū Mūsā al-Asha`rī: The Messenger of God mentioned: "Tribulation is before the Hour," so I said: "When the Book of God is yet in our midst?" He said: "When the Book of God is in your midst." I said: "When we have our intelligence?" He said: "When you still have your intelligence." [37]

115. Abū Mas`ūd al-Anṣārī[91] came to Ḥudhayfa b. al-Yamān and said: "Tell me of something that we can learn from after you." Ḥudhayfa said: "Error is truth, and error is when you approve

[91] `Uqba b. `Amr al-Anṣārī, Companion, d. either in al-Kūfa or Medina, 40, 41, or 42/660, 661, or 662.

what you should forbid, but forbid that which you should approve. So consider that in which you believe today, and hold fast to it, so that nothing will harm you later on."

116. Ḥudhayfa was asked: "Which of the tribulations are the worst?" He said: "Good and evil will be presented to your heart, but you will not know upon which to embark."
117. Ibrāhīm b. Abī `Abla[92]: It has reached me that the Hour will arise on people whose dreams are the dreams of birds.
118. `Alī: I will tell you of the types of jihad that predominate among you: There is the jihad with your hands, there is the jihad with your tongues, there is the jihad with your hearts, since whichever heart does not approve the good, and does not forbid the evil, its top becomes its bottom.
119. `Alī: When the heart does not approve the good, and forbid the evil, then it is inverted, its top becomes its bottom.
120. Abū Mas`ūd: What do you think of a heart that has been inverted?
121. `Abdallāh b. Busr[93] used to say: How will it be for you when you see twenty men or more together, without one of the fearing God Most High? [38]

Allowance for People's Desire to Die because of the Prevalence of Trials and Tribulations

122. Ibn `Umar: The Messenger of God said: The Hour will not arise until a man passes by a grave then says: "I wish that I were in place of the one inside!" because of the tribulations he has endured from the people.
123. Abū Hurayra: There will come upon you a time when a man will come across a tomb then lie down in it, saying: "Oh! would that I was in place of the one inside!" Not because of his

[92] Shimr b. Yaqẓān al-`Uqaylī, lived in Damascus, Ramla and finally in Jerusalem, d. 152 or 153/769 or 770.

[93] Correcting according to MM from `Abdallāh b. Bishr, `Abdallāh b. Busr al-Sakasakī, lived in Ḥimṣ, then in Baṣra, *fl.* 2nd/8th century.

desire to see God, but because of the intensity of the trial he is undergoing.

124. Abū Hurayra: The Messenger of God said: The Hour will not arise until a man passes by the tomb of his brother, then says: "I wish that I was in his place!"

125. Abū Hurayra: There will come upon the people a time when death is preferable during it than washing in cold water during a hot day, then not be able to die.

126. `Abdallāh: There will come upon the people a time when a man will come to a tomb, then roll over it like mounts roll over in the dust, wishing that he would be in the place of its owner—not because of desiring to see God, but because of the trial he is enduring. **(2)** [39]

127. Abū `Adhaba al-Ḥaḍramī[94]: If life is too much for you, a man from among you is about to go to the tomb of his brother, then rub himself on it, saying: "Oh! I wish that I was in his place!" You have been saved, you have been saved! So a young man from the people said: "Concerning what, O Abū `Adhaba?" He said: "You call to an enemy from one side, and while you are in that situation, you then call to another side and to another enemy, so when you are like that, when you are called to another enemy, you will not know to which enemy you should muster. On that day it will be like that." **(1)**

128. Ka`b: The sea is about to be too difficult for any boat to travel on it, while the land will be too difficult for anyone to be able to take refuge in a house.

129. `Abdallāh b. `Amr: There will come upon the people a time when a man will wish that he was in an overloaded open boat (*fulk*),[95] him and his family, being tossed around on the sea, because of the intense trial on the land.

130. `Abdallāh b. `Amr: Someone heard him say: There will come upon the people a time when a man with nobility, wealth and

[94] Probably `Amr b. Salīm al-Ḥaḍramī, lived in Ḥimṣ, *fl.* 1st/7th century.
[95] Cf. Q 10:73 (story of Noah's Ark).

children will wish for death because of the trial that he sees from their rulers.

131. Mu`adh b. Jabal: You will never see anything of this world other than trial and tribulation, and the matter will only get worse. You will never see anything other than rudeness in leaders (*a'imma*), and you will never see anything tempting to you without the disdain for it stronger afterwards. [40]
132. Abū Hurayra: Death is about to become preferable to the learned than red gold.[96]
133. `Umayr b. Isḥāq[97]: We used to discuss that the first thing which would be lifted from the people would be friendship.
134. Ibn Mas`ūd: I heard the Messenger of God mentioning the tribulation, so I said: When is that? He said: When a man cannot trust his companion.
135. Al-Ḥakam b. `Utayba[98]: A time will come upon the people which will not be pleasant for the wise man.
136. Mu`adh b. Jabal: When you see blood flowing without reason, wealth being given because of lying, and the appearance of doubt and mutual cursing, this is the apostasy, so whoever is able to die, let him die.
137. Abū Hurayra: A time is about to come upon the people in which death is preferable to the learned one than red gold.
138. `Abdallāh: The tribulation will have ebbs and flows, so whoever can die during its ebbs, let him. **(1)**
139. Ḥudhayfa: Its ebbs are when the sword is sheathed, its flows are when the sword is drawn.
140. Abū `Uthmān[99]: We were with `Abdallāh b. Mas`ūd sitting when some birdshit dropped on him, and so he took it with

[96] Considered to be the most valuable type of gold, e.g., Ghada Qaddumi (trans.), *Book of Gifts and Rarities* (Cambridge, MA: Harvard Center for Middle Eastern Studies, 1996), pp. 147, 243.

[97] `Umayr b. Isḥāq al-Qurashī, a *mawlā* of the Hashemites, no death date given, but *fl.* 1st/7th century.

[98] Al-Kindī, lived in Kūfa, a *mawlā*, d. 113, 114 or 115/731, 732, or 733.

[99] Probably Abū `Uthmān b. Sanna al-Khuzā`ī, lived in Syria, *fl.* 1st/7th century.

his finger and then said: "Truly, the death of my children and my wife is worse than this!" He [Abū `Uthmān] said: "By God, we did not used to know what he meant by that until the tribulation happened, and then we understood that was a warning about them." [41]

141. Abū al-Aḥwaṣ[100]: We entered in to Ibn Mas`ūd while his sons were with him, young men, like dinars by virtue of their handsomeness, and we began to admire their handsomeness, so `Abdallāh said: "I see that you are pleased with them?" We said: "By God, Muslim men are pleased with the likes of these!" So he lifted his head towards the low roof of his house, since a swallow had nested there after having laid an egg, and he said: "By the One who holds my soul in His hand, that I would have shaken the dust of their tombs off my hands is preferable to me than that the nest of this swallow would fall, breaking its egg." Ibn al-Mubārak[101] said: "In fear for them from the tribulations."
142. Ḥudhayfa b. al-Yamān: "How will it be for you during the tribulation of the best of people [will be] every wealthy, secretive person?" So Abū al-Ṭufayl said: "How indeed, when it is only the stipend of each of us that is thrown and tossed away?" Ḥudhayfa said: "Then, at that time, be like the son of a she-camel about to give birth, who has no teat from which to get milk, and no camel for riding on which to ride."
143. Al-Nu`mān b. Muqarrin[102]: The Messenger of God said: Worship during killing and tribulation is like performing emigration (*hijra*) to me.
144. Abdallāh b. `Amr: "The most preferable people to God are the strangers.' Someone said: 'Who are the strangers?" He said: "Those who flee with their religion, gathering [themselves] to Jesus son of Mary." [42]

[100] Ḥakīm b. `Umayr al-`Ansī, lived in Ḥimṣ, no death date, but *fl.* 1st/7th century.
[101] `Abdallāh b. al-Mubārak, one of the best-known of the jihadi-ascetics of the early `Abbāsid period, d. 181/797.
[102] Al-Nu`mān b. Muqarrin al-Muzanī, Companion, lived in Baṣra, d. 21/642.

The Regret of Some of the Prophet's Companions and Others with regard to the Tribulation

145. Abū Kināna[103]: al-Zubayr and his soldiers came upon us, while we were slave-soldiers (*mamlūk*) to [the tribe of] Rabī`a,[104] since our chiefs had joined `Alī, so we gathered together, and said: "It is possible that these [al-Zubayr] will force us to go out [to fight], but our chiefs will come with `Alī, so how can we fight them?" Then we said: "We will go out, but when we meet in battle, we will join them." Then some of us said: "We will not receive safe-conducts if we are not able to do this—so let us ask them, and so if they give us permission then we will go safely. But if not we will have to stay with our flag (side)." So we went to al-Zubayr b. al-`Awwām altogether and said to him: "On which side are the slaves (`*abīd*) [to fight]?" He said: "With their masters." We said: "But our masters are with `Alī." He said: It was as if we had silenced him, so we waited an hour, then he said: "This has warned us" [that they were considering desertion].
146. `Alī, when swords had had their way with the men, "I wish that I had died twenty years before this!"
147. Al-Ḥasan: `Alī wished that he had not done what he did, `Ammār[105] wished that he had not done what he did, Ṭalḥa wished that he had not done what he did, and al-Zubayr wished that he had not done what he did—the people of the End descended upon a group whose codices were entangled, and let the sword decide between them.
148. `Abdallāh b. `Umar: (but I did do not think that anybody was between him), I used to read this verse: "Surely you are mortal, and surely they are mortal, and surely in the Day of

[103] Mu`āwiya b. Qurra al-Muzanī, no death date given.
[104] A large tribal grouping, sometimes in opposition to Muḍar, eventually allying themselves with the Yemen, see *EI*[2] "Rabī`a" (H. Kindermann).
[105] Companion, devoted to `Ali, killed at the Battle of Ṣiffīn 37/657.

Resurrection you will dispute in the presence of your Lord,"[106] and I used to think that it was concerning the People of the Book, until some of us struck the faces of others with the sword, and then we knew that it was concerning us. [43]

149. Al-Ḥasan: concerning His Word, Most High, "Guard (yourselves) against trouble [*fitna*] which will smite not just the evildoers among you,"[107] he said: By God, people knew when it was revealed that it personified a group [in the tribulation].

150. Qays b. `Ubbād[108]: I said to `Alī, "Did the Messenger of God promise anything to you about this matter?" He said: "He did not promise anything to me that he did not promise to the people, but the people leapt upon `Uthmān to kill him, so they were worse in action and deed than me, so I believed that I had the better right to it. I seized it [power], so God knows best whether we sinned or not."

151. `Alī: He did not promise us the rulership that we would take it, but it was something I saw as right—if there is right in you, the it is from God, if there is wrong in you then it is from yourselves.

152. `Alī: Dissension struck us after Abū Bakr and `Umar, so it was what God willed.

153. Abū al-Ḍuḥā[109]: He mentioned on the authority of al-Ḥasan b. `Alī that he said to Sulaymān b. Ṣurad:[110] "You saw `Alī when the fighting was intense, when he hid himself against me, saying: 'O Ḥasan, I wish that I had died before this by twenty years!'"

154. Sulaymān b. Ṣurad: Ḥasan b. `Alī said to me: "I saw `Alī, when the swords were having their way with the men, cry for help

[106] Q 39:30–1.

[107] Q 8:25.

[108] Qays b. `Ubbād al-Qaysī al-Ḍuba`ī, lived in Baṣra, executed by al-Ḥajjāj (ruled Iraq 692–714).

[109] Muslim b. Ṣubayḥ al-Hamdānī, *mawlā*, lived in Kūfa, d. during the caliphate of `Umar b. `Abd al-`Aziz (717–20).

[110] A supporter of `Ali, fought at Ṣiffīn, killed 65/683: Ibn Ḥajar, *Isaba*, ii, pp. 75–6 (no. 3457).

to me, saying: 'O Ḥasan, I wish that I had died before this day by twenty years!'"

155. Ḥasan: The Commander of the Believers `Alī wanted something [the rule], then events followed, but he did not find a way out. [44]

156. Ḥasan: he heard `Alī saying when he looked towards the swords that had taken the people, "O Ḥasan, is this all because of us? I wish that I had died twenty or forty years before this!"

157. Masrūq[111]: When the people got entangled in the issue of `Uthmān, I went to `A'isha, and I said to her: "Be careful that they don't make you retract your view." She said: "How bad it is what you have said, my son! Because I would prefer to fall from the heavens to the earth, to something other than God's punishment, than to see the blood of a Muslim man. This is because I saw a vision, I saw as if I was on small hill, surrounded by flocks or cattle pasturing, when men burst in and began slaughtering them, until I did not hear any further bleating from them. So I began to descend from the hill, but I did not want to cross through the blood, lest some of it get on me, but I also did not want to lift my garments to reveal that which I did not want. While I was in that situation, two men or bulls came to me, and carried me until we had passed by this blood."

Ḥaṣīn—Abū Jamīla[112]: I saw on the Day [Battle] of the Camel, when they hamstrung her camel, `Ammār and Muḥammad b. Abī Bakr came and cut its saddle, then carried her in her palanquin until they were able to put her into the house of Abū Khalaf. I heard the people of the house (*dār*) weeping over a man who was struck [killed] that day. She said: "What are these?" They said: "They are supporting their leader." She said: "Get me out of here, get me out of here!"

[111] Probably Masrūq b. al-Ajdha` al-Hamadānī, lived in Kūfa, d. 63/682–3.

[112] .Maysara b. Ya`qūb al-Tuhawī, lived in Kūfa, was the standard-bearer for `Ali, *fl.* 1st/7th century.

158. `Ā'isha: She said that she was on a small hill, surrounded by flocks and cattle pasturing, and a man fell upon them. She told this to Abū Bakr, and he said: If your vision is truthful, a number of the people will be killed around you.

159. Jumay`[113]: I entered in to `A'isha with my mother, then my mother said to her: "What was [the purpose of] your journey on the Day of the Camel?" She said: "It was fate."

160. Abū Sa`īd al-Khudarī: that he was asked concerning Ṭalḥa and al-Zubayr, so Abū Sa`īd said: People who had precedence [in Islam], when the dissension struck them, so ask God about their issue.

161. Yazīd b. Abī Ḥabīb: The Messenger of God said: With regard to my Companions—meaning the dissension that was between them—God will forgive them because of their precedence in Islam. If people after them use them as an example, then God will throw them facedown into the Fire. [45]

162. `Alī: saying from the pulpit: The Messenger of God was first, then Abū Bakr prayed [as second], then `Umar as the third, but then tribulation trampled us, so whatever God wills.

163. Muḥammad b. Ḥāṭib[114]: It was said to `Alī: They will ask us concerning `Uthmān, so what should we say? He said: He was among those who believed and did righteous deeds, so then they were pious and believed, then they were pious and did well, and God loves those who do well.

164. Ibrāhīm al-Taymī[115]: The Prophet said to his wives: Which one of you will the dogs of al-Ḥaw'āb[116] bark for? When `A'isha passed the dogs barked, so she asked about it, and it was said: This is the oasis of al-Ḥaw'āb, [so] she said: I think that I should go. It was said to her: O Mother of the Believers, only you can make it right between the people.

[113] Jumay` b. `Umar al-`Ijlī, lived in Kūfa, *fl.* 1st/7th century.

[114] Muḥammad b. Ḥāṭib al-Qurashī al-Jumaḥī, a Companion, lived in Kūfa, d. 74/693–4.

[115] Probably Ibrāhīm b. Sālim al-Taymī, a *mawlā*, d. 153/770.

[116] An oasis on the road to Baṣra.

165. Ṭāwūs: The Messenger of God said to his wives: "Which of you is the one for whom the dogs of such-and-such an oasis will bark? [This is a] warning to you, little red one (*ḥumayra'*)," meaning `A'isha.[117]

166. Ibn Mas`ūd and Ḥudhayfa were sitting when they brought a woman by on a camel which voided itself of excrement, so one of them said to his companion: Is she the one? The other one said: No, it will be around this brilliant one, meaning `A'isha.

167. Qays b. `Ubbād said to `Alī: "This rule was something that the Messenger of God confided in you, or was it something that you saw fit to do?" So he said: "What do you mean by that?" He said: "Is it our religion, our religion?" So he said: "It is only something that I saw fit to do."

168. Ḥudhayfa b. al-Yamān: "If I related to you that your Mother [`A'isha] would raid you, would you believe me?" They said: "Is that really true?" He said: "True."

169. Al-Zubayr b. al-`Awwām[118]: This verse, "Guard (yourselves) against trouble [*fitna*] which will smite not just the evildoers among you," [Q 8:25] [46] on that day we were abundant (in numbers), so we were amazed at this tribulation, so we said: "This tribulation that is striking us, it is nothing other than what we saw" [from the verse].

170. `Alī: I hope that `Uthmān and I will be among those concerning whom God Most High said: "We shall strip away whatsoever rancor is in their hearts. (As) brothers (they will recline) on couches, facing each other."[119]

171. Ka`b: I heard the Messenger of God mention tribulation, and that it was near. Then he passed by `Uthmān b. `Affān, and said: "On that day this one will be guided." I rose to him and took his upper arm, turned his face to the Messenger of God, and uncovered his hair, since he was veiled by his

[117] The Prophet's nickname for `A'isha.

[118] Companion, one of the ten promised paradise, aided in the conquest of Egypt, killed at the Battle of the Camel in 36/657.

[119] Q 15:47.

garment, and said: "O Messenger of God, this one?" He said: "This one," it was `Uthmān b. `Affān.

172. Sahl b. Ḥunayf[120] said at Ṣiffīn: O people, suspect your own opinions, because by God, I saw myself on the Day of Abū Jandal,[121] and if I had been able to argue against the issue of the Messenger of God, I would have done so. By God, we have never put our swords on our shoulders going to a matter without it easing us into something that we knew, other than this matter (Islam). Al-A`mash: Shaqīq,[122] when someone would ask him: "Did you fight at Ṣiffīn?" he would say: "Yes, and what a terrible number of lines [of battle] that was!"[123]

173. `Alī that he said on the Day of the Camel, the Messenger of God did not promise us anything that we would take with regard to the rulership, but something that we saw from our souls—if it will be correct, then it is from God, if it will be wrong, then it is from our souls. He placed Abū Bakr as caliph, and he was upstanding, then he placed `Umar as caliph, and he was upstanding, until the religion [Islam] became established. Then people sought this world—may God pardon those who He wishes, and punish those who He wishes.

174. Abu Wā'il[124]: I heard `Ammār on this pulpit saying: `A'isha is the wife of your Prophet in this world and the next, but it [the battle] is a trial by which you will be tested. [47]

175. Sahl b. Ḥunayf rose at Ṣiffīn saying: O people, blame your souls, for we were with the Messenger of God on the Day of Ḥudaybiyya, and if we had thought war, we would have fought

[120] Companion, lived in Kūfa, d. 38/658–9.

[121] At the negotiation of the truce of Ḥudaybiyya (6/628), the fugitive Abū Jandal, who had converted to Islam, appeared from Mecca to join the Muslims, but was forcibly returned in accordance with the terms of the treaty, an event that angered a number of Muslims at the time.

[122] One of the people in the chain of transmitters.

[123] A pun on Ṣiffīn, sounding like "battle-lines", *ṣaffūn*.

[124] Shaqīq b. Salama al-Asadī, lived in Kūfa, d. after the Battle of the Jamājim in approximately 82/701.

concerning the truce (*ṣulḥ*) that the Messenger of God made with the polytheists.

176. Ḥudhayfa b. al-Yamān: The Messenger of God said: People will come down to the Pool[125] until when I know them and they know me, they will move away from me. then I will say: "O Lord, my Companions, my Companions!" But He will say: "You do not know what they innovated after you."

177. Al-Zuhrī: Tribulation was stirred when the Companions of the Messenger of God were abundant.

178. `Ā'isha: I entered in to the Messenger of God, while `Uthmān was before him, whispering to him, so I did not catch what they were saying, other than a phrase of `Uthmān, "injustice and aggression, injustice and aggression, O Messenger of God?" So I did not know what the meaning of that was until `Uthmān was killed, so then I knew that the Prophet had only meant his killing. `A'isha said: Every time I wanted to give `Uthmān something, he would always give me something similar, but God knows that I did not desire him to be killed—if I had desired to kill him, I would have killed him. That was when her palanquin was shot full of arrows so that it looked like a hedgehog.

179. Ibn `Abbās: I entered in to `Ā'isha, so I said: "Peace be upon you, O Mother [of the Believers]." She said: "And on you, my son." I said: "What made you want to go out with the hypocrites of Quraysh against us?"[126] She said: "That was just fate."

180. `Alī: I hope that Ṭalḥa and al-Zubayr and I are among those concerning whom God Most High said: "(As) brothers (they will recline) on couches, facing each other."[127]

181. Junayd b. al-Sawdā'[128] rose to [confront] `Alī, and said: "God is more just than this," so `Alī shouted at him such a shout that

[125] The Pool of Muḥammad is an eschatological locus for purification: Wensinck, *Concordance*, s.v. *ḥawḍ*.

[126] Ibn `Abbās fought on the side of `Ali at the Battle of the Camel.

[127] Q 15:47.

[128] Unidentified.

I thought the castle shuddered, "If we aren't them, then who are they?"[129]

182. Sulaymān b. Ṣurad: A little rumor[130] of something reached me concerning the Commander of the Believers `Alī [48], involving cursing and [threats of] exile, that had me worked up, so I traveled to him swiftly, and came to him just as he had lifted his hand from [the Battle of] the Camel, so I met al-Ḥasan b. `Alī, so I said: "A little rumor of something reached me concerning the Commander of the Believers, involving cursing and [threats of] exile, that had me worked up, so I traveled to him swiftly, and came to him to apologize to him or to clean my name before him," so he said: "O Sulaymān, by God the Commander of the Believers was more reluctant about this than any [other] blood spilled [lit. irrigated]—the Commander of the Believers desired the rule, but matters followed closely, and he did not find a way out. I will take care of you for the Commander of the Believers."

183. Sulaymān b. Ṣurad: I came to `Alī when he had finished with [the Battle of] the Camel, so when he saw me, he said: O son of Ṣurd, I have been remiss, removed and standing aside, so what do you think of what God has done? I said: "O Commander of the Believers, 'the race was to the limit,'[131] but God prolonged the issue as long as this so that you would know your enemy from your friend." When he rose, I said to al-Ḥasan b. `Alī: "I do not think that you have any need of me"—since I was eager to be a martyr with him—but he said: He said to you, "What would you say, when he said to me on the Day of the Camel, when the people went one against the other, O Ḥasan, may your mother be bereaved of you, or may you die before your mother, by God I do not look for any good to happen after this!"

[129] Meaning the "brothers" of the verse in no. 180.

[130] Ibn al-Athīr, *Nihāya*, ii, p. 159 gives this meaning.

[131] Abū Hilāl al-`Askarī, *Jamharat al-amthāl* (Beirut: Dār al-Fikr, 1988), i, pp. 554–5 (no. 1019) citing this tradition.

184. `Alī: If `Uthmān would have exiled me to Ṣirār,[132] I would have heard and obeyed.

185. `Awf b. Mālik al-Ashja`ī: The Messenger of God lifted a piece of gold chain as a remnant remaining from the spoils (*fay'*) at the end of his stick, then it fell, so he lifted it while he was saying: "How will it be on a day when there is a great deal of this?" No one answered him, then a man from the Companions of the Messenger of God said: "By God, we wish that God would make more abundant than that, so let endure he who endures, and let be tempted he who will be tempted." The Messenger of God said: "Perhaps you will be an evil, tempted, in it" [the time of abundance]. [49]

186. The daughter of Uhbān al-Ghifārī[133]: `Alī came to Uhbān, and said: "What prevented you from following us?"[134] He said: "My friend and paternal cousin, the Messenger of God, confided in me that there would be sects, tribulation and disagreement, so when that happens, break your sword, and sit in your house, and take up a sword of wood."

187. Abū Janāb[135]: I saw Ṭalḥa while he was saying: "I fought [the Battle of] Jamājim,[136] but I did not thrust with a spear or strike with a sword, so I wish that they," meaning his hands, "had been cut off from here, rather than I fought in it" [the Battle of the Camel].

188. Qays b. `Ubbād: We said to `Ammār [b. Yāsir]: "Do you think that this battle of yours is the wisest thing, since opinion is sometimes wrong or right, or a responsibility/covenant that the Messenger of God took from you?" He said: "The Messenger of God did not promise us anything that he did not promise to all people." [50]

[132] An oasis not far away from Medina on the road to Iraq.

[133] `Udaysa bint Uhban b. Ṣayfī, no death date given.

[134] The allusion is to Moses' saying to Aaron at the time of the golden calf, Q 20:92.

[135] Yaḥyā b. Abī Ḥayya al-Kalbī, lived in Kūfa, d. 147 or 150/764 or 767.

[136] A monastery close to the Euphrates where several major battles were fought, al-Bakri, *Mu`jam ma sta`jama* (Beirut: `Ālam al-Kutub, 1983), i, p. 573.

The Desirability of having Few Possessions and Children during the Tribulations

189. Abū al-Muhallab[137] and Abū `Uthmān[138]: The Messenger of God said: Whoever acquires camels at this time, or stores a treasure or a plot of land, fearing the troubled times, he will meet God on the Day of Resurrection disappointed, as a traitor.
190. Abū Hurayra: The Prophet said: A saddled she-camel on that day is better than a village (*daskara*) that yields 100,000 [dirhams].
191. `Abdallāh: The best wealth on that day is a good weapon and a good horse, upon which the servant [of God] can disappear wherever he wants.
192. Abū Sa`īd al-Khudarī: The Prophet said: The best type of wealth for the Muslim man is about to be flocks, which he can follow through the mountain peaks and rainy places, fleeing with his religion from the tribulations.
193. Ibn `Umar: The Prophet said: The most felicitous of the people during the tribulations is the master of sheep, on the top of a mountain, withdrawn from the evil of the people.
194. Ṭāwūs: The Messenger of God said: The best of people during the tribulations is a man who takes the head of his horse, frightening the enemy, as they frighten him, or a man who withdraws giving God his due. Ma`mar[139] said: Ibn Khuthaym[140] related to me that the Messenger of God said: The best of people during the tribulations is a man who eats from the spoils [conquered] by his sword in the path of God, and a man on the top of a lofty mountain, eating from the milk of his flocks. [51]
195. Sahl b. Ḥunayf: O people, suspect your own opinions, for by God we have never seized the supports (legs) of a matter that could separate us without it easing us into something that we

137 Probably Muṭṭariḥ b. Yazīd al-Asadī al-Kinānī, lived in Syria, *fl.* 2nd/8th century.
138 Probably the same as in no. 140.
139 His son.
140 `Abdallāh b. `Uthmān b. Khuthaym, a *ḥalīf*, lived in Mecca, d. 132/749–50.

knew (affirmed), other than this matter (Islam), since it will only get worse and more confusing. For I saw myself on the Day of Abū Jandal—if I could have found helpers against the Messenger of God, I would have rejected [the peace].

196. Al-Ḥasan: The Messenger of God said: By One who holds my soul in His hand, people who were my Companions will be raised before me on the Day of Resurrection, so that when I see them and know them, so they will be ashamed in front of me. Then I will say: Oh, Lord, my Companions, my Companions!! So He will say: You do not know what they innovated after you.

197. Arṭāt: The Sufyānī will kill all who disobey him, sawing at them with saws, and cooking them in pots for six months. He said: Then the easterners and westerners will meet [in battle]. [52]

The Number of the Caliphs after the Messenger of God in this Community

198. `Abdallāh b. Mas`ūd: The Messenger of God said: The number of caliphs after me will be the number of Moses' deputies (*nuqaba'*).[141]

199. Jābir b. Samura[142]: The Messenger of God said: This rule, glorious, will not disappear until there are twelve caliphs, all of them from Quraysh.

200. Abū al-Ṭufayl[143] said: `Abdallāh b. `Amr took my hand, and said "O `Āmir b. Wāthila, there will be twelve caliphs from Ka`b b. Lu'ayy [Quraysh], then breaking open and cracking

[141] See Uri Rubin, "Apocalypse and Authority in Islamic Tradition: The Emergence of the Twelve Leaders," *al-Qantara* 18 (1997), pp. 11–41 on this tradition.

[142] Jābir b. Samura, nephew of Sa`d b. Abī Waqqāṣ, lived in Kūfa, 74 or 76/693–4 or 695–6.

[143] `Āmir b. Wāthila al-Laythī, Companion, said to have been the last Companion to die, d. 100 or 108/718–19 or 726–7. He was the one who stood by while `Uthmān was murdered according to Ibn Bakkār, *al-Akhbār al-Muwaffaqiyyāt* (Beirut: `Ālam al-Kutub, 1996), pp. 154–5.

eggs.[144] The people will never agree on the matter of an imam until the Hour will arise."

201. `Abdallāh b. `Umar said, when a group of us, from Quraysh, all from Ka`b b. Lu'ayy, were with him: "There will be twelve caliphs from you, O Banū Ka`b."
202. Ibn `Abbās: They mentioned twelve caliphs around him and then the Commander, so Ibn `Abbās said: By God, after that, from our family there will be the Generous One (al-Saffāḥ),[145] the One Made Victorious (al-Manṣūr) and the Guided One (al-Mahdi), who will give it [the rule] over to Jesus son of Mary.
203. Ḥudhayfa b. al-Yamān: [53] After `Uthmān there will be twelve kings from the Umayyads; it was said to him: Caliphs? He said: No, kings.
204. Sarj al-Yarmūkī[146]: I find in the Torah that this community will have twelve lords, one of them their Prophet. When the number has been completed, they will become tyrannical and commit wrong, so then their might will fall among them [in fighting].
205. Ka`b: God Most High gave to Ishmael from his loins twelve righteous leaders, the best of them was Abū Bakr, `Umar and `Uthmān.
206. Reliable elders: Yashū` asked Ka`b concerning the number of kings for this community, so he said: In the Torah there are twelve lords. [54]

144 These terms, *naqf* and *niqāf* may be codes for *qatl* and *qitāl*, killing and fighting.

145 Al-Saffāḥ also means Blood-shedder, but it is difficult to believe that the first of the `Abbāsids would have taken this as his regnal title (see Lewis, "The Regnal Titles of the first `Abbasid Caliphs," in *Dr. M. Zakir Husayn Presentation Volume* [New Delhi: Matba` Jami`a, 1968], pp. 13–22). Alternatively, because of the purification of the Umayyads al-Saffāḥ could have benefitted from the dual meaning of his title (note the al-Saffāḥ b. Maṭar al-Taghlibī, al-Mizzī, *Tahdhīb*, iii, p. 231 [no. 2379] who probably dates from before the official name), see no. 1033 (if the name was universally understood then there would be no need for such "clarifying" traditions).

146 Perhaps originally a Christian, Sergius? Listed as Sarḥ al-Yarmūkī, Ibn `Asākir, *Tā'rīkh*, xx, p. 162 (tradition cited).

The Caliphs who were mentioned after the Messenger of God

207. Abū `Ubayda b. al-Jarrāḥ[147]: The Messenger of God said: The first of this community is prophecy and blessing, then caliphate and blessing, then biting kingship. One of them said: Biting, but in it is blessing, then bald tyranny (*jabrūt*), in which no one has any attachment, in which necks will be struck off, and hands and feet will be cut off, and in which wealth will be seized.
208. Ḥudhayfa b. al-Yamān: The Messenger of God said: This rule will begin with prophecy and blessing, then there will be caliphate and blessing, then biting kingship, in which they will drink wines, wear silk, and abuse women—they will be victorious and take sustenance until the rule of God comes.
209. Abū `Ubayda b. al-Jarrāḥ: The Messenger of God said: The first of this community is prophecy and blessing, then caliphate and blessing, then biting kingship, then it will become tyranny and pointlessness.
210. `Umar b. al-Khaṭṭāb: God began this rule on the day He began it as prophecy and blessing, then it returned to caliphate and blessing, then rulership (*sulṭān*) and blessing, then kingship and blessing, it will return to caliphate and blessing, then rulership and blessing, then kingship and blessing, then bald tyranny, in which you will bite one another like donkeys. [55]
211. Yaḥyā b. Abī `Amr al-Saybānī[148]: I heard Ka`b saying: The first of this community is prophecy and blessing, then caliphate and blessing, then rulership and blessing, then kingship tyranny, so when it is like that, the interior of the earth is better than its exterior.

[147] `Āmir b. `Abdallāh b. al-Jarrāḥ, Companion, one of the ten promised paradise, participated in the conquest of Syria, d. 18/639.

[148] Yaḥyā b. Abī `Amr al-Saybānī [correcting the name according to MM and al-Mizzī, *Tahdhīb*, viii, p. 74 [no. 7488]), lived in Ḥimṣ, "participated in the raid on Constantinople together with Maslama b. `Abd al-Malik," d. 145 or after 150/762 or after 767.

212. Ka`b: There will continually be a caliph who will unify them and an emirate existing for this community, which will dispense daily sustenance and [receive] the head-tax (*jizya*) until Jesus son of Mary, is sent, then he will unify them and break the emirate.

213. Abū `Ubayda and Bashīr b. Sa`d Abū al-Nu`mān[149] both mentioned, and said: There will be prophecy and blessing, then caliphate and blessing, then biting kingship and tyranny, corruption, abuse of women, drinking of wine, and wearing of silk—in spite of that they will be victorious and receive sustenance. [56]

Distinguishing the Caliphs from the Kings

214. An elder of the Banū Asad[150] in the land of the Byzantines—a man from his tribe who saw `Umar b. al-Khaṭṭāb, who asked his Companions, when Ṭalḥa, al-Zubayr, Salmān [al-Fārisī],[151] and Ka`b were among them, he said: "I will ask you concerning something, and a warning to you if you lie to me, for you will perish and cause me to perish, I implore you by God, what have you found in your books—am I a caliph or a king?" Ṭalḥa and al-Zubayr said: "You are asking us something that we do not know; we do not know what is a caliph, but you are not a king." So `Umar said: "If you say that, then you used to go and sit together with the Messenger of God!"

Then Salmān said: "It is that you deal justly with the subjects (*ra`ya*), and divide fairly between them, and are concerned about them like a man is concerned about his family." And Muḥammad b. Yazīd[152] said: "And you judge by the Book of God," whereupon Ka`b said: "I do not think that there is

149 Bashīr b. Sa`d [correcting from Sa`īd, al-Mizzī, *Tahdhīb*, i, p. 361 [no. 706]) al-Khazrajī, Companion, d. 13/634–5.

150 A northern Arab tribe.

151 Prototypical first Persian convert, saying to have been from Isfahan or Ramhurmuz, Companion, lived in Iraq, close to `Ali, d. 33 or 37/653–4 or 657–8.

152 One of Nu`aym's informants interjecting himself into the tradition.

anyone in this sitting who knows a caliph from a king other than me, but God has filled Salmān with wisdom and knowledge." Then Ka`b said: "I testify that you are a caliph, and not a king." `Umar said to him: "How is that?" He said: "I find you in the Book of God." `Umar said: You find me by my name? Ka`b said: "No, but by your description. I find prophecy, then caliphate and blessing," and Muḥammad b. Yazīd said: "caliphate after the manner of prophecy, then biting kingship." Hushaym[153] said: "Tyranny, and biting kingship." `Umar said: "I do not care since that is passing me by."

215. Ka`b: `Umar b. al-Khaṭṭāb said: "I implore you by God, O Ka`b, do you find me to be a caliph or a king?" He said: "Nay, a caliph, and one appointed," so then Ka`b said: "A caliph, and by God, the best of the caliphs, and your time the best of times."

216. Mughīth al-Awzā`ī[154]: `Umar b. al-Khaṭṭāb sent for Ka`b, then said [57] to him: "O Ka`b, what do you find as my description?" He said: "A caliph, a horn of iron—you do not fear before God the blame of anyone, then a caliph who his community will kill him wrongfully, then the trial will occur afterwards."

217. Sa`īd b. al-Musayyib[155]: "There are three caliphs, and the rest of them are kings, Abū Bakr, `Umar and `Umar." It was said to him: "We know Abū Bakr and `Umar, but who is the second `Umar?" He said: "If you live long enough, you will see him, and the finale is after [that for] you."

218. Elders: Whoever commands the good and forbids the evil is a caliph of God on the earth,[156] and the caliph of His Book, and of His Messenger.

[153] Hushay, b. Bashīr al-Sulamī, lived in al-Wāsiṭ, but originally from Bukhārā, d. 183/799 in Baghdād.

[154] Mughīth b. Sumayy al-Awzā`ī, lived in Syria, *fl.* 1st/7th century.

[155] Sa`īd b. al-Musayyib al-Qurashi, lived in Medina, one of the most important figures in jurisprudence, d. 93 or 94/711–12 or 712–3.

[156] Q 2:30, referring to Adam; 38:26, referring to David.

219. Abū Muḥammad al-Nahdī[157]: There will never be a king among the descendants of the Prophet.

220. Hammām[158]: A man from the People of the Book came to `Umar b. Khaṭṭāb and said: "Peace be upon you, O king of the Arabs." So `Umar said: "Is that the way you find me in your book? Don't you find the Prophet, then the caliphs, then the Commander of the Believers, and then the kings afterwards?" He said: "Yes, yes."

221. Abū Hurayra: Caliphate is in Medina, but kingship is in Syria.

222. Safīna the *mawlā* of the Messenger of God[159]: The Messenger of God said: "Caliphate after me among my community is for thirty years." Muḥammad b. Yazīd said concerning his tradition: "So they calculated that, and it came to the end of the rule of `Alī," then they said to Safīna: "They are claiming that `Alī was not a caliph." He said: "Who is claiming that? Are the Sons of the Blue-eyed Woman[160] more worthy and right?" [58]

223. Yaḥyā b. Abī `Amr al-Saybānī: Anyone who does not rule the two mosques, the Sacred Mosque (Mecca) and the Mosque of Jerusalem is not a caliph.

224. Ṣabbāḥ[161]: There is no caliphate after the carrying of the Umayyads until the Mahdi appears.

225. `Utba b. Ghazwān al-Sulami[162]: There has never been prophecy without it degenerating into kingship.

226. Ḥudhayfa b. al-Yamān: "Truly there will be after `Uthmān twelve kings from the Umayyads." It was said to him: "Caliphs?" He said: "No! Kings."

157 Unidentified.

158 Probably Hammām b. Munabbih, brother of Wahb (see no. 1426), author of one of the earliest collections to come down (*Ṣaḥīfat Hammām b. Munabbih*), from the descendents of the Persians in Yemen), d. 131/748–9.

159 A slave to Umm Salama, wife of Muḥammad, who freed him, *fl.* 1st/7th century.

160 The Umayyads.

161 Probably Ṣabbāḥ b. Muḥārib al-Taymi, who lived in one of the villages close to al-Rayy, *fl.* 2nd/8th century.

162 Probably (in al-Mizzī, v, p. 97 said to be al-Māzinī) Companion, d. 15 or 20/636 or 641.

227. `Utba b. Ghazwān al-Sulami, who was a Companion of the Messenger of God, said: There has never been prophecy ever without after it being kingship.

228. Sa`īd b. al-Musayyib: "The caliphs are three, the rest of them are kings." It was said: "Who are those three?" He said: "Abū Bakr, `Umar and `Umar." It was said to him: "We know Abū Bakr and `Umar, but who is the second `Umar?" He said: "If you live long enough, you will see him, and the finale is after [that for] you."

229. `Ā'isha, she said: "O Messenger of God, what will be the rule after you?" He said: "Among your people [= family] as long as there is good among you." I said: "Which of the Arabs will be destroyed the fastest?" He said: "Your people." I said: "How will that be?" He said: "Death will be pleasing to them, so the people will smite them." [59]

Naming those reigning after the Messenger of God

230. Safīna the *mawlā* of the Messenger of God: When the Messenger of God built the mosque of Medina, Abū Bakr brought a stone, and placed it, then `Umar brought a stone and placed it, then `Uthmān brought a stone and placed it, so the Messenger of God said: These will be in charge of the caliphate after me.

231. `A'isha: When the Messenger of God founded the mosque of Medina, Abū Bakr brought a stone and placed it, then `Umar brought a stone and placed it, then `Uthmān brought a stone and placed it, so the Messenger of God said: These will be in charge of the caliphate after me.

232. A man of the Banū al-Muṣṭaliq: My tribe, the Banū al-Muṣṭaliq,[163] sent me to the Messenger of God, so I could ask him to whom should we give our charity tax (*ṣadaqāt*) after him, so I came to him, but `Alī b. Abī Ṭālib met me, so he asked me [why I had come]. I said: "My tribe, the Banū al-Muṣṭaliq, have sent me

[163] Part of the Khuzā`a confederation, raided by the Prophet, 6/627–8.

to the Messenger of God to ask him to whom should they pay their charity tax after him," so `Alī said: "Ask him, then come to me to tell me." So I went to the Messenger of God, to tell him that my tribe had sent me[164] to ask him to whom should they pay their charity tax after him? So he said: "Pay it to Abū Bakr," so I went back to `Alī and informed him, so `Alī said: "Go back to him to ask him to whom should they pay it after Abū Bakr?" So I asked him, and he said: "Pay it to `Umar after him." So I came to `Alī, and informed him, but he said: Go back to him to ask him to whom they should pay it after `Umar? So I went to him and asked him, and he said: "Pay it to `Uthmān b. `Affān," so I returned to `Alī and informed him. `Alī said: "Go back to him to ask him to whom should they pay it after `Uthmān" but the man said: "I was too embarrassed to return to the Messenger of God after that."[165] [60]

233. `Amr b. Labīd[166]: The Messenger of God purchased a cow from a Bedouin at a loan on credit to him, so the Bedouin turned back, then met `Alī b. Abī Talib, and so `Alī said to the Bedouin: "If God takes His Messenger, who owes you?" So the Bedouin returned to the Messenger of God and said: "Who do I go to for my due if death comes upon you?" He said: "Abū Bakr al-Ṣiddīq will give you your due." So the Bedouin turned around, but `Alī met him again, and said: "Who did the Messenger of God say to you?" He said: "My due is with Abū Bakr al-Ṣiddīq." He said: "But if Abū Bakr dies?" So the Bedouin returned and said: "O Messenger of God, if Abū Bakr dies, who do I go to for my due?" He said: "To `Umar b. al-Khaṭṭāb," so the Bedouin turned around, but `Alī met him, and said: "Who did the Messenger of

164 The narrator has changed tenses here, but I am keeping the original first person for the sake of continuity.

165 Paralleling the repeat negotiation concerning the number of prayers, where Moses urges Muḥammad to ask God to lower the number of mandatory prayers for the Muslims during the Night Journey and Ascension to Heaven.

166 Unidentified, but relating to `Abd al-Malik b. Abī Karīma, who lived in the Maghrib, and moved to Egypt in 180/796.

God say to you?" He said: "My due is with `Umar." He said: "But if `Umar dies?" He said: "You are right!" so he returned, and said: "O Messenger of God, if `Umar should die, then who has it?" He said: "Your due is with `Uthmān," so the Bedouin turned around, but `Alī met him and said: "What did the Messenger of God say to you?" He said: "My due is with `Uthmān," but he said: "And if `Uthmān dies?" So he returned to the Prophet and said: "And if `Uthmān dies, O Messenger of God, to whom is my due?" He said: "To the one who sent you."

234. Jābir b. `Abdallāh[167]: A righteous man this evening saw as if Abū Bakr was attached to the Messenger of God, then `Umar to Abū Bakr, then `Uthmān to `Umar. Jābir said: When we arose, we said: The righteous man is the Messenger of God, and these are those in authority after him.

235. `Abdallāh b. `Amr: Abū Bakr al-Ṣiddīq, his name is exact. `Umar al-Fārūq, is an iron horn, his name is exact. Ibn `Affān Dhū al-Nūrayn (Possessor of the Two Lights),[168] who was killed unjustly, was given two portions of mercy, [then] the King of the Holy Land (*malik al-arḍ al-muqaddasa*) Mu`āwiya and his son [Yazīd].[169] They said: What! Are you not mentioning al-Ḥasan and al-Ḥusayn? But he repeated what he had said, until when he reached Mu`āwiya and his son, he added in al-Saffāḥ, al-Salām, al-Manṣūr, Jābir, al-Amīn, and the Commander of the Bands (*amīr al-`uṣab*), all of them without peer, and all of them from Banū Ka`b b. Lu'ayy, among them is a man from Qaḥṭān, and among them there is one who will only last two days. Among them is one to whom people will say: "Allow us to swear allegiance (*ba`ya*) to you or we will

[167] Jābir b. `Abdallāh al-Sulamī, Companion, lived in Medina, d. 72, 73 or 77/691, 692–3, 696–7.

[168] Because he married two of the Prophet Muḥammad's daughters, Ruqayya and Umm Kulthūm.

[169] It is fairly rare to find a Muslim text speaking favorably of Yazīd I, under whose rule the Prophet's grandson, al-Ḥusayn, was killed at Karbalā' in Iraq.

surely kill you," so when he did not allow them to swear they killed him. [63][170]

236. `Abdallāh b. `Amr b. al-`Āṣ: I found in some of the books on the day we raided the Battle of the Yarmūk [River][171] Abū Bakr al-Ṣiddīq, his name is exact, `Umar al-Fārūq an iron horn, his name is exact, `Uthmān Dhū al-Nūrayn, given two portions of mercy, killed unjustly, his name is exact. Then there will be al-Saffāḥ, then al-Manṣūr, then al-Mahdi, then al-Amīn, then Sīn and Salām, meaning righteous and clement, then the Commander of the Bands[172]—six of them from the descendants of Ka`b b. Lu'ayy and a man from Qaḥṭān, all of them righteous, without peer. Abū al-Jild said: Kings will be over the people because of their actions. **(2)** [64]

237. Unidentified: The Messenger of God said: `Umar and `Umar will rule you, and Yazīd and Yazīd, and al-Walīd and al-Walīd, and Marwān and Marwān, and Muḥammad and Muḥammad.

238. Ḥasan b. `Alī[173]: I heard the Messenger of God saying: There will not be many days and nights until the rule of this community will gathered under a man with a wide anus (buttocks), a gigantic gullet, eating without being satisfied, whose name is *m`wy* [Mu`āwiya].

239. Hilāl b. Yasāf[174]: The mail-post which Mu`āwiya sent to the Byzantine Emperor (*ṣāḥib al-*rūm) in order to find out who would be caliph after `Uthmān told me that the Byzantine Emperor called for a codex, to look in it, and said: "The caliph after him is Mu`āwiya, your master, who sent you."

240. Abū Ṣāliḥ: Mu`āwiya used to ride together with `Uthmān, so the camel-driver began to say: "The Commander after him is `Alī, and in al-Zubayr there is a satisfactory descendant."

170 Section break pp. 61–2.

171 In 15/636, the decisive battle in which the Byzantines were defeated in Syria.

172 Reading *amīr al-`uṣab* as in no. 235, together with the DKI and MM.

173 Grandson of Muḥammad, son of `Ali, according to Shi`ites, 2nd Imam, lived in Medina, d. 50/670.

174 Hilāl b. Yasāf al-Ashja`ī, *mawlā*, lived in Kūfa, *fl.* 2nd/8th century.

Ka`b said: While Mu`āwiya would ride to the side of the procession on a gray-colored donkey. Ka`b would say: "The commander after him [`Uthmān] is the one with the gray-colored donkey."

241. `Abdallāh b. `Amr: After the tyrants (*al-jabbārīn*) there will be al-Jābir, by whom God will compel the community of Muḥammad, then al-Mahdi, then al-Manṣūr, then al-Salām, then the Commander of the Groups. Whoever is able to die before then, should die.

242. Ka`b: God Most High gave to Ishmael twelve righteous leaders from his loins, the most meritorious and best of them was Abū Bakr al-Ṣiddīq, `Umar b. al-Khaṭṭāb, `Uthmān Dhū al-Nūrayn who was killed unjustly, given his reward twice, [then] the King of Syria [Mu`āwiya] and his son, and al-Saffāh, al-Manṣūr, Sīn and Salām, meaning righteous and clement. [65]

243. Tubay` b. `Āmir[175]: al-Saffāḥ will live forty years; his name in the Torah is "Bird of the heavens."[176]

244. Ka`b: Three will rule from the progeny of al-`Abbās, al-Manṣūr, al-Mahdi and al-Saffāḥ.

245. `Abd al-Raḥmān b. Qays b. Jābir al-Ṣadafī[177]: The Messenger of God said: After the tyrants (*al-jabābira*) there will be a man from my family who will fill the earth will justice, then the Qahtani after him, and by the One who sent me with the truth, he is not less than the other.

246. `Alī: The imams are from Quraysh, the best of them are over the best of them, the worst of them are over the worst of them, but after Quraysh there is nothing but *jāhiliyya.*

247. `Umar b. `Abd al-Raḥmān al-Dhimārī[178]: A stone was found on a tomb in Ẓafār[179] so `Abd al-Raḥmān said: "I reached it and in an ascending script was written on it: *khūri wa-ṭari kayl*

[175] Ka`b al-Aḥbār's stepson, lived in Ḥimṣ, d. in Alexandria 101/719–20.
[176] Perhaps a reference to Psalms 8:8.
[177] Probably Egyptian, *fl.* 2nd/8th century, related to no. 1172.
[178] Unidentified, appears to be a family tradition.
[179] Capital of Himyarite Yemen.

nask za`li wa-Jumādā wa-banlak ḥuli wa-maḥrizi baḥ* in the bull [when] it returns to being a parting: Ḥimyar the good ones, then the evil Ethiopians, then the Persian freedmen, then Quraysh the merchants, then *maḥār janaḥ ḥār* and every time the one with the two portions moans *wa-ha`di zajruhu `anhu mikhwār."[180]

248. Ka`b: To whom is the dominion of Ẓafār? To Ḥimyar the good ones. To whom is the dominion of Ẓafār? To the evil Ethiopians. To whom is dominion of Ẓafār? To the Persian freedmen. To whom is the dominion of Ẓafār? To Quraysh the merchants. To whom is the dominion of Ẓafār? To Ḥimyar of the seas.[181]

249. `Umar b. al-Khaṭṭāb: "There will be a man from my progeny, who will have a deformity on his face, who will rule, then fill it [the earth] with justice." Nāfi`: "I think that this could be none other than `Umar b. `Abd al-`Azīz."[182] [68]

250. `Umar b. `Abd al-`Azīz: I saw the Messenger of God in my sleep, when Abū Bakr, `Umar, `Uthmān and `Alī were with him, so he said to me: "Come close," so I came close until I stood in front of him, then he lifted his gaze to me, and said: "As for you, you will rule this community, and act justly towards them."

251. Al-Walīd b. Hishām[183]: A Jew met me and informed me that `Umar b. `Abd al-`Azīz will rule this matter, and act justly in it. Then I met him after, so he said to me: "Your master is drunk, so order him to regain his senses," so I met him, and mentioned that to him, but he said to me: "May God fight you! I will not inform him—I told him the time when you drank that if healing meant touching my earlobe, I would not do it, or bringing perfume to raise it to my nostrils, I would not do it."

180 Large sections of this are unintelligible. Perhaps there is some Old South Arabian that stands behind it, but the primary function of the reading is to emphasize the order of rule in Yemen: Ḥimyar—Ethiopians—Persians—Quraysh. See no. 1117 for another version.

181 All of which is a rhyme in Arabic.

182 Who was `Umar b. al-Khaṭṭāb's great-grandson.

183 Al-Walīd b. Hishām al-Mu`ayṭī, am Umayyad, governor of Qinnasrin for `Umar b. `Abd al-`Azīz, said to have been alive during the rule of Marwān II.

252. Al-`Uqaylī the muezzin of `Umar b. al-Khaṭṭāb[184]: `Umar sent me to one of the bishops, so I called him for him, then `Umar said to him: "Woe to you! Did you find my description among you[r books]?" He said: "Yes, Commander of the Believers." He said: "How did you find me?" He said: "I find you to be an iron horn." He [`Umar] said: "What is an iron horn?" He said: "Strong, powerful." `Umar said: "Praise be to God!" He said: "Then what?" He said: "The man who is after you has no backbone, since his relatives will influence him." So `Umar said: "May God have mercy on `Uthmān, may God have mercy on `Uthmān, woe to you—then what?" He said: "Then a crack in the rock." He said: "What is a crack in the rock?" He said: "A sword unsheathed, and blood spilt." This weighed on `Umar, so he said: "May he perish!" the rest of the day. The bishop said: "O Commander of the Believers, there will be unity after that," so `Umar said to me: "Rise and call to prayer!" But I do not know whether he asked him anything after that or not.

253. Ka`b: God has never sent prophecy without making a caliphate or kingship, except among the people of the villages and civilization—they did not desire it among the people of pillars or the waste. [69]

The Dominion of the Umayyads and Naming them after `Umar

254. A man of the Banū al-Muṣṭaliq: I asked the Messenger of God concerning the charity (*zakat*) of my tribe, to whom do we pay it after `Umar, and so he said: Pay it to `Uthmān after `Umar.

255. `Abdallāh b. `Amr: After `Umar, there is Ibn `Affān, then Mu`āwiya and his son.

256. Mughīth al-Awzā`ī: `Umar asked Ka`b who was after him, and he said: a caliph who his community will kill acting unjustly to him, meaning `Uthmān.

257. Ka`b: Yashū` asked me concerning the kings of this community, after its Prophet, and this was before `Umar became

[184] Probably `Abdallāh b. Shaqīq al-`Uqaylī, lived in Baṣra, died after 100/718–19.

caliph, so he said: "After `Umar there will be al-Amīn, meaning `Uthmān, and then the first of the kings," meaning Mu`āwiya.

258. Al-`Uqaylī, the muezzin of `Umar: that `Umar asked a bishop, when I was present, who was after him, so he said: "A man without any backbone, whose relatives will influence him." `Umar said: "May God have mercy on `Uthmān, may God have mercy on `Uthmān."

259. Hilāl b. Yasāf [70]: The mail-post which Mu`āwiya sent to the Byzantine Emperor to ask him who would be the caliph after `Uthmān told me he said: The Byzantine Emperor called for a codex, to look in it, and said: "After him is Mu`āwiya, your master, the one who sent you."

260. Abū Ṣāliḥ: Mu`āwiya used to ride together with `Uthmān, so the camel-driver began to say: "The Commander after him is `Alī, and in al-Zubayr there is a satisfactory descendant."

Ka`b said: While Mu`āwiya would ride to the side of the procession on a gray-colored donkey. Ka`b would say: "The commander after him [`Uthmān] is the one with the gray-colored donkey."

261. `Alī: I heard the Messenger of God say: It will not be long before the rule of this community is unified under Mu`āwiya.

262. Abū Sālim al-Jayshānī: I heard `Alī say in Kūfa: "I am fighting for a right that should prevail, but it will never prevail, because the rule belongs to them [the Umayyads]." I [Abū Sālim] said to my friends: "What is the point of staying here, when he informed us that the rule is not going to belong to them? Let's ask permission to go to Egypt," so permission was given to those he wanted from among us, and 1000 dirhams were given to each man of us, but a group of us stayed with him.

263. `Abd al-Raḥmān b. Abī `Awf al-Jurashī[185]: The Messenger of God mentioned Syria, so a man said: "How is it possible that we get Syria, when the Byzantines, possessors of horns, are in

[185] Lived in Ḥimṣ, served as a judge (*qāḍī*), *fl.* 1st/7th century.

it?" So the Messenger of God said: "Perhaps a youth (*ghulām*) from Quraysh will suffice for it," and the Messenger of God stretched with his stick towards the shoulders of Mu`āwiya.

264. `Umar b. al-Khaṭṭāb: "O Companions of the Messenger of God, give good advice to each other, because if you do not, then they will dominate it," meaning the caliphate, "like `Amr b. al-`Āṣ and Mu`āwiya b. Abī Sufyān."

265. Muḥammad b. Sīrīn[186]: "By God, I think that he was machinating for it, meaning Mu`āwiya, during the time of Abū Bakr and `Umar," meaning for the caliphate. [71]

266. `Ikrima: I was amazed at our brothers, the Umayyads—our call was the call of the believers, while their call was the call of the hypocrites, and yet they were victorious over us.

267. `Alī: "Mu`āwiya will defeat you." They said: "Shouldn't we fight?" He said: "The people need a commander, whether pious or impious." [72]

The End of the Umayyads' Dominion

268. Rāshid b. Sa`d[187]: When Marwān b. al-Ḥakam was born, he was given to the Messenger of God to pray over him, but he refused to do that, then he said: "Son of the Blue-eyed woman,[188] the destruction of most of my community will be at the hands of him and his descendants."

269. Some of our elders: When the Messenger of God gazed at him [Marwān] to pray over him, he said: "May God curse this one, and those in his loins, other than those who believe and perform good deeds—how few they are!"[189]

[186] Lived in Baṣra, was a *mawlā* of Anas b. Mālik, associated with the interpretation of dreams, d. 110/728.

[187] Rāshid b. Sa`d al-Maqrā'ī, lived in Ḥimṣ and Hebron, d. 108/726.

[188] Q 20:109 says that evildoers will be resurrected as "blue-eyed"; according to Amir Harrak (trans), *The Chronicle of Zuqnin* (Toronto: Pontifical Institute of Medieval Studies, 1999), p. 155 (years 724–5) there was an edict against blue-eyed people.

[189] Probably the exception was for `Umar II, see no. 288.

270. Al-Nazzāl b. Sabra[190]: "Have I not told you what I heard from `Alī b. Abī Ṭālib?" I said: "No," then he said: "I heard him say: Every community has a disaster, and the disaster of this community is the Umayyads."

271. `Abdallāh b. Mas`ūd: Every community has a disaster to corrupt it, and the disaster of this community is the Umayyads.

272. Abū Dharr: I heard the Messenger of God saying: "When the [number of] the Umayyads reaches forty they will take the servants of God as property, the wealth of God a gift, and the Book of God as confusion." [73]

273. Yazīd b. Sharīk[191] that al-Ḍaḥḥāk b. Qays[192] sent a garment with him to Marwān, so Marwān said: "Who is at the door?" He said: "Abū Hurayra," so permission was given to him [to enter], then I heard him after he had entered saying: "I heard the Messenger of God saying: The destruction of this community will be at the hands of a little youth from Quraysh." **(1)**

274. Ibn Wahb[193]: Mu`āwiya was with us sitting, together with Ibn `Abbās, when Marwān b. al-Ḥakam entered needing something. When he turned around, Mu`āwiya said to Ibn `Abbās: "Didn't the Messenger of God teach us that when the family of al-Ḥakam reaches thirty men they will take the wealth of God Most High as a well-bucket between them, His servants as property, and His Book as confusion?" Ibn `Abbās said: "O God! Yes!" Then Marwān had `Abd al-Malik returned for something. When `Abd al-Malik turned around, Mu`āwiya said: "I implore you, by God, O Ibn `Abbās, did you not know that the Messenger of God mentioned this one as the father of the four tyrants?" He said: "O God! Yes!" At that time Mu`āwiya adopted Ziyād b. Abihi.[194]

[190] Nazzāl b. Sabra al-Hilālī, lived in Kūfa, *fl.* 1st/7th century.

[191] Yazīd b. Sharīk al-Taymī, lived in Kūfa, *fl.* 1st/7th century.

[192] A Qurashite who lived in Damascus, commanded the army of Damascus for Mu`āwiya at Ṣiffīn, killed at Marj Rāhiṭ, 64/684.

[193] `Abdallāh b. Wahb al-Qurashī, lived in Egypt, a major jurisprudent, d. 197/812.

[194] Who became his viceroy over Iraq, after previously having been a supporter of `Ali, d. 53/673, known for his brutal methods (see nos. 399, 426).

275. Minā the *mawlā* of `Abd al-Raḥmān b. `Awf[195]: Every newborn was brought to the Prophet, so that he could pray over him, but when Marwān was brought to him, he said: "He is a coward son of a coward, a cursed one son of a cursed one."

276. Ka`b: Youths from Quraysh will rule your affairs, who will be on the level of long-tailed she-camels (`*ajājīl*)[196] at mangers—if they are left, they will consume everything that is before them; if they escape they butt whoever they come across.

277. Abū Sa`īd al-Khudarī: The Messenger of God said: The People of my House will encounter fierce slaughter after me, and the worst of our tribe in hatred against them will be the Umayyads, and the Banū al-Mughīra of the clan of Banū Makhzūm.[197] [74]

278. Bajāla b. `Abda[198]: I said to `Umar: Ibn Ḥaṣīn narrated to me concerning the most hateful of the people towards the Messenger of God, so he said: Conceal it for me until I die. I said: Yes. He said: The Umayyads, the Thaqīf[199] and the Banū Ḥanīfa.[200]

279. Tubay`: Four will be kings from the loins of one man: Sulaymān b.`Abd al-Malik, Hishām, Yazīd and al-Walīd.

280. Al-Ḥasan: The Messenger of God said: There will be a man named al-Walīd[201] who will constitute one of the supports of hell, or one of its corners.

281. Sa`īd b. `Abd al-`Azīz[202]: It reached me that the Messenger of

[195] Apparently lived in Medina, not considered reliable, *fl.* 1st/7th century.

[196] This phrase is difficult: Lane, p. 1965 (right col.) gives `*ajājīl* "a handful of dates;" the form `*ajūl* means "she-camels bereft of their young" (no. 1180 gives this form with the tradition; see al-Asma`i, *Kitāb al-ibl* [Damascus: Dār al-Bashā'ir, 2003], p. 65, but without the plural `*ajājīl* that appears in the tradition); the form *mudhannaba* appears as *murabbiya* in nos. 1097, 1144.

[197] A clan well known for its opposition to the Prophet Muḥammad during his lifetime.

[198] Bajāla b. `Abda al-Tamīmī, lived in Baṣa, considered an ascetic, *fl.* 1st/7th century.

[199] The tribe which dominated al-Ṭā'if, and supplied many Umayyad governors of Iraq such as al-Ḥajjāj b. Yūsuf al-Thaqafī.

[200] The tribe which dominated the central area of Arabia, whose most prominent member was the false prophet Musaylima.

[201] Presumably Walīd II.

[202] Sa`īd b. `Abd al-`Azīz al-Tanūkhī, lived in Damascus, considered to have been the pre-eminent jurisprudent of Syria, d. 167 or 168/783 or 784–5.

God said: "'Umar and 'Umar will rule you, Yazīd and Yazīd, al-Walīd and al-Walīd, Marwān and Marwān and Muḥammad and Muḥammad."

282. Yazīd b. Abī Ḥabīb: It used to be said that when the squint-eyed caliph[203] ruled the people, if you are able to leave Egypt for Syria, then do so, and that was before the caliphate of Hishām.

283. Abū Qubayl: that an informant came to 'Abd al-Malik to inform him that a boy had been born to him, and that his mother had named him Hishām, so he said: "May God crush her (*hashamahā*) in the Fire."

284. Makḥūl: It reached me that the Messenger of God said: "There will be four heretics (*zanādiqa*) from Quraysh." His father said: I heard Sa'īd b. Khālid[204] mention approximately the same from Ibn Abī Zakariyā,[205] then he said: "They are Marwān b. Muḥammad b. Marwān b. al-Ḥakam, and al-Walīd b. Yazīd b. 'Abd al-Malik b. Marwān b. al-Ḥakam, and Yazīd b. Khālid b. Yazīd b. Mu'āwiya b. Abī Sufyān, and Sa'īd b. Khālid who was in Khurāsān." **(1)** [75]

285. Ibn al-Musayyib: The brother of Umm Salama had a boy, and named him al-Walīd, so that was mentioned to the Messenger of God, who said: "You have named him with one of the names of your Pharaohs. Verily, there will be in this community a man called al-Walīd who will be more evil to this community than Pharaoh was to his people." Al-Zuhrī said: "Until al-Walīd b. Yazīd became caliph, they thought it was al-Walīd b. 'Abd al-Malik."

286. Someone who entered with al-Ḥajjāj[206] in to Asmā', daughter of Abū Bakr, so he said to her: "What have you heard from the

203 Probably Hishām.

204 Sa'īd b. Khālid al-Qurashī, lived in Sidon, *fl.* 1st/7th century.

205 'Abdallāh b. Abī Zakariyā al-Khuzā'ī, lived in Damascus, a jurisprudent, d. 117/735.

206 Al-Ḥajjāj b. Yūsuf al-Thaqafī, the brutal viceroy for the Umayyads who ruled Iraq until 96/714.

Messenger of God?" She said: "I have heard the Messenger of God saying: 'There will be a congenital liar from Thaqīf, and a destroyer'—as for the liar, we have known him;[207] as for the destroyer, it is you!" He said: "Yes, I am the destroyer of hypocrites."

287. Suhayl b. Dhakwān[208]: When al-Ḥajjāj killed Ibn al-Zubayr, he went in to see Asmā' daughter of Abū Bakr, so she said: "What did Ibn al-Zubayr do?" He said: "God killed him." She said: "Surely, by God, you have killed him when he was a fasting, praying man. I heard the Messenger of God saying: 'Three will come from Thaqīf: the liar, the long-tailed bull, and the destroyer.' As for the liar, he has passed, but as for the destroyer, it is you!" She said: "As for the long-tailed bull, we will see him later." Ibn `Umar passed by Ibn al-Zubayr crucified, and said: "The community has been successful, you are its worst."

288. `Umar b. al-Khaṭṭāb: "There will be a man from my descendants, who will have a deformity on his face, who will rule and fill it [the earth] with justice." Nāfi` said: "I would not think that it was anyone other `Umar b. `Abd al-`Azīz."

289. Ibn Shawdhab[209]: `Umar b. `Abd al-`Azīz entered a stable belonging to his father, when a horse belonging to his father knocked up against him, so he left with blood running down his face, so his father said to him: "Maybe you will be the hardest knocker of the Umayyads!"

290. Ḥudhayfa b. al-Yamān: "After `Uthmān there will be twelve kings from the Umayyads." It was said: "Caliphs?" He said: "No, kings." [76]

[207] Al-Mukhtār b. Abī `Ubayd al-Thaqafī, who ruled Kūfa briefly (63–5/683–5), and took vengeance upon the murderers of al-Ḥusayn (according to Ibn Abi al-Dunya, *Ishraf* [Cairo: Maktabat al-Qur'ān, 1990], p. 144 [no. 286] some thought him the Dajjal as well).

[208] Suhayl b. Dhakwān, lived in Wāsiṭ (hence his connection with Ḥajjāj), *fl.* 2nd/8th century.

[209] `Abdallāh b. Shawdhab al-Khurāsānī, originally from Balkh, lived in Baṣra, then moved to Jerusalem, d. 144 or 156/761–2 or 773.

291. Abū Umayya al-Kalbī[210]: He told them during the caliphate of Yazīd b. `Abd al-Malik, saying: When the people divided after Mu`āwiya and the dissension of Ibn al-Zubayr happened, a hoary elder who had lived during the *jāhiliyya* came to us, whose eyebrows had fallen over his eyes, so we said: "Tell us about this time, and the division of the people in it," so he motioned to us, and called for a band to fasten the skin of his eyebrows so that it was lifted above his eyes, and then studied us. He said: "I advise you to stay in your houses, since the rule will pass to a man from the Umayyads who will rule you twenty-two years then die.[211] Then after him caliphs will rule in succession for short periods of time, until a man with a mark in his eye—meaning Hishām b. `Abd al-Malik—who will gather wealth in a way no one previously had done, who will live [=rule] nineteen years and a bit, then die. Then a man from them, a young man, will give the people stipends the like of which were never given previously. Then a man from his family will urge against him[212] secretly, no one mentioning [it], and kill him, so then blood will be poured at this hands. Then *murrīn* [=Marwān] will come from there," and he pointed towards al-Jazīra.

292. Abdallāh b. Salām[213] said before the killing of `Uthmān: He will be killed at the end of two months, then Marwān [b. al-Ḥakam] leapt up angrily to go in to `Uthmān, but they were continuously on him until he was prevented from him, so `Abdallāh b. Qays said to al-Zuhrī: "This knowledge was concealed from the people, so do you have anything that you can tell us—and that was during the reign (*amāra*) of Hishām." Al-Zuhrī said:

210 Unidentified, but probably lived in Damascus, *fl.* 2nd/8th century (see nos.484, 507).

211 `Abd al-Malik.

212 Reading *yanushsh* (DKI); other editors suggest *yanshab* "to stick to" (SZ); *yunthi bihi* "to divulge news" (MM).

213 Early Jewish convert, Companion, is said to have participated in the conquest of Jerusalem, d. in Medina 43/663–4.

"Do you want a break from Hishām? It is as if that has happened. He will perish at the end of two years or so." It was said to him: "Natural death or being killed?" He said: "No, natural death," so it was said: "Who will come after him?" He said: "This youth from the people of his house." It was said: "How long will his time be?" He said: "Like the sleep of a boy." It was said: "Will he die naturally? Or be killed?" He said: "No, be killed." It was said: "Who will come after him?" He said: "The one who will come from there"—and pointed to al-Jazīra. Sulaymān b. Hishām was then the commander of al-Jazīra, so it was said: "Is it him?" He said: "His name and the name of his father have eight letters." It was said: "How long will his time be?" He said: "Like a worn-out garment—when one picks it up from one side, it falls apart on the other."[214]

293. Hilāl b. Yusāf: The mail-post that brought the head of al-Mukhtār to Ibn al-Zubayr informed me that when it was placed before him [Ibn al-Zubayr], he said: "Everything that Ka`b told me about my rule (*sulṭānī*) was just as he said, except for this, since he narrated that a man from Thaqīf would kill me, but it seems to me that I have killed him."[215] [77]

294. Abū Hurayra: The tribulation (dissension) of Ibn al-Zubayr was a zigzag (*ḥīṣāt*)[216] among the tribulations.

295. Abū Qubayl: When Ibn `Umar saw the heads of the supporters of Ibn al-Zubayr carried on spears and stalks, he said: They exchange heads amongst each other, but they do not know where the spirits have gone.

296. Abū Wā'il[217]: I met Abū al-`Alā' Ṣila b. Zufar,[218] so I said: "O Abū al-`Alā', did any of this pain"—meaning the plague—"strike

[214] A description of the multiple revolts that characterized the rule of Marwān II (127–32/744–50).

[215] The point of this comment was that Ibn al-Zubayr spoke too soon; he was indeed killed by al-Ḥajjāj b. Yūsuf al-Thaqafī.

[216] Ibn al-Athīr, *Nihāya*, i, p. 468.

[217] Shaqīq b. Salama al-Asadī, lived in Kūfa, d. 82/701.

[218] Ṣila b. Zufar al-`Absī, lived in Kūfa, d. during the rule of Mus`ab b. al-Zubayr (66–73/685–92).

your family?" He said: "I am more afraid that it will make them walk than that it will strike them."[219]

297. Abū Hurayra: I [Abū Salama] said: "O God! heal Abū Hurayra!" He said: "O God, do not repeat that!" Then he said: "A time is about to come upon the people in which death in it is more preferable to the knowledgeable one than red gold."

298. Abū Wā'il that `Abdallāh b. Mas`ūd mentioned `Uthmān one day, and said: "Stinginess caused him to perish, and what a poor protection!" We said to him: "Won't you go out, so we can go out with you?" He said: "It would be easier to move a deep-rooted mountain[220] than to move a king whose death is nigh." [78]

Protection from Tribulations and the Desirability of Holding Back and Withdrawing during them, and Undesirability of Looking out over them

299. `Abdallāh b. Mas`ūd: I heard the Messenger of God say: "There will be tribulation in which the sleeper is better than the one lying down, the one lying down is better than the one standing, the one standing is better than the one rising, the one rising is better than the one walking, the one walking is better than the one riding, the one riding is better than the one fully participating—those killed in it are all in Hell." I said: "O Messenger of God, when is this?" He said: "Days of killing." I said: "But when are the days of killing?" He said: "When a man will not be secure from his companion." I said: "What do you command me to do if I live in those days?" He said: "Hold yourself and your hand back and enter your house." I said: "O Messenger of God, and if they come into my house?" He said: "Go further into your house." I said: "But if they come in all the way?" He said: "Go to your mosque, and do like this"—then

[219] I.e., that they would participate in the tribulations.
[220] Cf. Q 79:32.

he grabbed his [left] elbow with his right hand, "and say: 'My Lord is God,' until you are killed doing this."

300. Ḥudhayfa b. al-Yamān: A warning to you about the tribulations! Let no one stare at them, because by God, anyone who stares at them will be carried away like the flood. They will seem to go forward, such that the ignorant might say: This seems [like it is forward] but it will be clear that it is backward, so gather together in your houses, break your swords, and cut your cords.

301. Abū Hurayra: The Messenger of God said: "Woe to the Arabs from an evil that has come close—so the one who holds his hand back succeeds." [79]

302. Abū Hurayra: "I am the most knowledgeable about a tribulation that is about to come is like the hop of a rabbit. And I am the most knowledgeable concerning the way out of them." They said: "What is it?" He said: "That I would hold my hand until they come to kill me."

303. Ḥudhayfa b. al-Yamān: [If there are] two groups of the Muslims—it does not matter which of the two of them has told you about their killed—their killed are those of the *jāhiliyya*.

304. Ibn `Umar: The Messenger of God said: The tribulation when it comes it has doubtful aspects, when it retreats it uncovers, and the tribulation pollinates by whispering and results in complaints, so do not arouse the tribulation when it is warming up, and do not offer yourself to it when it is offered. The tribulation is imposing in the lands of God, treading upon its halter. It is not permited to anyone among creation to awaken it until God Most High permits. Woe to the one who takes up its halter, then woe again, then woe again!

305. `Abdallāh: "The tribulation, when it comes, it is doubtful, when it retreats, it has consequences." Sufyān—Ḥudhayfa similarly, but he added: It was said to Ḥudhayfa: "What is its coming?" He said: "Drawing the sword" and it was said: "What is its retreat?" He said: "Sheathing the sword."

306. Ḥudhayfa: A man said to him: "How would you command

me when the prayers fight?" He said: "Enter your house, lock your door behind you, so anyone who comes to you, say: This way!"—Sufyān [b. `Uyayna] took his hand and encompassed [his neck]—"then say: Come back with your sin and my sin [on the Day of Resurrection]!"

307. Ibn `Umar: The Messenger of God said: Beware of tribulations, for the tongue during them is like a sword's blow.

308. Ḥudhayfa: The tribulation has been entrusted to three: to the experienced zealot, who every time something happens to him, he wants to subdue it with a sword, and to the preacher, who the events call to him, and to the aforementioned nobleman. As for the experienced zealot, struggle with him, but as for the other two, the preacher and the nobleman, incite them until you afflict that which they have. [80]

309. Ḥudhayfa b. al-Yamān: Watch out for two groups fighting over this world, for they are dragging [people] to hell.

310. Abū Idrīs al-Khawlānī: I heard Ḥudhayfa b. al-Yamān saying: I said to the Messenger of God: "How would you command me, if I live to see those, meaning the tribulations?" He said: "Stay with the community of the Muslims, and their imam." I said: "But what if they do not have an imam or community?" He said: "Withdraw from all of those factions, even if you have to bite on the root of a tree until death comes to you, while you are in this state."

311. Ḥudhayfa b. al-Yamān: The Messenger of God mentioned those who call to the gates of hell (*jahannam*)—whoever obeys them they will drag him inside, so I said: "O Messenger [of God], what is the means of salvation from this?" He said: "Stay with the community and the imam of the community." I said: "But what if there is no community or imam of the community?" He said: "Flee from all of these factions, even if death comes to you while you are biting on the root of a tree."

312. Ḥudhayfa b. al-Yamān: I said: "O Messenger of God, what is the protection from these," when he had mentioned the callers of error. He said: "If God has a caliph on the earth on that day,

then stay with him, even if they beat your back and take your wealth. If not, then flee the earth until death comes to you, while you are biting on the root of a tree."

313. Daughter of Uhbān al-Ghifārī: `Alī came to Uhbān one day and said: "What prevented you from following us?" He said: "My friend and your cousin [Muḥammad] instructed me that there would be tribulation, faction, and division, and that when they happen, break your sword, sit in your hourse, and take up a sword of wood."

314. Abū Janāb[221]: I heard Ṭalḥa saying: I fought in [the Battle of] Jamājim, but I did not thrust with my spear or strike with the sword. I wish that they had been cut off, meaning his hands, and that I had not fought in it. [81]

315. Mujāhid: His Word Most High, "Do not make us an (object of) persecution [*fitna*] for the people who are evildoers."[222] Do not allow them to rule over us, lest they decive us, and we be deceived by them.

316. Abū Qilāba[223]: When the dissension of Ibn al-Asha`th broke out, we were at a sitting, and Muslim b. Yassār was with us. Muslim said: "Praise be to God who has saved us from this dissension, for by God, I have not shot an arrow, thrust a spear or struck with a sword in it." Abū Qilāba: I said to him: "O Muslim, what do you think about one who is ignorant who looks at you [to kill you]?" He said: "By God, no Muslim is in this state without him having a right over the other, whether he kills or is killed." He said this and cried, "By the One who holds my soul in His hand, I even wished that I had not ever said anything to him."

317. Jundub b. `Abdallāh al-Bajalī[224]: A Syrian man attacked a man from the supporters of `Alī at [the Battle of] Ṣiffīn, and settled

[221] Yaḥyā b. Abī Ḥayya al-Kalbī, lived in Kūfa, d. 147/764–5.

[222] Q 10:85.

[223] `Abdallāh b. Zayd al-Jarmī, lived in Baṣra, moved to Dārayā, d. 104, 105, 106, or 107/722, 723, 724, 725.

[224] Companion, lived in `Iraq, *fl.* 1st/7th century.

down upon him to slaughter him, so I grasped my spear towards him to foil him, and he was foiled. Whenever I mention it, I grasp my throat.

318. Ḥudhayfa: O `Āmir, Let not those who you see deceive you, for those are about to be parted from their religion like a woman parts her pudenda, so when they do that, then you should stay as you are today.

319. Ṭāwūs: The Messenger of God said to Abū Dharr: "O Abū Dharr, I see that you are a seer, so how will it be for you, O Abū Dharr, when they expel you from Medina?" He said: "I will go to the Holy Land." He said: "How will it be for you when they expel you from it?" He said: "I will return to Medina." He said: "If they expel you from it?" He said: "I will take my sword, and strike with it until I am killed." He said: "No, but hear and obey, even to a black slave."[225] When he [Abū Dharr] came to al-Rabdha[226] he found a black slave belonging to `Uthmān, then the prayer was performed, and he said: "Go forward [to be the imam] O Abū Dharr." But he said: "I am ordered to hear and to obey, even to a black slave," so the slave went forward and led the prayer.

320. Ka`b: The mill of the Arabs will turn after twenty-five [years] after the death of their prophet, then dissension will develop. During it there will be killing and fighting [82] so hold back your hand and your weapons, then there will be another after a calmness, so hold back your hand and weapons, since I find it in the Book of God as the darkness that envelops everyone who has pride.

321. Ka`b: The mill of the Arabs will turn after the death of their prophet after twenty-five years, then dissension will be widespread in which there wil be killing and fighting, so hold back yourself and your weapons, until it passes, neither for you or

225 See Crone, "'Even an Ethiopian Slave': The Transformation of a Sunni Tradition," *Bulletin of the School of Oriental and African Studies* 72 (1994), pp. 59–67.

226 The oasis to which he was exiled.

against you. Then people will settle down like a rotation wheel (*dawwāma*) [for a mill], then dissension will develop, which I find in the revealed Book of God as "the darkness which does not pass until it envelops everyone who has pride," so hold back yourself and your weapons, and flee as fast as you can from them. If you only find a scorpion's stone in which to take refuge, go under it.

322. Abū Hurayra: The Messenger of God said, mentioning the fourth tribulation: "No one will be saved from it, except the one who prays the prayer of the drowning man. The happiest of its people are every god-fearer who hides—when he appears, he is not known, when he sits he is not missed. The most miserable of its people are every enthusiastic preacher and rider in the saddle."

323. `Abdallāh b. Abī Ja`far: The Messenger of God said: There will be dissension in which none will be saved other than the one who does not take its wealth, so whoever gains wealth in it is like one who sheds blood.

324. Abū Hurayra: The Messenger of God said: The happiest of people in it will be every concealer, who when he appears he is not known, when he sits [in an assembly] he is not missed.

325. Arṭāt b. al-Mundhir: It reached me that the Messenger of God said: In the fourth tribulation they will go towards unbelief in it, so the believer on that day will be the one who sits in his house, but the unbeliever will be one who draws his sword and spills the blood of his brother and neighbor.

326. `Uqba b. `Āmir[227] said: I heard the Messenger of God saying: Whoever dies without having associated anything with God, and is not wetted with blood, will enter into whichever gate of Paradise he wishes. [83]

327. Abū Mūsā al-`Asha`rī: There is no antagonist more hateful to me than to meet on the Day of Resurection with a man whose

[227] `Uqba b. `Āmir al-Juhanī, Companion, governor of Egypt for Mu`āwiya (44/664–5), then lived in Damascus, d. 58/678.

jugular veins are flowing with blood to reckon me on the Scales of Justice.[228] He will say: "O Lord, ask your servant here, by what right did he kill me?" So I will say: "He lied," but I will not be able to say that he was an unbeliever, so He will say: "Are you more knowledgeable about My servant than I am?"

328. Jundub b. `Abdallāh: No one of you who has a handful of blood of a man who says: "There is no God but Allāh" will meet God on the Day of Resurrection—even if he prayed the morning prayer, when he is in the protection of God (died)—God will not wait a moment before God will throw him prostrate, when He gathers the first and the last, into Hell (*jahannum*).
329. Muḥammad that [Mālik] al-Ashtar[229] asked `Alī permission, but was denied, but then he permitted him when a son of Ṭalḥa was present. He said: "So you denied me because of that?" He said: "Yes." He said: "If he was a son to `Uthmān would you have denied me for that?" He said: "Yes." He said: "I hope that I and `Uthmān will be among those concerning whom God Most High has said: 'We shall strip away whatsoever rancor is in their hearts. (As) brothers (they will recline) on couches, facing each other.'"[230]
330. Jundub b. `Abdallāh al-Bajalī: Fear God, every one of you, for a handful of Muslim blood shed will make it impossible for him to enter Paradise after he has looked at its gates.
331. A man of the Companions of the Messenger of God: I heard him [Muḥammad] saying: "A handful of Muslim blood shed will make it impossible for one of you to enter Paradise after he has looked at its gates."
332. Jundub b. `Abdallāh: If a trial descends, place your wealth below your religion, for the one battled is the one whose religion is battled, while the one stolen is the one whose religion is stolen, so know there are no riches after the Fire, and no

[228] E.g., Q 6:152.
[229] `Ali's most successful general.
[230] Q 15:47.

poverty after Paradise. The Fire does not release its prisoner, but it is not in need of its poor.

333. `Alī: "O God! Cast the killers of `Uthmān prostrate on their nostrils today!"

334. Abū Birza al-Aslamī[231]: "This one in [84] Syria," meaning Marwān (I), "by God, even if he is just fighting for this world, while this one in Mecca," meaning Ibn al-Zubayr, "by God, even if he is just fighting for this world, and those who you call Qur'ān reciters (*qurrā'*), by God, even if they are just fighting for this world . . ." so one of his sons said to him: "What do you command us [to do] then?" He said: "I consider the best people to be those staying at home," and he said [looking] to his hands: "With stomachs empty of the people's wealth, with backs light without their blood."

335. Umm Salama[232]: The Messenger of God said: "There will be imams who will rise over you who you will think well of or disapprove, so whoever disapproves is saved, whoever dislikes will be safe, but whoever approves and follows . . ." It was said: "O Messenger of God, shouldn't we kill or fight them?" He said: "As for those who come to prayer, no."

336. Al-Ḥasan: It was said: "O Messenger of God, shouldn't we fight them?" He said: "As for those who perform the prayer, no."

337. `Awf b. Mālik: I heard the Messenger of God saying: "The worst of your imams are those who you hate them so they hate you, and you curse them, so they curse you." We said: "O Messenger of God, can't we resist them at that time?" He said: "As for those who perform the prayer, no, other than the one who is ruled by a ruler, then sees him acting rebelliously against God, so let him disapprove of the rebellious act against God, but not remove a hand from obedience."

338. Ḥudhayfa: Have recourse to patience before trial descends

[231] Naḍla b. `Ubayd al-Aslamī, Companion, fought in Persia, perhaps died in either Nishapur, or between Herāt and Sijistān, d. approximately 64/683–4.

[232] One of Muḥammad's wives.

upon you, for nothing will afflict you that is worse than what afflicted us with the Messenger of God.

339. Abū Dharr[233]: The Messenger of God said to me: "O Abū Dharr, how will you act when the people are so hungry that you will be unable to rise from your sleeping-mat to go to the mosque? Or from the mosque to your sleeping-mat?" I said: "God and His Messenger know best." He said: "Go to someone close." I said: "What if they refuse me?" He said: "Enter your house." I said: "What if they refuse me?" He said: "If you fear that swords will flash in your direction, then meet a group, with your face under your garment,[234] [saying] come back with your and my sin [on the Day of Resurrection]." I said: "So I shouldn't bear weapons?" He said: "Then you would be participant."

340. Abū Salama[235]: Ḥusayn b. ʿAlī entered into the presence of ʿUthmān, while he was besieged, and said: "O Commander of the Believers, I am submissive to your hand, so command me [85] in what you wish." ʿUthmān said to him: "O nephew, return to your house and sit, and until God brings His decree—for there is no need for me to spill blood."

341. Ibn Masʿūd al-Anṣārī: My commanders have begun to force me to choose between staying according to that which humiliates me and makes my face ugly or that I should take my sword, fight and be killed, so enter the Fire, so I chose to stay according to that which humiliates me and makes my face ugly, and so I will not take my sword, fight and be killed, so enter the Fire.

342. ʿĀmir b. Maṭar[236]: Ḥudhayfa said to me: "O ʿĀmir, do not be deceived by what you see"—while the people were returning

233 No agreement about his name, perhaps Jundub b. Junāda, Companion, prominent ascetic, exiled to Rabdha, d. 32/652–3.

234 Reading *ridā'ika* with DKI, in place of *radhā'il*, also below, no. 389.

235 Probably Abū Salama b. ʿAbd al-Raḥmān al-Qurashī, lived in Medina, later in Baṣra, d. 94/712–3.

236 ʿĀmir b. Maṭar al-Shaybānī, said to have been close to Ḥudhayfa, *fl.* 1st/7th century.

to the mosque—"since those are about to be parted from their religion just as a woman parts her pudenda, so when they do that, you should stay with what you believe today."

343. Ḥudhayfa: Enjoining the good and forbidding the evil is meritorious, but it is not part of the way (*sunna*) [of the Prophet] to lift weapons against your imam.

344. Suwayd b. Ghafala[237]: `Umar said to me: "Perhaps you will live to see the tribulation, so hear and obey, even if an Ethiopian slave is placed above you—if he hits you, have patience, or if he does the forbidden or wrongs you, have patience. If he compels you do do something that would decrease your religion, then say: 'Hearing is obedience; my blood is below my religion.'"

345. `Abdallāh b. Salām, when the people were stirred up about `Uthmān: "O people, do not kill `Uthmān, for by the One who holds my soul in His hand, every time a community has killed its prophet, God does not set them aright until the blood of 70,000 of them has been shed. Every time a community has killed its caliph, God does not set them aright until the blood of 70,000 has been shed."

346. Abū Hurayra: I was with `Uthmān in the house, when a man from among us was killed, so I said: "O Commander of the Believers, is it appropriate for fighting? One of our men has been killed." He said: "I enjoin you to throw away your sword, for it is only me (my soul) that is sought, so I will protect the believers by my soul today." He said: "I threw away my sword, and I do not know where it landed."

347. Zayd b. Arqam[238] [86] said to `Alī: "I implore you by God, did you kill `Uthmān?" He was silent for a time, then said: By He who split the seed, and created breath, I did not kill or order his killing.

[237] Lived during the time of the Prophet, lived in Kūfa, fought at the Battle of Yarmūk, d. 80, 81 or 82/699, 700, 701.

[238] Companion, lived in Kūfa, d. 66/685.

348. Ka`b sent to `Uthmān while he was besieged: "Your right incumbent upon every Muslim today is like the right of a father upon his son. You are as good as dead, so restrain your hand, for it makes your case greater before God on the Day of Resurrection." When this reached him, he said to his supporters: "I enjoin upon everyone who sees themselves having a duty to me to depart from me." So Marwān was angry, and threw the sword from his hand, such that it left an impression in the wall. Al-Mughīra b. al-Akhnas[239] said: "I am determined for myself that I will be killed," so he fought until he was killed.

349. A man from among us: I saw `Uthmān after he was killed in the most beautiful manner I had ever seen him, in white clothes, so I said: "O Commander of the Believers, which matters have you found to be the firmest?" He said: "The straight religion, which does not have bloodshed in it," three times, so when it was the Battle of the Camel, I gird my weapons, rode my horse, took my spear, and was among the first ranks of the vanguard. While I was there, my vision came to me, so I said: "Didn't `Uthmān tell you in the dream such-and-such?" So I turned my horse towards the camp, threw down my weapons, and sat in my house until this issue had been decided, and did not come out for any reason.

350. Jābir b. Zayd al-Azdī[240]: I heard `Alī saying: "I never commanded the killing of `Uthmān, nor did I want it, but my cousins accused me of it, so I sent to apologize, but they refused to accept it, and refused to accept it, so I worshiped and was silent."

351. `Alī said: "O God! Scorn the killers of `Uthmān today as a disgrace."

352. Muḥammad b. Maslama: The Messenger of God gave me a sword, then said: "Fight the polytheists with it as long as you

[239] Al-Mughīra b. al-Akhnas al-Thaqafī, who mocked al-Zubayr, and was attacked by al-Mundhir b. al-Zubayr.

[240] Lived in Baṣra, d. 93/711–12.

are being fought, but when you see my community strike each other, then take it to someone, and strike it until it breaks, then sit in your house until a sinful hand comes to you, or a predetermined test." And so he did.

353. Abū Burda b. Abī Mūsā[241]: I entered into the presence of Muḥammad b. Maslama[242] in Rabdha, so I said to him: "Why aren't you going out to the people, when you have the status in this matter [87] of which we heard?" He said: "The Messenger of God said: 'There will be tribulation and division, so strike with your sword broadside, break your arrows, cut your bow-string, and sit in your house,' so I have done what he commanded me." There was a sword hanging on the tent-support, so he took it down, and drew it, but it was a sword of wood, then he said: "I have done to my sword what the Messenger of God commanded me, so this I use to frighten people."

354. Abū `Uthmān that the Messenger of God said: "O Khālid b. `Urfuṭa,[243] there will be events, tribulations and difference, so if you are able to be the one killed, and not the killer, then do so."

355. `Abdallāh b. `Amr—I did not see that there was anybody beyond him [in the chain of transmitters]: I used to read this verse: "and surely on the Day of Resurrection you will dispute in the presence of your Lord,"[244] and I used to think that it concerned the People of the Book, until we struck each other's faces with swords, and then we knew that it was concerning us.

356. Ḥarmala the *mawlā* of Usāma b. Zayd[245]: Usāma sent me to `Alī, then he said: "He will ask you: what has kept your master? So say: He says to you: By God, if you were in the jaw of a lion,

[241] Al-Ḥārith, son of Abū Mūsā al-`Asha`rī, lived in Kūfa, jurisprudent, d. 103/721–2.

[242] Companion, "brother" to Abū `Ubayda al-Jarrāḥ, d. 43, 46 or 47/663, 666 or 667–8.

[243] Companion, lived in Kūfa where he held a number of positions, d. 61/680–1.

[244] Q 39:31.

[245] Lived in Medina, *fl.* 1st/7th century

I would want to be in it with you, but this issue, I do not see it." So I went to `Alī, then I said to him what he said, but he did not give me anything, so I went to Ḥasan, Ḥusayn and Ibn Ja`far, they helped load my beast of burden. `Amr said: "I saw Ḥarmala, but I did not hear this narration from him."

357. `Umar b. Sa`d[246] went to his father Sa`d, while he was in al-`Aqīq,[247] withdrawn in his private land, then said: "Daddy, none of the fighters at [the Battle of] Badr are left other than you, nor of the People of the Council, so if you collected yourself, and placed it before the people, no two would differ over you," He said: "You came for this?? Yes, son, I sat it out, so nothing would remain for me other than [taking care of] the thirst of my mount—then go out, and have the community of Muḥammad strike each other! I heard the Messenger of God saying: 'The best type of sustenance is that which suffices, and the best type of remembrance [of God] is private.'"[248] [88]

358. Sa`d b. Mālik[249]: I was a Meccan man, in it my birthplace, my house, and wealth, and I continued in this manner until God Most High sent His Prophet, so I believed in him, and followed him. I stayed in that as long as God wished, then I departed from it, fleeing with my religion to Medina, and continued in it until God gathered for me my wealth and family in it. Today I am fleeing with my religion from Medina to Mecca, just as I fled with my religion to Medina.

359. Ibn `Umar: When `Uthmān was killed he met `Alī, so said: "O `Abū `Abd al-Raḥmān, you are a man who is obeyed by the Syrians, so I think that tribulation is burning its legs, so go, as I have appointed you commander over them." He said: "I would remind you of God, and your closeness to the Messenger of God, and my companionship to him, to let me off the hook,"

[246] Son of Sa`d b. Abī Waqqāṣ, commanded troops that killed al-Ḥusayn, d. approsimately 64/684–5.
[247] Close to Baṣra.
[248] Ibn Hanbal, *Musnad* (Beirut: Dār al-Fikr, n.d.), i, pp. 173, 180, 182.
[249] Abū Sa`īd al-Khuḍarī.

so he refused. Then he sought to persuade him using Ḥafṣa,[250] but still he refused, so he departed to Mecca, and then he [`Uthmān] sent after him, such that they came to the camel, and were making haste to muzzle him, thinking that he had gone to Syria, but then he was informed that he had gone to Mecca, so he gave it up.

360. Khālid b. Sumayr[251]: Mūsā b. Ṭalḥa b. `Ubaydallāh[252] fled from al-Mukhtār to al-Baṣra together with the notables of the Kūfans. At his time, people considered him to be the Mahdi, so he heard that one day, and mentioned the tribulation, then said: "May God have mercy on `Abdallāh b. `Umar! For by God, I used to consider him at the time of the Prophet the one who was promised. He was not tempted afterwards nor changed [in anything]. By God, Quraysh did not even arouse him in its first dissension (*fitnatuhā al-ulā*),"[253] so I said to myself: "This is the one who will rebuke his father for the killing [at the Battle of Ṣiffīn] which he did!"

361. Khālid b. Sumayr: One morning `Alī met Ibn `Umar, so he said: "These letters, we have finished with them, so ride with them to the Syrians," but he said: "I implore you by God, and I implore you by Islam." He said: "You are, by God, going to ride with them." He said: "I remind you of God and the Last Day, since this matter from the first of it, was not worth anything, and it will not at the end be worth anything. So I will not return anything from you to the Syrians. If, by God, the Syrians want you, their obedience will come to you. If they do not want you, I am not going to return anything to you." He said: "You will ride, obediently or disobediently." But Ibn `Umar entered his house, and `Alī departed from him, until he disappeared into

250 Daughter of `Umar, one of the wives of Muḥammad.
251 Baṣran, *fl.* 1st/7th century.
252 Son of Ṭalḥa, lived in Kūfa, as in the tradition, called al-Mahdi during his lifetime (al-Mizzī, *Tahdhīb*, vii, p. 264), held various governing positions in Kūfaa, d. 103/721–2.
253 The civil war between `Ali and Mu`āwiya.

the black of the night. He summoned his noble camels, sat upon them, and sent them to Mecca. [89]

362. Abū al-Dardā'[254]: "How beautiful it is to die believing in Islam before the tribulations!"

363. Sa`d b. Ibrāhīm from his father: When it reached `Alī that Ṭalḥa was saying: "I only swore allegiance when the weight was on my neck [pressuring me]," he sent Ibn `Abbās to the Medinans to ask them what he had said. So Usāma b. Zayd said: "As for the weight being on his neck, no, but he swore while he was reluctant," so the people leaped upon him, almost killing him.

364. Wāhib b. Abī Mughīth[255]: I entered with al-Mundhir b. al-Zubayr[256] in the presence of Ibn `Umar, while `Amr b. Sa`īd[257] was going at him over things about which he was exaggerating, so we said to him: "Will you not start to forbid the evil?" He said: "Of course, if you wish, so take us." They said: "If you only would lead us at the head of people, for we are fearing that something would happen unintentionally to you." So he said: "I am not going to do what you want."

365. Abū Hurayra: "The sultan does not speak today," which was during the time of Mu`āwiya.

366. Al-Walīd b. `Uqba[258] sent to Ibn Mas`ūd so that he would conceal these words: "The most truthful narrative is the Book of God, the most beautiful guidance is the guidance of Muḥammad, and the worst of things are the newest." Ibn Mas`ūd said: "As for differentiating between this and that, no." `Itrīs b. `Urqūb[259] rose and covered his sword. Then `Abdallāh came and stood next to his head, and he said: "Those who

[254] `Uwaymir b. Mālik, Companion, well-known ascetic, d. 32/652–3.

[255] Unidentified, but probably lived in Medina, *fl.* 1st/7th century.

[256] Son of al-Zubayr, grandson of Abū Bakr, Medinan, *fl.* 1st/7th century.

[257] `Amr b. Sa`īd b. al-`Āṣ, governor of Medina for Mu`āwiya and Yazīd I, killed in Damascus 69/688.

[258] Al-Walīd b. `Uqba b. Abī Mu`ayṭ, former opponent of the Prophet, Companion, held various positions during the time of `Uthmān died during the reign of Mu`āwiya.

[259] `Itrīs b. `Urqūb al-Shaybānī, Companion, *fl.* 1st/7th century.

would have been enjoining the good and forbiding the evil have perished." `Abdallāh said: "No, but those who would not enjoin good or forbid evil in their hearts have perished." `Itrīs said: "If you had said anything else, I would have walked to that man in order to strike him with the sword, so that they will not act disobediently towards God in the interiors of the houses." `Abdallāh said: "Go, throw your sword [away], come back and sit in the corner of this study-circle."

367. Abū al-`Āliya: `Abdallāh b. al-Zubayr and `Abdallāh b. Ṣafwān[260] were in a private room, when Ibn `Umar passed by them, so they sent for him, and he came to them. `Abdallāh b. Ṣafwān said to him: "What is preventing you, O Abū `Abd al-Raḥmān, from swearing to the Commander of the Believers"—meaning Ibn al-Zubayr—"when the people of the breadth,[261] the Iraqis, and most of the Syrians have sworn to him?" He said: "No, by God, I will not swear allegiance to you, while you [90] are placing your swords on your shoulders, so that one of you can obtain the blood of the Muslims."

368. Abū Hurayra: The Messenger of God said: Whoever fights under a banner of error, angered for tribal solidarity or giving aid to tribal solidarity or calling for tribal solidarity, and is killed, his death is that of the *jāhiliyya*. Whoever rebels against my community, striking its righteous and its iniquitious, not frightened of killing its believers, and not respecting the one with whom it has treaties, is not from me, and I am not from him. **(1)**

369. `Abdallāh: The Messenger of God rose among us the same way as I am among you, saying: "By the One who there is no God but Him, the blood of a man who testifies that 'there is no God but Allāh and that I am the Messenger of God' is not permitted, other than under three circumstances: as a soul for a soul, the fornicator, and the one who leaves the community,

[260] Companion, lived in Mecca, killed together with Ibn al-Zubayr in 73/691.
[261] The area of the Ḥijāz.

abandoning his religion." Ibn al-Mubārak said: "Or he said: Leaving Islam."

370. Al-Ṣunābiḥī[262]: I heard the Messenger of God say: I am the leader of you at the Basin, and I will contend with the [other] communities in terms of numbers, so do not fight after me.

371. Marḥūm al-Qaṭṭār[263]: When the dissension of Yazīd b. al-Muhallab happened, the people differed concerning him, so we went to Muḥammad b. Sufyān, and said to him: What do you think concerning this man? We said: What do you want to do? He said: Consider the most felicitious of the people when `Uthmān was killed, and follow his example. We said: That would be Ibn `Umar, who restrained himself.

372. `Abdallāh b. `Umar: The disappearance of this world in its entirety is less in God's eyes than blood of a Muslim man spilled without right.

373. Ḥumayd b. Hilāl[264]: It was said to Sa`d [b. Abī Waqqāṣ] during the days of these tribulations: "O Abū Isḥāq, will you not consider this matter, since you are one of the veterans of [the Battle of] Badr, and you are one of those left from the council,[265] so do you have [91] a solution?" He said: "In this here shirt (*qamīṣ*) I am not more worthy of the caliphate than I am, nor am I one who can fight, so that I can make my sword to differentiate the believer from the non-believer, and the non-believer from the believer, so to say: 'This is a believer, so do not kill him, while this is a non-believer, so kill him.'"

374. Abū Mūsā al-Asha`rī: on the authority of the Prophet, he said: "The Messenger of God mentioned that there will be tribulation before the Hour," then Abū Mūsā said: "By the One who

262 `Abd al-Raḥmān b. `Usayla al-Ṣunābiḥī, lived in Syria d. in Damascus, *fl.* 1st/7th century.

263 Listed as Marḥūm b. `Abd al-`Azīz al-`Aṭṭār, a *mawlā* of the family of Mu`āwiya, d. 187/803.

264 Lived in Baṣra, d. during the governorship of Khālid b. `Abdallāh al-Qaṣrī (724–38).

265 Appointed by `Umar on his deathbed.

holds my soul in His hand, there is no way out for me or for you concerning that which our Prophet promised us, other than we depart in the same way as we entered, without having innovated anything."

375. Abū Ḥāzim[266]: When al-Ḥasan b. `Alī's time had come, he instructed that he be buried with the Messenger of God, other than if there was conflict or fighting concerning that, in which case he should be buried in the graves of the Muslims. So when he died Marwān b. al-Ḥakam, leading the Umayyads and wearing weapons, came, and said: "He will not be buried with the Prophet—you prevented `Uthmān [from being buried with him], so we will prevent you." So they feared a fight between them. Abū Ḥāzim said: Abū Hurayra said: "I think that if Moses had a son, who instructed that he be buried with his father, and they prevented it, then would that not have been unjust?" I said: "Of course," so he said: "This son of the Messenger of God, they have prevented him from being buried with his father,"[267] then Abū Hurayra went to al-Ḥusayn, and spoke with him, imploring him by God, so he said: "Your brother instructed that if you feared fighting, then return me to the graves of the Muslims," and he kept at him until he did that, so they bore him to the Baqī` [al-Gharqad],[268] but not one of the Umayyads came to his funeral other than Khālid b. al-Walīd b. `Uqba—he emplored them by God and because of his close relationship (*qarāba*) [with Muḥammad], but they avoided him, so he attended the funeral with al-Ḥusayn.

376. Sufyān b. al-Layl[269]: I went to Ḥasan b. `Alī after his return from al-Kūfa to Medina, and I said to him: "O humiliator of the believers," since he was one of those who had argued with `Alī, saying: "I heard `Alī saying: I heard the Messenger of God

[266] Probably Abū Ḥāzim al-Anṣārī al-Bayāḍī, a *mawlā*, possibly a Companion, *fl.* 1st/7th century.

[267] Of course, al-Ḥasan was not really the "son" of Muḥammad; he was his grandson.

[268] The public cemetary of Medina.

[269] In Ṭabarī, *Tā'rīkh*, vi, p. 20 said to have been one of al-Mukhtār's followers.

saying: 'It will not be long before the rule of this community will be gathered to a man with a wide anus,[270] a mammoth [amount of] phlegm, eating without being sated,'—and this is Mu`āwiya, so I knew that the order of God had been fulfilled, but I was afraid that there would be blood between us. By God, when I heard this tradition, even if I had this world, and everything upon which the sun and moon rose, it would not have made me happy—since then I would meet God Most High with a letting-cup of blood belonging to a Muslim man, unjustly."

377. Al-Ḥasan: The Messenger of God said to al-Ḥasan b. `Alī: This, my son, is a lord, by whom God will make peace between two mighty groups of Muslims.

378. Al-Zuhrī: `Alī met Usāma b. Zayd or sent for him, then `Alī said to him: "We would never bring up something to you other than concerning ourselves, O Usāma, but why did you not join us [92] in this matter?" Usāma said: "O Abū Ḥasan, if you grasped the lip of a lion, I would grasp the other side with you, so that we would both perish or live together, but as for this matter in which you are, by God, I will never enter into it, ever."

379. Ibn `Umar said to a man who asked him concerning fighting with al-Ḥajjāj or Ibn al-Zubayr, so Ibn `Umar said to him: "Which ever of the two parties you fight with, if you are killed, you are in hell (*laẓā*)."[271]

380. `Abdallāh b. Salām: "Hold back from this old man," meaning `Uthmān, "for there is little life left to him, so I swear by God, if you kill him, God Most High will draw His sword, and will not sheathe it until the Day of Resurrection."

381. Abū Shurayḥ al-Ma`āfirī[272]: I said to Ibn `Umar or they said to him: "Do you not see what this group is doing? They are acting in opposition to the way of the Prophet, so will you not enjoin the good and forbid the evil??" He said: "Of course," they said:

[270] Mu`āwiya's large buttocks are attested in al-Ya`qūbī, *Tā'rīkh* (Beirut: Dār al-Kutub al-`Ilmiyya, 1999), ii, p. 166 (*`aẓīm al-iliyatayn*); see no. 238.

[271] Q 70:15.

[272] `Abd al-Raḥmān b. Shurayḥ al-Ma`āfirī, lived in Alexandria, d. 167/783–4.

"So we are afraid for you, all of us will come with you." He said: "So, come with the blessing of God." They said: "We are afraid, even though we are all bearing weapons." He said: "As for that, no."

382. `Alī b. Abī Ṭālib: It would not make me happy if I was [alive] seventy [years] from the killing of `Uthmān, even if I had this world and what is in it.

383. Ibn `Abbās: I heard `Alī saying: I never killed `Uthmān or ordered his killing.

384. Ibn Ṭāwūs from his father: When the dissension of `Uthmān happened, a man said to his family: "Bind me with iron, for I am crazy." So when `Uthmān was killed, he said: "Let me go, praise be to God, who healed me from the madness, and allowed me to avoid the killing of `Uthmān."

385. Abū Bakra[273] on the authority of his father: The Messenger of God said: Will you not go back after me into error, cutting each other's heads off?

386. Ibn Sīrīn: I was informed Sa`d used to say: I waged jihad when I knew what it was for, but I would not fight until you bring me a sword with two eyes, a tongue and lips, which can say: "This is a believer, but this is an unbeliever." [93]

387. Ibn `Umar: The Messenger of God said: "Whoever bears weapons against us, is not from us." Abū Mu`āwiya added: "Whoever draws weapons against us."

388. Ibn `Umar: Two men came to him during the dissension of Ibn al-Zubayr, and they said: "The people have done the things which you have seen, while you are [`Abdallāh] Ibn `Umar b. al-Khaṭṭāb, and the Companion of the Messenger of God, so what prevents you from going out [to fight]?" He said: "That God Most High forbade me from the blood of my brother Muslim," so the two of them said: "But did not God Most High say: 'Fight them until (there) is no persecution [*fitna*] and the

[273] Nufay` b. al-Ḥārith from al-Ṭā'if, Companion, lived in Baṣra, d. 50, 51 or 52/670, 671, or 672.

religion is God's.'"[274] He said: "We have fought until there is no dissension, and the religion is God's, but you want to fight until there is dissension, and that the religion would belong to other than God."

389. Abū Dharr: The Messenger of God said to me: "O Abū Dharr, when you see that the people are fighting until the oil stone is drowned in blood, what will you do?" I said: "God and His Messenger know best." He said: "Enter your house." I said: "But if they come to me?" He said: "Then go to whoever you are related." I said: "Should I bear weapons?" He said: "Then you would be participant with them." I said: "What can I do, O Messenger of God?" He said: "If you fear that the swords will flash in your direction, then meet an [enemy] group, with your garment over your face, [saying] 'Come back with your and my sin [on the Day of Resurrection].'"

390. `Abdallāh b. `Āmir b. Rabī`a[275]: `Uthmān said on the Day of the House:[276] "Among the mightiest of the people for whom I have use is a man who restrains his hand and weapons."

391. Abū Hurayra: I entered into the presence of `Uthmān on the Day of the House, so I said: "O Commander of the Believers, is it lawful for fighting?"[277] He said: "O Abū Hurayra, would it make you happy to fight all of the people and myself with them?" I said: "No." He said: "If you, by God, killed one man, it would be as if you killed all the people,"[278] so I returned and did not fight.

392. Abū Ṣāliḥ: I heard `Abdallāh b. Salām saying on the day `Uthmān was killed: "By God, for every cup of blood split, you are further away from God!" [94]

393. Jābir b. `Abdallāh: The Messenger of God said: "Your blood and

[274] Q 2:193.

[275] `Abdallāh b. `Āmir b. Rabī`a al-`Anzī, a *ḥalīf* of the Banū `Adī, Companion, d. approximately 85/704.

[276] When he was besieged in his house.

[277] For the phrase ṭāba *am ḍaraba*, see Lane, v, p. 1900 (right col.).

[278] Cf. Q 5:32.

wealth are forbidden you, just as this day, this month and this land are sacred to you."

394. `Abdallāh: A man continues to be in good standing (*fisḥat*)[279] with regard to his religion, as long as he does not spill forbidden blood, but when he spills forbidden blood, his modesty is stripped from him.

395. `Abdallāh b. al-Salām: We find `Uthmān in the Book of God Most High as a Commander over the deserter and the fighter.[280]

396. `Abdallāh b. `Āmir: I was with `Uthmān in the house, so he said: "I adjure every one who sees that he owes hearing and obeying to me to hold back their hand and weapons, for the best of you in my eyes are those who have no need of their hand and his weapons." Then he said: "Rise, O Ibn `Umar, and go among the people." So Ibn `Umar rose, together with men from his clan, from the Banū `Adī, Banū Sarāqa and Banū Muṭī`,[281] all rose with him. They then opened the door, whereupon the people entered and killed `Uthmān.

397. `Abdallāh b. `Āmir: `Āmir b. Rabī`a stayed the night in prayer when the people yearned to strike `Uthmān—praying the night. Then he slept, and a dream came to him, saying: "Rise, and ask God to grant you refuge from the dissension, from which God has granted refuge to His righteous servants," so he rose and prayed, then suffered, but did not go out, until his funeral.

398. Jundub: "There will be tribulations," so we said: "O Abū `Abdallāh, so what do you order us [to do]?" He said: "The earth, the earth, let each of you dwell in his house, not letting anyone come out without my upbraiding him."

399. Ibn `Abbās: When `Alī was assassinated, the people swore allegiance to al-Ḥasan. Ziyād said to me: "Would you like to have the rule?" I said: "Yes." He said: "So I will kill so-and-so

[279] Perhaps influenced by the Ethiopian *fsḥ* "to rejoice, be glad," Leslau, p. 168; also Biella, *Old South Arabian Dictionary* (Missoula, MT: Scholars Press, 1982), p. 412.

[280] Perhaps a reference to Q 3:160.

[281] Banū `Adī was the clan of `Umar; the other two were probably closely allied.

and so-and-so," three of his companions. I said: "Didn't they pray the morning prayers?" He said: "Of course." I said: "Then, by God, there is no way!" [95]

400. Ibn `Umar that he did not prepare to fight anyone of the people of the *qibla* (Muslims) other than Najda al-Ḥarūrī when he feared that he would block him from the House (the Ka`ba).

401. `Abd al-Raḥmān b. Abī Laylā[282]: I saw `Alī lifting his arms to his bosom (*ḥaḍīna*)[283] in one of the alleyways of so-and-so clan [in Medina] saying: "O God! I declare my innocence to You with regard to the blood of `Uthman."

402. Ḥudhayfa b. al-Yamān: "They will be killed at this wall," meaning two groups of Muslims, "their dead are the dead of the *jāhiliyya*."

403. Ḥudhayfa b. al-Yamān, when [the news of] `Uthmān's killing came to him, while he was sick, he said: "Sit me down," so they caused him to sit, then he lifted his hands, and said: "O God! I testify to You that I did not order, I did not associate, nor did I give approval," saying this three times.

404. Ibn al-Ḥanafiyya[284] and Ibn `Abbās: It was said to `Alī: This `Ā'isha is cursing the killers of `Uthmān, so he lifted his hands until they reached his face, and said: I curse the killers of `Uthmān, may God curse them on the plains and mountains. So he said that twice or three times, then Ibn al-Ḥanafiyya turned to us, and said: In us—meaning Ibn `Abbās—is there not a witness of justice?

405. Abū Mūsā: "Behind you there are tribulations like the falling of dark night, in which the man will wake a believer but go to bed a disbeliever, or go to bed a believer and wake a disbeliever. The one who sits during them is better than the one who rises,

[282] Lived in Kūfa, said to have been born during the caliphate of `Umar, so he could have been no more than fifteen when `Uthmān was murdered, a judge, d. 83/702–3.

[283] Leslau, p. 226.

[284] Muḥammad b. al-Ḥanafiyya, a son of `Ali, but not descended from the Prophet, a messianic figure for Mukhtāar (albeit unwillingly), d. 81/700.

the one who rises is better than the one who walks, and the one who walks is better than the one who rides." They said: "What would you command us to do?" He said: "Be people dwelling in houses."[285]

406. Ibn `Umar: On the day `Uthmān was killed he said: By God, if you have killed him, you will never pray together ever, nor wage jihad together, nor perform the pilgrimage or constitute a group together ever, but bodies and opinions will differ.

407. Khubāb b. al-Arat[286] said to his son when the people fell into the matter of `Uthmān, "It is as if I see these [in hell], who have departed [from Islam] at the least tribulation, so when you meet them, be like the best of humanity." [96]

408. Zurāra[287] and Abū `Abdallāh [that] they heard `Alī saying: "By God, I have not commanded, by God, I have not associated, nor killed, nor given approval," meaning to kill `Uthmān.

409. Ibn Abī Bakra from his father on the authority of the Prophet: "Do not return to being in error after me, cutting off people's heads; let the witness inform those absent, let your blood, wealth" and I think he said "sexual honor be forbidden to you like they are today in your land, in this [holy] month. You will meet your Lord, who will ask you concerning your deeds, so do not return to being in error after me, cutting people's heads off. Will not the witness inform those absent?"

410. Sayyār b. Salāma[288]: We entered into the presence of Abū Barza when the people were differing, so he said: "The happiest of people in my opinion are a band which sticks together, with empty stomachs with regard to their wealth, with light backs with regard to the blood [they have] shed."

411. Abū Hurayra: The Messenger of God said: Woe to the Arabs from an evil approaching; those who restrain their hand will prosper.

285 As opposed to *aḥlās al-khuyūl* "people dwelling on horseback."

286 Companion, a *mawlā* to Khuzā`a, a smith (*qayn*), lived in Kūfa, d. 37/657–8.

287 Probably Zurāra b. Awfā al-`Āmirī, lived in Baṣra, served as a judge, d. 93/711–12.

288 Sayyār b. Salama al-Riyāḥī, lived in Baṣra, *fl.* 2nd/8th century.

412. Muḥammad b. Sīrīn: Zayd b. Thābit entered into the presence of `Uthmān, and said: "These Helpers (Anṣār) are at your door saying, 'If you wish, we will be the Helpers of God twice [and help you].'" He said: "As for fighting, no."

413. Ribāḥ b. al-Ḥārith[289] said: I heard al-Ḥasan b. `Alī while he was preaching to the people in Ctesiphon (al-Madā'in), and he said: "Is not the command of God in force, even if the people dislike it, so I would not like to have a mustard-seed's weight from the community of Muḥammad flowing in it blood to the amount of a cupping-glass if I knew that which would benefit me from that which would harm me, but I do not find it for me or you. So join the best of you," meaning the place of safety for you.

414. `Umar b. `Abd al-`Azīz said: When you have an imam who acts according to the Book of God and the way (*sunna*) of the Messenger of God, then fight together with your imam, but if you have an imam over you who does not act according to the Book of God nor the way of the Messenger of God, then depart from him. [You should be] calling for the Book of God and the way of the Messenger of God, while sitting in your house.

415. Al-Aḥnaf b. Qays[290]: [97] I swore allegiance to `Alī b. Abī Ṭālib, so Abū Bakra saw me while I had a sword fastened, and he said: 'What is this, nephew?' I said: "I swore allegiance to `Alī." He said: "Do not do it, nephew, for the people are fighting for this world, but they are taking it without mutual consultation." I said: "But the Mother of the Believers (`Ā'isha)?" He said: "A weak woman, I heard the Messenger of God saying: 'No people that allows a woman to manage their affairs will succeed.'"[291]

416. Abū Hurayra: People will come down to the Basin until when I know them and they know me, they will move away from me.

[289] Possibly the Ribāḥ al-Kūfī in al-Mizzī, *Tahdhīb*, ii, p. 454 (no. 1833), said to have been a *mawlā*, and to have been associated with al-Ḥasan.

[290] Lived at the time of the Prophet, lived in Baṣra, conquered Marw, d. 67 or 72/686–7 or 691–2.

[291] See al-Bukhārī, *Ṣaḥīḥ*, viii, p. 124 (no. 7099).

then I will say: "O Lord, my Companions, my Companions!" But He will say: "You do not know what they innovated after you."

417. Ka`b b. Murra that the Messenger of God mentioned the future tribulation, then a man with his head veiled in the middle of the day in the intense heat passed by, so the Messenger of God said: "This man on that day will be in accord with the guidance," so I rose, and took him by the shoulders, removed the veil from his head, and turned his head to the Messenger of God, and said: "O Messenger, this man?" He said: "Yes," and it was `Uthmān.

418. Masrūq: The Prophet said: There is absolutely no soul killed unjustly without the son of Adam [Cain] having a portion of it, since he was the first to pave the way for killing. **(1)** Other than he said: "A portion of his blood."

419. `Abdallāh: The Messenger of God said: The first to be judged on the Day of Resurrection will be concerning [shed] blood, so a man will be brought taking the hand of a man, saying: "O Lord, this one killed me," so He will say: "For what did you kill him?" So he will say: "O Lord, I killed him for the glory of so-and-so," so then He will say: "It [the glory] is not for him, bring your deeds," so a man will be brought taking the hand of a man, saying: "O Lord, this one killed me," so He will say: "For what did you kill him?" So he will say: "That the glory be to God," so He will say: "Glory to Me!"

420. `Abdallāh: A man continues to be in good standing with his religion as long as his palm is clean from blood, so when he plunges his hand into forbidden blood, his modesty is stripped away from him. [98]

421. Abū Bakra: The Messenger of God said: "Whoever kills one covered by treaty improperly, God will forbid Paradise to him."

422. Abū Hurayra: The Messenger of God said: "Woe to the Arabs from an approaching evil, from blind, deaf, mute dissension, in which the sitter is better than the stander, the stander is

better than the walker, and the walker is better than the hasty one. Woe to the hasty one in it [dissension] from God Most High on the Day of Resurrection!"

423. Unidentified: that the Messenger of God said: "Whoever prays the morning prayer is in the company of God until the evening, and whoever prays the evening prayer is in the company of God until the morning. So do not betray God with regard to his company, since whoever breaks God's compact with regard to his company, God will seek him, then find him, then roll him on his nostrils in Hell."

424. `Umayr b. Hāni': I saw Ibn `Umar saying: "Ibn al-Zubayr, Najda, and al-Ḥajjāj are all falling into the Fire just like flies fall into soup, so when you hear the herald,[292] make haste to him."

425. Abū Ḥaṣīn: I saw Ibn `Umar prostrating at the Ka`ba in front of the [Black] Stone, while he was saying: "O God! I take refuge in You from the evil that Quraysh has mixed up."

426. Ibn `Abbās: When `Alī was killed and the people swore allegiance to his son al-Ḥasan, Ziyād [b. Abīhi] came to Ibn `Abbās and said: "Would you want for this matter [rule] to be firm with you?" He said: "Yes." He said: "Then send for so-and-so and so-and-so, and cut off their heads." Ibn `Abbās said: "Did they pray this morning?" He said: "Yes." He said: "Then there is no way to [kill] them, I believe they are under the protection of God." When what Ziyād did [later] reached Ibn `Abbās later he said: "I think he was alluding to that which he saw fit to do."

427. Ḥudhayfa: A warning to you concerning the tribulations—let them happen to no one, since by God, whenever they happen to anyone they will smash him like the flood smashes [in its wake]. They are an entanglement going forward, such that even the ignorant says: "This is an entanglement," and clear [way] going backwards. [99][293]

428. Abū Hurayra: The dissension of Ibn al-Zubayr is one

[292] Probably for the gathering to Syria, see nos. 1708–34.

[293] Section break for pp. 100–2.

of the zigzags of the tribulations. The Overshadowing Overwhelming one remains, whoever overlooks it, it overlooks him, and whoever is tossed by its waves, it tosses him.

429. Abū Hurayra: I am the most knowledgeable concerning a dissension that is to come which is like the hop of a rabbit. And I am the most knowledgeable concerning the way out of them. They said: "What is it?" He said: "That I would hold my hand [without a sword] until they come to kill me."

430. Jundub b. `Abdallāh, who detested some of these rulers during some of the dissensions, so he went out—he said: "A Syrian man stood out for combat, so he said: 'Who will do single combat?' So an Iraqi man stood out. He said: I attacked the Syrian with a spear, and God's oath, I didn't want to do anything other than intervene between them. So I said: 'Go, go,' and I went after him until he departed. He said: So by God, I remember my aggression after I sleep for a while, then the rest of my sleep for the night is denied me. I remember it after I place my food before me, so it [the pleasure of the food] is denied me, until I cannot reach it."

431. Mālik b. Dīnār[294]: When Medina was pillaged, Abū Sa`īd al-Khudarī took refuge on the mountain, but a Syrian followed him, so when Abū Sa`īd saw [104] that he was not departing, he advanced against him with a sword. He said: "Go, go," but he said that the Syrian refused to do anything other than fight him. When Abū Sa`īd saw that, he threw the sword [away], and said: "If indeed you stretch out your hand against me, to kill me, (still) I shall not stretch out my hand against you, to kill you. Surely I fear God, Lord of the worlds."[295] So when the Syrian took his hand, and led him off the mountain. Abū Sa`īd said: "You have seen me fight with the Messenger of God against the polytheists at this place."[296] So the Syrian said to

[294] Lived in Baṣra, well-known ascetic, d. 130/747–8.
[295] Q 5:28; Abel speaking to Cain.
[296] Presumably at the Battle of the Khandaq (5/627).

him: "Who are you?" He said: "I am Abū Sa`īd al-Khudarī." He said: "Go, may God bless you!"

432. `Alī: I never killed or gave orders, but I was overcome [by events].

433. Al-Ḍaḥḥāk that a man used to come in front of the commander to ask him: "If a man is brought to the commander, when I do not know what his condition is, then he commands me to cut off his head [should I do it]?" He said: "Do not cut off his head." He said: "But if the commander commands me?" He said: "Even if the commander commands you, do not obey him." He said: "Then he will cut off my head." He said: "Then you are the one with the head cut off."

434. Masrūq: The Messenger of God said during the Farewell Pilgrimage: "After me, do not return to being unbelievers, cutting each other's heads off."

435. Mujāhid: I was on a raid, so when I returned, Ibn `Umar said to me: "O Mujāhid, the people will be unbelievers after you—this Ibn al-Zubayr and the Syrians will kill each other."

436. Abū Ja`far al-Anṣārī[297]: I saw `Alī wrapped with a sword, sitting in the shadow of the women. He said: I heard him saying when `Uthmān was killed: "May they perish!" the rest of the day.

437. Kulthūm al-Khuzā`ī[298]: I heard Ibn Mas`ūd saying: "I do not like it that I shot an arrow at `Uthmān"—Musḥir said: "I thought that he was saying: 'to kill him'"—"even if I had gold more than anyone." [105]

438. Ka`b: Every time dissension rouses a group, they become its sacrifices.

439. Sa`īd b. al-Musayyib: The Messenger of God said: "Whoever aids the killing of a Muslim, by even part of a word, will come on the Day of Resurection with 'No hope of God's mercy' written between his eyes." **(1)**

[297] Lived in Medina, was a muezzin, *fl.* 1st/7th century.

[298] Companion, lived in Kūfa, *fl.* 1st/7th century.

440. Abū Mūsā al-Asha`rī: The likeness of the people during dissension is the likeness of people on a trip, when darkness overcomes them, some of them of them stand, while some of them stray [from the path], then when it passes, they have deviated from the path.

441. Al-Qāsim Abū `Abd al-Raḥmān: The Messenger of God said: "Have I not informed you of the treatment for the tribulation? God has not permitted anything that was forbidden before it, so what is with you that you ask for the door of your brother [to attack him], then in the morning come to him to kill him?"[299]

442. Muḥammad: When they gathered against the door of `Uthmān, it was said to him: "If you came out leading your squadron (*kutayba*)[300] perhaps when they saw it, they would go back." So `Uthmān went out leading his squadron, but a man from here and there drew [swords], then they struck each other, so it came time for `Uthmān to turn around. He said: "Concerning struggle over me and my being commander [of the believers] people are fighting," so he returned and entered the house, and I do not know whether he came out again after that until he was killed.

Muḥammad: Dissension happened when it happened, while the Companions of the Messenger of God were around 10,000 or more. If they had had permission they would have struck them until they expelled them from the quarters of Medina. Muḥammad said: Then Ibn al-Zubayr, Ibn `Umar and al-Ḥasan b. `Alī came to them—Ibn `Awn said and Nāfi` said: Ibn `Umar twice put on armor, and I was informed that Abū Hurayra used to circumambulate the house [of `Uthmān to protect it], saying: "Is it lawful to fight?"

443. `Abd al-Raḥmān b. Jubayr[301] that `Uthmān said on the day he was besieged, "On what basis do you allow killing me? Killing

[299] Reading *yaqtuluhu* with MM.

[300] Aramaic.

[301] `Abd al-Raḥmān b. Jubayr b. Nufayr al-Ḥaḍramī, lived in Ḥimṣ, d. 118/736.

is only allowed for three [reasons]: Whoever apostasizes after belief, commits fornication after correct sexual conduct, or kills someone without someone having been killed [unjustly] previously, and I do not fall under any of these categories. By God, verily, if you kill me, you will not pray together, you will not wage jihad against an enemy together, but with differing tendencies." [106]

444. `Abdallāh b. Salām: By God, people will be killed because of `Uthmān who are still in their fathers' loins, and who will never be born.

445. `Abd al-Raḥmān b. Faḍāla: When Cain killed his brother Abel, God transformed his intelligence, removed his heart, so he remained confused until the day he died.

446. Khalīfa b. al-Ḥasan[302]: The Messenger of God mentioned rulers, rulers of evil, and imams, imams of evil, and mentioned that the error of some of them would fill that which is between the heavens and the earth. He said: It was said: "O Messenger of God, can we not strike his face with a sword?" He said: "No, not as long as he prays." Or he said: "Not as long as they pray, no."

447. Abū al-Dardā': You will see matters you dislike, so be patient, do not change anything, or say: "We will change!" since God Most High is the Changer.

448. Ka`b: Fear the ruler, for the ruler only stays one day in his period [of rule], but the man and his family perishes during that day. Removal of a fixed mountain is easier than removal of a predestined king.

449. Ibn `Umar: We did not know that `Alī participated in the killing of `Uthmān either secretly or openly, but he was the head, so the people went frightened to him, so he took care of it, but [rumors] were attached to him of that which he did not do.[303] [107]

[302] Probably lived in Baṣra, *fl.* 1st/7th century.

[303] Because `Ali benefited from `Uthmān's murder, and confirmed a number of his assassins in various offices, in addition to letting them go unpunished, rumors spread that he was behind the murder.

Those who believed in Withdrawal during Tribulations

450. Usayyid b. al-Mutashammis b. Mu`āwiya: I heard Abû Mûsā al-Asha`rī, and he mentioned tribulation, then he said: "By God! If it is at the same time as me and you, I do not know of any way out for myself or you, according to what our Prophet entrusted us, other than to exit the way we entered." Al-Ḥasan said: "Safe." **(1)**
451. Abū Mūsā al-Asha`rī: There will be tribulations after you in which the one who is sitting is better the one who rises, the one who rises is better than the one who hurries—until he mentioned the rider—so be attached to your houses during [the tribulations].
452. Jundub: There will be tribulations, so stay close to the ground, and let each of you stay attached to his house. None will gush forth for the [tribulations] without them destroying it.
453. Abū Hurayra: The Messenger of God said: There will come upon the people a time when a man will have to choose between impotence and iniquity. Whoever lives in this time let him choose impotence over iniquity. **(1)**
454. Abdallāh b. Mas`ûd: [108] There will come upon the people a time when the believer in it is more lowly than a concubine; the cleverest of them, who moves stealthily with his religion like a fox. **(1)**
455. Kurz al-Khuzā`ī: The Messenger of God said: The best of people on that day is a believer who withdraws to the mountain paths, fearing his Lord, and leaving the people because of their evil.
456. Ḥudhayfa: There will come upon the people a time when none will be saved other than the one who prays the prayer of a drowning man.
457. Ibn Mas`ūd: The best of people during the tribulation are the people of black sheep, shepherding them on the mountain peaks and rainy places; the worst of people during [that time] will be every rider in the saddle and every enthusiastic preacher.

458. Mujāhid: Islam began as a stranger, and will return to being a stranger, so blessed are the strangers before the Hour.[304]

459. `Awn b. `Abdallāh[305]: When a man during the dissension of Ibn al-Zubayr threw his head down to the earth, another man came to him, saying: "What are you talking about to the earth, O Abü al-Dunyā?" He said: "Really, do you think about what has happened to the people—I am guilty of it!" He said: "God has saved you from it by your thinking about it. Who is it who asks God, but He does not give, or depends upon Him, but He does not suffice?"

460. `Abdallāh b. Hubayra: Whoever lives at the time of the dissension, let him break his leg; if he is compelled [to join] then let him break the other leg.

461. `Alqama: When the people of truth have been victorious over the people of untruth, then you are not in a tribulation. [109]

462. Ma`mar b. Ṭāwūs[306] from his father: The Messenger of God said: The best of people in the tribulation is a man who takes the head of his horse to frighten the enemy, and they frighten him, or the man who withdraws, giving God his due.

463. Ibn Khuthaym: The Messenger of God said: The best of people in the tribulation is the one who eats from the spoils (*fa'y*) of his sword in the path of God, and the man who is on a lofty mountain, eating from the milk of his flocks.

464. Ibn Ṭāwüs: There will come upon the people a time when the best dwelling is the desert.

465. `Abdallāh b. al-Zubayr sent to his mother, saying: "The people have discarded me, so these [Umayyads] have called me to give up, so what do you think?" She said: "If you rebelled to revive the Book of God and the Way (*sunna*) of His Prophet,

304 See al-Ajurrī, *al-Ghurabā' min al-mu'minīn* (Damascus: Dār al-Bashā'ir, 1992) for a discussion of this tradition.

305 `Awn b. `Abdallāh al-Hudhalī, lived in Kūfa, an ascetic, d. approximately 113/731–2.

306 Not listed, but like his father, a *mawlā* of Persian extraction, *fl.* 2nd/8th century.

then you will die in the truth, but if you only rebelled to seek this world, then there is no good in you, either alive or dead."

466. Abü Hurayra: The dissension of Ibn al-Zubayr was one of the zigzags of the tribulation. The overwhelming heaviness yet remains—whoever stays aloft, it will keep him aloft, whoever gets carried away, it will carry him. [110]

The Portents of the end of the Umayyads' Dominion

467. `Alī: The rule will continue with the Umayyads as long as they do not differ between themselves.
468. `Alī: The rule will be theirs until they kill their killed one, and quarrel among themselves. When this will happen, the God will send groups from the east against them, to kill them separately and to count them [down to the last one].[307] By God, for every year they rule, we will rule two; for every two they rule, we will rule four!
469. `Alī: "Those people [the Umayyads] will continue to grab the center of this rule as long as they do not differ between themselves. When they differ between themselves, it will depart from them, and not return until the Day of Resurrection," meaning the Umayyads.
470. Al-Ḥasan b. Muḥammad b. `Alī: The group will continue in the center of their rule, until one of four evils descends among them: God casts their misfortune amongst them, or the black banners come from the direction of the east and allow their [blood] to be shed, or the Pure Soul will be killed in the Sacred Enclosure, so God will get rid of them, or they will send an army to the land of the Sacred Enclosure, where it will be swallowed up by the earth.
471. Al-Hind daughter of al-Muhallab[308]: that `Ikrima the *mawlā*

[307] The curse of al-Khubāb when he was martyred: al-Bukhārī, *Ṣaḥīḥ*, v, pp. 15–16 (no. 3989).

[308] Al-Muhallab b. Abī Ṣufra, who served as a governor for the Umayyads, d. 83/702.

of Ibn `Abbās,[309] who used to frequent her, narrated to her that Ibn `Abbās said: [111] "The rule will continue among the Umayyads as long as two spears do not clash between them. When two spears clash between them, then it will leave them until the Day of Resurrection."

472. Tubay`, the step-son of Ka`b: The dominion of the Umayyads is 100 years; the Marwānids of that will have sixty some years. Their dominion will not go until they contest it with their hands, desiring to shore it up, but being unable [to do so]. Every time they shore it up from one side, then it collapses from the other. They will open with a *mim* [=Mu`āwiya] and close off with a *mim* [=Marwān II], and their dominion will not go until they overthrow a caliph from among them, and kill him and his retinue.[310] The reddish Ass of the Jazīra—Marwān—will be killed, then their dominion will be at an end. At his hands will be the destruction of the crowns.

473. Ibn Mas`ūd: The boy caliph will rule the people, who will receive the oath of allegiance when he has no sons, then he will be killed in Damascus by treachery, and the people will differ after him.

474. `Irbāḍ b. al-Sāriyya[311]: When the caliph is killed in Syria [=Damascus] spilled blood will be continue to be forbidden, since no imam would permit its sanctity until the rule of God comes.[312]

475. A man from the Sakāsik[313]: The Messenger of God said: When

309 Originally a Berber, an important figure in Qur'ānic exegesis, d. approximately 105/723–4.

310 Walīd II (d. 126/744); compare the version in Barbara Roggema (trans.), *The Legend of Sergius Baḥīra: Eastern Christian Apologetics and Apocalypse in Response to Islam* (Leiden: E.J. Brill, 2009), pp. 285–7: "And in the year 1055 [=744] of Alexander . . . the Arabs killed their king, and after that there was much unrest in the world during one week."

311 `Irbāḍ b. al-Sāriyya al-Sulamī, Companion, lived in Ḥimṣ, d. 75/694–5.

312 Cf. Q 11:76 (*amr rabbika*), 16:33 (*amr rabbika*), 40:78 (*amr Allāh*).

313 A Yemenite tribe, closely related to Kinda, allied with the Umayyads: Ibn al-Kalbi, *Jamharat al-nasab* (Cairo: Maktabat al-Thaqāfa al-Diniyya, 2010), ii, pp. 54–7.

Quraysh kills their lambs, then God will magnify the enmity between them, so that there will not remain anyone proud in themselves or a commander without being killed. The misfortune (*al-ṣaylam*) is in al-Jazīra.

476. `Alī: There is no tribulation more frightening to me that you will have to endure than that of the Umayyads, other than a blind dark-night tribulation.

477. Umm al-Dardā'[314]: I heard Abū al-Dardā' saying: "When the boy caliph from the Umayyads will be killed between Syria and Iraq unjustly, then obedience will continually be flouted, and blood shed on the face of the earth without right," meaning al-Walīd b. Yazīd. [112]

478. Yazīd b. Abī Ḥabīb: It was said: when a squint-eyed caliph rules the people, if you are able to leave Egypt for Syria, then do so. He said: That was before the caliphate of Hishām.

479. Sufyān al-Kalbī[315]: "When a man from the family of Marwān is made caliph, called al-Walīd—at that time the caliphate of the Umayyads will be broken, so when al-Walīd b. `Abd al-Malik became caliph, and then died," it was said: "What was it that you said?" He said: "Verily, a man from them [the Umayyads] named al-Walīd b. Yazīd will be made caliph."

480. Sufyān al-Kalbī: The departure of the Umayyads' rule will be when a youth from them is made caliph, then is killed, together with his mother, and so that that time their rule will be broken.

481. Tubay`: This rule will continue among the Umayyads until four will rule from the loins of one man: Sulaymān b. `Abd al-Malik, Hishām, Yazīd, and al-Walīd.

482. Mu`āwiya said to Ibn `Abbās, when Marwān b. al-Ḥakam came in to him with some need, then turned around [to leave]: "Do

[314] Wife of Abū al-Dardā', called Hujayma, received a proposal from Mu`āwiya after the death of her husband, still alive 81/700 when she is said to have made the pilgrimage.

[315] Unidentified, but probably Egyptian, *fl.* 1st/7th century.

you know that the Messenger of God said: 'When the clan of Banū al-Ḥakam reaches the number of 499 their destruction will be swifter than chewing a date?'" Ibn `Abbās said: "O God, yes!"

483. Kathīr b. Murra al-Ḥaḍramī: How beloved it would be for me if after the departure of the Umayyads nothing remained for me of this world other than my two shoes!

484. Abu Umayya al-Kalbī said that an elder who had lived during the time of the *jāhiliyya* during the caliphate of Yazīd b. `Abd al-Malik said: "After the death of Hishām a man from among them, a boy, will give the people stipends never before given, but then a man from his house would develop, secretively, without being mentioned, and kill him, so that blood would flow before him. Familial ties would be cut and wealth would be profuse at his hands. Then *murrīn* [=Marwān] from there—and he pointed to al-Jazīra—will come to you, and take it [the rule] by force with his sword. After *murrīn* the black banners will come to you, flowing." [113]

485. Al-Zuhrī: Hishām will die a natural death, then the youth from the people of his house will be killed unnaturally, then the one who comes from the direction of al-Jazīra—Sulaymān b. Hishām was in al-Jazīra then—will be killed. After that are the black banners.

486. `Alī: There will continue to be a fierce trial from the Umayyads until God sends the groups, like the autumn clouds, coming from everywhere. They will not appoint a commander or commanded, but when this happens, God will remove the dominion of the Umayyads.

487. Ka`b: There will be a dissension in Syria in which blood will be shed, familial ties will be cut, and wealth will be profuse, then after that will come the easterner (*al-sharqiyya*).

488. Ka`b: After his death [=Hishām] there will be a man who will rule for the length of a woman's pregnancy, and the weaning of her child. Then another will reign, though there won't be a bit until he perishes. Then a man will come who will be killed,

from Taymā',[316] whose time has come, and he and his son will be fifty years.

489. Tubay`: The last caliph from the Umayyads, his rule will be two years, not more.

490. Reliable elders: Yashū` and Ka`b met—Yashū` was a knowledgeable man, a reader of books from before the sending of the Prophet, so they asked each other [questions], then Yashū` asked Ka`b: "Do you have knowledge about the kings who will be after the time of the Prophet?" Ka`b said: "I find in the Torah twelve kings, the first of them *ṣiddīq* [Abū Bakr], then *al-fārūq* [`Umar],[317] then *al-amīn* [`Uthmān], then the beginning of the kings, then the Master of the Guard, then a tyrant, then the Master of the Groups—he is the last of the kings, who will die a natural death then the Master of the Sign [=Hisham][318], who will die a natural death.

As for the tribulations, they will be when the Son of the Gold Eraser (*ibn māḥiq al-dhahabiyyāt*) is killed.[319] Then the affliction will take over, and hope will be lifted. At that time there will be four kings from the people of the house of the Master of the Sign—two kings who will not read a book, a king who will die on his bed, with his staying-time being short, and a king who will come from the north (*jawf*)—at his hands there will be the affliction, and crowns will be destroyed. He will stay in Ḥimṣ (Emesa) 120 mornings, then a fright will come to him

[316] Oasis in northern Saudi Arabia.

[317] See Bashear, "The title al-*Fārūq* and its association with `Umar I," *Studia Islamīca* 92 (1990), pp. 47–70.

[318] This nickname is obscure.

[319] Presumably Walid II, whose father Yazid II issued an iconoclastic edict, and was responsible for the destruction of icons: A. A. Vasiliev, "The Iconoclastic Edict of the Caliph Yazid II, A.D. 721." *Dumbarton Oaks Papers* 9–10 (1956), pp. 25–47. The key to understanding this nickname is the fact that the word *maḥaqa* is used both in the Qur'ān (2:276, 3:141) in a favorable sense, as it is in the *ḥadīth* literature, cf. Wensinck, *Concordance* (Leiden: E. J. Brill, 1936–62), s.v., *maḥaqa*. Unlike other pejorative nicknames given to the Umayyads, apparently Yazīd II was remembered fondly in apocalyptic circles.

[114] from his land, and so he will go from it.[320] The affliction will occur in the interior, and between them, then their rule will be cut off, and come from the People of [the] House other than them, who will overcome them."

491. Abū `Āmir al-Ṭā'ī[321]: I was in Ḥimṣ when Marwān besieged Ḥimṣ for four months or approximately that long, until hunger and thirst reached them, and so constrained them that they desired to make a peace with him. He said: Marwān would order the people [soldiers] to dig outside the city, so that when they began to dig underneath its walls, other people from the people of Ḥimṣ opposite them dug inside the city, meeting each other in the tunnels. There was a Syriac-speaking Christian (*nabaṭī*) inside the city who, when Marwān's soldiers began to dig, ordered those in the city to dig opposite them. They continued to dig until they met each other [in the tunnels]. Often their diggings collapsed on them, and they would all die. Marwān was not able to order any digging against them from any direction without them counter-digging from inside the city. So it was said to Marwān: "There is a Syrian who, whenever an excavation is dug from outside the city, he directs them to dig opposite until both of us meet."

He said: So Marwān approached the Syrian, and [tried] to lure him with the promise of wealth that would be given to him, but the Syrian refused to come out to him. When he gave up on the Syrian, he said: "Cut all the water supplies going to them from every direction," so when the people of Ḥimṣ learned about this, they placed a black man on their walls naked, opposite the camp, and called: "O Marwān! If you are thirsty, we will give you to drink, if you are hungry we will feed you, and if you want we will do so-and-so to you,[322] so hold on to your army, so the water we send to you won't drown you!"

320 Marwān II. Note that Yāqūt, *Mu`jam*, ii, p. 188 states that the word *jawf* also means a donkey (*ḥimār*).

321 Probably `Abdallāh al-Alhānī, lived in Ḥimṣ, *fl.* 2nd/8th century.

322 Presumably some obscenity is being alluded to in the text.

Then they called inside the city to redirect al-Ḥarīs, their river,[323] to flow outside the city so as to encroach upon it [Ḥimṣ] and surround it. They poured the water from the wells into it, and water from it went out on to the camp of Marwān in earthenware jars. When it went by the camp of Marwān they were frightened of it, so Marwān said: "What is this?" They said: "Water sent out against you from the city of Ḥimṣ by the people of Ḥimṣ." He said: "I had thought that thirst was getting to them, but they have such an abundance of water that our camp is afraid of being drowned, so let's go." They went from them [the people of Ḥimṣ].[324] [115]

Appearance of the `Abbāsids

492. al-Zuhrī: It has reached me that the black banners will come out from Khurāsān, so when they have come down from the high road of Khurāsān they come down to remove Islam, so none but the banners of the non-Arabs from the Maghrib will be able to repel them.
493. `Uqba b. Abī Zaynab[325] that he went to Jerusalem to make a guarantee so I [Rajā' b. Abī Salama][326] said: "Perhaps you should be afraid of the westerners?' He said: 'No, their tribulation will never pass over them [the people of Jerusalem] as long as the black banners have not appeared. So, when the black banners appear, then fear their [the westerners'] evil."
494. Ibn `Abbās: I said to `Alī b. Abī Ṭālib: "When will our turn (*dawla*) be, O Abū al-Ḥasan?" He said: "When you see the banners of the youths of Khurāsān, you will get their sin, and we will get their piousness."

[323] Probably the same small fleuve for sewage mentioned in no. 1263.
[324] Al-Baladhuri, *Ansab*, vii, p. 175 states that Marwān II destroyed the walls of the city when he conquered it.
[325] Probably lived in Filasṭīn, listed with the informants of Rajā' in al-Mizzī, *Tahdhīb*, ii, p. 478 (no. 1878).
[326] Whose name was Mihrān, originally from Baṣra, lived in Ramla, d. 161/777–8.

495. Muḥammad b. al-Ḥanafiyya: A black banner will appear from Khurāsān belonging to the `Abbāsids.

496. Al-Zuhrī: The Messenger of God said: "An idiot son of an idiot will overcome this world." `Abd al-Razzāq[327] said: Ma`mar said: "This is Abū Muslim."

497. Abān b. al-Walīd b. `Uqba b. Abī Mu`ayṭ[328]: Ibn `Abbās went to Mu`āwiya while I was present, and asked him for provisions, so he gave them nicely [116], and then he said: "O Abū al-`Abbās, will you have a turn [ruling]?" He said: "Pardon me from that, O Commander of the Believers!" He said: "Tell me." He [Ibn `Abbās] said: "Yes, it will be at the end of time." He said: "Who will be your Helpers?" He said: "The Khurāsānians." He said: "There will be jousts for both the Umayyads and to the Hashemites, then the Sufyānī will appear."

498. Abū Hurayra: I was in the house of Ibn `Abbās, when he said: "Close the door." Then he said: "Is there anybody else but you?" They[329] said: "No," but I had been part of a group. So Ibn `Abbās said: "When you see the black banners coming from the direction of the east, then honor the Persians, for our turn is because of them." Abū Hurayra said to Ibn `Abbās: "Haven't I narrated to you what I heard from the Messenger of God?" He said: "You have something?" I said: "Yes," so he said: "Narrate!" I said: "I heard the Messenger of God saying: 'When the black banners appear the first part of them is dissension, the middle part is error, and the last part is unbelief.'"

499. Makḥūl: The Messenger of God said: What do I have to do with the `Abbāsids? They have divided my community, forced them to wear black clothes, so may God force them to wear clothes of fire!

327 Author of the *Muṣannaf*, a collection focusing upon the traditions from Yemen.

328 Abān commanded military operations during the 730s (al-Mizzī, *Tahdhīb*, vii, p. 478 [no. 7318]), son of al-Walīd, Companion, frequently appointed to financial positions, d. during the reign of Mu`āwiya (661–80).

329 It is not clear who the "they" are.

500. Abū Bakr b. Ḥazm[330]: The Prophet said: "This world will not go until it belongs to an idiot son of an idiot."

501. Ḥudhayfa: The Prophet said: "The Hour will not arise until the most felicitous of the people is an idiot son of an idiot."

502. Sa`īd b. al-Musayyib: The Messenger of God said: "The black banners belonging to the `Abbāsids will appear from the east, then they will stay as long as God wishes, then the small black banners will appear under a man from the progeny of Abū Sufyan and his supporters from the direction of the east."

503. Abū Hurayra: "Woe to the Arabs after 125 [=743], woe to them from a great killing of the wings. And what are the wings? And woe to the wings!! A wind following its blowing, a wind moving its blowing, and a wind slackening [117] its blowing! Is it not a woe to them from sudden death, from horrifying famine, from swift killing. God will impose a trial upon them because of their sins, which will cover their chests, uncover their curtains, change their happiness—is it not because of their sins that its pegs will be ripped out, its ropes be cut, its winds be made turbid, its disobedient one (*marrāq*)[331] will become perplexed! Is it not a woe to Quraysh from its heretic, who innovates things, making the religion turbid, and destroying its private dwellings, and turning against it its armies. The weeping, mourning [women] will rise up, crying, crying for this world, crying, crying for the humiliation of their servitude, crying, crying because of their sexual abuse, crying, crying because of the children in their bellies, crying, crying because of their children's hunger, crying, crying because of their humiliation after their haughty [station], crying, crying because of their men, crying, crying fearful about their soldiers, crying, crying desirous of their graves."

[330] Abū Bakr b. Muḥammad b. `Amr b. Ḥazm al-Anṣārī, lived in Medina, served as jurisprudent for Sulaymān b. `Abd al-Malik, d. 117 or 120/735 or 738.

[331] Presumably the reference to the tradition of Ali "I was ordered to fight the heretics, the oath-breakers, and the unjust," al-Sarakhsī, *Kitāb al-mabsūṭ* (Beirut: Dār al-Fikr, 2000), v, p. 1796; for an interpretation, Ibn Ṭāwūs, *Malāḥim*, pp. 24–5.

504. `Alī: "Woe to the Arabs after [the year] 125 from an evil encroaching! The wings, what are the wings? Woe and blessing (ṭūbā) are in the wings. A wind following its blowing, a wind blasting its blowing, and a wind slackening its blowing! Woe to them from swift killing, sudden death, horrifying famine, which will dump trial upon it, covering its chests, changing its happiness, and uncovering its curtains. Is it not because of its sins that its disobedient one has appeared, pulling up its pegs, and cutting its ropes. Woe to Quraysh from its heretic, who innovates things, making the religion turbid, pulling its dignity from it, destroying its private dwellings, turning against it its armies. At that the weeping, mourning [women] will rise up, crying, crying for this world, crying, crying for its religion, crying, crying because of their humiliation after their haughty [station], crying, crying because of their children's hunger, crying, crying because of the children in their bellies, crying, crying because of their forced servitude, crying, crying because of their sexual abuse, crying, crying because of the shedding of their blood, crying, crying because of their soldiers, crying, crying desirous of their graves."

505. Thawban[332]: The Prophet said: "What do I have to do with the `Abbāsids? They have divided my community, spilled its blood, forced it to wear black clothes—may God make them wear clothes of fire!"

506. Abū Umayya al-Kalbī during the caliphate of Yazīd b. Abd al-Malik said: An elder who had lived in the period of the *jāhliyya*, whose eyebrows had fallen in front of his eyes—we came to him to ask about our time, so he informed us concerning the Umayyads until he mentioned the appearance of Marwān: "Then after *murrīn* [Marwān II], who will appear from al-Jazīra, the black banners will flow to you until they will enter Damascus at three hours [118] into the day. They

[332] Thawbān b. Bujdud, Companion, *mawlā* of the Prophet, lived in Ramla, d. possibly in Ḥimṣ in 44/664–5.

will lift mercy from its people, then return it to mercy and lift the sword away from them, then go until they have reached the Maghrib."

507. Ka`b: After the Syrian eastern tribulation there will be the destruction of kings, the humiliation of the Arabs, until the people of the Maghrib appear.

508. Muḥammad b. `Alī: The Messenger of God said: "Woe to my community from the two parties (*shī`atayn*), the party of the Umayyads and the party of the `Abbāsids, and the banner of error."

509. Ka`b: Not many days will pass until black banners appear belonging to the `Abbāsids from the direction of the east. **(1)**

510. Al-Zuhrī: The black banners will advance from the east, men like Bactrian camels (*bukht*) covered in cloth, with hair, their genealogies are to their villages, their names are nicknames—they will conquer Damascus, lifting mercy from them for three hours.

511. Abū Ṭalḥa[333]: They will enter Damascus with great black banners, making a terrible killing in it, with their slogan being "kill, kill!"[334]

512. Abū Ja`far: When the year 129 [=746–7] was reached, the swords of the Umayyads differed [among themselves], and the Ass of al-Jazīra leapt upon Syria, the black banners appeared in the year 129, the Ram appeared with an unnoticed people—their hearts like iron anvils, their hair down to their shoulders, without compassion or mercy upon their enemy. Their names are nicknames, their tribes are villages, upon them are clothes the color of the black night. He will lead them to the `Abbāsids, since it is their turn (*dawla*). They will kill the prominent people of that time, until they flee into the

[333] Possibly Abū Ṭalḥa (Dira` b. `Abdallāh?) al-Khawlānī, who lived in Syria, who related traditions about Syria, *fl.* 2nd/8th century.

[334] Persian: *bukush, bukush.*

desert, and their turn will continue until the comet (star with a tail) appears, then they will differ between them. [119]

513. Abū Qubayl mentioned the Umayyads, and took them to task, then he said: "The supporters of the black banners will rule you after them, and their rule and period will be lengthy, until two youths from them have allegiance sworn to them. When it is that time, then they will differ between themselves, and this difference will be lengthy, until three banners will be raised in Syria. When these are raised that will be the reason for the end of their period. So when you read in Egypt 'from the servant of God, `Abdallāh, the Commander of the Believers,' do not wait to read for them another letter from 'the servant of God, `Abd al-Raḥmān, the Commander of the Believers,' who is the master of the Maghrib, since he is the worst person who has ruled. They will destroy Egypt and Syria, so when their rule is heavy in Syria, the black banners and the supporters of the three banners will gather against those from the Maghrib who are in it [Syria]—they will gather altogether and fight them. The victory will be for the people of the three banners, and the rule of the Berbers will be cut off. Then they will fight the supporters of the black banners until their rule will be cut off."

514. Ibn `Abbās: A man and Ḥudhayfa came to him, so he said: "O Ibn `Abbās, [what is the meaning of] His Word, Most High, '*ḥ-m `-s-q*'?"[335] so he remained silent looking down for a time, and he turned from him, then he repeated it, but he did not answer anything, so Ḥudhayfa said: "I would like to tell you that I know why he dislikes [discussing it]. It was only revealed concerning a man from the people of his house, who is called `Abd al-Ilāh or `Abdallāh, who will descend upon one of the rivers of the east, building two cities upon it, dividing the river between them. 'Every stubborn tyrant'[336] will be gathered in it."

[335] Q 42:1.
[336] Q 11:59.

515. Arṭāt: When a city is built on the shores of the Euphrates [Baghdad], then divisions and disasters will come to you, and you will be separated from your religion, just as a woman opens her pudenda, until you will resist the humiliation that will descend among you. When a city is built between the two rivers in a land connected to the land of Iraq, then the little darkness (*duhaymā'*) has come to you.

516. Yūsuf b. `Abdallāh b. Salām[337] passed by the house of Marwān b. al-Ḥakam, then said: "Woe to the community of Muḥammad from the people of this house! until the black banners appear from Khurāsān."

517. Ka`b: The black banners of the `Abbāsids will appear until they descend upon Syria, and so God will kill by their hands every "stubborn tyrant" or enemy of theirs. They will fasten [120] their camels (*adam*)[338] in its courtyard forty-five mornings, then 70,000 will enter it, with their slogan being "Die, die!" Then "the war will lay down its burdens"[339] and their dominion will last 9x7 [63 years]. Then their rule will come undone after seventy-three years.

518. `Abdallāh b. Abī al-Asha`th al-Laythī[340]: Two banners of the `Abbāsids will appear, one of them, the first of them, victory, and the last of them, a burden. Do not help them; God will not aid them; and the other, the first of them is burden, and the last of them is unbelief. Do not help them; God will not aid them.

519. Sa`īd b. Zur`a[341]: I heard Nawf al-Bikālī[342] say to his soldiers: "I see that this year you will drape Damascus with saddle-bags, pack-saddles and felt, and take their slain out quickly,

[337] Son of `Abdallāh b. Salām, *ḥalīf* to the Anṣār, lived in Medina, d. during the caliphate of `Umar b. `Abd al-`Azīz (717–20).

[338] Lane, *Arabic-English Lexicon*, i, p. 37 gives this meaning.

[339] Q 47:4.

[340] Probably Syrian, *fl.* 1st/7th century.

[341] Syrian, lived in Ḥimṣ, *fl.* 2nd/8th century.

[342] Nawf b. Faḍāla al-Bikālī, lived in Damascus, stepson of Ka`b al-Aḥbār, killed during a raid with Muḥammad b. Marwān, *fl.* 2nd/8th century.

and split the bellies of their women."[343] Ka`b said: Those are a people that will come from the east angry, with black banners—written on their banners is "Your covenant and your oath of allegiance, we have kept it"[344]—then they will break it. They will come until they camp between Ḥimṣ and the Masḥal Monastery,[345] whereupon a detachment will come out against them, but they will flatten it like leather. Then they will go to Damascus, and conquer it by force. Their slogan will be "Forward, forward!" and "Kill, kill!" Mercy will be lifted from them for three hours of the day [for sacking the city].

520. `Alī b. `Abī Ṭālib: When you see the black banners, stay close to the ground, do not move your hands or your feet. Then a weak group, hitherto unnoticed, will appear, their hearts like iron anvils, they are the soldiers of the turn (*dawla*), who do not keep a covenant or promise. They will call to the truth, but they are not from its people. Their names are nicknames, their genealogies are to their villages, their hair is loose like that of women—until they differ among themselves. Then God will bring the truth from where He wills.

521. Ibn Mas`ūd: A man from al-Jazīra will appear and tread on the people, and pour out blood. Then a Hashemite man from Khurāsān will appear after the killing of his brother, who is called `Abdallāh, who will rule approximately forty years, then perish. Two men from the people of his house will differ, who are called by the same name. There will be an apocalyptic battle at `Āqir Qūfā[346] where the both of them will be appearing to be close [121] to the caliphate (?). Then there will be a

343 Note this topos: Mordechai Cogan, "Ripping open pregnant women," *Journal of the American Oriental Society* 103 (1983), pp. 755–7.

344 Perhaps alluding to Q 33:23: "Among the believers are men who have been truthful to the covenant which they made with God . . ."

345 Bewteen Ḥimṣ and Ba`lbak.

346 Four leagues up from Baghdād on the Tigris River, next to the tell of Dur-Kurigaizu (Kassite period), mentioned by Ibn Jubayr.

sign among the Banū al-Aṣfar, and a comet will appear, but then will disappear and not return to them.

522. Ka`b: The people of Ḥimṣ are the happiest of Syria concerning the appearance of the black banners; the people of Damascus are the most miserable.

523. Abū Hurayra: We came to him visiting because of indigestion that afflicted him, so he mentioned Mu`āwiya, and was furiously angry with him, speaking about him rudely, then Abū Hurayra said to al-Ḥasan b. `Alī: "Do not let it get to you, since by the One who holds my soul in His hand, if there were only one day left in the world, God would lengthen that day so that the caliphate would belong to the Hashemites."

524. Rāshid b. Dā'ud al-Ṣanā`ānī,[347] giving the chain of transmitters, said: After the destruction of the Umayyads, the one who brings wild animals will come, the people of the earth will gather to him from all four corners, so then God will punish this community with them.

525. Sa`īd b. Marthad Abū al-`Āliyya[348]: I was sitting with Shuraḥbīl b. Dhī Ḥimaya[349] at the palace of Ibn Athāl[350] when a distinguished elder from the Christians passed by, whose eyebrows had fallen over his eyes, leaning on a stick, so he said: "Hey, you, elder!" So he sat with him, and said: "How far back do you remember?" He said: "Persians, I saw them in this city, sitting circle after circle, talking among themselves, saying: 'The Muslims will be victorious over this earth, so God will open (conquer) the storehouses for them, both on land and sea. They will be known by the length of their hair, and their spears, and their wearing a wrapping around the waist. Their

347 Rāshid b. Dā'ūd al-Barsamī, lived in Damascus, *fl.* 2nd/8th century.

348 Sa`īd b. Marthad al-Raḥabī, probably Syrian, maybe from Ḥimṣ, *fl.* 2nd/8th century.

349 Probably Shuraḥbīl b. Shufa`a al-Raḥabī, Syrian, *fl.* 2nd/8th century.

350 In Ḥīra, former capital of the Lakhmids, in south Iraq. Ibn Athāl was a Christian close associate of Mu`āwiya.

last king they will kill violently.[351] Wealth and many foodstuffs will be poured on their table, but they will not be satisfied.'" [122]

526. Ḥudhayfa b. al-Yamān: "A man from the east will appear calling for the family of Muḥammad, but he will be the farthest of people from them. They will raise black signs, the first of which is victory, the last of which is unbelief. The Arabs' garbage, the lowest of the *mawālī* (clients), runaway slaves, and the disobedient ones of all the horizons. Their signs are black, their religion is polytheism (*shirk*), and most of them are mutilated (*jud`*)." I said: "What is *jud`*?" He said: "Uncircumcised." Then Ḥudhayfa said to Ibn `Umar: "You will not be seeing him, O Abū `Abd al-Raḥmān?" `Abdallāh [b. `Umar] said: "But I will narrate about him to those who are after me." He said: "A tribulation called *al-ḥāliqa* (the encircling) because it will encircle the religion; the pure Arabs, the righteous *mawālī*, the posessors of treasures and the jurisprudents will perish during it, but the fewest of the few will make it through."
527. Al-Ḥasan b. Muḥammad b. `Alī: The Umayyads will continue to be in charge until the black banners appear from the east and declare them to be permitted (killed).
528. Al-Ḥasan and Ibn Sīrīn: A black banner will appear from the direction of Khurāsān, and it will continue to be victorious until their destruction will be from where they came: Khurāsān.
529. `Alī: Their destruction will be from where they came.
530. Abū Hurayra: The Messenger of God said: Black banners will appear from Khurāsān; nothing will stop them until they are raised in Jerusalem (*Iliyā'*),[352] meaning Bayt al-Maqdis (Jerusalem).
531. Ka`b: Verily, Iraq is about to be scraped like leather, Syria is

[351] Reading *ghasb* with DKI.
[352] From Aelia Capitolina, the Roman name for Jerusalem.

about to be split like hair, Egypt is about to be crumbled like dung—so at that time the rule [of God] will descend. [123]

The First Portent of the end of the Period of the `Abbāsids

532. Arṭāt: Their destruction will be from their differing, so the first sign of the end of their dominion will be differences between them.
533. Abū Qubayl: The people will continue to be well in ease as long as the dominion of the `Abbāsids does not fall apart. When their dominion falls apart, there will be continuous tribulations until the Mahdi appears.
534. Abū Umayya al-Kalbī: A man who had lived during the *jāhiliyya* whose eyebrows had fallen over his eyes, told me: The supporters of the black banners will continue to be strong-necked after they are victorious until they differ between themselves.
535. Abū Qubayl: Their rule will continue being triumphant until two youths from them have allegiance sworn to them, so if you live to see them differing between themselves, then their difference will be lengthy, until three banners are raised in Syria, so when they are raised, it will be the reason for the end of their dominion.
536. `Alī: Imams will rule you, the worst of imams, but when they have gone their separate ways according to three banners, know that it is their destruction.
537. Abū Umayya al-Kalbī: An elder who had lived during the *jāhiliyya* whose eyebrows had fallen over his eyes said: "The supporters of the black banners will continue to be strong-necked [124] until they differ between themselves. They will conflict one with another, then divide into three divisions—a division calling for the descendants of Fāṭima, a division calling for the descendants of al-`Abbās, and a division calling for themselves." I said: "What does that mean, 'themselves'?" He said: "I do not know, thus I heard."
538. Muḥammad b. al-Ḥanafiyya: The black banners will continue

until they depart from Khurāsān, victory will be in their spear-points, until they differ between themselves. When they differ among themselves three banners will be raised in Syria.

539. Ka`b: When the family of al-`Abbās differs among themselves, that is the first of the falling apart of their rule.

540. Ibn Mas`ūd The Prophet said: The seventh of the `Abbāsids will call the people to unbelief,[353] but they will not follow him, so the people of his house will say: Do you want to eject us from our livelihoods? So he will say: I am acting towards you like Abū Bakr and `Umar. But they will refuse him, then an enemy of his from the family of the Hashemites will kill him. When they attack him, they will differ among themselves—so he mentioned a long difference until the appearance of the Sufyānī.

541. `Alī: When the black banners differ between themselves, a village in Iram (Damascus) called Ḥarastā[354] will be swallowed up, and the appearance of the three banners in Syria.

542. Ka`b: When two men, who are chiefs, of the `Abbāsids throw off their allegiance, the first difference will occur between them, then the second difference will follow it, which is annihilation, and the appearance of the Sufyānī is at the time of the second difference.

543. Abū al-Jild: A man and his progeny from the Hashemites will reign seventy-two years. [125]

544. Ka`b: The `Abbāsids will reign 991 months[355]—woe to them after that, and double woe!

545. Muḥammad b. al-Ḥanafiyya: The `Abbāsids will reign until the people despair of any good, then their rule will be divided up. If you find nothing but a scorpion's stone, dive under it, because there will be a lengthy evil for the people, then their dominion will disappear and the Mahdi will arise.

353 Al-Ma'mūn, holding to the doctrine of the creation of the Qur'ān.

354 A village to the southeast of Damascus.

355 82 years and 7 months.

546. Ibn `Abbās: The Messenger of God said: When the fifth of the people of my house dies, then killing, killing. The seventh will die, then likewise until the Mahdi will arise.

547. Sharīk: It is Ibn al-`Afar,[356] meaning Hārūn [al-Rāshid], since he was the fifth, but we say that he was the seventh, and God knows best.

548. Abū Ḥassān b. Nūba[357]: It is necessary for three of the `Abbāsids to reign who the first [letter] of their names is *`ayn.*

549. Abū Wahb al-Kalā`ī[358]: The dominion of the `Abbāsids will continue victorious over any who oppose them until the westerners appear against them.

550. Ka`b: When there is a swallowing up by the earth of a village called Ḥarastā, two caliphs of the `Abbāsids throw off their allegiance, and the `Abbāsids differ among themselves, such that twelve flags and twelve banners will be raised—at this time the tribulations will overcome them from the center of their dominion, and they will gather there. At that time there is the End. They will cross [the River] Jayḥūn[359] (Amu Darya), and gather there. At that time will be the fall of their dominion, and the appearance of the Berbers in Syria.

551. Al-Zuhrī: Their dominion's falling apart will be their differences between themselves at the place where it began [Khurāsān].

552. Arṭāt: The last sign of the removal of the `Abbāsids' dominion will be three kings ruling, all of them having names of prophets—they will be after these kings. The period [126] of the `Abbāsids, of these three kings, will be forty years. When you see their difference between them, a gathering of the Hashemites between the two rivers, the governorship of an

[356] Hārūn is not known to have had this nickname.

[357] Probably Syrian, name appearing as Abū Ḥassān b. Tawba (no. 704), and Abū Ḥassān b. Būna/Devawayhi (nos. 704, 1932), *fl.* 2nd/8th century.

[358] `Ubaydallāh b. `Ubayd al-Shāmī, probably a *mawlā*, *fl.* 1st/7th century.

[359] Written *jayḥū.*

`Abbāsids man in the direction of the Maghrib,[360] the collision of the black and yellow banners in the navel of Syria, the killing of a governor of Egypt, and the refusal to pay its land-tax (*kharāj*), then this is the sign of the end of their period.

553. Shufay al-Aṣbaḥī[361]: Five of the progeny of al-`Abbās will rule, all of them tyrants. Woe to the earth from them! The fifth of the `Abbāsids will die[362]—an assassin like a lion will leap upon him, eating with his mouth, corrupting with his hands. The heavens will clamor to God Most High because of the blood flowing on the earth. He will reign two or three mornings, then a governor of one of the brothers of the camel will rule. Then a herald will call out from the heavens: "The earth, the earth is God's! The servants, the servants are God's!" The wealth of God will be [divided] between His servants[363] equally, and he will reign in this governorship ten years. [127]

The First of the Portents of the end of their Dominion will be the Appearance of the Turks after a dissension between them

554. Al-Walīd b. Muslim[364]: One who heard the messenger of al-Walīd b. Yazīd to Constantine [V], he heard al-Walīd b. Yazīd saying: "The apocalyptic battles between you are until the black banners come to you, then the Turks will appear against you, fighting them and killing them. Then the pack-saddles of your mounts will not be able to dry until the westerners appear."

555. Al-Walīd b. Muslim: A group that came from Armenia going to Syria narrated to me, since they met Abū Muslim there, saying: "We disliked `Abdallāh b. `Alī,[365] so we wanted to

[360] This may be a reference to the beginning of the Aghlabid dynasty in Tunisia.

[361] Shufay b. Māti` al- Aṣbaḥī, lived in Egypt, *fl.* 2nd/8th century.

[362] Which would have been Hārūn, who died a natural death.

[363] Reading *`abīdihi.*

[364] Al-Walīd b. Muslim al-Qurashī, *mawlā* to the Umayyads (then later to the `Abbasids), lived in Damascus, d. 174/790–1.

[365] First `Abbāsid governor of Syria, revolted at the accession of al-Manṣūr in 754, defeated and killed by Abū Muslim.

leave." He said: "You are right, the black banners will continue to be victorious over all who oppose them until the Turks enter through the Gate of Armenia." Al-Walīd said: "This is the first sign of the falling-apart of their rule after the difference between them."

556. Ka`b: It is as if I hear the rustle of the Turks' quivers between al-Aghila and Bāriq.[366]

557. Mu`āwiya b. Abī Sufyān: Those who ride the ear-pierced [mounts] will fall upon the hills of Syria and al-Jazīra.

558. Arṭāt: When one of the villages of Damascus is swallowed up, and [128] a part has fallen from the western part of its mosque,[367] at that point the Turks and the Byzantines will gather, fighting together. Three banners will be raised in Syria, then the Sufyānī will fight them until he bests them at Carchemish (Qirqīsiyā).[368]

559. Abū Ḥukayma[369]: I went out with my daughter when I was living in Syria, since it was said that those riding ear-pierced [mounts][370] will fall upon the hills of al-Jazīra and Syria, and take their women captive, until a man would see the whites of his wife's anklets and not be able to protect her.

560. Ka`b: The Turks will descend to al-Jazīra until they water their horses at the Euphrates [River]. Then God will send a plague against them, to kill them, so that only one man will escape.

[366] Aghila = al-Ubulla (?), the port of Baṣra; al-Bāriq, an oasis between Qādisiyya and Baṣra. These locations, however, would be much further to the south than other traditions involving Turks.

[367] Flood, *The Great Mosque of Damascus: Studies on the Makings of an Umayyad Visual Culture* (Leiden: E. J. Brill, 2001), Chapters 2–3; al- Suyūṭī, *Kashf al-ṣalṣala `an waṣf al-zalzala* (Beirut: `Alam al-Kutub, 1987), pp. 167–8.

[368] The ancient site of Carchemish was the crossing of the Euphrates.

[369] Unidentified, probably Syrian (there is an Abū Ḥukayma `Iṣma al-Baṣrī however), may be the same as no. 1865 (who also narrates about Turks).

[370] Prof. Ruth Meserve has suggested (through Devin DeWeese, communication of 3/4/2016) that the purpose of these piercings was to mark the ownership of the horse, although this practice is not documented so early in other texts. See Ruth Meserve, "Writing on Man or Animal," in *Writing in the Altaic World*, ed. Juha Janhunen and Volker Rybatzki, Studia Orientalia 87 (Helsinki: Finnish Oriental Society, 1999), pp. 171–86.

561. Ka`b: They will descend upon Amid[371] and drink from the Tigris and Euphrates [Rivers]. They will take themselves towards al-Jazīra when the people of Islam are in al-Jazīra, but unable to do anything to them. So God will send snow against them, in which there will be intense cold, wind[372] and ice, so they will suddenly be dying. So they will return and say that "God caused them to perish, and so took care of the enemy for you." None will remain, they will perish down to the very last one.[373]

562. Makḥūl: The Prophet said: The Turks will have two emergences: One emergence in which they will destroy Azarbayjān,[374] while in the second they will fasten their horses at the Euphrates [River]. There will be no further Turks afterwards.

563. Arṭāt: The Sufyānī will fight the Turks, then their final uprooting will be at the hands of the Mahdi. That will be the first flag the Mahdi will commission; he will send it against the Turks.

564. `Abdallāh b. `Amr: There is one remaining apocalyptic battle—the first of it will be the battle against the Turks in al-Jazīra.

565. Makḥūl: The Turks will have two emergences: one of them in which they will destroy Azarbayjān, while in the second they will go to the shores of the Euphrates.

566. `Abd al-Raḥmān b. Yazīd: The Prophet said: God Most High will send death against their horses, and force them to go on foot. Then will be God's greatest slaughter among them, and there will be no Turks afterwards. [129]

567. Ḥudhayfa: When you see the first of the Turks in al-Jazīra, fight them until you defeat them, or God takes care of their death, for they will dishonor the women in it [al-Jazīra]. This

371 The largest city in Diyarbakr, today southeastern Turkey.

372 Q 54:19, 69:6.

373 Although this account of the Turks' perishing from the extreme cold is exaggerated, note that the Turkish attacks of 762–3 are linked to an extreme bout of cold according to Theophanes, *Chronicle*, pp. 600–1; for their early raid in 731 in Azarbayjan, see Michael the Great, p. 500.

374 Eastern Turkey.

will be the sign of the appearance of the westerners, and the falling apart of their [the `Abbāsids'] dominion will be on that day.

568. Makḥūl: The Messenger of God said: The Turks will have two appearances: an appearance in al-Jazīra in which they will bag (=kidnap) those with beauty (women). God will cause the Muslims to be victorious over them, and God's greatest slaughter will be among them.

569. `Ammār b. Yāsir[375]: The People of your Prophet's House will have emirates, so stay close to the ground until the Turks come quickly during a dispute of a weak man, who will renounce his allegiance two years after taking his oath. The Turks will oppose the Byzantines, but be swallowed up by the earth east of the mosque of Damascus. Three men will emerge in Syria, and the destruction of their dominion will be when that begins. The beginning of the Turks will be in al-Jazīra, while the Byzantines are in Filasṭīn, so `Abdallāh should follow `Abdallāh[376] until their two armies meet in battle at Carchemish (Qirqīsiyā).

570. Ibn Mas`ūd: When the Turks and the Khazars[377] appear in al-Jazīra and Azarbayjān, while the Byzantines are in the valley (*al-`umq*)[378] and its sides, the one who fights the Byzantines will be a man from Qays, from the people of Qinnasrīn. The Sufyānī will be in Iraq, fighting the easterners, and each direction will be occupied by an enemy. When he fights them forty days, and no reinforcement comes to him, he will make a peace with the Byzantines on the condition that neither side give any aid to others.

571. Abū Ja`far: When the Sufyānī will be victorious over the

[375] Companion, supporter of `Ali, d. Battle of Ṣiffīn, 37/657.

[376] Or servant of God should follow servant of God.

[377] A Turkish people whose kingdom was based in the Volga River basin, and later converted to Judaism.

[378] The area to the north of Aleppo, see nos. 1215–1418, used for amassing troops during the middle Umayyad period.

Speckled One, and The Victorious Yemenite (al-Manṣūr al-Yamānī)[379] the Turks and the Byzantines will appear, but the Sufyānī will be victorious over them.

Portents in the Heavens concerning the end of `Abbāsids' Dominion

572. Ka`b: The sign of the end of the dominion of the `Abbāsids was a redness that appeared in the atmosphere of the heavens. This was between the tenth and the fifteenth of Ramaḍān, and a breaking-asunder (*wāhiya*)[380] between the twentieth and twenty-fourth of Ramaḍān, then a star rising from the east, giving light just as the moon does on the night of its fullness, then it will be bent.
573. Ka`b: A drought in the east, a breaking-asunder in the west, a redness in the interior, and spreading death at the *qibla* (Mecca).
574. Abū Ja`far: When the `Abbāsid reached Khurāsān, a horn, possessed of healing, rose in the east.[381] The first time it rose was for the destruction of the people of Noah,[382] when God flooded them, and then it rose during the time of Abraham when they threw him into the Fire.[383] Then when God caused Pharaoh and those with him to perish,[384] and when John son of Zachariah was murdered[385]—so when you see this, take refuge in God from the evil of the tribulations. Its rising will be after the eclipsing of the sun and the moon, then they will not be long until the Spotted One (*al-abqa`*) appears in Egypt.

[379] See C. L. Geddes, "The Messiah in South Arabia," *Muslim World* 57 (1967), pp. 311–20.

[380] Q 69:16. The term *wāhiya* is used for astronomical events throughout Nu`aym, cf. no. 591. It may be influenced by the Middle Persian.

[381] Probably a comet, cf. Kronk, *Cometography*, p. 115 (comet of 744); and note Bakhshal, *Tā'rīkh Wasit* (Beirut: `Ālam al-Kutub, 1986), p. 173 for the idea that a comet's appearance brings health and abundance.

[382] Cf. Q 11:25–50.

[383] Q 21:51–71.

[384] E.g., Q 2:50.

[385] Q 19:15; Mark 6:21–9.

575. Al-Zuhrī: At the appearance of the Sufyānī you will see a sign in the heavens.

576. Ibn Mas`ūd: The sign will be in [the month of] Ṣafar, and it will begin with the appearance of a comet.

577. Makḥūl: The Messenger of God said: In Ramaḍān there will be a sign in the heavens either two nights from the beginning or the end [of the month], then in Shawwāl, waste, and in Dhū al-Qa`da, an uproar, in Dhū al-Ḥijja, things coming down (*naza'il*), and in Muḥarram, what a Muḥarram! [131]

578. `Abd al-Wahhāb b. Bukht[386]: It reached me that the Messenger of God said: During Ramaḍān there will be a sign in the heavens like a long column, in Shawwāl there will be trial, in Dhū al-Qa`da annihilation, in Dhū al-Ḥijja the pilgrimage will be robbed, and then in Muḥarram, what a Muḥarram!

579. Sufyān al-Kalbī: In [the year?] seven there will be trial, in eight there will be annihilation, and in nine there will be famine.

580. Abū Hurayra: The Prophet said: There will be a sign in the month of Ramaḍān, then a group will appear in Shawwāl, then there will be annihilation, then in Dhū l-Ḥijja the pilgrimage will be pillaged, then sanctities will be violated in Muḥarram, then there will be a sound in Ṣafar, the tribes will fight in the [two] months of Rabī`, then there will be what an amazing thing in Jumādā al-Rajab! Then a saddled she-camel would be better than a village yielding 100,000 [dirhams].

581. Sa`īd b. al-Musayyib: There will come upon the Muslims a time when there will be a sound in Ramaḍān, waste in Shawwāl, then in Dhū al-Qa`da the tribes will join against each other, and in Dhū al-Ḥijja the pilgrimage will be robbed, and in Muḥarram, what a Muḥarram!

582. Shahr b. Ḥawshab: It reached me that the Messenger of God said: There will be a sound in Ramaḍān, waste in Shawwāl, in Dhū al-Qa`da, the tribes will gather into parties, in Dhū al-Ḥijja

[386] A *mawlā* of the Umayyads, lived in Syria, then married in Medina and lived there, killed 117/735.

the pilgrimage will be pillaged, and in Muḥarram, a herald will call out from the heavens: Is not God's chosen one from His creation so-and-so, so they will hear and obey him.

583. `Amr b. Shu`ayb[387]—grandfather: The Prophet said: There will be a sound in Ramaḍān, an uproar in Shawwāl, in Dhū al-Qa`da the tribes will gather into parties, and that year the pilgrimage will be pillaged. There will be a great apocalyptic war in Minā[388] in which there will be many killed. The blood will flow in it when they are on Pebble Pass (`Aqabat al-Jamra).[389]

584. `Abdallāh b. `Amr: The people will perform the pilgrimage together, and they will stand at `Arafāt together without an imam. While they are camped at Minā, suddenly something will take them like a dog, and the tribes will be calling out against each other. They will fight until the pass flows with blood. [132]

585. Khālid b. Ma`dān: A sign will appear, a pillar of fire, which will rise from the east—all of the people of the earth will see it. Whoever lives to see that, let him prepare food for his family for a year.

586. Kathīr b. Murra al-Ḥaḍramī: The sign (*aya*) of disaster in Ramaḍān will be a sign (*`alāma*) in the heavens. After that there will be differences between the people, so if you live to see that, prepare as much food as you can.

587. Al-Zuhrī: During the second rule of the Sufyānī and his appearance, you will see a sign in the heavens.

588. Kathīr b. Murra: I have expected the sign of disaster during Ramaḍān for seventy years. **(1)**

589. Ibn Mas`ūd: The Prophet said: "When there is a Shout[390] in Ramaḍān, there will be an uproar in Shawwāl, the separation of the tribes in Dhū al-Qa`da, blood will be shed in Dhū al-Ḥijja,

[387] `Amr b. Shu`ayb b. Muḥammad al-Qurashī al-Sahmī, lived in Mecca, d. 118/736.

[388] The plain located to the east of Mecca in which the hajj camped.

[389] Above the location where Satan (symbolized by a pillar) is stoned during the hajj festival.

[390] See Q 38:15, 54:31.

and Muḥarram—what a Muḥarram!"—he said it three times. "How far, how far! The people will kill in it, killing, killing (*harajan, harajan*)." We said: "What is the Shout, O Messenger of God?" He said: "A crash in the middle of Ramaḍān on Friday night, so it will be a crash that will wake the sleeper, cause the stander [in prayer] to sit down and cause young girls to emerge from their private quarters. On Friday night during a year with many earthquakes, when you have prayed the dawn prayer on the day of Friday, then enter your houses, lock up your doors, close up any apertures, and cloak yourselves,[391] close your ears. So when you feel the Shout, fall towards God in prostration, and say: Praise to the All-Holy, praise to the All-Holy, our Lord, All-Holy. Whoever does this will be saved, whoever does not do this will perish."

590. Walīd: We saw the earthquake that struck the people of Damascus during the first days of Ramaḍān, so that many perished in the month of Ramaḍān 137 [= February–March 755][392] but we did not see the breaking-asunder (*wāhiya*)[393] that had been mentioned, but it was the swallowing up by the earth that was mentioned in a village called Ḥarastā. I saw a comet (=a star with a tail) rise in Muḥarram 145 [=April–May 762][394] rising with the dawn from the east, and we would see it before the dawn through the rest of Muḥarram, then it disappeared. Then [133] we would see it after the sunset in the twilight, and after that in the interior and the west for two or three months, then it disappeared for two to three years. Then

[391] See Q 74:1 (directed towards Muḥammad).

[392] Theophanes, *Chronicle*, p. 594 dates this earthquake to March 9, 755. Al-Walīd, according to al-Mizzī, *Tahdhīb*, vii, p. 489 (no. 7332) was born in 117/735, so he would have been 20 years old when the earthquake struck.

[393] al-Sijistānī, *Gharīb al-Qur'ān* (Beirut: Dār Qutayba, 1995), p. 485 for this meaning.

[394] Most likely there is an error here for 143/760, in which case it would be a good fit from the months cited for IP/760 K1(appearing May 760), the earliest sighting of Halley's Comet in the Muslim sources; see Kronk, *Cometography: A Catalog of Comets (Volume 1: Ancient–1799)* (Cambridge: Cambridge University Press, 1999), pp. 116–18. Al-Walīd would have been approximately twenty-eight years old when this comet passed.

we saw a hidden star with a firebrand the size of cubit, according to what the eye saw, close to Capricorn, swirling around it with the rotation of the cosmos during both [the months of] Jumādā and some days of Rajab, then it disappeared.[395] Then we saw a star which did not glow, rise from the right of the direction of Mecca [the west] looking from Syria, with its blazing fire extending from the direction of Mecca towards the internior to Armenia.[396] I mentioned that to an old elder who was with us from the Sakāsik, who said: "That is not the expected star."

591. Walīd said: I saw a star during the few years left from [the reign of] Abū Ja`far [al-Manṣūr],[397] then it was folded until its two sides almost touched, and became like a ring, one hour of the night.

592. Ka`b: This is a star that will rise from the east, and light up for the people of the earth like the moon on the night of its fullness.

593. Walīd said: The redness and the stars we saw are not signs—the star of the signs is a star that will turn towards the horizons during Ṣafar and the two [months of] Rabī`, or during Rajab. At that time Khāqān[398] will lead the Turks, the Byzantines following him to the outer regions with banners and crosses.

594. Ka`b: A comet will rise from the east at the appearance of the Mahdi.

595. Sharīk: It reached me that before the appearance of the Mahdi the sun will be eclipsed in the month of Ramaḍān twice.

596. Ka`b: The destruction of the `Abbāsids will be at a star that will rise from the interior, and a crash and a breaking-asunder—all of this will be in the month of Ramaḍān. The redness will be between the fifth to the twentieth of Ramaḍān, while the

395 If the first comet is Halley from 760, then the second one is most likely the comet of 762, Kronk, p. 118.

396 Perhaps C/770 K1, May–July, 770, Kronk, pp. 119–20.

397 Perhaps the comet of 773 (Manṣūr died in 775), Kronk, p. 120.

398 The title of the leader of the Turks, ancestor of the title "khan."

crash will be between the twentieth to the twenty-fourth. The star will be seen, it will light up like the moon lights up, then coil like a snake coils until its two ends almost meet. The two earthquakes will be on the night of the two holy days.[399] The star which will be cast from a shooting star (*shihāb*) will shoot down from the heavens—with it will be a loud sound, such that it will happen even in the east. The people will be struck with a terrible experience.

597. Ṭāwūs: There will be three earthquakes: a terrible earthquake in the Yemen, an earthquake in Syria worse than that, and an earthquake in the east, which is the Torrent. The two in the Yemen and Syria have happened, but the one in the east has not. [134]

598. Abū Hurayra: "In Ramaḍān there will be a crash, because of which the sleeper will wake, and the young girls emerge from their private quarters. In Shawwāl there will be waste, in Dhū al-Qa`da the tribes will move against each other, in Dhū al-Ḥijja blood will flow, and in Muḥarram, what a Muḥarram!" And he said it three times. He said: "At that will be the end of the dominion of those [`Abbāsids]."

599. Ḥudhayfa b. al-Yamān: The Messenger of God said: "My community will never perish until discrimination (*tamāyuz*), variance (*tamāyul*) and uproar (*ma`āmi`*) appear among them." Ḥudhayfa said: "May my father and mother be your redemption, O Messenger of God, what is *tamāyuz*?" He said: "Tribal chauvinism (*`aṣabiyya*) which the people will renew in Islam after me." I said: "And what is *tamāyul*"? He said: "When a tribe tends against another tribe, and allows its sanctities to be violated unjustly." I said: "And what is *ma`āmi`*?" He said: "When the garrison cities march against each other, when their necks are intertwined in war."

600. Kathīr b. Murra: The sign of disaster in Ramaḍān, and the rabble-gathering in Shawwāl, a dispersement in Dhū al-Qa`da,

[399] Presumably `Id al-fiṭr at the end of Ramaḍān.

an uproar in Dhū al-Ḥijja, and a sign of this will be a flashing column in the heavens of fire.

601. Arṭāt: During the second time of the Sufyānī, the ugly one, there will be a crash in Syria such that every people will think that it is the destruction of what is beside them.

602. Khālid b. Ma`dān[400]: When you see the column of fire in the direction of the east during the month of Ramaḍān in the heavens, then prepare as much food as you can, for the year will be one of hunger.

603. Kathīr b. Murra al-Ḥaḍramī: I have been expecting the night of disaster in Ramaḍān for seventy years.

604. `Abd al-Raḥmān b. Jubayr: A sign will be in the heavens, there will be difference between the people, so if you live to see that time, then obtain as much food as you can.

605. Muhājir al-Nabbāl[401]: It will be during Ramaḍān, so their hearts will be burning, Shawwāl they will be angry, in Dhū al-Qa`da they will be asked to prepare for war, and in Dhū al-Ḥijja blood will be shed.[402] [135]

606. Shahr b. Ḥawshab: The disaster in Ramaḍān, the uproar in Shawwāl, the dispersement in Dhū al-Qa`da, cutting off of heads in Dhū al-Ḥijja, and in that year the pilgrimage will be attacked.

607. Kathīr b. Murra: The disaster in Ramaḍān, the rabble-gathering in Shawwāl, the dispersement in Dhū al-Qa`da, the uproar in Dhū al-Ḥijja, the judgment in Muḥarram, then he said: I have been expecting the disaster for seventy years.

608. Khālid b. Yazīd b. Mu`āwiya: When you see the argumentative, single-minded man, only interested in his own opinion, then his error will be complete. [136]

[400] Khālid b. Ma`dān al-Kalā`ī, lived in Ḥimṣ, close to the Umayyads, d. 104, 105, 106 or 108/722, 723, 724 or 726–7.

[401] Lived in Syria, *fl.* 2nd/8th century.

[402] All of these are puns on the names of the months.

Beginnings of the Tribulation in Syria

609. `Abd al-Raḥmān b. Jubayr b. Nufayr: Heraclius, the Emperor of Byzantium,[403] said: "The Arabs and us are like a man who had a house, and he gave it to some people to live, then said: 'Dwell in it as long as you are righteous, but watch out if you are corrupt lest I expel you from it.' So they have inhabited it for a time, then he looked carefully at them, and suddenly he realized that they were corrupting it, so he expelled them from it, and brought in others, settled them in it, and made their settlement conditional, just as had made it conditional on the ones before. The house is Syria, the Lord of it is God Most High, who caused the Israelites to dwell in it, for they were its people for a time. Then they changed and corrupted, and so He looked carefully at them, then expelled them from it, and caused us to dwell in it for a time after them. Then He looked carefully at us and found us having changed and corrupted, so He expelled us from it, and caused you[404] to dwell in it, O Arabs, so if you act righteously, you will be its people, but if you change and corrupt, He will expel you from it just as He expelled those before you."
610. Ka`b: There will be three tribulations in Syria: a tribulation of the spilling of blood, a tribulation in which familial ties are cut and wealth is stolen, and a tribulation from the Maghrib, which is the blind one.
611. Mu`āwiya b. Qurra from his father: The Prophet said: When the Syrians are annihilated, there will be no further good in my community.
612. Ibn Fātik al-Asadī[405]: The Syrians are the whip of God on His earth by whom He takes vengeance upon those of His serv-

[403] See Bashear, "The Mission of Diḥya al-Kalbī and the situation in Syria," *Jerusalem Studies in Arabic and Islam* 14 (1991), pp. 84–114.

[404] In place of *hum*.

[405] Probably Khuraym b. Fātik b. Faḍāla al-Asadī, Companion, lived in Raqqa, then moved to Kūfa, *fl.* 1st/7th century.

ants He wishes, and it is forbidden for its hypocrites to be victorious over its believers—they will only die in distress and worry. [137]

613. Ibn Mas`ūd: Every tribulation is of little worth, until it is in Syria, since when it is in Syria it is the misfortune (*al-ṣaylam*), which is the dark-night [tribulation].

614. Ka`b: Every tribulation [it is possible] to sleep during it, as long as it does not begin in Syria.

615. Abū al-`Āliyya: O people, do not count the tribulations to be anything until they come from the direction of Syria, which is the blind one.

616. Ṣafwān b. `Abdallāh[406]: A man on the Day of Ṣiffīn said: "O God, curse the Syrians!" But `Alī said to him: "Don't curse the Syrians altogether, for the *abdāl*[407] are among them."

617. Ka`b: God Most High created the world in the form of a bird, and placed the two wings as the east and the west, and made the head Syria, and the head of the head Ḥimṣ, which is its beak. When the beak is torn apart, then the people are split apart.[408] He made the breast Damascus, in which is the heart, so when the heart moves the body moves. The 'head' has two striking points: one from the east, which is towards Damascus, and one from the west which is towards Ḥimṣ, which is the most important of the two.[409] Then the 'head' turns to the two wings, and cracks them small stone by small stone.

618. Sulaymān b. Ḥāṭib al-Ḥimyarī[410]: Verily, there will be a tribulation in Syria in which you will be disquieted, like water is

406 Ṣafwān b. `Abdallāh al-Jumaḥī, lived in Mecca, *fl.* 1st/7th century.

407 The *abdāl* were originally those in Syria who supported the cause of `Ali (al-Hindi, *Kanz*, xiv, pp. 53–4 [nos. 37917, 37919]), and he said specifically two of them are from Beth-Shean (nos. 37919–20).

408 Like an egg.

409 Although this is local patriotism, note that in 724 the Christian pilgrim Willibald did visit Ḥimṣ as a matter of course on his way to Jerusalem (Wilkinson, *Jerusalem Pilgrims before the Crusades* [Oxford: Oxbow, 2002], pp. 236–7) when coming from the west.

410 Probably lived in Ḥimṣ, *fl.* 2nd/8th century.

disquieted in a water-skin. You will be exposed when you are regretting [the effects of] a terrible famine, so the smell of bread during that time will be better than the smell of musk.[411] [138]

619. Tubay`: When you see the white palaces in Syria, with their tops [reaching] toward the heavens, planted with trees that were never planted in the time of Noah, then you know that the rule [of God] has come.
620. Ka`b: The head of the world is Syria, while its two wings are Egypt and Iraq, and its tail is the Ḥijāz, since the falcon reclines on its tail.
621. Ka`b: "There will continue to be a period [of time] for the people until the head is struck, meaning Syria, and the people perish." It was said to Ka`b: "What is the head being struck?" He said: "That Syria would be destroyed."
622. Ka`b: The whole earth will be destroyed forty years before Syria.
623. Nawf al-Bikālī: Baṣra and Egypt are the two wings, so when they are destroyed then the rule [of God] will occur.
624. Abū Hurayra: The earth is likened to a bird, so Baṣra and Egypt are its two wings, so when they are destroyed then the rule will occur.
625. `Abdallāh b. `Umar: There will be tribulation in Syria that will lift its chiefs[412] and its nobles, then their idiots and low-lifes will multiply until their chiefs are like slaves, just as they made the former into slaves previously.
626. Sa`īd b. al-Musayyib: There will be a tribulation in Syria—every time it dies down on one side it flares up on the other, and will not cease until a herald calls out from the heavens: "Your Commander [of the Believers] is so-and-so."

[411] Musk is a smell that is associated with martyrdom (al-Bukhārī, *Ṣaḥīḥ*, iv, p. 269 [no. 2803]), so this might be alluding to preferring to eat rather than to fight and die.

[412] Replacing the text *rishi* "venal ones" for *ru'asa*, as at the beginning of the next section (an optional reading is *nisā'* "women.").

627. `Umar b. al-Khaṭṭāb: I heard the Messenger of God saying: God Most High created 1000 communities, 600 in the sea, and 400 on the dry land. The first community to perish was the locust, so when they perished, the [other communities] followed like a swarm when its string has been cut.[413] [139]

628. Ka`b: When tribulation flares up in Filasṭīn, then all of Syria is disquieted, like water is disquieted in a water-skin. Then it will be revealed when it is revealed, while you are few, regretful.

629. Abū Hurayra: The fourth tribulation is the blind one, dark-night, tossing like the sea, no Arab or non-Arab house will remain without being filled with humiliation and fear. It will cross Syria, strike Iraq, surround al-Jazīra with its hands and feet, flattening the community like leather. The trial will be intense during it until the good will be rejected while the evil will be known (affirmed), and no one will able to say: Hold on! Every time you patch it from one side it rips apart from the other. A man will wake up a believer, but go to bed an unbeliever—none will be saved other than one who prays the prayer of one drowning in the sea, it will last twelve years, revealing when it reveals, when the Euphrates will have uncovered a mountain of gold, they will fight over it until out of every nine, seven will be killed.

630. Ibn Sīrīn that when he was sitting, he said: "Has anything [good] come to you from the direction of Khurāsān? Has anything [bad] come to you from the direction of Syria?"

631. Ibn Sīrīn: "As for the bricks of al-`Alā' b. Ziyād,[414] who will expel them from Syria?" so we used to discuss how there was a tribulation there. [140]

413 Muḥammad is said to have cursed the locust, see al-Kinānī, *Tanzīh al-sharī`a al-marfū`a `an al-aḥādīth al-shanī`a wa-l-mawdu`a* (Beirut: Dār al-Kutub al-`Ilmiyya, 1981), ii, pp. 251–2 (no. 72).

414 Al-Balādhurī, *Ansāb*, x, p. 249.

The Triumph of the Lowliest and Weakest of Peoples

632. Bakr b. Sawāda[415]: The Banū Khatha`m[416] came to the the Messenger of God, so he said to them: "What did you see?" They said: "Nothing," so he said: "Tell me!" They said: "We saw a donkey whose legs were raised." He said: "How do you interpret that?" We said:[417] "The lowliest and vilest of people will be raised, while their nobles will be humbled." The Messenger of God said: "It will be as you have interpreted."

633. Abdallāh b. `Amr: There will be a tribulation in which their chiefs and their nobles will be raised, then after but a little time, their idiots and low-lifes will be raised until their chiefs are like slaves, just as they made the former into slaves previously.

634. Ka`b: "I would wish that every pearl on the face of the earth would become tar!" Then he said: "They will not stop until they have taken the flocks to milk and compete with each other concerning that, so that when they are many, the leave the cities, gatherings and mosques and start with that. God always has sent prophets with a caliphate, not a kingship, other than to the townsfolk and civilized people, since they do not desire to have it among the people of tent-poles or the desert [nomads]. When God saw their desire for gatherings and mosques, He sent against them those who took them as slaves (*malikat aymānihim*) as peoples who speak with them in Arabic, and hit them with Yemenite swords (*mashrafiyya*)[418] until they return to their gatherings and mosques, and do not seek many of the non-Arab captives. When you have taken

415 Bakr b. Sawāda al-Judhāmī, lived in Egypt, a mufti and jurisprudent, d. perhaps drowned crossing to Andalus, 108/726–7.

416 A Yemenite tribe, at the Prophet's time dwellng between Mecca and Yemen.

417 Changing person.

418 See Hoyland and Gilmour, *Medieval Islamic Swords and Swordmaking: Kindi's Treatise 'On Swords and their Kinds'* (Oxford: Gibb Memorial Trust, 2006), p. 96 describes how the villages of Mashraf to the south of Damascus made well-regarded swords at this time.

control [141] of the captives in your hands, you should kill nine out of every ten, and pay close attention to the tenth that remain, and exile them to the Dry Valley of Trees (Wadi al-Shajar), or the Dry Valley of Crows (Wadi al-`Araj) or the Dry Valley of `Ar`ar (Wadi `Ar`ar).[419] For by God, if they continue they will make your life difficult."[420]

635. Abū al-Zāhiriyya: How will it be for you when your desert-dwellers come in and share with you your wealth, and none can forbid them without somebody saying: "How long you have lived in comfort, while we lived in misery??"

636. Yaḥyā b. Jābir: You will continue doing well as long as your desert-dwellers do not need you; you will do well as long as you can find a back to carry things on.

637. Abū al-Zāhiriyya: Among the protected peoples, you will find none harsher towards you during these trials than the easterners, the possessors of salt and perfume [for the head]. One of their women would poke with her finger at the belly of a Muslim woman, and she would say: "Pay us the head-tax (*jizya*)!" gloating over her; she said: "Give [over] the head-tax."[421]

638. Ibn al-Musayyib: "If I went out and married with your people . . ." then he said: "God forbid that I should leave 125 prayers for five prayers!"[422] Then Sa`īd said: I heard Ka`b al-Aḥbār saying: "Would that this milk turned to tar!" So it was said: "Why is that?" He said: "Quraysh has followed the tails of

[419] Most probably these locations are in the area of the Dead Sea, although only `Ar`ar is listed.

[420] Reading *li-yamaran* with DKI; MM's *yamūt* seems unlikely.

[421] It is not clear which of the women is saying that to which; the translation is under the assumption that the two statements about the *jizya* are both from the Muslim woman, and that one is interpreting the other.

[422] Become a Muslim.

camels on the mountain paths.[423] Satan is with the single [person], but he is further away from two."[424]

639. Ibn `Umar: You will continue doing fine, as long as your desert-dwellers do not need your civilized dwellers; so when they come to you do not refuse them because of the many that will flow (come) to you saying: "How long we have been hungry while you have been satisfied, how long we have been miserable while you were comfortable, so soothe us today!"

640. Al-Ḥasan: The Messenger of God said: You should enjoin the good and forbid the evil lest God send the non-Arabs against you to strike off your heads, devour your spoils and be [like] a lion without fleeing. [142]

641. Muḥammad b. al-Asha`th: There is nothing that cannot be alternated—even the foolish get a turn in charge of the purse.[425]

642. Muḥammad b. al-Asha`th: There is nothing that cannot be alternated—even the foolish get a turn, and even idiots get control over the state.

643. `Abdallāh b.`Amr b. al-`Āṣ: Everything has a turn that happens to it, so the nobles over the vagabonds (*ṣa`ālik*) have a turn, then the vagabonds and low-lifes have a turn until the end of time, when they will alternate with the nobles. When that happens, watch out for the Dajjāl, then the Hour, "the Hour is grievous and bitter."[426]

644. Ibn `Abbās concerning His Word, mighty and majestic, "pushing back its borders,"[427] he said: the departure of the best people.

[423] Kister, "Land property and *jihād*," *Journal of the Economic and Social History of the Orient* 34 (1991), pp. 270–311.

[424] Al-Tirmidhī, *al-Jāmi` al-ṣaḥīḥ* (Beirut: Dār al-Fikr, n.d.), iii, p. 315 (no. 2254).

[425] Using the term *dawla*, which the `Abbāsids used for their revolution, most probably a hint at them.

[426] Q 54:46.

[427] Q 13:41.

645. `Abdallāh b. `Amr: Among the portents of the Hour are that the best people would be lowered, while the worst people would be raised, and that every people would be ruled by its hypocrites.

646. Ḥudhayfa b. al-Yamān: The Hour will not arise until those who do not weigh a feathersweight on the Day of Resurrection are over the people.

647. `Abdallāh b. `Amr: The Prophet said: How will it be for you during a time when the people will be sifted and the chaff of the people will remain? When it is like that, take that which is good, leave that which is evil, and go to the rule of the elite, leaving the rule of the populace.

648. `Abdallāh b. Qays: We used to hear that it was said: How will it be during a time when if you see twenty men or more, you will not see even one among them who fears God. [143]

649. `Uqba b. `Āmir: The Messenger of God said: Verily, I fear for my community milk more than wine. They said: Why is that, O Messenger of God? He said: They will love the milk, then go away from the gatherings, and lose them.

650. Kathīr b. Murra: Among the portents of the Hour is that one who reigns will not be worthy of it, the lowly will be raised, while the lofty will be lowered.

651. Ka`b: When you see the Arabs scorn the rule of Quraysh, then you see the *mawālī* scorning the rule of the Arabs, then you see the new Arab Muslims (*musallima*)[428] of the two lands[429] scorning the rule of the *mawālī* then the portents of the Hour are coming near.

652. Ḥudhayfa narrated to us a tradition concerning the two red ones, and he said: "That is when you are forbidden writing-pens and cushions." [144]

[428] See no. 1216 for this term.

[429] Probably Syria and Iraq.

Refuges from Tribulations

653. `Ammār b. Yāsir: When you see that Syria is united under Ibn Abī Sufyān [Mu`āwiya] then take refuge in Mecca.
654. `Alī: When the rule of the Sufyānī appears, none will be saved from the trial other than those who can endure a siege.
655. Sa`īd b. Muhājir al-Wiṣābī[430]: When the tribulation of the Maghrib occurs, then tighten the fronts of your shoes to the Yemen, because no other land will protect you from them.
656. Ibn `Abbās: The Prophet said: When a tribulation from the west occurs and another from the east, then take refuge in the heart of Syria—the interior of the earth is better then than its exterior.
657. Ka`b: The interior of the earth on that day is better than its back.
658. Abū Hurayra: None but every concealed [person] will be saved from them—when he appears, he is not known, when he sits (is present), he will not be missed (?)[431] or a man praying like the prayer of one drowning in the sea.
659. Ka`b: When it is like that, seek for yourself a place in private, leave like the ant preparing for winter. Let this be the way you behave (or gather), but do not publicize it. [145] Protection from that and other things is in Medina and the Ḥijāz that surrounds it. The coastlands are safer than other places.
660. Al-Najīb b. Sarī[432]: Jesus son of Mary passed by the hill of Hebron, and prayed on behalf of its inhabitants three prayers. He said: "O God, whoever is frightened, and comes to it, will be safe, let no animals oppress its people, and when the rest of the world is suffering a lack, it would not suffer."
661. Al-Waḍīn b. `Aṭā'[433]: The Messenger of God said: The hill of

[430] Sa`īd b. Muhājir, lived in Ḥimṣ, *fl.* 1st/7th century.

[431] Comparison with nos. 322, 324, 678 shows that part of this tradition has been garbled.

[432] Not listed, but probably lived in Ḥimṣ, *fl.* 2nd/8th century.

[433] Lived in Damascus, 147 or 149/764–5 or 766–7.

Hebron is a holy hill, since when dissension happened to the Israelites, God inspired His prophets to flee with their religion to the hill of Hebron.

662. `Umayr b. Hāni' al-`Ansī[434]: It reached me that a man from our brothers took a residence on the hill of Hebron and he was happy with it. It was said to him: "Why is that?" He said: "The Egyptians will settle it, either because of the Nile not flooding or because of its overflooding, so that they will divide upon the hill of Hebron between them with ropes."[435]

663. Al-Ḥārith b. `Abdallāh: None but him who endures a siege will be saved from its trial, and the refuge from the Sufyānī, with the permission of God Most High, are three non-Arab cities close to the frontierlands: a city called Antioch, a city called Coros (Qūrus)[436] and a city called Samosata.[437] The refuge from the Byzantines is Mt. Mu`taq.[438]

664. Ka`b: Ḥimṣ is the army-province (*jund*) whose martyrs will intercede for seventy [people], while the people of Damascus are known for their green clothes in Paradise. The people of al-Urdunn [Jordan] are those who will be in the shadow of the Throne on the Day of Resurrection, while the people of Filasṭīn are those who God looks at twice each day.

665. Abū Dharr: The Prophet said: "The first of the destruction will be in Egypt and Iraq, so then when building has reached [Mt.] Sal`[439] then go to Syria, O Abū Dharr!' I said: '[But] if they expel me from it?' He said: 'Follow wherever they lead you." [146]

666. Ka`b: The martyr from the people of Ḥimṣ will intercede for 70,000, while the people of Damascus, God will dress them in green garments on the Day of Resurrection. The people

434 Lived in Damascus, killed in Dārayā 127/744.

435 Presumably to make claims.

436 The ancient Cyrrhus.

437 In the mountains close to the Byzantine border.

438 Vocalized as Mu`naq in Ibn al-`Adīm, *Bughyat al-ṭalab*, pp. 499–501 (see no. 1217).

439 A little to the north of the oasis of Medina.

of al-Urdunn, God will shadow them in the shadow of His Throne, while the people of Filasṭīn, God looks at them three times each day. [149][440]

The Center of Islam is in Syria

667. Kathīr b. Murra: The Messenger of God said: The center for Islam is Syria; God will lead the pure of His servants to it. None but the blessed will be pulled to it, none will be deterred from it other than those tempted. God Most High has His eye on it from the first day of time until the end of time with dew and rain—so even if their wealth gives out, their bread and water will never give out.
668. Mu`āwiya asked Ka`b concerning Ḥimṣ and Damascus, so he said: "Damascus is the refuge of the Muslims from the Byzantines, and an ox's pen in it is better than a large house in Ḥimṣ. Whoever desires salvation from the Dajjāl, go to the Antipatris River (Nahr Abī Fuṭrus),[441] while whoever wants the dwelling of caliphs, go to Damascus. If you want struggle and jihād, then go to Ḥimṣ."
669. Ka`b: The refuge of the Muslims from the apocalyptic battles is Damascus, and from the Dajjāl is Nahr Abī Fuṭrus, and from Gog and Magog is the Mount [Sinai].
670. Ka`b: "Tribulation overshadows you like the falling of dark night, no house of the Muslims either east or west will remain unentered by it. None will be saved from it." He said: "The only ones who will be saved are those who are shadowed by [Mount] Lebanon, what is between it [150] and the sea. This is the safest place for people from this tribulation. When it will be the year 122 [=739–40] my house will be burned," and his house was indeed burned in that year.
671. Ḍamra b. Ḥabīb[442]: The safest people from the 'misfortune'

[440] Section break for pp. 147–8.
[441] Near Lydda, the classical Antipatris, where the Umayyads were slaughtered by the `Abbāsids.
[442] Ḍamra b. Ḥabīb al-Zubīdī, lived in Ḥimṣ, *fl.* 2nd/8th century.

tribulation are the people of the coast, and the people of the Ḥijāz.

672. Kathīr b. Murra: The Messenger of God said: Is not the center of Islam Syria? And he repeated it three times—God will lead the pure of His servants to it, none but the blessed will be pulled toward it, none deterred from it other than the tempted. God Most High has His eye on it from the first day of time until the end of time with dew and rain, so if their [the Syrians'] wealth gives out, then their bread and water will never give out.

673. Abū al-Zāhiryya: In the Book of God Most High [is written] that the earth will be destroyed forty years before Syria, and there will be no thunder or lightening in any other place, until it will be expanded for those who are gathered in it just as the womb is expanded for a child.

674. Ka`b: The most beloved of holy cities to God is Nablus, so there will come upon the people a time when they will divide it among themselves with ropes.

675. Miqdām b. Ma`dīkarib: The Messenger of God said: There will come upon the people a time when nothing but dinars and dirhams will benefit them.

676. Companions of Muḥammad: The Prophet said: The refuge of the Muslims from the apocalyptic battles is a city called Damascus, in a land called al-Ghūṭa (valley of Damascus).

677. Abū Hurayra: The Prophet said: The most felicitous of people during the tribulations is one concealed, clean, so if he appears, he is not known, but if he disappears he is not missed. The most miserable of the people during it is every enthusiastic preacher, or rider, placing [his saddle]. None will be saved from their [the tribulations'] evil other than one whose prayer is sincere like that of one drowning in the sea.

678. `Abdallāh b. `Amr: The Prophet said: When it is like that, take that with which you are familiar, and leave what you reject, and go to the rule of the elite, and leave the rule of the populace. [151]

679. Ibn `Abbās passed by them while he was going fast after his

sight had been afflicted, so he encroached, then said: "Where is Iram (Damascus)?" I[443] said: "Your road is to the west, at approximately twelve miles." He said: "And how far am I from al-Surāt?" I said: "Such-and-such miles." He said: "Do you have any knowledge of Tyre and Qarīn?" I said: "Yes, I am knowledgeable about them both." He said: "Is it possible to purchase them?" I said: "No." He said: "Why?" I said: "They belong to a man who does not have a residence in this area. He got them from relatives of his, so they are among his tribe, and he will never have a dwelling upon them." He said: "Who is that?" I said: "Rawḥ b. Zinbā`."[444] So he was silent, then I asked him: "May God have mercy on you, so tell me, what is this about?" So he said: "It is as if I see the camps at the end of time like the stars around Iram, so the best and most comfortable dwellings for the Muslims on that day will be Tyre and Qarīn."

680. Abū Sa`īd al-Khudarī: The Prophet said: It is on the verge of being true that the best type of wealth for a man would be flocks to follow on the peaks of mountains, or mountain-paths or rainy-places, by which he would flee with his religion from the tribulations.

681. Abdallāh: The best wealth for a man on that day will be his horse, and his weapons, to disappear with them wherever he disappears.

682. `Uqba b. `Āmir: The Prophet said: "I am more afraid of milk for my community than wine."[445] They said: "Why is that, O Messenger of God?" He said: "They will love the milk, and be distant from the gatherings (mosques?), and thus lose them."

683. Abū Sa`īd al-Khudarī: The Prophet said: It is on the point of being true that the best wealth for the Muslim would be flocks

443 It is not clear who is speaking.

444 See I. Hasson, "Le chef judhāmite Rawḥ ibn Zinbāʿ," *Studia Islamīca* 77 (1993), pp. 95–122.

445 Compare the questions about the Muslim community in al-Ṭabarī, *Jāmi` al-bayān `an ta'wīl ayy al-Qur'ān.* (Beirut: Dār Iḥya al-Turāth al-`Arabī, 2010), xv, p. 10f. (story of the Night Journey).

to follow on the peaks of mountains, and the rainy-places, fleeing with his religion from the tribulations.

684. `Awn b. `Abdallāh: When a man in Egypt threw his head to the ground during the dissension of Ibn al-Zubayr, another man came to him, and said: "What are you telling yourself, O Abū al-Dunyā?" He said: [152] "I am thinking about what has befallen the people." He said: "God has saved you from those [tribulations] by your thinking about them—who is it who asks God, then He does not give it? Or relies upon Him, but He does not suffice?"

685. `Abdallāh: The best form of wealth on that day is a good horse and good weapons, by which the servant can disappear wherever he disappears.

686. Shuraḥbīl b. Muslim al-Khawlānī[446] from his father: It was said: Whoever lives in the tribulation, let him speak with a soft voice during it.

687. Ibn Ṭāwūs: The Messenger of God said: The best of people in the tribulations is a man who takes the head of his horse, causing the enemy to fear, and fearing them or a man who withdras, fulfilling the duties of God Most High that are incumbent upon him.

688. Ibn Khuthaym: The Messenger of God said: The best of people during the tribulations is a man who eats from the spoils of his sword in the path of God, or a man on a mountain-peak eating from the milk of his flocks.

689. `Awn b. `Abdallāh: There will be matters, so whoever is pleased with them of those who are absent from them is like the one who witnessed them, but whoever dislikes them of those who witnessed them is like one who is absent from them.

690. `Abdallāh: A man who witnesses disobedience being done, then dislikes it, is like the one who is absent from it, while the one who is absent from it, but is pleased with it, is like the one who witnesses it.

[446] Syrian, *fl.* 2nd/8th century.

691. Ibn Mas`ūd: When you see a wrong, and you are unable to change it, then it is sufficient for you that God Most High knows that you dislike it in your heart.

692. It was said to `Alī b. Abī Ṭālib: "What is 'a doze' (*al-nawma*)?" He said: "A man who is silent during the tribulation, so that he reveals nothing."

693. `Alī: Every believer who dozes outwardly at that time will be saved. [153]

The First Portent will be the Portent of the Berbers and the Westerners

694. Abū Qubayl: When you come to this pulpit, then you will read [a letter belonging] to the servant of God `Abdallāh, the Commander of the Believers, then you are about to hear about the servant of God, `Abd al-Raḥmān, the Commander of the Believers.[447]

695. Abū Qubayl: When [a letter] Is read on the pulpit of Egypt from the servant of God `Abdallāh, the Commander of the Believers, it will not be long until you read from servant of God, `Abd al-Raḥmān, the Commander of the Believers, the master of the Maghrib, who is the worst of those who reigned.

696. Ḥudhayfa b. al-Yamān that he said to a group of the Egyptians: When a letter comes to you from the direction of the east, reading it to you from the servant of God `Abdallāh, the Commander of the Believers, then expect that you about to receive another letter from the west (Maghrib) to be read to you from the servant of God, `Abd al-Raḥmān, the Commander of the Believers. By the One who holds the soul of Ḥudhayfa in His hands, you and them will fight at the bridge,[448] and they will expel you from the land of Egypt and the land of

[447] `Abd al-Raḥmān al-Dākhil, the first Umayyad ruler of Andalus (757–88). Assuming that is the correct identification, the first `Abdallāh would be either al-Manṣūr or al-Mahdi. For that formula "the servant of God `Abdallāh" see Hoyland, *Seeing Islam*, pp. 690 (Mu`āwiya), 701 (al-Walīd I).

[448] The bridge across the Nile at Fusṭāṭ (Cairo).

Syria village by village, and an Arab woman will be sold on the Damascus road for 15 dirhams.

697. `Utba b. Tamīm al-Tanūkhī[449]: [154] Dominion will belong to the `Abbāsids until a letter will reach you in Egypt from the servant of God, `Abdallāh, the Commander of the Believers. When this happens then it is the first [sign] of the removal of their dominion, and the end of their period.

698. Ismā`īl b. al-`Alā' b. Muḥammad al-Kalbī on the authority of his father[450]: When a letter belonging to the `Abbāsids is read at the first part of the day from the servant of God `Abdallāh the Commander of the Believers, then expect a letter to be read to you at the end of the day from the servant of God `Abd al-Raḥmān the Commander of the Believers.

699. Ka`b: When a man from the `Abbāsids reigns who is called `Abdallāh, who will be the final *`ayn* among them[451]—with [this letter] they will open and with it they will close—he is the key to the sword of annihilation, so when a letter belonging to him is read in Syria from the servant of God `Abdallāh the Commander of the Believers, it will not be long until a letter to be read will reach you upon the pulpit of Egypt from the servant of God `Abd al-Raḥmān the Commander of the Believers. When it is like that, the easterners and the westerners will race to Syria like two running horses, seeing that the dominion will not be complete for whoever does not hold Syria. Each will say: "Whoever dominates it, will gain the dominion."

700. Jubayr b. Nufayr[452]: Woe to the servant of God from the servant of God; woe to `Abdallāh from `Abd al-Raḥmān.

701. Al-Zuhrī: When the yellow flags enter Egypt and have gathered on the bridge, then expect that the easterners will mobilize together with the westerners, and they will fight seven days in it [Egypt]. There will be blood between them the like of

[449] Lived in Syria, *fl.* 2nd/8th century.
[450] Unknown.
[451] The final one called `Abdallāh, which would be al-Mahdi.
[452] A Syrian relater of tradition, d. 80/699–700.

which was during all of the tribulations, but defeat will be for the easterners, until they will retreat to Ramla.[453]

702. Ḥabīb b. Ṣāliḥ[454]: Verily, a man called `Abd al-Raḥmān will appear leading the westerners until he ascends the pulpit of Ḥimṣ.

703. Abū Ḥassān b. Tawba[455]: It is necessary that three of the `Abbāsids rule, all of them with names beginning in *`ayn*. [155]

The Appearance of the Berbers and the Westerners

704. Al-Walīd b. Muslim: One who heard the messenger of al-Walīd b. Yazīd to Constantine [V] heard al-Walīd b. Yazīd saying: "When the Turks appear against the supporters of the black banners, then fight them. The pack-saddles of your mounts will not be able to dry until the westerners appear."

705. `Iṣma b. Qays al-Sulamī, the Companion of the Messenger of God, that he would take refuge in God from the tribulation of the east. It was said: "And the west?" He said: "That is greater and more overwhelming." **(1)**

706. Ibn al-Musayyib: It is necessary for the westerners to have a turn, a turn of unbelief.

707. Ka`b or one who narrated on the authority of Muḥammad b. Ka`b al-Quraẓī[456]: The westerners will reign, but they will be the worst of those who reign. [156]

708. Abū Qubayl: The ruler of the Maghrib is `Abd al-Raḥmān, but he is the worst of those who reign.

709. Abū Hurayra: The Prophet said: There is no creation under the canopy of the heavens worse than the Berbers. It is more preferable for me to donate the attachment of a whip in the path of God than to free 100 Berber slaves.

710. Abū Qubayl: `A'isha that she was ordered to give charity, so

[453] Capital of the province of Filasṭīn.

[454] Ḥabīb b. Ṣāliḥ al-Ṭā'ī, lived in Ḥimṣ, d. 147/764.

[455] See no. 548.

[456] A descendent of the Jewsh Banū Qurayẓa, lived in Kūfa, then moved to Medina, d. 117/735.

she said to the Messenger: Do not give anything of it to a Berber, even for you to have the dogs feed him.

711. Ka`b: The "strange" [tribulation] is the "blind" one, its people are rough, naked, not giving God His due, treading the earth like cattle which are threshing, so take refuge in God lest you would live during that time.

712. Tubay`: The ruler of the west (Maghrib) is `Abd al-Raḥmān b. Hind,[457] who has a long beard, and at his vanguard there is a man named Satan (Shayṭān)[458]—woe to whoever kills under his flag, his destination is hell.

713. Al-Ṣaqar b. Rustum[459] *mawlā* of Maslama b. `Abd al-Malik[460]: I heard Maslama b. `Abd al-Malik saying: "The westerners will rule Ḥimṣ sixteen months," so it is as if I can see him affirming sixteen [months].

714. Sa`īd b. Muhājir al-Wiṣābī: When it is the tribulation of the west, then fasten the fronts of your shoes for the Yemen, for no other country is protected. **(1)**

715. `Iṣma b. Qays,[461] Companion of the Prophet, that he used to take refuge from the tribulation of the east, then from the tribulation of the west, during his prayer.

716. Ibn `Abbās: The Prophet said: I warn you from a tribulation that will come from the east then a tribulation that will come from the west. [157]

717. `Abdallāh b. `Amr: Evil has been divided into seventy parts, but sixty-nine parts were placed among the Berbers, and only one among the rest of the people.

718. Some elders: The Messenger of God said: The Berber women are better than their men—a prophet was sent to them, but

457 Presumably `Abd al-Raḥmān I, whose mother was not named Hind, however. Perhaps the allusion is to a typical Umayyad female name.

458 Compare 1227 where the commander from the west is said to be son of a demon.

459 Lived in Damascus, *fl.* 2nd/8th century.

460 The most famous and dedicated Umayyad commander against the Byzantines during the period 710–38.

461 `Iṣma b. Qays al-Hawzanī, Companion, *fl.* 1st/7th century.

they killed him, then the women took care of him and buried him.[462]

719. Anas b. Mālik: I came to the Messenger of God when I had a Berber slave with me, so the Messenger of God said: The people of this fellow, a prophet came to them before me, but they slaughtered him, cooked and ate his flesh, and drank his juices.

720. Some elders who participated in the conquest of Ḥimṣ: The Byzantines who were in Ḥimṣ used to be afraid of the Berbers, and say *woe-s is-s you-s from the Berber-s.*[463] Ṣafwān said: They used to call Ḥimṣ "the date"[464] saying: "Woe to you, O date, from the Berbers." [158]

The Corruption and Fighting of the Berbers in Syria and Egypt, and whoever fights them, and the end of their appearance, and the evil conduct that will happen at their hands

721. Abū Qubayl: The ruler of the Maghrib, the Marwānids and Quḍā`a will gather together against the black banners in the heart of Syria.

722. Ḥudhayfa: When the servant of God {son of}[465] `Abd al-Raḥman comes to you from the west, you and they will fight at the bridge, and there will be 70,000 killed. They will expel you from the land of Egypt and the land of Syria village by village. An Arab woman will be sold on the Damascus road for twenty-five dirhams, then they will enter the land of Ḥimṣ, and stay there eighteen months, dividing up the wealth in it. They will kill male and female in it, and then the most evil man overshadowed by the heavens will come out against them, fight them, and defeat them, forcing them into the land of Egypt.

462 Probably an ethnic slur, but note the anonymous *Mafakhir al-Barbar* (c.705/1305) (Ribat: Dār Abi Raqraq, 2005), p. 174 for pseudo-prophets among the Berbers.

463 Mock Greek.

464 See no. 1354 for the meaning of this appellation, which could also be "fig."

465 The text reads `Abdallāh b. `Abd al-Raḥmān, which is inconsistent with the previous versions.

723. Al-Ṣaqar b. Rustum: I heard Maslama b. `Abd al-Malik say: The westerners will rule Ḥimṣ sixteen months.

724. Ḥudhayfa: When the westerners enter the land of Egypt, and stay in it for such-and-such [a time] they will kill and take its people captive. On that day the mourning [women] will rise, crying, crying about their sexual abuse, crying, crying about their humiliation after their haughty [station], crying, crying about the killing of their children, crying, crying about the killing of their men, crying, crying desirous of their graves. [159]

725. Abū Wahb al-Kalā`ī: When the westerners appear, and become powerful, then the Arabs will come out against them, and all of the Arabs will gather in the land of Syria under four banners: a banner for Quraysh and those with them, a banner for Qays and those with them, a banner for Yemen and those with them, and a banner for Quḍā`a and those with them. So the Arabs will say to Quraysh: "Advance and fight for your dominion or else go," so Quraysh will advance and fight, but not accomplish anything. Then Qays will advance and fight but not accomplish anything, then Yemen will advance and not accomplish anything. Then Abū Wahb struck the shoulder of Khālid b. Ẓuhayr al-Kalbī and said: "Your banner and the banner of your tribal confederation [Quḍā`a], the Piebald and Speckled on that day, by God, will be victorious over them!"

Al-Walīd said: On that day Quḍā`a will be victorious over the westerners, and among them those who followed them, then the tribes will pivot and fight the easterners.

726. Al-Zuhrī: The supporters of the black banners and the supporters of the yellow banners will meet in battle at the bridge, and fight until they reach Filasṭīn. The Sufyānī will attack the easterners, so when the westerners descend upon al-Urdunn, their commander will die. Then they will divide up into three groups: one group will return to where they came from, one group will go on pilgrimage, and one group will be constant and the Sufyānī will fight them, and defeat them, so they will enter into his service.

727. Muḥammad b. al-Ḥanafiyya: The first of the westerners will enter the mosque of Damascus, and while they are gazing at its wonders, the earth will tremble, so the western part of the mosque will sink, and a village called Ḥarastā will be swallowed up by the earth. Then the Sufyānī will appear in the midst of this, and kill them until he expels them to Egypt. Then he will return to fight the easterners until he returns them to Iraq.

728. Ka`b: When the Berbers appear and descend upon Egypt, there will be two conflicts between them: one in Egypt, and one in Filasṭīn. While this is happening they will be besieging Ḥimṣ, so woe to it from them! A fierce snow will hit them in it forty days, which will almost cause them to perish. Then they will conquer it, enter it and then expel everything between the western part and the bridge until the middle of the city. Then they will ride from it [160] and camp at Lake Fāmiya,[466] or close to it by a league. The people will come out against them, and they will kill them—their leader will be a man from the descendants of Ishmael. They will be killed in a village called Umm al-`Arab.[467] Then a rebellious man will rise up, kill the free, enslave the offspring, and slit the bellies of the women. He will defeat the gathering twice, then perish. Verily a woman of Quraysh will be slaughtered, while in it there will be Hashemite women whose bellies will be slit.

729. Al-Zuhrī: When the black banners differed amongst themselves, the yellow banners will come to them, and they will gather at the bridge of the Egyptians. The easterners and the westerners will fight for seven days, then there will be defeat for the easterners, such that they descend upon Ramla. Something will occur between the Syrians and the westerners, so the westerners will be angered, and say: We came to help you! Then they will do what they do, but God will divide

[466] The classical Apamea, located close to Ḥimṣ.

[467] Possibly the present-day town of Umm al-Kaṣab, to the west of Ḥimṣ.

between them and the easterners. So they will plunder you (the Syrians) because of the paucity of the Syrian population on that day in their eyes. Then the Sufyānī will appear, and the people of Syria will follow him, and fight the easterners.

730. Elders: The people of Ḥimṣ will be the most miserable of all the Syrians with the Berbers.

731. Ka`b: The most submissive and happy of the army-provinces of Syria with the yellow banners will be the people of Damascus; the most miserable of the Syrians will be the people of Ḥimṣ, so they will overflow from Syria the way water overflows a flask.

732. Ka`b: By the One who holds my soul in His hand, the Berbers will destroy Ḥimṣ in the latter of two flattenings—during the latter of which they will pull out the nails from the doors of its houses. They will have a battle in Filasṭīn, then they will go forth from Ḥimṣ to Lake Fāmiya or below it by a league, whereupon a rebel (*khārijī*) will appear against them and kill them.

733. Ka`b: When the Maghrib is victorious over Egypt and the interior of the earth at that time is better than the exterior for the people of Syria, woe to the two army-provinces of Filasṭīn and al-Urdunn, and the land of Ḥimṣ, from the Berbers, who will be striking with their swords to the gate for perfume (?),[468] while the ruler of the Maghrib is a man from Kinda, who is lame.[469]

734. Ḥassān[470] or another: It is said: When the yellow flags reach Egypt, then flee to the land of your effort,[471] so when it reaches you that they have descended upon Syria, which is the navel, if you can find a ladder to the heavens, or a hole in the groundin which to go then do so. [161]

735. Ḥassān b. `Aṭiyya: He would say: When you see the yellow banners, then the interior of the earth is better than its exterior.

468 Seems that it should be Bāb al-`Atar, but in BL it is *bāb lil-`aṭar.*

469 See nos. 809, 820, 919.

470 Ḥassān b. `Aṭiyya al-Muḥāribī, lived in Damascus, a *mawlā*, *fl.* 2nd/8th century.

471 The Ḥijāz.

736. Ka`b: The Berbers will descend from the black ships, then they will come out with their swords, following [the road] until they enter Ḥimṣ. It has reached me that their slogan that day will be: "O Ḥimṣ! O Ḥimṣ!"

737. Ka`b: When the Berbers leave Ḥimṣ for [Lake] Fāmiya, God will compel them to go on foot, and He will send a disease against their mounts so all will perish. Then he will expel them with rinder-pest and a stomach infection, so they will flee to the western part of the Black Mountain (Jabal al-Aswad),[472] and seek shelter there. But the Muslims will follow them, and kill them in a great slaughter until one man from them [the Muslims] would kill seventy or less than that, and none but a few would escape.

738. Ka`b: When you see the yellow flags descending on Alexandria, then descending on the navel of Syria, at that time a village of Damascus, called al-Ḥarastā will be swallowed up by the earth.

739. Ka`b: The Egyptians will divide up al-Jawn[473] with ropes among themselves, which will be because of the Nile not flooding or overflooding.

740. Shu`ayb from his father: I entered in to `Abdallāh b. `Umar when al-Ḥajjāj besieged the Ka`ba, then heard him say: When the black banners come from the east, and the yellow banners from the west, so that they will meet in battle in the navel of Syria, then will be the trial, then will be the trial!

741. Sulaymān b. `Aṭā' b. Yazīd al-Laythī[474] from the wife of his father: I heard his father say this.

742. Al-Najīb b. al-Sarī: The westerners will have two appearances: one in which they will end up at the bridge of Fusṭāṭ, fastening their horses on it, and another to Syria.

743. `Umar b. al-Khaṭṭāb said [162] to man from the Egyptians: The

[472] The Amanus Mountains, today the Nuayri Mountains, along the coast of Syria.
[473] Perhaps the black ships mentioned above no. 736.
[474] Unidentified.

Andalusians will come to you, such that they will fight you at Wasīm.

744. `Uqba b. `Āmir al-Juhanī[475]: When the westerners appear, the Byzantines will follow them, so Alexandria, Egypt and coastal Syria will be destroyed.
745. Ibn `Abbās: When tribulation approaches from the east and tribulation from the west, so they meet in the heart of Syria, then the interior of the earth is better than its exterior.
746. `Abdallāh that he ascended his house, and gazed toward Kūfa, and said: "It will be completely destroyed by a people that will surround it coming from the west."
747. Al-Najīb b. al-Sarī: `Abd al-Raḥmān will appear leading the people of the Maghrib when the Byzantines have already taken over Alexandria, so they are in it, then they will fight them [the Byzantines], defeat them, and expel them from it.
748. Elders: The Byzantines who were in Ḥimṣ used to fear the Berbers for it, and would say: "Woe to you, O date, from the Berbers," meaning "Woe to you, O Ḥimṣ from the Berbers!"
749. Ka`b: When the black banners and the yellow banners meet at the navel of Syria, then the interior of the earth is better than its exterior.
750. Ṣafwān[476]: The Berbers will pull the gates of Ḥimṣ away from [the walls] beside them.
751. Al-Zuhrī: When the easterners and the westerners with the yellow banners gather in Egypt, they will fight at the bridge for seven days, then reach Ramla.
752. Ibn Mas`ūd: When a Fihrī (from Quraysh) man appears gathering the Berbers, a man will appear from the progeny of Abū Sufyān. When it reaches the Mahdi that he has appeared they will divide into three groups: one group returning, one group remaining steadfast with him [163] going to Syria, and one group to the Ḥijāz, they will meet in the Valley of

[475] Companion, lived in Egypt, d. 58/677–8.
[476] Probably Ṣafwān b. `Abdallāh al-Jumaḥī.

the Sea-Onions (Wādī al-`Unṣul)[477] in Syria, and defeat the Berbers, then fight the Syrians.

753. Arṭāt: When the yellow and black banners collide at the navel of Syria, woe to its dwellers from the defeated army, then woe to it from the defeating army, then woe to it from the ugly, cursed one.[478]

754. Arṭāt b. al-Mundhir: The Berbers will come until they descend between Filasṭīn and al-Urdunn. Then groups from the east and from Syria will come to them, which will all camp at al-Jābiya.[479] A man will appear from the progeny of Ṣakhr (the Sufyānī) in [a time of] weakness, then the armies of the Maghrib will meet in the pass of Beth-Shean (Baysān)[480] but he will turn them away from it, then he will meet them the next day, and turn them away from it, so they will retreat beyond it. Then he will meet them on the third day, and turn them away to the Spring of the Wind (`Ayn al-Rīḥ)[481] where the [news of the] death of their leader will come to them.

Then they will divide into three groups: one group which will apostacize, one group will go to the Ḥijāz, and one group that will join al-Ṣakhrī, so go to the remainder of their gathering, until he comes to the Pass of Afiq.[482] They will meet there, and the Ṣakhrī will prevail over them, so then they will incline toward gatherings of the east and Syria, to meet them. They will prevail over them between al-Jābiya and the Ruin (al-Khirba),[483] until the horses wade in blood. The Syrians will kill their leader, so they will retreat joining the Ṣakhrī, so he

[477] Unidentified.

[478] The Sufyani.

[479] To the south of Damascus, traditionally one of the end-points of the caravan route from Arabia.

[480] Close to the Jordan River, destroyed by an earthquake January 18, 749.

[481] Unidentified, but presumably in or close to the northern Jordan Valley, below the Sea of Galilee.

[482] Near the present-day Golan Heights on the road to Damascus.

[483] To the south of Damascus, although there are many sites called al-Khirba in the region.

will enter Damascus, and use it as an example (by killing its people).

Blackened banners will appear from the east, and descend upon Kūfa, as their leader will be concealed there, but no one will know his hiding place.[484] This army will be unsuccessful, then the man who was hiding appear in the center of the valley, and take charge of that army. The reason for his appearance will be rage at what the Ṣakhrī has done to the people of his house. So he will lead the armies of the east towards Syria, and [the news of] his setting out will reach the Ṣakhrī, so he will send the troops of the easterners to him, and they will meet in battle at Mount Ḥaṣā (Jabal al-Ḥaṣā).[485] A great many will perish between the two of them, but the easterner will turn back, and the Ṣakhrī will follow him and catch up with him at Carchemish (Qirqīsiyā) at the meeting place of the two rivers [the Tigris and the Euphrates].

They will meet [in battle] and endurance (*ṣabr*) will be denied them—among the armies of the easterner seven out of ten will be killed. Then the Ṣakhrī will enter Kūfa, and treat its people horribly. He will dispatch an army from the westerners to the eastern troops that are in front of him, so they will bring him their captives. He will be occupied in this when news will come to him of the appearance of the Mahdi in Mecca, so he will send an expedition from Kūfa which will be swallowed up by the earth.

755. Arṭāt: Between the westerners and the easterners there will be seven days at the bridge of Fusṭāṭ. Then [164] they will meet at al-`Arīsh,[486] and the defeat will be for the easterners, so they will reach al-Urdunn. Then the Sufyānī will appear afterwards, and the Byzantines who were in Ḥimṣ. They had

[484] Possibly a reference to the `Abbāsid strategist Abū Salāma who indeed was hiding in Kūfa.

[485] Near Aleppo.

[486] Close to Gaza in the northern Sinai, on the road between Egypt and Syria.

been afraid for it from the Berbers, so they would say: "O date, be warned about the Berbers!"

756. Al-Najīb: `Abd al-Raḥmān will appear leading the westerners, after the Byzantines had already taken over Alexandria, since they were in it, so they will fight them, and defeat them, and expel them from it.

757. `Abdallāh b. `Amr: Evil was divided into seventy parts, and sixty-nine were placed among the Berbers, but one among the rest of the people.

758. Some elders: The Messenger of God said: The Berber women are better than their men—a prophet was sent to them, so they killed him, but the women took care of him, and buried him.

759. Anas b. Mālik: I came to the Messenger of God, when a Berber slave was with me, so the Prophet said: "The people of this fellow, a prophet before me came to them, but they slaughtered him, cooked him and ate his flesh, and drank his juices."

760. Ka`b: When the black and yellow banners meet at the navel of Syria, the interior of the earth is better than its exterior. Ṣafwān said: "The Berbers will rip the doors of Ḥimṣ off, in addition to everything else." [165]

The Description of the Sufyānī, His Name and Ancestry

761. An elder who had lived during the *jāhiliyya*: The beginning of the Sufyānī will be his appearance from a village to the west of Syria called Andrā, leading seven men.[487]

762. Abū Ja`far: The Sufyānī will reign the [length of] a woman's pregnancy.

763. Ibn al-Ḥanafiyya: Between the appearance of the black banner from Khurāsān, Shu`ayb b. Ṣāliḥ, the appearance of the Mahdi, and when the rule in its entirety will be given over to the Mahdi is seventy-two months.

764. Ibn Mas`ūd: A star will appear, then a man blind in one eye

[487] Presumably in northwestern Jordan, near the Dry Valley.

will move in Jerusalem (*iliyā'*), then there will be swallowing up by the earth afterwards.

765. Abū Ja`far: He will be squinty-eyed.

766. Sulaymān b. `Īsā[488]: It has reached me that the Sufyānī will reign three and a half years.

767. Ka`b: He will reign the [length of] a woman's pregnancy, his name is `Abdallāh b. Yazīd, and he is [called] al-Azhar Son of the Kalbite Woman, or al-Zuhrī Son of the Kalbite Woman, the ugly one, the Sufyānī.

768. Arṭāt: al-Azhar Son of the Kalbite Woman will enter Kūfa where a malignant growth will afflict him. So he will depart from it, but die on the road. Then another man will appear from them between al-Ṭā'if and Mecca, or between [166] Mecca and Medina, from Shabab, Ṭibāq and Shajar in the Ḥijāz,[489] very ugly in appearance, with a broad head, weak forearms, cross-eyed, and there will be a crash during his time.

769. Arṭāt: The Sufyānī who will die, the one who will fight from the first the black banners and the yellow banners in the navel of Syria, his appearance is from al-Māndarūn[490] to the east of Baysān, on a red camel, with a crown, defeating the gathering twice, then he will perish. He will receive the head-tax (*jizya*), take offspring captive, and slit open the bellies of pregnant women.

770. Ka`b: His rule is for nine or seven months.

771. Ḍamra and Dīnār b. Dīnār[491]: His rule will be [the length of a] pregnancy.

772. Muḥammad b. Ja`far b. `Alī[492]: The Sufyānī is from the progeny of Khālid b. Yazīd b. Mu`āwiya b. Abī Sufyān, a man with a huge

488 Probably lived in Dārayā, said to have been knowledgable concerning the tribulations according to no. 1144, *fl.* 2nd/8th century.

489 Not attested.

490 In the area of northeastern Jordan, near `Ajlūn.

491 A *mawlā* of `Abd al-Malik, commanded the summer raids during the 740s with Abān b. al-Walīd.

492 Perhaps the "caliph" of the 200/815–16 rising in Mecca, great-grandson of al-Ḥusayn.

head, on his face the scars of smallpox, and in his eye a white dot. He will appear from the direction of the city of Damascus, from a valley called the Dry Valley (Wādī al-Yābis)[493] leading seven men, with one of them having a commissioned flag, known as the Victory Flag. They will go before him for thirty miles; everyone who sees this flag and wants to attack it will be defeated.

773. Elders: The Sufyānī will appear from Wādī al-Yābis, the ruler of Damascus will come out to him to fight him, but when he sees his flag, he will be defeated.

774. `Abd al-Quddūs[494]: The governor of Damascus on that day will be a governor [appointed by] the `Abbāsids.

775. Ḍamra: The Sufyānī is a white man, with curly hair; whoever receives any of his wealth it will be a red-hot stone in his belly on the Day of Resurrection.

776. Al-Ḥārith b. `Abdallāh[495]: A man from the progeny of Abū Sufyān will appear from the Dry Valley leading red banners, with weak forearms, and calves, a long neck, and very yellow, on his [forehead] will be the sign of worship.[496] [167]

777. Jubayr b. Nufayr: Woe to `Abd al-Raḥmān from `Abdallāh, woe to `Abdallāh from `Abd al-Raḥmān!

778. Abū `Ubayda b. al-Jarrāḥ: The Messenger of God said: This rule will remain standing in justice until a man from the Umayyads defiles it.

779. Muḥammad b. `Alī: It reached me that the Messenger of God said: A man from the descendants of Abū Sufyān will rend apart Islam in a way that no one will ever be able to repair.

780. `Azra b. Qays[497]: A man rose to Khālid b. al-Walīd, when

[493] In present-day northwestern Jordan.

[494] Probably `Abd al-Quddūs b. al-Ḥajjāj al-Khawlānī, lived in Ḥimṣ, d. 222/837.

[495] Probably al-Ḥārith b. `Abdallāh al-Makhzūmī, grandson of Abraha, lived in Baṣra, *fl.* 1st/7th century.

[496] Presumably the permanent bruise on the forehead that develops from constant prayers.

[497] Correcting from Ibn `Asākir, *Tā'rīkh*, xxxx, p. 311, see no. 52 (note the similar content of the tradition).

he was speaking in Syria, and said: 'The tribulations have appeared,' but Khālid said: 'As long as Ibn al-Khaṭṭāb is alive, no. This will only happen when the people sin towards me, and sin to me.'[498] Then the man began to mention the earth, and that there was no likeness upon it of the one who fled to it, then no one could find him, and at that time would be the tribulations.

781. Ka`b: The name of the Sufyānī is `Abdallāh. [168]

The Beginning of the Appearance of the Sufyānī

782. Abū Qubayl: A man from the Hashemites will reign, and kill the Umayyads, so that none but a few will remain, not killing anyone else. Then a man from the Umayyads will appear and kill one out of every two men, not leaving any but the women,[499] then the Mahdi will emerge.
783. Khālid b. Ma`dān: The Sufyānī will emerge with three reeds in his hand—anyone who he strikes with them dies.
784. Elders: The Sufyānī will be approached in a dream, where it will be said: "Rise and emerge!" So he will rise, but not find anyone, then he will be approached a second time, and it will be said to him like the first, then it will be said to him a third time: "Rise and emerge! So look to see who is at the door of your house." So he will descend at the third [time] to the door of his house, and behold! There are seven men or nine, with a flag, so they will say: "We are your supporters." So he will emerge leading them, and the people of the villages around the Dry Valley will follow him. The ruler of Damascus will emerge to him, to meet him and fight him, but when he sees his banner, he will be defeated. The governor of Damascus on that day will be an `Abbāsid.
785. Abū `Ubayda b. al-Jarrāḥ: The Prophet said: This rule will

[498] This section is corrupt, reading with MM; as SZ and DKI read *tadanat lī wa-danat lī.*

[499] Q 7:127 (concerning Pharaoh and his killing of Israelite men, leaving the women).

remain standing in justice until a man from the Umayyads defiles it.

786. Abū Qubayl: The Sufyānī is the evilest of those who have reigned, he will kill the learned (*`ulamā'*) and the people of merit, annihilating them. He will seek help by them, so whoever refuses he will kill them.

787. Ibn [169] Mas`ūd: A man blind in one eye will move in Jerusalem, with much killing, and allowing taking of captives. He is the one who will send the army to Medina.

788. `Alī b. Abī Ṭālib: A man from the descendants of Khālid b. Yazīd b. Mu`āwiya b. Abī Sufyān will emerge leading seven men, with one of them having a commissioned flag, known as the Victory Flag. He will go before him at the distance of thirty miles, and no one who sees that flag will be undefeated.

789. Abū Subḥān: During the time of Hishām, you did not see any Sufyānīs until the westerners came; so if you see him emerge climbing the pulpit of Damascus, it is nothing until you see the westerners.

790. Tubay`: When there is the crash in Syria before the wasteland, then there will be no wasteland[500] and no Sufyānī.

791. Al-Layth[501]: There was a crash in Tiberias, so people woke up because of it even in Fusṭāṭ, throwing off wings (aftershocks) but the center was Tiberias.[502]

792. Abū Ḥabīb: The Messenger of God said: The emergence of the Sufyānī is after [1]39 [=756–7].

793. Ibn `Abbās: When the emergence of the Sufyānī happens in [1]37 his reign will be twenty-eight months, but if he emerges in [1]39 then his reign will be nine months.

794. Arṭāt: During the second time of the Sufyānī there will be the

500 Where the Sufyani's army will be swallowed up.

501 Probably al-Layth b. Sa`d al-Fahmī, Egyptian (although according to tradition of Persian descent, see al-Mizzī, *Tahdhīb*, vi, p. 184), one of the major jurisprudents, d. 176 or 177/792 or 793.

502 Most likely this was the great earthquake of January 18, 749.

crash, such that every people will think that what was next to it was destroyed. [170]

The Three Flags

795. Arṭāt: When the Turks and the Byzantines gather together and a village close to Damascus is swallowed up by the earth, a group falls from the western side of the mosque of Damascus, three banners will be raised in Syria: that of the Speckled One, the Piebald One, and the Sufyānī. A man will besiege Damascus, but he and those with him will be killed. Then two men will appear from the progeny of Abū Sufyān, and the victory will be for the second of these. So when the supplies of the Speckled One proceed from Egypt, the Sufyānī with his army will be victorious over them, and kill the Turks and the Byzantines at Carchemish, such that the beasts of the earth will be sated with their flesh. [171]

The Flags that will disperse in the Lands of Egypt and Syria, and other [countries], and the Sufyānī and his Victory over them

796. An elder who had lived at the time of the *jāhiliyya*, whose eyebrows had fallen over his eyes: When the black banners differ, then they will divide into three groups: one will call for the Sons of Fāṭima, one will call for the `Abbāsids, while one will call for themselves.
797. Muḥammad b. al-Ḥanafiyya: When they differ among themselves then three banners will be raised in Syria, a banner for the Speckled One, a banner for the Piebald One and a banner for the Sufyānī.
798. Abū Ja`far: When their beliefs have differed, and the malevolent horn has risen, there will only be a short while until the Speckled One will emerge in Egypt, killing the people until they reach Iram (Damascus). Then the ugly one will rise against him, and there will be a great apocalyptic war between them. Then the cursed Sufyānī will appear, and many will appear with him. Before that twelve known banners will be raised

in Kūfa, and a man from the descendents of al-Ḥusayn will be killed calling for his father. Then the Sufyānī will scatter his armies.

799. Dhū al-Qariyāt[503]: The people will differ concerning four men: two in Syria, a man from the family of al-Ḥakam, blue-eyed, piebald, and a man from Muḍar, short, tyrannical, and the Sufyānī, and the one who takes refuge in Mecca—those are the four.

800. Muḥammad b. `Alī: Four will be killed in Syria, all of them children of caliphs: a man from the Marwānids, a man from the family of Abū Sufyān, he said: The Sufyānī [172] will be victorious over the Marwānids, and kill them. Then the Marwānids will follow him, but he will kill them. He will then advance towards the easterners and the `Abbāsids until he enters Kūfa.

801. Abū Ja`far: The Sufyānī will contend with one of the Marwānids in Damascus, and be victorious over the Marwānid and kill him. Then he will kill the Marwānids for three months, then advance towards the east, until he enters Kūfa.

802. Al-Walīd: A *mawlā* of Khālid b. Yazīd b. Mu`āwiya informed me that he will emerge from Kūfa because of a sickness that will afflict him in it, so he will die between Arak and Tadmur,[504] from a frailty that will afflict him.

803. Ka`b: The worst of the people of that time will gather for al-Saffāḥ, until when they are where they can see their enemy, since they will think wrongly that they are the ones who are attacking their lands, the head of their tyrants previously unknown will advance—he is a rotund man with curly hair, cross-eyed, with eyebrows overhanging, jaundiced (*miṣfār*).[505] When he considers al-Manṣūr at the end of that year, in which he will gather the worst of the people of that time for al-Saffāḥ,

503 Dhū al-Qariyāt al-Ḥimyarī, possibly a Companion, close to Kab, lived in Syria, *fl.* 1st/7th century.

504 On the desert route between Damascus and `Iraq.

505 This form is not attested in Lane, but iv, p. 1008 (right col.), lists *ṣufār* "a disease as a consequence of which one becomes yellow."

al-Manṣūr will die naturally, they will have dispersed to many countries.

When the news reaches them, they will strike wherever they can, seeking to follow `Abdallāh, but the Sufyānī will return and call the westerners (Maghribis) on behalf of himself, so they will gather in a way that none has gathered according to the knowledge of God Most High previously. Then he will intercept an expedition from Kūfa, even though that expedition will come from Baṣra, so at that most its people will perish either from fire or drowning, and there will be a swallowing up by the earth in Kūfa.

When there is the expedition from the Maghrib, there will be a small battle, so woe at that time for `Abdallāh from `Abdallāh, who will rise up in Ḥimṣ, set Damascus alight, and a man will emerge in Filasṭīn who will be victorious over those who oppose him—the destruction of the easterners will be at his hands. He will reign for [the length of] a woman's pregnancy, and three armies belonging to him will be sent to Kūfa and Baṣra, by which houses of Quraysh will be struck, [but] they will be saved on that very day.

804. `Alī: When the supporters of the black banners differ one of the villages of Iram (Damascus) will be swallowed up by the earth, and the western side of its [Damascus'] mosque will fall. Then three banners will emerge in Syria, that of the Piebald, the Speckled One, and the Sufyānī, so the Sufyānī will emerge from Syria, the Speckled One from Egypt, and the Sufyānī will be victorious over them.

805. Dhū al-Qariyāt: The people will differ in Ṣafar, and the people will divide into four groups: one man in Mecca, the one who takes refuge there, two men in Syria, one of them is the Sufyānī, and the other from the descendants of al-Ḥakam, blue-eyed and piebald, and a man from the Egyptians, a tyrant—those are the four. [173]

806. Ibn Zuhayr: They will differ over four people, a tyrant who will swear for himself the oath of the caliphate, giving the

people 100 dinars. Two men in Syria, who will give that which none before have ever given—whichever of them dominates Damascus, he will possess Syria.

807. `Ammār b. Yāsir: Three men will emerge, all of them seeking the dominion: a speckled man, a piebald man, a man from the family of Abū Sufyān, who will emerge leading [the tribe of] Kalb, and he will besiege the people in Damascus.

808. `Alī: three banners will emerge in Syria: that of the Piebald One, the Speckled One and the Sufyānī. The Sufyānī will emerge from Syria, while the Speckled One emerges from Egypt, and the Sufyānī will be victorious over all of them.

809. Dhū Qariyāt: The people will differ in Ṣafar, and will divide over four men: a man in Mecca, the one who takes refuge there, two men in Syria, one of whom is the Sufyānī, while the other is from the descendants of al-Ḥakam, blue-eyed and piebald, and a man from the Egyptians, a tyrant—those are the four. A man from [the tribe of] Kinda will be enraged, and emerge against those in Syria, then bring the army to Egypt, killing that tyrant. Egypt will be crumbled like dung, then he will send an expedition to the one in Mecca.

810. Ḥudhayfa: When the Sufyānī enters the land of Egypt, he will stay in it four months, and kill and take captive its people. On that day the mourning [women] will rise, crying, crying about their sexual abuse, crying, crying about the killing of their children, crying, crying about their humiliation after their haughty [station], crying, crying desirous of their graves.

811. Abū Wahb al-Kalā`ī: The people will divide, the Arabs among the Berbers under four banners, so the victory will be for Quḍā`a, when a man from the descendants of Abū Sufyān is ruling over them.

812. Walīd: Then the Sufyānī will approach, and fight the Hashemites, and everyone he can contend with from those three banners and others, so he will be victorious over all of them, then go to Kūfa, and expel the Hashemites to Iraq. Then he will return from Kūfa and die very close to Syria. He will

appoint as his successor another man from the descendants of Abū Sufyān, so the victory will be his, and he will be victorious over the people, and he is the Sufyānī. [174]

813. Abū Ja`far: When the Speckled One appears with large people (*qawm dhūwī ajsām*), there will be a huge apocalyptic battle between them, then the squinty-eyed cursed Sufyānī will appear and fight all of them, and be victorious over all of them. Then al-Manṣūr al-Yamānī will will go towards them from Ṣana'ā'[506] leading his troops, with a burning rage, seeking to kill the people in the manner of the *jāhiliyya*. He will meet the squinty-eyed one and the yellow banners, wearing many-colored clothing, and there will be a fierce fight between them. Then the squinty-eyed Sufyānī will be victorious over him, but then the Byzantines will appear and emerge into Syria. {The squinty-eyed one will appear}[507] then the Kindī, looking good, will appear. When he reaches High Hill (Tall Samā) he will advance, then go towards Iraq, and raise well-known ascribed [to tribes] twelve banners before that in Kūfa. In Kūfa he will kill a man from the descendants of al-Ḥasan or al-Ḥusayn who will be calling for [the rights of] his father, and so a man from the *mawālī* will appear, but when his issue becomes clear, and he kills excessively, then the Sufyānī will kill him.

814. Ka`b: When there are the two earthquakes in the month of Ramaḍān, three men from one family will be deputized: one of them will seek it [the rule] by tyranny, one will seek it by asceticism, tranquility, and dignity, while the third will seek it by killing—and his name will be `Abdallāh. At the side of the Euphrates [River] there will be a great gathering, in which they will fight over wealth—seven out of every nine will be killed.

[506] Capital of Yemen.

[507] A phrase seems out of place.

815. Al-Zuhrī: When the supporters of the black banners and the people of the yellow banners meet in battle at the bridge [in Egypt], defeat will be for the easterners, so they will retreat until they reach Filasṭīn. Then the Sufyānī will emerge against the easterners, so when the westerners descend upon al-Urdunn, their ruler will die, and they will divide up into three groups: a group that returns to whence they came, a group that goes on pilgrimage, and a group that remains steadfast, and the Sufyānī will fight them, defeat them, and they will enter into his service.

816. Ibn al-Ḥanafiyya: When the Sufyānī is victorious over the Speckled One, he will enter Egypt, and at that time will be the destruction of Egypt.

817. \`Abdallāh b. \`Amr and Abū Dharr: Verily, everyone who leaves Egypt will be killed.

818. Khārija[508]: I said to Abū Dharr: "You mean that there is no imam at the time when he emerges?" He said: "No, since his peers will be cut off." [175]

819. Ka\`b: Verily, Egypt will be crumbled like dung.

820. Dhū al-Qariyāt: When you see a lame man from the Umayyads ruling Egypt, leave Fusṭāṭ with the first post-courier (*barīd*),[509] for a man from his family will kill him. Then the Syrians will send an army against them [the Egyptians], but a man from Kinda will meet them in battle at al-\`Arīsh, when the first and last of them will die obedient to them. He will say: "I will take care of this for you," so he will advance leading the army, but that man will be killed together with those who sought to follow him, such that the Egyptians will be sold in the Market of Māzin.[510] [176]

[508] Probably Khārija b. Zayd b. Thābit, lived in Medina, d. 100/718–19.

[509] Usually twelve miles, for an overall description see Adam Silverstein, *Postal Systems in the Pre-Modern Islamic World* (Cambridge: Cambridge University Press, 2007), Chapter 2.

[510] Presumably this is in Ḥimṣ, but otherwise unattested.

The Conflict between the `Abbāsids, and the Easterners, and the Sufyānī and the Marwānids in Syria towards Iraq

821. Thawban: The Prophet said to Umm Ḥabība[511] when he mentioned the `Abbāsids and their turn, so he turned to Umm Ḥabība and said: Their destruction will be at the hands of a man from this stock [the Umayyads].

822. Al-Walīd b. Muslim: When Quḍā`a has been victorious over the Maghribis, then their ruler will come to the `Abbāsids, whereupon their sister's son will enter Kūfa together with those with him, and destroy it. But then a malignant growth will afflict him, so he will depart from it, going towards Syria, but will perish between Iraq and Syria. Then a man from his family will rule them, who is the one who will do horrible deeds to the people, and be victorious in his rule. Then the Arabs will gather against in Syria, and there will be a fight between them until the fight turns towards Medina. The apocalyptic battle will be in Gharqad Ravine (Baqī` al-Gharqad).[512]

823. Al-Zuhrī: He will depart fleeing from Kūfa because of a malignant growth that will afflict him, then [he will] die. Then a man from them, whose name is the name of his father will rule after him, with his name having eight letters, with slumped shoulders, weak forearms and calves, a broad head, and cross-eyed. The people will perish after him.

824. Ka`b: He will light up his affair in Ḥimṣ, and set it ablaze in Damascus, but his desire will be the ruin of the `Abbāsids.

825. Al-Zuhrī: The Syrians will swear allegiance [177] to the Sufyānī, so he will fight the easterners and defeat them away from Filasṭīn, until they descend upon the Yellowish Field (Marj al-Ṣufar)[513] then they will meet in battle, but the defeat will be upon the easterners, so they will descend upon the Field

[511] Daughter of Abū Sufyān, sister of Mu`āwiya, wife of Muḥammad.

[512] The cemetary of Medina.

[513] The site of one of the conquest battles, south of Damascus.

of the Pass (Marj al-Thaniyya).[514] Then they will fight, but the defeat will be upon the easterners, so they will go to al-Ḥaṣ[515] where they will fight and again the easterners will be defeated. So they will go to the ruined city, meaning Carchemish, where they will fight and again will be defeated. Then they will end up at `Āqir Qūfā,[516] and yet again will be defeated.

The Sufyānī will gather the wealth, but then a malignant growth will appear on his throat, then he will enter Kūfa one morning, but depart from it in the evening leading his armies. While he will be at the entrance of Syria, he will pass away. Then the Syrians will rise up, and swear allegiance to the Son of the Kalbite Woman, whose name is `Abdallāh b. Yazīd b. al-Kalbiyya,[517] cross-eyed and ugly of face.

News of the Sufyānī's passing will reach the easterners, so they will say: "The turn of the Syrians has gone," so they will rise, but this will reach the Son of the Kalbite Woman, so he will rise at the head of his gathering against them. They will fight at the Flags[518] but defeat will be for the easterners, such that they [the Syrians] will enter Kūfa. He will kill the fighters, and take captive the offspring and the women, then destroy Kūfa. Then he will send an army from it to the Ḥijāz.

826. Arṭāt b. al-Mundhir: The ugly cursed one will emerge from near al-Mandarūn, east of Baysān on a red camel, with a crown, defeating gatherings twice, and then perish. He will kill the free men, take captive offspring, and split the bellies of women.

827. Ka`b: When the Sufyānī returns he will call to himself a gathering of the Maghribis, so they will gather for him a number never before seen, according to the knowledge of God Most

[514] Probably the pass to the north of Damascus.
[515] Close to Aleppo.
[516] One of the crossings of the Euphrates.
[517] Mu`āwiya's wife and Yazīd's mother was Maysūn from the tribe of Kalb. Another name for the Sufyani.
[518] Al-Alwiya', unidentified, but presumably in Iraq, close to Kūfa.

High. Then he will send an expedition to Kūfat al-Anbār,[519] but the two gatherings will meet in battle at Carchemish (Qirqīsiyā). Endurance will be lifted from the both of them, and victory as well so that they will both perish. When his expedition from the west is in the smaller battle, then woe at that time to `Abdallāh from `Abdallāh who will rise up in Ḥimṣ! He will be the worst of creation, and he will set Damascus ablaze—the destruction of the easterners will be at his hands.

828. Elders: The Prophet said: The Syrians and the [178] Iraqis will meet in battle at al-Ḥaṣ, and the defeat will be for the Iraqis. They will fight until they reach their land.

829. `Alī: `Abdallāh will follow `Abdallāh until the two armies meet in battle at Qirqīsiyā on the river [Euphrates].

830. Khālid b. Ma`dān: The Sufyānī will defeat a gathering twice, and then perish.

831. Ka`b: The Sufyānī will defeat the gathering twice, then kill the free men, take captive the offspring, and surely slaughter a woman from Quraysh in it—he will slit the bellies of those Hashemite women who he wants, then he will die. At that time a man from that woman's family will rise up after years, being called `Abdallāh, but he is not a servant of God Most High, at all. He is the worst of creation, the ugly, cursed one, whoever follows him and calls for him, the people of the heavens and the earth will curse them. He is the Son of the Liver-Eating Woman[520] and he will come to Damascus, and sit upon its pulpit, lighting up his rule in Ḥimṣ, and setting Damascus ablaze. This will be when two men throw off allegiance to the `Abbāsids, although they are nobles. At the difference of the second one, will be the emergence of the Sufyānī, young, curly haired, white with a long body, with his middle finger dried

[519] Presumably a suburb of al-Anbār, north of Baghdād.

[520] Hind, wife of Abū Sufyān, mother of Mu`āwiya, attempted to eat the liver of Ḥamza, when he was killed at the Battle of Uḥud in 4/625. Note al-Ya`qubi, *Tā'rīkh*, ii, p. 152 where Ziyād b. Abihi uses this title for Mu`āwiya in a speech (before he swore allegiance to the latter).

up. There will be battles between them in Syria, and he will take the women of the `Abbāsids captive, until he brings them to Damascus.

832. Arṭāt: The Sufyānī will kill everyone who disobeys him, and cut them up with saws, or grind them in kettles, for six months, and meet the easterners and the westerners in battle. [179]

The Conflict between the People of Syria, the `Abbāsid rulers at al-Raqqa, and what the Sufyānī will do

833. Al-Waḍīn b. `Aṭā': The fourth tribulation will begin in al-Raqqa.[521]

834. Al-Walīd: An informant told me that at the beginning of the difference between the `Abbāsids a banner will emerge from Khurāsān, so there will be an apocalyptic battle between them at the growing-places of saffron, which is in the pure city between the two rivers [Baghdad], and he will take out all of the wealth that has been gathered in it, until he descends upon the city of idols, meaning Ḥarrān,[522] then news will come to him that a king in the Maghrib had risen up, so he sent to him troops to be defeated by them, such that he will descend together with those with him upon Syria.

Then a herald from the heavens will call out: "Woe to the land of Ḥimṣ, the Garrisoned Spring (*al-`ayn al-shakhnā'*)[523] (spring of smoke)!" so every woman having a husband will carry him, every woman having a son will carry him, then they will go until they camp between the rivers. A great tyrant will be killed there, and it [Ḥimṣ] will be divided up. Then he will

[521] Classical Callinicum in northeastern Syria.

[522] Gen. 12:4–5, today in southern Turkey, close to the Syrian border. It was a center for sun-worship during the early Islamic period. See the Apocalypse of Weeks (no. 1949).

[523] SZ and DKI read *al-`ayīn al-sanja* "the smoky spring," while MM reads *al-`ayīn al-sanḥa* "sheltered spring." None of these are known from other sources. Compare no. 1949, the Apocalypse of Weeks.

go to the city of the idols, meaning Ḥarrān, so he will split the belly of its ruler, and deflower his people.

He will send to the east, so they will swear allegiance unwillingly, not obediently, and he will stay there eight months. Then he will go to the Khābūr [River][524] and stay there seven weeks (*sab` sābū`*), then go to the ox's pen, and leave it in flames. The ruler of the east will withdraw to the mountains of the interior (*jawf*), then a man from his family will betray him, and kill him. Then the ruler of the east will come until he camps between Ḥarrān and Edessa (al-Ruhā). Then the beardless boy will emerge from the Master's House (Bayt al-Ra's).[525] [180]

835. Abu Umayya al-Kalbī: While the supporters of the black banners fight between themselves, the seventh of seven will emerge, and he will send to the people of the towns (*qurā*) to help him, but they will refuse him. His appearance will reach a governor of the `Abbāsids over Tiberias, so he will send against him a mighty gathering, but when they confront him, they will go over to him in their totality, other than their commander who leads them, who will return to their ruler and inform him.

So the rebel (*khārijī*) and those with him will tend towards the lote-tree that is on the side of the hill, and camp under it. The people of the towns will come to him and swear allegiance to him, so he will lead them. Then the lord of Tiberias will meet them in battle at al-Uqḥawāna[526] so he will fight them at the Sea of Galilee until the surface of the lake is red with their blood, then he [the Sufyānī] will defeat them.

They will gather a great many at Jābiya for him, so woe to the people of Jābiya who are within a five-mile radius of this, and blessing to those whose families are beyond this

524 Close to the Euphrates River, in al-Jazīra, northern Iraq.

525 A location with this name is in present-day northwestern Jordan. Probably close to the Dry Valley.

526 In the Jordan River valley, close to the ascent to Afīq.

[distance]. He will defeat them then they will gather a gathering like that before at Damascus, and bring them inside, so they will fight there, until the horses will trample in blood up to their fetlocks, then he will defeat them.

836. Ibn `Abbās: A man will emerge from the east, but their dominion will shy away from him, so he will be killed between al-Raqqa and Ḥarrān. A man from Quraysh will kill him, and a man from the family of Abū Sufyān will emerge from the desert from the west, and kill the king of Kūfa in Ḥarrān.

837. Thawbān, the *mawlā* of the Messenger of God said: There will be a caliph to whom the people will be unable to swear allegiance, then there will be a disaster from an enemy, so he will not have a choice but to go by himself, but will be victorious over his enemy. The Iraqis will want hm to return to their Iraq, but he will refuse, and say: "This is the land of *jihād*," so they will throw off allegiance to him, and appoint a man over them. They will go to him until they meet him at al-Ḥaṣ, Mount Khunāṣira,[527] so he will send to the Syrians, and they will gather to him like one man.

He will kill by them in a fierce fight, until a man will rise upon his riding-camel, and almost be able to count the men from both sides. Then the Iraqis will be defeated, so they will pursue them until they have forced them into Kūfa, so they can kill everyone who is capable of carrying a weapon from among them. He will defeat them and kill any who are using razors. It was said to Abū Asmā'[528]: "Who did Thawban hear this from? Was it the Messenger of God?" He said: "Who else would it be from??"

838. Al-Walīd b. Hishām[529]: They will fight a fierce fight there [181], and while they are in that situation the Sufyānī will rise up among them, and defeat the two groups, until he forces them

[527] Between Aleppo and Qinnasrin, towards the desert.

[528] One of the chain of transmitters.

[529] One of the family of Abū al-Mu`ayṭ, governor for `Umar b. `Abd al-`Aziz over Qinnasrin, still alive during the reign of Marwān II (744–9).

into Kūfa. The first part of the day will be for him, but the last part against him.

839. A man from the Companions of the Messenger of God: A king will descend upon Iraq, to whom the Syrians will not want to swear allegiance, so there will be what is. Then it will reach him that his enemy has gone towards him, so he will find it necessary to go to him in Syria and meet him in battle, defeat him and kill him. Then he will say to those Iraqis who helped him: "This is my country, my land and my homeland, so return to your country, for I have no further use for you."

So they will return to their country, but say: "We made him king, and helped him, and killed people to protect him, but then he chose a land other than ours, so let's gather together and fight him." So they will go to him, and their gathering that day, I think, will be about 300,000, until they will meet in battle at al-Ḥaṣ, and fight there. There will be an apocalyptic battle the like of which the Arabs have never seen, and endurance will be taken from them, victory also, until a man will rise looking at the lines, and if he wished he would be able to count them because of the few that would be left.

840. Ka`b: When the last difference occurs between the `Abbāsids, which will be after the emergence of the Sufyānī, the Son of the Liver-Eating Woman, and during their last difference there will be annihilation. At that time, expect the battle of the Pass, and the battle of Tadmur, a village to the west of Salamiyya,[530] and a great battle at al-Ḥaṣ, so the `Abbāsids and the easterners will be dominated, until their women will be taken captive, and they will enter Kūfa.

841. Ya`qūb b. Isḥāq, who was a knowledgeable man concerning tribulations: A man from the descendants of al-`Abbās will settle in Raqqa and stay there two years, then raid the Byzantines. He will be more disastrous to the Muslims than he

[530] A town to the northeast of Ḥimṣ (and *to the west* of Tadmur); later a headquarters of the Ismaili movement.

will be to the Byzantines. Then he will return from his raiding to Raqqa, and something from the east will come to him that he does not like [news], so he will return to the east, but not return from it. Then he will nominate his son for a successor, and at his time will be the emergence of the Sufyānī and the falling apart of their dominion.

842. Al-Najīb b. al-Sarī: There will be a caliph from the east who will travel fleeing to al-Jazīra, then he will ask aid from the Syrians, so they will gather for him. He will kill the easterners, they will meet in battle at a hill called al-Ḥaṣ and a great number will be killed there.

843. `Alī b. Abī Ṭālib: The Sufyānī will send a man from the Banū Ḥāritha,[531] who has two locks of hair [182], called Nimr or Qamar b. `Ibād, against the army of Iraq. He will be a corpulent man; another man from his tribe, who is short and bald, with broad shoulders, will command his vanguard. Those Iraqis in Syria will fight him in a place called the Pass,[532] while the people of Ḥimṣ and their helpers are in the thick of fighting the [people of the] east. In it on that day there will be a great army from them, who will fight them along the way to Damascus. All of that will defeat them, then they will tactically retreat from Damascus and Ḥimṣ with the Sufyānī, and meet when the easterners are in a place called al-Yadayn,[533] which is to the east of Ḥimṣ. He will kill more than 70,000, three quarters of the easterners, so defeat will be on them. So the army that he sent will go to the east, until it descends upon Kūfa. How much blood there will be shed! And bellies slit! And children killed! And wealth plundered! Blood permitted! Then the Sufyānī will write to him to go to the Ḥijāz after that to scrape it like leather.

[531] There are many clans with this name; here presumably they are a northern tribe/clan.

[532] Probably the pass above Damascus, called Eagle's Pass (Thaniyyat al-`Iqāb).

[533] Probably the town of Aidoun, to the northeast of Ḥimṣ, southwest of Salamiyya.

844. Salmān b. Sumayr al-Alhānī[534]: A caliph will descend upon Kūfa who will defeat the Syrians, then he will be desirous of going to Syria, so it will be said to him: Go to Syria, for it is the holy land (*al-arḍ al-muqaddas*), and the land of the prophets, the residence of the caliphs, and to it wealth flowed, and from it expeditions would come out. So he will comply, then the easterners will take vengeance upon him, and say: We fought with him, and he endangered our blood, lives, and wealth, but now he chose against us. So they will throw off his allegiance. So the Syrians will go to Kūfa, to be scraped off like leather.

845. Ibn Mas`ūd: The seventh of the `Abbāsids will call the people to justice,[535] but they will not answer him in that, so he will say: "I will treat you the way that Abū Bakr and `Umar treated you, and divide the spoils fairly," so his family will say to him: "Do you want to expel us from our livelihoods?" So they will refuse him, and then he will kill a number from his family. They will differ among themselves, and at that a man from the descendants of Fihr will emerge, gathing the Berbers until he takes the pulpits in Egypt. Then a man from the descendants of Abū Sufyān will emerge, and when this reaches the Fihrī, they will divide into three groups . . . to the end of the tradition.

846. `Alī: The Sufyānī will be victorious over Syria, then there will be a battle between them at Qirqīsiyā, until the birds of the heavens and the animals of the earth are satisfied with their corpses. Then there will be a crack that will crack open behind them, so a group from them will approach until they enter the land of Khurāsān. The horsemen of the Sufyānī will approach in search of the Khurāsānis, then they will kill the Party of Muḥammad's Family (*shī`at Āl Muḥammad*) in Kūfa. Then the Khurāsānis will go out looking for the Mahdi. [183]

534 Lived in Syria, *fl.* 1st/7th century.

535 The Mu`tazilites, favored by al-Ma'mun (seventh `Abbasid ruler), were called the People of Monotheism and Justice.

847. `Ammār b. Yāsir: `Abdallāh will follow `Abdallāh and the armies of both of them will meet in battle at Carchemish on the river [Euphrates], so there will be a great fight. The lord of the Maghrib will go and kill the men and take the women captive, then return leading Qays until he descends upon al-Jazīra to the Sufyānī. The Yamānī will follow and kill Qays at Jericho (Arīḥā).[536]

The Sufyānī will gather those then go to Kūfa, and kill the helpers of the Family of Muḥammad. Then the Sufyānī will be victorious over the three banners in Syria, then there will be a battle after Qirqīsiyā, which will be huge. A crack will open up for them from behind them, so he will kill a group of them, until they enter the land of Khurāsān. The horsemen of the Sufyānī will approach like night and flowing water[537]—everything they pass they will cause to perish or destroy it, until they enter Kūfa. They will kill the Party of the Family of Muḥammad, and then they will search out the Khurāsānis at every point. So the Khurāsānis will go out in search of the Mahdi, calling for him, and seeking to help him.

848. Salmān b. Sumayr al-Alhānī: A caliph will descend upon Kūfa, and he will tread upon the Syrians in defeat. Then he will be desirous concerning them, so it will be said to him: "Go to the land of Syria, it is the holy land, the land of the prophets, the residence of the caliphs, to it wealth is brought, and from it expeditions are sent out." So he will comply, but when he complies to them, the Iraqis will take vengeance upon him, saying: "We endangered our blood, ourselves and our wealth with him, so now he prefers some people other than us." So they will oppose him, and the Syrians will go to Kūfa on that day to scrape it like leather. [184]

[536] Jericho, although perhaps another Arīḥā in northern Syria.
[537] Rhyming in Arabic.

What the Sufyānī will do in the Suburbs of Baghdad and Madinat al-Zawra' when his Expedition will reach Iraq, and the Destruction that will happen

849. Abū Ja`far: When the Sufyānī is victorious over the Speckled One, and over al-Manṣūr, al-Kindī, the Turks and the Byzantines, he will depart and go towards Iraq, then the ill-omened horn will arise. At that `Abdallāh will perish, and the cast-out one will throw off his allegiance, and accuse groups of ignorance in the Twisted City (Baghdad). Then the Squinty-eyed one will appear against the city with force, and have a huge killing in it. Six rams of the `Abbāsids will be killed, and there will be cold-blooded slaughter in it, then he will depart for Kūfa.

850. Ibn Mas`ūd: The Prophet said: When the Sufyānī crosses the Euphrates, and reaches a place called `Āqir Qūfā, God will wipe the belief from his heart, so he will kill 70,000 wearing girded swords in it to a river called the Tigris, and around it even more. They will come across a house of gold, and kill the fighters and the champions, splitting open the bellies of women—saying: "Perhaps they are pregnant with boy-children."[538] The women of Quraysh will shout out for help from the banks of the Tirgis [River] to those boats passing by, begging for the boatmen to transport them lest they would be thrown to the people, but the [boatmen] will not transport them out of hatred for the Hashemites. But they [the boatmen] did not hate the Hashemites, since the Prophet of Mercy [Muḥammad] and the Flyer in Paradise[539] was from among them [the Hashemites]. As for the women, when night came over them, they took refuge in caves fearing licentiousness, then [in the morning] succor from the helpers will come to

538 Fearing that those boys would grow up to take vengeance.

539 Ja`far al-Ṭayyār, brother of `Ali b. Abī Ṭālib, losing both of his arms at the Battle of Mu'ta in exchange for wings in paradise.

them. Then they will save those Baghdādi and Kūfan offspring and women from the Sufyānī.

851. Ḥudhayfa: [185] A man from his family called Abd al-Ilāh or `Abdallāh will descend upon one of the rivers of the east, where are two cities, divided by the river between the two of them, so when God gives permission to remove their dominion and to end their period God will send a fire at night against one of them [the two cities], so it will wake up black dark-night, having been set alight like it was not in its place. Its neighbor will awaken astonished that it disappeared, but it will not be more than a day until God will gather in it every stubborn tyrant, and God will cause them and it (the city) to be swallowed up by the earth completely. This is His Word, mighty and majestic, *ḥ-m-`-s-q*[540]—a disaster ordained by God, the *`ayīn* is *`adhab* (punishment), the *sīn* is meant "there will be bombardment in both of them," meaning the two cities.

852. `Abd al-Raḥmān b. Ghanm[541]: Two communities are on the verge of sitting on a skin placed under a mill to be ground: one of them will be swallowed up by the earth, while the other looks on. Then there will be two neighboring quarters divided by a river, from which all take water, each of them gaining from the other, then they will both wake up one day, when one of them has been swallowed up by the earth, while the other looks on.

853. Ḥudhayfa that he was asked concerning *ḥ-m-`-s-q*,[542] when `Umar, `Alī, Ibn Mas`ūd, Ubayy b. Ka`b, Ibn `Abbās and a number of the Companions of the Messenger of God were present, so he said: "The *`ayīn* is *`adhab* (punishment), the *sīn* is a hungry year, the *qāf* is a group bombarding at the end of time," so `Umar said to him: "Who are they?" He said: "From the descendants of al-`Abbās in a city called Twisted [Baghdad].

540 Q 42:1.

541 `Abd al-Raḥmān b. Ghanm al-Asha`rī, lived in Syria, d. 78/697–8.

542 Q 42:1.

There will be a huge killing in it, and upon them the Hour will arise." Then Ibn `Abbās said: "This is not concerning us [the `Abbāsids] but the the *qāf* is *qadhf* (bombardment), and swallowing up by the earth that will be." `Umar said to Ḥudhayfa: "As for you, your exegesis is correct, but Ibn `Abbās is correct in the meaning." A fever took Ibn `Abbās from what he heard from Ḥudhayfa, such that `Umar and a number of the Companions of the Messenger of God visited him [while he was sick].

854. Ibn `Abbās: The Sufyānī will emerge, then fight such that he will split open the bellies of women, and roast childen in caldrons. [186]
855. Ka`b: He will take the women of the `Abbāsids captive, until he will bring them to the villages of Damascus.
856. Arṭāt: When a city is built upon the Euphrates [River], then it is killing and fighting,[543] and when a city is built six miles from Damascus,[544] then brace for the apocalyptic battles. [187]

The Sufyānī and his Army enter Kūfa

857. Ka`b: Kūfa is safe from destruction until Egypt is destroyed.
858. Ka`b: Kūfa will be scraped like leather, then there will be the greatest apocalyptic battle after Kūfa.
859. Arṭāt: The Sufyānī will enter Kūfa and take captives in it for three days, and kill 60,000 of its people, then stay in it eighteen nights dividing its wealth. His entrance into Kūfa will be after he will fight the Turks, the Byzantines and [the easterners at] Carchemish. Then a crack will open up behind them, so a group of them will return to Khurāsan, so the horsemen of the Sufyānī will advance, destroying fortresses until they enter Kūfa. They will seek the Khurāsānis, and a group will appear in Khurāsān calling for the Mahdi.

    Then the Sufyānī will send to Medina, and a group of the

[543] Text: *naqf* and *niqāf*, codes, see no. 200.
[544] This is probably the town of Ḥarastā, later swallowed up by an earthquake.

family of Muḥammad, so as to bring them to Kūfa. Then the Mahdi and Manṣūr will depart from Kūfa fleeing, and the Sufyānī will send [an expedition] in their wake. When the Mahdi and Manṣūr reach Mecca, the army of the Sufyānī will camp in the wasteland, but it will swallow them up. Then the Mahdi will depart passing by Medina, so as to save those Hashemites in it. The black banners will advance until they camp at the water (the river?), so it will reach the Sufyānī's supporters in Kūfa that they are camped there, so they will flee.

Then he [the Mahdi] will descend upon Kūfa to save those Hashemites in it, a group will appear from the alluvial plain of Kūfa called the Bands (`*uṣab*), without very many weapons. There will be some people from Baṣra among them, so they will follow and reach the supporters of the Sufyānī, and liberate the Kūfan captives in their hands. The black banners will follow in swearing allegiance to the Mahdi. [188]

The Mahdi's Black Banners after the `Abbāsids' Banners, and what will happen between the Sufyānī's army and the `Abbāsids

860. Muḥammad b. al-Ḥanafiyya: A black banner belonging to the `Abbāsids will emerge, then another will emerge from Khurāsān, with their *qālansuwas* black,[545] their clothes white, at their vanguard, a man called Shu`ayb b. Ṣāliḥ b. Shu`ayb, from [the tribe of] Tamīm, defeating the supporters of the Sufyānī, until he settles at Jerusalem (*bayt al-maqdis*), preparing for the Mahdi his rule, supporting him with 300 from Syria. Between his emergence and the time when he gives over the rule to the Mahdi will be seventy-two months.
861. `Abdallāh: While we were with the Messenger of God, youth from the Hashemites came, and his color changed, so we said: "O Messenger of God, what has been revealed to you? We saw

[545] A type of turban, see Dozy, *Dictionnaire détailé des Noms des vêtements chez les Arabes* (Beirut: Librarie du Liban, 1843, reprint), pp. 365–71.

from your face that there is something that you dislike." He said: "We, the People of the House, God chose the Next World over this world, so the People of my House, these, will encounter[546] trial, expulsion, and scattering after me, until a group from from there, from the east, supporters of the black banners, who will ask for their due, but will not give it twice or three times. They will fight, and be victorious, so then they will receive what they asked for. They will not receive it until they give it to a man from my family, who will fill it with justice just as it has been filled with injustice. Whoever of you lives in that time, let him go to them, even crawling on the snow, for he is the Mahdi."

862. Thawbān: When you see the black banners emerging from the direction of Khurāsān, then go to them, even crawling on the snow, for among them is the caliph of God,[547] the Mahdi.

863. Al-Ḥasan: A man will emerge in Rayy[548] [189] corpulent, brown (*asmar*), a *mawlā* of Banū Tamīm, with a scraggly beard, called Shu`ayb b. Ṣāliḥ, leading 4,000 men, wearing white clothes, [having] black banners, while in their vanguard will be the Mahdi. Everyone he meets in battle flees.

864. `Alī: The Messenger of God said: A man from my family will emerge leading nine banners, meaning in Mecca.

865. `Ammār b. Yāsir: The flag of the Mahdi will be in the charge of Shu`ayb b. Ṣāliḥ.

866. Tubay`: The black banners will emerge from Khurāsān, with a group of weaklings, who will gather, God will aid them with His victory, then the Maghribis will emerge following that.

867. Abū Ja`far: A youth from the Hashemites will emerge, on his right hand will be a mole, from Khurāsān, leading the black banners, in front of him Shu`ayb b. Ṣāliḥ, fighting the supporters of the Sufyānī, and defeating them.

546 Reading *sa-yulqawuna* with BL.

547 On the significance of this phrase, see Crone and Hinds, *God's Caliph* (Cambridge: Cambridge University Press, 1986).

548 Present-day Tehran.

868. Sufyān al-Kalbī: "A youth young in age, with a thin beard, yellow"—although al-Walīd did not remember "yellow"—"will emerge with the flag of the Mahdi. If he fought the mountains, he would shake them"—Walīd said: "cause them to tremble"—"until he descends upon Jerusalem (*Iliyā'*)."

869. Ka`b: When one man reigns in Syria, and another in Egypt, then the two will fight, and the Syrians will take captive tribes from Egypt, so a man will approach from the east leading small black banners towards the lord of Syria, so he is the one who will give obedience to the Mahdi.

870. Abū Qubayl: There will be a commander in Ifrīqiyā (Tunisia) twelve years old, then after him there will be dissension, then a brown man will reign, ruling it with justice, then he will go to the Mahdi, and give him obedience, and fight for him.

871. Al-Ḥasan: The Messenger of God mentioned the trial that the people of his family will encounter until God sends the banner from the east, black—whoever helps it, God helps him; whoever forsakes it, God forsakes him—until they bring a man whose name is mine, then give him rule over them, so God will help him with victory. [190]

872. `Amr b. Murra al-Jamalī,[549] [on the authority of] a Companion of the Messenger of God: "Verily, a black banner will emerge from Khurāsān, until its horses are fastened it to this olive tree which is between Bayt Lihyā[550] and Ḥarastā." We said: "There is no olive tree between those two [villages]!" He said: "An olive tree will be planted so that the people of that banner can descend upon it, and fasten their horses upon it."

873. `Abdallāh b. Adam[551]: I narrated this tradition by `Abd al-Raḥmān b. Sulaymān, so he said: The one who will fasten are the people of the second black banner that will emerge, not the first banner. When they descend, a rebel will emerge

[549] Lived in Kūfa, was blind, d. 118/736.
[550] In the Ghūṭa (fertile plain) of Damascus, to the south of the city.
[551] Unknown.

from the people of these [villages]. He will only find concealment from the people of the first banner, then he will defeat them.

874. Sa`īd b. al-Musayyib: The Messenger of God said: Black banners belonging to the `Abbāsids will emerge from the east, and they will remain as long as God wills, then small black banners will emerge that will fight a man from the descendants of Abū Sufyān and his supporters from the direction of the east. They will give their obedience to the Mahdi.

875. `Alī: Black banners will emerge to fight the Sufyānī, among them a youth from the Hashemites, on his left shoulder there will be a mole, and in his vanguard there will be a man from Banū Tamīm called Shu`ayb b. Ṣāliḥ, so he will defeat his [the Sufyānī's] supporters.

876. `Ammār b. Yāsir: When the Sufyānī reaches Kūfa and he kills the helpers of the Family of Muḥammad, the Mahdi will emerge, in charge of his flag will be Shu`ayb b. Ṣāliḥ.

877. Abū Ja`far: The black banners that will emerge from Khurāsān will descend upon Kūfa, so when the Mahdi is victorious in Mecca, then the oath of allegiance will be sent.

878. Ka`b: When the mill of the `Abbāsids turns, and the the supporters of the black banners fasten their horses to the olive tree of Syria, God will destroy the Piebald One for them, killing him and most of his family at their hands, until there are no Umayyads who have not fled or hidden. Then two lightening strikes will fall, the Sons of Ja`far[552] and the `Abbāsids, while the Son of the Liver-Eating Woman sits on a pulpit in Damascus, and the Berbers emerge into the navel of Syria, this is the sign of the emergence of the Mahdi. [191]

879. Ibn Shawdhab: I was with al-Ḥasan, and we mentioned Ḥimṣ, and he said: "They will be the happiest of people at the first black [banner], but the most miserable at the second black

552 Presumably the descendents of the brother of `Ali, Ja`far al-Ṭayyār, who revolted during the 740s.

[banner]." We said: "Who are the second 'blacks' (*musawwada*), O Abū Sa`īd?" He said: "Abū al-Ṭuhawī[553] will emerge from the direction of the east leading 80,000 [troops], with their hearts stuffed with faith, just like pomegranates are with seeds. The destruction of the first 'blacks' will be at their hands." [192]

The Beginning of the End for the Sufyānī, and the Appearance of the Hāshimi from Khurāsān leading the Black Banners, and the Fighting between them until the Horsemen of the Sufyānī reach the East

880. `Alī b. `Abī Ṭālib: When the horsemen of the Sufyānī depart to Kūfa in search of the Khurāsānis, the Khurāsānis will emerge in search of the Mahdi, so he and the Hashemite will meet the black banners, which at its vanguard will be Shu`ayb b. Ṣāliḥ. Both he and the supporters of the Sufyānī will meet in battle at the Gate of Iṣṭakhr, and there will be a great apocalyptic battle between them, but the black banners will be victorious, and the horsemen of the Sufyānī will flee. At that time, people will desire the Mahdi and demand his appearance.
881. Abū Ja`far: The Sufyānī will scatter his troops to the horizons after his entrance into Kūfa and Baghdad. But his chief in [the province of] Transoxiana will inform him of the Khurāsānis, so the easterners will approach them killing. Their confidant will go, so when this reaches him, he will send a large army to Iṣṭakhr, under the command of an Umayyad. There will be a battle at Qūmas,[554] another one at Dawlāb[555] al-Rayy, and another one at Takhūm Zaranj.[556] At that time the Sufyānī

[553] Al-Ṭuhawī appears among the Baṣran rebels during the revolt of Ibrāhīm, brother of Muḥammad the Pure Soul (145/762), al-Ṭabarī, *Tā'rīkh*, vii, pp. 628, 637, 642. Presumably this name is a garbled version of his name.
[554] In northern Iran, close to Ṭabarīstan.
[555] Reading with the variants, meaning the waterwheels of Rayy.
[556] In southeastern Iran, Sijistan.

will order the killing of the people of Kūfa and the people of Medina, so the black banners will advance from Khurāsān.

Commanding all of the people will be a youth from the Hashemites, with a mole on his right hand. God will ease his matter and his way, then he will have a battle at Takhūm Khurāsān, and the Hāshimite will follow the Rayy road.[557] A man from the *mawālī* of Tamīm called Shu`ayb b. Ṣāliḥ will drive [the army] to Iṣṭakhr, to the Umayyad [193], and they will meet—him, and the Mahdi and the Hāshimite—at the wasteland (*bayḍā'*) of Iṣṭakhr. There will be a great apocalyptic battle between them, their commander will be a man from the Banū `Adī,[558] and God will grant victory to His Helpers and His troops. Then there will be a battle at al-Madā'in[559] after the two battles of Rayy, and at `Āqir Qūfā a "misfortune" battle[560] that everyone who is saved will tell about.

There will be a slaughter at Babylon (Bābil), and another battle in the lands of Niṣībīn,[561] then a group from its alluvial plain will emerge against the Squinty-eyed One—they are the bands—most of them are from Kūfa and Baṣra, so that they can liberate the captives from both cities who they are holding. [197][562]

The Sufyānī will meet the Black Banners in Battle, and there will be an Apocalyptic Battle between them, in which the People will desire the Mahdi and seek him

882. `Alī: The Sufyānī and the black banners, among them a youth from the Hashemites, who has a mole on his left palm, will meet in battle at the Gate of Iṣṭakhr. Commanding their vanguard there will be a man from the Banū Tamīm called Shu`ayb

[557] The northern road around the Great Salt Desert.
[558] Clan of `Umar.
[559] The ancient Sasanian capital of Ctesiphon, close to Baghdād.
[560] See no. 61.
[561] The classical Nisibis, in northern Iraq.
[562] Section break pp. 194–6.

b. Ṣāliḥ, and there will be a great apocalyptic battle between them, but the black banners will be victorious, and the horsemen of the Sufyānī will flee. At that time the people will desire the Mahdi and seek him.

883. Shurayḥ b. `Ubayd,[563] Rāshid b. Sa`d,[564] Ḍamra b. Ḥabīb and their elders: The Sufyānī will send his horsemen and troops, and they will reach most of the east in the land of Khurāsān, and the land of Persia, but then a man from the easterners will rise up against them, and fight them. There will be battles between them in a number of places. When the fighting lasts a long time between them, they will swear allegiance to a man from the Hashemites, who at that time will be at the very limit of the east, and he will emerge leading the Khurāsānis. Commanding their vanguard will be a man from Banū Tamīm, a *mawlā* of theirs, yellow, with a small beard, emerging on his behalf leading 5000. Then, when [news] of his emergence reaches him, he will swear allegiance to him, and he [the Mahdi] will place him [Shu`ayb] in command of his vanguard. If the firmly fixed mountains faced him he would shake them.[565] He and the horsemen of the Sufyānī will meet in battle, and he will defeat them and kill a great many of them. Then there will be victory to the Sufyānī, so the Hāshimī will flee, but Shu`ayb b. Ṣāliḥ will go secretly to Jerusalem (*bayt al-maqdis*) to prepare the dwelling for the Mahdi, when his emergence towards Syria reaches him.

884. Al-Walīd: It has reached me that this Hāshimī is the brother of the Mahdi on the father's side. But some of them said: He is his [198] paternal cousin, and some of them have said: He does

563 Lived in Ḥimṣ, related traditions on behalf of Maḥij, *fl.* 1st/7th century.

564 Lived in Hebron and Ḥimṣ, d. 108/726–7.

565 Compare the phrase to Ibn al-Muqaffa`, *Athar* (Beirut: Manshurat Dār Maktabat al-Hayat, n.d.), *al-Risāla fi al-sahaba,* pp. 347–8, where a similar idea is used to describe the fanatical loyalty of the `Abbāsid troops towards the caliph, that was to be turned against him during the Rawandiyya episode.

not die but after his defeat will depart to Mecca, so that when the Mahdi appears, he will go out with him.

885. Tubay`: The Sufyānī will send his troops to Marw al-Rūdh[566] so to possess that which is beyond it.

886. Al-Zuhrī: He [the Sufyānī] will send an expedition to Marv and an expedition to Mecca.

887. `Alī b. Abī Ṭālib: A man will emerge on the authority of the Mahdi from his family in the east, carrying the sword on his shoulders for eight months, killing and mutilating, and he will be turned to Jerusalem, but will not reach it before he dies.

888. Abū Ja`far: The black banners which approach from Khurāsān will descend upon Kūfa, so when the Mahdi appears in Mecca, he will send with the oath to the Mahdi. [199]

Sending the Troops to Medina and the Killing that will happen in it

889. `Alī b. Abī Ṭālib: The Sufyānī will write to the one entering Kūfa with his horsemen, after it was scraped like leather, ordering him to go to the Ḥijāz, so he will go to Medina, and place the sword on Quraysh—killing 400 men from them and the Helpers (Anṣār),[567] splitting bellies [of women] and killing children. He will kill two siblings from Quraysh, a man and his sister, called Muḥammad and Fāṭima, and crucify them both above the mosque gate.

890. `Alī: He will send an army to Medina, and take any of Muḥammad's Family that he can, and kill men and women of the Hashemites. At that time the Mahdi and the Whitening One (Mubayyiḍ)[568] will flee from Medina to Mecca, so he will send a detachment in search of them, but they will have taken refuge in the sanctuary of God, and its safety.

891. `Alī b. Abī Ṭālib: People will flee from Medina to Mecca when

[566] A suburb of Marw (today Marv), the major city of Khurāsān, where the `Abbāsids first proclaimed themselves.

[567] Descendants of the Helpers (Anṣār) from the Prophet Muḥammad's time.

[568] A figure carrying white banners, symbolic of the Umayyads.

the army of the Sufyānī reaches them, among them three men from Quraysh, under supervision.

892. Ka`b: Medina will be open for pillage at that time, and the Pure Soul will be killed. [200]

893. Ibn `Abbās: There will be a caliph from the Hashemites in Medina, but people from them will depart for Mecca, but when they arrive, the lord of Mecca will send to them: "What is bringing you here? Do you think that you will find messianic salvation (*faraj*) here?" So a man from the Hashemites will go back and forth with him, and be rude to him, so the lord of Mecca will be angry, and order him to be killed.

When the next morning happens, a man from them [the Hashemites] will arrive, having covered his sword with his garment, and say: "What brought you to kill our friend?" He will say: "He angered me," so he will say: "Bear witness, O Muslims, that this one only killed him because he angered him!" So he will unsheathe his sword, and strike him with it. Then they [the Hashemites] will withdraw to al-Ṭā'if, so the people of Mecca will say: "By God, if we allow these to inform the caliph of their story, we will be destroyed." So they will go towards them, and the Hashemites will implore them: O God, O God, for the sake of our blood and their blood! [answering] "You know that our lord was killed unjustly," so they would not return until they had fought them, but they [the Hashemites] defeated them [the Meccans] and overpowered Mecca.

The issue reached the lord of Medina, so they said: "By God, if we do not leave them, we will have a hard time with the caliph," so the lord of Medina will send an army to them, but they will defeat it, and then when the caliph does send an expedition to them, those are the ones who reward them.

894. Dhū Qariyāt: There will be a caliph in Syria, who will raid Medina, but when the people of Medina hear of the departure of the army against them, seven men of theirs will go out to Mecca, and hide in it. So the lord of Medina will write to the

lord of Mecca, "since so-and-so has come to you" naming them by their names "kill them." This will be too much for the lord of Mecca, so they wil take council between themselves, then come to him at night, and ask him for refuge, but he will say: Go out, in safety, so they will depart.

Then they will to two men of them, when one will be killed, while other looks on, then he will return to his companions, so them will depart to camp on one of the mountains of al-Ṭā'if. They will stay there, and send to the people, so then the people will come quickly to them. When this is happening, the people of Mecca will raid them, but they will defeat them, and enter Mecca, and kill its commander, and be in it until when the army [of the Sufyānī] is swallowed up, he[569] will be prepared and depart.

895. Ibn Shihāb: When they come to Medina, they will kill its people three days.

896. Abū Ja`far: It will reach the Medinans, then the army will depart for them, so those of the Family of Muḥammad who are in it will flee to Mecca, the strong carrying the weak, the older the weaker, so they [the army] will reach a soul from the Family of Muḥammad, and slaughter him at the Oil Stones.[570] [201]

897. Ibn `Umar: The sign of the battle of Medina is when the commander of Egypt is killed.

898. Abū Qubayl: The Sufyānī will send an army to Medina, and order the killing of all of the Hashemites in it, even the pregnant [women], and that will be because of what the Hāshimī who will emerge against his supporters from the east, saying: "This is not the complete story—since my supporters were killed, shoudn't those be killed?" So he will order them to be killed, and they will be killed, such that in all Medina not

569 It is not clear who "he" is here.

570 Where Muḥammad al-Nafs al-Zakiyya ("The Pure Soul") was killed, al-Isfahani, *Maqatil al-Talibiyyin* (Beirut: Mu'assasat al-A`la li-l-Matbu`at, 1987), pp. 207, 240.

one will be left. Some will divide away, fleeing from it, to the desert and the mountains, and to Mecca, even their women. The army will put the sword to them for days, then desist, but none will appear other than those afraid, until the rule of the Mahdi will appear in Mecca, then every rightly guided one of them will gather to him in Mecca.

899. Abū Hurayra: There will be a battle in Medina during which the Oil Stones will drown—the Battle of the Ḥarra,[571] in our opinion [comparatively] is nothing but a whipping, so then they will turn away from Medina the distance of two post-stops (*barīd*), then swear allegiance to the Mahdi. [202]

Swallowing up of the Sufyāni's Troops that he will send to the Mahdi

900. `Abdallāh b. `Amr: The sign of the Mahdi's emergence is a swallowing up by the earth of an army that will be in the wasteland—so this is the sign of his emergence.

901. Ibn `Abbās: The lord of Medina will send an army to the Hashemites in Mecca, but they will defeat them. Then the caliph in Syria will hear of this, and deputize an expedition, which will be 600 tribal leaders (*`arīf*), so when they come to the wasteland, and camp during a moonlit night, a shepherd will approach to look at them, and be amazed, thinking: Woe to the Meccans for what will strike them! Then he will go back to his flocks, and then return but not see anyone. They were all swallowed up! So he will say: "Praise be to God, they went in one hour!" and so he will go to their camp, and find a rough garment,[572] of which part has been swallowed up, part on the ground. So he will try to salvage it, but not be able to, because they were swallowed up. So he will go the lord of Mecca, to give him the good news, and then the lord of Mecca will say:

[571] The Battle of the Ḥarra between Yazīd I and the Medinans in 63/683 because of their reluctance to swear allegiance.

[572] Ibn al-Athīr, *Nihāya*, iv, p. 84.

"Praise be to God! This is the sign of which you have been informed," so they will go to Syria.

902. Tubay`: A refugee will seek refuge in Mecca, but be killed, then the people will remain for a time, then another refugee will seek refuge, so do not raid him, for this is the army that will be swallowed up.

903. Ḥafṣa, wife of the Prophet: I heard the Messenger of God saying: An army will come from the direction of the west, going towards this House [Mecca], until when they are [203] in the wasteland they will be swallowed up. So the one who was their leader will return to look at what the group did, and what happened to them will happen to him. The rearguard will catch up to them, to see what happened, and what happened to them will happen to them as well. Even those who were compelled, what happened, happened, then God Most High will raise each man from among them according to his intentions.

904. Muḥammad b. `Alī: There will be a refugee in Mecca,[573] so they will send 70,000 to him, with a man from Qays commanding them, until when they reach the pass, the last of them will enter, but the first will not exit. [Then] Gabriel will call out: "O wasteland, O wasteland!"—with its eastern and western parts hearing him—"take them, since there is no good in them!" None will be witnesses to their destruction other than a shepherd of flocks on a mountain, looking at them when they sink into the earth. So he will inform them [the Meccans], and when the refugee hears of it, he will depart.

905. Dhū Qariyāt: When it reaches the Sufyānī who is in Egypt, he will send an expedition to the one who is in Mecca, so they will destroy Medina [along the way] worse than at [the Battle of the] Ḥarra, such that when they reach the wasteland they will be swallowed up by the earth.

[573] See Madelung, "`Abdallāh b. al-Zubayr and the Mahdi," *Journal of Near Eastern Studies* 40 (1981), pp. 291–306.

906. Qatāda[574]: The Messenger of God said: An army from Syria will be sent to Mecca, so that when they are in the wasteland they will be swallowed up by the earth.
907. Ibn Mas`ūd: An army will be sent to Medina, then they will be swallowed up by the earth between the Jammā'wayn,[575] and the Pure Soul will be killed.
908. Abū Ja`far: They will be swallowed up and none will be saved from them other than two men from Kalb, whose names are Wabr and Wabīr, whose faces will be turned around towards their necks.
909. `Alī: When an army in search of those who departed to Mecca camps, they will camp in the wasteland and be swallowed up, and [he] will call out. This is His Word, mighty and majestic, "If (only) you could see when they are terrified and (there is) no escape, and they are seized from a place nearby"[576] from under their feet. A man from that army, seeking a she-camel belonging to him, will depart, and then return to the people, but not find any of them, and not sense them. He is the one who will narrate to the people their report.
910. Ka`b: An army of 12,000 will be directed to Medina, then they will be swallowed up in the wasteland. [204]
911. Al-Zuhrī: Two expeditions will be sent from Kūfa: one to Marw, and one to the Ḥijāz. One third of the expedition to the Ḥijāz will be swallowed up, one third metamorphosed—their faces turned back between their shoulder blades looking towards their buttocks, just as they had looked towards their genitals, walking backwards on their heels, like they used to walk on their feet, and one third will be left who will go to Mecca.
912. Abū Ja`far: When the news of the killing of the Pure Soul reaches the Sufyānī, since he was the one who wrote to him, most of the Muslims will flee from the *ḥaram* of the Messenger

[574] Probably Qatāda b. Di`āma al-Sudūsī, lived in Baṣra, famous scholar, d. 117 or 118/735 or 736.
[575] Two hills on the way between Medina and Mecca.
[576] Q 34:51.

of God [Medina] to the Sanctuary (*ḥaram*) of God Most High at Mecca. When that reaches him, he will send an army to Medina, commanded by a man from [the tribe of] Kalb, until when they reach the wasteland, they will be swallowed up by the earth, but their commander will escape. They said that he was from [the tribe of] Madhḥij,[577] but some say from Kalb.

913. Abū Ja`far: Only two men from Kalb, whose names are Wabr and Wabīr, will be saved from them, whose faces will be turned towards their backs.

914. Abū Qubayl: Only a proclaimer warner will escape from them, as for the proclaimer, he will come to the Mahdi and his supporters in Mecca, and inform them of what has happened, as he was a witness to this with his own eyes, as his face was turned towards his back, so they will believe him because of the change in his face that they see, so they will know that the people have been swallowed up. The second will be like that, having his face turned towards his back, he will come to the Sufyānī to inform him of what happened to his supporters. He will believe him and know that it is true because of the sign that he sees, so they are both men from Kalb.

915. `Abdallāh: God Most High will say: "O wasteland, annihilate your people!" so it will annihilate them other than a man from Bajīla[578] who God will turn his face towards his back, in order to inform the people of what happened.

916. Arṭāt: None will be saved from them other than one man, who God will turn his face towards his back, so he will walk the same way backwards. [205]

The Signs of the Mahdi in his Appearance

917. `Abdallāh b. `Amr: When the army is swallowed up in the wasteland, then that is the sign for the emergence of the Mahdi.

577 A Yemenite tribe, attested from the fifth century into early Islam.

578 A southern, Yemenite tribe, closely related to Banū Khatha`m.

918. `Alī b. `Abdallāh b. `Abbās: The Mahdi will not emerge until the sun rises . . .[579]
919. Ka`b: The sign of the Mahdis emergence are flags that will advance from the Maghrib, commanded by a lame man from Kinda.
920. Abū Hurayra: The Sufyānī and the Mahdi will emerge like two racing horses, but the Sufyānī will dominate over those around him, while the Mahdi over those around him.
921. Abū Ja`far: The Mahdi will appear during the year 200 [=815–16].
922. Al-Zuhri: During the second rule of the Sufyānī, you will see a sign in the heavens.
923. Abū Ṣādiq[580]: The Mahdi will not emerge until the Sufyānī rises upon its wood [pulpits] [206]
924. Abū Ja`far: The Sufyānī will not emerge until the unjust are higher.
925. Maṭar al-Warrāq[581]: The Mahdi will not emerge until God is disbelieved publicly.
926. Ibn Sīrīn: The Mahdi will not appear until seven out of nine are killed.
927. `Alī: The Mahdi will not emerge until a third are killed, a third die (naturally), and a third remain.
928. `Alī: The Mahdi will not appear until some of you spit in the faces of others.
929. `Abdallāh b. `Amr b. al-`Āṣ: The sign of the Mahdi's emergence is when an army gets swallowed up by the earth, so that is the sign of the Mahdi's emergence.
930. Abū Qubayl: "The gathering of the people for the Mahdi

[579] The ending seems to be a Qur'ānic verse, yet there is none which fits the context, or it could be a reference to the sun rising from the west, except that this is an event after which there is no history, so the Mahdi must be sent beforehand.

[580] Muslim b. Yazīd al-Azdī, lived in Kūfa, *fl.* 1st/7th century.

[581] Maṭr b. Ṭahmān al-Warrāq al-Khurāsānī, lived in Baṣra, was a scribe (*kāna yaktubu al-maṣāḥifa*), d. 129/746–7.

will happen in the year 204 [= 819–20]." Ibn Lahī`a[582] said: "According to the calcuations of the non-Arabs, not according to the calculations of the Arabs."

931. `Ammār b. Yāsir: The sign of the Mahdi is when the Turks come quickly upon you, and your caliph, who would collect the wealth, dies, appointing as caliph after him a weak man. After two years they will throw off allegiance to him, and there will be a swallowing up by the earth to the west of the mosque of Damascus. Three men will emerge in Syria, and the emergence of the Maghribis in Egypt, then will be the reign of the Sufyānī.

932. Abu Muḥammad[583] on the authority of a western man: The Mahdi will not emerge until a man takes out his drop-dead gorgeous slave-girl, and says: "Who will purchase her for her weight in food?"—then the Mahdi will emerge.

933. `Alī: [207] There will be tribulations, then there will be community under the leadership of a man from my family, who is no good, but will be killed or die, and then the Mahdi will arise.

934. Some Companions: The Mahdi will not emerge until every king (*qayl*) or son of a king has perished, and *al-qayl* is a chief.[584]

935. Abū Qubayl: A man will reign from the Hashemites, who will kill the Umayyads until none but a few remain of them, but not kill other than them. Then a man from the Umayyads will emerge, and kill one out of every two men, until none but women remain, then the Mahdi will emerge.

936. Abū Hurayra: The Prophet said: The Euphrates will reveal a mountain of gold and silver, so seven out of every nine will be killed for it, so if you live to see that, do not come near it.

937. Abū Hurayra: The fourth tribulation will last twelve years, being disclosed when it is disclosed, when the Euphrates

[582] `Abdallāh b. Lahī`a al-Ḥaḍramī, lived in Egypt, a prominent jurisprudent, d. 164/780–1.

[583] Probably Abū Muḥammad al-Nahdī.

[584] South Arabian, see Biella, *Dictionary*, p. 449.

reveals a mountain of gold, then seven out of every nine will be killed for it.

938. Ka`b: On the side of the Euphrates towards Syria or a little beyond it there will be a great gathering, and they will fight over wealth. Seven out of every nine will be killed, and that will be after a crash and a breaking-asunder (*wāhiya*) during the month of Ramaḍān. After that a division into three banners, each one seeking the dominion for himself, among them a man named `Abdallāh.

939. Abū Hurayra: The Messenger of God said: The fourth tribulation is eighteen years, then it will disclose what it discloses, when the Euphrates reveals a mountain of gold, the community will turn upside down over it, and then seven out of every nine will be killed for it. [208]

Another Sign at the Time of the Mahdi's Appearance

940. Sa`īd b. al-Musayyib: There will be tribulation, the first part of which is child's play, every time it is quiet from one side, then it flares up on the other, but it will not end until a herald from the heavens will call out: "Is not the commander so-and-so!" Ibn al-Musayyib intertwined his hands until they were shaking, then said: "This commander is true!" three times.

941. Abū Ja`far: A herald will call from the heavens: "Is not the truth with the Family of Muḥammad?" And then a herald will call from the earth: "Is not the truth with the Family of Jesus?" Or he said: "al-`Abbās," I am doubtful about it. The lesser voice is only from Satan to deceive the people; Nu`aym was doubtful.

942. Ibn Shihāb [al-Zuhrī]: A second commander from the family of Abū Sufyān will be appointed over the pilgrimage, and he will send an expedition with him. When they are at the pilgrimage, they will hear a herald from the heavens: "Is not the commander so-and-so?" And a herald will call out from the earth: "Lies!" While the herald from the heavens calls out: "Truth!" So this will lengthen, but no one will know which of them should be followed. The one from the heaven the first time

spoke the truth. So when you hear this, know that "the word of God is the highest,"[585] while the word of Satan is the lowest.

943. Al-Mughīra b. `Abd al-Raḥmān[586] on the authority of his mother, who was old: I said to her during the dissension of Ibn al-Zubayr: "This dissension, the people will perish during it." So she said: "No, my dear son, but after it there is a tribulation in which the people will perish. Nothing will be right until a herald from the heavens calls out: 'Go to so-and-so!'" [209]

944. Ibn al-Musayyib: There will be a tribulation in Syria, of which the first will be child's play, then nothing will be right for people, and there will be no community until a herald calls out from the heavens: "Go to so-and-so," and a hand will be apparent, pointing. Ibn al-Musayyib: same other than he said: A herald will call out from the heavens: "Your commander is so-and-so!" **(1)**

945. Shahr b. Ḥawshab: The Messenger of God said: During Muḥarram a herald will call out from the heavens: "Is not God's chosen one from His creation so-and-so?" So listen to him and obey him in a year of sounds and uproar.

946. `Ammār b. Yāsir: When the Pure Soul and his brother are killed, he will be killed pointlessly, a herald will call out from the heavens: "Your commander is so-and-so," and that will be the Mahdi who will fill the earth will truth and justice.

947. Sa`īd b. al-Musayyib: There wil be factionalism and division

585 Q 9:40.

586 Al-Mughīra b. `Abd al-Raḥmān al-Makhzūmī, a prominent army-commander under Maslama, who was suspected of being the Dajjal: "al-Mughīra would feed [the soldiers] when they camped, slaughtering a young camel and feeding whoever came. A Bedouin began to stare constantly at al-Mughīra, refusing to take his food, and so al-Mughīra asked him: 'Don't you want to eat this food? And why are you staring constantly at me?' He said: 'Your food impressed me, but your eye leaves me in doubt.' He said: 'What makes you doubt about my eye?' He said: 'I see that you are blind in one eye (*a`war*) and I see you feeding [people], and this is the description of the Dajjal.' al-Mughira said: 'The Dajjal won't have lost one of his eyes in the path of God!'" (Ibn `Asākir, *Tā'rīkh*, lx, p. 69; Ibn Ḥamdūn, *Tadhkira* [Beirut: Dār Ṣādir, 1996], ii, p. 390).

until a hand from the heaven is apparent, and a herald will call out: "Is your commander not so-and-so?"

948. `Alī: After the swallowing up by the earth, a herald will call out from the heavens: Truth is with the Family of Muḥammad, at the beginning of the day. Then a herald will call out at the end of the day: "Truth is with the Family of Jesus," but this is an exhortation from Satan.

949. Al-Zuhri: When the Sufyānī and the Mahdi meet in battle, on that day a voice will be heard from the heavens: "Are not the friends of God the supporters of so-and-so?" meaning the Mahdi.

950. Asmā' daughter of `Umays[587]: The emirate of that day will be a hand let down from the heavens, so that the people would look at it. [210]

951. Arṭāt: When the people are at Minā and `Arafāt, a herald will call after the tribes are assembled: "Is not your commander so-and-so?" But another voice will follow on its footsteps: "Did he not just lie?" And another voice will follow it: "Did he not just tell the truth?" So they will fight fiercely, with most of their weapons being pack-saddles—so this was the army of pack-saddles—and at that you will see a marked hand in the heavens, while the fighting will intensify until none will remain of the supporters of the truth other than the number of the fighters at Badr[588] so that they will swear allegiance to their lord. [211]

The People's Gathering Together at Mecca to swear to the Mahdi in it, and the Confusion, Fighting, Seeking the Mahdi that will happen that year in Mecca after the Battle and their Gathering to him

952. `Amr b. Shu`ayb on the authority of his grandfather: The Messenger of God said: During Dhū al-Qa`da, the tribes will

[587] Asmā daughter of `Umays al-Khatha`miyya, Companion, sister-in-law to the Prophet, *fl.* 1st/7th century.

[588] Usually said to have been 313 men.

divide into groups, during that year the pilgrimage will be pillaged, then there will be an apocalyptic battle at Minā, and there will be a great many dead. Blood will be shed there until their blood flows over Pebble Pass (`Aqabat al-Jamra), so that the [people's] lord will flee, then be brought back between the Corner (Rukn) and the Standing-Place (Maqām),[589] where he will have allegiance sworn to him, although he is reluctant. It will be said to him: "If you refuse, we will cut off your head," so the number of the fighters at Badr will swear to him. The inhabitants of the heavens and the earth will be pleased with him.

953. `Abdallāh b. `Amr: The people will perform the pilgrimage together and stand at `Arafāt together without an imam. While they are camped at Minā, suddenly it will take them like a dog—the tribes will rise up against one another, and fight until the pass flows with blood. So they will go frightened to the best of them, and bring him, while he is clinging his face to the Ka`ba, weeping—it is as if I am looking at his tears! They will say: "Come, let us swear allegiance to you." But he will say: "Woe to you! How many covenants have you broken!! And how much blood have you shed!!" So he will receive their allegiance reluctantly, so if you live at this time, then swear to him, for he is the Mahdi on the earth and the Mahdi in the heavens.

954. Sa`īd b. al-Musayyib: During Dhū al-Qa`da, the tribes will take sides against others, and in Dhū al-Ḥijja the pilgrimage caravan will be pillaged, and Muḥarram, what a Muḥarram!

955. Shahr b. Ḥawshab: The Messenger of God said: During Dhū al-Qa`da the tribes will be divided into groups, during Dhū al-Ḥijja the pilgrimage caravan will be pillaged, and in Muḥarram, a herald will call out from the heavens. [212]

956. Ibn `Abbās: God Most High will send the Mahdi after despair,

[589] The Rukn is one of the corners of the Ka`ba, and the Maqām is the standing place of Abraham (Q 2:125) where he is said to have prayed.

such that the people will say: "There is no Mahdi." His Helpers will be people from Syria, their number being 315 men, the number of the fighters at [the Battle of] Badr. They will go to him from Syria to take him out from the center of Mecca, from a house close to [the hill of] al-Ṣafā, and they will swear to him [when he is] reluctant. He will lead them in prayer two prayer-prostrations (*rak`as*), the Traveler's Prayer[590] at the Standing-Place, and then he will ascend the pulpit.

957. Abū Hurayra: The Mahdi will receive their allegiance between the Corner and the Standing-place, without waking a sleeper, without spilling blood.

958. Al-Zuhrī: There will be two heralds that year: a herald from the heavens: "Is the commander not so-and-so?" and a herald from the earth: "Lies!" So the helpers of the lower voice, until the bases of the trees are dyed with blood. This is the day about which `Abdallāh b. `Amr said: "An army will be called The Army of Pack-saddles, because they will divide their pack-saddles and use them as shields."

He said: "There will only remain of that voice's Helpers the number of the fighters at [the Battle of] Badr, 310 plus, so they will be victorious, then they will go to their master, and find him leaning his back to the Ka`ba, with his shoulder blades trembling, asking God for refuge from the evil to which they are calling, and so they will compel him to take their allegiance. The supporters of the lower voice will return to Syria, saying: 'We fought a group the likes of which we have never seen, even though they were a tiny band."

959. `Abdallāh b. `Amr: There will be dissension while the people are praying together, performing the pilgrimage together, standing at `Arafāt together, and celebrating the Sacrifice Festival (`Īd al-Aḍḥā)[591] together, then aroused like a dog, they will fight until the pass will flow with blood. Even the innocent

[590] A shortened form of the regular prayers.

[591] Which concludes the hajj ceremony.

will see that innocence will not save them, and the one who withdraws will see that his withdrawal is not useful. They will then seek to compel a youthful man, leaning with his back to the Corner, his shoulder blades trembling, called the Mahdi on the earth, and he is the Mahdi in the heavens, so whoever lives at his time, let him follow him.

960. Qatāda: The Messenger of God said: He will depart from Medina to Mecca, and the people will seek him out from among them, then swear allegiance to him between the Corner and the Standing-Place, while he is reluctant. [213]

961. Abū al-Jild: His rule will come to him easily, while he is in his house.

962. `Alī: When the black banners, among which is Shu`ayb b. Ṣāliḥ, defeat the horsemen of the Sufyānī the people will desire the Mahdi, and seek him. So he will emerge from Mecca with the banner of the Prophet, and pray two prayer-prostrations (*rak`as*), after the people will have despaired at his emergence, because of the lengthy trials. When he completes his prayers, he will depart, and say: "O people, the trial has beset the community of Muḥammad, and especially the People of the House—we were compelled and made to do iniquitous things."

963. `Alī: Three men from Quraysh will depart to Mecca, because the army of the Sufyānī is looking for them, so when the [news] of the swallowing up by the earth reaches them, they will gather in Mecca from the countries for those three men, and swear to one of them, [when he is] reluctant.

964. Al-Zuhri: The Mahdi from the descendants of Fāṭima will be taken out from Mecca, and have allegiance sworn to him.

965. Abū Ja`far: Then the Mahdi will appear in Mecca at the evening prayers with the banner of the Messenger of God, his shirt, his sword, signs, light and clear exposition. When he prays the evening prayer, then he will call out at the top of his voice: "I remind you of God, O people! And your place before your Lord. He has made proofs, sent prophets, revealed the Book,

commanded you not to associate anything with Him, to guard obedience to Him and to His Messsenger, to revive what the Qur'ān revives, and to cause to die what it causes to die, that you be helpers for the guidance, advisers for god-fearingness, since this world's annihilation and end have come near, and it has been given permission to say farewell. So I call you to God, to His Messenger, to action according to His Book, and to killing the prohibited, reviving His Sunna (way)."

So he will appear leading 313 men, the number of [the fighters at] Badr, without previous appointment, driven like the autumn clouds, and being like monks at night, lions during the day. God will conquer for the Mahdi the land of the Ḥijāz, and he will take out those Hashemites who are in prison. The black banners will descend upon Kūfa, then send their oath of allegiance to the Mahdi. The Mahdi will send his troops to the horizons, and kill injustice and its people. Countries will be set aright, and God will conquer Constantinople at his hands. [214]

966. `Abdallāh b. Mas`ūd: When commerce is cut—and roads, too—and tribulations multiply, then seven learned men will depart from different directions without previous appointment. 310 some men will have sworn to each of them, until they will gather at Mecca. The seven will meet, and say to each other: "What brought you?" And so they will say: "We came in search of the man who is appropriate to the task of calming these tribulations, and conquer Constantinople. We know his name and his father's and mother's names, and his description." So the seven will agree upon that, and seek him, and find him in Mecca, saying to him: "You are so-and-so son of so-and-so?" He will say: "No, I am a man from the Helpers (al-Anṣār)," so then he will disappear from them.

But they will describe him to the people in the know, and they will be told: "He is the one you are seeking, but he has gone to Medina," so they will seek him in Medina, but he will slip away from them back to Mecca, so they will seek him in

Mecca, and find him, and say: "You are so-and-so son of so-and-so, and your mother is so-and-so daughter of so-and-so, and you have this sign on you. You disappeared from us once, so then stretch out your hand so that we can swear to you."

But he will say: "I am not the one you are looking for. I am so-and-so of the Helpers. If you command me I will show you the one you are looking for." But then he will disappear again, so they will seek for him in Medina, but he will slip away from them again back to Mecca, where they will find him at the Corner, then say to him: "Our sin is upon you, and our blood is on your neck if you do not stretch out your hand to us so that we can swear to you. This army of the Sufyānī has been sent to find us, commanding it there is a man from Jarm,"[592] so he will sit between the Corner and the Standing-Place, and stretch out his hand so that they can swear to him. God will cast love for him into the hearts of the people, and he will lead the people, lions by day, but monks by night.

967. Qatāda: The Messenger of God said: Bands of Iraq will come to him, and the Substitutes (*abdāl*) of Syria, then they will swear to him between the Corner and the Standing-Place, and he will apply Islam in its totality. [215]

The Mahdi's Departure from Mecca to Jerusalem and Syria, after which they will swear to him, and His Traveling towards the Sufyāni and his Supporters

968. Muḥammad b. `Alī: When the refugee who is in Mecca hears of the swallowing up by the earth, he will depart with 12,000, among them the Substitutes (*abdāl*), until they descend upon Jerusalem (*Iliyā'*). Then the one who sent the army, when it reaches him about Jerusalem: "By God's life (*wa-`umri Allāhi*), God has placed in this man a lesson—I sent against him what I sent, so they sunk into the earth, so there is a warning and

[592] There are several different tribes by this name; probably these are related to Quḍā`a.

caution (*baṣīra*)," and the Sufyānī will give him obedience. But then he will depart and go to Kalb, as they are his maternal uncles, who will condemn him for what he did. They will say: "God dressed you in a shirt[593] so you took it off?" He will say: "Do you think that I should go back on my oath?" They will say: "Yes," so he will come to him [the Mahdi] in Jerusalem, and say: "Let me off," so he will say: "I am not going to do that." But he [the Sufyānī] will say: "Nevertheless," so he will say to him: "Do you want me to kill you?" He will say: "Yes," so he will say: "This man has thrown off his allegiance," so he will order him to be slaughtered at the flag-stones (*balāṭa*) of Jerusalem, then he will go to Kalb—and missing out is the one who misses the pillage of Kalb!

969. Dhū Qariyāt: He will go until he reaches Jerusalem, and swear to him at last, departing from him, then he [the Sufyānī] will regret it, and ask to go back on his oath, so he [the Mahdi] will release him, then order him to be killed because of his treachery.

970. Al-Zuhrī: The other will receive his oath of allegiance.

971. `Alī: He will depart leading 12,000 if less, or 15,000 if more, and fear will go before him.[594] Every enemy he meets in battle, he will defeat by the permission of God, their slogan will be "Kill, kill!" not fearing before God any condemner. Seven banners will come out against him from Syria, but he will defeat them all and reign. He will return to the people their love, grace [216], plenty and trade.[595] There will be nothing after them other than the Dajjāl. We said: "What are *fāḍa* (plenty) and *bazāza* (trade)?" He said: "The rule will be so plentiful that a man will be able to speak what he wants and not fear anything."

[593] Gave you power.

[594] Compare al-Bukhārī, *Ṣaḥīḥ*, iv, pp. 15–16 (no. 2977).

[595] *Bazāza* refers to the cloth trade. Interestingly, in the question as to the meaning of the two rare words in the tradition, the questioned figure does not define *bazāza*.

972. `Alī: God will send against the Syrians those who will break their grouping, until even if the foxes were to fight them they would overpower them (the Syrians). At that a man from the People of my House will emerge leading three banners—those who say more, 15,000, while those who say less, 12,000, their command being "Kill, kill!"—against a man who seeks the dominion under one banner, or in order to swear allegiance for the dominion, so God will kill them all, and then God will return to the Muslims their intimacy, plenty and trade. Ibn Lahī`a said . . . the same, other than he said: "Nine black flags."

973. Al-Walīd b. Muslim: Someone told me that the Mahdi and the Sufyānī and Kalb will fight at Jerusalem (*bayt al-maqdis*) when he [the Sufyānī] asks to be released from his oath, so the Sufyānī will be brought to him as a prisoner, and slaughtered at the Gate of Mercy,[596] then his women and spoils will be sold on the Damascus road.

974. Ali: When the Sufyānī sends an army to the Mahdi, and they are swallowed up by the earth in the wasteland, and that [news] reaches the Syrians, they will say to their caliph: "The Mahdi has emerged, so swear to him, and enter into his obedience—otherwise we will kill you!" So he will send his oath to him, and the Mahdi will go until he settles in Jerusalem, and the storehouses will be conveyed to him. The Arabs, the non-Arab Persians, the people of war, the Byzantines and others will enter into his service (obedience) without fighting, such that mosques will be built in Constantinople and other places. A man from his family will depart from before him leading the easterners, carrying his sword on his shoulders. Eight months he will kill and mutilate, and then turn towards Jerusalem, but not reach it before he dies.

975. Ka`b: I would have liked to have lived to see the pillage of the Bedouin, which is the pillage of Kalb—since missing out is the one who misses out on the pillage-day of Kalb.

[596] In Jerusalem, the eastern gate leading into the Sacred Enclosure.

976. `Alī: God will drive away the tribulations by a man from us, who will treat people unjustly, giving them nothing but the sword, placing the sword on his shoulders for eight months killing, until people will say: "By God, this guy is not from the descendants of Fāṭima! If he were from her descendants, he would have been merciful to us." God will raid the `Abbāsids and the Umayyads using him. [217]

977. Ibn `Abbās: When the army of the Sufyānī is swallowed up by the earth, the lord of Mecca will say: These are the signs of which you used to inform us! So they will go to Syria, and this will reach the lord of Damascus, so he will send him his oath and swear to him. Then [the tribe of] Kalb will come to him after that, saying: "What have you done? You came to get our oath, but then you have thrown it off, and given it to him??" So he will say: "What can I do? The people gave me over." So they will say: "We are with you, so give over your oath," so he will send to the Hashemite, asking to be released from his oath. Then he will fight him, but the Hashemite will defeat them, then on that day whoever rams his spear against a clan of Kalb, they will be his. Missing out is the one who misses out on the pillage-day of Kalb.

978. `Alī b. Abī Ṭālib: He will lead 12,000 if less or 15,000 if more, their slogan will be: "Kill, kill!" until the Sufyānī will meet him, then he will say: "Come out to me, cousin, so I can talk to you," so he will come out and talk to him, and then give him the rule, and swear to him. But when the Sufyānī returns to his supporters, [the tribe of] Kalb will make him regret this, so he will return and ask to be released from his oath, and he [the Mahdi] will do so. Then he will fight with the army of the Sufyānī, with seven banners, each master of a banner will hope for the rule for himself. The Mahdi will defeat him. Abū Hurayra said: The one who avoids the pillage of Kalb is himself to be avoided.

979. Abū Hurayra: The one who avoids the spoils of Kalb is himself to be avoided.

980. Al-Zuhri: The Mahdi will depart from Mecca after the swallowing up by the earth leading 314 men, the number of the [fighters at] Badr, and he and the commander of the Sufyānī's army will meet in battle—the Mahdi's supporters on that day will use pack-saddles as their shields (*junna*), meaning their shields (*tirās*), so it will be called the Day of the Pack-Saddles. It will be said that on that day a voice will be heard from the heavens, a herald calling: "Are not the friends of God the supporters of so-and-so the Mahdi?" So defeat will be on the supporters of the Sufyānī, and they will fight until only a few are left, then they will flee to the Sufyānī, to inform him. The Mahdi will depart to Syria, and the Sufyānī will meet the Mahdi with his oath, while the people everywhere make haste to him [the Mahdi], and he will fill the earth with justice just as it has been filled with injustice.

981. Ibn Mas`ūd: Seven men from the learned (*`ulamā'*) will swear an oath to the Mahdi, coming to Mecca from every direction without prior appointment—with each one of them having 310 some men sworn to him—so they will gather in Mecca, and swear to him [the Mahdi]. God will place love of him in the hearts of the people, so he will lead them. The horsemen of the Sufyānī commanded by a man from Jarm will have been sent to those who have sworn, so when he departs Mecca, he will leave his supporters, and walk in [218] a loincloth and an outer garment until he comes to the Jarmī and he swears to him. But then [the tribe of] Kalb will cause him to regret his oath, and come to him to ask him to get out of the oath, so he will release him from his oath, then will array his armies for battle. God will defeat the Byzantines, and will take away the tribulations at his hands, and he will settle in Syria.

982. Ka`b: When you see the caliph of Jerusalem, or the one before it, meaning Damascus, do not follow the one before him, for he is more astray than a donkey.

983. Abū Hurayra: The caliph who is in Jerusalem will kill the one who is before him.

984. Elders: The Sufyānī is the one who will give the caliphate to the Mahdi.

985. Arṭāt: The Ṣakhrī [Sufyānī] will enter Kūfa, then the appearance of the Mahdi in Mecca will reach him, so he will send an expedition to him from Kūfa, but it will be swallowed up by the earth, and none will be saved from it other than a proclaimer to the Mahdi and a warner to the Ṣakhrī. So the Mahdi will advance from Mecca, and the Ṣakhrī from Kūfa towards Syria like two racing horses. The Ṣakhrī will beat him, and then deputize another expedition from Syria to the Mahdi. They will meet the Mahdi in battle in the Ḥijāz, but they will swear to him an oath of guidance, and advance with him until they reach the border of Syria, which is between it and the Ḥijāz. He will stay there, so it will be said: "Carry forth!" but he will be reluctant to pass forward.[597]

Then he [the Mahdi] will say: "Write to my cousin and if he will throw off his obedience, then I will be your lord." So when his letter reaches the Ṣakhrī [Sufyānī], he will make peace with him [the Mahdi] and swear allegiance.

The Mahdi will go until he settles in Jerusalem (*bayt al-maqdis*). He will not leave a single little piece of land to any [Muslim] man in Syria, but return it all to the non-Muslims (*ahl al-dhimma*), and return the Muslims in their entirety to jihad.[598] He will remain doing this for three years, then a man will emerge from Kalb called Kināna, who will have a star in his eye, leading a clan of his tribe until they come to the Ṣakhrī, and say: "We swore to you, and helped you until when you reigned you swore to our enemy. Now, go out, you should fight!" He will say: "Leading who?" Then he [the envoy] will say: "Every female from `Āmir will join you, and none with foot or cloven hoof will stay behind."

So he will travel and [the tribe of] `Āmir in its totality will

[597] Reading with MM *majāz* in place of Ḥijāz.
[598] See Kister, "Land property" for the background to this idea.

travel with him until they descend upon Beth-Shean (Baysān). Then the Mahdi will send a banner to them—the biggest banner during the time of the Mahdi [219] will be 100 men—and then they will descend upon Fāthūr Ibrāhīm,[599] so Kalb will line up its horsemen and its infantry, its camels and flocks, but when the two groups of horses get wind of each other Kalb will turn and retreat. The Ṣakhrī will be taken and slaughtered on the stone that is across the face of the earth from the church that is at the bottom of the valley,[600] on the side of the road to the Mount of Olives, the bridge that is on the right side of the valley, on the stone that is across on the face of the earth from it.[601] He will be slaughtered like a sheep, then missing out is the one who misses out on the pillage-day of Kalb, where a virgin girl will be sold for eight dirhams.[602]

986. Arṭāt: He will swear to him, then the Mahdi will return to Mecca for three years, then a man from Kalb will emerge, and will cause those who are in the land of Iram (Damascus) to revolt unwillingly. Then he will go to the Mahdi in Jerusalem leading 12,000 men, but then the Sufyānī will be taken and killed at the Jayrūn Gate.[603] [220]

The Conduct and Justice of the Mahdi and the Plenty of his Time

987. Ka`b: The Mahdi will send to fight the Byzantines, having been given the jurisprudential knowledge (*fiqh*) of ten, and to remove the Ark of the Covenant (*tābūt al-sakīna*) from a cave at Antioch. In it there will be the Torah, which God revealed

599 Fāthūr usually means "a tray" (see no. 1552), but Yāqūt, *Mu`jam*, iv, p. 224 "a palace of marble." So perhaps this was a monumental or palatial structure in the area of Beth-Shean.

600 Either the Church of St. Mary (traditional burial spot for the Virgin Mary) or the Church of the Garden of Gethsemane.

601 Perhaps one of the group of Second Temple era tombs next to the Pillar of Absolom.

602 Note how much cheaper this is than the idealized price of a horse in the messianic era (nos. 1558, 1570, 1573).

603 Not attested for Jerusalem, but as the left gate leading out of the Great Mosque in Damascus.

to Moses, the Gospel which God revealed to Jesus, and he will judge between the people of the Torah [Jews] according to their Torah, and between the people of the Gospel [Christians] according to their Gospel.

988. Ka`b: He is only called the Mahdi because he guides to a hidden matter, so he will bring out the Torah and the Gospel from a land called Antioch.

989. Ja`far b. Sayyār al-Shāmī[604]: The Mahdi's fulfillment of justice will be such that if there was something under a molar tooth, he would yank it out and return it [to its owner].

990. `Abdallāh b. Sharīk[605]: The Prophet's Conquering Banner will be with the Mahdi—I wish that I would live to see it, and be young again!

991. Nawf al-Bikālī: On the Mahdi's banner will be written: "The oath belongs to God."[606] [221]

992. Ibn Sīrīn: it was said to him: Is the Mahdi better or Abū Bakr and `Umar? He said: He is better[607] than the both of them, and will act justly like a prophet.

993. Abū Ru'ba[608]: [During] the Mahdi's [time] it will be as if the impoverished will be able to lick butter.

994. Maṭar al-Warrāq: The Mahdi will take out the fresh, meaning new (*ṭriyya*), Torah from Antioch.

995. Ka`b: The leaders of the Mahdi will be the best of those who help and swear to him from the two Kūfas[609] and the Yemen, and the Substitutes (*abdāl*) of Syria. At their vanguard will be Gabriel, at their rearguard Michael, beloved among the

604 Unidentified, but probably *fl.* 2nd/8th century.

605 `Abdallāh b. Sharīk al-`Āmirī, lived in Kūfa, associated with extremism (*ghuluww*), *fl.* 1st/7th century.

606 Compare with the phrase on some pre-reform coins: *al-wafā' li-l-llah*, see Album, *Checklist of Islamic Coins* (Santa Rosa, CA: Stephen Album Rare Coins, 2011), p. 36 (no. 3523).

607 Reading *akhyar* instead of *akhbar* with MM and DKI.

608 Could he be the Murji'ite leader mentioned by al-Ṭabarī, *Tā'rīkh*, vi, pp. 593, 596, 598 (year 102)?

609 Kūfa and Baṣra.

created creatures, by whom God Most High will dampen the 'blind' tribulation, and make the earth safe, so that a woman could make the pilgrimage among five other women, without a man among them, and not fear anything other than God. The earth will give its charity, and the heavens will give their blessing.

996. Ṭāwūs: The sign of the Mahdi is that he will be harsh upon the governors, generous with wealth, merciful towards the indigent poor.

997. Abū Sa`īd: The Prophet said: A caliph will appear at the end of time who will give wealth without counting.

998. Maṭar: `Umar b. `Abd al-`Azīz was mentioned around him, and so he said: "It has reached me that the Mahdi will do something that `Umar b. `Abd al-`Azīz never did." We said: "What is that?" He said: "A man will come to him and ask him [for money], and so he will say: 'Go to the Treasury and take [what you want],' so he will go into the Treasury and take. He will depart and see the people satisfied, and regret so return to him, saying: 'Take what you have given to me,' then he will refuse, and say: 'We give, we do not take [in return].'"

999. Ka`b: I find concerning the Mahdi written in the books of the Prophets: "There is no injustice in his work, and no defect."[610]

1000. Ka`b: He is only called the Mahdi because he will guide to books of the Torah, taking them out of a mountain in Syria, calling the Jews to them so that they convert to Islam on the basis of those books, a great many of them, then he mentioned approximately 30,000.

1001. Muḥammad b. Sīrīn: He mentioned the tribulation to come, and said: "When it is like that, sit in your houses until you hear that ruling the people is someone better than Abū Bakr and `Umar." It will be said: "Better than both Abū Bakr and

[610] Perhaps an allusion to Ezekiel 28:15, although many biblical citations in the *ḥadīth* are fabricated.

`Umar?" He said: "He will be more meritorious than some of the prophets." [222]

1002. Qatāda: The Messenger of God said: He wil take out the treasures, divide the wealth, and set Islam aright.

1003. Abū Sa`īd al-Khudarī: The Prophet said: The dweller of the heavens and of the earth will be satisfied with him, the heavens will not avoid raining, nor the earth from bringing forth produce, such that the living and the dead will desire this.

1004. Abū Sa`īd al-Khudarī: The Prophet said: He will distribute wealth generously, not count it stingily, filling the earth will justice like it has been filled with injustice and wrong.

1005. Abū Sa`īd al-Khudarī: The Prophet said: His community will tend towards him like the female date palm tends towards the male, he will fill the earth with justice just as it has been filled with injustice, until the people come to be as in their first state, without a sleeper being awakened, without blood flowing.

1006. Abū Sa`īd: The Prophet said: He will fill the earth with justice just as it was filled previously with wrong and injustice, and reign seven years.

1007. Ibrāhīm b. Maysara[611]: I said to Ṭāwūs: "Is `Umar b. `Abd al-`Azīz the Mahdi?" He said: "No, he did not seek to actualize justice in its totality."

1008. Al-Walīd: I heard a man narrating to the people: "There are three Mahdis: The good Mahdi, who is `Umar b. `Abd al-`Azīz, [there is] the Mahdi of blood, who is the one who will calm the bloodshed, and [there is] the Mahdi of religion, who is Jesus son of Mary, who will convert his community [Christians] to Islam during his time." Al-Walīd said: It reached me from Ka`b that he said: "The good Mahdi will emerge after the Sufyānī."

1009. Ṭāwūs: When it is the Mahdi's time, the one who does good will increase in his good, the one who does evil will repent of

611 Ibrāhīm b. Maysara al-Ṭā'ifī, settled in Mecca, *mawlā*, d. approximately 132/749–50.

his evil. He will distribute the wealth, be harsh on governors, and have mercy on the indigent poor. [223]

1010. Ṭāwūs: I wish that I was not going to die, so I would live to see the time of the Mahdi, in which the one who does good will increase in his good, and the one who does evil will repent.

1011. Ṣabbāḥ[612]: The great during the time of the Mahdi will desire to be humble, and the humble great.

1012. Abū Sa`īd al-Khudarī: The Prophet said: My community will be blessed during the time of the Mahdi in a way never before seen. The heavens will send abundant rain upon them, and whatever is sown will produce. Wealth will be like something trampled, so a man will rise and say: "O Mahdi, give to me," so he will say: "Take."

1013. Abū Sa`īd on the authority of the Prophet, the same, other than he did not mention the wealth.

1014. Sulaymān b. `Īsā: It has reached me that at the hands of the Mahdi the Ark of the Covenant (*tābūt al-sakīna*) will appear from the Sea of Galilee, so that it will be carried, and placed before him in Jerusalem (*bayt al-maqdis*). When the Jews look upon it, they will convert to Islam other than a few of them, then the Mahdi will die naturally.

1015. From a man from the Maghrib: When the Mahdi emerges, God will cast sufficiency into the hearts of the servants, such that the Mahdi will say: "Who wants wealth?" but no one other than a man saying "I do" will come to him. He will say: "Distribute," and so he will pour it, carrying it on his back until he comes to the last of the people, he says: "Have I not been shown to be the worst of these?" So he will return, giving it back, saying: "Take your wealth, I have no need of it."

1016. Dīnār b. Dīnār: The Mahdi will appear when the immovable spoils have been distributed, so he will make peace between the people concerning that which comes to him. He will not

612 Probably Ṣabbāḥ b. Muḥārib a-Taymī, lived in some of the villages of Rayy, *fl.* 2nd/8th century.

prefer one over the other, and will act according to right until he dies, then the world after him will become murderous (*haraj*).

1017. `Alī b. Abī Ṭālib: The Messenger of God said: God Most High will make the Mahdi right during one night.

1018. Ṭāwūs: `Umar b. al-Khaṭṭāb left the House, then said: "By God, I do not see myself leaving the treasuries of the House, when there are no [224] weapons and wealth in it, while I could divide them in the path of God?" `Alī b. Abī Ṭālib said to him: "Go, O Commander of the Believers, for you are not its owner. Its owner is from us, a youth from Quraysh, who will divide it in the path of God at the end of time."

1019. Jābir b. `Abdallāh: the Prophet said: "There will be among my community a caliph will will distribute the wealth, not count it up."

1020. Abū Sa`īd al-Khudarī: The Prophet said: A man will emerge from my family at the completion of time, and the appearance of tribulations, whose stipends will be generous, who will be called al-Saffāḥ.

1021. An elder who narrated to them during the time of Ibn al-Zubayr, who had lived during the *jāhiliyya*: The caliphate will settle in Jerusalem, the oath of allegiance will be guidance, their women will be permitted [sexually] to the one who swears to him, so he will say: "Divorce or manumission will not be accepted from them."

1022. Ka`b: When you see a caliph in Jerusalem, and another below him, meaning in Damascus, do not follow the one who is below him, for he is more astray than the donkey of his family.[613]

1023. Abū Hurayra: The Prophet said: The caliph who is in Jerusalem will kill the one who is below him.

1024. Arṭāt: The first flag that the Mahdi will dispatch, he will send to the Turks, then defeat them, and take the prisoners and wealth that is with them, then go to Syria, and conquer it, then

613 Probably a reference to Marwān II.

manumit every slave (*mamlūk*) with him, and give his followers their value. [225]

The Description of the Mahdi

1025. Ka`b: The Mahdi will lower himself before God, the way the eagle lowers its wings.

1026. Abū Sa`īd on the authority of the Prophet . . .: The Mahdi is hook-nosed, hairless on the forehead. **(1)**

1027. Abū Sa`īd al-Khudarī: The Messenger of God said: The Mahdi is hairless on the forehead, hook-nosed.

1028. Abū Sa`īd al-Khudarī: The Prophet said: The Mahdi is hook-nosed,[614] hairless on the forehead.

1029. Ka`b: The Mahdi is fifty-one or fifty-two years old.

1030. `Abdallāh b. al-Ḥārith[615]: The Mahdi will emerge when he is forty years old, as if he is a man of the Israelites. [226]

1031. Ibn `Abbās: He is a youth (*shābb*).

1032. Abū al-Ṭufayl that the Messenger of God described the Mahdi, then mentioned a speech impediment on his tongue, and his [habit of] striking his left thigh with his right hand, when words came slowly. His name is my name and his father's name is my father's name.[616]

1033. Abū Sa`īd al-Khudarī: The Prophet said: A man will emerge at the end of time and the appearance of tribulations whose stipend will be generous, called al-Saffāḥ.

1034. Sufyān al-Kalbī: A youth (*ghulām*) will emerge under the flag of the Mahdi, young in age, with a sparse beard, yellowish hair (*aṣfar*)—but al-Walīd [b. Muslim] did not mention yellowish hair—when approaching the mountains, he would shake them, but al-Walīd said: he would cause them to tremble until he descends upon Jerusalem (*Iliyā'*).

614 On the nose, reading with DKI.

615 Probably `Abdallāh b. al-Ḥārith al-Qurashī, lived in Medina and Baṣra, d. 79/698–9.

616 These are descriptions of Muḥammad al-Nafs al-Zakiyya ("the Pure Soul"), d. 762; see al-Isfahani, *Maqātil*, pp. 214–15.

1035. Al-Ṣaqr b. Rustum on the authority of his father: The Mahdi is a man having fine eyebrows, parted eyebrows, with wide-eyes, who will come from the Ḥijāz until he will sit upon the pulpit of Damascus, when he is eighteen years old.[617]

1036. `Alī b. Abī Ṭālib: The Mahdi, his birthplace will be Medina, from the family (*ahl bayt*) of the Prophet, and his name my father's name,[618] his place of emigration is Jerusalem (*bayt al-maqdis*), with a spare beard, black-eyed, with incisor teeth flashing, a mole on his face, hook-nosed, hairless on the forehead, on his shoulder the sign of the Prophet.[619] He will emerge with the banner of the Prophet, of a square, black, fringed coarse-silk material (*mirṭ*),[620] with a stone on it, that has not been displayed with anyone since the Messenger of God died, and will not be displayed until the Mahdi will emerge. God will aid him with 3,000 angels,[621] striking the faces and buttocks of those who oppose him. He will be sent when he is between thirty and forty years old.

1037. `Alī b. Abī Ṭālib: He is a youth (*fatā*) from Quraysh, brown, lanky.

1038. Arṭāt: The Mahdi will be sixty years old. [227]

The Name of the Mahdi

1039. `Abdallāh: The Prophet said: The Mahdi and I will have identical names, and his father's and mine as well. I heard this

[617] Ibn Ṭāwūs, *Malāḥim*, p. 74 proposes that the difference between the Mahdi's age in no. 1035 and no. 1038 has to do with his appearance—he will be old, but appear youthful.

[618] One feels that there is a mistake here, perhaps this was meant to be a citation from Muḥammad. `Ali's father's name was `Abd Manāf or `Umrān (al-Samarqandi al-Maydani, *Tuhfat al-talib bi-ma`rifa man yantasib ila `Abdallāh wa-Abi Talib* [Qumm: Maktabat Ayatullāh al-`Uẓma al-Mar`ashli, 2011], p. 20); nowhere else is this name attested for the Mahdi.

[619] The *khatam al-nubuwwa* (some kind of a mole or growth on Muḥammad's shoulder): al-Bayhaqi, *Dala'il al-nubuwwa* (Beirut: Dār al-Kutub al-`Ilmiyya, 1985), i, pp. 259–67.

[620] See Ibn al-Athīr, *Nihāya*, iv, pp. 319–20.

[621] As at the Battle of Uḥud, see Q 3:124.

mentioned more than once without mentioning the name of his father.

1040. `Abdallāh: The Prophet said: The Mahdi and I will have identical names, and his father's and mine as well.

1041. Ka`b: "The name of the Mahdi is Muḥammad." He said: "The name of a prophet."

1042. Abū Thumāma[622]: I know his name, the name of his father and mother.

1043. Abū Sa`īd al-Khudarī: The Prophet said: The Mahdi's name is my name.

1044. Abū al-Ṭufayl: The Messenger of God said: The Mahdi, his name is my name, and his father's name is my father's name. [228]

The Ancestry of the Mahdi

1045. Qatāda: I said to Sa`īd b. al-Musayyib: "The Mahdi is truth, is he?" He said: "Truth." I said: "Where is he from?" He said: "From Quraysh." I said: "From which part of Quraysh?" He said: "From the Hashemites." I said: "From which part of the Hashemites?" He said: "From the descendants of `Abd al-Muṭṭalib." I said: "Which part of `Abd al-Muṭṭalib?" He said: "From the descendants of Fāṭima."

1046. Abū Sa`īd al-Khudarī: The Prophet said: "He is a man from my descendants," or he said: "From the People of my House."

1047. `Alī: He is a man from me.

1048. Ibn `Abbās: From us are al-Hādī (the guide) and al-Muhtadī (the one who seeks to guide), and from us are also the one who goes astray, and the one who leads astray.

1049. Ibn `Abbās: "The Mahdi is a youth from us, the People of the House." I said: "Your elders are incapable, but you hope for your youths?" He said: "God does what He wills."

1050. Abān b. al-Walīd: I heard Ibn `Abbās when he was with

[622] Lived in the Ḥijāz, dealt in wheat (*qamḥ*), *fl.* 1st/7th century.

Mu`āwiya saying: God will send guidance from us, the People of the House. [229]

1051. Ibn `Abbās: The Mahdi is from us, he will hand it [the rule] over to Jesus son of Mary.

1052. `Alī b. Abī Ṭālib: I said: "O Messenger of God, will the Mahdi be from us, the imams of guidance or from someone other than us?" He said: "From us, of course—by us the religion will be sealed just as by us it was opened, and through us they should seek salvation from the error of dissension, just as through us they sought salvation from the error of associating [other entities with God]. Through us God will unite their hearts in the religion after the enmity of dissension just as God united between their hearts and their religion after the enmity of associating."

1053. Abū al-Ṭufayl and `Alī on the authority of the Prophet, who said: "By us the religion will be sealed just as by us it was opened, and through us they seek salvation from associating." One of them said: "from the error," "and through us God will unite their hearts after the enmity of associating." One of them said: "The error and dissension."

1054. `Alī: The Prophet said: He is a man from my family.

1055. `A'isha: The Prophet said: He is a man from my descendents, who will fight for my way (*sunnatī*) just as I fought for the inspiration.

1056. Abū Sa`īd al-Khudarī: The Prophet said: He is a man from my community.

1057. Abū Sa`īd al-Khudarī: The Messsenger of God said: He is a man from my descendents.

1058. `Abdallāh b. `Amr: A man will emerge from the progeny of al-Ḥusayn from the direction of the east—if the mountains faced him, he would destroy them, and make roads through them.

1059. Aflat b. Ṣāliḥ[623]: I spoke to Muḥammad b. al-Ḥanafiyya

[623] Unknown.

concerning the Mahdi, [so] he said: "When he comes, he will be from the progeny of `Abd Shams."[624]

1060. Ibn `Umar that he said to Ibn al-Ḥanafiyya: "Who is this Mahdi of whom you speak?" [230] He said: "Just like you say 'the righteous man' when a man is righteous, you say of him *Mahdi*." So Ibn `Umar said: "May God make the idiots ugly!" as if he denied his words.

1061. Ash`ath b. `Abd al-Raḥmān[625] heard Abū Qilāba saying: "`Umar b. `Abd al-`Azīz is the Mahdi in truth."

1062. Al-Ḥasan was asked concerning the Mahdi, and he said: I think that the Mahdi is none other than `Umar b. `Abd al-`Azīz.

1063. Ṭāwūs said: `Umar b. `Abd al-`Azīz was a *mahdi*, but not the one. The Mahdi, when he is, the one who does good will increase, and the one who does evil will repent from his evil.

1064. Abū Qubayl: A man will emerge from the progeny of al-Ḥusayn—if the fixed mountains faced him he would cause them to tremble, and make roads through them.

1065. Abū Ja`far: He is from the Hashemites, from the progeny of Fāṭima.

1066. `Abdallāh b. `Umar: The Mahdi is the one upon whom Jesus will descend, and Jesus will pray behind him.

1067. Ibn Zurayr al-Ghāfiqī[626] heard `Alī saying: He is from the descendents of the Prophet.

1068. Ka`b: The Mahdi is from the progeny of al-`Abbās.

1069. Abū Sa`īd: The Prophet said: He is a man from me.

1070. Muḥammad: The Mahdi is from this community—he is the one who will serve as an imam to Jesus son of Mary.

1071. Al-Ḥasan: The Mahdi is Jesus son of Mary. [231] **(1)**

1072. Abū Hurayra: He is from the family of Muḥammad.

1073. Abū Sa`īd al-Khudarī: The Prophet said: He is a man from my family.

[624] Great-grandfather of Muḥammad, meaning the Hashemites.

[625] Ash`ath b. `Abd al-Raḥmān al-Yāmī, lived in Kūfa, *fl.* 2nd/8th century.

[626] `Abdallāh b. Zurayr al-Ghāfiqī, lived in Egypt, *fl.* 1st/7th century.

1074. Ka`b: The Mahdi is from the progeny of Fāṭima.

1075. `Alī b. Abī Ṭālib said: The Prophet named al-Ḥasan a lord (*sayyid*), and from his loins will emerge a man whose name is the name of your Prophet who will fill the earth will justice just as it has been filled with injustice.

1076. Al-Zuhrī: The Mahdi is from the progeny of Fāṭima.

1077. Ka`b: The Mahdi is from none other than Quraysh, as the caliphate is only with them, but he will have a root and a genealogical connection to Yemen.

1078. Sālim[627]: Najda wrote to Ibn `Abbās asking him concerning the Mahdi, so he said: "God Most High has guided this community with the first people of this family, and will bring salvation to it through the last of them. Two rams, hornless and with horns, will not butt during it." He said: "There are two Mahdis from the Banū `Abd Shams, one of the two of them is `Umar the Scarred [on the face]."[628]

1079. Zirr b. Ḥubaysh[629] heard `Alī saying: The Mahdi will be a man from us, from the descendents of Fāṭima. [232]

1080. `Alī b. Abī Ṭālib: The Messenger of God said: The Mahdi is from us, the People of the House.

1081. Al-Ḥasan: The Mahdi is Jesus son of Mary.

1082. Arṭāt: The Mahdi will stay forty years. [233]

The Length of the Mahdi's Reign

1083. Abū Sa`īd al-Khudarī: The Prophet said: The Mahdi will live during that, meaning after he reigns, seven, eight or nine years. **(2)**

1084. Qatāda: It reached me that the Messenger of God said: He will live during that seven years.

1085. Abū Sa`īd al-Khudarī: The Prophet said: He will live seven or nine years.

[627] Probably Sālim b. Abī Umayyad al-Qurashī, a *mawlā*, lived in Medina, d. 129/746–7.

[628] `Umar b. `Abd al-`Azīz.

[629] Zirr b. Ḥubaysh b. Ḥubāsha al-Asadī, lived in Kūfa, d. 81 or 82/700 or 701–2.

1086. Abū al-Ṣiddīq[630]: The Prophet said: He will live seven years then die [naturally].

1087. Abū Sa`īd: The Prophet said: He will reign seven years. [234]

1088. Abū Sa`īd al-Khudarī: The Messenger of God said: The Mahdi will be in my community at the least for seven, if not then eight, if not then nine years.

1089. Ṣabbāḥ: The Mahdi will stay among you for thirty-nine years, during which the young will say: "Oh! would that I was older!" and the elderly will say: "Oh! would that I was younger!"

1090. Ḍamra b. Ḥabīb: The life of the Mahdi will be thirty years.

1091. Al-Ṣaqr b. Rustum on the authority of his father: The Mahdi will reign seven years, with some two months and days.

1092. Dīnār b. Dīnār: "The Mahdi's length of staying will be forty years," but one of the two of them said once forty and another time twenty-four years.

1093. Al-Zuhrī: The Mahdi will live fourteen years then die naturally.

1094. `Alī: The Mahdi will manage the people thirty or forty years. [235]

What will happen after the Mahdi

1095. Dīnār b. Dīnār: It has reached me that the Mahdi, when he dies, the matter will go to killing (*haraj*) between the people, so that they kill (*yaqtul*) each other. The non-Arabs will appear, the apocalyptic battles will be continuous, without order, or unity until the Dajjāl will emerge.

1096. Ka`b: The Mahdi will die naturally, then a man from his house in whom there is good and evil, though his evil will be more than his good, will manage the people after him, and the people will be enraged as he will call them to division after their unity. He staying will be short, then a man from his family will rise up against him and kill him, so the people after him will fight fiercely. The staying of the one who killed him afterwards will be short, then he will die naturally. A man

630 Bakr b. `Amr al-Nājī, lived in Baṣra, *fl.* 2nd/8th century.

from Muḍar from the east will manage them, forcing them into unbelief and from their religion. He will fight the Yemenites fiercely between the two [Tigris and Euphrates] rivers, then God will defeat him and those with him.

1097. Al-Zuhrī: The Mahdi will die naturally, then the people after him will go into dissension, so a man from the Banū Makhzūm[631] will approach, and will receive the oath of allegiance, and stay for some time. Then he will forbid the daily sustenance, but no one will be found who can attack him, so then he will forbid the stipend (*ʿaṭāʾ*), but no one will be found who can attack him, when he is settling in Jerusalem (*bayt al-maqdis*) He and his supporters will be like fattened she-camels. Their women will walk with little gold shoe-slippers (*buṭayṭāt*)[632] and clothing that does not conceal them, but no one will be found who can attack him. He will order the expulsion of the Yemenites—[the tribes of] Quḍāʿa, Madhḥij, Ḥimyar, Azd, Ghassān, and everyone who is said to be from Yemen. He will expel them until they settle in the mountain paths of Filasṭīn, [236] so Jadīs, Lakhm, and the people as bands will bring to them food and drink from these mountains, constituting an aid for them, just as Joseph was an aid to his brothers.[633]

Then a herald from the heavens, who is neither human nor *jinn* will call out: "Swear to so-and-so! and do not return backwards after your emigration (*hijra*)." They will look, and not know the man, then he will call out three times, then they will swear allegiance to the Manṣūr. He will send ten delegations to the Makhzūmī; nine will be killed, but one will be left. Then he will send five, but four will be killed while one will be sent away. Then he will send three, so two will be killed, while one will be left. Then he will go to him, and God will help him against him, so God will kill him and those with him. None but

631 The richest clan of Quraysh during the time of Muḥammad, which opposed him bitterly.

632 See nos. 1126, 1152 for this meaning.

633 Cf. Q 12:88–9.

fugitives will manage to flee; he will not leave anyone from Quraysh alive. Qurashites will be sought at that time, but not found, just as they seek today men from [the tribe of] Jurhum, but are not found. In that way Quraysh will be killed and not found afterwards.

1098. Ka`b: The Yemenites will fight a fierce battle between the two rivers, then God will defeat them, so the easterners and those with them will be pleased with the dead who will float on the river, since they will inform [people] of their defeat. Their rider will approach Yemen, while they are settled between the rivers, then God Most High will make him and those with him victorious, and make the issue of the people right. Their beliefs will be united somewhat, then they will go until they descend upon Syria, and stay for a time in a righteous rule. But then Qays will rise against them, and the Yemenites will kill them until one might think that not one of Qays remained.

Then a man from the Yemenites will say: "O God, O God, take care of our brothers! [take care] of the rest, O God!"

Qays will go out leading those who remain from it, until they descend between the two rivers, whereupon they will gather a great gathering, while a man from Banū Makhzūm manages their affairs. Then the governor of the Yemen will die, so Qays will rejoice at his death, and the Makhzūmī will go until when the last of them has crossed the Euphrates [River] the Makhzūmī will die. Yemen will be on one side, Qays on the other [of the river], so the *mawālī* will be enraged by this, as they will be most of the people on that day.

They will say: "Let's appoint a man from the people of religion," so they will send about ten from the Yemenites, and about ten from Muḍar, and about ten from the *mawālī* to Jerusalem (*bayt al-maqdis*), whereupon they will recite the Book of God Most High [the Qur'ān], and ask of Him to choose. These small groups will return then, after they had appointed a man from the *mawālī*—so woe to the Syrians and their land from his rule! He will go to Muḍar, intending to fight them, then a man from the westerners will come, a tall, corpulent, broad-shouldered man, who will kill those who he meets, until he enters Jerusalem.

The Beast (*dābba*) will strike him, so he will die, then this world will be as evil as it has ever been, whereupon a man from Muḍar will rule after him, killing people having weapons, cursed, ill-fortuned, then after the Muḍarī, the `Umānī [who is also the] Qaḥṭānī will rule, acting as did his brother the Mahdi. At his hands, the city of the Byzantines [Constantinople] will be conquered. [237]

1099. Nu`aym: He will emerge from a village called Yaklā,[634] beyond Ṣan`ā' by a day's journey—his father being from Quraysh and his mother Yemenite.

1100. `Abd al-Raḥmān b. Qays b. Jābir al-Ṣadafī: The Messenger of God said: The Qaḥṭānī is not less than the Mahdi.

1101. Abū Hurayra: There will not be very many days and nights until a man from Qaḥṭān will drive the people.

1102. Abū Hurayra: The Prophet said: The Hour will not arise until a man from Qaḥṭān will emerge driving the people with his stick.

1103. `Umar b. al-Khaṭṭāb: The one who lives at the time of the Makhzūmī has no mother.

1104. Ka`b: The lesser apocalyptic battle of Acre will be at the hands of this Yemenite, and that will be when the fifth of Heraclius' family reigns.[635]

1105. Ka`b: The Yemenite will appear and kill Quraysh in Jerusalem (*bayt al-maqdis*), and at his hands will be the apocalyptic battles.

1106. `Abdallāh b. al-Ḥajjāj[636]: I heard `Abdallāh b. `Amr b. al-`Āṣ say: After the tyrants, there will be al-Jābir, then the Mahdi, then

[634] In Yemen.
[635] Either Constantine IV or Justinian II.
[636] A *mawlā* of `Abdallāh b. `Amr, *fl.* 2nd/8th century.

al-Manṣūr, then al-Salām, then the Commander of the Bands, then whoever can die after that, should.

1107. `Abdallāh b. `Amr: O Yemenites! You say that the Manṣūr is from you, but by the One who my soul is in His hand, his father is Qurashite. If I wished I could name him to the utmost degree, I would. [238]

1108. `Abd al-Raḥmān b. Qays b. Jābir al-Ṣadafī: The Messenger of God: There will be a man from my family who will fill the earth with righteousness just as it has been filled with unrighteousness, then after him al-Qaḥṭānī, and by the One who sent me in truth, the one is not less than the other.

1109. Arṭāt: At the hands of this Yemenite caliph and during his rule, Rome will be conquered.[637]

1110. Ibn `Umar: I heard the Messenger of God saying: The rule will remain among Quraysh as long as there are two men among the people.

1111. Ḥawshab: It reached me that `Alī said: There is nothing after Quraysh but *jāhiliyya*.

1112. `Ammār: There will come upon the people a time when if a man from Quraysh is found, they will do to him what they do to a wild ass while hunting—taking his headdress (*`amāma*) upon his head, and pulled it off so that his head will be cut off.

1113. `Alī: I wish that the soul which God humiliates and disgraces at the killing of Quraysh would be killed.

1114. Ka`b: When killing has increased among the people, the people said: "This fighting is among Quraysh, so kill them until you are liberated," so they will kill them until not one of them remains, and the people will raid each other, just as they did in their *jāhiliyya*. The people will crown one of the *mawālī*.

1115. Ka`b: When the Yemenite appears, Quraysh will be killed on that day in Jerusalem.

[637] Compare Armand Abel, "Une *ḥadīth* sur la prise du Rome," *Arabica* 5 (1958), pp. 1–14.

1116. Dhū Mikhbar[638]: The Prophet said: This rule was among [the tribe of] Ḥimyar, then God Most High yanked it away from them, and made it for Quraysh, but it will return to them (Ḥimyar).

1117. Abū Umayya [239] al-Dhimārī: A stone was found on a tomb in Ẓafār, on which was written: *khūri wa-ṭarbī kayl yask ri`l wa-humādā [=Jumādā] wa-naylak wa-maḥridhi thaj* arousing `Ād, it will be among you at mid-day: Ḥimyar the good ones, then the evil Ethiopians, then the Persian freedmen, then Quraysh the merchants, then *ḥāra maḥār janaḥ ḥār* and every time *dhan shu`batayn zaḥarahu wa-ma`dī zajruhu `amhu mikhwār.*[639]

1118. Ka`b: When the Yemenites have killed the lord of Jerusalem (*bayt al-maqdis*), they will advance against Quraysh and kill them until not one is left alive, until one of their shoes will be found, and it will be said: "This is the shoe of a Qurashite!"

1119. Ka`b: Dominion was among [the tribe of] Jurhum, but they were haughty, so they fought among themselves in envy for the dominion until they perished. So Quraysh will fight like them enviously for the dominion, until a man from Quraysh will be sought in Mecca and Medina, but no one will be able to find one, just as today no one can find any of the Jurhumites.

1120. Abū Bakr al-Azdī[640]: A king will settle in Jerusalem (*bayt al-maqdis*), then he will trample it, until he will wear the crown—he will be the one who will expel the Yemenites. It is as if I am looking at the Rock upon which the lord of Yemen sits! They will send a man to him [the king] as a messenger, but he will kill him, then another man, but he will kill him, too, so when they see this, they will deputize a man from them [with an army]. They will then go to him, find him and kill him.

1121. Arṭāt: The Mahdi will settle in Jerusalem then there will be

638 Nephew of the Negus of Ethiopia, according to no. 1227, *fl.* 1st/7th century.

639 See no. 247, although there are differences in the supposed South Arabian text.

640 Lived in Baṣra, *fl.* 2nd/8th century.

successors from his family after him, whose period will be lengthened. They will become tyrannical until the people will pray over the `Abbasids and the Umayyads as a result of what they are enduring. Jarrāh said: Their end will be around 200 years.

1122. Abū Qubayl: None of the family of the Mahdi after him will treat the people with justice, but their injustice will be lengthy for the people after the Mahdi, so that the people will pray over the `Abbasids, and say: "Would that they were in their place!" The people will continue like this until they raid Constantinople together with their leader. He will be a righteous man, who will pass the rule over to Jesus son of Mary. The people will continue in ease as long as the dominion of the `Abbasids does not fall apart, but when their dominion falls apart they will be in tribulation until the Mahdi arises.

1123. Ka`b: It will not be long until a caliph from Quraysh will settle in Jerusalem, gathering those of his people, the Quraysh, with their dwelling [240] and their redoubt, then they will exceed the boundaries in their rule, and lead decadent lives in their dominion, until they will make the lintels of their houses out of gold and silver. The lands will increase for them, and the peoples (*umam*) will serve them, yield the land-tax to them, and "the war will lay down its burdens."[641]

1124. Ka`b: A man from the Hashemites will settle in Jerusalem, his guard will be 12,000 [troops].

1125. Ka`b: His guard is 36,000, on every road to Jerusalem there will be 12,000.

1126. Arṭāt: His life will be lengthened, and he will be tyrannical, so his chamberlains (*ḥujjāb*) will be harsh towards the end of his time. His wealth and the wealth of those with him will increase until the leanest of them will be like the fattest of the rest of the Muslims. He will extinguish ways (*sunan*) that had been known (good), and innovate things that had not been,

[641] Q 47:4.

so fornication will appear, and he will drink wine openly, and frighten the learned (*`ulamā'*) so that a man would want to ride his mount then go to one of the garrison-cities, but not find a single man who will narrate *ḥadīth* in it. Islam during his time will be a stranger just as it began as a stranger. On that day the one who holds on to his religions will be like the one grabbing a coal. It will happen according to his order that a concubine would be sent, wiggling herself in the markets, with two little gold sheaths, meaning her shoe-slippers, together with the elite guard (*shuraṭ*), in clothes that do not conceal her either front or back, and if a man says a word about it, they will cut off his head.

1127. Al-Qāsim Abū `Abd al-Raḥmān[642]: He will circulate in your mosque with a concubine, whose pubic hair can be seen behind her garment, so then a man from the people will say: "By God, this is the worst guidance!" Then this man will be trampled until he dies, so would that I were that man!

1128. Arṭāt: In his time there will be trembling (earthquakes), metamorphosis, and swallowing up by the earth. The first part of his time will be for you, O Yemenites, but the last of it will be against you, such that he will order the expulsion of the Yemenites, the Syrians and the non-Arab foreigners (*ḥamrā'*) until they reach the extremities of the mountains from which they were expelled.

1129. Abū Hurayra: When the people gather in the valley of Jerusalem (*Iliyā'*), then Nizār will say: "O for Nizār!" and Qaḥṭān will say: "O for Qaḥṭān!" then endurance will be sent down, but victory lifted away, and the iron of each one will be set upon the other. [241]

1130. `Abdallāh b. `Amr: If you live during that time, be with the Yemenites, for they will have the victory.

1131. Abū al-Ṭufayl: I heard Ḥudhayfa b. al-Yamān saying to `Amr

642 Probably al-Qāsim b. `Abd al-Raḥmān, lived in Syria, a *mawlā* of the Umayyads, jurisprudent, d. 112 or 118/730 or 736.

b. Ṣulay`,[643] and `Amr b. Ṣulay` saying to him, Ḥudhayfa said: "Qays will continue to desire evil for God's religion until God will ride them with His troops—then absolutely nothing will stop them." `Amr said: "O one of [the tribe of] Muḥārib![644] When you see Qays ruling in Syria, then take precaution."

1132. Ka`b: When "the war lays down its burdens"[645] Muḍar will say to the Qurashite who is in Jerusalem (*bayt al-maqdis*): "God gave you what He never gave anyone previously, but you confined it to your cousins," so he will say: "Whoever is from the Yemenites, let him go to Yamna [= Yemen], while whoever is non-Arab (*a`ājim*) let him go to Antioch, since we have given everybody three [days? to leave?]. Whoever does not do that, his blood is permitted [to be killed]." So the Yemenites will go to Zīzā',[646] while the non-Arabs [go] to Antioch.

While the Yemenites are in Zīzā', they will suddenly hear a herald calling out in the night: "O Manṣūr, O Manṣūr!"[647] so the people will emerge to the sound of the voice, but not find anybody. Then it will call out the second night, and the third, so they will gather and say: "O people, will you return to being nomadic Bedouins after your emigration (*hijra*)? And return backwards, leaving your fighters, your lines, the home of your emigration and the graves of your dead?" So they will appoint that man [as leader].

1133. Arṭāt: They will gather, then look for [someone] to whom they can swear allegiance, so while they are in that state, they will a voice not either human or jinn "Swear allegiance to so-and-so" with his name, who does not have a *dhī* or a *dhū*,[648] but he is a Yemenite caliph.

[643] Companion, related *fitan* traditions from Ḥudhayfa, *fl.* 1st/7th century.
[644] Yemenite tribe, settled in Kūfa.
[645] Q 47:4.
[646] A village in northwestern Jordan on the hajj route.
[647] The battle-cry of the Yemenites.
[648] Many South Arabian names from the Umayyad period had these prefixes to their names.

1134. Ka`b: He will be Yemenite and Qurashite, he is the Commander of the Bands—among the bands there will be a lessening of the Yemenites and those who follow them from among the rest of those who left Jerusalem. That is the word of Tubba`:
And in the part of our tribe that I love, you lead by [being] a king after the disaster,
This remnant of the dying one, which has been broken into groups and the gathering of bands.[649]

1135. Ka`b: The Yemenites will emerge in the east of the land, then settle among Lakhm and Judhām, so they will share with them their livelihoods until all are equal. [242]

1136. Arṭāt: Lakhm, Judhām, Jadīs and `Āmila will be an aid to them on that day, just as Joseph was an aid to the family of Jacob, so the Yemenites and the non-Arabs foreigners (*ḥamrā'*), who are the *mawālī*, will send back and forth, then they will gather as a band just as driven [clouds] of autumn, meaning the intermittent clouds.

1137. `Alī: The religion will be destroyed until no one will say "There is no God but Allāh." Some of them will say: "until O God, O God" will not be said. The head-honcho (*ya`sūb*) of the religion will follow his tail, then God will send a people driven like the clouds of autumn—I know the name of their commander and the resting place of their rides.

1138. `Abdallāh b. `Amr b. al-`Āṣ: Whoever can die after the Commander of the Bands, should do so.

1139. `Abdallāh b. `Amr: Three commanders will attempt to conquer the lands, which will be under them, all them righteous: al-Jābir, then al-Mufarrij (the liberator), then the Possessor of the Bands. They will stay forty years, then there will be no good in this world after them.

1140. Ka`b: The one who expels the Yemenites will be a Hashemite, whose dwelling place is Jerusalem (*bayt al-maqdis*), his guard

649 Reading *yufaḍḍu* with MM; Tubba` was the title of the pre-Islamic kings of Ḥimyar (Yemen).

12,000 [troops], who will expel the Yemenites until they end up in the furthest part of the land, so they will settle among Lakhm and Judhām. So they will share with them their livelihoods until all are equal. Then the Yemenites will advance against each other, saying: "Where are you going? And to where are you returning?" So they will deputize a man from among them, so he will say: "I am your messenger to your ruler with your message." He will go until he brings him their letter and message in Jerusalem, that he should have clemency upon them and return them to their dwellings.

So he will order to have his head cut off, but since he took his time, they will send another man, so when he approaches them, he will order his head to be cut off. When he takes his time, they will send another man, but he will order his head to be cut off. But God Most High will free him so that he can come to them, to inform them of the killing of his friend, and the fact that he wanted to kill him. So they will gather, and appoint a commander from among them, then they will go towards him, fight him, then God Most High will grant victory to them over him, and they will kill him. Then they will advance against Quraysh, so there will not be a single Qurashite who survives, such that one of their shoes will be found, and someone will say: "This was a Qurashite's shoe." [243]

1141. Tubay`: Muḍar will gather, but I do not know whether Rabī`a will follow them or not, while the Yemenites are in the Valley of Jerusalem (*Iliyā'*),[650] so they will fight, then Muḍar will be killed until the valley flows with their blood.

1142. Al-Ṣunābiḥī: Qays will advance on that day until there will not remain from them enough to fill part of a valley or the top of a heap.

1143. Sulaymān b. `Īsā, who was knowledgeable concerning tribulations: It has reached me that the Mahdi wil stay fourteen years in Jerusalem (*bayt al-maqdis*), then die. Then after him there

[650] Most probably the Kidron Valley, which the Muslims called the Valley of Hell.

will be one noble of mention, of Tubba`'s people,[651] called al-Manṣūr, in Jerusalem, twenty-one years, fifteen of which are just, three of which are unjust, and three are [characterized by] confiscation of wealth, in which he will not give a dirham, and divide the Jews and Christians (*ahl al-dhimma*) among his fighters. He is the one who will exile the *mawālī* to the valley of valleys, and he will tread on the progeny of Ishamel just as cattle tread on the threshing floor (*andar*). A *mawlā* whose name and patronymic are that of a prophet will revolt against him. He will go up against him from the valleys until he will meet al-Manṣūr [in battle] in the interior of Jericho, then fight him and kill him.

Then the *mawlā* will reign, and exile the progeny of Qaḥṭān and Ishmael to the two treasure-cities of the Arabs: Medina and Ṣana`ā'. At his hands the Turks and the Byzantines will emerge, so that they will rule between the valley of Antioch and Mt. Carmel (*karmal*) in Filasṭīn, on the plain of the city of Acre. The *mawlā* will reign three years, then be killed. Then Hiyam[652] the second Mahdi will reign, who will kill the Byzantines, defeat them, and conquer Constantinople. He will stay there three years, four months and ten days, then Jesus son of Mary will descend, and he will give the dominion over to him.

1144. Ka`b: Youths (*ghilmān*) from Quraysh will manage your affairs who will be on the level of fattened she-camels at mangers—if they are left, they will consume everything that is before them; if they escape they butt whoever they come across.

1145. `Abdallāh b. `Amr b. al-`Āṣ sat in the Damascus Mosque, which had only Yemenites in it. He said: "O Yemenites, how will it be for you when we expel you from Syria, and take exclusive possession of it against you?" they said: "Will that really be?" He said: "Yes, by the Lord of the Ka`ba!" then he said: "What is

651 Yemenites.

652 This is a fairly unusual name, meaning "an extremely thirsty camel." Perhaps a mistake for Haytham?

with you, aren't you going to say anything?" Some of the group said: [244] "Do you really think that we are more unjust than you in it [the land]?" He said: "No, we are." The Yemenite said: "Praise be to God! 'Those who have done evil will come to know what a complete overturning they will suffer.'"[653]

1146. Ka`b: You will continue in ease of livelihood as long as the caliph does not settle in Jerusalem.

1147. Al-Walīd: The Mahdi will rule, manifest his justice, then die. After him one from his family will rule who will be just. Then those who are unjust and evil from among them will rule, until it [the rule] goes to a man from among them, who will exile the Yemenites to Yemen, so they will go to him and kill him. A man from Quraysh called Muḥammad will be appointed over them—some of the learned said that he was from Yemen—and at the hand of this Yemenite will be the apocalyptic battles.

1148. `Abdallāh b. `Amr: After the Mahdi, there is the one who will expel the Yemenites to their lands, then al-Manṣūr, then after him the Mahdi who at his hands the city of the Byzantines will be conquered.

1149. Ka`b: Both the Mahdi and the caliphate are from none other than Quraysh, but he will have a root and an ancestry in Yemen.

1150. Abū al-Zāhiriyya: The Messenger of God said: "Quraysh was given that which none other was given—it was given that upon which the heavens rained, the rivers flowed, the floods flooded—those who are past are better than those yet remaining. A man from Quraysh will continue to undertake this rule, either by theft or by desire [to rule]. I swear by God, if you obey Quraysh it will truly divide you up into tribes throughout the earth. O people, listen to the words of Quraysh, but do not act according to their actions."

1151. Ismā`īl b. Muḥammad b. `Amr b. Sa`d[654]: The Messenger of

653 Q 26:227.

654 Probably a mistake for the grandson of Sa`d b. Abī Waqqāṣ, lived in Medina, d. 134/751–2.

God said: "O Quraysh, you will continue to be managers of this affair as long as you obey God Most High, so when you disobey Him, He will peel you from the face of the earth, just as this, my rod, was peeled, then He will scatter a group of those He peeled and cast them down to the earth."

1152. Ka`b: After [245] the Mahdi there will be a caliph from the Yemenites, from Qaḥṭān, the brother of the Mahdi in his religion,[655] who will act according to his actions. It is he who will conquer the city of the Byzantines and obtain its spoils. Ka`b said: A man from the Hashemites will rule the people in Jerusalem, who will extinguish ways that were known, and innovate ones that were not, so that no learned man would be found able to narrate a single *ḥadīth*. During his time there will be swallowing up by the earth and metamorphosis. Islam will return to being a stranger just as it began as a stranger, so the one who holds fast on that day to his religion will be like one who grasps a coal, or like the one who has to pull off thorns during a black night. He will send his daughter wiggling herself in the markets, with the elite guard, and two gold shoe-slippers, concealing neither back nor front, but if a man says anything, they will cut off his head.

1153. `Amr b. al-`Āṣ: The Prophet said: The first people to perish will be Quraysh.

1154. Abū Hurayra: When Nizār says: "O Nizār!" and the Yemenites say: "O Qaḥṭān!" endurance will descend, victory will be lifted, and the iron of each of them will be set against the other.

1155. `Abd al-Raḥmān b. Qays al-Ṣadafī, from his father, then his grandfather: The Prophet said: The Qaḥṭānī is after the Mahdi, and by the One who sent me in truth, the one is not less than the other.

1156. Arṭāt: There will be a truce between the Mahdi and the Byzantines, then the Mahdi will perish. A man from his family will rule, performing minimal justice, then will unsheathe

[655] Cf. Q 33:5.

his sword against the people of Filasṭīn, so they will rise up against him, and ask assistance from the people of al-Urdunn. He will remain among them for two months, acting with the justice of the Mahdi, then unsheathe his sword against them. They will rise up against him, so he will depart, fleeing, until he settles in Damascus. Have you seen the lintels above the Jābiya Gate, where there the boxes for exchanging money (*tawabīt al-ṣarf*)? The round stone below these by five cubits—on it he will be slaughtered.[656] The remnant of his blood will not be dried before it will be said: 'The Byzantines have anchored in it [Syria] between Tyre and Acre!' and it will be the apocalyptic battles.

1157. `Abdallāh b. `Amr: "How will it be, O Yemenites, when Muḍar expels you?" We said: "Will that really happen, O Abū Muḥammad?" He said: "Yes, and by the One who holds my soul in His hand, they are wrong-doers to you." A man from the Yemenites said: "Those who have done evil will come to know what a complete overturning they will suffer."[657] `Abdallāh said: "If I live to see that time, I will be with you." [246]

1158. Murra b. Rabī`a Abū Shimr al-Ma`āfirī[658]: The head of the army-province on the Day of the Afīq Pass will be a youth from Madhḥij, on a female horse, with a mark on its thigh or on its leg.

1159. Abū Hurayra: Do not be in doubt about the perishing of Quraysh, for they are the first of those who perish, such that a shoe will be found in a garbage heap, so it will be said: "Take this shoe, for it was surely the shoe of a Qurashite."

1160. Ibn Shihāb that the Prophet said to `Ā'isha: "Your people are the fastest to be annihilated," so `Ā'isha cried, and so he said: "What is causing you to cry, butter-skin (`*ukak*)?[659] Do you

656 In 127/744–5 the rebel `Abd al-`Azīz b. Ḥajjāj was crucified upside down on this spot (Khalifa b. Khayyat, *Tā'rīkh*, pp. 297–8).

657 Q 26:227.

658 Unidentified.

659 Apparently another nickname for `A'isha; attested as a personal name:

think that the Bin Taym[660] is not part of Quraysh? I was not intending your clan specifically, but I meant Quraysh as a whole. God will conquer this world for them so that eyes will be lifted up to them, and the fates will be pleasant to them—thus they will be the fastest to be annihilated."

1161. Ka`b: "When you see the Arabs despised at the order of Quraysh, then you see the *mawālī* despised at the order of the Arabs, then you see the converts to Islam (*maslamat al-arḍīn*) despised at the order of the *mawālī*, then the portents of the Hour are overshadowing you." Kurayb[661] said: I said to him: "O Abū Isḥāq, Hudhayfa narrated to us a tradition (*ḥadīth*) concerning the two red ones."[662] He said: "That is when pens and cushions are forbidden." Abū `Abdallāh said: "The cushions are the governors, while the pens are the secretaries."

1162. Muḥammad b. al-Ḥanafiyya: When the caliph from the Hashemites settles in Jerusalem (*bayt al-maqdis*) he will fill the earth with justice, and build Jerusalem[663] in a way that it was never built before. He will reign for forty years, and the truce with the Byzantines will be at his hands with seven years left in his caliphate. Then they will betray him, and gather at the valleys (`*umuq*), so he will die there grieved. Then a man from the Hashemites will rule after him, then will be their defeat and the conquest of Constantinople at his hands. Then he will go to Rome conquer it, and take out its treasures and the table of Solomon, son of David.[664] Then he will return to Jerusalem,

al-Hamdānī, *al-Iklīl min akhbār al-Yamān* (Ṣan`ā': Wizārat al-Thaqāfa wa-l-Siyāḥa, 2004), x, p. 54.

660 `Ā'isha's clan, part of the larger tribe of Quraysh.

661 Kurayb b. Abī Muslim al-Qurashi, lived in Medina, a *mawlā*, d. 98/716–17.

662 Probably the tradition, "I was given the two treasures, the red and the white," by which the red is the gold of the Byzantines and the white is the silver of the Persians: Ibn al-Athīr, *Nihāya*, i, p. 438.

663 It is possible to understand this as *bayt al-maqdis* = the Temple, see also no. 1295.

664 Nicola Clarke, *The Muslim Conquest of Iberia* (London: Routledge, 2012), pp. 32–4, 38–9, 84–6, 88–98 on this item in Spain.

settle in it, and the Dajjāl will emerge during his time, Jesus son of Mary will descend, then pray behind him.

1163. Arṭāt: At the hands of that caliph, who is Yemenite, will be the raid on India, concerning which Abū Hurayra spoke.

1164. Unidentified: The Prophet said: A group from my community will raid [247] India, so God will conquer it for them such that when they bring back the kings of India fettered in chains, God will forgive for them their sins. They will return to Syria, and find Jesus son of Mary in Syria.

1165. Ibn `Abbās that they mentioned the twelve caliphs and the commander to him, so Ibn `Abbās said: "By God, from us after that is al-Saffāḥ, al-Manṣūr and al-Mahdi, who will give it over to Jesus son of Mary."

1166. `Abdallāh b. `Amr: al-Saffāḥ, then al-Manṣūr, then Jābir, then al-Mahdi, then al-Amīn, then Sīn, then the Commander of the Bands—six of them are from the progeny of Ka`b b. Lu'ayy, and a man from Qaḥṭān. None will be seen like them, all of them righteous.

1167. `Abdallāh b. `Amr: al-Saffāḥ, Salām, Manṣūr, Jābir, al-Amīn, the Commander of the Bands—all of them righteous, no one witnessed the like of them, all of them from Ka`b b. Lu'ayy—and a man from Qaḥṭān. Among them there are those who will only [rule] two days.

1168. Ka`b: al-Manṣūr, al-Mahdi, and al-Saffāḥ are from the progeny of al-`Abbās.

1169. Ka`b: al-Manṣūr is the Manṣūr of the Hashemites.

1170. Arṭāt: "The Commander of the Bands is a Yemenite." Al-Walīd said: "According to the knowledge of Ka`b, Yemenite and Qurashite—he is the Commander of the Bands."

1171. Jābir al-Ṣadafī[665]: The Messenger of God said: The Qaḥṭānī is after the Mahdi, and the one is not less than the other.

1172. Ka`b: al-Manṣūr is from Ḥimyar, the fifth of fifteen caliphs.

1173. `Abdallāh b. `Amr b. al-`Āṣ: al-Jābir, then al-Mahdi, then

665 Unknown other than as the grandfather of no. 245.

al-Manṣūr, then al-Salām, then the Commander of the Bands, so whoever is able to die after that, let him die. [248]

1174. `Abdallāh b. `Amr: Three caliphs will rule, all of them righteous, under them will be the conquest of the lands. The first of them is Jābir, the second is al-Mufarrij, and the third is the Commander of the Bands. They will stay forty years, there will be no good in this world after them.

1175. Abū Sa`īd al-Khudarī: The Prophet said: A man from my family will emerge called al-Saffāḥ, at the end of time and the appearsance of tribulations, whose stipends will be generous.

1176. Arṭāt: It has reached me that the Mahdi will live for forty years, then die on his bed, then a man from Qaḥṭān with pierced ears will emerge, according to the manner of the Mahdi, whose length of staying will be twenty years, then he will die, killed by al-Saffāḥ. Then a man from the family of the Prophet, guided, well-mannered, who will conquer Caesar's city.[666] He will be the last commander from the community of Muḥammad. Then the Dajjāl will emerge during his time, and Jesus son of Mary will descend in his time.

1177. Ka`b: A king in Jerusalem (*bayt al-maqdis*) will send an army to India and conquer it, taking its treasures, and bring them as a decoration for Jerusalem. They will come to him bringing the kings of India in fetters, this army will stay in India until the emergence of the Dajjāl.

1178. Ka`b: You will continue to live in ease until the caliphate settles in Jerusalem.

1179. Jubayr b. Nufayr: The Messenger of God said: Men from my community who are like you will live to see the Messiah son of Mary or the best of them are like you, or better.

1180. Ka`b: A man from Quraysh, among the worst of creation, will be appointed caliph in Jerusalem (*bayt al-maqdis*), and transfer to it the storehouses, and the nobles of the people. They will act tyrannically in it, and tighten their control, increasing

[666] Probably Constantinople.

their wealth, until one man from them will eat for a month, while another for two months, and three, until the leanest of them is like the fattest of the rest of the people. They will grow like a fattened she-camel at mangers. The caliph will extinguish ways that were known (affirmed), and innovate ways that never were. Evil wll appear during his time, fornication (*zinā*), drinking wine publicly, and the learned during his time will fear, such that if a man rode his mount, going around all of the cities, he would not find a single one of the learned who would narrate a tradition (*ḥadīth*) because of fear.

During his time there will be metamorphosis and swallowing up by the earth, and Islam will be a stranger. The one who clings to his religion will be like the one who grasps a coal, or [249] like the one who has to pull off thorns during a black night, such that among his issues, he will send his daughter to pass through the market, with the elite guard (*shuraṭ*), while wearing slipper-shoes of gold, and with a garment that neither conceals the front or the back because of its fineness. If any one of the people speak in disapproval with even one word, his head will be cut off.

He will start to deny the people their daily sustenance, then deny them the stipend, then after that order the expulsion of the Yemenites from Syria. So the elite guard will expel them dispersed, not leaving an army-province to which they can arrive, such that they will expel them from the mountains entirely, so they will end up in Buṣrā.[667] This will be at the end of his life. So then the Yemenites will send among themselves so that they can gather as the driven clouds of autumn, then placing themselves where they can be bands opposite each other [for battle]. Then they will say: "Where are you going? Are you leaving your land and the place of your emigration?"

So they will be united in their determination to swear allegiance to a man from among them. While they are saying: "Let

[667] Southern Syria, the end of the caravan route from the Hijāz.

us swear allegiance to so-and-so" they will hear a sound never uttered by either human or jinn: "Swear to so-and-so" naming him for them—and he is indeed a man with whom they are satisfied!

People who are not *dhī* or *dhī* (Yemenites) will be convinced by him, so they will send to the tyrant of Quraysh a delegation from them, but he will kill them. One man from it will return to inform them of what happened, then the Yemenites will go to him—but the tyrant of Quraysh will have 20,000 elite guards, so the Yemenites will set out, then Lakhm, Judhām, `Āmila and Jadīs will fight with them, bringing them food, drink, small and great. On that day they will be an aid to the Yemenites just as Joseph was an aid to his brothers in Egypt.

By the One who holds the soul of Ka`b in His hand, Lakhm, Judhām, `Āmila and Jadīs are part of the Yemenites, O Yemenites! So if they come to you, seeking [to take part in] your genealogy with you, then let them, for they are part of you. Then they will all go together until they overlook Jerusalem, meet the tyrant of Quraysh with this massive number, and the Yemenites will defeat him.

1181. Abān b. al-Walīd al-Mu`ayṭī who heard Ibn `Abbās narrate to Mu`āwiya saying: "A man from us will rule at the end of time for forty years. The apocalyptic battles will be during the seven last years of his caliphate, but then he will die in the valleys (*a`māq*) grieved. Then a man from them, the one with two black moles (*dhū al-sha'matayn*), and at his hands will be the conquest, on that day, meaning the conquest of the Byzantines in the valleys."

1182. Abū Qubayl: The [future] master of Rome will be a Hashemite, whose name will be al-Aṣbagh b. Zayd,[668] and he is the one who will conquer it.

[668] Probably identical with the Aṣbagh b. Yazīd in no. 1307. But the only Aṣbagh b. Yazīd listed is the son of Yazīd II; in general, neither Aṣbagh nor Yazīd were names favored by the Hashemites. Note that an early raider in Sicily (from 214/829, just

1183. `Abd al-Raḥmān b. Qays al-Ṣadafī from his father—his grandfather: The Messenger of God said: After the Mahdi will be the Qaḥṭānī, and by the One who sent me in truth, he is not less than him. [250]

1184. Thawban, *mawlā* of the Messenger of God: O Abū `Āmir [al-Alhānī], sharpen your sword, and take forty hairy goats, prepare a full load, cattle-girths (*ansā`*),[669] water-skins, since it is as if you were expelled from it village by village.

1185. `Umrān b. Sulaym al-Kalā`ī[670]: Woe to those fattened women, but blessed are the poor! Have your women wear light slippers as shoes, and tell them to walk in their houses, for they are about to be expelled from all of that.

1186. Ibn `Abbās: The Messenger of God said: The religion will last as long as there are twenty men from Quraysh remaining.

1187. Dhū Mikhbar: The Messenger of God said: The rule was with Ḥimyar, but God yanked it away from them and placed in Quraysh, but it will return to them.

1188. Ḥudhayfa: The tyrants of Muḍar will continue tempting each righteous servant of God, and killing him, until God, His angels and the believers strike them with those who are with him. No part of a hillside will protect them.'[671] `Amr b. Ṣulay` said to him: "What is with you, they are not Muḍar, and what is with you, mentioning other than them?" He said: "Are you from [the tribe of] Muḥārib?" He said: "Yes," so he said: "Do you think that Muḥārib is a mother's palm-basket (*khaṣafat umm*) from Qays?" He said: "Yes," {so he said:}[672] "When you see Qays ruling Syria, then take your precaution."

1189. Abū Arṭāt heard `Alī saying: "... those who have exchanged the blessing of God for disbelief, and caused their people to

after Nu`aym) was named Aṣbagh, although he was Berber (Alex Metcalfe, *The Muslims of Medieval Italy* [Edinburgh: Edinburgh University Press, 2009], p. 12).

669 Reading with MM.

670 Unattested, but probably lived in Ḥimṣ, *fl.* 2nd/8th century.

671 Reading *tala`a* as in no. 1194 for *balaghahu.*

672 Addition from MM.

descend to the home of ruin,"[673] then he said: "People are innocent of them, other than Quraysh." Then he said: "It will not be long until a man from Quraysh will be brought, then the headdress will be snatched from his head, nothing different, because of the evil of their trial."

1190. Abū Hurayra heard the Messenger of God saying: Perishing of my community or the corruption of my community will be upon the heads of commanders, [who are] foolish youths from Quraysh. [251] **(1)**

1191. Ḥudhayfa: "O `Amr b. Ṣulay`, when you see Qays ruling in Syria, take your precaution." Then he said: "Muḍar are about to kill the believers and tempt them, until God, His angels and the believers strike them, such that no part of a hillside will protect them."

1192. Ka`b: "To whom is the dominion of Ẓafār?" He said: "To the good Ḥimyarites. To whom is the dominion of Ẓafār?" He said: "To the free Persians. To whom is the dominion of Ẓafār?" "To the trader Quraysh."

1193. Abū Ḥalbas[674]: The Messenger of God said: Quraysh has been given that which no other people has been given—given that upon which the heavens rain, upon which the rivers flow, and upon which the floods overflood. Those are past are better than those yet remaining. A man from Quraysh will continue to undertake this rule, either by theft or by desire [to rule]. I swear by God, if you obey Quraysh it will truly divide you up into tribes throughout the earth. O people, listen to the words of Quraysh, but do not act according to their actions. The best of people are followers to the best of Quraysh, just as the worst of people are followers to the worst of Quraysh. Flags will come from them as long as you pay the fifth (*khums*), as long as you do not betray the trust, break the covenant, as long

673 Q 14:28.

674 One who was unknown to Muslim scholars (al-Mizzī, *Tahdhīb*, viii, pp. 292–3 [no. 7921]).

as you divide [spoils] equitably, and are just in judgments—so when mercy is sought of you, then give mercy! Whoever does not do that, the curse (*bahla*) of God is upon him.[675]

1194. `Amr b. al-`Āṣ: The Messenger of God said: the first of the people to perish will be Quraysh, and the first of them will be the people of my family.

1195. Arṭāt: After the Mahdi, there will be a man from Qaḥṭān with pierced ears, according to the manner of the Mahdi. His life will be twenty years, then he will die, killed by weapons. Then a man from the family of Aḥmad will emerge, with a good manner, conquering the city of Caesar, and he will be the last king or commander of the community of Aḥmad.[676] The Dajjāl will emerge in his time, and Jesus will descend in his time.[677]

The Raid on India

1196. Ka`b: A king in Jerusalem will send an army to India, and conquer it, so that they will tread on the land of India and take its treasures.[678] These will be made into decoration for Jerusalem, and that army will come to it, bringing the kings of India in chains. [The army] will conquer the east and the west, but their staying in India will be until the appearance of the Dajjāl.

1197. Abū Hurayra: The Messenger of God said, and mentioned India: An army of yours will raid India, with God conquering for them, until they bring its kings in weighted down in chains. God will forgive their sins, so they will depart wherever, then find [Jesus] son of Mary in Syria.

1198. Abū Hurayra: "If I live at the time of that raid, then I will sell everything, small and large, to be on that raid, for when God conquers for us, and we have left, then I, Abū Hurayra, the devoted one, will go to Syria and find Jesus son of Mary

[675] Perhaps a reference to Q 3:61.
[676] Muḥammad, cf. Q 61:6.
[677] A rare occurance of Jesus without being called "son of Mary."
[678] It is difficult to say which section of India is referenced here; most probably the northern, wealthier Ganges plains were the focus of this family of traditions.

in it. I would desire to get close to him, so to tell him that I was a Companion of yours, O Messenger of God." He said: The Messenger of God smiled, and laughed, saying: "Indeed!"

1199. Abū Hurayra: The Messenger of God promised us the raid on India, so if I live to see it, I would spend everything, myself and my money, so if I was martyred, I would be among the most meritorious of martyrs, but if I returned, then I would be Abū Hurayra the devoted one.

1200. Arṭāt: At the hands of the Yemenite caliph who will conquer Constantinople and Rome, at his hands the Dajjāl will appear, [and] Jesus son of Mary [253] will descend. At his hands there will be the raid on India—he will be from the Hashemites—the raid on India concerning which Abū Hurayra spoke.

1201. Unidentified: The Prophet said: a group of my community will raid India, with God conquering it for them, until they bring back the kings of India weighted down in chains, so God will forgive them their sins, then they will go to Syria, and find Jesus son of Mary in Syria. [254]

What will happen in Ḥimṣ during the administration of the Qaḥṭānī, and between Quḍā`a and Yaman after the Mahdi

1202. Ka`b: During the rule of the Qahtani Quḍā`a and Ḥimyar will fight in Ḥimṣ, when a man from Kinda, {Quḍā`a},[679] will be charge of it [the city].[680] Quḍā`a will kill him and hang his head on a tree. So Ḥimyar will be enraged on his behalf, so they will fight fiercely, until every house near the mosque will be destroyed in order to widen their lines for battle. At that point, woe to the easterner from the westerner, and other than those in Ḥimṣ. The most miserable Yemenite tribe will be Sakūn,[681] because they are their neighbors.

1203. Ka`b al-Aḥbār: Ḥimyar and Quḍā`a will fight in Ḥimṣ over a

[679] Thus in BL but it seems to be misplaced.

[680] Who unfortunately cannot be identified, as we have no city history for Ḥimṣ from this period.

[681] A tribe associated with Kinda.

gray donkey, so Quḍā`a will urge on [those tribes] between them and the Euphrates [River] against Ḥimyar, so they will fight in the Rastan Market. Two horses will go through the two markets, with neither of them seeing the other—as this was prior to the building of the shops—so we were amazed at how the two horses would not see the other, when the market was an open court until the shops were built. But then we knew that was the explanation (*ta'wīl*) and verification of the tradition that we would hear, "Two horses would fight fiercely, then an angel would come out against them from the cotton aisles [of the market]"—in the narration of Ṣafwān, "the perfume aisles"—"on a gray nag pony (*birdhawn*), and interpose between them. Then the two groups will depart, while they are few and regretful. Woe to `Ād from Ayim and to Ayim from `Ād! as `Ād are the Yemenites, and Ayim are Quḍā`a." In the tradition of Ṣafwān, "then and there the Quḍā`a-ness will perish." Ḥarīz b. `Uthmān[682] said: "Quḍā`a and Ḥimyar will fight in Ḥimṣ between the Rastan Gate and the Dome (*qubba*),[683] and there will be a great slaughter among them." [255]

1204. Tubay`: The battle will be fierce in Ḥimṣ, such that what is between its markets will be destroyed, and such that aid for Quḍā`a will come from between the Euphrates [River] and below it, then they will lose, when they fight under the Dome of Ḥimṣ.

1205. Ka`b: Ḥimyar and Quḍā`a will fight in Ḥimṣ until Quḍā`a will destroy those houses around its market up to the Rastan Gate in order to widen the area for the line of battle. The Yemenites will destroy the houses around the markets, in order to widen the area for the line of battle. Then each tribe from Ḥimyar will sit with its banner west and east of Ḥimṣ, and gather at

682 Ḥarīz b. `Uthmān al-Raḥabī, lived in Ḥimṣ, d. 163/779–80.

683 A dome mentioned by al-Muqaddasi, *Ahsan al-taqasim* (Beirut: Dār Sadir, n.d. [reprint of Leiden: E. J. Brill, 1909]), p. 156, trans. Basil Collins, *The Best Divisions for Knowledge of the Regions* (Reading: Garnet Publishing, 2001), p. 133, near the marketplace.

the place where the markets conjoin. The fighting will be fierce in Ḥimṣ, and there will be a great bloodshedding such that the horses' hooves will stick to the paving stones because of the blood, such that the blood will flow towards the conjoining of the markets and there will be a great slaughter in it. Whoever is present, and is able to leave Ḥimṣ should do so. Blessed is the one who lives in a village or close towards the direction of the *qibla* (south) in Ḥimṣ on that day! Ḥimyar will press Quḍā`a so as to expel them through the Rastan Gate, and the fighting will be fierce until an angel on a horse, seen by the people, will come, when they had almost annihilated each other, and interpose between them. Quḍā`a will ask for aid[684] from the tribes in the region (*ahl al-ḥāḍirīn*),[685] and the Quḍā`a [tribes] around the Euphrates [River] against Ḥimyar, so they will advance with a mighty army, and the tribulations and fighting will increase in Syria.

1206. Ḥarīz b. `Uthmān: I heard that during the rulership of Yazīd b. `Abd al-Malik Quḍā`a and Yemen will fight as tribal chauvinism, such that the two sides will destroy that which is between the two markets to the Rastan Gate in order to widen them for fighting. At that time there were no shops in Ḥimṣ, then they built them after Hishām. So we said: "These were destroyed on that day." Ḥarīz said: "We used to hear when four mosques were built for Ḥimṣ that this, and that mosque was the one built by Mūsā b. Sulaymān, the head of the land (*kharāj*)-tax of Ḥimṣ[686] as the third mosque."

1207. Ka`b: In Ḥimṣ there were three prayer-places (*masājid*)[687]: a prayer-place (*masjid*) belonging to Satan and his people,

684 All of the manuscripts and editions favor *yashtaddu* over *yastamaddu*, but the context and the comparison with the previous traditions demands this emendation.

685 Lane, ii, 590 (mid. col.) for this meaning.

686 Possibly Mūsā b. Sulaymān b. Mūsā al-Qurashī al-Umawī, who lived in Damascus and Beirut, who is cited for a financial tradition (al-Mizzī, *Tahdhīb*, vii, p. 262 [no. 6858]), *fl.* 2nd/8th century.

687 Because of the inclusion of a Christian church as one of the *masājid* one is forced to go back to the original meaning rather than translate "mosque."

meaning to Satan,[688] a prayer-place belonging to God, but its people were Satan's, and a prayer-place belonging to God and its people belonging to God. As for the prayer-place belonging to Satan, and its people were Satan's, it is the Church of Mary,[689] and as for the prayer-place which belongs to God but its people to Satan, it is our prayer-place,[690] and its people are a mixture (*akhlāṭ*). The prayer-place which belongs to God and its people as well is the prayer-place at the Church of Zacharias[691]—its people are Ḥimyar, and the Yemenites pray the Friday prayers there.

1208. Abū Zāhiriyya: [256] No water flows to the house of al-`Abbās, because it has been taken as a mosque recently since your mosque fell (was occupied), so they were fighting over it [the house], then you took it as a mosque, so do not urinate in it.

1209. Ka`b: Woe to `Ād from Ayam, when [the tribe of] Kalb has grown in Ḥimṣ and the children.

1210. The elders: There will be a Shout in Ḥimṣ, so let everyone stay in their houses, and not come out for three hours.

1211. Baqiyya[692]: I saw the Messenger of God in a dream having tucked up his clothes [in preparation], so I said: "O Messenger of God, what is it that I see you have tucked up your clothes!" He said: "Prepare for the return of Jesus son of Mary." [257]

688 Presumably these are Christians; see the account of Willibald on this church (called the Church of St. John): Wilkinson, p.236. However, Yāqūt, *Mu`jam*, ii, pp. 303–4 states that the Church of St. John was the one that was divided between Christians and Muslims.

689 This church was divided between the Christians and the Muslims for several centuries, see Thomas Carlson, "Contours of Conversion: The Geography of Islamization in Syria 600–1500," *Journal of the American Oriental Society* 135 (2015), pp. 791–816, at p. 799.

690 Who exactly are the "our" is difficult to say, since the tradition appears to be extolling the non-official third prayer-place.

691 Apparently completely converted to a mosque (perhaps the one listed in 1208).

692 Baqiyya b. al-Walīd al-Kalā`ī, lived in Ḥimṣ, key traditionalist, d. 197/812–13.

Al-Āʿmāq and the Conquest of Constantinople

1212. ʿAbdallāh b. ʿAmr: The Byzantines will reign [the type of] dominion in which almost no one will be able to disobey, and it will go to them until they descend on such-and-such a land for a number of days which I have forgotten. He said: It is written on the gate that the believers will receive aid from ʿAdan Abyan on their young she-camels, so they will come and fight for ten [days], without eating anything except for what was in their small skins (*adawāt*), without anything interposing between them other than the night. Their swords will not be blunted, nor their arrows or their short-spears while you are in this situation.

God will place defeat upon them, so they will be killed in numbers the like of which have never been seen, such that the birds will pass on the sides of [this slaughter] then die from the reeking stench. The martyr of that day is equivalent to those martyrs from previously, or the believers on that day are equivalent to the believers from previously. The remainder will never, ever be shaken, and this remainder will fight the Dajjāl.

1213. ʿAbdallāh b. Salām: If I live to see it, but I do not have strength, then carry me on my sickbed so as to place me between the two lines [of battle].

1214. Kaʿb: God has two great slaughters among the Christians (*naṣārā*): one has passed but the other remains [to come].

1215. Maslama b. ʿAbd al-Malik, while he was besieging Constantinople,[693] when suddenly a young man with a beautiful garb and a swift mount came to him, then said to him: "I am Tiberius,"[694] so he honored him [258], brought him to

[693] During 715–17.

[694] Known as "the false Tiberius" or possibly Tiberius III Apsimaros see Theophanes, *Chronicle*, pp. 529–30; there is a later incident from 737 in which a man presented himself to Sulaymān son of the caliph Hishām, see Michael the Great, pp. 501–2. See also Sidney Griffith, "Bashīr/Bešer: Boon companion of the Byzantine

his council, and kept him close. Then he sent for Abū Muslim al-Rūmī, who was from the *mawālī of* the Marwanids, a captive from the Byzantines, who had converted to Islam, became knowledgeable about jurisprudence and Islam, and his primary loyalty was to Islam. He [Maslama] said: "O Abū Muslim, this one claims that he is Tiberius." So he said: "He is lying, may God make the commander righteous. I of all people know Tiberius well, so if he were between 10,000 I would be able to pick him out. Tiberius is a ruddy man with a broad forehead, bad teeth, who will appear when he is sixty years old—known by blood, drinking water. He will say: 'How long will we allow the camel-eaters to stay in our country and our land? Take us to the camel-eaters so we can do whatever we like to them.'"

So they will come to him in a gathering the like of which has not been seen previously, such that they will settle in the valleys. The Muslims will learn of his coming and his settling [in the valleys], so they will ask for aid, such that from the furthest Yemen they will come, helping Islam. The Christians of al-Jazīra and Syria will aid those Christians [the Byzantines], so the Muslims will go towards them. Victory will be lifted from them, but endurance will descend upon them, and the iron of each of them will be set against the other. It will not harm a man to have a sword that would not cut off a nose, to not have al-Ṣamṣāma[695] in its place—everything he touches [with his sword] will be cleft. A group of the Muslims will desert them, then go to a land overflowing with sand—they will never see Paradise or their families ever! A group will be killed, and then God will send down His help upon a group, who will be the best people on earth on that day. A martyr from among them will receive the reward of seventy martyrs

Emperor Leo III: the Islamic recension of his story in Leiden Oriental Ms. 951 (2)," *Le Musèon* 103 (1990), pp. 225–64.

695 Sword of ʿAmr b. Maʿdikarib (d. *c.*21/641), Hoyland, *Swords*, pp. 27, 60 (the ʿAbbāsid caliph Hārūn supposedly still had the sword in the early ninth century).

from previous [battles],[696] while the remaining will get a double portion of reward. When they meet [in battle] a man will take the banner, and be killed, then another and be killed, then another and be killed,[697] until a ruddy man, with curly hair, a broad forehead, and a hooked nose will take it, and God will conquer for him. So he will kill them, defeat them, and sell their wealth, while holding on to his flag, not letting any one else bear it, until he reaches the bay [Bosphorus]. When he reaches the bay, he will advance to perform the ritual ablutions, then the water will retreat from him. He will come close, but the water will retreat yet further, so when he sees this, he will return to his mount, take it, then cross the bay, while the water is divided—half on his right and half on his left.[698] He will indicate to his supporters that they should cross, as God Most High has parted the sea for them just as He parted it for the Israelites. So they will cross, and come to a spring near a church on that side of the bay.[699] Abū Zura`a: "I saw this spring, and did my ritual ablutions in it—a sweet-water spring, so I did the ritual ablutions in it, and prayed two prostrations."[700] He[701] will say to his supporters: 'This is a matter for which God Most High has given permission, so say *allāhu akbar!* and *lā ilaha illā allāhu!* and *al-ḥamdu li-llāhi!* They will do it, and he will turn towards twelve towers (*burj*) of it [Constantinople], and they will fall to the ground. So they will enter it, and on that day kill its fighters, divide up its plunder, and leave it in ruins, never to be inhabited again. [259]

696 See my *Martyrdom in Islam* (Cambridge: Cambridge University Press, 2007), pp. 32–8 for those rewards.

697 Recalling the Battle of Mu'ta (6/627) in which three commanders successively took the flag, but were each killed until Khālid b. al-Walīd became commander: al-Bukhārī, *Ṣaḥīḥ*, iv, p. 268 (no. 2798).

698 Like Moses parting the Red Sea (Ex. 14; Q 20:78, 97, 28:40, 51:40).

699 Probably the Blachernae, to the northwest of Constantinople, which had a holy spring (thanks to Michael Decker for this identification).

700 This is the *ṣalāt al-khawf* (fear prayer), see al-Bukhārī, *Ṣaḥīḥ*, i, p. 256 (no. 942).

701 The commander of the Muslim army.

1216. `Abdallāh b. Mas`ūd: The Prophet said: There will be a truce between the Muslims and the Byzantines such that they will fight with them an enemy, and divide between them their spoils. Then the Byzantines will raid Persia (*Fāris*) with the Muslims, and kill their fighters and take their offspring captive. The Byzantines will say: "Divide the spoils with us, just as we divided with you," so they will divide the wealth and the pagan offspring, but the Byzantines will say: "Divide your offspring who you have taken," but they will say: "We will never divide the offspring of Muslims with you, ever!" So they will say: "You have betrayed us," and the Byzantines will return to their lord in Constantinople, then say: "The Arabs betrayed us, but we are more numerous than they, better prepared, and stronger, so aid us that we can fight them." He will say: "I do not like to betray them, for they have been victorious over us through the ages (*fī ṭūl al-dahr*)." So they will go the ruler of Rome[702] and inform him of this, whereupon he will send eighty banners[703]—under each banner there will be 12,000 [troops]—in the sea. Their lord will say to them: "When you have anchored on the coastlands of Syria, burn your boats so that you [are forced] to fight for your lives." So they will do that, and take the land of Syria, all of it, land and sea, other than Damascus and Mt. Mu`taq, and they will destroy Jerusalem.

Ibn Mas`ūd: "How many Muslims can Damascus contain?" The Prophet said: "By the One who holds my soul in His hand, it will contain as many Muslims as come to it, just as the womb contains a child." I said: "What is al-Mu`taq,[704] O Prophet of God?" He said: "A mountain in the land of Syria, close to Ḥimṣ, on a river called the Orontes. The offspring of the Muslims will be on the highest part of al-Mu`taq, while the Muslims are on the River Orontes and the polytheists are behind the

[702] Perhaps the pope.

[703] This is the Yemenite dialect word *ghayāya*, which appears for the more common *rāya* (see no. 1218).

[704] Changing from *mu`naq* for consistency; see no. 663.

River Orontes, fighting them day and night. So when the lord of Constantinople perceives this, he will send [troops] on the land to Qinnasrin[705] 600,000 [troops]. Then Yemenite provisions will come to them [the Muslims], a total of 70,000, who God has united their hearts in belief, together with 40,000 from Ḥimyar, such that they will come to Jerusalem (*bay al-maqdis*), fight the Byzantines, defeat them, and expel them from army-province to army-province, until they come to Qinnasrin, and the *mawālī*'s provisions will come to them."

I said: "What are the *mawālī*'s provisions, O Messenger of God?" He said: "They are your freedmen, and they are part of you—a group coming from the direction of Persia. They will say: 'You have acted in a chauvinistic/tribal manner, O Arabs, so we will not be with either of the two factions until you unite in your belief (*kalima*)'—so they will fight Nizār one day, Yemen one day, and the *mawālī* one day. Then the Byzantines will emerge into the valleys, and the Muslims will descend upon a river called so-and-so[706][260] bearing up patiently, while the polytheists are at a river called al-Ruqayya, which is the Black River,[707] so they will fight them [the Byzantines], while God Most High lifts His victory from both armies, and causes endurance (*ṣabr*) to descend on them, until a third of the Muslims are killed, a third flee and a third are left.

As to those killed, they are martyrs [with a rank of] ten of the martyrs of [the battle of] Badr,[708] as one of the martyrs of Badr will intercede for seventy, while the martyr of the the apocalyptic battles will intercede for seven hundred. As to the third that flee, they will divide into three groups: one third will join the Byzantines, saying: 'If God had any need of this religion [Islam], He would have aided it.' These are the

705 In northern Syria, southwest of Aleppo.
706 Most likely the Orontes River,
707 The River Halys (classical), today the Karasu (thanks to Michael Decker for this identification).
708 First major battle of Islam, 2/624, described in Q 8.

Arabs' deserters (*musallimat al-`arab*): [the tribes of] Bahrā', Tanūkh, Ṭayyī' and Salīḥ.[709] One third will say: 'The dwellings of our fathers, and grandfathers are better—they will never reach us there, and we will pass into the desert'; these are the Bedouin. One third will say: 'Everything is like its name, and the land of Syria (*sha'm*) is like its name, ill-omened (*shu'm*), so let us go to Iraq, the Yemen, and the Hijaz, where we will not fear the Byzantines.'

As to the third that will remain [on the battlefield], each one will go to the other, and will say: 'O God, God—put aside the tribal chauvinism (*`asabiyya*), and unite your belief together to fight your enemy, since you will never be victorious as long as you act in a tribal manner.' So they will gather together, and will swear allegiance that they will fight until they have joined their brothers who were killed. When the Byzantines will see those who joined them and [the number of] those killed, and the small number of the Muslims, a Byzantine will stand up between the two rows [of fighters], who will have with him a flag with a cross at the top of it, and cry out: 'The Cross is victorious, the Cross is victorious!' Then a Muslim who will have a flag will stand up between the two rows and cry out: 'Nay, God's Helpers (*anṣār Allāh*) and His friends (*awliyā'*) are victorious!'[710]

God Most High will be angered because of those who blasphemed by saying that the cross is victorious, then say: 'O Gabriel, support My servants!' so Gabriel will descend at the head of 100,000 angels, then He will say: 'O Michael, support My servants!' so Michael will go down at the head of 200,000

[709] All of whom were Christian originally, and most of whom had federate status with the Byzantines previously.

[710] Although this is an idealization, according to Ibn A`tham al-Kūfī, *Futūḥ* (Beirut: Dār al-Nadwa al-Jadīda, n.d. reprint of Haydārabād edn), vii, p. 302 after the failure at Constantinople in 717, Maslama was allowed to enter the city, where he took the cross from the major church (Hagia Sophia), and spirited it out of the city, to be speared by the soldiers.

angels, and He will say: 'O Isrāfīl, support My servants!' so Isrāfīl will go down at the head of 300,000 angels.[711] God will cause His help to descend upon the believers, and His wrath upon the unbelievers, so they will be killed and defeated.

The Muslims will go through the land of the Byzantines until they reach Amorium, while there will be a great number of people on its walls, saying: 'We have never seen a more populous nation than the Byzantines—how many we have killed and defeated, and yet how many there are in this city and on its walls!' But they will say: 'Give us safe conduct on the condition that we pay the head-tax (*jizya*) to you,' so they will accord the safe conduct to them and to all of the Byzantines on the condition they pay the head-tax.

Their outer regions will gather, then say: 'O Arabs, the Dajjāl is behind you, in your homes!' But the report will be false—so whoever of you will be among them, let him not throw away what he has, for it will be necessary for what remains. They will depart, but find the repart to be false.

The Byzantines will rise up against those Arabs in their lands, and kill them—not even leaving a single male or female Arab or child alive in the land of the Byzantines. This will reach the Muslims, so they will return, enraged for God, mighty and majestic, kill their fighters, and take their offspring captive. They will gather wealth, and every single city or fortress to which they lay siege [261] will be conquered for them in three days. Then they will descend upon the Bay, and the Bay will overflow, so the people of Constantinople will begin to say: 'The Cross has aided our sea for us, and the Messiah is our Helper!' But then they will wake to the Bay being dry, so that tents will be pitched on it, and the sea will withdraw from Constantinople. The Muslims will surround the city of unbe-

711 Gabriel, Michael (cf. Rev. 12:7) and Isrāfīl (see S.R. Burge [trans.], *Angels in Islam: Jalāl al-Din al-Suyūṭī's al-Ḥabā'ik fī akhbār al-malā'ik* [London and New York: Routledge, 2012], pp. 120–31).

lief on Friday night with praising God, saying *allāhu akbar*, and *lā ilaha illā allāhu* until the morning—there will not be a single sleeper or sitter among them. When the dawn rises, the Muslims will let out one *allāhu akbar!* and that which is between the two towers will fall down.

The Byzantines will say: 'Before we were merely fighting the Arabs, but now we are fighting our Lord, as He has devastated our city, and destroyed it for them.' So they will stay [be controlled] under their [the Muslims'] hands, and [the Muslims will] weigh out the gold in shields—dividing up the offspring until the portion of each man will be 300 virgins, taking pleasure with them as long as God wishes. Then the Dajjāl will emerge truly. God will conquer Constantinople at the hands of people who are the friends (*awliyā'*) of God, and God will lift death, sickness, and disease from them, until Jesus son of Mary descends upon them, and they will fight the Dajjāl together with him."

1217. Ka`b: After the conquest of Rome, no [war] ship will ever sail on the seas ever. He said: The fighting of the valleys (*al-a`māq*)[712] will be placed together with the tribulations because three tribes in their totality will join unbelief with their banners and a section of the non-Arabs (*ḥamrā'*)[713] will manifest [its true loyalty] and join with them also. Ka`b said: If it were not for three [things] I would not like to have lived an hour: The first of them is plunder of the Bedouin. They will be called to war during some of the apocalyptic battles, but they will say just as they said at the beginning of Islam the first time they were called to war: "Our wealth and our families kept us busy."[714] Those who answered, answered, but those who left, left; so when they will be called up a second time during the time of the apocalyptic battles they will refuse—then God will permit

[712] Correcting from *al-a`māl.*

[713] According to Ibn al-Athīr, *Nihāya*, i, p. 438 one of the preferred names for the non-Arabs.

[714] Q 48:11.

what He promised them in His Book: "Say to those of the Arabs who stayed behind: 'You will be called to (fight) a people of harsh violence.'"[715] This is the plunder of the Bedouin—and the one who misses out on the pillage-day of [the tribe of] Kalb will miss out indeed! And the second is that if I did not participate in the greatest apocalyptic battle—God has forbidden any metallic object from cowardice, so that even if a man strikes on that day with a skewer he will cut, and the third is that if I do not participate in the conquest of the city of unbelief; before it, the lowly will be great.

Ka`b: Who are those tribes who will join unbelief? Tanūkh, Bahrā', and Kalb, and more from Quḍā`a, and most of those *mawālī*. The *mawālī* of those tribes are the rebels (*yafa`āniyya*) of Syria,[716] meaning their deserters. [262]

1218. Ḥudhayfa: "The Messenger of God conquered conquests unlike any others since God Most High sent him." I said to him: "O Messenger of God, may you enjoy the conquest! so 'the war will lay down its burdens.'"[717] He said: "But, no! By the One who my soul is in His hand, before it there will be six characteristic [events] O Ḥudhayfa. One is my death." I said: "We belong to God and to Him we return!" "Then Jerusalem (*bayt al-maqdis*) will be conquered, then there will be a dissension in which two great bands will fight, and in which there will be much killing (*qatl*) and killing (*haraj*), even though their belief (*da`watuhumā*) will be the same. Then death will overcome you, and it will kill you suddenly like flocks die. Then wealth will be multiplied, and overflow such that a man will be called to 100 dinars, but scorn to take it.

Then a youth from the sons of the kings of the Banū al-Aṣfar will grow." I said: "Who are the Banū al-Aṣfar, O Messenger

[715] Q 48:16.

[716] This appears to be the Old South Arabian verb *yaf`*, "to rebel, to rise up against," (Biella, pp. 233–4; also Ibn al-Athīr, *Nihāya*, v, p. 299); which may also be Aramaic, cf. Jastrow, i, p. 586 "to lift one's face up against, to have the courage to rebuke."

[717] Q 47:4.

of God?" He said: "The Byzantines. He will grow up in a day the way a young boy grows in a month, and will grow up in a month the way a young boy grows in a year. When he reaches maturity, they will love him and follow him the way they never loved a king previously. Then he will rise in the midst of them, and say: 'Until when will we leave this band of Arabs continuing to target parts of you, when we are more in number and in provisions on land and sea than they? Until when will this be? So tell me what you think.'—and their nobles will begin to speak in their midst, and say: 'Yes, to whatever you think! the command is yours!'

So he will say: 'By the One by whom we swear[718] we will not leave them until we have caused them to perish.' So he will write to the islands of the Byzantines[719] and they will throw (supply) eighty banners (*ghayāya*) at him, under each banner 12,000 fighters—and *ghayāya* means 'banner'—so they will gather 760,000 fighters with him. He will write to each island, and they will send 300 ships, so he will sail in one of the ships, him and his fighters, with bravery and weapons, and everything, until they are thrown between Antioch and al-`Arīsh.[720]

The caliph of that day will send his horsemen with numbers, provisions, and what cannot be counted, so a preacher will speak among them saying: 'What do you think, give me your opinion, for I see this as a dreadful matter. I know that God Most High carries out His promise, and gives our religion victory over all religions.[721] But this is a terrible trial, and I think that maybe I and those with me should depart for the city of the Messenger of God [Medina]. I will send to Yemen and to all the Arabs[722] wherever they are. God helps those who He helps, and it will not harm us to leave this land for them

718 A rather clumsy cover for what would have been a Christian oath.
719 Presumably Sicily.
720 In the northern Sinai on the way to Egypt.
721 Cf. Q 9:33.
722 *Ilā al-`Arab . . . wa-ilā al-A`ārīb.*

until you see that which is prepared for you.'" The Messenger of God said: "Then they will expel you until you settle in my city [Medina], whose name is Ṭayyiba,[723] for it is the dwelling of the Muslims."

So they will settle [in it] and write to those Arabs who are around them. When their letter arrives, then they will answer it, such that Medina will be crowded. Then they will depart, as one gathering, as a military detachment, having sworn allegiance to their imam unto death. God will conquer for them, so they will break the sheaths of their swords, then they will pass as a military detachment, and the lord of the Byzantines will say: "These people desire death for this land, and they have come to you, when they are not hoping for life. So I am writing to them that [263] they should send me the non-Arabs who they have, and we can leave this land for them, as we have no need of it. If they do that, we will do that, but if they refuse, we will fight them until God decides between us."

When this issue will reach the ruler of the Muslims on that day, he will say to them: "Whoever of the non-Arabs who wants to go to the Byzantines from among us, let them do it." So a speaker from the *mawālī* will say: "God forbid—we desire Islam as a religion and as a substitute,"[724] then they will swear to the death as the Muslims had done previously. They will all go as one gathering, so when the enemies of God see them, they will desire [to fight], be angry, and energized. The Muslims will draw their swords, and break their sheaths—and the tyrant will be enraged at his enemies.

The Muslims will kill such numbers of them that the blood will reach the fetlocks of the horses. Then the rest of them will sail under an easy wind day and night until they think that they are powerless, but then God will send a gale-force wind against them, to return them to the place from which they

[723] A nickname for Medina.
[724] Cf. Q 3:85.

came. The hands of the Emigrants (*muhājirīn*) will kill them, so that not one will escape. At that, O Ḥudhayfa, "the war will lay down its burdens," and then you will live as long as God wishes. Then a report will come from the east of the Dajjāl, that he has emerged among us. [264] [725]

1219. Ka`b: The imam of the Muslims will be in Jerusalem, then he will send to Egypt and the Iraqis to ask them for aid, but they will not aid him. His post-courier will pass by the city of Ḥimṣ, and find its non-Arabs having locked up all the offspring of the Muslims who are inside. This will horrify him, so he will go leading those Muslims he can gather until he meets them[726] on the plains of Acre. Then he will fight them, and God will defeat them. The Muslims will demand that they take them to their own land, so he will go to Ḥimṣ and God will conquer it at his hands.

1220. Ḥassān b. `Aṭiyya[727]: The Byzantines will descend on the plain of Acre, and overcome Filasṭīn, the center of al-Urdunn, Jerusalem (*bayt al-maqdis*)—but they will not pass the Pass of Afīq—for forty days. Then the imam of the Muslims will go to them, and drive them to the Field of Acre. They will fight there until the blood reaches the fetlocks of the horses, then God will defeat them and kill them other than a small number who will go to Mt. Lebanon, then to a mountain in the land of the Byzantines.[728]

1221. Makḥūl: The Byzantines will traverse Syria for forty mornings—nothing will be safe from them other than Damascus and the high peaks of the Balqā'.[729]

1222. `Abd al-Raḥmān b. Salmān[730]: One of the Byzantine kings will

[725] Section break for pp. 264–6.

[726] Apparently a Byzantine landing expedition, see no. 1223.

[727] Ḥassān b. `Aṭiyya al-Muḥāribī, lived in Damascus, a *mawlā* of Persian extraction, lived also at Beirut, *fl.* 2nd/8th century.

[728] Here we see the route that subversive groups such as the Mardaites/Jarājima would use to get back and forth between along the coast the two empires.

[729] al-Muqaddasī, *Aḥsan al-taqāsim* (Beirut: Dār Ṣādir, n.d.), s.v.

[730] `Abd al-Raḥmān b. Salmān al-Ḥajarīal-Ru`aynī, lived in Egypt, *fl.* 2nd/8th century.

overcome all of Syria other than Damascus and `Ammān,[731] then they will be defeated, and will rebuild Caesarea in Anatolia.[732] It will be made into one of the army-provinces of the Syrians. Then a light will be manifest from `Adan Abyan.[733] [268]

1223. Tubay`: Then the Byzantines will send to you asking you for a peace (*ṣulḥ*), and so you will make peace with them. On that day a woman will cross the path to Syria in safety, and the city of Caesarea in Anatolia will be rebuilt. During that peace, Kūfa will be scraped like leather—that will be because of their failure to aid the Muslims. God knows whether in addition to their desertion there will be another event that will make raiding them permissible. You will ask the Byzantines for aid against them, and they will aid you, so you will set out until you camp on a field with hills (*marj dhī tulūl*), then one of the Byzantines will say: "By our Cross you have overcome, so give us our portion of the spoils—namely the women and the offspring." But they [the Muslims] will refuse to give to them the women and offspring, so they will fight, then set off and gather for the apocalyptic battle.

1224. Dhū Mikhbar, the nephew of the Negus [of Ethiopia]: I heard the Messenger of God saying: You will make a secure peace with the Byzantines, such that you and they will raid an enemy behind them.

1225. `Abdallāh b. `Amr: You will raid Constantinople three times: the first disaster will strike you, the second there will be a peace between you such that you will build a mosque in their city, and you will raid together an enemy beyond Constantinople. Then you will return, then raid it the third time, when God will conquer it for you.

1226. Dhū Mikhbar heard the Prophet saying: So you will set out,

[731] The future capital of Jordan.
[732] The present Turkish city of Kayseri in central Anatolia.
[733] Perhaps from a volcano.

after having been victorious and taken spoils, and settle on a field with hills. One of them will say: "The Cross is victorious!" but a Muslim will say: "Nay, God is victorious!" so the issue will be passed back and forth for a time, then the Muslim will leap upon their cross—since he is not far from it—and break it. They will rise up against him and kill him, so the Muslims will rise to their weapons, and then God will honor this band of Muslims with martyrdom. They will come to their king and say: "We have taken care of the bravery of the Arabs, then they betrayed us" so they will gather for the apocalyptic battle.

1227. Ka`b: The Byzantines will betray those in it [Constantinople?], then they will gather, and bring an army via the sea from Rome. Its commander will be called Camel (*al-jamal*), and one of his parents will be a jinn or it is said, a demon (*shayṭān*), and he will come in his ships until he descends at a monastery called Valley (`Umq) at Acre.

1228. Arṭāt b. al-Mundhir: When a city is built six miles from Damascus, then gird yourself for the apocalyptic battles. [269]

1229. Ka`b: He will emerge leading 6000 ships, then he will order the ships to be burned.

1230. Abū Hurayra: They will be burned until they will light the necks of camels during the night in the waste (*jusham*)[734] of Judhām.

1231. Abū Mūsā al-Asha`rī said to his people in Syria: "O [tribe of] Asha`rites, this is a warning to you with regard to farms and homes, for they are almost not appropriate for you. You should go with goats, roan horses, horses and long spears [instead]."

1232. Ibn Shihāb: The blue-eyed ones[735] of Rome are about to expel the community of Muḥammad from the growing places of wheat.

1233. Biṭrīq b. Yazīd al-Kalbī[736]—his uncle: `Urwa b. al-Zubayr said

[734] Lane, ii, pp. 427–8; read as *ḥismā* "unlucky" by Ibn `Asākir, *Tā'rīkh*, ii, p. 214.

[735] *Azāriq* most likely on the form of *afā`il*, but not attested as a color, so could be an otherwise unattested plural for *zawraq*, "small boat."

[736] Syrian, *fl.* 2nd/8th century.

to me, when his head and beard were snow-white, "O you of Syria, the Byzantines will surely expel you from your Syria, and horsemen from the Byzantines will stop on this mountain"—when he was on that day upon Mt. Sal`[737]—"so let the Medinans manage! Then God will send His help upon them."

1234. Ka`b: Twelve non-Arab kings will be present at the greatest apocalyptic battle, the least of them and [one with the] smallest army will be the lord of the Byzantines. God Most High has two treasures in Yemen—one of them He brought at the Battle of Yarmūk, as [the tribe of] Azd was a third of the people, and He will bring the other on the day of the greatest apocalyptic battle—70,000 carrying swords in sheaths of palm-fiber.

1235. `Abdallāh b. `Umar: "When the idol of Dhū al-Khalṣa[738] is worshipped [again], the Byzantines will be victorious over Syria. On that day they will send to the people of the acacia tree (Medina) asking them for aid, so they will come upon their young she-camels, meaning the Hijāzis." Al-Walīd said: "Yemen." Nu`aym said: "I doubt it." [270]

1236. `Abdallāh b. `Amr: Aid will come from the army-province, and area in between.

1237. Ka`b concerning His Word Most High, "You will be called to (fight) a people of harsh violence,"[739] he said: "The Byzantines on the day of the apocalyptic battle." Ka`b: "God scared the Bedouin at the beginning of Islam when they said: "Our wealth and our families kept us busy . . ."[740] so He said: "You will be called to (fight) a people of harsh violence," on the day of the apocalyptic battle. So they will say, just as they said at the beginning of Islam: "Our wealth and our families kept us busy

[737] Just to the north of Medina.

[738] An idol worshipped in the region between Mecca and Yemen in the pre-Islamic period (see no. 1639), venerated by the Yemenite tribes including Azd, Bajīla and Khatha`m Ibn al-Kalbī, *Kitāb al-aṣnām* (Cairo: Maṭba`at Dār al-Kutub al-Miṣriyya, 1995), pp. 34–7.

[739] Q 48:16.

[740] Q 48:11.

. . ." so the following verse will apply to them: "He will punish you (with) a painful punishment . . ."'[741] `Abd al-Raḥmān b. Yazīd narrated on that day, saying: "He spoke the truth." Continuing with his narration: "If I do not participate in the conquest of the city of unbelief, then I do not want to live, for God Most High on that day will forbid each metallic object from cowardice."

1238. Elders: There will be Bedouin on that day who will apostacize, and among them those who will turn away from helping Islam and their army in doubt, so when the Muslims conquer on that day, they will send a raid against those who deserted, the unbelieving, apostacizing band, and the deserting, doubting band, so the missing out is the one who misses out on despoiling them on that day.

1239. `Abdallāh b. Mas`ūd: At that fighting there will be a severe apostasy.

1240. `Abdallāh b. `Amr: "God will make that group which is victorious, victorious, but those who rule them will incite them to attack their enemy, but [also] men will rush into unbelief." Muḥammad: "I do not know whether the apostasy from Islam and the rushing into unbelief are separate."

1241. `Abdallāh b. `Amr: "Arab tribes in their entirety will join the Byzantines." I said: "Really, in their entirety?" He said: "Even their shepherds and their dogs." He said: "If God wills, O Abū Muḥammad," and rose angrily. So he said: "God has willed," and he wrote it.

1242. Sulaymān [271] b. `Abd al-Raḥmān b. Sunna[742] heard the Prophet saying: "A third will disbelieve, a third will doubt, and be swallowed up."

1243. Al-Qāsim Abū `Abd al-Raḥmān said: The deserting band of the Muslims in the valleys of Acre and Antioch—the earth will

[741] Q 9:39.

[742] Lived in Damascus, a *mawlā* to the Umayyads, d. 142/759–60.

open up for them, so they will enter it and never see paradise or return to their families ever.

1244. `Abdallāh b. `Amr: A third will be defeated—those are the worst of creation in the eyes of God, mighty and majestic.

1245. Abān b. al-Walīd al-Mu`ayṭī heard Ibn `Abbās narrating to Mu`āwiya, and asking him concerning the time, so he informed him, that a man from among them would rule at the end of time for forty years. The apocalyptic battles would be for the last seven years of his caliphate, but that he would die in the valleys grieved. Then a man from them with two moles would rule, and the conquest would be at his hands on that day.

1246. Ka`b: The caliph of the Muslims will be killed on that day leading 1400, every one of them a commander and the possessor of a flag—the worst disaster to happen to the Muslims after the time of the Prophet.

1247. Ibn `Abbās that he mentioned twelve caliphs, then the commander, and said: "By God, after that there are al-Saffāḥ, al-Manṣūr and al-Mahdi, who will hand it [the rule] over to Jesus son of Mary."

1248. Ka`b: They will fight fiercely in the valleys, so then victory will be lifted, and even endurance will be exhausted. Iron will be set against each other, until the horse will wade in blood up to his fetlocks for three days straight. Nothing will give them a break except for the night, until groups (*`amā'ir*) of people—meaning groups (*ṭawā'if*)—will say: "Islam was only for a (set period of) time and an end, so its time and end have been reached, so let's go back to homes of our fathers!" They will join unbelief, but our sons the Emigrants will remain, and a man from them will say: "O you, do you not see what these ones have done? Rise with us, and let us join God!" But no one will follow him, so he will walk to them coming towards them [the Byzantines], so they will rain spears upon him until his blood spatters on their armor. Then God will defeat them.

1249. Ka`b: This is the greatest [272] martyr ever in Islam other than Ḥamza b. `Abd al-Muṭṭalib,[743] so the angels will say: "O our Lord, will you not give us Your permission to help Your servants?" He will say: "I am more worthy of helping them!" and on that day he will pierce with His spear and strike with His sword—for His sword is His command[744]—and God Most High will defeat them, and He will present them their shoulders [in defeat],[745] and tread on them like a press is trod, so there will be no further Byzantines after it, either as a group or as a dominion.

1250. Arṭāt: When the lord of the roan horse appears in Alexandria and the land of Egypt, the Arabs will betake themselves to Yathrib (Medina) and the Ḥijāz, and will be exiled from Syria. Each tribe will join with its family, so God will send them an army. When it ends up between the two islands (Jazīratayn),[746] then a herald will call out: "Every pure (Arab) or one who is taking refuge with us among the Muslims should come out to us!" So the *mawālī* will be enraged, then swear allegiance to a man called Ṣāliḥ b. `Abdallāh b. Qays b. Yassār,[747] who will lead them out and encounter an army of the Byzantines, and kill them. Death will strike the Byzantines while they are on that day in Jerusalem (*bayt al-maqdis*), as they had taken it over, so they will die like locust. The lord of the roan horse will die, then Ṣāliḥ leading the *mawālī* will descend upon the land of Syria (*sūriya*), and enter Amorium after having laid it to siege.

Then they will besiege Qamūliya,[748] and conquer Byzantium

[743] See no. 1294.

[744] It is interesting that Nu`aym, who was imprisoned for his anti-Mu`atazilite beliefs, would allow such a tradition that avoids anthropomorphism of God's "sword" and instead interprets it as "His command" (see also no. 1349) much the same way as the Mu`tazilites were interpreting the anthropomorphisms in the Qur'ān.

[745] See Ibn Māja, *Sunan*, ii, p. 1296 (no. 3930) for this phrase with the meaning of "put them to flight."

[746] Northern Iraq.

[747] Otherwise unknown. The name might be chosen because of its meaning: Righteous one, son of the Servant of God, son of Qays, son of the Straight One.

[748] Probably Camuliana in Cappadocia (thanks to Michael Decker for this identification).

(*bizanṭiya*)—the voices of his army praising God in it will be loud, and he will divide its wealth among them in containers. He will be victorious over Rome, and take out from it the Gate of Zion,[749] an ark (*tābūt*) of onyx, in which are the earring of Eve and the cotton wrapper of Adam[750]—meaning his garment—and the decoration of Aaron. While they are in this state, a report [of the Dajjāl's appearance] will come to him, but it is false, then he will return.

1251. Arṭāt: So the first apocalyptic battle according to the word of Daniel will be in Alexandria,[751] they will appear with their ships, so the Egyptians will ask the Syrians for help, then they will meet in battle, and fight fiercely. The Muslims will defeat the Byzantines after a great effort, then they will stay in it [Alexandria], and gather a great number, advance, and descend upon Jaffa [in] Filasṭīn at the distance of ten miles. Its inhabitants will take protection with their offspring in the hills, then the Muslims will meet them in battle, be victorious over them, and kill their king.

The second apocalyptic battle: they will gather after their defeat a number greater than their first gathering, then advance and descend upon Acre, when their king, son of the one killed, will perish. Then the Muslims will meet in battle at Acre, but victory will be held back from them for forty days. So the Syrians will ask for help from the people of the garrison-cities,[752] but they will be slow about giving their help. But there will not be a single free or slave polytheist Christian who does not render aid to the Byzantines. A third of the Syrians will flee, a third will be killed, but then God will help the rest,

749 It is difficult to associate this with any specific Temple artifact.

750 The variants suggest that *kaghūta* should be read as *katūna* (probably from the Hebrew *kutonet*); see discussion in my *Studies in Muslim Apocalyptic*, pp. 56n84 (variants), p. 349.

751 No Daniel apocalypse known to me mentions Alexandria.

752 Presumably in Iraq.

and the Byzantines will be defeated in a way that no one has heard of previously, and they will kill their king.

The third apocalyptic battle in which those who had returned on the sea will return and those of them who had fled on land would join together, and they will crown the son of their king who was killed, who will be under-aged, not yet having night-emissions, but the love of him will be placed in their hearts. So he will advance leading all of those [273] did not advance with their first two kings.

They will descend upon the valleys of Antioch, while the Muslims will gather opposite them, then they will fight for two months. Then God will cause His victory to descend upon the Muslims, so they will defeat them and kill them, while they are fleeing, climbing the pass.[753] Then aid will come to them, so they will stop, slowing the Muslims, but there will be an attack against them [the Byzantines], and they [the Muslims] will kill them and their king. So the remainder of them will retreat, but the Emigrants will search after them, and kill them in a sweeping manner.

At that time the Cross will be seen to be false, and the Byzantines will depart to the peoples beyond them in Andalus,[754] but they will kill them, until they descend upon the paths. The Muslims will divide up into two halves: one half on the land towards the pass, while the other half sail on the sea. The Emigrants who are on the land will meet their enemy in the pass, but God will grant them victory over their enemy, defeating them more completely than in their earlier defeats.

The proclaimer (*al-bashīr*) will be sent to their brothers on the sea that "We will meet you at the City" [Constantinople] so God will cause them to travel in the easiest manner, until they besiege the City, conquer it, and destroy it. After that will be Andalus and the peoples, so they will gather and come to

[753] The Cilician Gates.

[754] Probably meaning Europe as a whole here.

Syria, but the Muslims will meet them in battle, where God, mighty and majestic, will defeat them.

1252. Ka`b: The Byzantines will cause seventy crosses to enter Jerusalem (*bayt al-maqdis*) until they destroy it. Obedience will continue, being under the control of a governor, as long there is a caliphate in the land of Jerusalem (*arḍ al-quds*) and in Syria and the lower part of the coastal region.

1253. God will be enraged against him,[755] and al-Ṣārifiyya,[756] Caesarea, and Beirut will be swallowed up by the earth because of it. The Byzantines will rule in Syria for forty days from the sea-coasts to Al-Urdunn and Baysān. Then there would be victory for the Muslims over them, so they will make it right such that their governance will roll over and all the land will be safe for seven [or] nine [years?].

Ka`b: The Iraqis will throw off their allegiance and obedience, and kill their commander from the Syrians. So the Syrians will raid them, and ask for aid from the Byzantines. After having made peace with the Byzantines before asking their aid, so they will give aid of 10,000 [troops] such that they will reach the Euphrates [River] and meet [in battle]. The victory will be for the Syrians over them [the Iraqis], then they will enter Kūfa and take its people prisoner. Then the Byzantines will say to the Syrians: "Let us participate [in dividing] the prisoners you have taken," but they will say: "As for the Muslims, there is no way! But we will divide up the wealth with you." The Byzantines will say: "You were only victorious because of the Cross," but the Muslims will say: "Nay, through God and His Messenger we were victorious over them." So this matter will pass back and forth between them, so the Byzantines will be enraged. A man from the Muslims will go to the Cross and break it, so they will dis-

[755] It (or him, in which case it would more likely be the caliph) is not clear here. This text may be garbled.

[756] Probably Sarefa, later called Sarafand, between Sidon and Tyre in Lebanon.

perse, and the Byzantines will retreat to a river that separates between the two [armies].

The Byzantines will break the peace, and kill the Muslims in Constantinople,[757] then the Byzantines will depart [274] to the plain of Ḥimṣ. The people of Ḥimṣ will come out to them, but the non-Muslims (*a`ājim*) will lock the gates of the city of Ḥimṣ against them. The king of the Byzantines will lay siege, as the protective [defenders] will not be able to pass the bridge below the Monastery of Bahrā'.[758] The Byzantines will say to the Muslims: "Leave us Ḥimṣ, for it is the place of our fathers," and so they will fight until the blood reaches the middle seven stones, the speckled ones—then they will defeat the Byzantines.

The Muslims will return to Ḥimṣ and fasten their horses to the olive trees, then place mangonels (*majānīq*) against them (the walls), and destroy the Masḥal Monastery's church.[759] Then the Muslims will conquer Ḥimṣ because of a Jewish man [opening] its furthest right western gate or through the stopped-up gate between the Damascus Gate and the Jews' Gate. The Emigrants will enter it [Ḥimṣ], and a group of its defenders will flee to the Monastery of Banū Asad.[760] The Muslims will kill the non-Muslims who are in it, destroy a third, burn a third, and then drown a third. Syria will continue to be settled as long as Ḥimṣ is [settled].

1254. Elders: A spring in the hill of Dhū Mayyan[761] will burst and it will overflow, drowning Ḥimṣ or most of it, and it is to the east of Ḥimṣ by ten miles.

1255. Abū `Āmir al-Alhānī: I was in a village, and then al-Ḥārith

757 Al-Muqaddasi, *Ahsan al-taqasim*, p. 124–5; trans. Collins, *The Best Divisions*, pp. 124–5 states that Maslama b. `Abd al-Malik built a mosque in Constantinople; also Ibn al-Faqih, *Buldan*, p. 190.

758 According to nos. 1258-59 located on a hill to the northwest of Ḥimṣ.

759 According to Ibn `Asākir, lx, p. 399 Mu`āwiya stayed there.

760 Note how both this and the Bahrā' Monastery are named for Christian Arab tribes from the area of Ḥimṣ.

761 Unidentified other than through the text.

b. Abī Ana`m came to me when it was noon, and the sun's heat was beating down, so I said: "O uncle, what is bringing you at this time?" He said: "I was exploring this river which passes by the Jews' Gate, then I lost its course, which got mixed up in some fields. So, in your village is there a man who has seniority and age?" I said: "Yes, there is an elderly shaykh, who does not go out because of age," so we went to him. Al-Ḥārith asked him about this river-branch, so the shaykh said: "I heard my father saying: "Its water is clear; if a pregnant woman drinks from it, then what is in her belly (womb) will go mad, and if it touches a tree then the leaves will fall off." This perturbed the people, so they sought after it, then a [work]man came and they agreed upon a wage for him. He called for a chunk (lit. a brick) of lead, suet, pitch and wool, then they went to Sarbal,[762] and made what they made, so that the water was concealed/blocked up.

Abū `Āmir said: I heard some of the Companions of the Prophet saying: "This is one of the valleys of Hell" (*jahannam*), and Ḥimṣ will be half drowned because of it—the other half will be struck with fire.

1256. Ka`b: The Byzantines will ask for aid from the second-tier nations, and [peoples speaking] different tongues will gather forces for them. The people of Rome, Constantinople and Armenia will gather for them—even the shepherds and the ploughmen—will be enraged for the king of the Byzantines, and they will come with many peoples—other [275] than the Byzantines there will be ten kings, their sum total will reach 180,000.

The Arabs will come together one to another from the corners of the earth, and the two wings of Egypt and Iraq will gather in Syria, since it is the head.[763] The king of the Byzantines will advance on a platform carried upon [between?] two mules, so

[762] Mentioned as being to the southeast of Ḥimṣ in no. 1273.

[763] See no. 617.

they will send their armies and surround Syria entirely, other than Damascus. The Muslims will come to them, their foot-soldiers, and meet them in such-and-such a valley [with] four battlefields.[764] The two groups will go to a river whose waters are cold in the summer and warm in the winter.[765] Its waters will be deep and copious on that day, and the Emigrants will camp near it [the river], while the Byzantines are on the other side of it. They will tie their horses to trees near their packs and prepare for battle so that they can move to the land of Qinnasrin. Their camp will be between Antioch and Ḥimṣ, while the Arabs are between Buṣrā and Damascus, and what is behind them.[766] The Byzantines will burn every single piece of wood, firewood or tree. The two gatherings will meet near a small river between Aleppo and Qinnasrin.[767]

Then they will go to a valley where there is room for fighting. Whoever fights that day, let him be in the first charge, if not then in the second, third, fourth or the last—if he has no choice, then let him stay in the common camp (*fusṭāṭ al-jamāʿa*) and not leave it, for the hand of God will be upon them.[768] Whoever flees that day will not breathe the breath of paradise. The Byzantines will say to the Muslims: "Give us our land, and return to us every non-Arab foreigner (*aḥmar*)[769] and half-breed (*hajin*) of yours, and the sons of the concubines."

The Muslims will say: "Whoever wants to join you can; whoever wants to defend his religion and himself can," so the half-breeds, the [sons of] concubines and the non-Arab foreigners (*ḥamrāʾ*) will be enraged.

They will assign a banner to a man of the non-Arab

764 Perhaps Dābiq, but not stated explicitly.
765 The Orontes River?
766 Northern Jordan.
767 Probably the Quwayq or Aleppo River, a little to the north of Qinnasrin (present day Ḥāḍir).
768 Presumably the Byzantines.
769 Lane, ii, p. 642 (left col.), or emancipated slaves.

foreigners (*ḥamrā'*)—he is the sultan Abraham and Isaac promised would come at the end of time —and they will swear allegiance to him. Then they will fight one by one with the Byzantines and be victorious over the Byzantines. The emigration of the Arabs will turn toward the Byzantines [then], and their hypocrites (*munāfiqūn*), when they see the victory of the *mawālī* over the Byzantines. Tribes in their totality, most of them Quḍā`a and the non-Arab foreigners (*ḥamrā'*), will flee until they place their banners among them [the Byzantines]. Then companions will cry back and forth to distinguish [between them]—those who joined what they joined will cry: "The Cross is victorious."

The best Arabs on that day are the Yemenites, the Emigrants—Ḥimyar, Alhān, and Qays. Those will be the best of people on that day. Qays on that day will kill but not be killed, and Jadīs the same. Al-Azd will kill but not be killed, but the army of the Muslims will divide into four groups: one will be martyred, one will endure, one will raid [the enemy], and one will join the enemy.

The Byzantines will be fierce against the Arabs, so their righteous Qurashi Yemenite caliph[770] will advance leading 3000 [troops], so they will appoint a commander over them. He will have seventy commanders with him, all of them righteous, and in possession of banners. The one who will be killed, and the one who is patient on that day will receive the same reward. Then God will set upon the Byzantines a wind and birds, who will strike their faces with their wings and gouge out their eyes. The earth wil be split asunder for them, so they will stutter in a ravine after lightening strikes and earthquakes hit them.

God will support the patient ones, and necessitate for them a reward just as He necessitated for the Companions of Muḥammad, and He will fill their hearts and breasts with

770 See no. 1099.

courage and bravery, so that when the Byzantines will see the fewness of the patient group they will desire [to fight them] and say: "Ride every hoofed animal, run them down, and finish them off!"

A rider from the Muslims will rise upon his saddle, and look right, left and forward, but not see any edge [276] or end [to their armies], so he will say: "The mass of people has come, and there is no aid for you other than God, so die and cause [others] to die!" They will swear caliphal allegiance to a man from among them, so he will order them to pray the morning prayers, then God Most High will look at them, and cause His victory to descend upon them, saying: "None other than Myself, My angels and My Emigrant servants remain. Today is the feast of the birds and the wild animals—surely I will feed them them flesh of the Byzantines and their helpers, and give them their blood to drink."

So your Lord will open His weapons armory (*khizānat silāḥihi*), which is in the fourth heaven,[771] and His weapons of might and power (*jabrūt*), and cause the angels to descend upon them. The Muslims will draw their bows, and break the sheaths of their swords, pointing them at them [the Byzantines], and turn the tips of their spears towards them.

Your Lord will reach out His hand to the weapons of the unbelievers and take it so that it will not cut, and tie their hands to their necks. The weapons of the Unitarians (*al-muwaḥḥidīn*) will be set against them, so that even if a believer struck with a tent-peg, he would cut [the enemy].

Gabriel and Michael will come down, and defend them, leading angels, so God will defeat them and drive them like flocks until they end up back with their kings. Their kings will fall down upon their faces from fear, and tear their crowns

771 Traditionally the heaven associated with Enoch (or Idrīs), see al-Ṭabarī, *Jami` al-bayan*, xv, pp. 14–15 (Night Journey and Ascension to Heaven), but in other versions Aaron.

from their heads, then horse-riders and foot soldiers will tread upon them until they kill them, until their blood reaches the fetlocks of the horses—the earth will not be able to absorb it—and all the blood will reach the fetlocks of the horses, as it is an apocalyptic battle. This is the slaughter which will be the end of the Byzantines' dominion, so then God Most High will send angels to all of its islands to inform them of the killing of the Byzantines.

1257. `Imrān b. Sulaym al-Kalā`ī: What a woman prepares normally is better for her than a tank for ablution and two shoes—woe to those fattened (women), but blessed are the poor. Have your women wear light slippers as shoes, and tell them to walk in their houses, for they are about to be expelled from all of that.

1258. Abū al-Zāhiriyya:The Byzantines will end up at the Monastery of Bahrā', and at that there will be the ring (*ḥalqa*),[772] so they will not pass it going towards Ḥimṣ, then the Muslims will return towards them and defeat them.

1259. Abū Baḥriyya[773]: The Byzantines will go until they descend upon the Monastery of Bahrā', until their king will place his Cross and his standards (*bunūd*)[774] on this hill, the Hill of Faḥmāyā (Coal-Hill).[775] Then the first part of their destruction will be at the hands of a man from Antioch, who will summon the people, then delegate Muslim men, so he will be the first one to attack them, then God Most High will defeat them.

1260. Elders: When it is like that, then stay in your homes, O people of Ḥimṣ, for your perishing will be at the Hill of Faḥmāyā—it will not come to you! So whoever is steadfast will be saved, but whoever goes to Damascus will die of thirst. [277]

1261. Abū `Āmir al-Alhānī: I went out with Tubay` from the Rastan

[772] Presumably some type of defensive or armored ring.

[773] `Abdallāh b. Qays al-Kindī al-Tarāghimī, lived in Ḥimṣ, a leader of raids against the Byzantines, said to have been a loyalist to `Uthmān, *fl.* 1st/7th century.

[774] Persian.

[775] Perhaps the present-day Mushrifiyya, a small hill located to the northeast of Ḥimṣ

Gate, so then he said: "O Abū `Āmir, when these two garbage heaps are scattered, then take your family out of Ḥimṣ." I said: "Do you think that I wouldn't?" He said: "When Tortosa[776] is entered (conquered)[777] and 300 martyrs are killed beneath the grapevine, then take your family out of Ḥimṣ." I said: "Do you think that I wouldn't?" He said: "So when you see the Camel's Head {from Andalus}[778] leading the naval forces (*qiṭa`*),[779] then they sink[780] between Jaffa and the Bald Mountain (al-Aqra`),[781] then take your family out of Ḥimṣ." I said: "Do you think that I wouldn't?" He said: "Then what happens to the people of Ḥimṣ will happen to you." I said: "And what will happen to them?" He said: "At that time they will be locked up."[782] Then he walked until we came to the Masḥal Monastery. He said: "O Abū `Āmir, do you see this wood? It will be [used as] mangonels for the Muslims on that day." I said: "How long between entering Tortosa and the emergence of the Camel's Head?" He said: "There will not be more than three years completed—this will be the first apocalyptic battle."

1262. Ka`b: I met Abū Dharr when he was walking from a

[776] Present-day Ṭartus—from the Umayyad period: "Mu`āwiya took out the war spoils of Cyprus to Ṭarṭūs (Tortosa) of the plain of Ḥimṣ. Then he placed them in a church (*kanīsa*) called the Church of Mu`āwiya. Then he began to speak to the people, and said: 'I am dividing your war spoils into three portions: a portion to you, a portion to the ships [sailors, Christians], and a portion to the Copts—since there would be no power to raid by sea if it were not for the ships and the Copts.' Abū Dharr [al-Ghifārī] began to speak: 'I swore to the Messenger of God that no blame would take me in the sight of God—O Mu`āwiya, are you dividing a portion to the ships, when they are our property, and a portion to the Copts when they are part of us (*ajzā'unaā*)?' Mu`āwiya divided according to what Abū Dharr said." (al-Ṭabarānī, *Musnad*, ii, pp. 73–4 (no. 940), also 120–1 (no. 1029).

[777] Presumably by the Byzantines.

[778] Addition from MM and DKI. Presumably the Camel's Head was a name for a Byzantine or foreign commander, see nos. 1227, 1267.

[779] This appears as *qila`*, "ships' sails" in no. 1268.

[780] Appearing as *farraqaha* "to disperse" in no. 1268, which is more plausible.

[781] A mountain close to the mouth of the Orontes River in northern Syria (see nos. 1267, 1288).

[782] Both MM and DKI read: 'Its non-Arabs (*a`ājim*) will lock them [the gates] against the offspring and women of the Muslims.'

sitting-session of Abū `Irbāḍ, while he was crying, so Ka`b said to him: "What is causing you to weep, O Abū Dharr?" He said: "I weep for my religion." So Ka`b said: "Today you weep, but I just parted from the Messenger of God a bit ago, while the people were well and Islam was new" until he departed from the Jews' Gate, then he rose upon the garbage heap, and said: "O Abū Dharr, there will come upon the people of this city a day in which a fright will come to them from the coast-land, so they will go to them [the enemy], and meet them at Solomon's Pass[783] and fight them. God will defeat them, so they will kill them in its dry valleys and mountain paths. While they are doing this, a report will come to them from behind them that its people have locked up inside of it the offspring of the Emigrants, so they will leave for it, then they will cordon it until God will conquer it for them."

If the people of this city knew of the benefit in the Masḥal Monastery for them on that day, they would visit it with oil with which to dowse its wooden beams. When God conquers it, there will not be a single possessor of books who will remain—such that an Emigrant man will kill a Christian man, even if he has just been yanked from his mother's breasts, until the canal from Ḥimṣ in which (sewage) water flows will run with blood in such a way that nothing else has ever mixed with it.

1263. Some of our elders: A man came to us, while I was living with one of my son-in-laws at `Arqa[784] and said: "Is there a place to stay for the night?" so they brought him in, and suddenly he was a man worthy of good [278] when you looked at him, as if he was seeking knowledge. He said: "Do you have knowledge of Sūsiya?"[785] They said: "Yes." He said: "Where is it?"

[783] Presumably the Ḥimṣ Gap, the major route between the sea-coast and the interior of Syria. The area of Ba`lbak was sometimes known as "Solomon's cities," so this may have been the origin of the term.

[784] A town about twenty miles to the east of Tortosa.

[785] Possibly the town of Sūsiya [= Hippos] in northern Lebanon.

We said: "It is a ruin towards the sea." He said: "Does it have a spring to which one descends on steps, and whose water is cold, sweet?" They said: "Yes." He said: "Is there a ruined fortress on the side of it?" They said: "Yes." We said: "Who are you, O `Abdallāh?" He said: "I am a man from [the tribe of] Ashja`." They said: "What do you care about what you have mentioned?" He said: "The Byzantine boats will advance from the sea until they will descend close to that spring, whereupon they will burn their ships.[786] Then the people of Damascus will send to them, and they will stay three [days], with the Byzantines calling them to evacuate this land.

But then they will refuse, so the Emigrants will fight them. On the first day the killing will be in both groups, but the second among the enemy, and on the third God will defeat them. None but a few will reach their ships from among them, since they will have burned many of them. They will say: 'We will not leave this land,' but God will defeat them. The line of the Muslims on that day will be facing the ruined tower. While they are in that situation, after God has defeated their enemy, then somebody will come from behind them and inform them that the people of Qinnasrin have started to advance towards [i.e. retreating towards] Damascus, that the Byzantines have attacked them. There is an appointment with them on land and sea. The refuge of the Muslims on that day will be Damascus."

1264. Ka`b narrated to him[787] that in the west there is a queen who reigns over one of the nations—that nation flaunts its Christianity,[788] and she will construct ships intending to

[786] According to al-Musharraf b. al-Murajjā', *Faḍā'il*, p. 226 (no. 333) when the caliph Sulaymān heard of a Byzantine raid on these plains, taking a female captive, he decided to attack Constantinople.

[787] Jubayr b. Nufayr al-Ḥaḍramī.

[788] One is tempted to see this tradition as perhaps being a distant echo of a powerful Carolingian (such as Bertrada of Laon, d. 783, mother of Charlemagne) or perhaps an English queen (such as Eadburh of Wessex, d. 802), or more distantly Lampagie, daughter of Duke Eudes of Aquitaine (who is said to have been sent to Damascus as a captive, see http://fmg.ac/Projects/MedLands/AQUITAINE.htm).

attack this community (Muslims), such that after they will have finished building them and garrisoning them with soldiers, she (the queen) will say: "We will sail whether God wills or not!" Therefore, God will send a gale-force wind and destroy her ships. She will continue to build [ships] like this and to speak like this—and God will continue to act like this towards her—until He will wish to permit her to sail. She will say: "We will sail if God wishes!" so she will sail with her ships—they will be 1000 ships the like of which has never been put to sea—and they will sail until they have passed the land of the Byzantines.

The Byzantines will be terrified of them, and they will say: "Who are you?" They will say: "We are a nation claiming [to believe in] Christianity, intending [to attack] a community which overcomes nations—whether [it be] to plunder them or to be plundered by them." The Byzantines will say: "These (the Muslims) are those who have destroyed our country, killed our men and enslaved our sons and women—so help us against them!" Thus they will aid them (the Byzantines) with 350 ships, and so they will sail until they have anchored at Acre. They will disembark from their vessels and burn them, saying: "This is our land; we will live here and die here."

Then the crier will to the imam of the Muslims, who on that day will be in Jerusalem (*bayt al-maqdis*), and say: "An enemy has descended against whom we have no ability," so he will send a post-courier to Egypt, and to Iraq asking them for aid.

Most probably if there is a historical kernel to this tradition it focuses upon three major themes: a powerful queen, who is obviously Christian, who has access to sea-power, and who is unknown to the Byzantines, and should be identified with the region of France. This story also is topically related to the traditions about a king (no. 1288) or the One with the Mane (nos. 1300, 1857), which may be echoes of Charlemagne. If one would make the claim that France is distant from Syria, then one should note that both the Venerable Bede (d. 735) in England, and the historian called Fredegar (up till 642) were quite well informed about the Islamic Empire in spite of the distance.

The post-courier will come from Egypt saying: "The Egyptians say: 'We are in the presence of the enemy, but your enemy has only come from the direction of the sea, while we are on the coastline of the sea, so would we fight for your offspring, but leave our offspring to the enemy?'" Likewise, the Iraqis will say: "We are in the presence of the enemy, so would we fight for your offspring, but leave our offspring to the enemy?"

So the post-courier will pass by the one who is coming from Iraq in Ḥimṣ, and find that those non-Muslims (*a*`ājim) in it have locked in the offspring of the Muslims, as the report had come to them that the Arabs had [279] perished—even though they disbelieved in the report that had come to them, it came to them three times.

The ruler will say: "Should we expect anything other than that every city in Syria will lock up those who are inside?" He will rise among the people, praising and extolling God, then saying: "We have sent to your brothers, the Iraqis and the Egyptians, to aid you, but they have refused to aid you." He will conceal the issue of Ḥimṣ and say: "There is no aid for you other than from God Most High. Go toward your enemy," so they will meet in battle on the plain of Acre. By the One who holds the soul of Ka`b in His hand, they will not be wait for the Syrians for as much time as it takes to wrap yourself in your cloak until they are defeated.

They will come to the coastlands and not find any succor there, so it is as if I am looking at the Muslims striking at their necks on the plain of Acre until they reach Mt. Lebanon [fleeing]. Only about 200 men from among them will get away, reaching Mt. Lebanon so they can reach the mountains of the Byzantines' lands. The Muslims will turn to Ḥimṣ, and besiege it. They surely will cast the heads of those who you know from it towards you [using the mangonels]—although perhaps it will just be one or two heads—so let it be left in ruins from that day, uninhabited. They will say: "How can we dwell in a place in which our women were ravished!"

1265. Al-Saybānī[789]: Twelve kings, the least of whom is the Byzantine king, will gather under the sycamore trees of Jaffa.[790]

1266. Ka`b: al-Manṣūr is a Mahdi, upon whom the inhabitants of the heavens and the earth will pray, and the birds of the heavens. He will be tested for twenty years by fighting the Byzantines and the apocalyptic battles, then will be killed as a martyr during the greatest apocalyptic battle—he and 2000 with him, all of them commanders and possessors of banners. The Muslims will not be struck with a greater disaster than this after the [death of the] Messenger of God.

1267. Abū `Āmir al-Alhānī: I went out with Tubay` from the Rastan Gate, then he said: "O Abū `Āmir, O Abū `Āmir, when these two garbage heaps are scattered, then take your family out of Ḥimṣ." I said: "Do you think that I wouldn't?" He said: "When Tortosa is entered (conquered) and 300 martyrs are killed, then take your family out of Ḥimṣ." I said: "Do you think that I wouldn't?" He waid: "So when the Camel comes from al-Andalus leading 1000 ships' sails, then he disperses them between Bald Mountain and Jaffa, then take your family out of Ḥimṣ." I said: "What is going to happen to them?" He said: "Its non-Muslims will lock it with the offspring and women of the Muslims inside." He said: Then we went around the walls, until we entered the Masḥal Monastery, so he said: "Do you see this wood? On that day it will be mangonels for the Muslims." I said: "How much time is it between the Camel's Head and Tortosa?" He said: "There will not be more than three years in total."

1268. Then he said: There will be three expeditions for the Byzantines, so that is the first one. In the second an army will come from the sea in 1000 ships' sails, and they will disperse to each army-province its share, and set a time for them to

[789] Yaḥyā b. Abī `Amr al-Saybānī.

[790] Nasir-i Khusraw (in the 1040s), Wheeler Thackston, trans., *Nasir-i Khusraw: Book of Travels* (Costa Mesa, CA: Mazda, 2001), p. 25 mentions the groves of figs and olives around Jaffa.

emerge on a single day. When it is that day, then each group will emerge towards the Muslims who are beside them, burn their boats, and make their sails into tents, then [280] fight. The trial and fighting will be intense in the entirety of Syria, so that neither side wll be able to dominate the other. God will hold back His victory, set the weapons [against each other], and the people will weaken—to such a state that the Muslims will fortify themselves in al-Madā'in.[791]

The letter of the Byzantines will order [them] to be enclosed[792] in the midst of al-Madā'in, and at that time the non-Muslims (*a`ājim*) will lock the gates of Ḥimṣ with the Muslims' offspring and women inside.

The fighting in the land of Filasṭīn will rage for four days consecutively. Abū al-Zāhiriyya said: "If you want, I will inform you about the first and the last day of the four, so God Most High will conquer for the Muslims on the fourth day, and the Byzantines will be defeated. Then the Muslims will follow them and kill them in every plain and mountain until the remnants of the Byzantines enter Constantinople. It will not be long then until they send to you asking you for a peace."

1269. Ka`b: You will make a peace with them for ten years and during this peace (*ṣulḥ*) a woman will cross the pass[793] in safety, and you together with the Byzantines will raid beyond Constantinople against an enemy of theirs and be victorious over them. When you have finished and seen Constantinople and seen that you have reached your families and people of your peace [the Byzantines?], then you together with them will raid al-Kūfa and scrape it like leather. Then you together with the Byzantines will also raid some of the easterners, and you [pl.] will demonstrate patience against them—take their offspring and women prisoners, and take wealth. Then

791 No Syrian city is known with this name. Presumably it is a fortified location not identical with any of the major Muslim settlements in Syria.

792 Reading *yuḥẓar* with MM in place of SZ *yakhṭuru*.

793 Or the path, of the Cilician Gates.

while you are camped returning, you will begin to divide the spoils. The Byzantines will say: "Give us our portion of the offspring and the women," but the Muslims will say: "This is not possible for us in our religion; but take from the rest of the things." The Byzantines will say: "We will only take from the sum total." The Muslims will say: "You will never get it." The Byzantines will say: "You were only victorious because of us and our cross," but the Muslim will say: "Nay, because God aided his religion." While they are doing this, wrangling back and forth, they will lift up the cross so the Muslims will be enraged, and a man will leap upon it and break it. Some of the group will move away; and there will be a short fight between them.

The Byzantines will depart angrily to their king and say: "The Arabs betrayed us and denied us our rights, broke our cross and slaughtered among us." Their king will be terribly enraged and gather together a huge gathering of the Byzantines and make peace with all the peoples (*umam*) they could. This is the first of the great apocalyptic battles—then they will come and the Muslims will hasten towards them. Their caliph then will be a Yemenite. Ka`b said: "He is a Yemenite, and is also from Quraysh." They will fight on the forward part of the land[794]—the Byzantines will have the upper hand over the Muslims so they will expel them from their camp, and it will be like that every time they meet in battle: the Byzantines will have the upper hand over the Muslims, until the news [of their defeat] reaches Ḥimṣ. They will continue until the people of Ḥimṣ see the dust (*al-ghabara wa-l-rahj*) [of the advancing Byzantine armies] with their own eyes; then the people of Ḥimṣ—the offspring and the women, among them the weak—will flee pell-mell towards Damascus. Between Ḥimṣ and Eagle's [281] Pass[795] thousands of the people will die of barefootness and

[794] Presumably the border regions.
[795] Above Damascus, to the north, on the road to Ḥimṣ.

thirst. A woman will beg, just as she would beg a horseman, "Have you not seen so-and-so daughter of so-and-so?" and the man will say: "O servant of God (`*abd allāh*) I saw her in such-and-such a place where she had bound her feet with her veil since they were dripping with blood."

The fight between the Byzantines and the Muslims will rage—victory will be held back and weapons will be set upon each other—nothing struck will be unaffected. The caliph of the Muslims will be killed then among seventy commanders on one day, and the people will swear allegiance to a man of Quraysh. Every single possessor of a plot of land (*faddān*)[796] or tent-pole (`*amūd*)[797] will join the Byzantines, and tribes in their entirety with their banners will join the Byzantines. The Muslims will be patient/constant—until one part will join with unbelief, another will be killed and a third will flee, [but a fourth] will be victorious. The Byzantines will say: "O Arabs, we know that you don't want to fight us—come and surrender to us those who are from us (*man kāna aṣluhu minnā*) originally, and go to your lands with your *mawālī*." The Arabs will say to the Byzantines: "They heard what you have to say; they know [what you want]." Then the *mawālī* will be enraged—this is the wrath of the *mawālī* which is known—and the *mawālī* will say to the Arabs: "Did you think that we have something of Islam in us?" and they will swear allegiance to a man of them, and turn away and fight from their side while the Arabs fight from [their] side, and God will grant the victory—the king of the Byzantines will perish then and the Byzantines will be defeated.

Men will rise from their saddles on the backs of their horses and cry out with loud voices: "O Muslims! God will never grant a victory like this again if we turn from it," and so the Muslims will catch them, and kill them in every plain and

796 Syriac, "a yoke, plough."
797 Peasants and nomads.

hill. Not a single buried treasure nor city will distract them until they camp in front of Constantinople. The Muslims will find a community of the people of Moses[798] there to join the victory with them. The Muslims will say *allāhu akbar!* from one side, and the wall will be split. The people will rise and enter Constantinople, and while they are guarding their possessions and captives, fire will fall from the heavens on a side of the city, and it will blaze up. The Muslims will leave with what they gathered and camp in Chalcedon (al-Qarqadūna).[799] While they are dividing up the spoils God has granted them, they will hear that the Dajjāl has appeared in the midst of their families, and so they will leave and find the news false. They will go to Jerusalem (*bayt al-maqdis*) and it will be their refuge at the Dajjāl's appearance.

1270. Abū al-Zāhiriyya: The Byzantines will end up at the Bahrā' Monastery, and at that time will be the pell-mell flight—but they will not pass it towards Ḥimṣ, then the Muslims will return to them and God Most High will defeat them.

1271. Ka`b said [282] to Mu`āwiya b. Abī Sufyān: An issue will overcome the people in Ḥimṣ so that it will terrify them into stampeding, such that they will leave it in a rush, having left everything from this world behind them—to the extent that a woman will leave, being followed by her girl, yanking on her garment, saying: "Where? Where?" 70,000 of them will die of thirst between Damascus and the Eagle's Pass.[800] [It will be] such that a man will begin to seek his family in the Vale of Ghūṭa,[801] "Who saw her, who noticed her??" So someone will say: "I saw her in a waste, carrying her child on her shoulder, having wrapped her veil around her leg, but I do not know

[798] Jews?

[799] In the text *farqadūna*.

[800] This is a change from nos. 1269 and 1273, and there may be a mistake here for Ḥimṣ in place of Damascus. The people would be coming from Ḥimṣ, and the Eagle's Pass is just above Damascus.

[801] Valley of Damascus.

what she did after that." "How will it be with you, O people of Ḥimṣ, when you will ride with those lighter women of yours in front of you, but leave the heavier women behind for your enemy?" When the people heard this narration in that time, when they saw a heavier woman, they would curse her with the curses of God.

1272. Ka`b: The Byzantine king will descend upon the Bahrā' Monastery, so there will be a battle such that the blood will reach the speckled (*abraṣ*) white huge stone.

1273. Ka`b: Between Ḥimṣ and the Eagle's Pass 70,000 will perish from turmoil, so whoever from among you lives to see that, let him go on the eastern road from Ḥimṣ to Sarbal, then from Sarbal to al-Khumayrā',[802] and then from al-Khumayrā' to al-Dhukhayra, then from al-Dhukhayra to al-Nabk,[803] then from al-Nabk to al-Quṭayfa,[804] and from al-Quṭayfa to Damascus. Whoever takes this road will have a continuous supply of water.

1274. Ka`b: You will continue to be well, as long as the people of al-Jazīra do not ride down the people of Qinnasrīn, and the people of Qinnasrīn do not ride down the people of Ḥimṣ—it is like that, then there will be a pell-mell stampede, and the people will go terrified to Damascus. **(1)**

1275. Abū al-Tiyāḥ[805] from my father: My father said to me: "My little son, we used to narrate that a people, their families will prevent them from perishing." [. . .] `Abdallāh b. `Amr: "There will be an emigration after the Emigration.[806] The people of the lands will traverse to the Emigration-place of Abraham, until none but the evilest of its people will remain on the earth."

[802] This may be the present-day town of al-Ḥamrat, located to the south of Ḥimṣ off the main road.

[803] Today on the main Damascus-Ḥimṣs road, approximately the halfway mark.

[804] On the main Damascus-Ḥimṣ road.

[805] Yazīd b. Ḥumayd al-Ḍuba`ī, lived in Baṣra, d. 128/745–6.

[806] Meaning the Emigration to Medina during the time of the Prophet (Q 4:89) would be followed by an emigration to Syria, the Emigration-place of Abraham (Gen. 12:1).

1276. `Abdallāh b. `Amr: When you hear from the pulpit a message from `Abdallāh to `Abdallāh then depart from Egypt.

1277. Ḥudhayfa: [283] I said: "O Messenger of God, is the Dajjāl first or Jesus son of Mary?" He said: "The Dajjāl, then Jesus, then if a man breeds his horse, he would not have time to ride the colt until the Hour rises."

1278. `Abdallāh b. `Amr b. `Amr: There will come upon the people a time a time when a man will wish he and his family were in an overloaded open boat (*fulk*), being tossed around by the waves, rather than on the land because of the intensity of the trial.

1279. Companions of the Prophet: An idiot son of an idiot is about to take over this world. [284]

The Imam of the Muslims in Jerusalem and his Victory on the Plain of Acre, and the Conquest of Ḥimṣ

1280. Ka`b: I have heard that [the destruction of] Constantinople is in return for the destruction of Jerusalem, since she [Constantinople] waxed proud and tyrannical, and so is called "the haughty."[807] She said: "The throne of my Lord is built upon the waters,[808] and I am built upon the waters." God Most High has promised punishment [for it] on the Day of Resurrection, and said: "I will tear away your decoration, your silk, and your veil, and I will leave you when there is [not even] a rooster crowing in you. I will make you uninhabited except for foxes {and jackals},[809] and unplanted except for mallows, and the

[807] Note the similar tradition about Damascus: "When Ka`b al-Aḥbār came to Syria, he gazed at Damascus and said: 'O city of whores (*zawānī*), you have become proud over [other] cities; by the One who has the soul of Ka`b in His hand, 70,000 drawn swords will enter you; God will lift mercy from them for three hours of the day. They will then stay for a time and destroy its wall—when its wall is destroyed, the Hour is close'" (Ibn `Asākir, *Tā'rīkh*, xxvi, p. 245).

[808] Compare Rev. 19:18–19; note that Satan's throne is said to be on the waters, see Muslim, *Ṣaḥīḥ*, viii, p. 190; and al-Tirmidhī, *Jāmi`*, iii, p. 353 (no. 2349).

[809] Ibn al-Faqīh, *al-Buldān* (Beirut: `Ālam al-Kutub, 2009), pp. 190–1 adds "jackals" but deletes the vegetation following.

thorny carob. I will cause to rain down upon you three [types] of fire: fire of pitch, fire of sulfur and fire of naphtha. I will leave you bald and bare, with nothing between you and the heavens. Your voice and your smoke will reach Me in the heavens, because you have for such a long time associated [other deities] with God Most High, and worshipped other [deities] than Him."[810]

Girls who will have never seen the sun because of their beauty will be deflowered, and none of you who arrive will be able to walk to the palace (*balāṭ*) of their king [because of the amount of loot]—you will find in it the treasure of their twelve kings, each of them more and none less than it [the one before], in the form of statues of cows or horses of bronze, with water flowing on their heads—dividing up their treasures, weighing them in shields and cutting them with axes. This will be because of the fire promised by God which will make you hurry, and you will carry what of their treasures you can so you can divide them up in Chalcedon.[811]

Then someone will come from the direction of Syria, [telling] you that the Dajjāl has emerged, [285] so you will reject that which is in your hands![812] When you reach Syria, you will find that it is false, and was only a lying whisper. Abū Ayyūb said: Which he whispered. And he said: In al-Qarqadūna. A man will not rise from his house to one of your walls in order to urinate on you.

1281. Ka`b: When it is the greatest apocalyptic battle, the apocalyptic battle of the Byzantines, a troop of you will flee and join with the enemy, then another troop will depart, then give you up, so God will have the earth swallow some of them up, and for the rest He will send birds to pluck out their eyes—then the third troop will remain. O servants of God, whoever

810 Ibid, p. 191, "For so long other deities were associated with me in you, and worshipped in you."

811 Ibid, p. 191, *ghadqadūniyya*.

812 Throw it down.

of you reaches this, then his soul has overcome coercion, so let him enter under his pack-saddle, or hold on to the pole of his tent (*fusṭāṭ*), and be constant, for God Most High will help the remaining troop. This will be when the Byzantines will consider you to be weak, and desire [to attack] you. The lord of the Byzantines will say: "When you get up, ride every hoofed beast, then ride them down completely, so that this religion"—meaning Islam—"will never be mentioned again on the earth."

So God, mighty and majestic, will be enraged at that point, so that He will be in the fourth heaven, which has God's armory and His [means of], so He will say: "There is only Myself, and My religion, Islam—the Yemenites and Qays—so I will surely help My servants today!" so the Hand of God will be between the two lines, so when He tends it against a people, then they will lose. "O Yemenites, do not hate Qays, and O Qays, love the Yemenites!" since Qays is among the best of people, in themselves and in ethics (*akhlāq*), by the One who holds the soul of Ka`b in His hand, only you, Yemenites and Qays, will be fighting on behalf of Islam on that day! Qays on that day will kill the enemies but not be killed, while al-Azd will kill the enemies but not be killed, and Lakhm and Judhām will kill the enemies and not be killed.

1282. Ka`b: Constantinople will be conquered at the hands of the progeny of Sheba and Qedar.[813]

1283. Ka`b: There will be a battle at Jaffa, in which the Muslims will fight them on Wednesday, Thursday, Friday, Saturday, and Sunday, then on Monday God will conquer for them.[814]

[813] Cf. Gen. 10:26 (Sheba said to be the son of Joktan, identified with Qaḥṭān), 25:13 (Kedar, son of Ishmael, said to be the ancestor of the northern Arabs). The tradition means that Constantinople will be conquered through an alliance of northern and southern tribes.

[814] See al-Bayhaqī, *Fadā'il al-awqāt* (Beirut: Dār al-Kutub al-`Ilmiyya, 1997), pp. 141–3 for the importance of Mondays for battles.

1284. Ṣafwān said: I asked Khālid b. Kaysān[815] concerning this, and he said: "My father told me that when God defeats the Byzantines at Jaffa, they will go and gather at the valleys, then it will be the apocalyptic battle, the apocalyptic battle of the valleys." [286]

1285. Ka`b: Caesarea in Anatolia will be inhabited, such that the Muslims will divide it with ropes and cubits [for farming], such that a woman can depart, going to Jerusalem (*bayt al-maqdis*) in safety on her donkey, being followed by the things that she needs, asking which path is the closest to Jerusalem without her fearing anything. The people will be safe, and the stick will be tossed [aside].

1286. `Abdallāh b. `Amr b. al-`Āṣ: The Byzantines will expel you village by village until you reach the waste (*jusham*) of [the tribe of] Judhām, until they place you in the outback (lit. shin bone) of the earth.[816]

1287. Ka`b: God Most High will aid the Syrians when the Byzantines fight them during the apocalyptic battles with two breaks: one a [group] repelling of 70,000, and one of 80,000 from the Yemenites, carrying their swords in sheaths of palm-fiber, and saying: "We are truly, truly the servants of God, we fight the enemies of God!" God will lift plague (*ṭā`ūn*), pains, and illnesses from them, so there will be more healthy land than Syria. But those pains and plagues that were in Syria will be in other places.

1288. Ka`b: 'In the west for the [duration of the] pregnancy of a sheep there will be one of their kings who will prepare 1000 sails (ships) for the Syrians, but every time he prepares them, God will send a gale-force wind against them until God gives him permission to set out. Then they will anchor between Acre and the [Orontes] River, so each army-province will be busy aiding the other.' So I asked him: "Which river is that?"

[815] Lived in the Ḥijāz, *fl.* 1st/7th century.
[816] See no. 1230.

He said: "The fleuve Orontes, the river of Ḥimṣ, since its fleuve is between Bald Mountain and Maṣīṣa."[817]

1289. Bashīr b. `Abdallāh b. Yassār[818]: `Abdallāh b. Busr al-Māzinī, companion of the Messenger of God, took my ear, and said: "O nephew, perhaps you will live to see the conquest of Constantinople, so a warning to you, if you do live to see it, do not leave your share of the spoils from it, because between its conquest and the emergence of the Dajjāl is seven years."

1290. Abū `Amr al-Saybānī: The Byzantines will beat the clappers (*nawāqīs*)[819] in Jerusalem (*bayt al-maqdis*) for forty days until the army of the Muslims and the army of the Byzantines meet in battle on the Mount of Olives. The Muslims will defeat the Byzantines, and force them to the Jericho Gate,[820] then force them from David's Gate,[821] and will [287] continue to kill them until they cause them to reach the sea. The [area] between them and Jerusalem will be called the Corpse Valleys until the Day of Resurrection.

1291. More than one of the Companions of the Messenger of God: There will be a truce between the Muslims and the Byzantines on the condition that the Muslims send an army to them, to be in Constantinople, as succor for them. Then an enemy from behind them will come to them, fighting them, so the Muslims and the Byzantines with them will come out, and God will help them against them, defeat them, and kill them, so that someone of the Byzantines will say: "The Cross is victorious!" But one of the Muslims will say: "Nay, God is victorious!" The people will bat this back and forth between them, then the Muslim will rise to the Byzantine, and cut off his head, so the Byzantines will feel that violation such that when they return

[817] In Cilicia, on the Byzantine border.

[818] Unidentified, but probably lived in Ḥimṣ, *fl.* 2nd/8th century.

[819] An activity that is forbidden according to the Pact of `Umar.

[820] Probably the present-day St. Stephen's Gate, on the eastern side of the Old City of Jerusalem, facing the Mount of Olives.

[821] Present-day Jaffa Gate, on the western side of the Old City.

to Constantinople, and are safe, they [Byzantines] will kill them [Muslims], while they are secure. When they kill them, they will know that the Muslims will seek vengeance for their blood, so the Byzantines will emerge with eighty banners, under each banner will be 12,000 [troops].

1292. Abū Qubayl: When the Byzantines come the people will have no further support—with them will be the Turks, the Burjān[822] and the Slavs (*saqāliba*).[823]

1293. Al-Muhājir b. Ḥabīb[824]: The Messenger of God said: "The fifth of the family of Heraclius; at his hands will be the apocalyptic battles." Heraclius reigned, then his son Constans (II), then his son Constantine (IV), son of Constans, then Iṣṭafān,[825] son of Constantine, then the rule of the Byzantines departed from the family of Heraclius to Leo [the Isaurian] and his progeny after him. The rule will return to the fifth of the family of Heraclius, at whose hands the apocalyptic battles will happen.

1294. `Abdallāh b. `Amr: The Messenger of God said: "The best killed under the shadow of the heavens since God Most High created His creation, the first of them was Abel, killed by the cursed Cain, wrongfully, then the prophets, who were killed by the peoples to whom they were sent when they said: 'Our Lord is God' and called to Him, then the believer of Pharoah's family,[826] then the [unnamed] one of [*sūra*] *yā sīn*,[827] then Ḥamza b. `Abd al-Muṭṭalib,[828] then the slain of [the battle of] Badr, then the slain at [the battle of] Uḥud, then the slain at Ḥudaybiyya,[829] then the slain at [the battle of] Ḥunayn, then

822 Probably Burgundy.

823 It is not easy to know who is meant by "Slavs" in the early ninth century (or possibly eighth century), perhaps a reference to the peoples of southeastern Europe, or to Europeans in general.

824 Al-Muhājir b. Ḥabīb b. Ṣuhayb, lived in Ḥimṣ, *fl.* 2nd/8th century.

825 Probably Justinian II.

826 Q 40:28.

827 Q 36:13–30, esp. 20.

828 The paradigmatic martyr of Islam, killed at the Battle of Uḥud, 4/625.

829 A bit odd, as Ḥudaybiyya was actually a peace negotiation in which no one was killed.

the slain who will be killed after me by the dissenting, iniquitous Kharijites. Then [288] return your hand to what ever God wishes, to the fighters in His path, such that the slain during the apocalyptic battle of the Byzantines will be like the slain of Badr, then the slain of the apocalyptic battle of the Turks will be like the slain of the Battle of the Aḥzāb (Confederates), then as to the apocalyptic battle of battles, its slain will be like the Battle of Ḥunayn. Afterwards there will be no further apocalyptic battle in Islam for its people until the Day in which the trumpets are blown."

1295. Abū Qubayl: When you have conquered Rome, enter its great eastern church through its eastern gate.[830] Then count seven paving stones (*balāṭāt*), then lift up the eighth, and under it there will be the Rod of Moses, the original Gospel, and the decoration of Jerusalem (*bayt al-maqdis*).[831]

1296. \`Abdallāh b. \`Umar: Constantinople will be conquered by a man whose name is my name.[832]

1297. \`Abdallāh b. \`Amr b. al-\`Āṣ: You will raid Constantinople three raids. As for the first you will encounter trial and hardship, and for the second, there will be a peace (*ṣulḥ*) between you and them, such that the Muslims will build mosques in it [Constantinople], and you will raid together with them beyond Constantinople. Then you will return to it, and during the third raid God will conquer it for you with [shouts of] *allāhu akbar!* It will be divided up into thirds: one third will be destroyed, one third will be burned, and the last third weighed [and looted].

1298. Abū Qubayl and Yusayr b. \`Amr[833] both said: Alexandria and the apocalyptic battles of the valleys will be at the hand of

[830] St. John's Lateran?

[831] Here *bayt al-maqdis* could mean the Temple (the original meaning of the term).

[832] It is difficult to place this tradition; presumably it originally was intended to be from the Prophet with his name (see no. 1318).

[833] Yusayr b. \`Amr al-Muḥāribī, a chieftain (*\`arīf*) in Kūfa, d. 85/704.

Tiberius son of Isṭbiyān [Justinian II] son of the Slit-nosed,[834] son of Constantine son of Heraclius. He said: "I have heard that it is in Rome."

1299. `Abdallāh b. `Amr b. al-`Āṣ: "The Andalusians will come on the sea,[835] and the length of their ships' [fleet] in the sea will be fifty miles, its breadth will be thirteen miles, until they descend upon the valleys." Ibn Wahb said: "On land and sea."

1300. `Abdallāh b. `Amr b. al-`Āṣ: There is a man from among the enemies of the Muslims in Andalus called the One with the Mane (Dhū al-`Arf),[836] who will gather the tribes of polytheism massively, knowing that the Muslims of Andalus will have no ability to withstand him. So the Muslims in it will flee, the strong Muslims will sail in ships to Tangiers (Tanja), while the weak and the majority will not have any ships to cross. So God will send a mountain goat to them, and God Most High will make a path in the sea for them to cross it. The people will perceive it and follow that mountain goat, crossing in its wake. Then the sea will return to the same way it was previously.

The [289] enemy will cross in boats (*marākib*) in pursuit of them, so when the people of Ifrīqiyyā (Tunisia) and the Muslims who were already there learn about them they will set out until they reach Egypt. The enemy will follow them until they camp between Maryūṭ and the Pyramids, a distance of five post-stops. A banner of the Muslims will come out against them, then God will grant them [the Muslims] victory over them, and defeat them, killing them [as they flee] to Libya

834 Justinian II was nicknamed the Slit-nosed. No. 1401 retains the correct order of the Byzantine rulers, leaving out the "son of" the Slit-nose.

835 If there is any historical value to this tradition, the "Andalusians" must be Aquitainians or French.

836 Could this be a distant rumor of Charlemagne? See *The Fourth Book of the Chronicle of Fredegar*, trans. J.M. Wallace-Hadrill (Westport, CT: Greenwood, 1960), pp. 93–5 (note that in this account, the Muslims flee in boats, just as the description in the apocalypse, although of course not from southern Spain. This tradition, however, could be an echo of the battle of 737 or one of Charlemagne's campaigns in northern Spain in the 780s or 790s).

(*lūbīya*), a distance of ten nights' travel. The Egyptians will transport their goods and their tools in their carts (*`ajal*) for a period of seven years.

The One with the Mane will flee, having a book with him, written for him, in which he should not look until he arrives in Egypt. So he will look into it once he has been defeated, and then find mention of Islam in it—and be ordered to enter into it. So he will ask for safe-conduct for himself and those of his supporters who have responded to the call to Islam, so he will convert to Islam and become part of the Muslims.

When it is the next year, a man from the Ethiopians called Eusebius (*isīs/usīs*)[837] will approach, after having gathered a huge number. The Muslims will flee from Aswān[838] until there are no Muslims in it or around it left who have not gone to al-Fusṭāṭ (Cairo). The Ethiopians will travel until they descend upon Memphis.[839] Then the Muslims will come out to them with their banners, and God will give them [the Muslims] victory over them. They will fight them, and take them captive, so that a black will be sold on that day for a cloak.

1301. `Abdallāh b. `Amr: "Arab tribes in their totality will join with the Byzantines." I [Abū Muḥammad al-Juhanī[840]] said: "In their totality?" He said: "With their shepherds and dogs." Sulaym b. `Umayr said to him: "If God wills, O Abū Muḥammad," but he got up angrily, saying: "God has already willed, and has foreordained it."

1302. `Abdallāh b. `Amr: When Dhū al-Khalṣa is worshipped, at that time will be the appearance of the Byzantines in Syria.

1303. Abū Hurayra: The Messenger of God said: When the apocalyptic battles happen a delegation of the *mawālī* will depart from Damascus—they are the noblest of the Arabs in horseman-

837 See nos. 1851, 1855.

838 The southernmost border of Egypt at the First Cateract.

839 The classical site, a bit to the southeast of present-day Cairo.

840 Unidentified.

ship, and have the most prowess in weapons. God will aid the religion by them.[841]

1304. Ka`b: If it were not for the clamor of the people of Rome,[842] you would have heard the setting (*wajabat*) of the sun when it sets. [290]

1305. Ka`b: The first city for Christianity is Rome; were it not for the unbelief of its people, they would hear the rustling sound of the sun when it falls.

1306. `Abdallāh b. `Amr: The conquest of Constantinople, then you will raid Rome,[843] then God will conquer it for you.

1307. Abū Qubayl: A man from the Yemenites will rule Tunisia (Ifrīqiyā) called Muḥammad b. Sa`īd,[844] and there will be a man from the Hashemites called Aṣbagh b. Zayd[845] after him—he is the lord of Rome and the one who will conquer it.

1308. An elder from [the tribe of] Ḥimyar: From your enemy, at this Ramla, the Ramla of Ifrīqiyā,[846] there will be a battle-day in which the Byzantines will advance with 800,000 ships (!), so they will fight you over this Ramla. Then He[847] will defeat them, so you will take their ships, and sail them to Rome. When you have come to it, then you will shout out *allāhu akbar!* three times, so the fortress will quake from your shouting—and then collapse at the third to the distance of a mile. So you will enter it, then God will send a blinder upon them[848] to cover them, so that you will not be restrained until you have entered it. The dust will not be revealed until they are on their sleeping-mats.

841 Ibn Māja, *Sunan*, ii, p. 1370 (no. 4090).
842 Presumably during their worship. This detail probably came from a traveler.
843 The Muslims did raid Rome in 846, after Nu`aym's time.
844 Unidentified.
845 Reading with MM, and see no. 1182.
846 Perhaps mentioned in the fourteenth century account of `Abdallāh b. Muḥammad al-Tijānī, *Riḥlat al-Tijānī* (Beirut: Dār al-Ma`ārif l-l-Kitāb, 2005), p. 207 as being next to Tripoli.
847 Probably God is the doer of the action here.
848 Apparently the people of Rome.

1309. `Abdallāh b. `Amr: The apocalyptic battles are five, two have passed, and three remain. The first of these is the apocalyptic battle of the Turks in al-Jazīra, then the apocalyptic battle of the Byzantines, and then the apocalyptic battles of the Dajjāl. There will be no further apocalyptic battles after these.

1310. `Abdallāh b. `Amr b. al-`Āṣ: A youth (*ghulām*) will grow among the Byzantines, developing during a year the growth of a youth in ten years, so he will be in the land of the Byzantines, ruling them among themselves, then he will say: "Until when, while we have been dominated by these [Arabs] in places in our land, will we wait for them be expelled? So I will surely fight them until I dominate that which they have come to control, or they dominate me over what is left beneath my feet?" So he will emerge leading 7000 ships, until they are between Acre and al-`Arīsh. Then he will set fire to his ships, and the Egyptians will emerge from Egypt and the Syrians from Syria, so they make for the Arabian Peninsula.

This is the day concerning which Abū Hurayra used to say: "Woe to the Arabs from an approaching evil." Rope and pack-saddle on that day are more desirable for a man than his family or his wealth. So the Arabs will ask their Bedouin for aid, then they will go until they reach the valleys of Antioch. There will be the greatest of the apocalyptic battles, such that the horses will be wading [in blood] up to their fetlocks.

God will remove His help from everyone until the angels say: "O Lord! Will You not help Your servants, the believers?" He will say: "[Not] until their martyrs increase," so a third will be killed, a third return [backwards], but a third will be constant. Let God have the earth swallow up those who return!

The Byzantines will say: "We will continue to fight you until you bring out to us everyone among you who is foreign." [291] So the non-Arabs (*`ajam*) will emerge and say: "God forbid that we go back into unbelief after Islam!" At that God, mighty and majestic, will be enraged and strike with His sword and pierce with His spear, so everyone will be killed, even those informing [of news]. Then they [Muslims] will roll over them, conquering every single city they pass with *allāhu akbar!* until they reach the city of the Byzantines. They will find its gulf overflowing, but God Most High will conquer it for them. Such-and-such a number of virgins will be raped, and its spoils will be divided weighed out in sacks.

Then it will come to you that the [false] messiah has emerged, so they will advance until they meet him in Jerusalem (*bayt ilīyā'*),[849] and they will find it besieged. There will be 8000 women and 12,000 [male] fighters—the best of those who remain, like the righteous of those past. While they are under a mist of clouds, when the mist will clear for the morning, and suddenly Jesus son of Mary will be among them.

1311. Abū Dharr: I heard the Messenger of God saying: "There will be a pug-nosed man from the Umayyads in Egypt, who will rule a government (*sulṭān*) but his government will be overcome, or it will be taken from him, so he will flee to the Byzantines. Then the Byzantines will come to the people of Islam, and that will be the first of the apocalyptic battles."

1312. `Abdallāh b. `Amr: "When you see or hear of a man from the sons of the tyrants (*al-jabābira*) in Egypt having a government, when his government is overthrown, then he will flee to the Byzantines. This will be the first of the apocalyptic battles. The Byzantines will come to the people of Islam." It was said to him: "The Egyptians will be taken prisoner, according to what we were told, when they are our brothers. Is that true?" He said: "Yes, when you see the Egyptians having killed their imam among them, then depart if you can, and do not come close to the palace (*qaṣr*) for they will be inside of it allowing the taking of captives."

1313. Ka`b: "At the conquest of Rome, an army will emerge from the Maghrib on an eastern wind in which not a single oar will

[849] This is probably the oddest combination of the four possible names of Jerusalem in Nu`aym.

break, no rope will be cut, no sail will blow away, and not a single vessel (*qaraba*)[850] will be cracked until they anchor at Rome and conquer it."[851] Ka`b said: "It has a tree in the Book of God which serves as a sitting for 3000 [people], so whoever hangs their weapons on it or fastens his horse to it, in the eyes of God Most High, he is among the best of martyrs."

1314. Ka`b: Amorium will be conquered before Nicea, Nicea before Constantinople, and Constantinople before Rome.

1315. `Abdallāh b. `Amr: [292] We were with the Messenger of God, and he was asked which of the two cities would be conquered first: "Rome or Constantinople?" The Prophet said: "The city of the son of Heraclius will be first, which is Constantinople."

1316. `Abdallāh b. `Amr: "The Hour will arise when the Byzantines are the largest number of people." `Amr b. al-`Āṣ wanted to drive him away, then `Amr said: "If you say that, then they are the firmest people during a disaster, the fastest to recover from a defeat, the best to the old and the weak, and the most efficient at forbidding the tyranny of kings."

1317. Ibn Muḥayrīz[852]: The Messenger of God said: "As for Persia, one or two blows, and then there is no Persia; after the many-horned Byzantines—every time a horn goes, another horn replaces it. Masters of stone and sea, how far they proceed to the end of time! They will be your companions as long as there is good in life."

1318. Abū Qubayl: "The one who will conquer Constantinople will have the name of a prophet." Ibn Lahī`a said, and related it from their books, meaning the Byzantines, "his name is Ṣāliḥ."[853]

1319. Khuthaym al-Ziyādī[854]: Rome will be conquered with the ropes

850 Reading with MM.

851 The raid that sacked Rome in 846 did come from the west.

852 `Abdallāh b. Muḥayrīz al-Jumaḥī, lived in Jerusalem, one of the most respected religious figures in Syria, d. approximately 100/718–19.

853 Perhaps because the prophet Ṣāliḥ was the messenger to Thamūd, who like the Byzantines, "took palaces from its plains and carved houses out of the mountains" (Q 7:74) in their arrogance.

854 Possibly Khuthaym b. Thābit, *fl.* 2nd/8th century.

of Baysān, the wood of Lebanon, the nails of Marīs,[855] and you will take the Ark of the Covenant.[856] The Syrians and the Egyptians will cast lots for it, and it will go to the Egyptians.

1320. Al-Mustawrid al-Qurashī[857]: I heard the Messenger of God saying: "The Hour will arise when the Byzantines are most of the people," then this reached `Amr b. al-`Āṣ, so he said: "What are these traditions that are mentioned on your authority? Are you stating them on the authority of the Prophet?" al-Mustawrid said: "I said that which I heard from the Messenger of God." `Amr said: "If you said that, they are the most restrained people during the tribulation, the firmest people during a disaster, and the best of people to their indigent and weak ones."

1321. Ka`b: The apocalyptic battles are at the hands of a man from the family of Heraclius, the fourth and fifth, called Tiberius (Ṭayāra). Ka`b said: The commander of the people on that day will be a man from the Hashemites, to whom aid from the Yemen will come: 70,000 with swords in sheaths of palm-fiber. [293]

1322. Abū Tha`laba al-Khushanī, Companion of the Messenger of God, said: "When you see Syria as a feast or a table for one man and his family[858] then at that time will be the conquest of Constantinople." I think that Ibn Wahb said: "Table."

1323. Ka`b: The Messenger of God mentioned the apocalyptic battle—and it is named *malḥama* (apocalyptic battle) because of the number of people [fighting in it]—so I will interpret it for you: Twelve kings will be present at it, and the Byzantine king will be the least of them, with the smallest number of

[855] Perhaps Maras, today Kahramanmarash in southeastern Turkey (in Ibn `Asākir, *Tā'rīkh*, iii, p. 389 a Christian man is said to come from Marīs) or somewhere on the Via Maris (Way of the Sea) (thanks to Michael Decker for this identification). There is no source that indicates whether the region of Maras was known for nail manufacture.

[856] Correcting the name according to no. 1332.

[857] Al-Mustawrid b. Shaddād al-Qurashī, lived in Kūfa, *fl.* 1st/7th century.

[858] Probably a reference to the Umayyads. See al-Ṣāliḥī, *Subul al-hudā*, x, p. 129.

fighters, but they will be the ones to call for it [to happen], as they will have called the nations to give them aid. It will be forbidden to anyone who considers Islam to be true to not help Islam on that day. So on that day aid for the Muslims will come from the army-province of Ṣana`ā' (Yemen).

It will be forbidden to anyone who considers Christianity to be true to not help it on that day, so al-Jazīra will aid them with 30,000 Christians. A man will abandon his plot of land (*faddān*), saying: "I will go to help Christianity," so iron will be set against each other. It will not harm a man to have a sword that would not cut off a nose, to not have al-Ṣamṣāma in its place[859]—every armor or anything his sword touches that day will be cut. It will be forbidden for an army to leave off help. Endurance will be cast upon those and those, and iron will be set against another in order to make the trial severe.

A third of the Muslims will be killed on that day, a third will flee, and will fall into a pile of sand on the earth—meaning those will never see paradise or their families again, ever—and a third will be constant. They will guard them three days so they will not flee like their fellows who fled. On the third day, a man from among them will say: "O people of Islam, what are you waiting for? Rise and let us enter paradise just as our brothers have entered it!"

Then God Most High will cause His help to descend and be enraged for His religion. He will strike with His sword, pierce with His spear, and shoot with His arrow. It will not be permitted for a Christian to carry weapons after that day until the Hour arises. The Muslims will strike at their necks while they are fleeing. Every single fortress and city they pass by will be conquered until they reach Constantinople. They will say *allāhu akbar!* and bless God, and praise Him, so God will cause that which is between the twelve towers to collapse, so the Muslims will enter it on that day, kill its fighters, and rape its virgins.

[859] See no. 1215

God will order it to reveal its treasures, to take and leave—so the one who takes and the one who leaves will both be regretful. They will say: "How can they both be regretful?" He said: "The one who takes will regret that he could not take more, while the one who leaves will regret that he was not the one taking." They said: "You want us to be desirous of this world at the end of time?" He said: "What you obtain from it [Constantinople] will be a succor to you during the hard years and the years of the Dajjāl." He said: "Someone will come to them while they are there, saying: 'The Dajjāl has emerged in your lands' so they will leave off in confusion and find him having not emerged, but it will not be long until he does emerge."

1324. Abū Qubayl: Abū Firās, *mawlā* of `Amr b. al-`Āṣ, Mūsā b. Nuṣayr and `Iyāḍ b. `Uqba[860] gathered together, so they mentioned the conquest of Constantinople, and the mosque which [294] would be built in it. Abū Firās said: "I know the place where it will be built." Mūsā b. Nuṣayr said: "I know that place," so `Iyāḍ b. `Uqba said: "From your mouth to my ear," so both of them informed him, then he said: "You are both right." Abū Firās said: "I heard `Abdallāh b. `Amr b. al-`Āṣ saying: You will raid Constantinople three times. As for the first raid, it will be a disaster, as for the second one there will be a peace such that the Muslims will build a mosque in it. You will raid beyond Constantinople, then they will return to Constantinople. As for the third, God will conquer it for you with [shouts of] *allāhu akbar!*, and a third of it will be destroyed, God will burn a third, and they will weigh out the last third [as spoils]."

1325. `Umayr b. Mālik[861]: We were with `Abdallāh b. `Amr b. al-`Āṣ in Alexandria one day, so they mentioned the conquest of Constantinople and Rome. Some of the people said: "Constantinople will be conquered before Rome," while

[860] Presumably Egyptian, *fl.* 2nd/8th century.
[861] Presumably Egyptian, *fl.* 2nd/8th century.

others said: "Rome will be conquered before Constantinople." `Abdallāh b. `Amr called for a chest (*ṣundūq*) belonging to him, in which there was a book. He said: "Constantinople will be conquered before Rome, then you will raid Rome after Constantinople and conquer it, if not, then I, `Abdallāh, are among the liars, which he said three times."

1326. Yazīd b. Ziyād al-Aslamī, who was one of the Companions[862]: "Ibn Maurice (*mawruq*),"[863] meaning the king of the Byzantines, "will come leading 300 ships until he anchors at Sarsinā."[864]

1327. `Abdallāh b. `Amr: The apocalyptic battle and Alexandria will be at the hands of Tiberius, son of Justinian (II) son of the Slit-nose. When a boat lands at the lighthouse, not half the day will pass until 400 boats will come to you, then another 400 until they land at the lighthouse.

1328. `Abdallāh b. `Amr on the authority of the Prophet: When the two freedmen, the freedman of the `Arabs, and the freedman of the Byzantines rule, then at their hands will be the apocalyptic battles. **(2)**

1329. Abū Dharr: I heard the Messenger of God saying: There will be a pug-nosed man from the Umayyads in Egypt, who will rule the government, then his government will be overthrown or taken from him, so he will flee to the Byzantines. Then the Byzantines will come to the people of Islam, and that will be the first of the apocalyptic battles.

1330. `Urwa b. Abī Qays: [295] A man from the Umayyads—if you wanted his description, so that when he is seen he would be known by his description [I would give it]—will flee to the Byzantines as a result of a rage that he will feel. His government

862 Ibn Ḥajar notes that he is completely unknown other than from this tradition.

863 The false Tiberius (no. 1215) claimed to be the son of Maurice [named Flavius Mauricious Tiberius Augustus] (ruled 582–602).

864 Perhaps a village in the Fayyum, Egypt, although it is not clear why the Byzantines would dock there. One wonders whether this is a memory of the Byzantine-Persian wars.

in Egypt will be overthrown or taken from him, so he will lead the Byzantines to them.

1331. Khuthaym al-Ziyādī: I heard Tubay` saying, and I asked him concerning Rome, and he said: "When you see the island that is near Fusṭāṭ, that they are building ships on it or he said a ship whose wood is from Lebanon, its rope is from Maysān,[865] and its nails are from Marīs, then order an army and raid it. No rope will be cut and no wood will break [on these ships], so they will conquer Rome. They will take the Ark of the Covenant (*tābūt al-sakīna*), but the Syrians and the Egyptians will dispute over the Ark as to which one will bring it to Jerusalem (*ilīyā'*). They will cast lots for it, so the Egyptians will win it, so take it to Jerusalem." He said: I asked him about Constantinople, so he said: "Men who weep and humbly beseech God Most High will raid it, so when they land there they will fast three days, praying to God, and beseeching Him, so God will cause its eastern side to collapse. The Muslims will enter it and build mosques in it."

1332. Rabī`a b. al-Fārisī[866]: An army from among you will go to Rome and conquer it, taking out the decoration of Jerusalem (*bayt al-maqdis*), the Ark of the Covenant, the table, the Rod [of Moses] and the ornament of Adam. A youthful boy will command this, so he will bring it to Jerusalem.

1333. Al-Ḥārith b. Ḥarmal[867]: I heard `Abdallāh b. `Amr saying: "The quivers of the Byzantines will snap back and forth in the alleyways of Jerusalem (*ilīyā'*)." I said to `Abdallāh b. `Amr: "Wasn't it destroyed already once?" He said: "Yes, such that they do not have a plough-furrow in the mountains. But the Byzantines will say: 'Until when will those [Arabs] eat from the [produce of the] sides of your mountains?' He said: So your speakers will rise, and some of you will say: 'Patience, stay behind from

[865] Appears as Baysān in no. 1319;

[866] Unidentified, but probably Egyptian, maybe *fl.* 1st/7th century.

[867] Al-Ḥārith b. Ḥarmal al-Ḥaḍramī, originally from Edessa, was a judge in Damascus, *fl.* 2nd/8th century.

your enemy until you see your banner.' But some of them will say: 'Nay, let's go forward against them, so that God can decide between us.' A group of you will go and advance toward them, then fight in a valley in which there is a river."[868]

I said: "I know the valley, but there is no water in it, other than when it is a river [seasonally]." He said: "When God wills to make it, He will make it manifest." He said: "God will defeat them." He said: "They will go, and none will reach them. Donkeys will be expensive on that day in a way never before seen nor will again—until they reach the city [Constantinople], where the body of water [Bosphorus] will have taken a group of them. A group will remain, and then conquer it, and every people will take [spoils] according to their position."

1334. Tubay`: The one who will defeat the Byzantines on the battle-day of the valleys will be the caliph of the *mawālī.* [296]

1335. Ka`b: Then the Byzantines will send asking you for a peace, so you will make peace with them. On that day a woman will cross the path to Syria in safety, and the city of Caesarea in Anatolia will be rebuilt.

1336. Tubay`: Between the destruction of Rhodes (*rawdhas*) and the emergence of the Hashemite will be seventy years.

1337. Sa`īd b. Jubayr concerning His Word, Most High, "For them (there is) disgrace in this world,"[869] he said: "A city among the Byzantines that will be conquered."

1338. Ka`b concerning His Word, Most High, "When the promise of the Hereafter coms, We shall bring you (all together) as a mob,"[870] he said: "Two tribes of the Israelites that will fight on the day of the greatest apocalyptic battle, helping Islam and its people," then Ka`b recited: "After that we said to the Sons of Israel: 'Inhabit the land, and when the promise of the Hereafter comes, We shall bring you (all together) as a mob.'"

[868] Presumably in northern Syria.
[869] Q 5:41.
[870] Q 17:104.

1339. Ka`b: In Filasṭīn there will be two battles concerning the Byzantines. One is [called] "the Plucking" and the other one is "the Harvest."

1340. Abū Hurayra: You will conquer Rome until the sons of the Emigrants will hang their swords on the *acacia mimosa* of Rome,[871] so that the traveler will return from Constantinople and find that it [Rome] is locked up.

1341. `Abd al-Malik b. `Umayr: I heard al-Ḥajjāj b. Yūsuf saying: Someone who heard Ka`b narrated to me: If it were not for the people in Rome, the passing of the sun would be heard as a dragging like the dragging of a saw.

1342. Abū [297] al-Zāhiriyya and Ḍamra b. Ḥabīb both said: The Byzantines will bring [armies] from Rome to Romania[872] on the sea against you, then they will overcome you on your coastline with 10,000 sails, and dwell between the Rock Face (*wajh al-ḥajar*)[873] and Jaffa. One and all will alight at Acre, then the Syrians will flee to their harbors (*mawāḥīz*)[874] and run away. Then they will send to the Yemenites asking them for aid, so they will aid them with 40,000 carrying swords in sheaths of palm-fiber.

So they will go until they occupy Acre and around it, every single last one of the people, so then God will conquer for them, killing them and following them until those who can, will join the Byzantines. They will kill those opposite them,

871 Ibn Waḥshiyya, *al-Falāḥa al-Nabaṭiyya* (Damascus: Institut Français de Damas, 1995–8), ii, pp. 1279, 1305 states that the *labakh* tree either grows exclusively in Egypt, or best in Egypt, and the Arab lands (*bilād al-`arab*). Although this does not absolutely preclude that there were acacias to be found in Rome during this period (because Ibn Waḥshiyya was writing about the `Abbāsid empire, not about the Mediterranean basin), it raises questions about whether a tradition like this represents genuine knowledge about Rome.

872 In the text, *rumāniya*, perhaps the Balkans (thanks to Michael Decker for this identification).

873 Probably the outcropping of Naqoura or Rosh ha-Niqra, what Willibald called "the Head of Lebanon" (Wilkinson, *Pilgrims*, p. 247).

874 This is probably the Aramaic word *maḥoz* "harbor, trading-place," cf. Jastrow, *Dictionary*, p. 757.

and those are the ones who will be present for the greatest apocalyptic battle at the valley.

The Christians will gather altogether from the Syrians, until no one is left who is not aiding the people of the valley. Then the Muslims will go towards them, every single last one of them. The Yemenites are the ones who will advance to Acre, where they will fight a fierce battle. Iron will be set against iron, and not even a tool of iron will act cowardly on that day. A third of the Muslims will be killed, but most will join with the enemy, and a group of them will depart. Whoever departs from the camp of the Muslims has gone astray and will continue to be astray until he dies.

Whoever of the Muslims is cowardly on that day, let him lie down on the earth, then order his pack-saddle to be placed upon him, with his food-sacks (*jawālīq*) above him. Then the people will call to each other for a peace, so they will say: "The Yemenites are going to their Yemen, Qays is going to the desert!" Then those devoted to God (*muḥarrirūn*) will rise and say: "What about us? Should we join unbelief?" The chief of the devotees will rise and incite his people, and charge the Byzantines, striking the head of their chieftain with his sword until his head is cloven in two. The fight will ignite and God will cause victory to descend upon them. God will defeat them and they will be killed in every plain and mountain such that one of their men will hide behind rocks and trees, but they will say: "O believer! There is an unbeliever behind me, so kill him!"

1343. Ka`b: Blessed are Ḥimyar and the lesser Ḥimyarites on the day of the greatest apocalyptic battle, for God will give them this world and the next, even if the people do not like it.[875]

1344. Abū Daws al-Yaḥṣubī[876]: I heard Khālid b. Ma`dān saying: "The Byzantines will surely expel you from Syria village by village

[875] Presumably an echo of Q 9:33.

[876] `Uthmān b. `Ubayd al-Yaḥṣubī, lived in Syria, *fl.* 2nd/8th century.

and their seal (*khatam*) will run for forty days, meaning the post-couriers".

1345. Yūnis b. Sayf al-Khawlānī[877]: You will make peace with the Byzantines, a secure peace, such that you will raid together with them the Turks and the Kirmān,[878] and God will conquer for you. Then the Byzantines will say: "The Cross is victorious!" but the Muslims will be enraged, so they will each disengage from the other, then fight a fierce battle on a field with hills. Then God will conquer them for you, whereupon the apocalyptic battles will follow.

1346. Dhū Mikhbar, the nephew of [298] the Negus: I heard the Messenger of God saying: You will make peace with the Byzantines for ten years—a secure peace. They will keep it for two years, but betray in the third, or keep it four years and betray in the fifth. One of your armies will land at their city, so you and them will turn away to an enemy behind them, and God will conquer for you, and help you in the reward and spoils that you will gain.

You will camp on a field with hills, and your spokesman will say: "God is victorious!" but their spokesman[879] will say: "The Cross is victorious!" So you will bat this back and forth for a time, then the Muslims will be enraged—and the cross will not be far away—so a Muslim will arise to their cross and crush it. Then they will arise to the breaker of the cross, and cut off his head.

So that band of Muslims will arise to their weapons, and the Byzantines to theirs. Then will fight, then God will honor this band of Muslims, so they will be martyred. They [the Byzantines] will come to their king, and say: "We have taken care of the Arabs, so what do you think?" Then they will gather

[877] Probably Yūnis b. Sayf al-`Ansī al-Kalā`ī, lived in Ḥimṣ, d. 120/738.

[878] In central Persia.

[879] In Abū Dā'ūd, *Sunan*, iv, p. 107 (no. 4292) "a Christian man" (*rajul min ahl al-naṣrāniyya*).

for the duration of a woman's pregnancy, coming to you with eighty banners, under each banner 12,000.

1347. Ka`b: If it were not for three [matters], I would not want to live: the first is the greatest apocalyptic battle, as God Most High has on that day forbidden every iron tool from being cowardly—if a man struck with a spit, he would cut—and secondly, if it were not for that I would participate in the conquest of the city of unbelief. Before it there is lowliness and terrible humiliation.

1348. `Ulayy b. Ribāḥ[880]: While `Abdallāh b. `Amr was on his farm in al-`Ajlān,[881] to the [south] side of Caesarea in Filasṭīn, suddenly a man passed, riding swiftly on his warhorse, touching his weapons, informing him that the people were terrified, hoping that he would be able to participate in the apocalyptic battle of Caesarea. He said: "That is not in my time nor in yours, not until you see a man from the sons of the tyrants in Egypt, with his government overthrown, then fleeing to the Byzantines, so he will lead the Byzantines—that is the first of the apocalyptic battles."

1349. `Abd al-Raḥmān b. Sunna[882]: I heard the Messenger of God saying: By the One who holds my soul in His hand, the faith will coil up to that which is between the two mosques[883] just as a snake coils itself in its hole. The faith will go past the city, just as the flood passes through ruins—so while they are in this situation, the Arabs will ask succor from their Bedouin, as an assembly for them—like the righteous ones of previously and the best of those who yet remain. So they and the Byzantines

[880] `Ulayy (nickname) or `Ali b. Ribāḥ b. Qaṣīr al-Lakhmī, lived in Egypt, then in Ifrīqiyā, d. 114/732–3.

[881] Close to Beer-Sheva, in southern Israel, where he retreated when he fell out of favor with `Uthmān in 656.

[882] Father of no. 1242, so presumably lived in Damascus. He related to Maymūna, the grandmother of Yūsuf b. Sulaymān, who was presumably also Syrian, and is the grandmother mentioned at the end of the tradition.

[883] Mecca and Medina.

will fight, and the wars will turn them upside down, until they reach the valley of Antioch.

They will fight there three days, so God will lift His victory from both of the sides, until the horse will wade in blood up to its fetlocks. Then the angels will say: "O Lord, will You not help Your servants?" He will say "Not until their martyrs are numerous," so then a third will be martyred [299], a third will be constant, and a third will return doubting, and will be swallowed up by the earth.

Then the Byzantines will say: "We will never leave you until you hand over to us all of those whose origin is from us," so the Arabs will say to the non-Arabs (`*ajam*): "Join the Byzantines," but the non-Arabs will say: "Should we become unbelievers after belief?" and they will be enraged at that. They will attack the Byzantines and fight, so God will be enraged at that and strike with His sword, and pierce with His spear.

It was said: "O `Abdallāh b. `Amr, what are the sword and spear of God?" He said: "The sword and spear of the believer—until you cause the Byzantines to perish entirely. None but an informer [of news] will be able to flee. Then they will depart to the land of the Byzantines, conquering its fortresses and cities with [shouts of] *allāhu akbar!* until they reach the city of Heraclius (Constantinople). They will find its gulf overflowing, but then they will open it with *allāhu akbar!* —shouting it out one time, so that one of its walls falls, then shouting it out another time, so that another wall will fall. Its sea-wall will remain without falling. Then they will pass over to Rome, and conquer it with [shouts of] *allāhu akbar!* Then they will weigh out their spoils in sacks on that day. Other than al-Walīd did not mention his grandmother."[884]

1350. Sa`īd b. Jābir[885]: A man from the family of Mu`āwiya said to

[884] Al-Walīd b. Muslim, one of Mu`aym's major informants, was one of two who related this tradition to him through the figure of the grandmother of Yūsuf b. Sulaymān, Maymūna.

[885] Unattested, but certainly a Syrian, probably lived in Damascus, *fl.* 1st/7th century.

him: "Have you not read one of the codices of your brother Ka`b?" So he presented me with a codex in which the following was written:

> *Say to Tyre, the city of the Byzantines—she who is called by many names, say to Tyre: In what way have you rebelled against My command, and become arrogant with your arrogance? You vie with Me by your arrogance, and you imagine your cosmos [*falak*] to be like My throne.*
>
> *I will surely send My servants, the unlettered, the children of Sheba and the Yemenites, against you, who will come to the invocation of God, just as the starving birds come to meat, just as the thirsty flocks come to water.*
>
> *I will close up the hearts of your people, I will constrict their hearts (from pity), and make the voice of one of you at the time of hardship like the voice of the lion emerging from the den. Then shepherds will shout at it, but their voices will only increase in boldness and harshness.*
>
> *I will make the hoofs of their horses like iron on soft stones on a day of hardship, and I will fasten the strings of their bows. I will leave you bald to the sun, and without inhabitants other than the birds and wild animals. I will make your stones into sulphur, and your smoke swirl below the birds of the heavens. All the islands of the sea will hear your voice in great promise, but be unable to save it (from Me).*[886]

1351. `Abdallāh b. `Amr: The best of the martyrs in God's sight are the martyrs of the sea, the martyrs of the valleys, and the martyrs of the Dajjāl.
1352. Ka`b: The graves of the martyrs of the greatest apocalyptic battle will shine light among the graves of the martyrs of those who killed them. [300]
1353. Ka`b: If I participate in the day of the greatest apocalyptic

[886] This appears to be a collage of Ezekiel 28:2, 7, perhaps influenced by Rev. 18. However, there are no identifiable verses translated in it.

battle, I will not be distressed about the things [sins] that have passed previously, nor would I care about what would follow afterwards, since fighting one day in the greatest apocalyptic battle is better than fighting the Dajjāl. There will be but one sword with the Dajjāl, but many with the fighters in the apocalyptic battle, plus the swords of all the nations.

1354. Ka`b: God Most High has with the Byzantines three slaughters: the first of them at Yarmūk, the second at Fīnqus, meaning the date,[887] which is Ḥimṣ, and the third is the valleys.

1355. Ka`b: "Constantinople will not be conquered until its loin (or kidney) [will be]." It was said: "What is its loin?" He said: "Amorium."

1356. Ka`b: "Constantinople will not be conquered until its fang [will be]." It was said: "What is its fang?" He said: "Amorium." Abū Bakr told me on the authority of Ka`b the same, other than he said: "Its dog."

1357. Ka`b: Amorium is the bitch of Constantinople, from the perspective that it will crumble first.

1358. Ka`b: How much I would love to remain after the conquest of the city of Heraclius, that the gates of evil would open at that time, and how much humiliation and lowliness [for its people] there will be at the moment of its conquest!

1359. Abū al-Dardā': Do not wish the conquest of the city of Heraclius to be quick, for how much humiliation and lowliness there will be at the moment of its conquest!

1360. Ka`b: When a man from Quraysh runs away to Cosntantinople, then the matter [of the end] is at hand. The commander of the army that will conquer Constantinople—there will be no thieves, fornicators or illegal looters. The apocalyptic battles will be at the hands of a man from the family of Heraclius.

1361. Ka`b: "It will be conquered at the hands of a man from the Hashemites." [. . .] Ka`b: "It will be conquered at the hands of the progeny of Sheba and Qedar." [. . .] [301] Ka`b: "The one

[887] Presumably *ficus*, see nos. 720, 748, 755.

at whose hands will be the apocalyptic battles will be a man from the family of Heraclius named Tibr," meaning Tiberius. **(1)** (second half of the tradition)

1362. Al-Muhājir b. Ḥabīb: The Messenger of God said: The fifth from the family of Heraclius, called Tibr [Tiberius]—at his hands will be the apocalyptic battles.

1363. Jubayr b. Nufayr: You will conquer the city of unbelief with *allāhu akbar!* at which God Most High will lay low a third of its walls. After three days while you are in that situation the report of the Dajjāl will come to you, but do not be alarmed by that, as it is false, so carry your spoils [with you].

1364. `Abdallāh b. Busr al-Māzinī: When the report of the Dajjāl comes to you, while you are in it [Constantinople] do not put aside your spoils, for the Dajjāl has not emerged.

1365. Abū Tha`laba al-Khushanī: When what is between the path [over the Cilician Gates] and al-`Arīsh is a feast for one family, then the conquest of Constantinople is close.

1366. `Awf b. Mālik al-Ashja`ī: The Messenger of God said: "The sixth tribulation is a truce that will be between you and the Banū al-Aṣfar, so they will come to under eighty banners (*ghay*āya)." I said: "What is a *ghay*āya?" He said: "A banner, and under every banner there will be 12,000 [troops]."

1367. Abū al-Dardā', when he was told the tradition: "They will expel you from it village by village," then Abū al-Dardā' said: "Did not God, mighty and majestic say, 'Certainly We have written in the Psalms, after the Reminder: The earth—My righteous servants will inherit it.'[888] Who are the righteous servants if not us?"

1368. `Abdallāh b. `Amr: A third of the Muslims will retreat on the day of the apocalyptic battle, and those are the worst of creation in God's sight. [302]

1369. `Abdallāh b. `Amr: When Dhū al-Khalṣa is worshipped—an

[888] Q 21:105, citing Psalms 37:9, 11.

idol belonging to Daws during the *jāhiliyya*—that will be the sign of the appearance of the Byzantines in Syria.

1370. Ka`b: "O Qays, love Yemen! And O Yemen, love Qays! For there is about to be a time when none but the both of you will be killed for this religion."

1371. Al-Awzā`ī: It reached me that the Messenger of God said: Qays are the horsemen of God on the day of the apocalyptic battles, while Yemen is the hope of Islam.

1372. Abū Hurayra: The Prophet said: When the apocalyptic battles happen, a delegation of *mawālī* will depart from Damascus, who are the noblest of the Arabs[889] in horsemanship and having the most prowess in weapons by whom God will support this religion.

1373. `Abd al-Wāḥid b. Qays al-Dimashqī[890]: The Byzantines during the days of the apocalyptic battles will not leave a single watering hole on the coastlands without an army camp beside it.

1374. `Aṭiyya b. Qays[891]: The Messenger of God said: When the apocalyptic battles happen, a delegation will depart from Damascus who are the best of God's servants, the first and the last.

1375. Rāshid b. Sa`d: The Messenger of God said: God Most High promised me Persia, then the Byzantines, then their women, their sons, their low-born, and their treasures, and He aided me with Ḥimyar as helpers.

1376. Abū al-Dardā': The Byzantines will expel you from Syria village by village until they force you to the Balqā'.[892] At that this world will perish and be annilated, but the next [world] will remain.

[889] Since the *mawālī* were not Arabs, perhaps this means the equal of the Arabs, or even superior to them, although it is difficult to see why they would be praised in two categories concerning which the Arabs considered themselves to be without peer.

[890] Al-Sulamī, snub-nosed, a *mawlā*, lived in Damascus, was the teacher for the children of Yazīd II, *fl.* 2nd/8th century.

[891] `Aṭiyya b. Qays al-Kilābī or al-Kalā`ī, lived in Ḥimṣ and Damascus, raided during the period of Mu`āwiya, d. 110/728–9.

[892] Compare Ibn `Asākir, *Tar'ikh*, ii, p. 214.

1377. Ka`b: The greatest apocalyptic battle, the destruction of Constantinople and the emergence of the Dajjāl will occur within seven months, if God wishes this.

1378. Makḥūl: The apocalyptic battles are ten, the first of which is the apocalyptic battle of Caesarea in Filasṭīn, and the last of which is the valley of Antioch.

1379. `Abd al-Raḥmān b. Abī Bakra[893]: I heard `Abdallāh b. `Amr saying: "There is about to emerge the duration of a sheep's pregnancy" [303] three times. I said: "What is the duration of a sheep's pregnancy?" He said: "A man one of whose parents is a demon (*shayṭān*), who will rule the Byzantines, and lead 1,500,000 [troops] on land, and 500,000 on the sea until they land at a place called the valley. Then he will say to his supporters: 'I have a need for your ships.' So when they land, he will order them to be burned. Then he will say to them: 'You have no further Constantinople or Rome!' Whoever wants, let him rise and aid the Muslims," then he mentioned the tradition until Constantinople the whore will be conquered, "I find it to be called 'the whore' in the book of God Most High.[894] Their commander will say: 'There is no illegal pillaging today.'"

1380. Ka`b: During the greatest apocalyptic battle, the coastlands of Syria will be destroyed, such that the coastlands will weep over their destruction like the cities and the villages.

1381. Ḥassān b. `Aṭiyya: The Byzantines will overcome the plain of Al-Urdunn[895] and Jerusalem (*bayt al-maqdis*) during the lesser apocalyptic battle.

1382. Abū Zaynab[896]: When Cyprus is destroyed, then weep for the days of your life over yourself.

1383. Al-Muhājir b. Ḥabīb: The Messenger of God said: "The fifth of the family of Heraclius, at his hands will be the apocalyptic battles." Arṭāt said: "But four of the family of Heraclius have ruled."

[893] Nufay` b. al-Ḥārith al-Thaqafī, lived in Baṣra, *fl.* 1st/7th century.

[894] Probably the reference is to Rev. 19, with Constantinople = Babylon.

[895] Most likely the lowland areas of Galilee or the Plain of Esdraelon.

[896] Ḥāzim b. Ḥarmala al-Ghifārī, Companion, *fl.* 1st/7th century.

The Companions of the Messenger of God said: "So the fifth is remaining." Arṭāt said: "Until now there has not been a fifth."

1384. Ka`b: A woman will rule the Byzantines,[897] who says: "Build for me 1000 ships, the best type of ship that has been made on the face of the earth. Then depart for those, the ones who have killed our men, and taken our women and sons captive." When they will finish with it, she will say: "Board, if God wills or not," so God will send a wind against them to dash them into pieces because of her word "If [he does] or does not wish." Then they will build for her another 1000 ships like them, and she will say the same thing, and God will send a wind against them to dash them into pieces. Then they will build for her another 1000, so she will say: "Board, if God wishes."

They will depart and go until they end up at the hill of Acre,[898] so they will say: "This is our land, the land of our fathers." Then they will set fire to their ships to burn them. The Muslims on that day will be in Jerusalem, so the ruler will write to the Iraqis, the Egyptians, and the Yemenites, but his messengers will come saying: "We are afraid of what has happened to you will happen to us." [304] His messengers will pass by Ḥimṣ, while its people will have locked its gates against the Muslims inside of it. They will kill a woman in it, and throw her from the section close to the wall outwards.

So the ruler will conceal the matter of Ḥimṣ, then say to the Muslims: "Go out to your enemy; die and kill!" So they will fight a fierce battle, and a third of the Muslims will be killed, a third will be defeated, and fall into a pile of sand on the earth, and the remaining third will advance until they end up in Jerusalem (*bayt al-maqdis*). Then they will depart from it, going to al-Mawjib[899] in the land of al-Balqā'. Al-Mawjib is

897 The Empress Irene (regent 780–97)?

898 Presumably the ancient tell of the city located a short distance to the east of the port city.

899 In between Jerusalem and the Balqā', so presumably somewhere in the Jordan Valley.

a land in which there are springs, and grass (*ḥashīsh*) of the earth's vegetation is produced, so the Muslims will descend there.

The enemies of God will advance until they end up in Jerusalem, then he[900] will say: "Go and fight the remains of my slaves who are left." Then the ruler of the Muslims will say to those who are with him: "Go out to your enemy." So they will weep and beseech God, mighty and majestic. On that day, God will be enraged for His religion, so He will pierce with His spear, and strike with His sword, and God will set iron against each other—so that a man would not care whether al-Ṣamṣāma was with him or something else.

They will be killed in the Jordan River valley (*al-ghūr*), so they will fight a fierce battle, and the enemy will be killed on that day. None but a minute remnant will be left from them which will take refuge in Mt. Lebanon, while the Muslims are right behind them, driving them on until they end up at Constantinople.

Commanding the Muslims will be a brown (*ādam*) man, having his spear thrust down between his thigh and his saddle,[901] until they reach the body of water[902] that is near Constantinople. Then the ruler will make his ablutions, and pray, then the waters will retreat from him. He will go after them, but they will retreat, so when he sees this, he will mount his ride, then say: "O everyone! This is something that God wants, so go and cross!" So they will cross until they end up at the wall of Constantinople. Then they will shout *allāhu akbar!* one time as one man, and twelve towers on it will fall down. On that day its men will be killed, its women will be taken captive and its wealth taken. While they are in that situation someone will come and say: "The Dajjāl has emerged in Syria,"

900 It is not clear who "he" is here.

901 Lane, v, p. 2114 (mid. col.).

902 Presumably the Bosphorus separating the Muslims from Constantinople.

so the people will depart—the one who will take something will regret that he did not take more because of the years that will be under the Dajjāl. But they will that he did not emerge, although it will only be a little time until he does.

1385. Khālid b. Ma`dān: I said to `Abdallāh b. Busr: "When will Constantinople be conquered?" He said: "It will not be conquered until there is a peace between the Muslims and them, so that you raid together. They will depart after having taken spoils, then descend upon its field. A man from among them will lift the cross, and say: 'The Cross is victorious!' but a man from the Muslims will rise, strike the cross and crush it. So the Muslims and them will arise, fight, and God will have them conquer. At that time will be its conquest."

1386. `Abdallāh b. Sa`d: The Messenger of God said: God gave me Persia—its bowmen, sons, wealth, and weapons, and He gave me the Byzantines—their women, their sons, their weapons, and their wealth—and aided me with Ḥimyar. [305]

1387. Khālid b. Ma`dān: The Byzantine enemy will surely enter Tartosa at the morning prayer, and kill 300 Muslim men under its water-wheels, whose light will reach the Throne.

1388. Some of the elders of his [al-Faraj b. Yaḥmad's][903] people: We were with Sufyān b. `Awf al-Ghāmidī[904] until we came to the Gate of Constantinople, the golden gate, leading 3000 horsemen from the sea side until we had passed the body of water or the gulf.[905] So they were terrified and beat their clappers (*nawāqīs*), then they said: "What is with you, O Arabs?" We said: "We have come to 'this town of evildoers'[906] that God would destroy it at our hands." They said: "By God, we do not know whether the Book has lied or whether the calculation is mistake, but you have come too fast. By God, we know that it

903 Unidentified, but presumably Syrian.

904 `Amr b. `Abdallāh al-Azdī, appointed by Mu`āwiya over the summer raids against the Byzantines, killed by the Byzantines 55/675.

905 The Bosphorus.

906 Q 4:75.

will be conquered one day, but we do not think that this is the time."

1389. Ka`b: "When you see [the tribe of] Hamdān of the east, when it has descended between Rastan and Ḥimṣ, then that is the presence of the apocalyptic battle and the emergence of the Dajjāl." I[907] said: "What will cause it to descend at Rastan?" He said: "An enemy from behind it."

1390. `Abdallāh b. `Amr: Both Madhḥij and Hamdān will pass over from Iraq until they settle in Qinnesrin.

1391. `Abdallāh b. `Amr: The Byzantines will mobilize an army, so the Syrians will ask for aid, and beg for succor, so no believer will stay back from them. So the Byzantines will be defeated until they end up at a pillar (*usṭawāna*) whose location I know.[908] When they are there, a crier will come to them: "The Dajjāl is behind you among your families!" so they will toss everything that is in their hands, and advance towards him.

1392. Abū Tha`laba al-Khushanī: When you see that which is between al-`Arīsh and the Euphrates [River] a feast for one family, then that is the sign of the apocalyptic battles.

1393. Ka`b: At the hands of the Yemenite who will kill Quraysh.

1394. Ka`b: At the hands of that Yemenite will be the lesser apocalyptic battle of Acre, and that will be when the fifth of the family of Heraclius rules. [306]

1395. Abū Qubayl: The apocalyptic battles will be at the hands of Tiberius, son of Justinian (II) son of the Slit-nose son of Constantine son of Heraclius.

1396. Ḥudhayfa b. al-Yamān: The Messenger of God said: There will be a truce between you and the Banū al-Aṣfar, the Byzantines, but they will betray you during [the duration of] a woman's pregnancy. They will come leading eighty banners on land and sea, under every banner will be 12,000 [troops], until they land between Jaffa and Acre. The lord of their realm will burn

907 Abū al-Yamān al-Hawazanī.

908 Could this be one of the pillars of the Stylites?

their ships, saying to his soldiers: "Fight for your lands!" so the fight will be desperate. The army-provinces wll aid each other such that from Ḥaḍramawt in Yemen they will aid you. On that day the Merciful One will pierce with His spear, strike among them with His sword, and fire among them with His arrows, so there will be the greatest slaughter among them because of Him.

1397. Ka`b, that he came to a gathering of the people at the Jews' Gate for the [Feasts of] Fiṭr and the Aḍḥā, faced the city, and wept, then went until he came to the locked gate, faced it and wept violently. Then he came to the locked gate below the Rastan Gate, faced it, and wept violently. Then he came to the Eastern Gate, stood between its vault and the gate, and laughed loudly, and rejoiced obviously.[909]

He said: "O God, You have the praise!" so he said "*lā ilaha illā allāhu, al-ḥamdu li-l-llāhi, subḥ*ān allā*h*, and *allāhu akbar*," so I said to him: "O Abū Isḥāq, what caused you to weep and laugh in the places where you did, and what caused you to rejoice?" He said: "The people of this city will receive a call to arms from the people of Islam for the coastal area, because of an enemy who will come to them from that direction. Every single person who can bear arms will make haste to the coastal area."

So its people, the unbelievers, will gather and say: "Your aid and force has come to you from your city, so lock the gates to keep in the offspring and families of the Muslims." God will conquer for the Muslims, and give them victory over their enemy that had come to them, but then they will be informed that their women and offspring are locked in, so they will advance until they are standing on the place I was at first. They will implore them by God concerning the covenant and

[909] Compare Ibn `Asākir, *Tā'rīkh*, ii, p. 218 where Ka`b acts in the same manner in Damascus as he is leaving the Jābiya Gate, saying that a house for the Dajjāl will be built there.

protection (*dhimmi?*), but they will not return anything to them or open up to them. So they will come to my second place, and implore them by God concerning the protection and the covenant, but they will not return anything to them or open up to them.

Then they will bombard them [the Ḥimṣis] with the head of a woman from the [tribe of] Banū `Abs. Whereupon they will come to my third standing place, and implore them by God and the protection, but they will not return anything to them or open up for them. So then they will come to my fourth place, which is this one. When the Muslims see that, they will lift up their hands to God Most High, and ask succor from Him and call Him to arms. I swear by God that neither wood nor iron nor nails will remain of this gate: they will come off and fall down. So the Muslims will come in and will cut off the head of every single one of the unbelievers upon whom a razor has passed.[910] On that day their blood will reach the fetlocks of the horses below the confluence of markets. [307]

1398. Arṭāt: There will be a peace between the Mahdi and the tyrant of the Byzantines after his killing of the Sufyānī, and the pillage of [the tribe of] Kalb, such that your merchants will go back and forth to them, and theirs to you, and then they will build ships for three years. Then the Mahdi will perish, and a man from his family will rule, performing minimal justice, then acting wrongly. He will be killed, but his memory will not be extinguished until the Byzantines moor [their ships] between Tyre and Acre, and that will be the apocalyptic battles. [308][911]

[910] Passed puberty.

[911] Section break pp. 308–10.

Concerning the Appearance of the Byzantines in Alexandria, the Edges of Miṣr and its Harbors (*mawāhīz*)[912]

1399. \`Abdallāh b. \`Amr b. al-\`Āṣ that he was in Alexandria, so it was said to him: "Boats have been seen, so the people were terrified." \`Abdallāh b. \`Amr b. al-\`Āṣ said: "Saddle up." Then he said: "From which direction were they seen?" They said: "From the direction of the lighthouse." So he said: "Hold on, we will only fear them if they are from the direction of the west."

1400. Shufay b. \`Ubayd al-Aṣbaḥī[913]: Alexandria will have two apocalyptic battles: one of them the greater and the other the lesser. As for the greater, the sea will recede from the lighthouse the distance of one or two post-stops, then the treasures of Dhū al-Qarnayn[914] will be taken out. His treasures will span the east and the west. The sign of the lesser [apocalyptic battle] will be that Alexandria will drip blood.

1401. Abū Qubayl: The apocalyptic battle of Alexandria will be at the hands of Tiberius son of the Slit-nose son of Constantine son of Heraclius.

1402. \`Abdallāh b. \`Amr b. al-\`Āṣ: "The Byzantines will prepare 700 ships, then advance in them to Alexandria, when a man from Quraysh will be ruling Alexandria. They will deceive the Muslims with their ships, directing them to the lesser arsenals to the west [312] of Alexandria.[915] So the Qurashite will divide his horse, and send them to those western ships, but keep some with him." \`Abdallāh said: "You idiot! Do not divide your horse! They will land and the Muslims will fight them, until the Byzantines force the Muslims to the Fish Market. They will fight until the blood will reach the fetlocks of the

912 Probably the Aramaic *maḥoz*, with an Arabic plural, see no. 1342.

913 Egyptian, *fl.* 1st/7th century.

914 Usually identified with Alexander the Great.

915 These are probably the old Byzantine arsenals from the time of Justinian (thanks to Michael Decker for this identification).

horses. Then a banner will come to the Muslims as aid, so when the Byzantines will see it, they will turn to their boats and board them. They will push and go, until the weak-eyed one [with bad vision] would say: 'I cannot see them,' but the clear-eyed one [with good vision] would say: 'I see the last of them.' Then God will send a gale-force wind against them, which will return them to Alexandria, and their boats will be broken up between Alexandria and the lighthouse. They will be taken captive in their entirety, other than one boat, which will save its people until they reach their land so as to inform them of what happened. Then God will send a gale-force wind and return it to Alexandria where it will be broken and those in it taken."

1403. Abū Qubayl: The sign of the apocalyptic battle of Damietta (Dimyāṭ) will be flags that will emerge from Egypt to Syria—those flags will be called "Error."

1404. `Abdallāh b. `Amr: When you see two land-holders (*dihqānayn*) of the Arabs flee to the Byzantines that is a sign, of the battle of Alexandria.

1405. `Abdallāh b. Ta`lā said to his daughter[916]: "When it reaches you that Alexandria has been conquered, if your veil is in the west, do not take it so that you can take refuge in the east." `Abdallāh b. Ta`lā was learned.

1406. Shufay: The first part of the harbors (*mawāḥīz*) of Egypt that the enemy will destroy will be Nikiu (Niqiwūs).

1407. Abū Zura`a that he heard Shufay saying: "O Egyptians, your harbors/trading-posts (*mawāḥīz*) will be cut from you, during the winter as well as the summer. So choose for yourselves the best of them." They said: "What are the best of them?" He said: "Every [313] harbor/trading-post that is not surrounded by water. Then the enemy will desire you like a rabid dog, so they will fasten you to your harbors/trading posts, such that one of you would be looking at the smoke of his kettle [in his house],

[916] Unknown, although presumably Egyptian.

but be unable to get to it, out of concern that the enemy would come to his family in his absence."

1408. `Abdallāh: The apocalyptic battle of Alexandria will be at the hands of Tiberius son of Justinian (II). When a boat lands at the lighthouse, and lowers [its sails], then lifts them three times, suddenly in the middle of the day 400 boats will come to you, then another 400 to land at the lighthouse.

1409. Tubay`: The idiot of Quraysh will be in charge of Alexandria on that day for its apocalyptic battle, so the battle will be in the Fish Market, and the kings of the Byzantines will lower their thrones at Caesarea, at the Green Dome,[917] at Yuḥnas[918] and so the Muslims will retreat to the Praying-place (*masjid*) of Solomon,[919] until a vanguard of the Arabs overtakes them. Among them will be a horseman on a horse with a blaze, tractable, with a bit of motley color on it, [who will be] upon the prominence of the lighthouse.

1410. `Abdallāh b. Rāshid: I heard my father say: A man known for his ancestry through both father and mother from Quraysh will depart angrily to the Byzantines, so they will greet him, and give him a position of honor. From the day of his departure for the Byzantines there will be twenty months, then he will lead the Byzantines to Alexandria in their ships. A fierce wind will greet them, so that none but one informing will return to the land of the Byzantines. His father: If I wanted to I could tell you where the commander of the Byzantines will place his banner on that day, as he will land between the old Green [Dome] and the lighthouse, which is beside Alexandria.

1411. `Abdallāh b. `Amr: The sign of the apocalyptic battle of Alexandria is when you see two land-holders of the Arabs

[917] Mentioned in Alexandria, Ibn Zawlaq, *Faḍā'il Miṣr wa-akhbāruhā wa-khawaṣṣuhā* (Cairo: Maktabat al-Khanjī, 2000), p. 72 as being covered in copper.

[918] This is probably St. John the Baptist Church, at Pompey's Pillar, destroyed in the 10th century.

[919] Mentioned in Ibn Zawlaq, *Faḍā'il* p. 51; Ibn Ẓahīra, *al-Faḍā'il al-bāhira fī maḥāsin al-Qāhira* (Cairo: Wizārat al-Thaqāfa, 1969), p. 102.

depart for the Byzantines, so this will be the sign of the apocalyptic battle of Alexandria.

1412. Abū Firās: We were with ʿAbdallāh b. ʿAmr in Alexandria, and it was said to him: "The people are terrified," so he called for his weapons and his horse, so a man came to him saying: "Where is this fright coming from?" He said: "A ship from the direction of Cyprus." He said: "Let go of my horse." We said: "May God make you righteous, have the people ridden?" So he said: "This is not the apocalyptic battle of Alexandria, they will only come from the west, from the direction of Anṭablus.[920] They will come with 100, then 100," until he counted 700.

1413. ʿAmr b. Jābir al-Ḥaḍramī: I heard Shufay al-Aṣbaḥī [314] saying: Alexandria will have two apocalyptic battles: one of them the lesser while the other is the greater. As for the lesser, 500 sails will come it, but as for the greater 100 sails.[921] Seventy chieftains (*ʿarīf*) will be killed[922] during the lesser, but 400 will be killed during the greater. The sign of the lesser is that the sea will retreat from the lighthouse the distance of two post-stops. Then the treasures of Dhū al-Qarnayn will be taken out—his treasures will encompass both the easterners and the westerners.

1414. ʿAbdallāh b. ʿAmr: In the apocalyptic battle of Alexandria the Byzantines will approach from the west from the direction of Anṭablus, until when they reach the Slaughter-place of the Nag Pony (Minḥar al-Birdhawn) from the land of Libya (*lūbiya*) the report of them will reach the lord of Alexandria, so he will send his vanguard to them, but they will not [be able to] return to him until the Byzantines land in Alexandria—so I wish that I could cleave to Quraysh on that day here and say: "O idiot! Keep your horsemen close to you! For they [the Byzantines] overshadow you."

920 Close to Barqa, in present-day Libya; see no. 67.
921 One wonders whether this is a mistake for 100,000.
922 With MM, in place of "will advance."

1415. Ka`b: "I wish that I would not die until I could participate in the day of Alexandria!" It was said to him: "Hasn't it been conquered already?" He said: "That was not its day, but its day will be when 100 ships come to it, and in their wake another 100, until it reaches 700, then in the wake of that the same—that will be its day! By the One who holds the soul of Ka`b in His hand, they will fight until the blood reaches between the shanks and the forelegs of the horse." [315]

What will happen to People previous to the Appearance of the Antichrist

1416. Abū Umāma al-Bāhilī[923]: The Messenger of God spoke to us, and most of his speech of what he told us was warning us about the Dajjāl. From his words: "O people, there has not been any tribulation on the earth greater than that of Dajjāl. Every prophet sent by God Most High has warned his community concerning him. I am the last of the prophets and you are the last of communities, so he will emerge among you, without any doubt. If he emerges while I am among you, then I will be the defender (*ḥajīj*) of every Muslim; if he emerges after me, then every man will be the defender of himself. God will be my successor for every Muslim—so whoever of you meets him, let him spit in his face, and read the opening verses of *sūrat al-kahf*."[924]

1417. Ka`b al-Aḥbār used to say: The dog of the Hour is the Dajjāl, whoever is constant at the tribulation of the Dajjāl will not be tempted, nor will be tempted in life or death. Whoever lives in his time but does not follow him, will receive paradise absolutely. If a man is saved, and calls the Dajjāl a liar one time—saying: "I know who you are: you are the Dajjāl!"—then reads the opening of *sūrat al-kahf*, and does not fear him, he will not be able to tempt him. This verse is like an amulet

[923] Ṣudayy b. `Ajlān al-Bāhilī, Companion, lived in Ḥimṣ, d. 81/700–1.
[924] Q 18.

(*tamīma*) against the Dajjāl. Blessed are those who are saved by their faith before the tribulation of the Dajjāl, his lowliness and humiliation—he will meet people like the best of the Companions of Muḥammad.

1418. Shurayḥ b. `Abd[925] that the Messenger of God warned his Companions about the Dajjāl, saying: "Know, O people, that you will not meet your Lord until you die, and that your Lord is not blind in one eye, that the Dajjāl, blind [lacking an eyeball] (*maṭmūs*) in one eye, lies concerning God, is not [316] deep or cavernous (*ḥujrā'*).[926] Written between his eyes is 'Unbeliever' which every believer will be able to read. If he emerges while I am with you, I will be your defender; if he emerges after me and I am not with you, then every man will be his own defender. God will be my successor over every Muslim, so whoever meets him, let him read the opening of *sūrat al-kahf*."

1419. Abū Qilāba: I saw the people crowding around a man, so I pressed up against the people, until I was close to him, so I asked concerning him. They said: "A man from the Companions of the Messenger of God," so I heard him saying: "After you will be the liar, the one who leads astray, and behind his head [his hair] is plaited doubly (*ḥubukan ḥubukan*). He will say: 'I am your lord' so anyone who says: 'You lie, you are not our lord, but God is our Lord, upon Him we have relied, and to Him we return; we take refuge in God from you,' he [the Dajjāl] will have no way to get to him."

1420. Hishām b. `Āmir[927]: I heard the Messenger of God saying: "There is no matter greater between the creation of Adam and the arising of the Hour than the Dajjāl."

[925] Probably Shurayḥ b. `Ubayd al-Ḥaḍramī, lived in Ḥimṣ, *fl.* 2nd/8th century.

[926] This phrase, *nāt'a . . . ḥujrā'*, the latter of which is also read as *juḥrā'*, is probably corrupt, and was difficult for scholars: Ibn al-Athīr, *Nihāya*, i, pp. 240, 343.

[927] Companion, lived in Baṣra, *fl.* 1st/7th century.

1421. Ṭalḥa b. `Aṭā'[928]: The Messenger of God said: The Dajjāl will emerge during a rage that he feels.[929]

1422. Jābir: The Messenger of God said before his death by a month: Before the Hour there will be liars, among the lord of the Yamāma,[930] among them the lord of Ṣana`ā', al-`Ansī,[931] among them the lord of Ḥimyar, and among them the Dajjāl, but the Dajjāl is the greatest of them in his temptation.

1423. Wahb b. Munabbih: The first of the signs is the Byzantines, then the second is the Dajjāl, the third is God [and Magog], while the fourth is Jesus son of Mary. **(1)**

1424. `Ubāda b. al-Ṣāmit[932]: The Messenger of God said: I have told you of the Dajjāl until I fear that you will not comprehend. The [False] Messiah, the Dajjāl is a short man, walking with his toes turned in, curly hair, blind in one eye, lacking an eyeball, not deep or cavernous, so if he deceives you know that your Lord is not blind in one eye, and that you will never see your Lord until you die. [317]

1425. Anas: The Messenger of God said: "The Dajjāl is blind in his left eye, on his forehead is written 'unbeliever' and on his eye there is an obvious growth over his eye." Sahl said: "He is *k f r* [*kāfir* = unbeliever] with the letters written together, like cursive."

928 Probably Ṭalḥa b. al-`Alā' al-Aḥmasī, lived in Kūfa, *fl.* 1st/7th century.

929 A real fear during the Umayyad period, e.g., "Ibrāhīm b. Hishām said to Hishām b. `Abd al-Mālik: 'O *amir al-mu'minin*, I came to `Abd al-Raḥmān b. `Anbasa b. Sa`īd b. al-`Āṣ one day, and with me was Ibrāhīm b. `Abdallāh b. Muṭī`. `Abd al-Raḥmān b. `Anbasa was wearing green clothes, an upper garment, a gown and a headdress (`amama), and Ibrahim said: "Ibn `Anbasa has come with the decoration of Korah (Qārūn)" and I laughed. `Abd al-Raḥmān said: "What made you laugh, O commander?" I said: "Ibrāhīm said thus-and- thus when you came in." `Abd al-Raḥmān said: "If it were not that I fear for you and me, and for the Muslims if he is angered, I would have answered." I said: "What makes you frightened of his anger?" He said: "I have heard that the Dajjal will appear during a rage, and Ibrāhīm is blind in one eye (*a`war*)—and I think that he is the Dajjal!" (al-Balādhurī, *Ansāb*, vii, p. 351).

930 Musaylima.

931 Al-Aswad al-`Ansī, revolted in Yemen after the death of the Prophet.

932 Companion, lived in Jerusalem, died in Ramla, d. 34/654–5.

1426. Anas b. Mālik: The Messenger of God said: There will be approximately seventy deceivers (Dajjāls) before the emergence of the Dajjāl.

1427. Abū Sa`īd al-Khudarī: There will be a woman together with the Dajjāl called Ṭayyiba—every village he comes to she will preceed him saying: "This man is entering into your presence, so watch out!"[933]

1428. `Alī: A man who has made light of traditions, every time he puts out an outrageous tradition (*uḥdūtha*) he lies, and then its measure is cut by something longer—if he lives to see the Dajjāl, he will follow him.

1429. Sālim from his father: The Messenger of God rose among the people, then praised God in the way that was appropriate, then mentioned the Dajjāl, and then said: "I am warning you of him; every single prophet has warned his people concerning him. Noah warned his people, but I will say to something that no prophet has said previously to his people: Do you know that he is blind in one eye? Your Lord is not blind in one eye."

1430. Some of the Companions of the Prophet that the Prophet said one day to the people while he was warning them concerning his tribulation: "Do you know that not one of you will ever see his Lord until he dies, and that between his eyes is written 'unbeliever,' which can be read by every believer who disapproves of his actions." [318]

Signs before the Appearance of the Antichrist

1431. `Abdallāh b. Busr, Companion of the Prophet: The Prophet said: Between the apocalyptic battle and the conquest of Constantinople there are years, then the Dajjāl will emerge on the seventh year.

1432. Ka`b: The Dajjāl will not emerge until the conquest of Constantinople.

[933] Probably the virgin Tabitha mentioned in Frankfurter, *Elijah in Upper Egypt* (Minneapolis: Fortress Press, 1993), p. 316.

1433. Kathīr b. Murra: Whoever is present at Constantinople, let him carry what he can and take it, for the Messenger of God said: "Its conquest and the emergence of the Dajjāl are in seven years."

1434. Ka`b: The news will come to you while you are dividing your spoils that the Dajjāl has emerged, but it is only a lie. Take what you can, for you will stay six years, then he will emerge in the seventh.

1435. Ka`b: The Dajjāl will not emerge until the city [Constantinople] is conquered.

1436. Bashīr b. `Abdallāh b. Yassār said: `Abdallāh b. Bishr al-Māzinī, Companion of the Messenger of God, took my ear, then said: "O nephew, perhaps you will live to see the conquest of Constantinople, so a warning to you if you do see its conquest from leaving its spoils, because between its conquest and the emergence of the Dajjāl are seven years." [319]

1437. `Abdallāh b. `Amr: The Dajjāl will emerge after the conquest of Constantinople, but before the descent of Jesus son of Mary at Jerusalem.

1438. Ka`b: The Messenger of God said: The news will come to them that the Dajjāl has emerged after their conquest of Constantinople, so they will turn back, but not find him; then it will be but a short time until he emerges.

1439. Abū Hurayra: The Messenger of God said: Before the emergence of the [false] messiah the Dajjāl there will be years of treachery, in which the truthful will be called liars and the liars truthful, and the traitor will receive trust, while the reliable one will be accused of treachery. Mean (*ruwaybīḍa*), contemptible ones among the people will speak forth.

1440. Ḥudhayfa b. al-Yamān: There will be a raid on the sea—whoever joins the raid will be wealthy, and never be poor again, but whoever does not join it, his wealth will not grow after it, except that [wealth] which was from before—then the sea will be difficult after the raid for six years, then the sea will return to what it was previously for six years, then be difficult for six years, a total of eighteen years, then the Dajjāl will emerge.

1441. Ka`b: Before the emergence of the Dajjāl there will be three tribulations: the tribulation of `Uthmān, the tribulation of Ibn Zubayr, and the third,[934] then the Dajjāl will emerge.

1442. Tubay`: Before the Dajjāl there are three signs: three years of hunger, in which the rivers will decrease, the aromatic plants become yellow, the springs dry up, so [the tribes of] Madhḥij and Hamdān will move from Iraq to settle in Qinnasrin and Aleppo, so then they will fight the Dajjāl in their homelands morning and evening.

1443. Mu`ādh b. Jabal: [320] The Messenger of God said: The greatest apocalyptic battle, the conquest of Constantinople, and the emergence of the Dajjāl are within seven months.

1444. Ḍamra b. Ḥabīb: `Abd al-Malik b. Marwān wrote to Abū Baḥriyya that it had reached him that 'you are narrating on the authority of Mu`ādh concerning the apocalyptic battle, Constantinople and the emergence of the Dajjāl.' So Abū Baḥriyya wrote back to him that he heard Mu`ādh saying: "The greatest apocalyptic battle, the conquest of Constantinople and the emergence of the Dajjāl are within seven months."

1445. Ibn Muḥayrīz: The greatest apocalyptic battle, the destruction of Constantinople and the emergence of the Dajjāl are within the duration of a woman's pregnancy.

1446. `Abdallāh b. Busr on the authority of the Prophet: Between the apocalyptic battle and the conquest of Constantinople there are six years, and the emergence of the Dajjāl is in the seventh.[935]

1447. Ka`b said: "The Dajjāl will emerge in the year 80," but God knows best which 80, whether 280 [893–4] or another.

1448. Ka`b: The Messenger of God said: God will never link the

[934] Presumably this is the emergence of the `Abbāsids, but the writer did not dare to say it explicitly.

[935] Abū Dā'ūd, *Sunan*, iv, p. 108 (no. 4296).

sword of the Dajjāl with the sword of the apocalyptic battle [at the same time] for this community.

1449. Asmā` daughter of Yazīd al-Anṣāriyya[936]: The Messenger of God was in my house, and he mentioned the Dajjāl, and said: "Before him there are three years: a year in which the heavens will hold back a third of their water, and the earth a third of its produce, and the second, in which the heavens will hold back two-thirds of their water, and the earth two-thirds of its produce, and the third in which the heavens will hold back their water, and the earth its produce entirely, so that every possessor of hoof and tusk among the quadrupeds will perish."

1450. Ibrāhīm b. `Abla: It is said that before the emergence of the Dajjāl a boy will be born in Beth-Shean (Baysān), of the tribe of Levi son of Jacob, with an image of weapons on his body: a sword, a shield, a javelin and a knife.

1451. `Umayr b. Hāni': The Messenger [321] of God said: When the people go into two camps—the camp of belief in which there is no hypocrisy, and a camp of hypocrisy in which there is no belief—when they both gather, then look out for the Dajjāl that day or the next.

1452. Ibn `Umar on the authority of the Prophet that he was filled with fear about the Dajjāl, and mentioned his signs, characteristics and precedents, until the crowd thought that he would arise against them, from among them from the palm-grove, or from outside of the palm-grove to them.[937] He [Muḥammad] then went to some of his business, then returned, and the fear and weeping of those present increased, so he said: "Why?" he said it three times "what is making you weep?" They said: "You mentioned the Dajjāl and how close he is, so we thought that he was going arise among us, that he was coming out of the palm-grove to us!" The Messenger of God said: "If he

[936] Asmā' daughter of Yazīd b. Sakan al-Anṣāriyya, said to have participated in the Battle of Yarmūk (636) and killed nine of the Byzantines, *fl.* 1st/7th century.

[937] See no. 1507; the reference is to the palm-grove associated with the Jewish Dajjāl, Ibn Ṣayyād.

emerges while I am among you, then I am a defender [for you], but if he emerges while I am not among you, then each man is his own defender, but God is my successor for every believer. One of his eyes is blinded, while the other is mixed with blood, as if it was shining."

1453. Arṭāt: Constantinople will be conquered then the news of the Dajjāl's emergence, but it will be false, so they will stay three-sevenths of a week (*sābū`*), then the heavens will hold back that year a third of their water, then in the second year two-thirds of it, and in the third year then hold back its water entirely. Every possessor of claw and tooth will perish them, and hunger will occur, with sixty out of every seventy dying. The people will flee to the interior mountains (*jibāl al-jawf*), to Antioch. Among the signs of the Dajjāl's emergence will be an eastern wind, neither hot nor cold, which will destroy the idol of Alexandria,[938] and cut the olive trees of the Maghrib and Syria down to their bases. The Euphrates [River], springs and bodies of water will dry up. The times of days and months will be postponed, and times of the new moons.

1454. Sulaymān b. `Īsā: It reached me that the Dajjāl will emerge after the conquest of Constantinople, and after the Muslims will stay there three years, four months and ten [months? days?].

1455. Ka`b: A Bedouin asked concerning Abū al-Dardā', and advanced until he came to a sitting-session for completion of the new moon (*mutimm*), and suddenly there were Abū al-Dardā' and Ka`b sitting, while people were with them. So he said: "Which of you is Abū al-Dardā'?" They said: "Him." So he said: "When will the Dajjāl emerge?" He said: "O God (*allāhumma*), leave this question!" but he repeated it twice, so when he saw his reluctance to answer what he had asked him, he said: "By God, I did not come, O Abū al-Dardā', to ask con-

938 Uncertain, but perhaps Pompey's Pillar (which was actually that of Diocletian) (thanks to Michael Decker for this possible identification).

cerning your wealth, but concerning your knowledge." So he slapped Ka`b's shoulder and then said: "O [322] questioner! When you see the heavens drying up, not raining at all, when you see the earth is barren, not producing anything, and the rivers and springs have sunk back into the earth, and the aromatic plants are yellowish, then look out for the Dajjāl to come either morning or night."

1456. Abū Hurayra: The Hour will not arise until the city of Caesar or Heraclius [Constantinople] is conquered, muezzins sound in it, and they divide up its wealth in shields, so they will advance with most of the wealth on the earth. A crier will meet them, "The Dajjāl is behind you among your families!" so they will throw away what they have, and go to fight him.

1457. Elders: Ibn Mas`ūd called out a call, but did not whisper a secret, and said: "The riverbank, the shores of the Euphrates [River] will be the road for the remnant of the believers, fleeing from the Dajjāl, as they are not expecting to move quickly—is this the emergence of the Dajjāl? What a bad observer, whether the Hour . . . 'and the Hour is grievous and bitter.'"[939] Then he took a handful of small pebbles, and said: "His emergence is not more harmful to a believer" then he took the pebbles onto a fingernail, "than the diminishing of these pebbles is to my fingernail."

1458. Ka`b: They will conquer Constantinople, then the news of the Dajjāl will come to them, so they will depart for Syria, and find that he has not emerged, but then very little time remains until he does emerge.

Where will the Antichrist appear?

1459. Abū Umāma al-Bāhilī: The Messenger of God said: The Dajjāl will emerge from a direction between Syria and Iraq.

1460. Ka`b: The news will come to them after its conquest—meaning Constantinople—so they will reject what is in their hands, and

939 Q 54:46.

depart, finding that it is false, as the Dajjāl will only emerge after that, with a snake attached to him, from the edge of the sea, then he will emerge.

1461. Ka`b: A snake will cause the Dajjāl to be attached to the seashore, then he will emerge.

1462. Abū Hurayra: The Dajjāl will emerge from a village in Iraq, then the people will split at his emergence, with some of them saying: "Let's go to Syria, let's go to our brothers!"

1463. Abū Bakr al-Ṣiddīq: The Dajjāl will emerge from Marv, from its Jewish quarter.

1464. Abū Bakr al-Ṣiddīq: The Dajjāl will emerge from Khurāsān.

1465. Ka`b: The birthplace of the Dajjāl is a village of Egypt called Qawṣ[940] which is Basrā.[941] [324]

1466. Jubayr b. Nufayr, Shurayḥ, al-Miqdām,[942] `Amr b. al-Aswad, and Kathīr b. Murra said: He is not human, he is a demon.

1467. Sālim: He is Ibn Ṣā'id[943] who was born in Medina.

1468. `Abdallāh: The Dajjāl will emerge from Kūthā.[944]

1469. Al-Ḥasan: An army will emerge from Khurāsān, followed by the Dajjāl.

1470. `Abdallāh b. `Amr: The Dajjāl will emerge from Kūthā.

1471. Al-Haytham b. al-Aswad[945]: `Abdallāh b. `Amr said to me, while he was with Mu`āwiya: "Do you know of a land before you called Kūthā, which has many salt-flats?" I said: "Yes." He said: "From it the Dajjāl will emerge." **(1)**

1472. Ṭāwūs: The Dajjāl will emerge from Iraq. **(1)**

1473. `Abdallāh b. `Amr heard the Prophet saying: "People will emerge from the direction of the east, reading/reciting the Qur'ān, but it will not pass their clavicles. Every time a horn

940 Today Qus, a little to the north of Luxor.

941 Presumably the pre-Islamic name for Qus. How and why the birth of the Antichrist became associated with the town is a mystery.

942 Probably Miqdām b. Shurayḥ al-Ḥārithī, lived in Kūfa, *fl.* 2nd/8th century.

943 Ibn Ṣayyād.

944 In `Iraq, a center for Jewish learning for centuries.

945 Al-Haytham b. al-Aswad al-Nakha`ī, lived in Kūfa, joined Maslama in the attack on Constantinople, *fl.* 2nd/8th century.

emerges from them, it is cut" until the Prophet counted them more than ten times. "Every time a horn emerges from them it is cut off until the Dajjāl will emerge from their remnant."[946] [325]

The Appearance of the Antichrist, his Conduct, and the Corruption at his hands

1474. Ka`b: The first water-hole that the Dajjāl will come to will be the peak of a mountain overlooking Baṣra, and the water to the side of it is full of clay or sand, so this is the first watering-hole to which the Dajjāl will come.

1475. Abū Bakr: The Dajjāl will emerge from the direction of the east, from a land called Khurāsān.

1476. Ḥudhayfa b. al-Yamān: I heard the Messenger of God saying: The Dajjāl will emerge, then Jesus son of Mary.

1477. `Abdallāh: The first families to be terrified of the Dajjāl will the people of Kūfa. [326]

1478. Asmā' daughter of Yazīd al-Anṣāriyya: The Messenger of God was in my house, then mentioned the Dajjāl, and said: "One of the worst temptations is that he would come to a Bedouin and say: 'If I raised your camel to life, would you not know that I am your lord?' So he will say: 'Yes.' Demons will impersonate the approximation of his camel, in the best way that its udders were, and with the biggest humps. He will come to a man whose father and brother had died and say: 'If I raised your father and brother to life, would you not know that I am your lord?' So he would say: 'Of course.' Demons will impersonate the approximation of his father and brother."

Then the Prophet went out to the toilet, and returned, while the people were in a state of intense interest and distress at what he had said. So he took the warp of the door and said: "Are you perplexed, Asmā'?" Asmā' said: "O Messenger of God, you have disturbed our hearts by mentioning the Dajjāl." He

[946] This tradition is usually associated with the appearance of the Kharijites.

said: "If he emerges while I am among you, then I will be a defender, but if not, then my Lord is my successor for every believer." Asmā' said: "O Messenger of God, by God, we are kneading our dough, so we can bake it lest we be hungry. So how will the believers be on that day?"[947] He said: "They will be satisfied with what the inhabitants of heaven are, with praise and magnification [of God]."

1479. Abū al-Za`rā'[948]: The Dajjāl was mentioned in the presence of `Abdallāh b. Mas`ūd, and he said: People will be divided into three groups at his emergence. One will follow him, one will join the lands of their fathers, the growing-places of wormwood, and one will take the shore of the Euphrates [River], with him fighting them and them fighting him, until the believers will gather in the western part of Syria. They will send a vanguard against him, among them a horseman on a roan or motley horse. They will be killed, not one human will return.

1480. `Abdallāh b. Mas`ūd: "A roan horse," then `Abdallāh said: "The People of the Book claim that the Messiah Jesus son of Mary will descend to kill him." Abū al-Za`rā' said: "I never heard `Abdallāh mention another tradition on the authority of the People of the Book other than this one." He said: "Then Gog and Magog will emerge."

1481. Abū Umāma al-Bāhilī: The Messenger of God said: When the Dajjāl emerges he will lurch right and left. O servants of God, be steadfast, for he is just beginning. So he will say: "I am a prophet," but there is no prophet after me. Then he will praise and say: "I am your lord," but you will never see your Lord until you die, and he is blind in one eye, but your Lord is not blind. Between [327] his two eyes there is written "unbeliever" which every believer will be able to read. Part of his temptation is that he will have with him "paradise" and "hell", but his "hell" is paradise, while his "paradise" is hell. Whoever

[947] What will they eat?

[948] Probably `Abdallāh b. Hāni' al-Kindī, lived in Kūfa, *fl.* 1st/7th century.

is tempted by his hell,[949] let him read/recite the opening verses of *sūrat al-kahf* and ask for succor from God, so it will be "coolness and peace"[950] just as the fire was "coolness and peace" upon Abraham. Among his temptations is that he will have demons with him who will impersonate the forms of people, so he will come to a Bedouin and say: "If I raise for you your father and mother will you testify that I am your lord?" so he will say: "Yes," and then his demons will impersonate for him the forms of his father and mother. They will then say to him: "O dear son, follow him for he is your lord."

Among his temptations will be that he will possess someone's soul, and then kill it, raise it back to life, but it will not come back again after that, and that will only happen with one soul. He will say: "Look, my servant, I will raise him not, so he will claim that he has a lord other than me." So he will raise him, then say: "Who is your lord?" He will say to him: "My Lord is God, and you are the Dajjāl, the enemy of God."

Among his temptations is that he will say to a Bedouin: "Do you think if I raised your camels, would you testify that I am your lord?" So he will say: "Yes." Then demons will impersonate for him the form of his camels. Among his temptations is that he will order the heavens to rain and they will, and he will order the earth to bring forth produce, and it will. He will pass by a tribe and they will call him a liar, so every single one of their cattle will perish, but he will pass by another tribe and they will accept him as true, so he will order the heavens to rain upon them, and the earth to bring forth produce for them. So their quadrupeds will go in the morning from that day in the best possible shape, the fattest, with the most extended flanks, and the most productive udders.

1482. Ka`b: When the Dajjāl camps in al-Urdunn he will cause Mt.

[949] One would expect for them to be tempted by his false "paradise" but perhaps the meaning is his false paradise that is really hell.

[950] Q 21:69.

Tabor[951] and Mt. Jūdī to butt together fighting, while the people are watching just as two oxen or two rams would butt, then he will say: "Return to your places."

1483. Ḥudhayfa: The Messenger of God said: The Dajjāl, the enemy of God will emerge, while with him are armies of Jews, and different types of people. He will have a "paradise" and a "hell" with him, and men who he will kill, then raise from the dead. He will have a mountain of *tharīd*[952] and a river of water. I will describe to you what he looks like: he will emerge with with one eye smooth, on his forehead written "unbeliever", which will be read by anyone who can read (*kullu man yuḥsinu al-kitāba*), and whoever cannot. His "paradise" is hell, while his "hell" is paradise. He is the [false] messiah, the monstrous liar. 13,000 Jewish women will follow him so God will stone/ curse a man who prevents his foolish [girl] from joining him.

The power over him on that day will be from the Qur`ān, since his issue is an intense trial. God will send demons from the east and west of the earth, so they will say: "Use us in any way you want." So he will say to them: "Go, inform the people that I am their lord, and that I have brought my 'paradise' and my 'hell.'"

So the demons will go [328] and more than 100 demons will enter into the presence of a man, and impersonate for him his parents, his children, his brothers, his clients (*mawālī*) and his friend. They will say: "O so-and-so, do you know us?" So the man will say: "Yes, this is my father, this is my mother, this is my sister, and this is my brother," so the man will say: "What is your news?" they will say: "You first, what is your news?" The man will say: "The enemy of God, the Dajjāl, has emerged," but the demons will say: "Slow down! Don't say that! He is your lord, desiring justice among you. He is bringing his 'para-

[951] In northern Israel, the traditional site of the transfiguration of Jesus.
[952] A meat and bread stew, beloved by Muḥammad.

dise' and his 'hell' and he has with him rivers and food. The food from before was nothing other than what God wanted."

So the man will say: "You are lying! You are nothing but demons, and he is the Liar. It has reached us what the Messenger of God related to us, warning us, informing us of him. There is no return for you, you are demons while he is the enemy of God! God will drive Jesus son of Mary until he kills him, so get out, turn over as you are frustrated!" The Messenger of God said: "I am only narrating this for you for you to think, be knowledgable, and aware, acting against him, and narrating concerning him to those who come after you. So let one narrate to the other, for his temptation is the worst of temptations."

1484. \`Abdallāh b. \`Amr: "The vanguard of the Dajjāl will be 70,000 who are faster and bolder than tigers." A man said: "Who can handle the likes of these?" He said: "None but God."

1485. Al-Haytham b. Mālik al-Ṭā'ī,[953] who raised the tradition [to the Prophet]: The Dajjāl will rule in al-\`Iraq for two years, in which he will be praised for his justice, and the people will stretch their necks out to him. One day he will ascend the pulpit to speak from it, then he will come to them and say: "What is with you, do you not know your lord?" Someone will say: "Who is our lord?" He will say: "I am," so one of the servants of God from the people will disapprove his words, but they will take him and kill him. Two angels will descend upon him from the heavens, then one of them will say when he says: "I am your lord" "He is lying" and his companion will say to him: "You are telling the truth," confirming what his companion said.

Whoever God desires to guide [329] He makes him firm, and causes him to know that the angel is only confirming his companion. Whoever God desires to lead astray He causes him to doubt. So [that person] would think: the angel when he

[953] Lived in Syria, blind in one eye, *fl.* 1st/7th century.

confirmed his companion was only confirming what the Dajjāl [said], augmenting his error. Then the Dajjāl will go, so whoever answers him, the heavens will order them to receive rain, while whoever opposes him, will be awoken, as the Dajjāl will have confiscated their wealth. Most of his followers will be Jews and Bedouin. He will lie in wait for the Muslims and press against them, until they are in extremity. Even families who have a large number [of animals] will live off just one goat.

1486. Ḥassān b. `Aṭiyya: 12,000 men and 7000 women will be saved from the Dajjāl.

1487. Ka`b: Whoever is constant during the tribulation of the Dajjāl, will never be tempted again living or dead, and whoever lives during his time, and does not follow him, paradise is his. When a man is saved and declares the Dajjāl to be a liar one time, he says: 'I know who you are, you are the Dajjāl,' then reads/recites the opening of *sūrat al-kahf* cannot be tempted, and that verse will be an amulet against the Dajjāl. Blessed are those who are saved through their faith before the tribulations of the Dajjāl, his humiliation and lowliness, and surely people will live during the Dajjāl who are like the best of the Companions of Muḥammad.

1488. Yazīd b. Khumayr,[954] Yazīd b. Shurayḥ,[955] Jubayr b. Nufayr, al-Miqdām b. Ma`dikarib,[956] `Amr b. al-Aswad and Kathīr b. Murra all said: The Dajjāl is not a human, but he is a demon, on one of the islands of the sea. He is bound with seventy links—it is not known who bound him, whether Solomon or someone else. At the first of his appearance, God will break one of his links each year. When he comes forth, he will ride a she-donkey (*atān*), the breadth between its ears will be forty cubits, according to the *al-jabbār* cubits,[957] which is a *farsakh*

[954] Yazīd b. Khumayr al-Raḥabī, lived in Ḥimṣ, *fl.* 2nd/8th century.

[955] Yazīd b. Shurayḥ al-Ḥaḍramī, lived in Ḥimṣ, *fl.* 2nd/8th century.

[956] al-Miqdām b. Ma`dikarib al-Kindī, Companion, lived in Ḥimṣ, d. 87/706.

[957] Not listed in *EI*[2] for measurements. Perhaps it is the equivalent of the "royal cubit" but issues with measurements from this period are quite problematic.

[three miles] for a hard rider. He will place a pulpit of copper on its back, and sit on it. Tribes of jinn will swear allegiance to him, and they will bring out the treasures of the earth for him, and kill people on his behalf.

1489. Ka`b: The Dajjāl is a human, born of a woman, and although he is not mentioned in the Torah or the Gospels, but there is mention of him in the books of the Prophets. He will be born in a village in Egypt called Qūs. There will be thirty years between his birth and his emergence. When he appears, Idrīs and Enoch (*khanūk*)[958] will emerge [330] crying in the cities and villages: "The Dajjāl has emerged!" When the Syrians advance because of his emergence he will turn towards the east. Then he will camp near the eastern gate of Damascus. He will try [to enter], but be unable to. Then he will be seen at the tower (*manāra*) which is near the Kuswa River.[959] Then he will be sought, but it will not be known where he has gone, so the remembrance of him will be forgotten.

He will go to the east, and appear, act justly, and be given the caliphate, and deputize [subordinates]. This will be at the time of the emergence of the [false] messiah. He will heal those born blind and lepers, so that people will be amazed. Then he will manifest sorcery, claim prophecy, and people will be divided concerning him. The Syrians will abandon him, but the easterners will divide into three groups: one group will take refuge in Syria, one will join the Bedouin, and one will join him [the Dajjāl], so he will advance leading those with him.

1490. Ka`b: They are 40,000, and some of the learned have said: 70,000. The nations will come to give aid to them against the Syrians, then organize them into armies. The Jews will gather

Merely the fact that the text needed to specify which type of cubits demonstrates this fact.

958 Usually the Qur'ānic prophet Idrīs (Q 19:56) is identified with the biblical Enoch.

959 A river flowing from the Balqā region of Jordan, presumably into the Yarmuk River.

to him altogether. He will send his vanguard, the eastern band, towards Syria, among them the Bedouin of Jadīs, wearing ṭaylasāns.[960] The Syrians will be terrified, and 12,000 men and 7000 women will flee to the hills and the refuges of wild animals—most of them to the mountains of the Balqā'. They will fortify themselves there, but not find anything to eat, except the salty trees, and the wild animals will flee from them into the marginal regions (*sahl*). Among them will be those who will come to Constantinople and dwell[961] in it.

Then they will send back and forth, so that the others would come quickly, so that they can settle in the west of al-Urdunn, at the Antipatris (Abī Fuṭrus) River, so that every refugee from the Dajjāl will tend towards them. They will prepare weapons at the tower (*manāra*) that is on the western part of al-Urdunn.[962] Then the Dajjāl will advance, and descend the Pass of Afīq, and camp on the eastern part of al-Urdunn. He will besiege them for forty days, and command the Antipatris River, so it will flow against them.

Then he will say: "Return," so it will return to its place, and will say: "Dry up!" so it will dry up. He will command Mt. Thawr[963] and the Mt. of Olives to butt each other fighting, so they will do so. He will command the wind, so clouds will rise from the sea, raining on the earth so that it brings forth produce. The greatest Devil will order his offspring to follow him [the Dajjāl], and so they will extract the treasures for him. Every time they pass by a ruin or a land in which there is treasure, they will note that to him.

He will have a tribe of the jinn with him who will imperson-

[960] A type of semicircular head-covering usually associated with the religious elite of Islam: Dozy, *Noms*, pp. 278–80. Presumably the infraction here is that the Bedouin would be arrogating to themselves honor that they did not deserve; see no. 1875 for a similar tradition about the Turks, and no. 1551 where the Jews are said to be wearing crowns.

[961] Reading with MM.

[962] Presumably near the coast.

[963] One of the mountains of Mecca.

ate the dead people, and he will say: "I am going to raise your dead," then they will impersonate their dead. So one relation will say to another: "Didn't I die, but now I am raised." He will enter the sea during the day three times, but it will not reach his waist. He will distinguish between the believers, the hypocrites and the unbelievers, and fleeing from him is better than staying in front of him. The one who speaks a word by which he is saved on that day will receive a reward that is like the sands of this world. He will fight the people for unbelief, and so one of them who is killed, his grave will shine during the darkest night, and during the night without any light.

1491. Ka`b: When the believers see that they cannot kill him or his followers, they will go to the western part of the Jordan River,[964] which is Jerusalem (*bayt al-maqdis*), so its fruits will bless them, and they will be filled after eating a little because of the great blessing. They will also be filled with bread and olives. The Dajjāl will follow them, and two angels will come to him, so he will say: "I am the lord," but one of them will say to him: "You lie!" and the other will say to his companion: "You tell the truth." His description is that he walks with his toes turned in, is gray [331], of a mixed complexion, with his right eye blind (and covered with skin). One of his hands will be longer than the other, so that he will plunge the longer of the two into the sea, and it will reach the bottom, extracting fish from it. He will go to the ends of the earth, and its closest areas during two days, his step will be the distance of his vision. Mountains, rivers, and clouds will be subjected to him, so that a mountain will come to him, then he will lead it and bring its agriculture forth in one day. He will say to the mountains: "Turn away from the road," and they will do it, and he will come to the earth and say: "Produce the gold in you," and so it will be gleaned as from the [seed of the] male palm tree, or as

[964] Literally al-Urdunn, but due to the geography the Jordan must be the intention.

from [round] locust-eyes.[965] With him will be a river of water and a river of fire—his "paradise" is green, while his "hell" is red. But his "hell" is paradise, while his "paradise" is hell. And a mountain of bread. Whoever is thrown into his "hell" will not be burned. He will appear at the Upper [part of Medina] once, at the gate of Damascus once and at the Antipatris River once, then Jesus son of Mary will descend.

1492. Al-Ḥārith b. ʿAbdallāh: The Prophet said: Between the ears of the Dajjāl's donkey (*ḥimār*) there are forty cubits, and each step of his donkey is a three-day journey. He will enter the sea on his donkey, just as one of you enters a small stream on his horse. He will say: "I am the lord of the worlds, and this sun orbits with my permission—so would you like for me to stop it [in its place]?" So then he will stop the sun, until he makes a day like a month and a week. He will say: "Would you like for me to change it for you?" so they will say: "Yes," and he will make a day like an hour.

A woman will come to him and say: "O lord, will you raise my son, my brother, and my husband?" so she will be able to hug a demon, and have intercourse with a demon, so that their houses will be filled with demons. The Bedouins will come and say: "O our lord, will you raise for us our flocks and our camels?" So he will give them demons with the forms of their flocks and camels, exactly the same age and type as what they had lost, sleek and fat. They will say: "If he was not our lord, then our dead camels and flocks would not be raised for us."

He will have a mountain of broth (*maraq*) and meat soup (*ʿurāq al-laḥm*)—which will be hot, never cold—a flowing river, a mountain of produce and green vegetables, and a mountain of fire and smoke. He will say: "This is my paradise, while this is my hell; this is my food, while this is my drink." Elisha will be with him, warning the people, and saying: "This

[965] Apparently the simile is to round beads of gold that will be produced by the earth.

is the [false] messiah, the liar, so beware of him. God has cursed him. God will give to anyone quickly and nimbly, as long as he does join the Dajjāl." So when he says: "I am the lord of the worlds," the people will say: "You are lying." Elisha will say: "The people are telling the truth."

He will pass by Mecca, where there will be a great creature, so he will say: "Who are you? This is the Dajjāl who has come to you!" So he will say: "I am Michael; God Most High has sent me to forbid him from His sanctuary." So he will pass by Medina, where there will be a great creature, so he will say: "Who are you? This is the Dajjāl who has come to you!" So he will say: "I am Gabriel; God Most High sent me to forbid you from the sanctuary of the Messenger of God."

So he will pass by Mecca again, but when he sees Michael, he will turn fleeing, and not enter the sanctuary. He will let out a screech, as a result of which every male and female hypocrite in Mecca will come out to him [332], then he will pass by Medina, and when he sees Gabriel so he will turn fleeing, then let out a screech, as a result of which every male and female hypocrite will come out to him.

The warner will come to the group by whom God conquered Constantinople, and those Muslims connected with them in Jerusalem (*bayt al-maqdis*), and say: "This deceiver (*Dajjāl*) has come to you!" so they will say: "Sit down, for we want to fight him." But he will say: "Nay, return, so that I can inform the people of his emergence." But when he will set off, the Dajjāl will catch up with him, and then say: "This is the one who is claiming that I cannot handle him, so kill him in the worst possible way." They will saw him with saws.

Then he will say: "If I raise him for you, will you know that I am our lord?" They will say: "We already know that you are our lord, but it would be nice for us to increase in certainty (*yaqīn*)." He will say: "Yes." Then he will rise with the permission of God Most High—as God does not grant permission to any soul other than that for the Dajjāl to be raised—he will say: "I put you to death, and now I have raised you, am I your lord?"

But he will say: "I am increased in certainty that I am the one about whom the Messenger of God proclaimed that you would kill me, then I would be raised with the permission of God Most High. God will not raise another soul other than me." Strips of copper will be placed upon the skin of the warner, but no weapons were allowed to leave a mark upon him—neither the striking of a sword, nor knife, nor stone—all were turned away from him and did not harm him at all.

Then he will say: "Throw him in the fire," and then God will move that mountain of produce and vegetables upon the warner, so the people would be in doubt concerning him. He [the Dajjāl] would hasten to Jerusalem, but when he would ascend the Pass of Afīq, his shadow will fall upon the Muslims, so they will string their bows to fight him. The strongest of the Muslims on that day will kneel or sit as a result of hunger and weakness. Then they will hear the call: "O people, succor has come to you!"

1493. Abū al-Ḥasan[966]: The Messenger of God said: The food of the believers on that day will be praise, saying *lā ilaha illā allāhu*, and saying *al-ḥamdu li-llāhi.*

1494. `Ubayd b. `Umayr al-Laythī[967]: The Dajjāl will emerge and the people will follow him, saying: "We testify that he is an unbeliever, but we only follow him to eat his food, and to use the firewood." When the wrath of God descends, it will descend upon all of them.

1495. Ma`mar: It reached me that he will place a strip of copper on his throat, and that al-Khiḍr[968] is the one who the Dajjāl will kill and then raise from the dead.

966 Probably Muhāhir al-Taymī, lived in Kūfa, *mawlā*, *fl.* 1st/7th century.

967 A *mawlā* of Ibn `Abbās, *fl.* 1st/7th century.

968 Frequently identified with the mysterious guide in Q 18:65; see *Encyclopedia of the Qur'ān*, s.v. "Khaḍir/Khiḍr" (John Renard).

1496. Yaḥyā b. Abī Kathīr[969]: Most of the followers of the Dajjāl will be the Jews of Iṣfahān. **(1)**

1497. Ḥudhayfa: The Prophet said: The Dajjāl is blind in his left eye, with wild hair, who has a "paradise" and a "hell" with him—but his "paradise" is hell. [333]

1498. Ḥudhayfa: The Dajjāl in my view is not more of a difficulty than a meaty billy goat.

1499. Abū Wā'il[970]: Most of the followers of the Dajjāl will be the Jews [and][971] children of prostitutes (*mawāmis*).[972]

1500. `Ubayd b. `Umayr: The Messenger of God said: Groups will accompany[973] the Dajjāl, saying: "We are accompanying him, even though we know that he is an unbeliever, but we are accompanying him to eat from the food, and use the wood." When the wrath of God Most High descends, it will descend upon all of them.

1501. Ibn `Umar: The Prophet said: The Dajjāl has one of his eyes blinded, and other mixed with blood, as if it is Venus. Two mountains will travel with him: a mountain of rivers and fruits, and a mountain of smoke and fire. He will part the sun just like a hair is parted, and he will catch the birds in the air.

1502. Ibn `Umar: The Messenger of God said: "Have you seen a ruddy man with curly hair, blind in the right eye, looking most like Ibn Qaṭan?"[974] I asked: "Who is that?" He said: "The [false] messiah, the Dajjāl."

1503. `Abdallāh b. `Amr: The apocalyptic battles for the people are five, so two have passed, but three will happen in this community: the apocalyptic battle of the Turks, the apocalyptic battle

969 Al-Ṭā'ī, lived in al-Yamāma, *mawlā*, d. 129 or 132/746–7 or 749–50.

970 Probably Shaqīq b. Salama al-Asadī, lived in Kūfa, *mawlā*, d. approximately 82/701–2.

971 Addition from MM.

972 This is probably the Greek μίμος "actor", but then by extention, "prostitute."

973 Reading *la-yaṣḥabanna* with MM.

974 `Abd al-`Uzzā b. Qaṭan al-Khuzā`ī, see Ibn Ḥajar, *Isaba*, iii, p. 239 (no. 7125),

of the Byzantines, and the apocalyptic battle of the Dajjāl. After the apocalyptic battle of the Dajjāl there will not be any other.

1504. `Abdallāh: The ear of the Dajjāl's donkey will shade 70,000. **(1)**

1505. `Abdallāh: 70,000 will seek shade under the ear of the Dajjāl's donkey.

1506. Sālim from his father: The Messenger of God said that he passed by Ibn [334] Ṣayyād[975] among a bunch of his followers, among them `Umar, while he was playing near the fortified house (*utum*) of Banū Maghāla[976] while he was a youth. He did not notice until the Messenger of God struck his back with his hand, then said: "Do you testify that I am the Messenger of God?" so Ibn Ṣayyād looked at him, and said: "I testify that you are the messenger of the trusted one." Then Ibn Ṣayyād said to the Prophet: "Do you testify that I am the messenger of God?" So the Messenger of God said: "I believe in God and His messengers." Then the Messenger of God said: "What is coming to you?" Ibn Ṣayyād said: "A truthful person and a liar are coming to me." The Messenger of God said: "The issue is mixed up for you." Then the Messenger of God said: "I have concealed something for you." He had concealed "the Day when the sky will bring a visible smoke."[977] Ibn Ṣayyād said: "It is smo. . ."[978] The Messenger of God said: "Get out! For you will never pass your ability." `Umar said: "O Messenger of God, permit me, and I will cut off his head." But the Messenger of God said: "If it is he, then you do not have what it takes, but if not, then there is nothing good for you in killing him."

[975] For a thorough discussion of the traditions concerning him, see Wim Raven, "Ibn Ṣayyād as an Islamic 'Antichrist', A Reappraisal of the Texts," in Wolfram Brandes and Felicitas Schmeider (eds), *Endzeiten: Eschatologie in den monotheistischen Weltreligionen* (Berlin: Walter de Gruyter, 2008), pp. 261–91.

[976] See version in al-Bukhārī, *Ṣaḥīḥ*, iv, p. 40 (no. 3055). Medina was divided up into clan and sub-tribal units dispersed throughout the oasis, with Jewish families and clans mixed in between. Most had a fortified house for protection.

[977] Q 44:10.

[978] Shortened form of the word *dukhān*, "smoke," *dukh*.

1507. Ibn `Umar: The Messenger of God and Ubayy b. Ka`b[979] set out walking towards the palm-grove where Ibn Ṣayyād was, so when the two of them entered, the Messenger of God began to be wary of the palm-trunks, while he was approaching Ibn Ṣayyād stealthily, so that Ibn Ṣayyād would not hear anything before he would see him. Ibn Ṣayyād was lying on a sleeping mat, in the midst of a grove belonging to him humming (*zamzama*). The mother of Ibn Ṣayyād saw the Messenger of God while he was being wary of the palm-trunks, so she said: "O Ṣāf!" which was his name "Here is Muḥammad!" The Messenger of God said: "If she had left him be, the issue would have been clarified."

1508. Ḥusayn b. `Alī: The Messenger of God concealed smoke for Ibn Ṣayyād or asked him concerning what he had concealed for him, so he said: "Smo. . ." So the Messenger of God said: "Get out! For you will never pass your ability." When the Prophet turned, then the Prophet said: "What did he say?" Some of them said: "Smo. . ."; others said: "*Dīkh* or smo. . ." Then the Prophet said: "You are disagreeing while I am still in your midst; afterwards you will be subject to further disagreement."

1509. Hishām b. `Urwa[980] on the authority of his father: Ibn Ṣayyād was born blind in one eye and circumcised.[981]

1510. Abū Bakr: The people spoke much about Musaylima before the Messenger of God said anything about him. Then the Prophet rose and spoke: "Now to the point, concerning this man, you have spoken much about him, so he is surely a liar, one of thirty liars who will emerge before the [335] [false] messiah. Every land will be subject to the terror of the [false] messiah, other than Medina. On every one of its aperatures

[979] Companion, Qur'ān reader, lived in Medina, d. approximately 22/642–3.

[980] One of the major historical sources, a member of the family of al-Zubayr, d. 155/772.

[981] See M. J. Kister, "'. . . And he was born circumcised . . .': Some notes on circumcision in *Ḥadīth*," *Oriens* 34 (1994), pp. 10–30.

there are two angels protecting it from the terror of the [false] messiah."

1511. Abū Sa`īd al-Khudarī: The Messenger of God narrated to us a long tradition concerning the Dajjāl, and he said according to what he narrated to us: "The Dajjāl, it is forbidden to him to enter the aperatures of Medina, so a man will come out to him, the best of people on that day, or among the best of people on that day, and say: 'I testify that you are the Dajjāl concerning whom the Messenger of God narrated to us his tradition.' So the Dajjāl will say: 'Do you all think that if I killed this man, and then raised him from the dead, would you doubt the issue?' They will say: 'No.' So he will kill him, then raise him, then he will say at the time when he is raised: 'By God, I never have seen more clearly than I do right now!' So the Dajjāl will want to kill him a second time, but not be able to do that."

1512. Ma`mar: It has reached me that he will place a strip of copper on his throat, and it has reached me that Khiḍr is the one who the Dajjāl will kill then raise from the dead.

1513. Abū Sa`īd al-Khudarī: The Prophet said: From my community 70,000 wearing red head-coverings will follow the Dajjāl.

1514. One of the Anṣār who was a Companion of the Messenger of God: The Messenger of God said: He will come to the salt-flats of Medina, but it is forbidden for him to enter its aperatures, so Medina with its people will be shaken (*tantafiḍu*) once or twice, which is an earthquake (*zalzala*). Every male and female hypocrite will go out to him, then the Dajjāl will turn towards Syria, and besiege them [the Muslims]. The remnant of the Muslims on that day will be fortified on one of the mountain peaks in Syria, so the Dajjāl will besiege them while camping at its base so that the trial will be extended for them. A man from the Muslims will say: "O Muslims, until when are you going to be like this, while the enemy of God is camped at the foot of your mountain like that? There are really only two great outcomes for you: you could ask God for martyrdom, or He could give you victory, then you can swear allegiance to the death, an oath that God Most High knows is true, from yourselves." Then a darkness will take them, so that a man will not be able to see his palm, then he mentioned the descent of Jesus. [336]

1515. Al-Mughīra b. Abī Shu`ba: No one asked the Messenger of God more than I did concerning the Dajjāl, so he said: "Why did you ask him?" I said: "The people claim that he will have food and drink." He said: "He is more contemptible to God Most High than that."

1516. A man from the Companions of the Messenger of God: The Messenger of God rose among us, then warned us concerning the Dajjāl, then he said: "He will have a 'paradise' and a 'hell', but his 'hell' is paradise, while his 'paradise' is hell. He will have a mountain of bread and a river of water, and he will cause rain to fall, and for the eath to produce vegetation. He will take over a soul, kill it, and then raise it, but not be able to do that again." [337]

The Length of the Antichrist's Staying

1517. Abū Umāma al-Bāhilī: The Messenger of God said: The days of the Dajjāl are forty, so a day like a year, a day less than that, a day like a month, and a day less than that, a day like a week, and a day less than that, a day like [regular] days, and a day less than that. The last of his days will be like sparks of fire on a stripped-down palm tree (*jarīda*). A man will start in the gate of a city, but not reach its other gate before the sun goes down. They said: "O Messenger of God, how will we pray during these extremely short days?" He said: "You will measure proportionally just like in these very long days, and then pray."

1518. Abū `Amr al-Saybānī: I heard Ḥudhayfa saying: The tribulation of the Dajjāl is forty days.

1519. Asmā' daughter of Yazīd b. al-Sakan al-Anṣāriyya: I heard the Messenger of God saying: The Dajjāl's life will be extended to forty years, with a year like a month, a month like a week, a week like day, and a day like the burning of a palm tree in the fire.

1520. Ka`b: Salmān al-Fārisī said that the Dajjāl's days would be the amount of two and a half years. [337]

1521. Abū `Amr al-Saybānī: I was with Ḥudhayfa b. al-Yamān in the mosque, when a man came running until he squatted right in front of him, so he said: "Has the Dajjāl emerged?" So Ḥudayfa said: "I am more afraid of what is before the Dajjāl than of the Dajjāl himself—his tribulation is only forty days."

1522. Ḥudhayfa: The Dajjāl will emerge during the fourth tribulation; his length of staying is forty years, during which God will protect the believers, so a year will be like a day.

1523. One of the Companions of the Messenger of God: I heard the Messenger of God say: "The Dajjāl will remain forty mornings."

Jesus son of Mary will kill the Antichrist at the Gate of Lydda at the distance of sixteen Cubits

1524. Abū Hurayra: The Messenger of God said: Jesus son of Mary will kill the Dajjāl short of the gate of Lydda by seventeen cubits.

1525. Abū Umāma al-Bāhilī: The Messenger of God said: Jesus son of Mary will catch the Dajjāl after he flees from him, so when his descend reaches him, he will catch him at the eastern gate of Lydda and kill him.

1526. `Abdallāh b. `Amr: When Jesus descends upon Jerusalem (*bayt al-maqdis*) as the Dajjāl will have been besieging the people in Jerusalem, he will walk towards him after he prays the morning prayer, he will walk towards him while he is taking his last breath, and strike him, killing him.

1527. Ka`b: When Jesus descends, his spirit and his breath will cause every unbeliever it finds to die. His breath will reach the distance of his sight, so his breath will reach the Dajjāl at the distance of a span from the gate of Lydda. He will have descended at the spring that is in the lower part of the path to drink from it,[982] then he will melt like a candle and die.

1528. Majma` b. Jāriya[983] heard the Messenger of God saying: The son of Mary will kill the Dajjāl at the gate of Lydda. [342]

1529. Ka`b: When the Dajjāl hears of the descent of Jesus son of Mary he will flee, but Jesus will follow him and catch him at the gate of Lydda and kill him. Everything will point out the followers of the Dajjāl, and say: "O believer, here is an unbeliever."

1530. `Abdallāh b. Mas`ūd: The People of the Book claim that Jesus son of Mary will descend and kill the Dajjāl and kill his followers.

1531. Sulaymān b. `Isā: It reached me that Jesus son of Mary will kill the Dajjāl on the hill of apocalyptic battles, which is the Antipatris River, then return to Jerusalem.

1532. Abū Ghālib[984]: I was going with Nawf {b. Faḍāla}[985] [al-Bikālī] until I ended up at the Pass of Afīq when he said: "This is the place where the Messiah will kill the Dajjāl."

1533. Majma` b. Jāriya: I heard the Messenger of God saying: The son of Mary will kill the Dajjāl at the gate of Lydda or at the side of Lydda.

1534. Sālim from his father that `Umar b. al-Khaṭṭāb asked a Jewish man, who spoke to him, so `Umar said to him: "You have been

[982] Epiphanius the Monk (travelling before 692) mentions "the waters of proof" four miles to the west of Lydda: Wilkinson, *Jerusalem Pilgrims*, p. 210 (his directions are problematic as right afterwards he states that Ashkelon is to the west of Lydda); Nasir-i Khusraw (in the 1040s), p. 26 mentions a water source just before ascending from Lydda into the highlands going to Jerusalem.

[983] Companion, lived in Medina, *fl.* 1st/7th century.

[984] Possibly Nāfi` or Rāfi`, nothing known of him.

[985] According to the version in Ibn Isḥāq, *Fitan*, pp. 165–6 (no. 50), with the additional ending: "I said: 'Who are you?' He said: 'I am Nawf,' so I said: 'May God have mercy on you! Why didn't you tell me, so that I could chat with you, mention God with you, and learn from you!' He said: 'Who are you?' I said: 'From the people of Baṣra,' so he said: 'Do you have a mountain next to you called Sanīr [see no. 1757]?' So I said: 'Sanām.' He said: 'That's it!' then said: 'Do you have a river next to you called al-Ṣafī?' so I said: 'Ṣafwān.' He said: 'That's it! The both of them will go with the Dajjal as food and water. It is a cursed mountain, and it was the first mountain placed on the earth.'"

truthful with me, so inform me of the Dajjāl," so he said: "The god of the Jews; the son of Mary will kill him in the open-place of Lydda." [343]

Refuges from the Antichrist

1535. Abū Umāma al-Bāhilī: The Messenger of God said: There will be no part of the earth upon which the Dajjāl will not tread and overcome other than Mecca and Medina. Any time he comes to one of its aperatures he will be met by an angel with drawn sword until finally he will settle at the Red Rock (al-Ẓarb al-Aḥmar)[986] at the end of the salt flats near the confluence of the torrents. Then Medina with its people will feel three quakes, and every male and female hypocrite will go out to him. On that day Medina will remove the waste, just as the blast furnace removes the dross from iron. That day will be called the day of purity. Umm Sharīk said: "Where will the Muslims be on that day?" He said: "In Jerusalem (*bayt al-maqdis*)—he will depart and besiege them until it reaches him that Jesus has descended and then he will flee."

1536. Ibn `Umar: The Messenger of God said: The protected towns: Mecca, Medina, Jerusalem (*ilīyā'*) and Najrān. Every night 70,000 angels descend upon Najrān wishing peace upon the People of the Trench,[987] never to return to it ever.

1537. Ka`b: The refuge from the Dajjāl is the Antipatris River. [344] **(1)**

1538. Ka`b: The refuge of the Muslims when the Dajjāl emerges will be Jerusalem (*bayt al-maqdis*).

1539. Ka`b: "A space of a cloak in Jerusalem during the days of the Dajjāl is better than this world and all that is in it, according to the word of the Messenger of God: 'The refuge of the Muslims

[986] In Ibn Māja, *Sunan*, ii, p. 1361 (no. 4077), *al-ẓurayb al-aḥmar* "the Little Red Rock"; in Ibn `Asākir, *Tā'rīkh*, ii, p. 225 *al-ḍarb al-aḥmar*, "the Red Formation."

[987] Cf. Q 85:4–7.

from the Dajjāl is Jerusalem—they will not be expelled [from it] nor overcome.'"

1540. A man from the Companions of the Prophet said: The Messenger of God rose speaking, and said: "The Dajjāl will reach every watering place other than four mosques: The Sacred Enclosure Mosque, the mosque of Medina, the mosque of Mt. Sinai and the al-Aqṣā Mosque [in Jerusalem]."

1541. Abū Sa`īd al-Khudarī: Whoever reads/recites *sūrat al-kahf* as it was revealed, what is between him and Mecca is lit up, and whoever reads/recites the end of it, and lives to see the Dajjāl, will not be overpowered.

1542. `Abdallāh b. Salām: The angels of God Most High guard Medina from every direction. Every one of its aperatures has an angel with drawn sword, so do not be scared away by God's angels who are protecting you.

1543. Asmā' daughter of Yazīd b. al-Sakan al-Anṣāriyya: I heard the Messenger of God saying: The Dajjāl will come to every watering place other than the two mosques.

1544. Abū Sa`īd al-Khudarī: Whoever reads/recites *sūrat al-kahf* as it was revealed, then when the Dajjāl emerges will not be overcome by him, he will have no way to get him.

1545. Abū Sa`īd al-Khudarī: It is forbidden for the Dajjāl to enter the aperatures of Medina. [345]

1546. Abū Bakra: The Prophet said: The fear (*ra`b*) of the Dajjāl will enter every area other than Medina—over each of its aperatures there are two angels protecting it from the fear of the [false] messiah.

1547. Companions of the Prophet: The Dajjāl will come to the salt-flats of Medina, but it is forbidden him to come into any of its aperatures. Every male and female hypocrite will come out to him, then he will turn towards Syria.

1548. Asmā' daughter of Yazīd al-Anṣāriyya: I heard the Prophet saying: The believers will be recompensed for their hunger on that day, just as the people of the heavens are recompensed for their praising and magnifying [God].

1549. Al-Ḥasan: The food of the believers on that will be praising, glorifying, saying *lā ilaha illā allāhu*, magnifying [God] and saying *allāhu akbar!*

1550. Ibn `Umar: The Prophet that he said, when the Muslims said: "What will the food of the believers be during the time of the Dajjāl?" He said: "The food of the angels." They said: "But how are angels fed?" He said: "Their food is to surround themselves with praising and magnifying God, so whoever is surrounded on that day with praising and magnifying, God will cause hunger to leave him, and so he will not feel it." [346]

Jesus' Return and his Conduct

1551. Abū Umāma al-Bāhilī: The Messenger of God mentioned the Dajjāl, so Umm Sharīk said: "Where will the Muslims be on that day, O Messenger of God?" He said: "In Jerusalem (*bayt al-maqdis*), he will emerge to besiege them. The imam of the people on that day will be a righteous man." It is said: "He will pray the morning prayer. When he will say *allāhu akbar!*, and begin it [the prayer] Jesus son of Mary will descend. When that man sees him he will know him intuitively, and walk backwards.[988] But Jesus will come forward and place his hand between his shoulders then say: 'Pray, [as] I am appointing you.' So Jesus will pray behind him."

Then he will say: "Open the gate," so they will open the gate. With the Dajjāl on that day will be 70,000 Jews, all of them wearing crowns and having drawn swords. When he looks towards Jesus he will melt like lead melts, or dissolve like salt in water. He will depart, fleeing, then Jesus will say: "I have one blow against you, from which you will never recover," so he will catch him and kill him. Every creation of God Most High behind which a Jew will conceal themselves will be granted speech by God. Every rock, every tree, every mount will say: "O servant of God, Muslim, there is a Jew, so kill him!" with the

[988] Giving up his position as prayer-leader for the people in favor of Jesus.

exception of the *gharqad*,[989] because it is their tree, so it will not speak.

Jesus will be judging justly among my community, and a just imam, crushing the cross, killing the swine and imposing the head-tax, but leaving aside the charity-tax. One will not busy oneself with lust, grudges and mutual hatreds will be lifted, and the animal nature of mounts will be removed, such that a boy will be able to put his hand on a serpent, and it will not harm him, and a girl will be able to meet a lion, and it will not harm her,[990] and it will be among camels as if it were their guard dog. The wolf will be among the flocks as if it were their guard dog. The world will be filled with Islam, and the unbelievers will be deprived of their dominion. There will be no dominion other than Islam. The earth will be like a silver tray (*fāthūra*),[991] so its vegetation will grow [347] just as it grew during the time of Adam. People will be able to gather to a single bunch of grapes that will satisfy everyone, people will be able to gather to a single pomegranate that will satisfy everyone. An ox will cost such-and-such amount, and a horse will cost a small number of dirhams.

1552. Ka`b: The Messiah, Jesus son of Mary will descend at the White Bridge near the eastern gate of Damascus at the edge of the trees.[992] A cloud will carry him, and he will place his hands on the shoulders of two angels, with two thin white cloths around him, one wrapping around his loins, while the other is covering him.[993] When he bends his head downwards water drips from him like pearls (*jumān*).[994] The Jews will come to

989 Usually said to be the boxthorn; in Ibn `Asākir, *Tā'rīkh*, ii, p. 225 "a thorn located close to Jerusalem."

990 Compare Is. 11:6, 8.

991 Aramaic, Jastrow, *Dictionary*, ii, p. 1250; in Ibn `Asākir, *Tā'rīkh*, ii, p. 226 *qānūr*.

992 A number of travelers mention the encirclement of Damascus by orchards (e.g., the Bishop Arnulf *c.*683), Wilkinson, *Jerusalem Pilgrims*, p. 195.

993 The *rayṭa* is occasionally used for dress in paradise, Wensinck, *Concordance*, s.v., *rayṭa*.

994 Persian.

him saying: "We are your supporters," but he will say: "You are lying." Then the Christians will come to him saying: "We are your supporters, but he will say: 'You are lying—my supporters are the Emigrants, the remnant of the fighters of the apocalyptic battle.'"

The gathering of the Muslims will come as they are, and find their caliph leading them in prayer. The Messiah will hold back when he sees him, so he will say: "O Messiah of God, pray for us," but he will say: "Nay, rather you pray for your supporters, for God is pleased with you, so I was only sent as a counselor (*wazīr*)." So the caliph of the Emigrants will perform the prayers for them, two prayer-prostrations (*raka`as*) one time, while the son of Mary is among them. Then the Messiah will pray for them after him, and remove their caliph.

1553. Ḥudhayfa b. al-Yamān: The Messenger of God said: While the demons with the Dajjāl are deceiving some of the humans into following the Dajjāl, those who reject him, some of them will say to him: "You are demons, but God Most High will drive Jesus son of Mary towards him [the Dajjāl] in Jerusalem (*ilīyā'*)." While you are in that situation Jesus son of Mary will descend in Jerusalem, when there will be a gathering of the Muslims with their caliph. When the muezzin calls for the morning prayer, he will hear from the people a collective gasp (*`aṣ`aṣa*).[995] Suddenly Jesus son of Mary will be there!

Jesus will descend, and the people will welcome him, rejoicing at his descent, because of the verification of the tradition of the Messenger of God. He will say to the muezzin: "Perform the prayer," then the people will say to him: "Pray for us," but he will say: "Go to your imam, so he can pray for you, for he is the best imam." So their imam will lead them in prayer, and Jesus will pray with them. Then the imam wil go his way, and give Jesus obedience.

He will lead the people until when the Dajjāl sees him he

[995] Ibn al-`Athīr, *Nihāya*, iii, p. 248 (extrapolation).

will flow like a pitch flows. Jesus will walk towards him, then kill him with the permission of God Most High, and kill among those who are with him as many as God wishes. Then they will disperse and secret themselves behind trees and rocks, until the tree will say: "O servant of God, O Muslim, come here, there is a Jew behind me, so kill him!" The rock will call out the same, except for the *gharqad* tree, the tree of the Jews, which will not give away anyone who is near it. Then the Messenger of God said: "I only narrate this to you that you would consider it, understand and be aware of it, act against it and narrate about it to those who are after you. Let each one narrate to the other, for his tribulation is the worst of tribulations. Then you will live afterwards for as long as God Most High wishes together with Jesus son of Mary." [348]

1554. Ka`b: When Jesus son of Mary emerges, the emirate will be at an end.

1555. Abū Hurayra: The Prophet said: The coming of Jesus at this end is not like his first coming. The fear of death will be upon him, he will wipe the faces of men, and he will tell them the glad tidings of the levels of paradise.

1556. Abū Hurayra: Whoever lives from among you is about to see Jesus son of Mary as an imam and a Mahdi, and judging justly, so he will break the cross, kill the swine, put aside the head-tax and "the war shall lay down its burdens."[996]

1557. Muḥammad, but I think that it was from none other than Abū Hurayra: He will descend between two calls to prayer, with his robe dripping water, with two yellowish robes on him or two cloaks. Muḥammad said: "I thought that they had found him a book, but they did not know what his color was," so then Jesus will pray behind a man from this community.

1558. `Abdallāh b. `Amr b. al-`Āṣ: The emergence of the Dajjāl will reach those who will conquer Constantinople, so they will advance until they meet him at Jerusalem (*bayt al-maqdis*). He

[996] Q 47:4.

will have besieged 8000 women and 12,000 fighters, who are the best of those who remain, as righteous as those of the past. While they are under the mist of a cloud, suddenly the mist will be rolled away for them by the morning, and Jesus son of Mary will be in their midst.

Their imam will avoid him so that he [Jesus] could lead them in prayer, so Jesus son of Mary will come so as to pray in order to honor this band. Then he will walk to the Dajjāl when he is at his last gasp, strike him and kill him. At that time the earth will shout, and every rock and tree, and everything else, will say: "O Muslim, here is a Jew behind me, so kill him," except for the *gharqad* tree, for it is a Jewish tree.

He will descend, judging justly, break the cross, kill the swine, and put the head-tax aside. Quraysh will stripped of the emirate, and "the war shall lay down its burdens."[997] The earth will be like a silver tray—enmity, grudges and hatred will be lifted, together with the animal nature of all. The earth will be filled with peace just as a vessel is filled with water and overflows from its edges.

A girl will tread on the lion's head, the lion will come among the cattle, or the wolf among the flocks [349], and a horse will be sold for twenty dirhams. The ox will reach a high price, and people will be righteous. The heavens will be ordered to rain, and the earth to produce vegetation such that it will be like its previous state when Adam first descended upon it. Many people will be able to eat from one pomegranate, and from a cluster of grapes as well, until people will say: "Would that our fathers lived this life!"

1559. Ibn `Umar: The Messenger of God said: I was shown from the Ka`ba on the part that is beside the Standing-place a ruddy man, with lank hair, resting his hands on two men, with his head pouring water, or having his head drip water, so I asked: "Who is that?" Someone said: "This is Jesus son of Mary."

[997] Ibid.

1560. `Abd al-Raḥmān b. Jubayr: The Messenger of God said: People from my community will live to see the son of Mary, who are like you or better, like you or better.

1561. Ka`b: While they are dividing up the spoils of Constantinople the news of the Dajjāl will come to them, so they will reject what is in their hands, then advance and take refuge in Jerusalem (*bayt al-maqdis*), so he [Jesus] will pray behind the one taking care of the Muslims. Then God Most High will inspire Jesus son of Mary to go to Gog and Magog, then the earth will produce its charity/bounty according to what it was at the first of this world. He will stay seven [years], then God will send a wind and take the spirits of the believers.

1562. Ka`b: Jesus son of Mary will descend at the tower (*manāra*) that is near the eastern gate of Damascus.[998] He will be a ruddy youth, with him will be two angels—he will be leaning on their shoulders. Every unbeliever that his breath and spirit finds will die. This will be because his breath will reach the distance of his vision, so his breath will find the Dajjāl, so he will melt like a candle melts, and die. The son of Mary will go to the Muslims in Jerusalem (*bayt al-maqdis*), and inform them of his killing, and then pray one prayer behind their commander. Then the son of Mary will pray for them, which is the apocalyptic battle, and the remainder of the Christians will convert to Islam. Jesus will stay and give them good tidings of their levels in paradise.

1563. Abū Hurayra: "The mosques will be renewed because of the descent of Jesus son of Mary so he will break the cross, kill the swine, put aside the head-tax," then he turned and saw that I was the youngest member of the group, and said:

[998] Ibn Jubayr in 1185, Roland Broadhurst (trans.), *The Travels of Ibn Jubayr: A Medieval Spanish Muslim visits Makkah, Madinah, Egypt, cities of the Middle East and Sicily* (London: Goodward, 1952, reprint 2004), p. 295 notes the white minaret; also Ibn Battuta in 1326, *Travels of Ibn Battuta*, trans. H. A. R. Gibb (Cambridge: Cambridge University Press, 1958), i, p. 144 claimed to have seen the white tower.

"O nephew, if you live to see him, give him my greetings." [350]

1564. `Abdallāh: The Messenger of God said: When the Dajjāl will reach the Pass of Afīq, his shadow will fall upon the Muslims, so they will string their bows to fight him. They will hear a call: "O people, succor is coming to you!" when they were weakened by hunger. So they will say: "These are the words of a man who is well-fed!" They will hear the call three times, then the earth will shine with its light, and Jesus son of Mary and the Lord of the Ka`ba will descend, and call out: "O Muslims, praise your Lord, say *subḥān* allā*h*, *lā ilaha illā allāhu*, and *allāhu akbar!*," and they will do so. Then they[999] will make haste desiring to flee, rushing, but God will tighten the earth upon them until they come to the gate of Lydda in half an hour.[1000] There they will meet Jesus son of Mary having descended upon the gate of Lydda. When he [the Dajjāl] will look at Jesus, who will say: "Perform the prayer," the Dajjāl will say: "O prophet of God, I have performed the prayer." Jesus will say: "O enemy of God, you performed it for yourself, so come forward and pray." When he will come forward to pray, Jesus will say: "O enemy of God, you claimed that you were the Lord of the Worlds, so why are you praying?" Then he will strike him with a club he has with him, and kill him. Every one of his helpers who will be under or behind something, it will call out: "O believer! Here is a deceiver (*dajjāl*), so kill him!"

1565. Some of the Companions of the Messenger of God: While the Muslims are in Syria, after the Dajjāl had besieged them on one of its mountains, desiring to kill the Dajjāl, when a darkness will come to them, in which a man will not be able to see his palm, then the son of Mary will descend, and uncover their sight. Among them will be a man upon whom there is a breastplate, so they will say: "Who are you, O servant of

[999] Apparently the Dajjāl's followers.

[1000] Afīq is at least a two-day journey from Lydda.

God?" He will say: "I am the servant of God, His Messenger, His Spirit and His Word,[1001] Jesus son of Mary so choose among three possibilities: one that God Most High would send a punishment upon the Dajjāl and his soldiers from the heavens, (two), that the earth would swallow them up, or (three) that He would set your weapons against them, and hold back their weapons." They will say: "The last one, O Messenger of God, is more healing to our hearts and souls."[1002] So on that day the large, tall, well-fed and sated Jew will not be able to hold a sword in his hand because of fear, so they will descend upon them, and the Dajjāl will melt when he the son of Mary just like lead melts, until he comes to him or catches up with him and kills him.

1566. Sālim from his father: The Prophet said: The Jews will fight up, but you will overpower them until the rock says: "O Muslim, this Jew is behind me, so kill him."

1567. Abū Hurayra: The Messenger of God said: By the One who holds my soul in His hand, the son of Mary is about to descend among you, as judging justly, and a just imam, breaking the cross, killing the swine, putting the head-tax aside, spreading wealth until no one would want to receive it. [351]

1568. Abū Hurayra: The Messenger of God said: "How will it be for you when the son of Mary descends among you, and serves as your imam?" or he said: "an imam from among you?"

1569. Abū Hurayra: The Messenger of God said: By the One who holds my soul in His hand, the son of Mary will shout the *labbayka*[1003] from the Mountain-road of al-Rawḥā'[1004] at the pilgrimage or on the off-season pilgrimage (*'umra*) or the both of them.

1570. Ṭāwūs: The son of Mary will descend as a imam guide, judging justly, and when he descends he will break the cross, kill the

[1001] Cf. Q 4:171.
[1002] Cf. Q 9:14.
[1003] "Here I am, at your service!" the call that one makes at the pilgrimage to Mecca.
[1004] Fajj al-Rawḥā' between Mecca and Medina.

swine, put aside the head-tax, so the nation/belief (*milla*) will be one,[1005] and safety will be placed throughout the earth. The lion will be with the cattle, so that one would think that he was an ox, and the wolf with the flocks, so that one would think he was their dog. The animal nature will be removed from everything, so that a man could tread on the head of a serpent, and it would not harm him, so that a girl could have a lion as a pet just as a boy might a small dog, and the Arabian horse will cost twenty dirhams.

1571. Abū Hurayra: The Messenger of God said: The prophets are brothers to different wives, their religion is one, but their mothers are different. The one most worthy of me among them is Jesus son of Mary as there was no messenger between myself and him, and he will descend among you, so you should know him. He is a round man, tending towards whitish-red, who will kill the swine, break the cross, put aside the head-tax, and not accept anything but Islam.[1006] The summons will be one, to God, Lord of the Worlds, and the matter during his time will reach the extent that the lion will be with the cattle, the wolf with the flocks, and the little boys will play with snakes, without any of them harming the other.

1572. Abū Hurayra: The Hour will not arise until Jesus son of Mary will descend, as a just imam, judging justly, so Quraysh will stripped of the emirate, and he will kill the swine, break the cross, put aside the head-tax, and there will be one prostration to God, the Lord of the Worlds. "The war shall lay down its burdens,"[1007] and the earth will be filled with peace just as a vessel is filled with water. The earth will be like a silver-leaf tray;[1008] grudges, enmity, and hatred will be lifted, and the wolf will be with the flocks as their dog, and the lion with the camels as if he was their calf (*ʿijl*).

1005 Cf Q 5:48, using the similar word *umma*.
1006 Cf. Q 3:85.
1007 Q 47:4.
1008 Reading *fāthūrā* with MM.

1573. Ṭāwūs: The Arabian horse will cost twenty dirhams, but the ox will be appraised at such-and-such a price.[1009] The earth will return to its first appearance at the time of Adam, so a large number will be able to eat from a grape cluster, and a large number will be able to eat from a pomegranate. [352]

1574. Ibn `Umar: The Messenger of God said: I was shown from the Ka`ba, what is beside the Standing-place, a ruddy man, with lank hair on his head, placing his hands upon two men, with his head pouring water, or having his head drip water, so I asked: "Who is that?" They said: "Jesus son of Mary" or "the Messiah son of Mary."

1575. Abū Hurayra: The Prophet said: The son of Mary is about to descend among you judging justly, breaking the cross, killing the swine, putting aside the head-tax, and spreading wealth until no one would want to receive it.

1576. `Abdallāh b. `Amr: Jesus son of Mary will descend, so when the Dajjāl sees him, he will melt like lard melts. Then he will kill the Dajjāl, and the Jews will disperse from him until the rock says: "O servant of God, the Muslim, this guy with me is a Jew, so come and kill him."

1577. Ka`b: The Dajjāl will besiege the believers in Jerusalem (*bayt al-maqdis*), and a terrible hunger will hit them such that they will eat their bow-strings from hunger. While they are in that situation, suddenly they will hear a voice in the darkness just before dawn, so they wil say: "That voice is one of a well-fed man!" So they will be looking, and suddenly Jesus son of Mar, will be there. He will say: "Perform the prayer," so the imam of the Muslims, the Mahdi, will return, but Jesus will say: "Return, because you should perform the prayer," so that

[1009] Apparently the apocalyptic informants were annoyed by the fact that a warhorse cost dramatically more than an ox, so desired to up-end the prices (note the additional conversation in al-Hindī, *Kanz*, xiv, p. 295 [no. 38742] to this tradition in which the Prophet was asked why horses would be so cheap: "no one would ride for war again, ever"), but could not decide how much an ox should be worth ideally.

man will lead them in prayer for that prayer-time. Then Jesus would be imam after him.

The Length of Jesus' Staying after his Return

1578. Ka`b: When Jesus saw the few number of people with him, he complained to God Most High, so God said: "I am going to raise you to Myself and take you,"[1010] and so one who I have lifted to Me will not die, but I will send you against the one-eyed Dajjāl, so you can kill him. Then you will live after that twenty-four years, then I will take you in true death.

1579. Ka`b: This is something that confirms the words of the Messenger of God: "How could a community whose beginning is me and whose ending is the Messiah perish?"

1580. Ka`b: Jesus son of Mary will undertake ten pilgrimages, giving glad tidings to the believers about their [relative] levels in paradise.

1581. Sulaymān b. `Īsā: It has reached me that Jesus son of Mary when he will kill the Dajjāl will return to Jerusalem (*bayt al-maqdis*), and marry into the tribe of Shu`ayb, the in-law of Moses, which is [the tribe of] Judhām, and have children among them. He will stay for nineteen years, where there will not be any commander, any police (*shurṭī*) or king.

1582. Ka`b: There will come a gentle wind which will take the spirits of Jesus and the believers.

1583. Tubay`: Jesus and those with him will depart to Jerusalem, saying: "Now 'the war shall lay down its burdens.'"[1011] Then the earth will produce [354] its charity with the permission of God Most High in accord with what was at the beginning of this world. Jesus and the believers will stay for years in Jerusalem until God sends a wind to take their spirits.

1584. Al-Ḥārith b. `Abdallāh: The Prophet said: When Jesus son of

[1010] Q 3:55, though one should note that the order of the two phrases is reversed from the Qur'ānic one, so the citation is a mistake.

[1011] Q 47:4.

Mary descends and kills the Dajjāl, you will take pleasure until you come to the night of the sun's rising from the west. You will even take pleasure at the emergence of the Beast. For forty years no one will die or get sick. A man will say to his flocks and mounts: "Go and pasture in such-and-such a place, and come back at such-and-such a time." Quadrupeds will pass by planted fields without eating even an ear (*sunbula*), and not breaking a stalk with their hoofs. Snakes and scorpions will be visible without injuring anyone, with the wild animal being at the gates of [people's] houses seeking food, without hurting anyone. The righteous man growing wheat and barley will take and scatter on the face of the earth—without tilling or ploughing—and a single measure[1012] will yield 700 measures.

1585. Tubay`: Jesus son of Mary will stay forty years.

1586. Yūsuf b. `Abdallāh b. Salām from his father: "We find in the Torah that Jesus son of Mary will be buried with Muḥammad." Abū Mawdūd said: "There is one further grave in the house."[1013]

1587. Abū Hurayra: Jesus son of Mary will descend and stay on the earth forty years.

1588. Abū Hurayra: Jesus son of Mary will continue on the earth, staying on the earth forty years. If he said to a [river-] torrent: "Flow with honey," it would flow with honey. [355]

1589. Ka`b: "Jesus son of Mary after he descends will stay forty years." Al-Walīd said: "I read the same in front of Daniel."[1014]

1590. Arṭāt: Jesus son of Mary will stay after the Dajjāl thirty years, each year of which he will go to Mecca and pray there, and say *lā ilaha illā allāhu.*

The Appearance of Gog and Magog

1591. Ka`b: God created Gog and Magog according to three types: one type whose bodies are [thin] like rice, one type who are

[1012] Perhaps approximately eighteen dry liters.

[1013] As Muḥammad, Abū Bakr and `Umar are already buried there.

[1014] It is not clear who Daniel is here.

four cubits [tall], with their breadth the same, who are strong, and one type which treads upon their ears and wraps the other around them—they eat the placentas of their women.

1592. Ka`b: The refuge from Gog and Magog is the Mount [Sinai], and from the apocalyptic battles, Damascus.

1593. Ka`b: There are seven times more of Gog and Magog than there are of other people.

1594. Ka`b: The breadth of the lower threshold of Gog and Magog's gate, which will open for them, is twenty-four cubits, the [area that] the points of your spears would cover.

1595. Ibn `Abbās: The earth is in seven parts, six of which belong to Gog and Magog, while the remaining part belongs to the rest of creation.

1596. Ḥassān b. `Aṭiyya: Gog and Magog are two communities. In each community there are 100,000 sub-communities, not one of them like any of the others. Not a single man of them dies without looking at 100 ones of his progeny.

1597. Zayd b. Aslam on the authority of his father[1015]: The Messenger of God said: "Gog and Magog when they emerge, the first part of them will emerge at at the lake, the Sea of Galilee, then they will drink it, then the last part of them [357] will come to it, and say: 'There was water here once.' When they have overcome the entire earth, they will say: 'We have overcome the earth, come, we will fight the people of the heavens.'" They said: "O Messenger of God, where will the Muslims be then?" He said: "They will fortify themselves [in fortresses]. God will send clouds called *`anān*[1016]—which is its name with God—so they will shoot it with their arrows. But their arrows will come back down to them dripping with blood."

So they will say: "We have killed God!" but God will fight them. So they will remain as long as God wishes, then God Most High will inspire the coulds, so they will rain a type of

[1015] Al-Qurashī, lived in Medina, a *mawlā*, d. 136/753–4.

[1016] Hebrew, "clouds."

worm like a *naghaf* (worm found in camel's nostrils), the *naghaf* of camels. These will emerge from the [clouds] and each one of them will attach themselves to their necks, and kill them. While they are in that state, a man from the Muslims will come, and say: "Open the gate, and come out to see what God's enemies have done—perhaps God has caused them to perish!" so he will depart, then come to them, and find them standing one against the other, dead, so he will praise God and call to his friends: "God has caused them to perish!" So then God will send rain, and cleanse the land from them. The Muslims will use their bows and arrows to burn as tinder with for such-and-such a number of years, and the quadrupeds of the Muslims will eat from their corpses and grow large and fat on them.

1598. Qatāda: A man said: "O Messenger of God, I have seen the barrier of Gog and Magog, but the people call me a liar." The Prophet said: "How did you see it?" He said: "I saw it looked like an embellished garment (*burd*)." He said: "You are right, by the One who my soul is in His hand, you saw a barrier, a brick of which is gold and a brick of which is lead."

1599. Tubay`: When Jesus son of Mary will kill the Dajjāl, God Most High will inspire him: "Go, you and the believers with you, to the Mount [Sinai], for servants have emerged over whom no one can handle other than Me." The believers on that day will be 12,000 men not including the offspring and women. Gog and Magog will emerge, "they come swooping down from every height."[1017] They will drink dry every water-source they pass—the water on that day will be minimal, as it will have sunk down in the earth at the emergence of the Dajjāl—until they end up at the Sea of Galilee. The last of them will say: "There was water here once."

Some of them will advance against some others, saying: "Until when? since we have conquered the people of the

[1017] Q 21:96.

earth—let's go and attack the people of the heavens!" So they will shoot their arrows towards the heavens, but their arrows will return dripping with blood. Then God will send a disease upon them, called *al-naghaf*, which will attach itself to their necks, so God will make them perish, until the earth is reeking with their corpses.

The suffering will get to the believers, wherever they are, so the believers will approach Jesus and say: "There is a stench, which we cannot endure, and cannot abide," so Jesus and the believers will pray to his Lord, whereupon God will send birds in flocks (*abābīl*) upon them to carry them and throw them into a depression in the earth, which will become like a cavity, from [358] their blood and fat.

The people will remain some years gathering their weapons, remaining seven years, then God will send a wind which will take th spirits of the believers.

1600. Ḍamra b. Ḥabīb: I heard Jubayr b. Nufayr saying: "Gog and Magog have three types: one type whose height is like a [stalk of] rice and two small troughs (*sharabayn*)." Abū Ja`far said: "A stalk of rice is something like a tree, which in this way goes towards the heavens 100 cubits, or 120 cubits, or a bit less or more." "Then a type whose height and breadth are the same, and a type who the man among them walks on his ear while covering himself in the other, which conceals the rest of his body."

1601. Ka`b: The sea-dragon (*tinnīn*)[1018] is a snake, which harmed the land-dwellers of the earth's people, so God threw it from the dry land into the sea. When the sea creatures shouted because of it, God sent those who will convey it from the sea to the earth, to Gog and Magog, so it became sustenance for them.

1602. Azdād b. Aflaḥ al-Muqrā'ī that he and Jābir b. Azdād

[1018] Aramaic to Heb., cf. Ezekiel 29:3, 32:2. For the description, see al-Damīrī, *Kitāb al-ḥayawān al-kubrā* (Beirut: Dār al-Fikr, n.d.), i, pp. 165–6.

al-Muqrā'ī[1019] were on their way to their dwelling after [the Battle of the Field of] Rāhiṭ[1020] by a short time—that means after the raid called Rāhiṭ—Jābir said to him: "Would you like to visit `Amr al-Bikālī?" He said: "Yes." He said: "We went until we entered his dwelling, and we found that the troops were visiting him, while he was sitting conversing with them. A man mentioned the sea-dragon (*tinnīn*), and so `Amr said: 'Do you know what the *tinnīn* is like?' They said: 'What is it like?' He said: 'It is a snake that attacks another snake and eats it, then it begins to eat the snakes, so it grows bigger and more bloated, and increases its heat until it burns. Since it attacked land-creatures causing them to perish, God directed it to a river to cross it, then the current of water hit it, so it entered the sea. It treats the sea-creatures the same way it treated the land-creatures, so it grew and increased in its heat until the sea-creatures cried out to God concerning it. So God sent an angel to it, throwing it until its head stuck out of the water. Then the clouds and the lighting closed in on it to carry it, to toss it to Gog and Magog, so be sustenance for them. They watch over it, just like you watch over camels and cattle." [359]

1603. Ka`b: The same, but he added: They have a sea which they call the Sea of Blood, in which there is putrefaction. Among them there are those who eat their women's after-births. In spite of the number of humans, humans do not outnumber them by more than seven people. The total area of the [human-inhabited] earth and the seas do not outsize them [that of Gog and Magog] by more than an ox-pen.

1604. Ka`b: Gog and Magog will emerge when "they come swooping down from every height."[1021] They have no king or ruler

[1019] Both of them unknown, but probably Syrian, probably *fl.* 1st/7th century. One should note that these brothers in no. 1604 use the verbal form of their name, *tazdād* several times.

[1020] In 64/684 in Syria, Marj Rāhiṭ was the battle that established the beginnings of the Marwānid branch of the Umayyad dynasty.

[1021] Q 21:96.

(*sulṭān*); birds will go with them on their heads, but not cut them until they march, then will fall and be taken [and eaten]. Their vanguard will pass by the Sea of Galilee, with its regular level of water, so they will drink from it. Then their rearguard will come, and fix their spears in it, saying: "There was once water here."

Jesus will say: "A community has come to you who no one but God can handle," so his followers will come to the Mount [Sinai] and then will be hungry there, until the [price of the] head of a donkey will reach 100 dinars.

Gog and Magog will say: "We have killed the people of the earth, so come, let us fight the people of the heavens!" so they will fire their arrows at the heavens, and they will return dripping with blood. Then they will say: "We have killed the people of the heavens." Jesus and the believers will pray imprecations against them. They will invite them [the believers, to go out and fight], but not more than twenty men will respond. Each man will gird himself in such-and-such a way. Then Jesus and the believers will pray so God will send flocks [of birds],[1022] whose necks are like the necks of Bactrian camels (*bukht*), their dwellings being in the air, laying their eggs in the air, which stay in the air for a year before hatching, When they burst from the egg, they fall through the air, [then] fly until they rise to the place from which they fell.

They [the birds] will carry their bodies, and throw them into a pit (*ukhdūd*), and a very low place in the earth, so them God will cause rain to fall upon them, then purify the earth from them, so that it will become like an oyster-shell (*zulfa*), and return to the way it was during the time of Noah. Every community on that day will be at peace, even the wild animals and the carnivores, and rage will be removed from everyone possessing it. Humans, snakes, wolves, lions and sheep will all eat together, and a youth will ride on the back of a lion,

[1022] Cf. Q 105:3.

while twisting a snake in his hand. This is His Word Most High: "whoever is in the heavens and the earth has submitted to Him, willingly or unwillingly, and to Him they will be returned."[1023]

A company will eat from the grape cluster and a pomegranate, and a man will sow, reap and eat from his harvest in one day. The milk-camel will more than suffice for a family, and the cattle and sheep also. Gold and silver will be depreciated, such that a man will take 100 dinars, and not find anybody who will take it from him. A woman will be able to take her finery and not find a market that will compete for it, nor one who looks, holds out his hand or grabs [the merchandise]. A man will go on his way to his dwelling, and his stick and stone will tell him what his family was doing.

1605. Sulaymān b. `Īsā: It reached me that when Jesus son of Mary will kill the Dajjāl, and settle in Jerusalem (*bayt al-maqdis*), Gog and Magog will appear. They are twenty-four communities: Gog [360], Magog, Yanājīj, the Jij, the Ghasalā'-ites, the Sabatt-ites, the Fazān-ites, the Qūṭ-ites—who are the ones who wrap themselves in one ear, and walk on the other—the Zuṭṭ, the Kana`ān-ites, the Difarā'-ites, the Khākhū'-ites, the Anṭār-ites, the Maghāsha'-ites, the Dog-Heads, and all of them are twenty-four communities.[1024] Everything which they will

[1023] Q 3:83.

[1024] This list should be compared with the one in Ps. Methodius, trans. Martinez, *Eastern Christian Apocalyptic Literature*, p. 134; trans. Reinink, *Die Syrische Apokalypse des Pseudo-Methodius*, i, pp. 24–6; trans. Aerts, and Kortekaas, *Die Apokalypse des Pseudo-Methodius*, i, pp. 116–17; and trans. Garstad, *Apocalypse: Pseudo-Methodius*, pp. 27 (Greek), 101 (Latin). In spite of the text twice stating otherwise, there are only fifteen of the expected twenty-four listed (out of the twenty-two in the Ps. Meth text). The first four are exact matches, the correspondence and endings on the Ghasalā', the Difarā', the Khākhū' and the the Maghāsha' indicate that the immediate source-language is Syriac. Of the further peoples listed, Prazaye = Fazan-ites, Canaanites = Kana`ān-ites, Saltaraye = Anṭār-ites, and the Dog-Heads = Cynocephalians are clear. The ones not listed by the Syriac are more problematic: Qūṭ = Goths, Zuṭṭ = Jatts (archers from India), both well known). Other identifications are more tentative. Note also the list in Keagan Brewer, *Prester John: The Legend and its Sources* (Aldershot: Ashgate, 2015), p. 70

pass, whether living or dead, they will eat, every water they will drink—their vanguard will drink the water of the Sea of Galilee, then their rearguard will pass but not find any water. They will gather at the lowland of Jericho. When Jesus and the believers who are with him hear [of this] they will go terrified to the Rock [in Jerusalem], and he will rise as a speaker to them, praising God and glorifying Him, saying: 'O God! Help the few who obey You against the many who disobey You! Are there any volunteers?' So a man from Jurhum will volunteer, and a man from Ghassān, so they will descend to the bottom of the pass, so the Ghassānid will descend, whereupon the Jurhumite will say to him: "I am not there."

1606. Jubayr b. Nufayr: The Prophet said: The refuge of the Muslims from Gog and Magog is the Mount [Sinai].

1607. Ka`b: At the emergence of Gog and Magog, they will dig until those who are next to them will hear the banging of their hoes. When it is night they will say: "Tomorrow we will open [the barrier] and emerge," but God returns it to the state in which it was. So they will dig until those next to them will hear the banging of their hoes. Then when it is night they will say: "Tomorrow we will open and emerge," but God will return it to the state in which it was. So they will dig until those next to them will hear the banging of their hoes, but when it is night then [the words] will be placed on the tongue of one of their men the third time, so he will say: "Tomorrow we will emerge, if God wills," so they will dig the next morning and find that it was as they had left it, so dig, then emerge.

The first grouping of them will pass by the Lake of Tiberias, and drink its water. Then the second grouping will lick its clay, then the third grouping will say: "There was water once here." The people will flee from them, and nothing will stand up to them. They will fire their arrows at the heavens, which

(the original letter of "Prester John" from the 1140s), which is a closer fit to some of the names.

will return dripping with blood. Then they will say: "We have killed the people of the earth and the heavens!"

Jesus son of Mary will imprecate against them, saying: "O God! We cannot handle them, so take care of them for us in the way You wish." God will give them over to creatures called *al-naghaf*, which will prey upon their necks. God will send birds to take them in their talons and toss them into the sea. Then God will send a spring called Life, and purify the earth from their putrefaction, until a pomegranate will satisfy the dwellers in a house (*al-sakn*).[1025] Ka`b said: *al-sakn* is a family.

1608. `Abdallāh b. `Amr b. al-`Āṣ mentioned Gog and Magog saying: Every one of them begets 1000 from his loins before he dies. Beyond them there are three other communities, of whom none but God knows their number: Mansak, Tāwīl and Tārīs(h).[1026] [361]

1609. `Abdallāh b. Salām: Every one of Gog and Magog leaves 1000 and upwards offspring before he dies.

1610. Zaynab daughter of Jaḥsh[1027]: The Messenger of God woke up from sleep, while he was red-faced, and saying: "There is no god but Allāh! Woe to the Arabs from an evil approaching! The barrier of Gog and Magog has opened today this much" and Sufyān [b. `Uyayna] locked his ten [fingers] together, so I said: "O Messenger of God, are we to perish, when righteous people are still among us?' He said: 'Yes, when filth grows."

1611. `Abdallāh b. Mas`ūd mentioned the mergence of the Dajjāl and the descent of Jesus son of Mary and his killing of the Dajjāl. He said: "Then Gog and Magog will emerge, so they will crash like waves across the earth, and corrupt it." Then `Abdallāh recited: "they come swooping down from every height."[1028]

[1025] This might be the Aramaic cognate *shaken*, Jastrow, ii, p. 1575.

[1026] Mansak = Meshech, Tāwīl = Tubal and Tārīs(h) = Tashish (Ez. 36:2, 13). Compare also `Abd al-Razzāq, *Muṣannaf*, (Beirut: al-Maktab al-Islamī, 1983), xi, p. 385 (no. 20810; and al-Maqdisī, *al-Bad' wa-l-tā'rīkh*, ii, p. 204.

[1027] One of Muḥammad's wives, mentioned Q 33:37.

[1028] Q 21:96.

Then God will send a creature like this *naghaf* which will insert itself into their ears and nostrils, so they will die from it. The earth will stink because of their putrefaction, so it [the earth] will beseech God, then God will purify the earth from them.

1612. Abū al-Zāhiriyya: Gog and Magog will besiege the people in the Mount [Sinai] until the head of an ox will be better than 100 dinars.

1613. Ka`b and Shurayḥ b. `Ubayd both said: Gog and Magog are three types. One type whose height is like that of a rice stalk, one type whose height and breadth are the same, and one type who walks on one ear while wrapping [themselves] in the other, and concealing the rest of his body.

1614. Ka`b: The refuge of the people on the Day of Gog and Magog will be Mount Sinai.

1615. Ḥassān b. `Aṭiyya: Gog and Magog are two communities, in each one there are 100,000 that do not resemble any other community. Each man does not die until he can gaze upon 100 ones of his progeny, meaning 100 of his progeny. [362]

1616. Ibn `Umar: The Messenger of God said: My community is a community which has received mercy—there is no punishment upon it in the next world; its punishment is in this world. The earthquakes, the trial, so when it is the Day of Resurrection, God will give each man from my community a man from the unbelievers, from Gog and Magog, then it will be said: "Here is your redemption from hell." The man said: "O Messenger of God, where is the justice [in that]?" but he was silent.[1029]

1617. Ibn Mas`ūd: Each man from Gog and Magog leaves 1000 offspring and upwards before he dies.

[1029] This tradition represents a trend by which Gog and Magog would be punished in the next world for the sins of humanity. Not surprisingly, the Mu`tazilites opposed such a patently injust solution to the question of hell's torments, and one that would allow people to avoid responsibility for their actions. See also no. 1688.

1618. `Aṭiyya b. Qays and Ḍamra both said: The earth is broader than the sea by an ox's pen.

1619. Ibn `Abbās: The Prophet said: God Most High sent me when He took me by night[1030] to Gog and Magog, so I summoned them to the religion and worship of God, but they refused to answer me. So they are in hell together with those who rebelled from the progeny of Adam and the progeny of the Devil.

1620. Wahb b. Munabbih: The Byzantines are the first of the signs, then the Dajjāl, and the third is Gog and Magog, then Jesus.

1621. `Abdallāh on the authority of the Prophet: When Jesus kills the Dajjāl and those with him, then the people will continue until the barrier of Gog and Magog will be broken, so then they will crash like waves over the earth, corrupting it—everything they will pass they will corrupt—and causing it to perish. Every water-source, spring or river they pass by they will drink dry. They will pass the Tigris and Euphrates [Rivers], so they will go to the bottom of the Tigris or the Euphrates, and say: "There was water here once." Whoever hears this tradition, let them not destroy any fortresses or cities in Syria or in al-Jazīra, for the fortress of the Muslims from Gog and Magog will be Mount Sinai. The people will ask for succor from their Lord by having Gog and Magog perish, but He will not answer them.

Then the people of Mount Sinai, who are those at whose hands God conquered Constantinople, will pray to their Lord, so God will send to them a creature with four legs, which will enter their [Gog and Magog's] ears, so they will all become dead. The earth will stink because of them, and the stench will harm the people worse than when they were alive, so they will ask for succor from God. God will send a dusky Yemenite wind and a thick smoke, which will make the people blind, whereupon will be a rheum (cough) over the believers. They will ask for succor from their Lord. The people of Mount Sinai will

[1030] Cf. Q 17:1–2.

pray, and so God will reveal what has happened after three days, so Gog and Magog will have been tossed in the sea. [363]

1622. \`Abdallāh b. \`Amr: 'The vanguard of Gog and Magog will pass by a river like the Tigris, and then their rearguard will pass, and they will say: "There was a river here once." Every single man of them will die leaving 1000 of his offspring and upwards. Beyond them are three communities, but no one other than God knows their number: Tāwīl, Tārīs(h) and Nāsik or Nasak.' The doubt [about this last name] is from [the narrator] Shu\`ba.

1623. \`Abdallāh who said: "When God gets rid of Gog and Magog, God will send an intensely freezing cold wind (*zamharīr*) which will take every single believer on the face of the earth. Then the Hour will arise on the worst of the people, then the blowing of the horn. There will no longer remain any of Gods creation in the heavens or on the earth who has not died, other than those who your Lord wishes. The time between the two blowings will be as long as God wishes, then God will send down semen, like men's semen, by which their bodies and flesh will grow through that water."

1624. Junāda b. \`Īsā al-Azdi[1031] and Ka\`b, though some said just to Tubay\`, not to Ka\`b: When Jesus son of Mary and the believers depart from Gog and Magog to Jerusalem (*bayt al-maqdis*), then they will stay years in Jerusalem, they will see something on the shape of killing and dust from the interior, so they will send some of them to see what it is—and it will be a wind that God has sent to take the spirits of the believers. This will be the last band of believers to be taken, but the people will remain after them for 100 years, without knowing either religion or way (*sunna*) of the Prophet, excited in the way that donkeys are excited. Upon them the Hour will arise, while they are in their markets, buying and selling, bringing forth and meeting, but not able to bequeath anything, nor return to their families.

[1031] Junāda b. Abī Umayya al-Azdī, lived in Syria, d. 75 or 86/694–5 or 705.

1625. Ḥudhayfa b. al-Yamān on the authority of the Prophet: Even if a man brings forth a horse, he will not ride its colt after Jesus until the Hour arises.
1626. Abū Hurayra and `Abdallāh b. `Amr: Then God will send after Gog and Magog a gentle wind to take the spirit of Jesus and his friends, and every believer on the face of the earth.
1627. `Abdallāh b. `Amr: The remnants of the unbelievers will remain, while they are the worst of people from the first and the last 100 years. [364]
1628. Abū Hurayra: The unbelievers do not have a long time after the believers until the Hour will arise upon them, and that is according to the word of the Messenger of God: "A band of my community will continue believing in the truth, standing on the command of God, without the opposition of those who oppose them harming them—every time a party of them goes, another one grows—until the Hour shall arise."
1629. Ka`b: The people will remain after Gog and Magog in prosperity, abundance and ease for ten years, until two men will carry one pomegranate [because of its size], and will carry one grape-cluster between them, and they will continue in that situation for ten pilgimages. Then God Most High will send a gentle wind which will take the spirit of every believer. Then the people will remain after that, excited like donkeys in a field, so then the command of God will come to them and the Hour, while they are in that situation.
1630. Wahb b. Munabbih: The Byzantines, then the Dajjāl, then Gog and Magog, then Jesus and then the smoke.
1631. `Abdallāh b. `Amr: How delightful it will be for the people at the time when Jesus is with them! A Yemenite wind, whose touch is softer than silk, and its smell is that of musk, will approach, so it will take out the spirit of every Muslim. Then the people will say: "Until when will we believe in this religion?" So they will return to the religion of their fathers, so that they will return to what their fathers worshipped. This is the word of Abū Hurayra: "It is as if I see the buttocks of

the women of [the tribe of] Daws shaking, worshipping Dhū al-Khalṣa."

1632. Abū Hurayra on the authority of the Prophet: "God will send a wind from Yemen softer than butter, and sweeter than honey, which will not leave any man who has a verse of the Qur`ān in his heart."

1633. Ḥudhayfa b. al-Yamān: Islam will disappear just as the embroidery of a cloak disappears, until none will know what fasting, charity or the rites [of pilgrimage]. A night will befall the Book of God Most High, without leaving one verse from it on the earth. Groups of people will remain, among them elderly elders, and old women who will say: "Our fathers saw the time of 'there is no god but Allāh' so we say it." Ṣila b. Zufar[1032] said to him, while he was sitting with him: "Will 'there is no god but Allāh' be sufficient for them, when they do not know fasting, charity or rites?" Ḥudhayfa turned from him three times, then said: "O Ṣila, it will save them" twice or three times. [365]

1634. Abū `Awf al-Ḥimṣī[1033]: The smoke will fill the heavens and the earth until the people will not pray, and will not know east from west, while the unbeliever is swollen from all of his orifices, while the believer will have a rheum (cough).

1635. `Abdallāh b. `Amr: The Hour will not arise until the Arabs worship that which their fathers worshipped 120 years after the descent of Jesus and after the Dajjāl.

1636. Al-Ḥārith b. `Abdallāh: The Prophet said: When God kills Gog and Magog, the earth will stink because of them, so the believers will ask for succor from their Lord from the stench. So God will send a dusky Yemenite wind, and it will be sultry and smoky for the people. A rheum (cough) will come upon the believers, although God will remove it from them after three days.

1637. Ibn Mas`ūd: This Qur`ān which is among you is about to be

[1032] Ṣila b. Zufar al-`Ansī, lived in Kūfa, d. during the rule of Muṣ`b b. al-Zubayr (685–90)

[1033] Unidentified, but presumably *fl.* 1st/7th century.

taken by night, and what is in your hearts will be taken as well, and lifted from your codices. Then he declaimed: "If we (so) pleased, We could indeed take away what We have inspired you (with)."[1034]

1638. Ka`b: Jesus will send a vanguard to the Ethiopians who are coming to the House (Ks`ba), but once they are on the way, God will send a gentle Yemenite wind and take the spirit of every believer by it. Then the people will mount each other on the road, so the likeness of the Hour is like a man circumambulating on his horse, looking for a place to get off, so whoever worries about anything after this knowledge of mine, is just a worrier!

1639. Abū Hurayra: The Prophet said: The Hour will not arise until the women of Daws shake their buttocks in front of Dhū al-Khalṣa, which was an idol that Daws used to worship in the *jāhiliyya* at Tubāla.[1035] Ma`mar: Other than al-Zuhrī have said that this rock is a constructed house today. [366]

1640. `Ayyāsh b. Abī Rabī`a[1036]: I heard the Messenger of God saying: Before the Hour a wind will come to take the spirit of every believer.

1641. Al-Qāsim b. Abī Bazza[1037] asked Ṭāwūs concerning the signs which are before the Resurrection, and he said: "I do not know what they are, but a delightful wind will come before the Day of Resurrection that will take the spirit of every believer, even if it is in the center of a rock."

1642. Al-Sha`bī concerning His Word, Most High, "the former ignorance" (*jāhiliyya*),[1038] he said: "That was between Jesus and Muḥammad."

[1034] Q 17:86. The tradition uses the verb *asrā*, "to travel by night", which is related to the name of the *sūra.*

[1035] In the Asir province of Saudi Arabia.

[1036] `Ayyāsh b. `Amr al-Makhzūmī, Companion, emigrated to Syria, killed in a battle (either Yarmūk or another).

[1037] Lived in Mecca, *mawlā*, originally from Hamadhan (Persia), d. 114, 115 or 120/732, 733 or 738.

[1038] Q 33:33.

1643. Masrūq: While a man is narrating in the mosque, he said: "When it is the Day of Resurrection, smoke will be seen in the heavens, but the hearing and eyesight of the hypocrites will be taken, the believers will be taken with a type of rheum (cough)." Masrūq said: "I entered into the presence of `Abdallāh and informed him of this, so `Abdallāh said: 'Quraysh sought to disobey the Prophet, so he said: 'O God! Torment them with years like the years of Joseph!'"[1039] So a year [of famine] took them in which they ate bones and the dead, until one of them would see that which is between him and the heavens in the form of smoke as a result of hunger. They said: "Our Lord, remove the punishment from us! Surely we are believers."[1040] It would be said to him: "If We remove it from you, then you will return," so it was removed, and then they returned, so God took vengeance upon them the battle-day of Badr,[1041] and this was His Word Most High: "So watch for the Day when the sky will bring a visible smoke, covering the people. This is a painful punishment!" to His Word: "you are going to revert."[1042]

1644. Sa`d b. Abī Waqqāṣ: The Messenger of God said: The westerners will continue being victorious, staying with the truth, until the Hour rises. [367]

1645. Rāshid b. Sa`d: The Messenger of God said: The best of the earth are its western parts.

1646. `Abdallāh: We were with the Prophet at Minā when the moon was split into two parts, so part of it went behind the mountain, so the Messenger of God said: "Testify, testify!"

1647. Anas: The Meccans asked the Prophet for a sign so he split

[1039] See M. J. Kister, "O God, Tighten Thy Grip on Muḍar . . .' Some Socio-Economic and Religious Aspects of an Early Ḥadīth," *Journal of the Economic and Social History of the Orient* 24 (1981), pp. 242–73.

[1040] Q 44:12.

[1041] The curse upon Quraysh took place according to the sources at least four years after the Battle of Badr.

[1042] Q 44:10–11, 15.

the moon in Mecca twice, and said: "The Hour has drawn near and the moon has been split open! Yet if they see a sign, they turn away and say: 'Non-stop magic!'"[1043] saying: "Magic is happening."

1648. Mu`āwiya: I heard the Messenger of God saying: "A group of my community will remain believing in the truth, victorious over the people, not caring who opposes them, until the rule of God (*amru allāhi*) will come, while they are victorious."

1649. `Ikrima: The moon was split at the time of the Messenger of God into two pieces. The polytheists said: "It's magic," so "The Hour has drawn near and the moon has been split open! Yet if they see a sign, they turn away and say: 'Non-stop magic!'" was revealed.

1650. Ibn Mas`ūd: The moon was split at the time of the Messenger of God into two pieces, so the Prophet said: "Testify!"

1651. Ḥudhayfa: Hasn't the moon already been split?

1652. Ibn Mas`ūd: "The first thing that you will lose from your religion is your faith, but the last that you will lose will be the group prayer. The Qur`ān that is among you is about to be lifted." They said: "How will that be when God has established it in our hearts, and we have established it in our codices?" He said: "In the darkness of night, what is in your hearts and on your codices will be taken," then `Abdallāh read/recited: "If We (so) pleased, We could indeed take away what we have inspired you (with)."[1044] [368]

1653. `Abdallāh: The moon was split while we were with the Messenger of God at Minā, so that part of it disappeared behind the mountain, so the Messenger of God said: "Testify!"

1654. Ibn `Umar on the authority of the Prophet: "The Hour will not arise until idols are erected, and the first who will erect them will be the people of Ḥuḍayr[1045] in the Tihāma."[1046]

1043 Q 54:1.

1044 Q 17:86.

1045 Approximately sixty miles to the south of Mecca.

1046 Central Yemen.

1655. `Abdallāh: Five [tribulations] have passed: The smoke, the continuous,[1047] the overwhelming, the Byzantines and the moon. **(1)**

1656. `Abdallāh b. `Amr: God will send a dusky wind before the Day of Resurrection, then take the spirit of every believer. It is said: So-and-so, his spirit will be taken when he was in the mosque, and so-and-so, his spirit will be taken when he was in the market. [369][1048]

Swallowing up by the Earth, Earthquakes, Tremors, and Metempsychosis

1657. Ka`b: The Lord will come close to the heavens, and return the water to its [original] element, and the earth will quake, the people falling on their faces, bowing, and many will manumit their slaves. Then it will be calm for a time, but return and shake its people worse than the first time, so that most will be with their arms held around their bodies. Then it will crack open, and a group from the earth and its dry valleys, and the people will be swallowed up. It will be such that a man would be traveling by night and pass by a tribe when they are safe, but others are swallowed up, and that two men would be grinding [at a mill], then one would be struck by the lightening bolt, and one of them would die, or both of them in their sleep.

The earth will be difficult with earthquakes like a young difficult nag pony, so that the people of the cities and vilages will take refuge in the mountains, then be with the wild animals. The beauty of the earth will be gathered, its gold and silver, to Jerusalem (*bayt al-maqdis*) such that a man and a woman will open a woman's chest (*safaṭ*)[1049] and jewelry-jar (*jawna*) an not find any of their jewelry. The wood and roofs of Jerusalem

[1047] Interpreted as the Battle of Badr.

[1048] Section break pp. 369–70.

[1049] The Aramaic *sifaṭā*, see Jastrow, ii, p. 985 "a bag, luggage."

(or the Temple) will tremble, and the pastures and quadrupeds will perish.

The kingship of al-Jazīra and Armenia will be cut off, its trees will dry up, and its quadrupeds will perish from the earthquake—both of them will cause famine. A man will desire to be uprooted from his place, then flee three times—[but] in each case will be returned to his place. His final uprooting and fleeing will be to Tiberias, so he will be based in it, and take refuge in God by His Most Holy Name to not return him, but to establish him there. The [prices of] horses (*khayl*) will be exorbitant, so a riding horse (*faras*) would be sought for much wealth and not be obtained.

1658. Qabīṣa b. Dhu'ayb[1050]: The Messenger of God said: "A group from this community will be turned (*la-yu'fikanna*)[1051] into monkeys and swine, and they will awaken [372] and then it will be said: 'The houses of so-and-so and so-and-so have been swallowed up.' While two men are walking along, one of them will be swallowed up." They said: "O Messenger of God, because of what?" He said: "Because of drinking wines, wearing silk, strumming musical instruments and [playing] flutes (*zamāra*)."[1052]

1659. \`Urwa b. Rūaym[1053] said: The Messenger of God said: God Most High is saying: "I will shake the earth upon my servants at the best of nights, so whichever believers I take during it, it will be a mercy to him, and it was the end that was foreordained for them. Whichever unbelievers I take will be a punishment for them, and it was the end that was foreordained for them."

1660. Ṭāwūs: There will be three quakes: a quake in Yemen, a quake

[1050] Al-Khuzā\`ī, lived in Medina, then moved to Syria, d. 89/707.

[1051] Probably related to the Hebrew *hafoq* "to change." The Qur'ānic root seems to be related, but is not used for metamorphosis.

[1052] Compare al-Ṭabarānī, *Musnad*, iii, p. 193 (no. 2061).

[1053] Correcting from al-Mizzī, *Tahdhīb*, v, p. 153 (no. 4493), al-Lakhmī, lived in al-Urdunn, but had a house in Damascus on the side of the Sinan Bridge, d. 131/748–9.

in Syria stronger than that, and a quake in the east, which is the Sweeper (*al-jāḥif*). Two of those have passed, other than the one in the east.

1661. Ka`b: The earth will be difficult for its people such that it will be more difficult than the back of a difficult nag pony. Then it will tend against you another time (an aftershock), until you will think that it is the Overturning,[1054] such that people will manumit their slaves. Then it will be calm for a time until those holding [slaves] will regret that which they are holding, then it will tend against you another time, so that one of the people will say: "O our Lord, we are manumitting, we are manumitting!" But God Most High will say: "You are lying—I am the One who manumits!"

1662. `Abdallāh b. `Amr: Different mines will emerge close, called Pharoah of Gold. The worst of people will go to them, so while they are working in it (a mine), when suddenly the gold will be disclosed to them, amazing those working it when both they and it will be swallowed up by the earth.

1663. Abū Hurayra: You are on the verge of not being able to find houses that will be firm for you, as the quakes will cause them to be destroyed, nor quadrupeds that will take you on your journeys, as the lightening bolts will cause them to be destroyed.

1664. Khālid b. Ma`dān: The Prophet said: My community, there is no punishment for it in the next world; its punishment is the earthquakes and tribulations in this world.

1665. Abū Hurayra: The Prophet said: Only a few days until the Euphrates [River] will reveal a mountain of gold, so killing will multiply around it such that in every 100 such-and-such a number will be killed—so if you live to see that, do not go near it.

1666. Sa`īd said: The earth quaked at the time of `Abdallāh. He said:

[1054] Cf. Q 53:53.

"What is with you?? [earth]" Then he said: "As for it, if it spoke, the Hour would arise." [373]

1667. Abū al-`Āliyya concerning His Word, Most High, "Our Lord, obliterate their wealth!"[1055] he said: "It became stones."

1668. Sa`d b. Abī Waqqāṣ: The Prophet concerning His Word, Most High, "He is the One able to raise up punishment against you, from above you or from beneath your feet . . ."[1056] the Messenger of God said: "It will happen," but did not give any exegesis afterwards.

1669. Ṣafwān on the authority of a man from Mu`āwiya's guard who heard Abū Hurayra: "The earthquakes, trial, killing and tribulations promised to this community are beyond [the year] 200 and below [the year] 100."[1057] And he repeated that three times.

1670. Zuhayr b. Sālim[1058]: `Umar asked Ka`b: "Do you fear an enemy that will be victorious over this community?" He said: "No," [then] he said: "O God! But an enemy and earthquakes, it will be tested through them, and this will happen! As for the dome (*qubba*, totality) of Islam, and its core, no."

1671. Shurayḥ b. `Ubayd: "There will be earthquakes and apocalyptic battles that will move the people from their places until [the price of] shoes will be exhorbitant." One of them said: "Donkeys—so you will not be able to get the better of your enemy, and your steps will be shortened."

1672. Salama b. Nufayl al-Sakūnī[1059]: I heard the Messenger of God saying: It was inspired to me [by God] that I will not be staying among you, and you will not be staying after me but a short time. Then you will stay until you will say: "Until when, when you will come as groups (*afnād*) to annihilate each other.

[1055] Q 10:88.
[1056] Q 6:65.
[1057] Beyond 815–16, and under 718–19.
[1058] Al-`Ansī, lived in Syria, *fl.* 1st/7th century
[1059] Companion, originally from Yemen, lived in Ḥimṣ, *fl.* 1st/7th century.

Before the Hour there is a terrible death, and after that years of earthquakes."

1673. Abū Hurayra said to Mu`āwiya: "The trial, earthquakes and killing will be beyond the 80s before 100 [=718–19]," but only God knows which 80s. [374]

1674. Abū Burda[1060] on the authority of his father: The Prophet said: My community is one that has received mercy: it will have no punishment in the next world, its only punishments in this world are earthquakes, tribulations and killing.

1675. Ibn `Umar: The Prophet: The earth will turn difficult for you until your settled people will envy your nomadic people, just as today your nomadic people envy your settled people because of the difficulty of the earth. The earth will tend against you (aftershock) in a way that will cause those to perish who perish, and those to remain who remain, such that they manumit the slaves. Then the earth will calm down, so that those who manumitted will regret it, and it will tend against you again, so those who perish will perish, while those who remain will reamin, saying: "Our Lord, we are manumitting! Our Lord, we are manumitting!" But God will call them liars, saying: "You are lying, you are lying! It is I who manumit."

The very last ones of this community will be tried by quakes, so if they repent, then God will repent to them (accept their repentance), but if they return [to their actions] then God will return to them with quakes. Bombardament, metamorphosis and lightening bolts. When it is said: "The people have perished, the people have perished!" three times, they have [truly] perished. God will never punish a community until their excuser makes a plea for them, until they know their sins, but refuse to repent, and let their hearts be calm with the right and wrong that is in them, just as a tree is calm with what is inside of it. One who does good (*muḥsin*) will not be able to increase in doing good, while one who does evil will

[1060] Al-Ḥārith b. Abī Mūsā al-Asha`rī, lived in Kūfa, jurisprudent, d. 103/721–2.

not be able to be reproved. This is what God Most High said: "By no means! No! What they have earned has rusted on their hearts."[1061]

1676. Mu`ādh b. Jabal: The Prophet said: My community is one that has received mercy—there is no punishment upon it in the next world, but its punishment is in this world, tribulations, earthquakes and trials.

1677. Abū Hurayra: The Euphrates [River] will uncover a treasure, so if you live to see it, do not take anything from it.

1678. `Abdallāh b. `Amr b. al-`Āṣ: You will surely be swallowed up by the earth going from house to house when there are the misdeeds (*maẓālim*).

1679. Qabīṣa b. al-Barā'[1062]: "When such-and-such is swallowed up [375] by the earth, then a group will appear who color using black. God will not look upon them [with favor]." Mujāhid said: "I have seen that place on the earth which was swallowed up."[1063]

1680. Al-Zuhrī: The Messenger of God said: The Hour will not arise until a group in cattle pasturages is swallowed up by the earth, the Hour will not arise until a wealthy and prolific man is swallowed up by the earth.

1681. A man from the Companions of the Messenger of God: The Prophet said: "When the Dajjāl encamps at the salt-flats of Medina, Medina will shake once or twice," meaning an earthquake, "so then every male and female hypocrite will depart from it."

1682. Abū Hurayra: A mountain of gold will be uncovered at the Euphrates [River]—out of every 100 ninety-nine will be killed there, and only one will remain.

1683. `Abd al-Raḥmān b. Sābiṭ[1064]: The Messenger of God said: "Metamorphosis, swallowing up by the earth and

[1061] Q 83:14.

[1062] Probably a mistake for Qabīṣa b. Burma al-Asadī, *fl.* 1st/7th century.

[1063] Presumably the village of Ḥarastā, see nos. 542, 551, 739.

[1064] Al-Jumaḥī, lived in Mecca, d. 118/736.

bombardament will happen among you." They said: "O Messenger of God, while they are testifying 'There is no god but Allāh'?" He said: "Yes. This will be because they will have taken singing girls (*quyūn*) and musical instruments, be drinking wines and wearing silk."

1684. Ubayy b. Ka`b concerning His Word Most High: "He is the One who is able to raise up punishment against you, from above you or from beneath your feet . . ."[1065] he said: "They are four, all of them punishments. Two of them were lasting after the death of the Messenger of God by twenty-five years: 'to confuse you (into different) parties, and make some of you taste violence from others.'[1066] But two of them remain, and it is necessary that they occur: swallowing up by the earth and bombardment." **(1)**

1685. Abū Hurayra: The Messenger of God said: The Euphrates [River] will uncover a mountain of gold, so then the people will fight over it, and out of every 100 ninety or he said "nine" will be killed, all of them thinking they should be [the one who will be] saved.

1686. Al-Ḥasan concerning His Word Most High: "He is the One who is able [376] to raise up punishment against you, from above you" he said: "That is for the polytheists," "or to confuse you (into different) parties, and to make some of you taste violence from others."[1067] He said: "That is for the Muslims."

1687. Shurayḥ b. `Ubayd, Ḍamra and Abū`Āmir: The Prophet said: Swallowing up by the earth and metamorphosis will happen in my community after the 210s [=825–35].

1688. Abū Burda on the authority of his father: The Prophet said: This community is one that has received mercy, its punishment is at its own hands, and so a man will be taken from the

[1065] Q 6:65.
[1066] Q 6:65.
[1067] Q 6:65.

family of the king, and another man given to him, saying: "This is your redemption from the Fire."

1689. Abū Hurayra: The Hour will not arise until the Euphrates [River] uncovers a mountain of gold, and the people fight over it. From every 100 ninety-nine will be killed, and from every 100 one will remain, so every man will say: 'I will be the one who is saved.'

1690. Ibn `Abbās: The seventy who Moses chose from his people—they were taken by the quake because they were not satisfied with the [golden] calf, but did not forbid it [either].[1068]

1691. Ibn `Umar: The Prophet that he would say: "O God! I take refuge in You from sudden death beneath me!" meaning swallowing up by the earth.

1692. Abū Sa`īd al-Khudarī: When the time approaches lightening bolts will increase.

1693. Ḥassān b. `Aṭiyya that he disliked looking towards the sun when it was eclipsed, fearing the loss of his sight if he did this.

1694. A female *mawlā* to the Messenger of God[1069]: The Prophet entered into the presence of `Ā'isha or one of his wives, while I was with her, and said: "When evil appears and is not forbidden, God will cause His wrath to descend among you." So I said: "O Prophet of God, even if there are righteous ones among them?" He said: "Yes, what will strike the others will strike them, too, then they will go to the forgiveness and mercy of God."

1695. Anas b. Mālik: "I entered into the presence of `Ā'isha while a man was with me,[1070] so the man said: 'O Mother of the Believers! Narrate to us concerning [377] the earthquake,' but she turned her face from him." Anas said: "I said to her: 'Narrate to us, O Mother of the Believers, concerning the earthquake,'" but she said: "O Anas, If I narrated to you concerning

[1068] Cf. Q 2:54; Ex. 32:27–38.

[1069] Possibly Barīra or Khulaysa, listed with the other female servants of the Prophet, al-Ṣāliḥī al-Shāmī, *Subul al-hudā*, xi, p. 412.

[1070] Reading with MM.

that, I would live and die sad, and would be raised when you would be raised—that is the fear in my heart." He said: "O handmaiden! Narrate to us!" So she said: "When a woman removes her clothing in someplace other than her husband's house, every veil between her and God is ripped away. When she puts on perfume for anyone other than her husband it is fire and disgrace upon her. When they play the stud in illicit sexual relations, drink types of wine with someone and strum musical instruments, God goes into His heavens, and says: 'Shake for Me!' If they repent and pull away [then it is accepted]—but if not, then God will destroy them." Anas said: "As a punishment for them?" She said: "No! As a mercy, blessing and lesson to the believers, and as an exemplary warning and punishment for the unbelievers." Anas said: "I never heard a tradition after the Messenger of God over which I was happier than this tradition. I live and die of happiness, and will be raised when I am raised. That was happiness in my heart," or he said: "in my soul."

1696. Jābir: "He is the One who is able to raise up punishment against you, from above you" was revealed to the Messenger of God, so the Messenger of God said: "I take refuge in Your Face." "Or from beneath your feet" so the Messenger of God said: "I take refuge in Your Face." "Or to confuse you (into different) parties, and to make some of you taste violence from others."[1071] So the Messenger of God said: "These two are more degrading, so bring the first two and forbid the last one."

1697. Ṣafiyya[1072]: Medina quaked during the time of `Umar, while Ibn `Umar was standing [the night in prayer], not aware [of the earthquake] until the water-troughs vibrated. So when `Umar woke, he said: "O people, how quickly what you were

[1071] Q 6:65.

[1072] Ṣafiyya daughter of Abū `Ubayd b. Mas`ūd al-Thaqafiyya, wife of `Abdallāh b. `Umar and sister of al-Mukhtār b. Abī `Ubayd, lived in Medina, *fl.* 1st/7th century.

told [happened]." Ibn `Uyayna said, in a tradition not that of Nāfi`, "If[1073] it returned I will depart from amongst you."

1698. Abū Hurayra: When[1074] mines appear at the end of time, the worst of people will come to you.

1699. `Ā'isha: The Prophet said: "When evil appears on the earth, God Most High will cause His wrath to descend upon the people of the earth." I said: "When there are those obedient to God among them?" He said: "Yes, then they will be taken to the mercy of God."

1700. Zaynab daughter of Jaḥsh: I said: "O Messenger of God, will we perish while the righteous are among us?" He said: "Yes, when the filth has increased."

1701. `Umar b. `Abd al-`Azīz [378]: God Most High does not take the common people because of the actions of the elite, but when rebellious actions appear, and are not disapproved of, then God takes both the common people and the elite.

1702. Al-Qāsim: `Abdallāh said when a man said "The people have perished" "He [God] is the one who caused them to perish." Ibn `Uyayna on the authority of Mālik that Ibn `Umar heard a man saying: "The people have perished" so he said: "The iniquitous have perished."

1703. Ibn `Umar: The Prophet said: "When mines appear the worst of people will join you."

1704. Arṭāt: During the time of the Hashemite, who will be a tyrant in Jerusalem (*bayt al-maqdis*) after the Mahdi, who will send a girl whose clothes do not conceal her [to the marketplace]; during his time there will be quakes, metamorphosis and swallowing up by the earth.[1075]

[1073] Reading with MM.

[1074] Reading with MM.

[1075] Note the Iranian cleric Hojatoleslam Kazem Sedighi who in 2010 stated that "many women who do not dress modestly . . . lead young men astray, corrupt their chastity and spread adultery in society, which increases earthquakes," See http://www.theguardian.com/world/2010/apr/19/women-blame-earthquakes-iran-cleric (accessed March 23, 2016).

1705. Ka`b: The earth will become difficult for its people such that it will be more difficult than the back of a difficult nag pony. Then it will tend against you (aftershock), so you will manumit your slaves, then be calm for a time. So then those who manumitted will regret that, whereupon it will tend against you another time so that one will say: "Our Lord, we manumitted, we manumitted!" but God Most High will say: "You are lying, it is I who manumitted."

1706. Abū Tha`laba al-Khushanī: The Prophet said: When you see the astonishment of everyone possessed of an opinion, then take yourself, and leave the matter of the common people.

1707. A *mawlā* belonging to `Adi b. `Adi al-Kindī[1076] heard his grandfather saying: I heard the Messenger of God saying: God Most High does not punish the common people, but the elite, until they see the despicable [actions] amongst themselves—while they are able to disapprove but do not disapprove. When they act like this, then God will punish both the common people and the elite. [379]

Concerning the Fire that will Gather [People] to Syria

1708. `Umar b. al-Khaṭṭāb said one day in Mecca at the pilgrimage: "O Yemenites! Emigrate before the two darknesses. As for the first of them, it is the Ethiopians who will emerge until they reach this place here, and the second is a fire that will emerge from `Adan that will lead the people, the quadrupeds, the [domestic] animals and the wild animals, both the delicate and majestic quadruped, so when it rises they will rise, and when it moves they will go."

1709. Ka`b: When either a man or his mount stumble, the fire will say to him: "You stumbled and fell on your face—if you had wished, you could have emigrated before today, so that you would have ended up in Buṣrā, and stayed there forty years."

[1076] Lived in al-Jazīra, serving as governor of Armenia and Azarbayjan for Sulaymān, and of Mosul for `Umar II, d. 120/738.

None will be roasted in it [the fire] other than those upon whom is written "denizen of hell-fire" (*jahannamī*). The unbeliever will ask, and say: "This is the fire of which we were promised!" So how will it be for you when you see this great sign. The one looking will look to the eastern parts of the earth and see those places with their green fertile land; they will have sex together and join [it]. Do you think you are abandoning your deeds that you are doing today, while you are looking at this greatest sign? By the Lord of the Ka`ba, you will do your deeds while you are looking at it! **(1)**

1710. `Abdallāh b. `Amr: God will send a fire to the spirits of the believers, with this gentle wind, that will emerge from the sides of the earth, after taking Jesus son of Mary and gather the people, the quadrupeds and the minute particles (*dharr*)[1077] to Syria.

1711. Ka`b: This fire will emerge from Constantinople—fire and sulphur, of which its flame and smoke will reach the heavens, and it will settle at the pass between the Jayḥān and Sayḥān [Rivers].[1078] There will be another fire from Adan reaching Buṣrā. It will rise when they rise [380] and go when they go. During the first part of the day the Euphrates [River] will flow with water, but by the evening it will flow with sulphur and fire. Fire will emerge from the direction of the west and reach al-`Arīsh, and another from the direction of the east and reach such-and-such a place. It will stay a time, without dying out, until the doubter will doubt, and the ignorant will say: "There is no paradise or hell; just this."

It will avoid Mecca and Medina, and the entire Sacred Enclosure in its way, until it penetrates Syria. All of the people will be gathered other than two Bedouin from Qays in their wasteland, one of them going in the footsteps of the people

1077 Cf. Q 34:3.

1078 Flowing in eastern Turkey, the Sayḥān entering the Mediterranean Sea close to Adana.

until he becomes weary, as he is not finding anybody, so he will return to his friend, and tell him. So they will proceed to Medina and find it filled with wealth, flocks and food, but without any people. They will say: "We will stay in this easy situation," but they will be gathered, dragged on their faces to Syria. This is the word of Mu`ādh b. Jabal.

They will be gathered in three ways: a third on the backs of horses, a third carrying their children on their shoulders, and a third on their faces like monkeys and swine to Syria. In it is the place of gathering and from it is the place of raising [from the dead].

Those who are gathered to Syria will not know the truth or obligation, nor will they act according to the Book of God Most High, or the way (*sunna*) of His Prophet. Modesty and dignity will be lifted from them, and indecency will appear among them. A man will not know his wife, nor a wife her husband, but they will mount each other, them and the jinn, for 100 years, just as donkeys and dogs mount each other. They will forget God Most High and not be cognizant of Him, such that the one will say to his friend: "There is no god in the heavens!" The worst, first and last.

Mu`ādh said to Ka`b: "The first of the issue of the Hour that will surprise the people will be that God Most High will send a wind at night and take every dinar and dirham, and convey them to Jerusalem (*bayt al-maqdis*). The building of Jerusalem (or the Temple) will be split, and it will be flung into the Dead Sea (*al-buḥayra al-muntina*)."

1712. Qays b. Abī Ḥāzim: The Messenger of God said: I know of the last two men from my community who will be gathered. They will be in one of these ravines with their flocks. When the people are flown they will leave their flocks and come to Medina, and so one of them will say to his friend: "Didn't you know the road of the Ihāb Path?"[1079] The other will say: "Of

[1079] On the western side of Medina, at the edge of the settled area.

course." So they will direct themselves to Medina but not meet any people in it—other than wild animals lying on the furnishings of the people. They will follow in the wake of the people.

1713. Sālim b. `Abdallāh b. `Umar said, while we were descending from [381] Harshā,[1080] and he was looking to a mountain off to his left, "The people will be gathered, and none will remain but two men on that mountain. One of them will say to his friend: 'O so-and-so, go and see what the people are doing.' So when they are opposite that pass, the Pass of Harshā, they will be gathered on their faces."

1714. `Abdallāh b. `Amr: There will be an emigration after the Emigration (*hijra*) for the best of the people of the lands, to the Emigration-place of Abraham, so that only the worst of the people will be left in the land. Their land will reject them, the breath of God will be hateful for them[1081] and the fire will gather them with the monkeys and swine—they will rest with them when they rest, sleep the night with them when they sleep, and they will get whoever falls from among them.

1715. A man from Medina: I heard Abū Hurayra saying: The people will be gathered in three types: one type on their faces, one type on camels and one type on their legs.

1716. `Ikrima: The gathering place for the people is in the direction of Syria, and the first of those who will be gathered from this community will be [the tribe of] al-Naḍīr.[1082]

1717. Abū Hurayra: Fire will emerge from the direction of the east, and another fire from the direction of the west which will gather the people—before them will be the monkeys who will go during the day but hide during the night, until they gather at the Bridge of Manbij. **(1)** [1083]

[1080] Located about two miles from Medina, towards the coast.

[1081] See the variant no. 1732.

[1082] Not attested; however, the tribe of Naḍāra, which was a southern tribe, allied to Khatha`m.

[1083] The classical Mabbogh or Hieropolis, the bridge is over the Euphrates River.

1718. Ka`b: Truly, the Ka`ba will be gathered to Jerusalem (*bayt al-maqdis*).

1719. `Abd al-Raḥmān b. Salmān: When Caesarea in the land of the Byzantines will be built, it will become an army-province for Syria, and fire from `Adan Abyan will emerge after that.

1720. Ka`b: Fire is about to appear in Yemen which will drive the people to Syria. It will wake when they wake, rest when they rest and sleep when they sleep. It will light up the necks of the camels in Buṣrā. When you hear of it, depart for Syria! [382]

1721. Mu`ādh b. Jabal: "Depart, Yemenites, before the rope is cut from you, and before you find no sustenance other than locust." He said: "I saw the rope of which he spoke—it is the fire that will emerge from it, driving the Yemenites."

1722. Abū Sarīḥa al-Ghifārī, Companion of the Messenger of God[1084]: I heard the Messenger of God saying: Two men from [the tribe of] Muzayna[1085] will be gathered who will be the last of the people to be gathered. They will approach from a mountain they had ascended, until they come to signs of settlement, but find the earth abandoned. So they will come to Medina, and when they have come close to Medina, they will say: "Where are the people?" as they will not see anybody. One of them will say to his friend: "Surely the people are in their houses," so they will go into the houses, but not find anybody. There will be foxes and cats (*sanānīr*) on the furnishings. So they will say: "Where are the people?" one of them will say to the other: "The people are in the mosque," so they will go to the mosque but not find anybody there. They will say: "Where are the people?" One of them will say: "I think that they must be in the market; the markets are keeping them busy." So they will go out and come to the market and not find anybody. They will go around until they come to the pass, but there will be two angels on it, who will take them by their legs and drag

[1084] Ḥudhayfa b. Usayyid al-Ghifārī, Companion, lived in Kūfa, *fl.* 1st/7th century.

[1085] A northern tribe, located close to Medina during the time of the Prophet.

them to the land of gathering. They will be the last people gathered.

1723. Abū Hurayra: The Prophet said: The last ones who will be gathered will be two shepherds from Muzayna who are going to Medina, screeching at their flocks, and find it abandoned, until they come to the Farewell Pass, being dragged on their faces.

1724. Shahr b. Ḥawshab: I came to Jerusalem (*bayt al-maqdis*) at the time when Mu`āwiya died, and allegiance was sworn to Yazīd. I was early to the prayer, so I took a place close to Nawf al-Bikālī—and suddenly there was a huge man, white, with bad eyes, having a black cloak (*khamīṣa*)[1086] on him, stepping in between people's slaves, until he sat before Nawf. I said: "Who is that?" They said: "`Abdallāh b. `Amr b. al-`Āṣ," but Nawf refrained from talking. Then Nawf said to him: "I enjoin you by God, won't you narrate to us a tradition you have heard from the Messenger of God?" He said: "Yes, I will. The Messenger of God came out to us and said: 'Surely the people will emigrate after the Emigration (*hijra*) to the Emigration-place of Abraham. The Hour will only arise upon the worst of people, upon a people who loath the Spirit of God [=Jesus]. Their earth will reject them, so the fire will gather them with the monkeys and the pigs, camping where they camp, sleeping where they sleep, and getting (eating) whoever of them falls behind.'" [383]

1725. Mu`ādh b. Jabal: "Depart from Yemen before the breaking of the rope!" meaning the road, "before you do not have any provisions other than locust and before a fire gathers you to Syria."

1726. `Abdallāh b. Ma`qil[1087]: The son of `Abdallāh b. Salām wanted to raid, but he [`Abdallāh] said: "My son, do not cause me

[1086] See Dozy, *Noms*, pp. 170–5.

[1087] `Abdallāh b. Ma`qil b. Muqarrin al-Muzanī, lived in Kūfa, *fl.* 1st/7th century.

distress with this. Every believer will come when the crier of Syria [calls]."

1727. Abū Umāma: The Hour will not arise until the best of the Iraqis turn towards Syria, and the worst of the Syrians turn towards Iraq, as the Prophet said: "Go to Syria!"

1728. Mu`ādh b. Jabal: Depart from Yemen before three things happen: the emergence of the fire, before the breaking of the rope, and before there is no provision for its people other than locust. Ṭāwūs said: The fire will emerge from Yemen driving the people, it will go out in the morning, come back in the evening and set out at nightfall.

1729. Al-Zuhri: A fire will emerge that will light up the necks of the camels in Buṣrā.

1730. Shahr b. Ḥawshab: I heard `Abdallāh b. `Amr, while he was with Nawf, saying: "I heard the Messenger of God saying: 'There will be emigration after the Emigration for the best of people to the Emigration-place of Abraham, until none but the worst of its people will be left in the land. Their land will reject them, the breath of God Most High will bridle them and a fire will gather them with the monkeys and swine—sleeping with them when they sleep, resting with them when they rest and eating those who fall behind.'"

1731. Al-Zuhri: The Messenger of God said: You will leave Medina in the best state it has been, and none will overshadow it but prowlers such as birds and wild animals. The last to be gathered will be two shepherds from Muzayna, who will be screeching at their flocks, then they will find it [Medina] abandoned, until they come to the Farewell Pass, they will be gathered on their faces.

1732. `Abdallāh b. `Amr: I heard the Messenger of God saying: There will be emigration after Emigration such that [384] the people will emigrate to the Emigration-place of Abraham. None but the worst of people will be left on the earth. The spirit of God Most High will loathe them, their land will reject them and a fire from Adan will gather them with the monkeys and swine, sleeping with them wherever they sleep, resting with them wherever they rest, and they will get whoever falls from them.

1733. Arṭāt: There will be fire and smoke in the east for forty nights.

1734. Ibn `Abbās: A herald will call out before the Hour: "O people, the Hour has come to you!"—the living and the dead will hear it. [385]

Among the Portents of the Hour

1735. Al-Ḥasan: The Messenger of God said: "The likeness of you and I, and the Hour is like a people who feared an enemy, so they sent a scout-troop (*rabī'a*) toward them [to obtain news]. When it came near to them [the enemy], suddenly they were at the horses' manes [ran into them], and feared that the enemy would beat them back to their fellow-troops." Then he flapped his cloak, and called out: "Woe for the morning, since the Hour has almost beaten me to you!"

1736. Abū Sa`īd al-Khudarī: The Messenger of God said when the sun was close to setting: "What has passed and what remains of this world of yours is like what has passed and what remains of this day of yours."

1737. Qasāma b. Zuhayr: It reached me that the Messenger of God said: A likeness of you and I, and the Hour is like a people who fear an enemy, and so sent out a scout-troop of theirs close by, but when the scout-troop saw the invasion of the people, it [the scout-troop] feared if it descended from its place, it would warn the invaders that it had stumbled upon their invasion, so began to wave a cloak from the place [of concealment] and calling: "Woe for the morning!"

1738. Elders of the Helpers: The Messenger of God said: "I was sent together with the Hour like this," and he twisted his pointer and index fingers together "at the same time." Or he said: "The breath[1088] of the Hour."

1739. Jābir b. `Abdallāh: [386] The Messenger of God said: "The Hour

[1088] See readings of MM.

and I were sent together like these"—and when he would mention the Hour, his cheeks reddened, his voice raised, and his anger became fierce like he was the warner of an army: "Either your morning or your evening [it could happen]!"

1740. Abū Hurayra: The Hour will surely arise upon two men with their scales in their hands.

1741. Ibn `Abbās: The Messenger of God said: The Hour will arise when two men have spread a garment between them, but they will not be able to sell it nor wind it up when the Hour arises. A man will have raised a mouthful but not be able to put it in his mouth when the Hour arises. A man will be plastering his cistern, but not be able to fill it with rainwater when the Hour arises. Then the Messenger of God read/recited: "Yet it will indeed come upon them unexpectedly, when they do not realize (it)."[1089]

1742. Abū Hurayra: The Hour will arise upon two men having spread out a garment to sell it between the two of them, but then the Hour will arise upon the both of them.

1743. Abū Sa`īd al-Khudarī: The Prophet said: "How will I be at ease when the One with the Horn has already put (lit. devoured) his horn [to his mouth], and I have heard with the ear that the [trumpet] blowing has been ordered to blow?" This was hard for his Companions, so the Messenger of God said: 'Say: God suffices for us, and what a good One to rely upon! We have relied upon God!'

1744. `Abdallāh b. `Amr: A Bedouin said: "O Messenger of God, what are the trumpets?" He said: "A horn in which one blows."

1745. `Alqama: "Surely the earthquake of the Hour is a great thing."[1090] He said: Before the Hour.

1746. Al-Sha`bī: Gabriel met Jesus, so Jesus said to him: "O Gabriel, when is the Hour?" But he shook with his wings, then said: "The one being asked is not more knowledgable than the

[1089] Q 29:53.

[1090] Q 22:1.

questioner. It is difficult (lit. heavy) in the heavens and the earth, it will only come to you unexpectedly." He said: "He is the only One who reveals its time." [387]

1747. `Umar: A man asked the Messenger of God concerning the Hour, and he said: "The one being asked its not more knowledgable than the questioner." He said: "What are its portents?" He said: "That a handmaiden/concubine would give birth to her mistress or master, and that you would see the barefoot, naked, destitute [Bedouin] sheep-herders building tall buildings."

1748. `Urwa: The Prophet continued to be asked concerning the Hour until "What do you have to do with the mention of it? To your Lord is its (ultimate) goal."[1091] [388]

The Portents of the Hour after the Rising of the Sun from the West

1749. Jābir: The Prophet that he said before his death by a month: "You ask me concerning the Hour, but knowledge of it is only with God."

1750. Kathīr b. Murra, Yazīd b. Shurayḥ and `Amr b. Sulaymān said: The last of the rising of the sun from the west is only one day, and the guardians (*ḥafaẓa*)[1092] will be lifted, and ordered that they not write anything. When this happens, they will prostrate to God, and the angels will be lonely at the presence of the Hour. The sun and moon will be frightened, and the heavens will mount a strong guard, so that no demon (*shayṭān*) or jinn can come near. The jinn will be lonely, and the jinn, humans, birds, animals and wild animals will toss about like waves against each other. The flashing jinn and demons will come to try to listen in, but will be pelted by fireballs (meteors),[1093] so they will not hear anything.

[1091] Q 79:43–4.

[1092] Burge, trans. of al-Suyuti, pp. 159–74 describes the function of these guardian scribes

[1093] Cf. Q 72:8–9.

The color of the heavens will change, the earth will tremble and the mountains will be shattered other than four: Mount Sinai, [Mt.] Jūdī, Mount Lebanon and Mount Tabor, which is above Tiberias. God has situated them as green gardens with trees between paradise and hell. Upon them is a building of pearl (*lu'lu'*), emerald, pearl (*durr*) and rubies, and God has placed His throne upon them in order to judge creation.

The leg of the angel, the one with the trumpet, will be at Qulzum[1094] and he will blow the first blowing crashing against those in the heavens and the earth, continuing for forty years.

The heavens will be rent asunder and its stars spread apart, and God will send the Water of Life, so humanity will regenerate. Every human among them will look like the eye of a locust because of the cognizance of sin, and like [the size of] the grain in the belly button.

`Abdallāh b. `Amr said: "Then he will blow the final trumpet-blast at the Western Judgment Gate, and suddenly they will all stand, looking, risen amongst the smoke and darkness." Abū al-Dardā' said: "Whoever has a good deed will be happy at [389] the smoke and the darkness, such that he will go into a state of ease. Light will be divided among the people in accord with their deeds."

1751. Wahb b. Munabbih: At the time of the rising of the Hour the mountains of the sea will emerge to the dry land, and the mountains of the dry land into the sea. The sea will emerge and overflow onto the earth. Every single building and mountain on the face of the earth will be destroyed and fall down. The stars will be scattered, and the heavens changed. The earth will be split asunder in fear from the rising of the Hour, then the Hour will rise.

1752. Jābir: The Messenger of God said before his death by a month: I swear by God, no living soul today on the earth will see 100 years.

[1094] Classical Clysma, the area of the Suez.

1753. Sa`d b. Abī Waqqāṣ: The Prophet said: "I hope that my community will not be impotent before my Lord if it is delayed a half a day." It was said to Sa`d: "How much is half [a day]?" He said: "500 years."[1095]

1754. Jubayr b. Nufayr: The Jews and others frequently asked at the time of the Messenger of God concerning the Hour, so Gabriel came to him and he said: "O Gabriel, the Jews and others are frequently asking me about the Hour," so he said: "The one being questioned does not know more than the questioner."

1755. Abū Ḍamra al-Kalā`ī[1096]: "The people of this city," meaning Ḥimṣ, "will go to bed, and surely wake up, so one will go out from the Eastern Gate and be unable to see [Mount] Sanīr,[1097] as it will be gone from its place, so he will tell himself he is dreaming (lit. lying). He will do the call to prayer for the people, so they will emerge and gaze at what he was gazing. Suddenly [Mt.] Lebanon will be in its place, and suddenly [Mount] Sanīr will be gone from its place! They will stay [gazing] like that for as long as God wishes during the day, until someone comes from Ḥawārīn[1098] saying: 'Sanīr has moved from us completely, so we do not know where it has gone.'" It is said that it is one of the pegs[1099] of hell (*jahannam*).

1756. Wahb b. Munabbih: The seventh sign is when God sends angels on piebald horses flying between the heavens and the earth, announcing the demise of the earth and those upon it. The eighth sign is that every tree on the earth will weep blood, and the ninth sign is that every single stone will lament like women lament. The tenth is the rising of the sun from the west. [390]

[1095] Cf. Q 22:47.
[1096] Lived in Ḥimṣ, *fl.* 2nd/8th century.
[1097] The Biblical name for Mt. Hermon (cf. Ez. 27:5).
[1098] One of the towns.
[1099] Cf. Q 78:7.

1757. Al-`Uryān b. al-Haytham[1100]: I went as part of a delegation with my father to Yazīd b. Mu`āwiya, so I heard `Abdallāh b. `Amr, and I said to him: "Did you claim that the Hour will rise at the beginning of the 70s?"[1101] So he said: "They tell lies about me, it is not like that. But I said: 'The 70s will not pass without disasters and important events.'"

1758. Anas b. Mālik: The Prophet said: The Hour will not arise until a year is like a month, a month is like a week (*juma`*), and a week is like a day, and a day is like a kindled fire.

1759. Abū Hurayra: "The Hour will not rise until the people screw each other on the roads, just as mounts screw, with the men only needing men and the women women—do you know what lesbianism (*tasāḥuq*) is?"[1102] They said: "No." He said: "When a woman mounts a woman, then she rubs her (*tasḥaquhā*)."

1760. Sa`īd b. Masrūq: The Messenger of God said: The waters will all sink deep and return to their places, other than the Jordan River and the Nile of Egypt.

1761. Makḥūl: A Bedouin said: "O Messenger of God, when is the Hour?" The Messenger of God said: "The one being questioned does not know more than the questioner, but its portents [are]: the close building of markets, rain without vegetation, the appearance of slander, the appearance of children of error (*ghayya*), extolling the one possessed of wealth, for iniquitous people to raise their voices in the mosques, the victory of those who do wrong over those who do good—whoever lives in this time, let him flee with his religion, and remain close (*aḥlās*) to his house."

1762. `Abdallāh b. Mas`ūd: When you see that the people have killed

[1100] Al-`Uryān b. al-Haytham al-Nakha`ī, lived in Kūfa, blind, in charge of the *shuraṭ* of Kūfa, then its governor, *fl.* 2nd/8th century. He was teased about his name ("Naked") by the local wits: see al-Anbārī, *al-Mukhtār min nawādir al-akhbār* (Beirut: al-Maktaba al-`Aṣriyya, 1994), p. 110.

[1101] Yazīd ruled 680–3; the 70s began at 70/689.

[1102] Probably one of the earliest datable mentions of lesbianism in the Muslim sources, see Samar Habib, *Arabo-Islamic Texts on Female Homosexuality 850–1780 A.D.* (Youngstown, NY: Teneo, 2009).

off the prayer, squandered trust, permitted lying, taking oaths of alliance (*ḥilf*) frequently, consuming interest, taking bribes, building high buildings, following their whims and selling the religion for the sake of this world, then salvation, salvation! May your mother be bereaved of you!

1763. `Ā'isha: When the first signs emerge, the pens are thrown aside, the angel-guardians sit down and the bodies testify about the deeds. **(2)** [391]

1764. `Abdallāh b. `Amr: The Hour will not arise until people screw each other on the roads like donkeys screw each other.

1765. It was said to Nawf: `Abdallāh b. `Amr would say: "The people will not remain very long after the 90s." So Nawf said: "I think that they will remain living for a long while after that, but most of those living will be in Syria." It was said: "Kūfa and Baṣra?" He said: "Those are new."

1766. Shahr b. Ḥawshab: The Prophet said: It is almost to the point where a man will be departing from his house, then his stick and his whip will inform him of what his family have done in his house.

1767. `Abdallāh b. `Amr: The evil ones after the good ones for 120 years, but not one of the people know when the first of that [period] is.

1768. Mujāhid: The Messenger of God said: The Hour will not arise upon those who say: "There is no god but Allāh." When the angel wishes to blow in the trumpets, then hears somebody saying: "There is no god but Allāh" he delays it by seventy autumns.

1769. Anas: The Prophet said: The Hour will not arise upon anyone who says: "God, God!"

1770. `Alī: The worst or among the worst of the people are those who will live to see the Hour while they are still alive.

1771. Zayd b. Aslam: The Messenger of God said: The likeness of me and the Hour are like a group that has sent a spy, and has seen the enemy, but feared that they would beat him back to his friends, so he used his sword to flash [a signal] to them that they were about to be ambushed. I was sent just before the Hour.

1772. `Abdallāh b. `Amr: There are demons (*shayāṭīn*) who are imprisoned, who are on the verge of being set free, so recite the Qur`ān for the people [for the sake of protection].

1773. Al-`Uryān b. al-Haytham: I went on a delegation to Mu`āwiya, so while I was with him, a man who had two rich garments on came in, and Mu`āwiya welcomed him, and sat him on the throne with him [392] so I said: "Who is that, Commander of the Believers?" He said: "Don't you know him? This is `Abdallāh b. `Amr b. al-`Āṣ!" I said: "So this is the one who says: 'People will not live past 100 years'?" So he approached me, saying: "That was you will find them living past 100 for a long time, but this community was given a time span of 130 years."

1774. Abū Hurayra: The Prophet said: The Hour will arise while two men are selling a garment, but they will not have time to roll it up or sell it until the Hour arises. A man will be milking, but not have time to put the container to his mouth before the Hour arises. And a man will be filling a pool, but not have time to drink from it until the Hour arises.

1775. Abū al-Firās, a man from Aslam[1103]: A man said to the Messenger of God: "When is the Hour?" He said: "The one being questioned concerning it is not more knowledgable than the questioner, but it has signs: when the sheep-herders raise tall buildings, when the barefoot and naked are kings, who are the little Arabs (*`urayb*)."

1776. Ibn Mas`ūd: The Hour has portents, and it will never arise until its portents come.

1777. Abū Hurayra: The Prophet said: "The Hour will not arise until it rains upon the people such a raining that permanent houses will not be able to stand, but tents of hair will." Suhayl said: "My father never left tents of hair until he met God Most High (died)."

[1103] A northern tribe, living close to Medina at the time of the Prophet.

1778. Sahl b. Sa`d[1104]: The Prophet said: "I was sent together with the Hour like this" and he showed with his two fingers, the pointer and the middle intertwined.

1779. Ibn Abī al-Hudhayl: If one of you has to urinate, let him do his ablutions with sand (*tayammum*), fearing that the Hour would overtake him.

1780. Ḥanash b. al-Ḥārith[1105] on the authority of his father: We arrived at Qādisiyya, and during the night one of us had a colt born, but when it was morning he slaughtered his colt. This reached `Umar [b. al-Khaṭṭāb], so his letter came to us that we should be equitable to that which God has given us for sustenance, as the matter (the Hour) is coming (lit. smiting).

1781. Abū Sa`īd al-Khudarī: The Hour will not arise until no one does the pilgrimage to the House (Ka`ba). [393]

1782. A *qāṣṣ* [popular storyteller] who used to narrate in Medina from a gathering of other *quṣaṣ*: I heard Anas b. Mālik saying: Among the [signs of the] nearness of the Hour is the appearance of mines, the proliferation of rain, but the paucity of vegetation, that a man would walk with an ounce or two [of gold] but not find anyone who will accept it, such that everyone will not need anything—while on that day they will be the most desirous of this world of theirs. These are signs that will appear, so the rich man will go terrified to the poor man saying: "What will I do with this [wealth], when this Hour will arise?" and a man will be walking with a loaf (*raghīf*), not owning anything other than that, wandering with it, but not find anybody who will take it. This is the day when "belief will not benefit anyone who did not believe before, or (who did not) earn some good through his belief."[1106]

[1104] Companion, lived in Medina, d. 91/709–10, said to have been the last of the Companions in Medina.

[1105] Ḥanash b. al-Ḥārith al-Nakha`ī, lived in Kūfa, *fl.* 2nd/8th century.

[1106] Q 6:158.

1783. Rajā' b. Ḥaywa al-Kindī[1107]: There will come a time upon the people when only one date will be on a palm tree.

1784. Anas b. Mālik: The Prophet said: Gabriel came to me and brought me a white woman with a black dot on her, so I said: "Who is this?" He said: "This is Friday," so I said: "And what is the black dot?" He said: "On it the Hour will arise."

1785. Abū Sa`īd al-Khudarī: When the Hour nears lightening bolts will increase.

1786. Another one: I heard the Prophet say: "The Hour and I were sent together like these two," meaning his two fingers.

1787. Ibn `Umar: The Prophet said: The Hour will not arise until the number of porticoes and buildings increase, and the gum-acacia leaves (*al-sumar al-waraq*)[1108] do not grow. [394]

1788. `Abdallāh: The Hour will arise on the worst of people, then an angel will blow in the trumpets, a horn between the heavens and the earth. Every creation between the heavens and the earth will die at that time, other those those who your Lord wishes. Then between the two trumpet blasts there is [however much time] God wishes. Then God will send water from under the Throne as sperm like men's sperm. Every single human in the earth will be given some of it, so their bodies and flesh will regenerate from this water just as the earth regenerates from the soft rains. Then `Abdallāh read/recited "(It is) God who sends the winds, and it stirs up a cloud, and We drive it to some barren land, and by means of it give the earth life after its death. So (too) is the raising up."[1109] Then the angel will rise between the heavens and the earth, and blow in it, so every soul will go to its body, and enter it, then they will stand and be alive as one man, standing before the Lord of the Worlds.

[1107] Rajā' b. Ḥaywa al-Kindī, originally from Beth-Shean, lived in Filisṭīn, a prominent supporter of the Umayyads, d. 112/730–1.

[1108] Collected from the leaves of *Acacia nilotica*, and used in both edibles and for adhesive.

[1109] Q 35:9.

1789. Ka`b: The Hour will not arise until a man manages the affairs of fifty women.
1790. Ḥudhayfa: If a man fastened a warhorse and birthed a colt from it at the first of the signs, he would not be able to ride the colt before the last of them.
1791. Ka`b: The Hour will not arise until the year is like a month, a month like a week, a week like a day, and a like an hour, and an hour like the burning of an ulcer (*sa`fa*).
1792. Abū Hurayra: The Prophet said: "Between the two trumpet-blasts there are forty." They said: "O Abū Hurayra, forty days?" He said: "I refuse," so they said: "forty months?" He said: "I refuse," so they said: "forty years?" He said: "I refuse." Then water will descend from the heavens by which it will grow just as vegetables grow—there will only be one bone for the [reconstituted] human, which will be the spine—and from it [the water] creation will be constituted on the Day of Resurrection.
1793. `Abdallāh: There will come a day for the Euphrates [River] [395] in which if a basin of water was sought, it would not be found, as all the waters will return to their sources. The remainder of the water and the believers will be in Syria.
1794. Ibn Mas`ūd: The worst of the nights, days, months and times are those closest to the Hour.
1795. `Abdallāh: The Hour will arise on the worst of people, who will not command the right and forbid the wrong, mounting each other like donkeys mount each other. A man will take the hand of a woman, be alone with her, and do what he wants with her, then return to them while they laugh at him, and he at them.
1796. Kathīr b. Murra: Among the signs of the trial, and the portents of the Hour are that a voice from the heavens will come to them by night, and the voice will scare them. In the midst of their fright, suddenly God will send voices like lions from the heavens to scare the people's hearts, and to take hold of souls. In the midst of their fright, a sign will happen in the heavens, making both believer and unbeliever take haste to believe.

1797. Ibn `Abbās: The end for the community of Muḥammad is 300 years like the years of the Israelites.

1798. `Abdallāh b. `Amr: What is between the signs is like from week to week, the first of it and the last of it, or seven difficult stitch-holes (*khurazāt*) with a weak thread—when it snaps the rest unravels.

1799. Ibn Mas`ūd: When the Qur`ān is lifted from the breasts of men, they will filled up with poetry.

1800. Ibn `Umar: The Prophet said: When the sun rises from the west all of the people will believe, but on that day "belief will not benefit anyone who did not believe."[1110] [396]

The Rising of the Sun from the West

1801. Kathīr b. Murra, Yazīd b. Shurayḥ and `Amr b. Sulaymān said: The last part of the rising of the sun from the west is only one day, so on that day whatever is in peoples' hearts will be stamped upon them. The angel-guardians and the actions will be completed, the angels will be commanded not to write/record actions, and the sun and moon will be terrified from the rising of the Hour.

1802. Abū Hurayra: The Messenger of God said: Five are among the signs, I do not know which one is first, and which one of them has come—"belief will not benefit anyone who did not believe before, or (who did not) earn some good through his belief"[1111]: the rising of the sun from the west, the Dajjāl, Gog and Magog, the smoke and the Beast.

1803. Wahb b. Munabbih: The rising of the sun from the west is the tenth and final sign, then "every nursing woman will forget what she has nursed . . ."[1112], every possessor of wealth will throw it aside, and every merchant will be distracted from his merchandise.

[1110] Q 6:158.
[1111] Q 6:158.
[1112] Q 22:2.

1804. `Abdallāh concerning His Word: "On the Day when one of the signs of your Lord comes belief will not benefit anyone who did not believe before,"[1113] he said: "The rising of the sun from the west." [397]

1805. `Abdallāh on the authority of the Prophet said: Jesus and his friends [prayers] will be answered concerning Gog and Magog, then they will live until one night they will greet the rising of the sun from the west, and until they will enjoy forty years after the appearance of the Beast of the Earth in plenty and security.

1806. `Abdallāh on the authority of the Prophet: You will only remain a short while after Gog and Magog until the sun will rise from the west. Those who have no happiness will say: "We do not care as long as God returns His light upon us whether it rises from the east or the west." They will hear a call from the heavens: "O you who believe! Your belief has been accepted from you, and actions have been lifted from you. O you who have disbelieved! The doors of repentance have been locked against you, the pens have ceased to write, and the codices have been rolled up, so no repentance or belief will be accepted from anyone other than those who believed previously."

A believer will only be born of a believer, and an unbeliever from an unbeliever. The Devil will fall prostrate, crying: "My God! You commanded me to prostrate myself to whom You wished, and what You wished!" The demons will gather to him, saying: "O our master, to whom should we go in our terror?" He will say: "I only asked my Lord to look upon me until the Day of Resurrection, and to a known time.[1114] Now the sun has risen from the west, so it is the known time—and there are no actions counted after today." So the demons will go openly to the earth, such that a man will say: "This is my spirit-double (*qarīnī*) who used to deceive me. Praise be to God who has

[1113] Q 6:158.

[1114] Cf. Q 15:38.

disgraced him and given me rest from him." The people will look at the jinn and demons, their food and drink, their living and dying, but the Devil will continue to be prostrate, weeping until the Beast from the Earth will emerge and kill him.

1807. Ibn `Abbās: The Prophet said: When the sun rises from the west, mothers will forget their children and loved ones because of the fruits of their hearts. Every soul will be occupied with what comes to it, and no repentance will be accepted after it from anyone, other than those who were doing good in their belief, as after that nothing will be recorded for them as was previously done. As for the unbelievers, it will be a loss and regret for them, so that even if a man brought forth a horse, he would not be able to ever ride it until the Hour rises because of the proximity of the rising of the sun from the west to the rising of the Hour. The Hour will surely rise while the people are in their markets, with two men having spread a garment, but being unable to sell it or even roll it up, while a man has lifted his mouthful to his mouth, but will not be able to taste it. Then he declaimed: "Yet it will indeed come upon them unexpectedly, when they do not realize (it)."[1115] [398]

1808. `Abdallāh b. `Umar: The sun and the moon with be combined in the heavens at its station during the evening prayer, and the day will be perpetual (*sarmad*) for twenty years.

1809. Wahb b. Jābir al-Khaywānī[1116]: I was with `Abdallāh b. `Amr, so he began to narrate to us, saying: "The sun when it sets gives the peace greeting, prostrates, and asks permission—so permission is granted to it until the day when it sets, it [the sun] will say: 'O Lord, the way is long, so if permission is not granted to me, I will not make it.' So it will hold back as long as God wills, then it will be said to it: 'Rise from the direction from which you set,' so from that day until the Day

[1115] Q 29:53.

[1116] Lived in Kūfa, then went to live in Jerusalem, in Ibn `Asākir, *Tā'rīkh*, lxiii, p. 355 relates tradition on Gog and Magog, *fl.* 2nd/8th century.

of Resurrection 'belief will not benefit anyone who did not believer before.'"[1117]

1810. `Amr b. `Ubayd b. `Umayr: "A day (in which) one of the signs of your Lord will come."[1118] He said: The rising of the sun from the west.

1811. `Abdallāh: The rising of the sun from the west will be like two conjoined camels.

1812. `Abdallāh b. `Amr: The people will remain after the sun rising from the west 120 years.

1813. Ṣafwān b. `Assāl al-Murādī: The Messenger of God narrated to us: In the west there is a door for repentance, whose length and breadth are seventy or forty years. It will not be locked until the rising of the sun from the west is before it. Then he declaimed: "On the Day when one of the signs of your Lord come belief will not benefit anyone who did not believe before or (who did not) earn some good through his belief."[1119,1120]

The Appearance of the Beast (*Dābba*)

1814. Abū Sarīḥa: The Messenger of God said: The Beast has three appearances in the age (*dahr*): it will emerge once in the furthest Yemen, so the mention of it will be widespread among the nomads but will not reach the settled people, meaning Mecca. It will stay for a long while after that, then it will emerge again close to Mecca, so mention of it will be widespread among the nomads. It will stay for a long while after that, then while the people on that day are in the holiest and best of mosques in God Most High's eyes, and the most noble mosque to God, the Sacred Enclosure Mosque. It will not frighten them except in the direction of the Mosque; it will grow between the Black Corner and the Gate of Banū Makhzūm[1121] to the right of the

[1117] Q 6:158.
[1118] Paraphrase of Q 6:158.
[1119] Q 6:158.
[1120] Section break pp. 399–400.
[1121] One of the nineteen gates of the Sacred Enclosure.

exit from the Mosque. The people will reject it separately and together, with a band of Muslims standing firm against it.

They will know that they are incapable against God, so it will emerge in front of them, with the dirt shaking from its head, then it appears to them. Their faces will be shining such that they will be left looking like twinkling stars. Then it will turn in the earth, no one coming after it will be able to catch it, and no one will be able to flee from it. Even a man who will take refuge from it in prayer, it will come to him from behind him, saying: "O so-and-so, right now you are praying," so he will approach facing it, and it will mark him on his face. Then it will go and visit people in their houses, accompany them on their trips, and associate with their businesses, to distinguish the unbeliever from the believer. The unbeliever will say to the believer: "O believer, fulfill my trust!" and the believer will say to the unbeliever: "O unbeliever, fulfill my trust." [402]

1815. `Abdallāh b. `Amr b. al-`Āṣ: The Beast will emerge from a mountain path at Ajyād,[1122] with its head touching the clouds, even though its two legs will not have fully emerged from the earth, until he comes to a man while he is doing the prayer, and says: "Your prayer is not from personal necessity, it is just for the sake of taking refuge and showing off," so he will mark him.

1816. Wahb b. Munabbih: The first of the signs is the Byzantines, then the Dajjāl, the third is Gog and Magog, the fourth is Jesus son of Mary the fifth is the smoke and the sixth is the Beast.

1817. `Aṭiyya b. `Umar[1123] concerning His Word Most High: "When the word falls upon them, We shall bring forth for them a creature from the earth, (which) will speak to them."[1124] He said: "When they do not command the right and do not forbid the wrong."

[1122] A location near Mecca.

[1123] Probably a mistake for `Aṭiyya b. `Urwa al-Sa`dī, Companion, lived in the Balqā', *fl.* 1st/7th century.

[1124] Q 27:82.

1818. `Abdallāh b. Mas`ūd: The Dajjāl, Gog and Magog, the Beast and the rising of the sun from the west.

1819. `Abdallāh: The Prophet said: "The friends of Jesus son of Mary who fought the Dajjāl with him, will enjoy themselves after the emergence of the Beast of the Earth forty years in comfort and security."

1820. `Abdallāh: The Prophet said: The emergence of the Beast is after the rising of the sun [from the west], so when it emerges the Beast will kill the Devil, while he is prostrating himself. Then the believers will enjoy themselves on the earth after that for forty years. Everything they wish for will be given to them or found, there will be no injustice or wrong. Everything will submit to the Lord of the Worlds willingly or unwillingly—the believers willingly, while the unbelievers unwillingly, and the wild animals and the birds unwillingly. But then the wild animals will not harm a quadruped or a bird, and the believer will be born but not die until forty years have been completed from the emergence of the Beast of the Earth. Then death will return to them, and they will stay in that situation for as long as God wishes. Then death will be speedy among the believers, and no believer will remain.

So the unbeliever will say: "We were fearful of the believers, but now not one of them remains. No repentance will be received from us, so there is nothing for us but to act wantonly." So they will act wantonly in the roads like animals, one will mount his mother, his sister or his daughter. They will have sex in the middle of the road—one will mount her and another will dismount. No one will disapprove or be jealous; [403] the best of them on that day will say: "If you moved off the road it would be better!"

They will act like this until there are none left who are children of [legitimate] marriages; all will be children of fornication (*awlād al-sifāḥ*). They will be like this as long as God wishes. Then God will make the women's wombs infertile for thirty years, so that no woman will give birth and there will be no children on the earth. All of them will be children of illicit sexual relations (*awlād al-zinā*), the worst of people. Upon them the Hour will arise.

1821. Umar said: The Beast will not emerge until there are no believers on the earth, so read/recite if you wish "When the word falls upon them, We shall bring forth for them a creature from the earth."[1125]

1822. `Abdallāh b. `Amr: The Beast will emerge from a crack on the [Hill of] Ṣafā[1126] the height of a warhorse for three days, without a third of it emerging. **(1)**

1823. Ḥammād b. Salama[1127]: The Prophet said: The Beast will emerge with the stick of Moses and the seal of Solomon. He will polish the face of the believer with the stick, but mark the nose of the unbeliever with the seal so that faithless people will gather, saying: "Hey, you believer!" or "Hey, you unbeliever!"

1824. Ibn `Abbās concerning His Word Most High: "We shall bring forth for them a creature from the earth"[1128] He said: "It will have soft hair and feathers, and have four legs. It will emerge from the some of the dry valleys of the Tihāma." `Abdallāh b. `Amr said: "It will dot the face of every unbeliever with a black dot, which will spread over his entire face making it black, while he will dot the face of every believer with a white dot, which will spread over his entire face making it white. The people of a family will sit at the table, and know the believer from the unbeliever, and when they buy and sell in the markets, they will know the believer from the unbeliever."

1825. `Āmir al-Sha`bī[1129]: The Beast of the Earth will have the speed of a weasel, and its face will touch the heavens. [404]

1826. `Ā'isha said: The Beast will emerge from Ajyād.

[1125] Q 29:82.

[1126] One of the two hillocks contained within the Sacred Enclosure, cf. Q 2:158.

[1127] Lived in Baṣra, a *mawlā*, an important traditionist, d. 167/783–4

[1128] Q 29:82.

[1129] `Āmir b. Shurāḥbīl al-Sha`bī, lived in Kūfa, visted Constantinople as an emissary of `Abd al-Malik, d. 105/723–4.

1827. Ibn `Umar: The Beast will emerge on the night of [the gathering at] Muzdalifa, where they will gather, then the Beast will emerge when its neck is erect because of its length. It will find every hypocrite and mark him.

1828. Ibn `Umar: The Beast will emerge from a crack in [the Hill of] Ṣafā.

1829. Ibn `Umar: "When the word falls upon them, We shall bring forth for them a creature from the earth, (which) will speak to them."[1130] He said: "When they do not command the right and do not forbid the wrong."

1830. Ḥudhayfa: "The Beast has three emergences: emergences in which it will emerge from the deserts, then be concealed (*tankami*)," meaning be hidden, "and an emergence from one of the towns, such that when it is mentioned blood will flow. Then it will be concealed, so when the people are at the most noble, greatest and most meritorious mosque," which we think is called the Sacred Enclosure, but he did not name it, suddenly the earth will be lifted up for them, so the people will get out fleeing. A band of Muslims will remain, who will say: "Nothing will save us from the command of God."

So the Beast will emerge to them, and make their faces shine like twinkling stars. Then it will go, and no one who is trying to catch it will be able to, and no one fleeing it will be able to avoid it. It will come to a man while he is praying, and say: "By God you are not among those praying!" It was said: "What are the people doing on that day, O Ḥudhayfa?" He said: "Neighbors in the pastures, business associates, traveling companions."

1831. Ibn `Umar: The Messenger of God said: When the promise that God Most High said: "We shall bring forth for them a creature from the earth, (which) will speak to them,"[1131] he said: "This will not be discourse or talk, but it will be a mark that it will

[1130] Q 29:82.
[1131] Q 29:82.

make at the command of God Most High. Its emergence will be from [the Hill of] Ṣafā on the night of Minā, so they will wake up between its head [405] and its tail. No one will enter or exit until it has completed that which God Most High has commanded it. Those who perish will perish, those who are saved will be saved. The first step it takes will be at Antioch."

1832. Ḥudhayfa b. al-Yamān: No group has ever cursed each other without the words coming back to bite them.

1833. Unidentified: "The Beast will emerge and the signs after Jesus by seven months." `Amr b. al-`Āṣ said: "The Beast will emerge from [the Hill of] Ṣafā which is next to [the Hill of] Marwa. It will mark whoever tells lies concerning God Most High and His Messenger." [406]

The Ethiopians

1834. Abū Hurayra: The Prophet said: The Ka`ba will be destroyed by the One with Two Small Shanks (Dhū al-Suwayqatān) from the Ethiopians.[1132]

1835. `Abdallāh b. `Amr heard him said: it is as if I am looking towards the Ka`ba while an Ethiopian, bald and crooked-boned is destroying it. Mujāhid said: When Ibn al-Zubayr destroyed it, I came to look to see what he had said, but I did not see anything of it.

1836. `Alī: Circumambulate this house [the Ka`ba] frequently, for it is as if I see a bald and small-eared, narrow-shanked man, with an iron shovel (*misḥāt*)[1133] destroying it.

1837. Abu `Utba,[1134] the *mawlā* of `Amr b. al-`Āṣ: Egypt will perish when it is shot by [the shooting of] four bows: the bow of the Turks, the bow of the Byzantines, the bow of the Ethiopians and the bow of the Andalusians. [407]

[1132] The area of Mecca was raided by the Ethiopians in 702, and they occupied its port, Jeddah, briefly.

[1133] See Wolf Leslau, *Comparative Dictionary of Ge`ez*, p. 495 "to scrape off."

[1134] Abū `Utba al-Khawlānī, *fl.* 2nd/8th century.

1838. `Ubayd b. Rafī`: `Umar b. al-Khaṭṭāb: "How far is the distance between you and Wasīm?" I said: "It is exactly one post-stop (*barīd*) [away]." He said: "The Andalusians will come and fight you there." Ḥāṭib b. Abī Balta`a[1135] that he heard `Umar b. al-Khaṭṭāb say: "The Andalusians will come to you and fight you at Wasīm until the horses will move in blood up to their fetlocks, then God will defeat them." [408]

The Emergence of the Ethiopians

1839. `Umar b. al-Khaṭṭāb rose in Mecca during the pilgrimage, and said: "O Yemenites, emigrate before the two darknesses—as for the first of them, it is the Ethiopians who will come out until they reach this place I am standing."

1840. Ka`b: The Ethiopians will come out all at once, and end up at this house [Mecca], then the Syrians will come out against them, and find them having spread themselves on the ground, and will fight them in the dry valleys of Banu `Alī, which are near to Medina,[1136] until an Ethiopian will be sold for a cloak (*shamla*).

1841. Ka`b: They will destroy the house, and take the Standing-place, and tread upon it whereupon God will kill them.

1842. `Abdallāh b. `Amr: The Ethiopians will come out after the descent of Jesus son of Mary whereupon Jesus will send a vanguard [against them] and they will be defeated.

1843. Abû Qatāda: The Prophet said: The Ethiopians will come and destroy the House (Ka`ba) completely, such that it will not be inhabited again, and they are the ones who will take out its treasures.

1844. Abû Hurayra: The One with the Two Small Shanks from the Ethiopians will destroy the Ka`ba. [409]

1845. Abû Hurayra: The Prophet said: It is as if I see a bald,

[1135] Companion, supposedly used as a messenger to Egypt by the Prophet, d. 30/650–1.

[1136] See al-Fākihī, *Akhbār Makka* (Beirut: Dār Khiḍr, 1998), i, p. 358 (no. 746).

crooked-boned, bandy-legged [one] at the back of the Ka`ba, striking it with a great pickax (*karzana*).[1137]

1846. Abû Hurayra: The One with Two Small Shanks, the Ethiopian, will destroy the House of God.

1847. `Abdallāh b. `Amr: The Ka`ba will be destroyed twice, and the [Black] Stone will be lifted on the third time.[1138]

1848. `Abdallāh b. `Amr: It is as if I see an Ethiopian, narrow-shanked, sitting against the Ka`ba with his iron shovel, while it is being destroyed.

1849. Ka`b: Truly, an Ethiopian will destroy the house [Ka`ba], and will take the Standing-place, then tread upon it, whereupon God will kill them.

1850. Wardān[1139] went out one day from the presence of Maslama b. Mukhallad, while he was governor of Egypt, then passed by `Abdallāh b. `Amr making haste. So he called him, saying: "Where are you going, O Abû `Ubayd?" He said: "The governor has sent me to Memphis so I can bring out the treasure of Pharaoh." He said: "Return to him and greet him with the peace greeting, and say to him: The treasure of Pharaoh is not for you, nor for your soldiers, but it belongs to the Ethiopians, who will come in their ships (*sufun*) to al-Fusṭāṭ, and proceed until they camp at Memphis. Then God will reveal to them the treasure of Pharaoh, so they will take of it what they will. Then they will say: 'Don't we desire booty better than this?' So they will return, and the Muslims will come out following them until they catch them. God will defeat these Ethiopians; then the Muslims will kill them, and take them prisoner, until an Ethiopian will be sold on that day for a garment (*kisā'*)."

1851. `Abdallāh b. `Amr: You and the Andalusians will fight at Wasīm,

[1137] Ibn al-Athīr, *Nihāya*, iv, p. 162, evidently related to the Heb. *garzen* (cf. Deut. 19:5, 20:19, Is. 10:15).

[1138] The theft of the Black Stone actually happened in 930, when the Kharijites took it for twenty-three years.

[1139] A *mawlā* of Maslama b. Mukhallad, from the captives of Iṣfahān, lived in Damascus, killed in Egypt by the Byzantines at al-Barlas on the shores of the Nile in 55/675.

so you will bring your supplies from Syria. When the first of them will land, God will defeat your enemy and continue to kill them into Libya. Then they will return whereupon the Ethiopians will come with 300,000 [troops], led by Eusebius (*usbus*).[1140] You and the Syrians will fight them; then God will defeat them, whereupon you will return to the Copts, and tell them: "You did not aid us against our enemies." So they will say [410]: "You did this to us, you took our power, and did not leave us any weapons.[1141] You are the most beloved of people to us." He said: "So they will pardon them [the Copts]."

1852. `Abdallāh b. `Amr that a man from among the enemies of the Muslims in Andalus, which is the tradition of the One with the Mane—a long tradition, which I have written under the Byzantines.[1142]

1853. `Abdallāh b. `Amr: The Andalusians will fight you at Wasīm, but your supplies will come from Syria, so God will defeat them.

1854. `Umar b. al-Khaṭṭāb: They will fight you at Wasīm, then God will defeat them, then the Ethiopians will come to you the following year.

1855. `Abdallāh b. `Amr: The Ethiopians will come with 300,000 [troops], led by a man called Eusebius, so then you will fight them together with the Syrians, then God will defeat them.

1856. `Abdallāh b. `Amr: They are the ones who will take out the treasure of Pharaoh from a city called Memphis. The Muslims will come out against them, fight them, and they will plunder those treasures, until an Ethiopian will be sold for a cloak (*`abā'a*).

1857. Layth and Ibn Lahī`a: The one who will lead the Andalusians will be a king from the non-Arabs, called the One with the Mane, who will exile the Andalusians and Maghribi Muslims

[1140] Compare no. 1300.
[1141] According to the Pact of `Umar.
[1142] See no. 1300.

until the Egyptians will fight him, whereupon God will defeat him, then the One with the Mane will convert to Islam after the defeat.

1858. `Abdallāh b. `Amr: Banū Qanṭūrā b. Karkarā[1143] are about to emerge. They will lead the Khurasanians harshly, until they fasten their horses at the palm tree of al-Ubulla.[1144] Then they will send to the Basrans: Either you join us, or [411] you leave it empty for us. A third will join them, a third to the Arabs, and a third to Syria.

1859. Ka`b: When God will kill Gog and Magog, when the people are in that situation, a caller will come to them: "The One with the Two Small Shanks has raided the house [the Ka`ba], intending [to attack it]," so Jesus son of Mary will send a vanguard of either 700 or between 700 and 800 until when they are part of the way God will send a soft Yemenite wind to take the spirit of every believer. Only the lowest people will remain, mounting each other like animals. The likeness of the Hour is like a man who circles his horse, seeking a way to ride; whoever undertakes anything after my words here or after knowledge of me, will be an undertaker.

1860. Ḥārith b. Mālik [known as] b. Barṣā'[1145]: I heard the Prophet say on the Day of Mecca's Conquest: "Do not raid each other after today until the Day of Resurrection."

1861. Mujāhid: When Ibn al-Zubayr destroyed the Ka`ba we went out for three days, expecting the punishment [from God].

1862. `Abdallāh b. `Amr: It is as if I see a crooked-boned, small

[1143] The Banū Qanṭūrā are mentioned six times in the text (nos. 1868, 1869, 1873, 1882, 1891), all of which are associated with the Turks, horses, the east, and so this tradition seems misplaced as it does not relate to Ethiopians at all. It is not clear how the Banū Qanṭūrā got associated with the Turks, as the name seems to be related to Keturah, the concubine of Abraham (Gen. 25:1–4). Even that association is tentative (nor did Muslims know what to make of it: Ibn Abī Shayba, *Muṣannaf*, vii, p. 482 [no. 37393] "thus we found it in the book; as for the description it is that of the Turks").

[1144] The port of Baṣra.

[1145] Al-Laythī, Companion, *fl.* 1st/7th century.

shanked Ethiopian sitting against the Ka`ba, with his iron shovel, while it was being destroyed. [412]

The Turks[1146]

1863. Ka`b: The Turks will descend upon Amid, drink from the Tigris and the Euphrates Rivers, and they will run amok in al-Jazīra, while the people of Islam are in al-Ḥīra,[1147] unable to do anything to them. God will send snow against them—a heavy snow, with gale-force winds, and bitter cold, so that they will be dying off. After they will be staying for a number of days, the commander of the people of Islam will rise before the people, and say: "O people of Islam, is there not a people willing to give themselves to God?" so they will see what the people do. They will deputize ten horsemen, who will go out to them [the Turks] and find them having died away, so they will return and say: "God has caused them to perish, and has sufficed for them!" So they will perish to the very last one.

1864. Ka`b: The Turks will descend upon al-Jazīra until their horses will drink from the Euphrates [River]. God will send a plague against them, and kill them, without leaving even one man of them.

1865. Abū Ḥukayma al-Ghunawī[1148]: They will stand on the mounds of al-Jazīra to take the women captive, until a man will see the white of his wife's anklets and not be able to do anything about it.

1866. Al-Ḥakam b. `Utayba: They will emerge, and nothing that is struck by their battles (*malāḥim*) will stop them short of the Euphrates, but the people's horsemen on that day will be Qays

1146 See my "Image of the Turk in Classical and Contemporary Muslim Apocalyptic Literature," in Felicitas Schmeider (ed.), *Peoples of the End-Time* (Berlin: de Gruyter, 2016), pp. 225–35; also Ibn al-Faqīh al-Hamdānī, *Nuṣūṣ lam tuḥaqqaq min Kitāb akhbār al-buldān* (Riyāḍ: Wizārat al-Ta`līm, 1997), pp. 115–32.

1147 Former capital of the Lakhmid dynasty before Islam, largely eclipsed by the rise of Kūfa.

1148 Reading with MM (variant) in accord with the name in no. 560, probably Syrian, *fl.* 2nd/8th century.

`Aylān,[1149] so they will uproot them—there will be no Turks afterwards. [413]

1867. Makḥūl: The Turks will have two emergences: an emergence which will be the destruction of Azarbayjān, and an emergence in which they will appear in al-Jazīra snatching up [on horses] those with anklets [women]. God will give victory to the Muslims; among them [the Turks] will be God's greatest slaughter, and there will be no Turks afterwards.

1868. `Abdallāh b. `Amr: The Banū Qanṭūrā are about to emerge driving the people of Khurāsān and Sijistān[1150] before them brutally, until they fasten their mounts at the palm of al-Ubulla. They will send to the people of Baṣra: "Either give us your land, or we will descend upon you!" So they will divide into three groups: one will join the Bedouin, one to Syria, and one to its enemy. This rule, when it covers the earth will be the rule of idiots.

1869. Abū Bakra: The Prophet said: A land called Baṣra or Buṣayra, the Banū Qanṭūrā will come to it, until they come to a river called the Tigris, with palm trees, then the people will divide into three groups: one will join their original [tribes] and perish, one will take itself and apostasize, and one will place their families behind their backs, and fight them—God will conquer through the remnant of them.

1870. Abū Qilāba: The Prophet said: They will divide into three groups: one group will stay, one will join with their fathers in the growing places of wormwood (*shīḥ*) and santonin (*qayṣūm*), and a group will join up [with those] in Syria, and this is the best group.

1871. Abū Hurayra: Their eyes are like moles, and their faces are stripped, they will have a battle between the Tigris and the Euphrates, and a battle at the Donkeys' Field (Marj Ḥimār),[1151] then a battle at the Tigris so that the [cost of the] crossing at

[1149] A northern Arab tribe.

[1150] In far eastern Persia.

[1151] Unattested, but seems to have been close to Baṣra.

the beginning of the day will be 100 dinars to go to Syria, then it will increase at the end of the day.

1872. `Abdallāh b. Burayda from his father[1152]: The Prophet said: "A wide-faced, small-eyed people, as if their faces were stripped, will drive my community until they reach the Arabian Peninsula three times. As for the first, the ones who flee will be saved, as for the second some will perish, some will be saved, but the third will uproot. They are the Turks—and by Him who holds my soul in His hands, they will fasten their horses to [414] the pillars of the Muslims' mosque." Burayda used to never be far away from two or three camels, and traveling-gear for fleeing, because of what he had heard of the Turks.

1873. `Abdallāh b. `Amr: "The Banū Qanṭūrā are about to expel you from the land of Iraq." I said: "We will return." He said: "Do you want that?" I said: "Yes," so he said: "Yes, then you will have ease in life."

1874. `Abdallāh b. `Amr: There are five apocalyptic battles for the people: Two have already passed, and three are for this community. [One is] the apocalyptic battle of the Turks, and [the second] is the apocalyptic battle of the Byzantines, then [the third] is the apocalyptic battle of the Dajjāl. There will be no more apocalyptic battles after the Dajjāl.

1875. Abū Salama b. `Abd al-Raḥmān: The Messenger of God said: The Dajjāl will come down upon Jur [= Khūz] and Kirmān[1153] leading 80,000, as if their faces were beaten shields, wearing *ṭaylasāns*, and shoes made of hair.

1876. Mu`āwiya: Leave the herders alone as long as they leave you [alone],[1154] meaning the Khazars.

1152 Burayda b. al-Ḥuṣayb b. `Abdallāh al-Aslamī, Companion, lived in Medina, then moved to Marw, d. 63/682–3, the last of the Prophet's Companions in Khurāsān.

1153 The Khūz could be from southeastern Persia (today Khuzistan) or the word could be a mistake for Khazar (`Abd al-Razzāq, *Muṣannaf*, xi, p. 375 [no. 20782] reads it like that); the Kirmān are probably from Central Persia.

1154 See the common popular tradition: "Leave the Turks alone as long as they leave you alone," Abū Dā'ūd, *Sunan*, iv, p. 110 (no. 4302)

1877. Ka`b: The Turks will surely make an appearance; nothing will stop them short of al-Qaṭī`a.[1155] God's greatest slaughter will be among them.

1878. Ḥudhayfa said to the people of Kūfa: A small-eyed, snub-nosed people, as if their faces were beaten shields, wearing shoes of hair, will expel you from it [Kūfa], and will fasten their horses on the palm of Jūkhā [River],[1156] and they will drink from the mouth of the Euphrates.

1879. Mu`āwiya: Leave the herders as long as they leave you alone, for they will appear until they end up [415] at the Euphrates, so the first of them will come to it to drink, but the last of them will come and say: "There was once water here."[1157]

1880. `Abdallāh b. `Amr: We came to him and he said: "Where are you from?" We said: "From the people of Iraq." He said: "By God, who there is no god but He, the Banū Qanṭūrā from Khurāsān and Sijistān will surely drive you brutally before them until they settle in al-Ubulla. They will not leave a single palm tree to which they have not fastened a horse. Then they will send to the people of Baṣra: 'Either you leave our country or we descend upon you!'" He said: "They will divide into three groups: one group will go to Kūfa, one to the Ḥijāz, and one to the desert of the Arabs. Then they [Banū Qanṭūra] will enter Baṣra and dwell in it for a year, whereupon they will send to Kūfa and say: either you depart from our country or we descend upon you! So they will divide into three groups: one will go to Syria, one to the Ḥijāz, and one to the desert-land of the Arabs. Iraq will then be without either *qafīz* or dirham [in taxes], and this will be the 'rule of children.' By God, this will surely happen!" And he repeated it three times.

1881. Abū Hurayra: The Prophet said: The Hour will not arise until

[1155] Close to Damascus, according to Ibn `Asākir, *Tā'rīkh*, lxiii, p. 153.

[1156] Close to Baghdād.

[1157] Similar to what Gog and Magog said, see no. 1597.

you fight the Turks, red-faced, small-eyed, snub-nosed, as if their faces were beaten shields.

1882. Abū Hurayra: The first roll-back of the Arabs' lands will be to a red-faced people, as if their faces were beaten shields.

1883. `Umar used to say to the Muslims: You will find their faces to be like leather shields, their eyes like moles, so leave them alone as long as they leave you alone.

1884. Ibn Dhū al-Kalā`[1158] said: I was with Mu`āwiya when the post came from Armenia, from its master, so he read the letter, and was angered. Then he called his secretary, and said: Write an answer to his letter: "You mentioned that the Turks have raided the outskirts of your land, and gotten the best of it, so you sent men to search after them to liberate what they had taken. May your mother be bereaved of you!! Do not do this again! Do not move against them, do not liberate anything from them, for I heard the Messenger of God say that they will force us back to the growing-places of wormwood." [416]

1885. More than one of the Companions of the Prophet: He said: The Byzantines will appear in the greatest apocalyptic war, with them the Turks, the Burjān and the Slavs.

1886. `Abdallāh b. `Amr: The apocalyptic battles are three: two have passed, but one remains: the apocalyptic battle of the Turks in al-Jazīra.

1887. Makḥūl: The Prophet said: The Turks will have two emergences: one of them in which they will emerge in Azarbayjān, and the other one in which they will drink on the shores of the Euphrates.

1888. Ka`b: The Turks will make their way along the Euphrates River, so it is as if I see those [women] who wear red dye (*mu`aṣfarat*)[1159] lined upon along the Euphrates River [to be sold as slaves].

[1158] Shurāḥbīl b. Dhī al-Kalā` Usamayfi`, lived in Ḥimṣ, killed in al-Jazīra 67/686–7 supporting Ibn al-Zubayr.

[1159] Forbidden for men (like gold and silk) but allowed for women (see the case of `Ā'isha, al-Bukhārī, *Ṣaḥīḥ*, ii, p. 179 [no. 1545]).

1889. Makḥūl: God will send death upon their straw, meaning their mounts, forcing them [the Turks] to go on foot, so then will be God's greatest slaughter among them—there will be no Turks afterwards.

1890. Ibn Mas`ūd: It is as if I see the Turks, upon their nag ponies with pierced ears,[1160] until they fasten them on the shores of the Euphrates.

1891. `Abdallāh b. `Amr: "The Banū Qanṭūrā are about to expel you from the land of Iraq." I said: "Then we will return?" He said: "Would you like that? Then you will return, and have ease of life."

1892. Al-Ḥasan: The Messenger of God said: Among the portents of the Hour are that you fight a people whose faces are like beaten shields, and that you fight a people whose shoes are hair. I have seen the first, they are the Turks, and we have seen those, who are the Kurds. Al-Ḥasan said: "When you are in the midst of the portents of the Hour, it will be as if you see them eye-to-eye."

1893. Ḥudhayfa: The people of Iraq are about to not receive either dirham or *qafīz* further, since the non-Arabs (*`ajam*) will prevent them from receiving it. The Syrians are about to not receive either dinar or bushel (*muddan*), since the Byzantines will prevent them from receiving it. [417]

1894. Ibn Mas`ūd: "How will it be for you, when you depart from this land here to the Arabian Peninsula, the growing-place of wormwood?" They said: "Who will expel us?" He said: "The enemy."

1895. Abū Hurayra: The Prophet said: The Hour will not arise until you fight a people as if their faces were beaten shields; the Hour will not arise until you fight a people whose shoes are hair.

1896. Abū Hurayra: The Prophet said: The Hour will not arise until

[1160] Ibn al-Athīr, *Nihāya*, ii, p. 16, see nos. 557, 559; also `Abd al-Razzāq, *Muṣannaf*, xi, p. 380 (no. 20798).

you fight a people snub-nosed, small-eyed, their faces are beaten shields. [418]

The Times, Months, and Days that are Dated in the Tribulations

1897. Ka`b: The mill of the `Arabs will turn after 125 years from the death of their prophet, then tribulations.[1161] **(1)**

1898. Al-Mustawrid b. Shaddād: I heard the Messenger of God say: Every community has an end, and my community has 100 years. When 100 years has passed for my community, then what God has promised it will come about.

1899. `Alī: The rule of the community of Muḥammad after his death is 176 years and thirty-one days [=187/803]. Then God will place fear over them.

1900. Ḥudhayfa: Tribulations are after the death of the Messenger of God until the Hour arises, four tribulations: the first five [years], the second twenty [years], the third twenty [years], and the fourth, the Dajjāl.

1901. Safīna, the *mawlā* of Muḥammad: The caliphate in my community [419] will be for thirty years, so reckon that, and it will be the end of the rule of `Alī.[1162]

1902. Abū Umayya al-Kalbī: When the people differed after Mu`āwiya, and the dissension of [`Abdallāh] b. al-Zubayr, an old man came to us, whose eyebrows had covered his eyes, and had lived during the *jāhiliyya*. We said: "Tell us about our time!" He said: "Rule will pass to a man from the Umayyads, who will govern you for twenty-two years, then die.[1163] Caliphs will follow [him] reigning for short times, then a man whose sign (*`alāma*) is in his eye"—meaning Hishām b. `Abd al-Malik—"will gather wealth in a way no one had previously, and will live nineteen some years, and then die."

1903. Some shaykhs: The Messenger of God said: When 125 years

[1161] Placing this date 136/753–4, the ascension of al-Manṣūr.

[1162] Almost exactly correct, dating from 11/632 to 41/661.

[1163] `Abd al-Malik.

have come upon my community, then will be the apocalyptic battles, and everything that has been mentioned at the end of time.

1904. Ka`b: After Mu`āwiya a man will govern the length of a woman's pregnancy and the weaning of her child,[1164] then another who will not be anything, until he will perish,[1165] then a man from Taymā',[1166] whose time has come [for death], will govern,[1167] him and his progeny, for fifty years.

1905. Tubay`: The last of the Umayyad caliphs, his rule will be two years, not even reaching that, but approximately eighteen months.

1906. Abū Hurayra: Woe to the `Arabs, after 125 years! **(2)**

1907. Muḥammad b. al-Ḥanafiyya: The rule of the `Abbāsids will be disunited in the year [1]97 or [1]99, and the Mahdi will arise in the year 200.

1908. Abū al-Jild: Two men will rule, a man and his progeny from the Banū Hāshim seventy-two years. [420]

1909. Abū Sa`īd: The Prophet said: The Mahdi will reign seven, eight, or nine [years].

1910. Ṣabbāḥ: They will continue thirty-seven years, Banū Hāshim for seventy years.

1911. Al-Walīd: I read, according to Daniel, the totality of this community after its prophet Muḥammad until Jesus will be 174 years. The Umayyads will have a period of eighty years. The rulers—they will be twelve, and have 100 years, then the tyrants will reign forty years, then the people will remain without a ruler for seven years, then the Dajjāl will emerge for seven years, then Jesus son of Mary will emerge, and he will have forty years.

1912. Al-Naḍr b. Shumayṭ[1168]: "When the truth will be stripped

[1164] Yazīd I.

[1165] Mu`āwiya II.

[1166] An oasis in northern (present-day) Saudi Arabia.

[1167] Marwān I.

[1168] Probably al-Naḍr b. Shumayl al-Māzinī, lived in Baṣra, moved to Marw, d. 203/818–19.

away, then 1335 days will be given to its people, 1295 days.[1169] Blessed are those who are patient! The trial during it will cause the ruler to wrap [his head] with a crown—then the righteous one, then the one between the two of them." I said: "Why are forty days missing from the first count?" He said: "There are tremors, casting of stones, and swallowing up by the earth during it. Then [will be] a just imam, then a dominating imam, then a just imam—they will all reign twenty some years. Then a just imam [will reign] for fifteen years."

1913. Al-Haytham b. al-Aswad: I heard `Abdallāh b. `Amr say: The evil people will be after the good people for 120 years, but no one knows when the beginning of [the period] is.

1914. Ibn Mas`ūd: A man will appear from the *mawālī* of Marv, and call towards the Hashemites, perhaps named `Abdallāh, who will rule for four years, and then perish.[1170] [421]

1915. Yazīd b. Abī Ḥabīb: The Messenger of God said: The emergence of the Sufyānī will be in the year [1]37, and his reign will be for twenty-eight months. If he appears [in the year] [1]39, then his reign will be nine months.

1916. Ibn `Abbās: If it [happens], the emergence of the Sufyānī will be [in the year] [1]37.

1917. Abū Hārūn: I said to Nawf: `Abdallāh b. `Amr said: "The people will not stay more than a short while after [the year] 70." He said: "I think that they will live considerably after that."[1171]

1918. Sa`d b. Abī Waqqāṣ on the authority of the Prophet, who said: "I hope that my community will not be incapable with regard to my Lord, that He will grant them a delay of a half a day." Sa`d said: "A half a day is 500 years."[1172]

[1169] Compare Rev. 11:3, 12:6, where 1260 days are mentioned.

[1170] Most likely this is Abū Muslim (d. 754), the `Abbāsids' general.

[1171] Note that several traditions in Muslim, al-Bukhārī, *Ṣaḥīḥ*, viii, pp. 209–10 indicate that those in the Prophet's generation would not have a chance to grow old because of the end of the world.

[1172] Cf. Q 22:47; compare Ibn Kathīr, *al-Nihāya fi al-fitan wa-l-malāḥim* (Cairo: al-Maktab al-Thaqafī, n.d.), i, p. 25.

1919. Ka`b: "Tribulation overshadows you, like the falling of dark-night, neither east nor west will be saved from it, other than the one who seeks shelter in Lebanon, between it and the sea. They are safer than the others. This was when my house burns." It burned in the year 122 [=740].

1920. `Abdallāh b. Busr, the Companion of the Messenger of God, said: Between the conquest of Constantinople and the emergence of the Antichrist is seven years.

1921. Abū Hurayra: The fourth tribulation will last eighteen months, then the Euphrates [River] will uncover a mountain of gold, whereupon they will fight over it, until out of every nine, seven will be killed.

1922. Baḥīr b. Sa`d[1173]: Tribulation will emerge from Sidon to the heights of Syria and remain four years among them.

1923. Ibn Mas`ūd: The Messenger of God said: "The mill of Islam will come to an end [in the year] [1]35, [1]36 or [1]37, so if they perish, it will be like others who perished, if [they] continue, then for seventy years." They said: "O Messenger of God, is it concerning those who have passed, or those who are present?" He said: "No, concerning those who are present." [422]

1924. `Abdallāh b. Salām that he said to `Alī: You asked my advice concerning land to buy, the best of lands, but I forbade you. But if you have need of it, then buy it, for at the point of forty [years] there will be peace and unity. **(1)**

1925. Ibrāhīm b. `Abdallāh b. al-Ḥasan: "In the year [1]67 there will be famine, in [1]68 death, in [1]69 dissension, and in 170 they will be robbed. Then a man from my family will be pleased after [1]70, so that he will double the stipend, the produce will double in his time, and the people will desire commerce." Ḥudhayfa said: "Due to what [will the] people of that time [get this]?" He said: "The mercy of your Lord and the request of your Prophet."

1926. Jubayr b. Nufayr: It was said: "O Messenger of God! Tell us

[1173] Correct from al-Mizzī, Baḥīr b. Sa`d al-Saḥūlī, lived in Ḥimṣ, *fl.* 2nd/8th century.

about what will happen!" He said: "I will tell you that after your Prophet there will be dissension for some few years. Then at 133 [years] the self-controlled (*ḥalīm*)[1174] will not rejoice in his progeny, at 150 [years] heretics will appear, at 160 [years] store up food for two years, at [1]66, salvation, salvation!, at 190 the kings will rob its dominion from [the years 1]80 until [1]90—trial for wrongdoers—and at 192 [years] pebbles with rocks, swallowing up by the earth, metempsychosis, appearance of indecency, at 200 [years], judgement, torment that will come suddenly upon the people in their markets."

1927. Jubayr b. Nufayr: The dissension of my Companions after me will be for twenty-five years, they will kill each other. At 125 [years] there will be terrible hunger, and the Umayyads will kill their Caliph. At 133 [years] raising a dog cub will be better for you than raising a child. At 150 [years] will be the appearance of heretics, at 160 hunger for a year or two. Whoever lives at that time, let him store up food! There will be a falling star from the east to the west, and this crash will be heard by everyone. At 166 [years] whoever has an outstanding loan, let him collect it, and whoever has a daughter, let him marry her off. Whoever is a bachelor, let him hold off [423] on marriage, and whoever has a wife, practice *coitus interruptus* with her. At 170 [years] will be the kings' theft of their dominion, at 180 will be trial, at 190 will be perishing, and at 200 will be judgement.

1928. Ḥudhayfa: The Prophet said: At the year 150, the best of your children will be daughters.

1929. Ka`b: The dominion of the Umayyads will be for 100 years, for the Marwānids sixty some years of that. They will have a wall of iron, against which no one will aspire [to attack], until they tear it down themselves. Then they will wish to plug it [back up] but be unable to do so. Every time they will plug one part, another part will be destroyed, until God causes

[1174] Perhaps should be read as *ḥakīm*, "wise."

them to perish. They will open with *mim* [Mu`āwiya] and close with *mim* [Marwān II], and their mill will come to an end, their dominion will fall, but their dominion will not fall until they remove one of their caliphs to be killed, and his pregnant women will be killed. Then the Reddish Ass of al-Jazīra will approach, together with Satan and the worst of the people, from the north—he is Marwān (II). At his hands will be the destruction of crowns, meaning the destruction of cities, at his hands there will be tremors.

1930. Al-`Uryān b. al-Haytham heard `Abdallāh b. `Amr speaking, and I said to him: "You claimed that the Hour will arise exactly on 70 [years]?" He said: "They lie concerning me. This is not what I said, but I said: 'When it is 70 there will be hardships and terrible matters, but the Hour will not arise until the `Arabs worship what their ancestors worshipped 125 years.'"

1931. Ibn `Abbās: The end of the community of Muhammad is 300 years, like that of the Israelites.[1175] [424]

1932. Abū Ḥassān Būna/Devawayhi[1176]: It is necessary for three of the `Abbāsids to rule, all of whose names start with *`ayn*.[1177]

1933. Ka`b al-Aḥbār sat together with a monk called Yashū`—who was knowledgeable, a reader of books, and they discussed the issue of the world and what will happen in it.

Yashū` said: "O Ka`b! A prophet will appear, with a religion, and his 'religion will triumph over all others.'"[1178] Then Yashū` said to him: "Tell me of their kings, O Ka`b, so that I can believe you and enter into your religion." Ka`b said: "I find in the Torah twelve kings of theirs will rule, the first of them will be [Abū Bakr] *al-Ṣiddīq*, who will die naturally, then [`Umar] *al-Fārūq*, who will be killed, then the Commander [`Uthmān], who will be killed. Then the first of their kings will die natu-

1175 Compare al-Tawḥīdī, *al-Baṣā'ir wa-l-dhakhā'ir* (Beirut: Dār Sadir, 1999), i, pp. 15–16 (21). Why exactly the Israelites were associated with 300 years is unclear.

1176 Unknown, see no. 548.

1177 Most likely al-Saffāḥ, al-Manṣūr and al-Mahdi.

1178 Cf. Q 9:33.

rally, then the Commander of the Guard[1179] will die naturally, then a tyrant will die naturally. Then the Commander of the Bands, who will be the last of the kings, will die naturally, then the Possessor of the Sign[1180] will reign, and he will die naturally."

Yashū` said: "Tell me about your 'deaf' tribulation, in which you will shed blood, and during which the trial will multiply." Ka`b said: "This will happen when the Son of the Gold Eraser will be killed,[1181] and at his killing, the trial will fall, abundance will rise, a learned and humble group will cause it to break out, and they will have four kings from the family of the son of the Possessor of the Sign—two kings unable to read, one king who will die on his bed, and stay but a little, and a king who will come from the north.[1182] At his hands there will be trial, and by his hands crowns will be broken. He will stay in Ḥimṣ four months, then a fear will come to him from his land, so he will hasten to it. The trial will happen in the north, and when this happens, there will be killing (*haraj*) between them, and the tribulation of the `Abbāsids will occur. They will send twelve riders to the east, but God will not be pleased with their works, and he will test the people of that time by them. They will enter every single Arab family's tent, and they will proceed from the east like a bridal procession. At that time their banners will appear, the black banners, they will fasten their horses to the olive tree of Syria. God will kill at their hands every tyrant, or enemy that they have, until there is none left except refugees or hidden. There will be three from their family: al-Manṣūr, al-Saffāḥ and al-Mahdi."

Yashū` said: "So who will be their commander, and who will be in charge?" He said: "Those who walk as groups, dress as groups, and then al-Saffāḥ will treat the westerners unjustly,

1179 Probably Mu`āwiya.

1180 `Abd al-Malik? Or Hishām?

1181 See note 319.

1182 Marwān II.

and garrison Iram [Damascus] for forty-five mornings. Then 70,000 drawn swords will enter it, with their slogan: 'Kill, kill!' After that al-Saffāḥ will have two further battles, one in the west, and the other in the north (*jawf*), and then 'the war will lay down its burdens.'"[1183]

Yashū` [425] said: "How long will their dominion last?" Ka`b said: "Nine times seven [63 years], and at the end of that is woe." Yashū` said: "What will be the sign of their perishing?" He said: "A drought in the east, a crash in the west, a redness in the north, and sudden death in the south. Then the worst of the people of that time will gather for al-Saffāḥ—they will take their religion lightly, as a joke, selling it for their dinars and dirhams. When they will look upon their enemy, they will think that they are attacking their land. The head of their tyrant will advance, who would be unknown previously—a corpulent man, with curly hair, and hollow eyes, with overhanging eyebrows, jaundiced."[1184]

Manṣūr, at the end of this year, in which the people will gather for al-Saffāḥ —Manṣūr will die. So they will disperse to more than one place, and so when the newes comes to them, they will stop wherever they are, and swear allegiance to `Abdallāh.

Then the Sufyānī will return, and summon to himself a gathering of the westerners, so they will gather to him in a number never previously seen. Then he will furnish a military detatchment from Kūfa, even if there is not one from Baṣra, and at that most of them will perish from fire and drowning. There will be swallowing up by the earth in Kūfa, and the two groups will meet in battle at a land called Carchemish. Endurance will be provided, while victory will be lifted, until the two [groups] are annihilated.

If there is a detachment from the west, there will be smaller

[1183] Q 47:4.

[1184] Reading *miṣfār* with MM, in place of *miṣghār.*

battle, so woe then to `Abdallāh from `Abdallāh! I fear for you the yellow banners when they descend from the west. Egypt, they will have two battles, one in Filasṭīn, and one in Syria. Then the Emigrants will turn against them after a woman from Quraysh is slaughtered. If I wished to name her, I could name her. Then they will perish.

A rebel will arise called `Abdallāh, the most disgusting of creation, who will spark his rule in Ḥimṣ, light it up in Damascus, and then emerge in Filasṭīn, victorious over all who oppose him. The easterners will perish at his hands, but his message is the worst of messages, and his killed are the worst of those killed. He will rule for the duration of a woman's pregnancy, emerging against three armies to Kūfa and Baṣra, striking the houses of Qays in them who were seeking to escape on that day. And an army to Mecca and Medina, which will be struck by swallowing up by the earth. Only two men from Juhayna will escape from them—one of them returning to Syria, while the other proceeds to Mecca.

1934. `Alī b. Abī Ṭālib: "A man will emerge from among the progeny of Ḥusayn, whose name is the name of your Prophet—the people of heaven and earth will rejoice at his appearance." A man said: "O Commander of the Believers, the Sufyānī, what is his name?" He said: "He is from the progeny of Khālid b. Yazīd b. [Mu`āwiya] b. Abī Sufyān, a large portly man, with scars of smallpox on his face, and with a white spot in his eye. His and the Mahdi's appearance will not have the duration of a ruler between them—he is the one who will give the caliphate to the Mahdi. He will appear from Syria, from a seasonal river [426] close to Damascus called the Dry Valley (Wadi al-Yābis).

He will appear leading seven followers, with a man among them carrying a deputized flag, known as 'the Victory Flag,' who will proceed before him for a total of thirty miles—everyone who intends [to attack] that flag will be defeated. He will come to Damascus, and sit upon its pulpit, and the jurisprudents and Qur'ān reciters will come to him. He will put the sword to the merchants, and the wealthy, but closely accompany the Qur'ān reciters, and ask their aid for his affairs.[1185] Anyone who tries to forbid them access to him, he will kill. He will equip an army for the east, another for the west, and yet another for the Yemen. The commander of the Iraqi army will be a man from the Banū Ḥāritha called Qamarī b. `Ibād or Qamar b. `Ibād—a corpulent man, with two locks plaited down his front, a man from his people, short, bald, broad-shouldered, who will fight from Syria to Iraq.

There will be a great army in it belonging to them, which will fight them between Damascus and a place called al-Bathaniyya,[1186] while the people of Ḥimṣ are fighting the easterners and their helpers—all of them will be defeated by the Sufyānī. Then they will retreat hastily away from Damascus and Ḥimṣ with the Sufyānī, and will meet the easterners at a place close to Ḥimṣ called Laydīn,[1187] toward the direction of Salamiyya. More than 60,000 will be killed there, three-quarters of them from the people of the east. So the loss will be on them.

The army that he [the Sufyānī] will send to the east will go and besiege Kūfa, and there will be fierce fighting, with many dead. Then the defeat will be on the people of Kūfa—how much blood poured out! And bellies cut open, and children killed! And wealth stolen, women sexually abused! The people will flee to Mecca, and the Sufyānī will write to the commander of that army to go to the Ḥijāz, so he will go to scrape it like leather.

He will besiege Medina, and put Quraysh to the sword, and kill 400 men from them and from the Anṣār, and cut open bellies, kill children, and kill two siblings from Quraysh, from the Hashemites. He will crucify them both at the door of the

[1185] SZ reads *hum* "their."
[1186] A village between Damascus and Adhri`āt.
[1187] Possibly the town of Latmin north of Shayzar.

mosque, a man and his sister, who are called Muḥammad and Fāṭima. The people will flee from him to Mecca, so he will lead his army to Mecca, intending to attack it, then will camp in the wasteland. God will command Gabriel, so he will shout out with his voice: 'O wasteland, annihilate them!'[1188] They will perish to the last of them, other than two men who Gabriel will meet, making their faces face their buttocks, so it is as if I see them, walking backwards, telling the people what happened."

1935. Ka`b: There has never been a community which has not been tempted after the death of its prophet, up till thirty-five years—if you are saved, you will be tempted for thirty-five years, but if not, then you will be tempted at thirty-five years—what befell you has befallen the [other] communities. [427]

1936. Ḍamra b. Ḥabīb: It has reached us that the Messenger of God said: My community has five levels (*ṭabaqāt*), each level will have forty years. The first level is that of myself and those who are with me, people of knowledge and certainty, then the second level are people of piety and loyalty, then the third level are people of fulfilling the ties of kinship. The fourth level is that of people who cutting the ties of kinship, while the fifth level is that of people of happiness and mirth, killing and killing.

In the 210s there will be bombardment, swallowing up by the earth, and metamorphosis. In the 220s there will be death among the *`ulama'* of the earth, until there will only be left a couple of men. In the 230s the heavens will rain hail the size of eggs, so that cattle will be killed, and in the 240s the Nile and the Euphrates will dry up so that people can sow [crops] in their river beds. In the 250s the roads will be cut [by robbers], and animals will rule over humans, so that each people will stay in its city. In the 260s the sun will stop shining for half an hour, so that half of humanity and jinn will perish. In the 270s no one will be born, and no female will become pregnant,

[1188] Similar to phraseology in Q 21:69 (ordering the fire to be cool to Abraham), 11:44 (ordering the rain to stop during the Flood).

and during the 280s women will become like donkeys, until a woman will have sex with forty men, and not think anything of it. In the 290s a year will be like a month, a month like a week, a week like a day, a day like an hour, and an hour like a burning ulcer, such that a man will go out of his house, and not reach the city gate until sunset. At 300 the sun will rise from the west, and every heart will be stamped with what is in it. "Belief will not benefit anyone who did not believe before, or (who did not) earn some good through his belief,"[1189] so do not ask about what is beyond that.

1937. `Abdallāh b. `Amr: The people will continue after the rising of the sun from the west 120 years.

1938. `Abdallāh b. `Amr: The Messenger of God said: "Do you see this night of yours, at the passing of 100 years none will be left on the face of the earth of those present." Ibn `Amr said: "Are the people talking about what the Messenger of God said, some of these traditions enumerating 100 years, but the Messenger of God only said: 'None who are present right now on the face of the earth will be left,' meaning then this generation will be swept away." [428]

1939. Abū Hurayra: Woe to the Arabs from an evil closing in at exactly 60 [years] securities will turn into booty, charity will turn to indemnity, and bearing witness by knowledge to judgement on the basis of whim.

1940. Ibn Mas`ūd: When it is the year 35 [=656] there will be a terrible event—if they perish, it will be barely, if he is saved, then it befits [him]. When it is the year 70 [=689–90], you will see that which you reject.

1941. Al-`Uryān b. al-Haytham: I heard `Abdallāh b. `Amr say, when Mu`āwiya was present, that this community was foreordained 130 years.[1190]

[1189] Q 6:158.

[1190] Ibn Abī Shayba, *Muṣannaf*, vii, p. 466 (no. 37262): "`Abdallāh b. `Amr said: If it is the year 130 and you do not see a sign, then curse me in my grave."

1942. Al-Najīb b. al-Sarī: The Messenger of God said: When it is 150 years, then the best of your women will be barren.

1943. Ḥudhayfa: I would not care after the year 70 if a stone rolled down on top of the mosque, and ten of you were killed in it.

1944. Ibn `Umar: "Do you know how long Noah stayed in his community?" I said: "Yes, 950 years." He said: "Those who were before him lived longer, but people have continued to decline in creation, morals and lifespan until the present day."

1945. Sa`īd b. Jubayr: Every prophet lives half of what the previous prophet lived, so Jesus lived 140 years.

1946. Ibn `Umar: "Do you know the longest-lived person?" I said: "God mentioned Noah, and he said: 'He stayed among them 950 years,' but I do not know what was before then." He said: "The people continue to decrease in creation, morals, and lifespan." [429]

1947. Ibn `Umar: Between every two, there are forty years, forty months and forty days of repentance, a matter of just saying verses, until the sun rises from the west.

1948. `Abdallāh b. `Amr: The evil people after the good people for 120 years, but no one knows when the first of this is.

1949. "The Apocalypse of Weeks"

Artāt b. Mundhir: It has reached us that Nāth[1191] was a prophet, and that he mentioned the age. He said: The age is seven weeks, and the last week is 7000 years. The period (*adān*) is 1000 years, and he described the previous centuries, and clarified all that had happened in them, until he reached the last of the centuries.

He said: At the end of four periods of the final week, the virginal virgin (*al-`adhrā al-batūl*) gave birth, then brought signs, resurrecting the dead, and then was raised into the heavens. Sects differed after him, thereupon the son of the rejected

[1191] Perhaps Baba the Harranian, cf. F. Rosenthal, "The Prophecies of Baba the Harranian," in *A Locust's Leg: studies in honour of S. H. Taqizadeh*. London: Percy Lund, Humphries, 1962, pp. 220–32. The apocalypse is, however, based upon Daniel-style apocalypses, with the framework of "weeks" (cf. Daniel 9:24–7).

community (*al-umma al-ṭarīda*) will appear,[1192] with twelve flags. The first of them is his birth in the *ḥaram* [Mecca], with the heavens praising God at his birth, and the angels rejoicing at his appearance. He will be victorious over all communities, whoever believes in him will be safe, whoever rejects him will be a disbeliever. He will be victorious over Persia and its kingdom, Ifrīqiyā [and its kingdom], and Syria (*sūriya*), and then there will be three weeks less a seventh of a week. Then God will take him, praised.[1193]

Umayya will reign after him, weak, trustworthy, short of life, and hunger will be intense in Egypt during his caliphate, and the king of India will perish. His life will be a seventh of a week. Then after him will reign the strong one, the just, and conquer Syria; the loss of him will be a disaster, and his life will be a week and two-thirds of a week, less half a week. Then the rich man will rule after him, and will be killed, [but] his killer will not be victorious. His life will be two weeks less one seventh of a week.

Then after him, the "head" will rule in the great house, collecting wealth. There will be many apocalyptic battles during his time. Woe to the head from the wings and woe to the wings from the head! His life will be three weeks, less three-sevenths of a week. Then the beardless youth of his loins (descendants) will rule; during his time the produce of Syria will dry up and the king of Rome will perish. His life is half of a week less three-sevenths of a week. After him the chief of the second house of the "head" will rule, wise and staid [in judgment]; four kings will appear from his loins. His life is three weeks less one seventh of a week. After him the [one with] smallpox from his loins will rule; the multitude of Byzantines will perish during his time, and there will be an earthquake in Syria, such

[1192] Such a derogatory reference to the Muslim community may be an echo of Gen. 16:12, but one can be certain that with a description like this the apocalypse did not originate among Muslims.

[1193] Muḥammad.

that the buildings are destroyed. His life will be one week and a third of a week less half of a seventh of a week.

After him the satiated one, who did not achieve what he hoped, the master of the great army in the land of the Byzantines. His life will be a third of a week. Then the [one] scarred in the face will rule; there is no deceit in his faith, he will enjoin justice [430], his life will be short and his death is a disaster. His life will be one third of a week.[1194]

The braggart will reign after him, the one who destroys buildings and who alters shapes (or pictures). His life will be three weeks less a third of a week. Then the youth, the possessor of the two cubs will reign, and be killed, [though] his murderer has no length [of life]. During his time death will spread from Egypt to the Euphrates River. His life will be a seventh of a week and three-sevenths of a week. Then a wind will blow from the north with a tyrant (*jabbār*) leading it, with killing following it for one week less a seventh of a week; his destruction is in the land of Bābil (Babylon, Iraq).

Then an east wind will blow against him, whose leaders are non-Arab Persians, and whose followers are mongrel half-castes. They are led by [a man with] hairy eyebrows, encamping together between the two rivers and then he will move his army expeditiously towards the bull. The tyrant will come out and the men will take bridges [to cross the rivers], encamping in the waterless desert of Syria, and Syria will be conquered forcefully with swords. The [man with] red eyebrows will administer it three weeks and two-thirds of a week. The names of both of them are the same; one will perish on his bed and the other in battle after denying his Lord. When their injustice multiplies, then the wind of the east will blow upon it and its foundations will split at the growing places of saffron. The bull will rise up in fear from what is coming to him, and will leave his land and settle in the city of idols [Ḥarrān]. The

[1194] `Umar b. `Abd al-`Azīz, see no. 1078.

master of the east will settle down, sickened, and the bull will rise up between the two rivers; his sign is [a] brown [man], fleshless, with colored eyes, preferring to till [the ground] twenty-one weeks. This will be 147 years after the conquest of Syria by [the tribe of] Quraysh.[1195]

The western king will be roused to anger, and the nations will stretch out their necks. While they are doing this, when tidings of the west are on the point of scattering the dust upon the east, then the bull will send armies to him [the western king], with him leading them, and they will encounter him face to face, and be revealed (or made manifest), and render it spoil [the west?] together with him [the western king], and shake the east thoroughly. He will encamp at the Yellowish Field (Marj Ṣufar),[1196] and the brown [man], [having] joined [eyebrows], and small eyes will meet him there in battle, whereupon God will disperse his army.

Then he will move away from this place, and when he is between the Garrisoned Spring (al-`Ayn al-Shaḥnā')[1197] and Kharqadūna,[1198] a divine herald will call out from the heavens: 'Woe to those who are between Kharqadūna and the Garrisoned Spring! Every eye will weep its grief.' Then he will travel and encamp in the midst of the rivers [Mesopotamia], and the men will wade through them [the rivers] and kill the tyrant upon them and divide up the wealth. Then they will rush upon the city of idols, and conquer it by force. The bull will be gored in it; his belly will be split open, his army dispersed, and his posterity will be cut off in it. What is between the gate of Niṣībīn will be destroyed, and he will send to the east what it [the city] contained, unwillingly, not obedient[ly].

[1195] Approximately 782–3.

[1196] The site of an early battle between the Muslims and the Byzantines, close to Damascus.

[1197] According to the reading of no. 835 another name for Ḥimṣ.

[1198] Probably in northern Syria, not Chalcedon in the Byzantine Empire.

He will stay two-sevenths of a week; eight months the east will be obedient to him.

A truce of seven weeks between him and the ruler of the Byzantines will take place, and he will travel to the city of slaves,[1199] and make a great killing there. Then he will go out from it and settle in the populous village (*al-rabūdh*),[1200] giving out wealth and distributing the fifth part of the booty. The land of Persia will suffer humiliation, and a great destruction will occur in the alluvial plain [of southern Iraq]. His horsemen [431] will reach Abrāshahar, and he will rule the area between China and the Sea of Tripoli (the Mediterranean Sea?). The ruler of the east will withdraw towards the direction of the mountains of the north, not seeking [battle] and not sought [in battle], whereupon a man of his immediate family (*ahl baytihi*) will betray him, and come towards him, and this [news] will reach the ruler of the east, and he will advance until he reaches the area between Ḥarrān and Edessa.

Woe to Ḥarrān! The beardless youth from the sons of the head will meet him there, and there will be an apocalyptic battle between them with many killed. The ruler of the east will come in the morning; then he is humiliated and his army lessened, and the beardless youth will go out until he settles in Syria, and he will change the existing things that were in it, and prepare [other] things. The Byzantines will go out to the valleys [in northern Syria] and the one with the two prominent cheekbones (*dhū al-wajnatayn*) from the descendants of Nizār[1201] will meet them in battle there, and kill from among them [a number] like the slaughter of `Ād. Their emperor (*ṭāghūt*) will flee with a lance thrust [in him?],

1199 Probably Kūfa.

1200 Prehaps another name for Baṣra, remembering its famous open-area called al-Rābiḍa.

1201 Northern Arabs.

and the Byzantines will split into two groups: one will take the River Sawas (Sūs), and the other the pass of Jayḥān.[1202]

Quraysh will renounce their truce, Egypt will refuse [to send] its land-tax, and the Franks will make their weapons manifest. The land of Yemen will be ruled by a man from the descendants of Qaḥṭān called Manṣūr, possessor of a nose [a man of high honor], a mole and two locks of hair. His horsemen will reach Ramla and the land of Ḥarrān. The beardless youth at that time will rule the Byzantines, managing, not feared and he will rise up against him with Ka`b and Ḥawāzin, and Qaḥṭān will be killed in every ravine. Their progeny will be divided among the lands, and he [the beardless youth] will go until he encamps in the mountains of Sanīr [Hermon] and Lebanon, while Manṣūr is in Ramla. He will go towards him until he encamps in the Field of the Virgin (Marj `Adhrā')[1203] and the two armies will meet in battle there. Endurance will be poured out upon the both of them and Manṣūr will be defeated, and his horsemen will be slain, and the beardless youth will conquer all of al-Urdunn.

He will stay there seven weeks and five-sevenths of a week, then a man from the descendants of the wise, staid man will appear,[1204] and will lead the Egyptians and the Copts. When he encamps in al-Jifār,[1205] the land will become desolate because of him, without giving battle, [since] news comes to him from the land of the Berbers about the advance of the ruler of Andalus (Spain) leading Berbers, Franks (*Ifranja*) and lions' whelps (Arabs).

The ruler of Andalus will come until he encamps on the Jordan River, and the beardless youth will fight him and kill

1202 One in northern Anatolia and the other in southern Anatolia.

1203 Located twelve miles from Damascus, according to al-Ṭabarī, *Tā'rīkh*, v, pp. 271–3.

1204 Probably `Abd al-Malik.

1205 Located on the road between Egypt and Syria in the Sinai Desert, see Ibn `Asākir, *Tā'rīkh*, xx, p. 19.

him, and then encamp in Egypt and al-Jifār. Then a clamor from behind him will reach him that the Master of the Black Horse has appeared in Alexandria and gained the mastery over Egypt.

The Arabs will stay close to Yathrib (Medina) in the Ḥijāz at that time, and the master of the black horse will advance leading his army, and he will encamp in Syria, exiling its people, and al-Jazīra will be desolate. Each tribe will stay close to its nearest relations (*ahl*). He will send an army and when they reach the [area] between the two Jazīras their herald will proclaim: "Let every pure-blooded or stranger who is of us (apostates) among the Muslims come out and join us!" The *mawālī* will be enraged/filled with zeal, and they will swear allegiance to a man called Ṣāliḥ b. `Abdallāh b. Qays b. Yassār. He will go out leading them and meet in battle the army of the Byzantines sent against them [432] and they will kill them. Death will occur among the army of the master of the black horse, of the Byzantines, and Ṣāliḥ will encamp with the *mawālī* in the land of Syria, and enter Amorium and encamp in Qamūliya,[1206] and conquer Byzantium.

The voices of his army in it will be openly [proclaiming] the unity of God, and its wealth will be divided in containers. He will be victorious over Rome and take out from it the "gate of Zion" and a bejeweled container inside of which is [the] earring of Eve, and the *kutūna* of Adam—meaning his garment—and his gown, and the vestments of Aaron.

While he is occupied with this, news will reach him, which will be false, that the ruler of Tyre has appeared,[1207] and he will return until he encamps in the Field of Jawmṭīs.[1208] He

1206 See note 748. Note the identical phraseology with no. 1250, paired with Byzantium (rather than the more common Constantinople).

1207 Apparently a reference to the Dajjal, see no. 1350.

1208 Unidentified, but perhaps conveying the Greek word κόμητες, "count[s]" or even the Latin "campus" if one could envision this location as being an army staging-ground.

will remain there three-sevenths of a week, and the skies will withhold [from raining] that year one third of their rain, and during the second year two-thirds of it and during the third year all of it. Not a [creature] with claws or a toothed [creature] will remain—all will perish. Starvation and death will occur such that only ten out of every seventy will remain, and the people will flee to the mountains of the north. Then the Dajjāl will appear.

1950. Ḥudhayfa: The Messenger of God said: "The best of your children after 145 years are daughters, and the best of your women after 160 years are barren. When it is the year 168, then call in your loans, then the year 173, pay off your loans. At the year 190, killing, killing (*haraj, haraj*)." They said: "O Messenger of God, what will be salvation and deliverance?" He said: "Killing, killing, killing, until the Hour arises."

1951. Abū Hurayra: The Prophet said: "My community will follow exactly in the footsteps of the communities from before it," so a man said: "Just like Persia and the Byzantines?" The Messenger of God said: "Are there any other people?"

1952. Maslama b. Makhrama[1209]: When Ibn Abī Ḥudhayfa rushed to evil[1210] in Egypt, and rebelled against `Uthmān, he called the people to give him allegiance, but I refused to take it from him, so I rode to `Uthmān, and said to him: "Ibn Abī Ḥudhayfa is an imam of error, just as you know, and he has rushed to it [error] in Egypt, so he called us to give him allegiance, but I refused to take it from them." So he [`Uthmān] said: "You were powerless, so that is your only right." [433]

1953. Tubay`: When the yellow flags have entered Egypt, overcoming it, and sitting on its pulpit, let the Syrians dig conduits in the earth, for it is the trial.

1954. Tubay`: "When there is a shaking in Syria before the

[1209] Unattested, probably Egyptian, *fl.* 1st/7th century.

[1210] Muḥammad b. Abī Ḥudayfa, revolted in 656 against `Uthmān.

'wasteland',[1211] there will be no wasteland and no Sufyānī." Layth said: "This 'shaking' happened in Tiberias, and people woke up because of it in Fusṭāṭ. It took wings [had aftershocks], so it was the night of Tiberias."[1212]

1955. `Abdallāh b. `Amr: The Prophet that he rose onto the pulpit, speaking, and said: "The first people to be annihilated will be Quraysh, and the first of them killed will be the People of my Family."

1956. Ibn `Umar: I will not fight during a tribulation, but I will pray behind whoever wins.

1957. Ṭāwūs: The Messenger of God said: When it is time for the stranger[1213] to die, let him turn to the right and to the left, and if he only sees a stranger, let him breathe in the Books of God—with every breath he will gain 100,000 good deeds, and 100,000 evil deeds will be erased from him, so that he dies a martyr.

1958. Ibn `Abbās: Dying as a stranger constitutes martyrdom.[1214]

1959. Al-Mu`allī b. Rāshid al-Nabbāl[1215]—grandfather: Nabīsha al-Khayr[1216] came in to us—who was one of the Companions of the Messenger of God—while we were eating from a large dish, and said: I hear the Messenger of God say: "Whoever eats from a large dish, and then licks it, the dish asks forgiveness for him."[1217] [434]

This is the end of the Nu`aym b. Hammād al-Marwazī's *Book of Tribulations*, and praise to God, Lord of the Worlds, and prayers

[1211] The disappearance of the Syrian army in the wasteland, see nos. 901–17.

[1212] Probably the earthquake of January 18, 749.

[1213] Stranger in this world, see no. 458.

[1214] See al-Suyūṭī, *Abwāb al-sa`āda fi asbāb al-shahāda* (Cairo: Maktabat al-Qiyāma, 1987), p. 56 (no. 35).

[1215] Lived in Baṣra, *fl.* 2nd/8th century.

[1216] Companion, *fl.* 1st/7th century.

[1217] This is an odd tradition on which to finish a book about tribulations. The traditions following the Apocalypse of Weeks have the feel of some randomness about them; perhaps Nu`aym never had the opportunity to integrate them into the text, and left it in an unfinished state.

and peace of God upon our master Muḥammad, and his family, and Companions, in their totality. The completion of his book corresponds with the `Id al-Aḍḥā, year 706 [1306] in the shade of Mt. Qāsyūn in Damascus, at the hand of the impoverished one to God, Muḥammad b. Muḥammad b. `Alī al-Ṣayrafī al-Anṣārī.[1218]

[1218] In Ibn Ḥajar, *al-Durar al-kāmina* (Beirut: Dār al-Jīl, 1993), iv, pp. 198–9 (no. 538), d. 722/1322.

Bibliography

Primary Sources

`Abd al-Razzāq al-Ṣan`ānī (d. 211/826), *al-Muṣannaf.* Ed. Habib al-Rahman al-A`ẓam, Beirut: al-Maktab al-Islamī, 1983 (11 vols).

Abū Dā'ūd = al-Sijistānī, Abū Dā'ūd Sulaymān b. al-Asha`th (d. 275/888–9), *Sunan*. Beirut: Dār al-Jīl, 1988 (4 vols).

Abū Zur`a al-Dimashqī, `Abd al-Raḥmān b. `Amr (d. 281/894), *Kitāb al-tā'rīkh*. Ed. Luṭfi Maḥmūd Manṣūr, Beirut: Dār al-Fikr, 2008 (2 vols).

al-Ajurrī, Muḥammad b. al-Ḥusayn (d. 360/971), *al-Ghurabā' min al-mu'minīn*. Ed. Ramaḍān Ayyûb, Damascus: Dār al-Bashā'ir, 1992.

al-Anbārī, Muḥammad b. Aḥmad (*c.*4–5th/10–11th cent.?), *al-Mukhtār min nawādir al-akhbār*. Beirut: al-Maktaba al-`Aṣriyya, 1994.

al-`Askarī, Abū Hilāl al-Ḥasan b. `Abdallāh (d. 395/1004–5), *Jamharat al-amthāl*. Ed. Muḥammad Abū al-Faḍl Ibrāhīm, Beirut: Dār al-Fikr, 1988 (2 vols).

al-Asmā`ī, `Abd al-Malik b. Qurayb (d. 216/831), *Kitāb al-ibl*. Ed. Ḥātim Ṣāliī al-Ḍāmin, Damascus: Dār al-Bashā'ir, 2003.

al-Baghdādī, Aḥmad b. `Alī b. Thābit al-Khatīb (d. 463/1070–1), *Tā'rīkh madīnat al-salām*. Ed. Bashshār `Iwāḍ Ma`rūf, Beirut: Dār al-Gharb al-Islamī, 2001 (17 vols).

Bakhshal, Aslam b. Sahl al-Bazzāz al-Wāsiṭī (d. 292/905), *Tā'rīkh Wāsiṭ*. Ed. Kirkīs `Awwād, Beirut: `Ālam al-Kutub, 1986.

al-Bakrī, `Abdallāh b. `Abd al-`Azīz al-Andalusī (d. 487/1094), *Mu`jam mā sta`jama*. Ed. Muṣṭafā al-Saqā', Beirut: `Ālam al-Kutub, 1983 (2 vols).

al-Balādhurī, Yaḥyā b. Aḥmad (d. 279/892), *Ansāb al-ashrāf*. Ed. Muḥammad Firdaws al-`Aẓm, Damascus: Dār al-Yaqẓa al-`Arabiyya, 1997 (26 vols).

______ *Futūḥ al-buldān*. Ed. `Abdallāh Anīs al-Tabbā` and `Umar Anīs al-Tabbā`, Beirut: Mu'assasat al-Ma`ārif, 1987.

Bar Hebraeus, *Chronography*. Trans. E. A. W. Budge, Piscataway, NJ: Gorgias Press, 2003.

al-Bayhaqī, Aḥmad b. al-Ḥusayn (d. 458/1066), *Dalā'il al-nubuwwa*. Ed. `Abd al-Mu`ṭī Qala`jī, Beirut: Dār al-Kutub al-`Ilmiyya, 1985 (7 vols).

______ *Faḍā'il al-awqāt*. Ed. Khilāf Maḥmūd `Abd al-Samī`, Beirut: Dār al-Kutub al-`Ilmiyya, 1997.

Brewer, Keagan (trans.), *Prester John: The Legend and its Sources*. Aldershot: Ashgate, 2015.

al-Bukhārī, Muḥammad b. Ismā'īl (d. 256/870), *Ṣaḥīḥ*. Ed. `Abd al-`Azīz b. Bāz, Beirut: Dār al-Fikr, 1991 (5 vols).

Burge, S. R. (trans.), *Angels in Islam: Jalāl al-Dīn al-Suyūṭī's* al-Ḥabā'ik fī akhbār al-malā'ik. London and New York: Routledge, 2012.

al-Damīrī, Kamāl al-Dīn, Kitāb al-ḥayawān al-kubrā. Beirut: Dār al-Fikr, n.d.

al-Dhahabī, Muḥammad b. Aḥmad b. `Uthmān (d. 748/1347), *Siyar a`lām al-nubalā'*. Ed. Shu`ayb al-Arnawā'ūṭ, Beirut: Mu'assasat al-Risāla, 1992 (25 vols).

______*Tadhkirat al-ḥuffāẓ*. Beirut: Dār al-Kutub al-`Ilmiyya, 2012.

al-Fākihī, Abū `Abdallāh Muḥammad b. Isḥāq (d. 353/964), *Akhbār Makka fi qadīm al-dahr wa-ḥadīthihi*. Ed. `Abd al-Mālik b. `Abdallāh b. Dāhish, Beirut: Dār Khiḍr, 1998 (3 vols).

Fredegar = *The Fourth Book of the Chronicle of Fredegar*. Trans. J. M. Wallace-Hadrill. Westport, CT: Greenwood, 1960.

al-Ghassānī, `Alī b. Dā'ūd b. Yūsuf (d. 764/1362–3), *al-Aqwāl al-kāfiya wa-l-fuḍūl al-shāfiya fī al-khayl*. Ed. Yaḥyā Wāhib al-Jabūrī, Beirut: Dār al-Gharb al-Islamī, 1987.

Ḥajjī Khalīfa Muṣṭafā b. `Abdallāh, Katip Çelebi (d. 1067/1657), *Kashf al-ẓunūn `an asāmī al-kutub wa-l-funūn*. Ed. Gustavus Flügel, Beirut: Dār Ṣādir, n.d. (1852 reprint) (8 vols).

al-Hamdānī, al-Ḥasan b. Aḥmad (d. 322/934), *al-Iklīl min akhbār al-Yamān wa-ansāb Ḥimyar*. Ṣan`ā': Wizārat al-Thaqāfa wa-l-Siyāḥa, 2004 (vols 1, 2, 8, 10).

Harrak, Amir (trans.), *The Chronicle of Zuqnin*. Toronto: Pontifical Institute of Medieval Studies, 1999.

Ibn Abī Shayba, `Abdallāh b. Muḥammad (d. 235/849–50), *Kitāb al-muṣannaf*. Ed. Muḥammad `Abd al-Salām Shāhīn, Beirut: Dār al-Kutub al-`Ilmiyya, 1995 (9 vols).

Ibn `Asākir, `Alī b. al-Ḥasan b. Hibatallāh (d. 571/1176), *Tā'rīkh madīnat Dimashq*. Ed. `Alī Shīrī, Beirut: Dār al-Fikr, 1995–8 (80 vols).

Ibn A`tham al-Kūfī, *Futūḥ* (Beirut: Dār al-Nadwa al-Jadīda, n.d. reprint of Haydārabād edn) (7 vols).

Ibn al-Athīr, al-Mubārak b. Muḥammad al-Jazarī (d. 606/1209–10), *al-Nihāya fī gharīb al-ḥadīth*. Ed. Ṭāhir Aḥmad al-Zāwī and Maḥmūd Muḥammad al-Tanāhī, Beirut: Dār Iḥya al-Kutub al-`Arabiyya, n.d. (5 vols).

Ibn Bakkār, al-Zubayr (d. 256/870), *al-Akhbār al-Muwaffaqiyyāt*. Ed. Sāmī Makkī al-`Alfī, Beirut: `Ālam al-Kutub, 1996.

Ibn Baṭṭūṭa, Muḥammad b. `Abdallāh (d. 779/1377–8), *The Travels of Ibn Battuta*. Trans. H. A. R. Gibb, ed. C. Defremery and B. R. Sanguinetti, index by C. F. Beckingham and A. D. H. Bivar, Cambridge: Cambridge University Press (for the Hakluyt Society), 1958–2000 (5 vols).

Ibn al-Faqīh al-Hamdānī, Abū Bakr Aḥmad b. Muḥammad b. Muḥammad b. Isḥāq (d. *c.*290/903), *Kitāb al-buldān*. Ed. Yūsuf al-Hādī, Beirut: `Ālam al-Kutub, 2009.

_______ *Nuṣūṣ lam tuḥaqqaq min Kitāb akhbār al-buldān*. Ed. Ḍayfallāh Yaḥyā al-Ẓahrānī, Riyāḍ: Wizārat al-Ta`līm, 1997.

Ibn Ḥajar al-`Asqalānī, Aḥmad b. `Alī (d. 852/1438–9), *al-Iṣāba fī tamyīz al-ṣaḥāba*. Beirut: Iḥya al-Turāth al-`Arabī, n.d. (4 vols).

_______ *al-Durar al-kāmina fī a`yān al-mī'a al-thāmina*. Ed. Hāshim al-Nadūrī, Beirut: Dār al-Jīl, 1993 (4 vols) (reprint).

Ibn Ḥamdūn, Muḥammad b. al-Ḥasan (d. 562/1166–7), *al-Tadhkira al-Ḥamdūniyya*. Ed. Iḥsān `Abbās, Beirut: Dār Ṣādir, 1996 (10 vols).

Ibn al-`Imād, `Abd al-Ḥayy b. Aḥmad b. Muḥammad (d. 1090/1679), *Shadharat al-dhahab fī akhbār man dhahab*. Ed. `Abd al-Qādir al-Arnawā'ūṭ and Maḥmūd al-Arnawā'ūṭ, Damascus: Dār Ibn Kathīr, 1992 (11 vols).

Ibn Isḥāq al-Shaybānī, Ḥanbal (d. *c.*3rd/9th cent.), *al-Fitan wa-yalihi Juz Ḥanbal b. Isḥāq*. Ed. `Āmir Ḥasan Ṣabrī, Beirut: Dār al-Bashā'ir al-Islamiyya, 1998.

Ibn al-Jawzī, Abū al-Faraj `Abd al-Raḥmān (d. 597/1200), *al-Muntaẓam fi tā'rīkh al-mulūk wa-l-umām*. Ed. Muḥammad `Abd al-Qādir `Aṭā' and

Muṣṭafā `Abd al-Qādir `Aṭā', Beirut: Dār al-Kutub al-`Ilmiyya, 1993 (19 vols).

Ibn Jubayr (d. 614/1217) = Roland Broadhurst, trans., *The Travels of Ibn Jubayr: A Medieval Spanish Muslim visits Makkah, Madinah, Egypt, cities of the Middle East and Sicily*. London: Goodward, 1952, reprint 2004.

Ibn al-Kalbī, Hishām b. Muḥammad b. al-Sā'ib (d. 204/819–20), *Jamharat al-nasab*. Ed. `Alī `Umar, Cairo: Maktabat al-Thaqāfa al-Dīniyya, 2010 (2 vols).

______ *Kitāb al-aṣnām*. Ed. Aḥmad Zākī Pasha, Cairo: Maṭba`at Dār al-Kutub al-Miṣriyya, 1995.

Ibn Kathīr, Abū al-Fidā' b. `Umar (d. 774/1372–3), *al-Nihāya fi al-fitan wa-l-malāḥim*. Ed. Muḥammad Aḥmad `Abd al-`Azīz, Cairo: al-Maktab al-Thaqāfī, n.d. (2 vols).

Ibn Khayyat al-`Usfuri, al-Khalifa (d. 240/854–5), *Ta'rikh*. Ed. Suhayl Zakkar, Beirut: Dar al-Fikr, 1993.

Ibn Māja al-Qazwīnī, Muḥammad b. Yazīd (d. 275/888–9), *Sunan*. Ed. Muḥammad Fū'ād `Abd al-Bāqī, Beirut: Dār al-Fikr, n.d. (2 vols).

Ibn al-Mubārak, `Abdallāh (d. 181/797), *Kitāb al-zuhd wa-l-raqā'iq*. Alexandria: Dār Ibn Khaldūn, n.d.

Ibn al-Muqaffa`, `Abdallāh (d. 142/759), *Athār*. Beirut: Manshūrāt Dār Maktabat al-Ḥayāt, n.d.

Ibn Rajab al-Ḥanbalī, `Abd al-Raḥmān b. Aḥmad (d. 795/1392–3), *Faḍā'il al-Shām*. Ed. Sāmī b. Muḥammad b. al-Bashar b. Jādallāh, al-Riyāḍ: Dār al-Waṭan li-l-Nashr, 1999.

Ibn Sa`d al-Baṣrī, Muḥammad (d. 230/844–5), *Kitāb al-ṭabaqāt al-kubrā*. Ed. Aḥmad Shams al-Dīn, Ibrāhīm Shams al-Dīn and Yaḥyā Maqlad, Beirut: Dār al-Kutub al-`Ilmiyya, 1990 (9 vols).

Ibn Ṭāwūs, `Alī b. Mūsā b. Ja`far (d. 664/1265–6), *al-Malāḥim wa-l-fitan fi ẓuhūr al-ghā'ib al-muntaẓar*. Beirut: Mu'assasat al-Wafā', 1992.

Ibn Waḥshiyya al-Kasadānī, Aḥmad b. `Alī b. Qays (*fl. c.*4th/10th cent.), *al-Falaha al-Nabaṭiyya*. Ed. Toufic Fahd, Damascus: Institut Français de Damas, 1995–8 (3 vols).

Ibn Zawlaq, al-Ḥasan b. Ibrāhīm (d. 387/997), *Faḍā'il Miṣr wa-akhbāruhā wa-khawaṣṣuhā*. Ed. `Alī Muḥammad `Umar, Cairo: Maktabat al-Khanjī, 2000.

Ibn Ẓahīra, Muḥammad b. Muḥammad (d. 888/1483), *al- Faḍā'il al-bāhira fī maḥāsin al-Qāhira*. Ed. Muṣṭafā al-Saqā' and Kāmil al-Muhandas, Cairo: Wizārat al-Thaqāfa, 1969.

al-Iṣfahānī, Abū al-Faraj (d. 356/967), *Maqātil al-Ṭālibiyyin*. Ed. Aḥmad Saqr, Beirut: Mu'assasat al-A`lā li-l-Maṭbū`āt, 1987.

al-Kinānī, `Alī b. Muḥammad b. `Iraq (d. 963/1556), *Tanzīh al-sharī`a al-marfū`a `an al-aḥādīth al-shanī`a wa-l-mawḍū`a*. Ed. `Abd al-Wahhāb `Abd al-Laṭīf, Beirut: Dār al-Kutub al-`Ilmiyya, 1981 (2 vols).

al-Kindī, `Umar b. Muḥammad b. Yūsuf (d. 350/961–2), *Wulāt Miṣr*. Ed. Ḥusayn Naṣṣār, Beirut: Dār Ṣādir, n.d.

Mafākhir al-Barbar (ca. 705/1305). Ed. `Abd al-Qādir Babaya, Ribāṭ: Dār Abī Raqrāq, 2005.

al-Maqdisi, al-Mutahhir b. Tahir (*fl. c.*355/966), *Kitab al-bad' wa-l-ta'rikh*. Ed. Clement Huart, Beirut: Dār Ṣādir, n.d. (reprint) (3 vols).

Martinez, Francisco Jarvier, *Eastern Christian Apocalyptic Literature*. Unpublished Ph.D. dissertation, Catholic University of America, 1985.

al-Marwazī, Nu`aym b. Ḥammād (d. 229/844), *Kitāb al-fitan*. Ed. Suhayl Zakkār, Beirut: Dār al-Fikr, 1993.

______ *Kitāb al-fitan*. Ed. Suhayl Zakkār, Beirut: al-Maktaba al-Tijāriyya, n.d. (=SZ)

______ *Kitāb al-fitan*. Ed. Sumayr b. Amīn al-Zuhayrī, Riyāḍ: Maktabat al-Ma`ārif, 2010 (2 vols). (=MM)

______ *Kitāb al-fitan*. Ed. Majdī b. Manṣūr b. Sayyid al-Shūrī, Beirut: Dār al-Kutub al-`Ilmiyya, 2004. (=DKI)

Michael the Great, *The Syriac Chronicle of Michael Rabo (the Great)*. Trans. Matti Moosa, Teaneck, NJ: Beth Antioch Press, 2014.

al-Mizzī, Abū al-Ḥajjāj Yūsuf (d. 742/1341–2), *Tahdhīb al-kamāl fi asāmī al-rijāl*. Ed. Bashshār `Iwāḍ Ma`rūf, Beirut: Mu'assasat al-Risāla, 1998 (8 vols).

al-Muqaddasī, Muḥammad b. Aḥmad (b. *c.*335/946), *Kitāb aḥsan al-taqāsim fi ma`rifat al-aqālīm*. Ed. M. J. de Goeje, Beirut: Dār Ṣādir, n.d. (reprint of Leiden: E. J. Brill, 1903). Trans. Basil Collins, *The Best Divisions for Knowledge of the Regions*. Reading: Garnet Publishing, 2001.

al-Musharraf b. al-Murajjā' al-Maqdisī, (*fl. c.*492/1098), *Faḍā'il Bayt al-Maqdis wa-l-Khalīl wa-faḍā'il al-Shām*. Ed. Ofer Livne-Kafri, Shafar`am: Dār al-Shurūq, 1995.

Muslim = al-Qushayrī al-Naysābūrī, Muslim b. Ḥajjāj (d. 261/875), *Ṣaḥīḥ*. Beirut: Dar Jīl, n.d. (4 vols).

al-Mutaqqī al-Hindī, *Kanz al-`ummāl*. Beirut: Dār al-Risāla, 1982.

Nāṣir-i Khusraw, Wheeler Thackston (trans.), *Nāṣir-i Khusraw: Book of Travels*. Costa Mesa, CA: Mazda, 2001.

Palmer, Andrew (ed.), *The Seventh Century in the West-Syrian Chronicles*. Liverpool: Liverpool University Press, 1993.

Penn, Michael (trans.), *When Christians first met Muslims*. Berkeley: University of California Press, 2015.

Ps. Methodius, see Martinez, F. J., *Eastern Christian Apocalyptic*. Unpublished Ph.D. thesis, Catholic University of America, 1985.

Qaddumi, Ghada al-Hijjawi (trans.), *Book of Gifts and Rarities*. Cambridge, MA: Harvard Center for Middle Eastern Studies, 1996.

al-Ṣāliḥī al-Shāmī, Muḥammad b. Yūsuf (d. 942/1535), *Subul al-hudā wa-l-rashād fi sīrat khayr al-`ibād*. Ed. `Ādil Aḥmad `Abd al-Mawjūd and `Alī Muḥammad Mu`awwaḍ, Beirut: Dār al-Kutub al-`Ilmiyya, 2013 (14 vols).

al-Samarqandī al-Maydānī, Ḥusayn b. `Abdallāh al-Ḥusaynī (d. 996/1587–8), *Tuḥfat al-ṭālib bi-ma`rifa man yantasib ilā `Abdallāh wa-Abī Ṭālib*. Ed. Al-Sayyid Mahdī al-Rajā'ī, Qumm: Maktabat Ayatullāh al-`Uẓmā al-Mar`ashlī, 2011.

al-Sarakhsī, Abū Bakr Muḥammad b. Aḥmad (d. *c*.483/1090), *Kitāb al-mabsūṭ*. Ed. Khalīl Muḥyī al-Dīn al-Mīs, Beirut: Dār al-Fikr, 2000 (15 vols).

al-Sijistānī, Abū Bakr Muḥammad b. `Uzayr (d. 330/941–2), *Gharīb al-Qur'ān*. Ed. Muḥammad Adīb `Abd al-Waḥīd Jamrān, Beirut: Dār Qutayba, 1995.

al-Suyūṭī, Jalāl al-Dīn `Abd al-Raḥmān b. Abī Bakr (d. 911/1505–6), *Abwāb al-sa`āda fī asbāb al-shahāda*. Ed. Najm `Abd al-Raḥmān Khalaf, Cairo: Maktabat al-Qiyāma, 1987.

______ *Kashf al-ṣalṣala `an waṣf al-zalzala*. Ed. Muḥammad Kamāl al-Dīn `Izz al-Dīn, Beirut: `Ālam al-Kutub, 1987.

al-Ṭabarānī, Sulaymān b. Aḥmad (d. 360/971), *Musnad al-Shāmiyyīn*. Ed. Ḥamdī `Abd al-Majīd al-Silafī, Beirut: Mu'assasat al-Risāla, 1996 (4 vols).

al-Ṭabarī, Muḥammad b. Jarīr (d. 310/923), *Jāmi` al-bayān `an ta'wīl ayy al-Qur'ān*. Ed. Maḥmūd Shākir al-Ḥarastānī, Beirut: Dār Iḥya al-Turāth al-`Arabī, 2010 (16 vols).

______ *Tā'rīkh al-rusul wa-l-mulūk*. Ed. Muḥammad Abū al-Faḍl Ibrāhīm, Beirut: Rawā'ī` al-Turāth, n.d. (11 vols).

al-Tamīmī, Muḥammad b. Aḥmad b. Tamīm (d. 333/944–5), *Kitāb al-miḥan*. Ed. Yaḥyā Wāhib al-Jabūrī, Beirut: Dār al-Gharb al-Islamī, 1988.

al-Tawḥīdī, Abū Ḥayyān `Alī b. Muḥammad (d. 414/1023), *al-Baṣā'ir wa-l-dhakhā'ir*. Ed. Wadād al-Qāḍī, Beirut: Dār Ṣādir, 1999 (6 vols).

al-Tijānī, Abdallāh b. Muḥammad (*c.*706/1306), *Riḥlat al-Tijānī*. Beirut: Dār al-Ma`ārif l-l-Kitāb, 2005.

al-Tirmidhī, Muḥammad b. `Īsā (d. 279/892), *al-Jāmi` al-ṣaḥīḥ*. Ed. `Abd al-Wahhāb `Abd al-Laṭīf, Beirut: Dār al-Fikr, n.d. (5 vols).

Theophanes = Mango, Cyril, and Roger Scott (trans.), *The Chronicle of Theophanes Confessor: Byzantine and Near Eastern History AD 284–813*. Oxford: Clarendon Press, 1997.

Wakī` = Ibn Ḥayyān, Muḥammad b. Khalaf (d. 306/918–9), *Akhbār al-quḍāt*. Beirut: `Ālam al-Kutub, n.d. (3 vols).

Yāqūt b. `Abdallāh al-Ḥamāwī (d. 628/1229), *Mu`jam al-buldān*. Beirut: Dār al-Fikr, n.d. (5 vols).

______ *Mu`jam al-udabā'*. Ed. Iḥsān `Abbās, Beirut: Dār al-Gharb al-Islamī, 1993 (7 vols).

al-Ya`qūbī, Aḥmad b. Isḥāq (d. 284/897?), *Tā'rīkh*. Ed. Khalīl al-Manṣūr, Beirut: Dār al-Kutub al-`Ilmiyya, 1999.

Secondary Sources

Abel, Armand, "Une *ḥadīth* sur la prise du Rome," *Arabica* 5 (1958), pp. 1–14.

Aerts, W. J., and Kortekaas, G. A. A. (eds), *Die Apokalypse des Pseudo-Methodius: Die ältesten Griechischen und Lateinischen übersetzungen*. Louvain: Peeters, 1998 (CSCO vols. 56–70) (2 vols).

Aguade, Jorge, *Messianismus zur Zeit der frühen Abbasiden: das Kitāb al-fitan des Nu'aim ibn Ḥammād*. Unpublished Ph.D. dissertation, University of Tübingen, 1978.

Album, Stephen, *Checklist of Islamic Coins*. Santa Rosa, CA: Stephen Album Rare Coins, 2011.

Alexander, Paul, "Medieval Apocalypses as Historical sources," American Historical Review 73 (1968), pp. 997–1018.

Bashear, Suliman, "Early Muslim apocalyptic materials," *Journal of the Royal Asiatic Society* 1991, pp. 173–207.

______ "The mission of Diḥya al-Kalbī and the situation in Syria," *Jerusalem Studies in Arabic and Islam* 14 (1991), pp. 84–114.

______ "Muslim apocalypses and the Hour: a Case-Study in Traditional Interpretation," *Israel Oriental Studies* 13 (1993), pp. 75–99.

______ "The title *al-Fārūq* and its association with `Umar I," *Studia Islamica* 92 (1990), pp. 47–70.

Biella, Joan Copeland, *A Dictionary of Old South Arabian*. Missoula, MT: Scholars Press, 1982.

Carlson, Thomas, "Contours of Conversion: The Geography of Islamization in Syria 600–1500," *Journal of the American Oriental Society* 135 (2015), pp. 791–816.

Clarke, Nicola, *The Muslim Conquest of Iberia*. London: Routledge, 2012.

Cobb, Paul, *White Banners: Contention in `Abbasid Syria, 750–880*. Albany, NY: SUNY Press, 2001.

Cogan, Mordechai, "Ripping open pregnant women," *Journal of the American Oriental Society* 103 (1983), pp. 755–7.

Cook, David, *Martyrdom in Islam*. Cambridge: Cambridge University Press, 2007.

______ *Studies in Muslim Apocalyptic*. Princeton: Darwin, 2002.

______ "The Image of the Turk in Classical and Contemporary Muslim Apocalyptic Literature," in Felicitas Schmeider (ed.), *Peoples of the End-Time*. Berlin: de Gruyter, 2016, pp. 225–35.

______ "Tamīm al-Dārī," *Bulletin of the School of Oriental and African Studies* 61 (1998), pp. 20–8.

Cook, Michael, "A Muslim Apocalyptic Chronicle," *Journal of Near Eastern Studies* 52 (1993), pp. 25–9.

Crone, Patricia, "'Even an Ethiopian Slave': The Transformation of a Sunni Tradition," *Bulletin of the School of Oriental and African Studies* 72 (1994), pp. 59–67.

Crone, Patricia and Martin Hinds, *God's Caliph*. Cambridge: Cambridge University Press, 1986.

Donner, Fred McGraw, *Muhammad and the Believers at the Origins of Islam*. Cambridge, MA: Harvard University Press, 2010.

Dozy, Reinhart (d. 1883), *Dictionnaire détaillé des noms des vêtements chez les Arabes*. Beirut: Librarie du Liban, 1843 (reprint).

Droge, A. J. (trans.), *The Qur'ān: A New Annotated Translation*. Sheffield: Equinox, 2014.

Fierro, Maribel, "al-Aṣfar," *Studia Islamica* 77 (1993), pp. 169–81.

______ "al-Aṣfar again," *Jerusalem Studies in Arabic and Islam* 22 (1998), pp. 196–213.

Flood, Finbarr Barry, *The Great Mosque of Damascus: Studies on the Makings of an Umayyad Visual Culture*. Leiden: E. J. Brill, 2001.

Frenkel, Yehoshua, *The Turkic Peoples in Medieval Arabic Writings*. New York: Routledge, 2014.

Frankfurter, David (trans.), *Elijah in Upper Egypt: The Apocalypse of Elijah and Early Egyptian Christianity*. Minneapolis: Fortress Press, 1993.

Garstad, Benjamin (trans.), *Apocalypse: Pseudo-Methodius; An Alexandrian World Chronicle*. Cambridge, MA: Harvard University Press, 2012.

Geddes, C. L., "The Messiah in South Arabia," *Muslim World* 57 (1967), pp. 311–20.

Griffith, Sidney, "Bashīr/Bešer: Boon companion of the Byzantine emperor Leo III: the Islamic recension of his story in Leiden Oriental Ms. 951 (2)," *Le Muséon* 103 (1990), pp. 225–64.

Habib, Samar, *Arabo-Islamic Texts on Female Homosexuality 850–1780 A.D.* Youngstown, NY: Teneo, 2009.

Hasson, I., "Le chef judhāmite Rawḥ ibn Zinbāʿ," *Studia Islamīca* 77 (1993), pp. 95–122.

Hoyland, Robert, *Seeing Islam as Others Saw It*. Princeton: Darwin Press, 1997.

Hoyland, Robert, and Brian Gilmour (eds and trans), *Medieval Islamic Swords and Swordmaking: Kindi's Treatise 'On Swords and their Kinds.'* Oxford: Gibb Memorial Trust, 2006.

Jastrow, Marcus, *A Dictionary of the Targumim, the Talmud Bavli and Yerushalmi, and the Midrashic Literature*. New York: Title Publishing Co., 1943 (2 vols).

Kister, M. J., "'. . . And he was born circumcised . . .': Some notes on circumcision in *Ḥadīth*," *Oriens* 34 (1994).

______ "Do not assimilate yourselves: *Lā tashabbahū*"; with an Appendix by M. Kister, *Jerusalem Studies in Arabic and Islam* 12 (1989), pp. 321–71.

______ "Land property and *jihād*," *Journal of the Economic and Social History of the Orient* 34 (1991), pp. 270–311.

______ "'O God, Tighten Thy Grip on Muḍar . . .' Some Socio-Economic and Religious Aspects of an Early Ḥadīth," *Journal of the Economic and Social History of the Orient* 24 (1981), pp. 242–73.

Krenkow, F., "The book of strife (i.e., the *Kitāb al-fitan* of Nu`aim b. Hammad al-Marwazi)," *Islamic Culture* 3 (1929), pp. 561–8.

Kronk, Gary, *Cometography: A Catalog of Comets (Volume 1: Ancient–1799).* Cambridge: Cambridge University Press, 1999.

Lane, E. W., *An Arabic-English Lexicon.* Cambridge: Islamic Texts Society, 1984 (2 vols).

Lecker, Michael, "Biographical Notes on Ibn Shihāb al-Zuhrī," *Journal of Semitic Studies* 41 (1996), pp. 121–64.

Leslau, Wolf, *Comparative Dictionary of Ge`ez.* Wiesbaden: Otto Harrassowitz, 1997.

Lewis, Bernard, "The Regnal Titles of the first `Abbasid Caliphs," in *Dr. M. Zakir Husayn Presentation Volume.* New Delhi: Matba` Jami`a, 1968, pp. 13–22.

McCormick, Michael, *Origins of the European Economy: Communications and Commerce AD 300–700.* Cambridge: Cambridge University Press, 2002.

Madelung, Wilferd, "`Abdallāh b. al-Zubayr and the Mahdi," *Journal of Near Eastern Studies* 40 (1981), pp. 291–306.

______ "Apocalyptic prophecies in Ḥimṣ during the Umayyad age," *Journal of Semitic Studies* 41 (1986), pp. 141–85.

______ "The Sufyānī," *Studia Islamica* 63 (1986), pp. 5–48.

Meserve, Ruth I., "Writing on Man or Animal," in *Writing in the Altaic World.* Ed. Juha Janhunen and Volker Rybatzki, Studia Orientalia 87, (Helsinki: Finnish Oriental Society, 1999), pp. 171–86.

Metcalfe, Alex, *The Muslims of Medieval Italy.* Edinburgh: Edinburgh University Press, 2009.

Payne-Smith, Jesse, *A Compendious Syriac-English Dictionary.* Oxford: Oxford University Press, 1988.

Raven, Wim, "Ibn Ṣayyād as an Islamic 'Antichrist', A Reappraisal of the Texts," in Wolfram Brandes and Felicitas Schmeider (eds), *Endzeiten: Eschatologie in den monotheistischen Weltreligionen.* Berlin: Walter de Gruyter, 2008, pp. 261–91.

Reinink, Gerrit J. "'Ismael, der Wildesel in der Wuste.' Zur Typologie der Apokalypse des Pseudo-Methodius," Byzantische Zeitschrift 75 (1982), pp. 336–44.

______ "Ps. Methodius: A Concept of history in response to the rise of Islam," in A. Cameron and L. Conrad (eds), *The Byzantine and Early Islamic Near East.* Princeton: Darwin, 1992, pp. 149–87.

______ (ed. and trans.), *Die Syrische Apokalypse des Pseudo-Methodius.* Louvain: Peeters, 1993 (CSCO vos 540–1) (2 vols).

Roggema, Barbara (trans.), *The Legend of Sergius Bahira: Eastern Christian Apologetics and Apocalypse in Response to Islam.* Leiden: E. J. Brill, 2009.

Rosenthal, Franz, "The Prophecies of Baba the Harranian," in *A Locust's Leg: studies in honour of S. H. Taqizadeh.* London: Percy Lund, Humphries, 1962, pp. 220–32.

Rubin, Uri, "Apocalypse and Authority in Islamīc Tradition: The Emergence of the Twelve Leaders," *al-Qantara* 18 (1997), pp. 11–41

Savvides, Alexis, "Some notes on the terms *Agarenoi*, *Ismaelitai* and *Sarakenoi* in Byzantine sources," *Byzantion* 67 (1997), pp. 89–96.

Sezgin, Fuat, *Geschichte des Arabische Schriftums.* Leiden: E. J. Brill, 1967 (13 vols).

Silverstein, Adam, *Postal Systems in the Pre-Modern Islamic World.* Cambridge: Cambridge University Press, 2007.

Taragan, Hannah, *Patronut ve-omanut bi-armon ha-Umayyi bi-Yeriho* (*Patronage and Artwork in the Umayyad Palace at Jericho*). Jerusalem: Yad Yitzhak Ben Zvi, 1997.

Vasiliev, A. A., "The Iconoclastic Edict of the Caliph Yazid II, A.D. 721." *Dumbarton Oaks Papers* 9–10 (1956), pp. 25–47.

Wensinck, A. J. (ed.), *Concordance et indices de la Tradition Musulmane.* (Leiden: E. J. Brill, 1936–62).

Wilkinson, John (trans.), *Jerusalem Pilgrims before the Crusades.* Oxford: Oxbow, 2002 (reprint).

Index

Muḥammad is only referenced when he is mentioned explicitly.
The definite article *al-* is disregarded for alphabetization.
Numbers in italics refer to the relater of a tradition on that page; other materials referring to that person may also appear on the referenced page.
Numbers in roman refer to any other appearances on a given page.

Aaron, 260, 443
Abān b. al-Walīd b. `Uqba b. Abī Mu`ayṭ, *101, 211, 234, 258*
`Abbās, 50, 110, 213, 241
`Abbāsids, 16, 104, 110, 111, 112, 121, 122, 163, 172, 177, 221, 426, 431
  black banners and, 100, 101, 102, 103, 105, 106, 109, 114, 149–50, 155, 157, 164, 174, 177
  supporters of, 167
Abdāl, 125
`Abdallāh (unidentified), *10, 12, 15, 27, 28, 39, 62, 76, 82, 86, 136, 137, 147, 187, 210, 211, 317, 328, 329, 356, 371, 372, 376, 378, 404, 405, 407, 409, 411*
`Abdallāh b. `Abbās, *7, 36, 41, 80, 82, 83, 87, 100, 105, 112, 130, 132, 135, 141, 147, 154, 166, 173, 182, 184, 193, 200, 209, 211, 212, 231, 235, 258, 362, 371, 385, 395, 396, 406, 408, 412, 427, 445*; 55, 95, 101, 172
`Abdallāh b. Abī al-Asha`th al-Laythī, *106*
`Abdallāh b. Abī Ja`far, *66*
`Abdallāh b. Adam, *176*
`Abdallāh b. `Alī, 113
`Abdallāh b. `Āmir b. Rabī`a, *81, 82*
`Abdallāh b. `Amr, *4, 5, 27, 29, 48, 49, 50, 52, 72, 115, 119, 128, 130, 131, 135, 141, 150, 160, 184, 187, 188, 193, 194, 212, 219, 222, 224, 225, 227, 228, 229, 231, 232, 242, 254, 256, 257, 258, 280, 283, 285, 286, 287, 288, 289, 290, 291, 292, 296, 304, 306, 312, 315, 316, 317, 318, 323, 328, 333, 341, 346, 353, 359, 369, 372, 373, 374, 378, 380, 383, 389, 391, 394, 396, 401, 402, 406, 409, 412, 414, 416, 417, 418, 420, 421, 422, 423, 424, 436, 437, 445*; 40, 218, 279, 293, 297, 302, 303, 308, 394, 398, 400, 408, 427
`Abdallāh b. Burayda, *421*
`Abdallāh b. Busr, *26, 306, 322, 324, 428*

`Abdallāh b. Ḥajjāj, *218*
`Abdallāh b. al-Ḥārith, *209*
`Abdallāh b. Ḥawwwāla, xxix
`Abdallāh b. Hubayra, *18, 93*
`Abdallāh b. Ma`qil, *393*
`Abdallāh b. Mas`ūd, *7, 16, 23, 24, 28, 34, 40, 55, 61, 69, 92, 107, 111, 116, 118, 119, 125, 138, 147, 150, 154, 169, 171, 186, 196, 201, 245, 257, 330, 347, 369, 370, 374, 377, 400, 402, 405, 406, 411, 424, 427, 428, 436*; 75, 89, 172
`Abdallāh b. al-Mubārak, 29, 77
`Abdallāh b. Qays, *131*; 59
`Abdallāh b. Rāshid, *317*
`Abdallāh b. Sa`d, *311*
`Abdallāh b. Ṣafwān, 76
`Abdallāh b. Salām, *59, 70, 79, 82, 91, 242, 349, 369, 428*; 81, 393
`Abdallāh b. Sharīk, *204*
`Abdallāh b. Ta`lā, *316*
`Abdallāh b. `Umar, *1, 3, 10, 22, 26, 30, 39, 41, 62, 63, 73, 77, 79, 80, 83, 84, 91, 126, 130, 183, 213, 219, 286, 325, 341, 343, 348, 350, 354, 359, 370, 377, 382, 385, 387, 404, 406, 408, 413, 437, 445*; 74, 75, 82, 87, 90, 109, 146
`Abdallāh b. Wahb, *55*
`Abdallāh b. Yazīd, 151, 162; *see also* al-Sufyānī
`Abdallāh b. al-Zubayr, 10, 14, 15, 58, 59, 60, 76, 80, 87, 90, 137, 208, 324, 414, 418, 425
`Abd al-Malik (caliph), 324
`Abd al-Malik b. `Umayr, *299*
`Abd al-Muṭṭalib, 211
`Abd al-Quddūs, *152*
`Abd al-Raḥmān (ruler of Spain), 138n, 140, 141, 150
`Abd al-Raḥmān b. Abī `Awf, *53*
`Abd al-Raḥmān b. Abī Bakra, *308*
`Abd al-Raḥmān b. Abī Laylā, *83*
`Abd al-Raḥmān b. Faḍāla, *91*
`Abd al-Raḥmān b. Ghanm, *172*
`Abd al-Raḥmān b. Jubayr, *90, 123, 124, 355*
`Abd al-Raḥmān b. Qays b. Jābir al-Sadafī, *50, 218, 219, 228, 235*
`Abd al-Raḥmān b. Sābiṭ, *383*
`Abd al-Raḥmān b. Salmān, *253, 392*
`Abd al-Raḥmān b. Sulaymān, 176
`Abd al-Raḥmān b. Sunna, *302*
`Abd al-Raḥmān b. Yazīd, *115*
`Abd al-Wahhāb b. Bukht, *118*
`Abd al-Wāḥid b. Qays al-Dimashqī, *307*
Abdāl (substitutes), 197, 204
Abel, 91
Abraham, 117, 266, 331
  emigration-place of, 279, 391, 393, 394
Abū `Adhaba al-Ḥaḍramī, *27*
Abū al-Aḥwaṣ, *29*
Abū al-`Āliyya, *7, 76, 125, 381*
Abū `Āmir al-Alhānī, *263, 268, 274*
Abū `Āmir al-Ṭā'ī, *99, 384*
Abū Arṭāt, *235*
Abū Asmā', 166
Abū `Awf al-Ḥimṣī, *374*
Abū Baḥriyya, *268*; 324
Abū Bakr (caliph), *328, 329, 343* 31, 33, 35, 41, 44, 47, 111, 204–5, 430
Abū Bakr al-Azdī, *220*
Abū Bakr b. Ḥazm, *102*
Abū Bakra, *80, 84, 86, 349, 420*; 85
Abū Birza al-Aslamī, *68*; 84
Abū Burda b. Abū Mūsā, *72, 382, 384*
Abū Ḍamra al-Kalā`ī, *399*
Abū al-Dardā', *75, 91, 96, 305, 306, 307*; 326, 398
Abū Daws al-Yaḥṣubī, *300*
Abū Dharr al-Ghifārī, *69, 81, 133, 160, 291, 296*; 65, 269n, 270
Abū Dharr `Abd al-Raḥmān b. Faḍāla, *23, 55*
Abū al-Ḍuḥā, *31*
Abū Fīrās, *318, 402*
Abū Ghālib, *347*
Abū Ḥabīb, *154*
Abū Ḥalbas, *236*
Abū Hārūn al-Madanī, *23, 427*
Abū al-Ḥasan, *340*
Abū Ḥaṣīn, *87*
Abū Ḥassān b. Nūba, *112, 140, 430*

Abū Ḥāzim, *78*
Abū Ḥukayma, *114*, *419*
Abū Hurayra, *2*, *10*, *16*, *17*, *24*, *25*, *26*, *27*, *28*, *39*, *45*, *60*, *61*, *62*, *66*, *76*, *81*, *84*, *85*, *86*, *87*, *88*, *92*, *94*, *101*, *102*, *108*, *109*, *116*, *122*, *126*, *127*, *132*, *140*, *184*, *188*, *189*, *190*, *194*, *200*, *201*, *208*, *213*, *218*, *222*, *228*, *229*, *236*, *237*, *238*, *255*, *288*, *299*, *307*, *323*, *327*, *328*, *346*, *353*, *355*, *357*, *358*, *359*, *361*, *373*, *375*, *380*, *382*, *383*, *384*, *385*, *387*, *391*, *393*, *396*, *400*, *402*, *405*, *406*, *414*, *415*, *416*, *420*, *422*, *423*, *426*, *428*, *436*, *444*; 8, 78, 90
Abū Idrīs al-Khawlānī, *4*, *63*
Abū Ja`far al-Anṣārī, *89*, *104*, *116*, *117*, *150*, *155*, *156*, *159*, *171*, *175*, *181*, *183*, *186*, *188*, *190*, *195*, *213*
Abū Janāb, *38*
Abū Jandal, 35, 40
Abū al-Jild, *9*, *20*, *111*, *195*, *426*
Abū Khalaf, 32
Abū Kināna, *30*
Abū Mas`ūd al-Anṣārī, *25*, *26*
Abū Muhallab, *39*
Abū Muḥammad al-Juhanī, 288
Abū Muḥammad al-Nahdī, *45*, *189*
Abū Mūsā al-Asha`rī, *3*, *9*, *12*, *23*, *24*, *25*, *66*, *77*, *83*, *90*, *92*, *255*; 21
Abū Muslim (`Abbāsid general), 101, 113
Abū Muslim al-Khawlānī, 4
Abū Muslim al-Rūmī, 243
Abū Qatāda, *415*
Abū Qilāba, *64*, *320*, *420*; 213
Abū Qubayl, *12*, *57*, *60*, *105*, *110*, *138*, *140*, *142*, *153*, *154*, *176*, *183*, *187*, *188*, *189*, *213*, *221*, *234*, *285*, *286*, *289*, *292*, *295*, *312*, *315*, *316*
Abū Ru'ba, *204*
Abū Ṣādiq, *188*
Abū Sa`īd al-Khudarī, *1*, *17*, *33*, *39*, *56*, *136*, *205*, *206*, *207*, *208*, *209*, *211*, *212*, *213*, *214*, *215*, *232*, *322*, *344*, *349*, *385*, *395*, *396*, *403*, *404*, *426*; 88
Abū Salama, *421*; 69
Abū Ṣāliḥ, *49*, *53*, *81*; 4
Abū Sālim al-Jayshānī, *6*, *53*
Abū Sarīḥa al-Ghifārī, *392*, *409*
Abū Shurayḥ al-Ma`āfirī, *79*
Abū al-Ṣiddīq, *215*
Abū Subḥān, *154*
Abū Sufyān, 152, 166, 169, 177, 190
Abū Ṭalḥa, *104*
Abū Tha`laba al-Khushanī, *23*, *24*, *293*, *306*, *312*, *388*
Abū Thumāma, *211*
Abū al-Tiyāḥ, *279*
Abū Ṭufayl, 29
Abū al-Ṭufayl, *40*, *209*, *211*, *212*, *222*
Abū al-Ṭuhawī, 178
Abū `Ubayda b. al-Jarrāḥ, *42*, *43*, *152*, *153*
Abū Umāma al-Bāhilī, *319*, *327*, *330*, *345*, *346*, *348*, *350*, *394*
Abū Umayya al-Dhimārī, *220*
Abū Umayya al-Kalbī, *59*, *97*, *103*, *110*, *165*, *425*
Abū `Utba, *414*
Abū `Uthmān, *28*, *39*, *72*
Abū Wahb al-Kalā`ī, *112*, *143*, *158*
Abū Wā'il, *35*, *60*, *61*, *341*
Abū Zāhiriyya, *23*, *129*, *135*, *227*, *241*, *268*, *278*, *298*, *370*
Abū al-Za`rā', *330*
Abū Zaynab, *308*
Abū Zura`a, *316*; 244
Acre, 226, 229, 253, 255, 257, 260, 272–3, 283, 290, 299, 309, 312, 314
Adam, 260, 297, 320, 351, 354, 359, 443
`Adan Abyan, 19, 388, 392
Adī b. `Adī al-Kindī, *388*
Afīq, pass of, 148, 253, 336, 340, 347, 356
Aflat b. Ṣāliḥ, *212*
Al-Aḥnaf b. Qays, *85*
`Ā'isha, *33*, *36*, *212*, *387*, *401*, *412*; 32, 34, 36, 83, 85, 140, 229, 385
`Ajlān, 302
Ajyād, 410, 412
Al-`Ālā' b. Ziyād, 127
Alexandria, 147, 259, 260, 286, 295
  attacks upon, 315–16

Fish Market in, 315, 317
idol of, 326
lighthouse of, 315, 317
Alhān (tribe), 266
Aleppo, 324
`Alī b. `Abdallāh b. al-`Abbās, *188*
`Alī b. Abī Ṭālib, *14, 17, 20, 24, 26, 30, 31, 33, 34, 35, 38, 50, 53, 54, 68, 71, 80, 89, 94, 96, 97, 103, 107, 109, 110, 111, 132, 138, 154, 157, 158, 163, 168, 169, 175, 177, 178, 179, 181, 186, 188, 189, 192, 195, 198, 199, 200, 210, 211, 212, 214, 219, 224, 322, 401, 414, 425*; 6, 87, 91, 100, 125, 172, 208, 235
killing of `Uthmān and, 36–7, 45, 46–7, 55, 67, 82, 83, 84
`Alqama, *93, 396*
Al-A`mash, *9*
Amid, 115, 419
`Āmila (tribe), 224, 234
Al-Amīn (title), 48
`Āmir (tribe), 202
`Āmir b. Maṭar, *69*
`Ammān, xvi, 254
`Ammār b. Yāsir, *116, 132, 158, 170, 175, 177, 189, 191, 219*; 30, 32, 35, 38
Amorium, 248, 259, 292, 305, 443
`Amr b. al-`Āṣ, *237*; 21, 54, 295, 414
`Amr b. al-Aswad, *334*
`Amr b. Jābir al-Ḥaḍramī, *318*
`Amr b. Labīd, *47*
`Amr b. Murra, *176*
`Amr b. Sa`īd, 75
`Amr b. Shu`ayb, *119, 192*
`Amr b. Sulay`, 223
`Amr b. Sulaymān, *397, 406*
`Amr b. `Ubayd b. `Umayr, *409*
`Āmir al-Sha`bī, *375, 396, 412*
Anas b. Mālik, *9, 142, 150, 321, 322, 376, 385, 400, 401, 403, 404*
Andalus, 261, 269, 417
Andalusians, 287, 414–15, 416–17, 442
Andrā, 150
Anṣār (Helpers), 181, 196, 434
Anṭablus, 15, 318
Antioch, 133, 203, 204, 223, 251, 257, 261, 265, 268, 290, 303, 308, 326
Antipatris River (Nahr Abī Fuṭrus), 134, 336, 338, 347, 348
`Aqabat al-Jamra (Pebble Pass), 119, 193
`Aqīq, 73
`Āqir Qūfā, 107, 162, 171, 179
Al-Aqṣā Mosque, 349
Arabs, 2, 13, 19, 62, 65, 86, 124, 246, 277, 311, 442–3
betrayal of, 248, 251–3, 301
loss of status and, 102, 103, 302–3, 402, 426, 436
`Arafāt, 194
Arak, 156
Al-`Arīsh, 149, 160, 251, 290, 306, 312, 389
Ark of the Covenant, 203, 207, 293, 297
Armenia, 113, 264, 379, 423
`Arqa, 270
Arṭāt b. Mundhir, *17, 40, 66, 106, 110, 112, 114, 115, 123, 148, 149, 154, 155, 162, 164, 173, 187, 192, 202, 203, 208, 210, 214, 219, 220, 221, 222, 223, 224, 228, 231, 232, 237, 238, 255, 260, 326, 361, 387, 395, 437*
`aṣabiyya (tribal chauvinism), 7, 122, 246–7
Aṣbagh b. Zayd, 234, 289
Asha`th b. `Abd al-Raḥmān, *213*
Ashja` (tribe), 271
Asmā' daughter of Abū Bakr, 57
Asmā' daughter of `Umays, *192*
Asmā' daughter of Yazīd al-Anṣāriyya, *325, 329, 345, 349*
Aswān, 288
`Aṭiyya b. Qays, *307, 371*
`Aṭiyya b. `Umar, *410*
`Awf b. Mālik al-Ashja`ī, *12, 13, 20, 38, 68, 306*
`Awn b. `Abdallāh, *93, 137*
Al-Awzā`ī, *307*
`Ayn al-Rīḥ (Spring of the Wind), 148
Al-`Ayyāsh b. Abī Rabī`a, *375*
Azarbayjān, 115, 420, 423
Azd (tribe), 216, 256, 266, 282

Azdād b. Aflaḥ, *364*
`Azra b. Qays, *152*

Babylon, 179, 439
Badr, Battle of, 73, 77, 192, 196, 201, 246, 285
Baghdad, 106, 164
  destruction of, 171, 172
Baḥīr b. Sa`d, *428*
Bahrā' (tribe), 247, 250
  Monastery of, 263, 268, 279
Bajala b. `Abda, *56*
Bajīla (tribe), 187
Bakr b. Sawāda, *128*
Bakhtrian camels, 104, 366
Balqā', 253, 307, 309
Banū `Abs (tribe), 314
Banū `Adī (clan), 82, 179
Banū `Alī, valleys of, 415
Banū Asad (tribe), 43
  Monastery of, 263, 278
Banū al-Aṣfar (Byzantines), 13, 250–1, 306, 312
Banū al-Ḥakam (clan), 97
Banū Ḥāritha (tribe), 168, 434
Banū Khatha`m (tribe), 128
Banū Maghāla (clan), 342
Banū Makhzūm (clan), 216–17
  Gate of, 409
Banū al-Muṣṭaliq (tribe), 46
Banū Muṭī`, 82
Banū Qanṭūrā b. Karkarā, 418, 420, 421–2, 424; *see also* Turks
Banū Sarāqa (clan), 82
Baqī` al-Gharqad, 78, 161
Baqiyya, *241*
Bashīr b. `Abdallāh b. Yassār, *284, 323*
Bashīr b. Sa`d, *43*
Baṣra, 74, 126, 157, 174, 179, 329, 347n, 401, 420, 422, 432
Bathaniyya, 434
Baysān/Maysān (Beth-Shean), xvi, 148, 151, 162, 203, 262, 293, 297, 325
Bayt Lihyā, 176
Bayt al-Ra's, 165
Beast of the Earth (*dābba*), 218, 407, 408, 409–14
Bedouin, 256–7, 290, 302, 331, 334, 389, 420
Beirut, 262
Berbers, 112, 140, 141–2, 144, 145, 147, 150, 169, 177, 442
Biṭrīq b. Yazīd al-Kalbī, *255*
Black Mountain, 146
Black Stone, 416
Book of Tribulations, themes of, xvii–xxix
Burayda, 421
Burjān (Burgundians), 285, 423
Buṣrā, 233, 265, 388, 389, 392, 394
Byzantines, xxx, 13, 20, 43, 49, 53, 116–17, 121, 124, 147, 199, 272, 290, 293, 321, 438–9
  alliance with Syrian Muslims, 245, 254, 262, 275–6, 284, 301, 311
  attacking Egypt, 315–19, 414
  attacking Syria, 149, 155, 159, 229–30, 247, 251–3, 260–1, 263, 271, 274–5, 290–1, 294, 299–300, 305, 307, 308–10, 312
  defeat of, 167, 201, 203, 218, 226, 228, 260, 266–8, 303, 443
  other attacks, 289
  valleys and, xxx–xxxi, xxxv, 234, 242–87, 300, 440–1

Caesar, City of (prob. Cosntantinople), 232, 237
Caesarea (in Palestine), 262, 302, 308, 317
Caesarea in Anatolia, 254, 283, 298
Cain, 23, 86, 91
Camel, Battle of, 32, 33, 38, 71
Carchemish *see* Qirqīsiyā
Chalcedon, 278, 281
China, 441
Christianity, 271, 294
Christians, 206, 242, 260, 270, 294, 300, 301n, 352, 355
Church of Mary, 241
Church of Zacharias, 241
Comet, Halley's, 120
Constantine IV (emperor), 285
Constantine V (emperor), 113, 140

Constantinople, 5n, 221, 242, 264, 322–3, 336
Bay of, 244, 248, 311
destruction/conquest of, xxxv, 196, 218, 226, 228, 230, 244–9, 261, 275, 277, 280–1, 284, 292, 294–5, 297, 303, 304–5, 306, 308, 310, 311, 322–3, 325–7, 353
Mosque/s built in, 199, 254, 286, 295
Copts, 269n, 417, 442
Cyprus, 308, 318

Dābiq, xxxv–xxxvi
Ḍaḥḥāk b. Qays, *89*; 55
Dajjāl (Antichrist), 15, 16, 17, 20–1, 130, 231–2, 237, 242, 249, 278, 280–1, 290, 295, 308, 310, 312, 319, 321, 444
description/appearance of, 191n, 320–1, 322, 328–9, 334–5, 426
followers of, 332, 334–5, 336, 341, 357, 421
identification of, 191n, 321n, 323, 326, 330–1
opponents of, 304, 305, 322, 330, 334, 337, 340, 346–8, 350, 354, 355–6
refuges from, 134, 290, 339, 343–4, 348–50, 383
temptations of, 329, 331–3, 336–7, 338–40, 345, 352
Damascus, 95, 103, 104, 106, 107, 108, 125, 133, 134, 173, 177, 253, 265, 271, 276, 279, 288, 362, 433
destruction of, 163, 280n
Mosque of, 116, 144, 154, 157, 210, 226
ruler of, 152, 153, 208, 229
Tower of, 335, 338, 355
White Bridge, 351
Damietta, 316
Ḍamra b. Ḥabīb, *134, 151, 152, 180, 215, 299, 324, 364, 371, 435*
Daniel, 260, 361, 426
David's Gate, 284
Daws (tribe), 307, 375
Dead Sea, 390
Dhū al-ʿArf (One with the Mane), 287–8
Dhū al-Khalṣa, 256, 288, 306, 375
Dhū Mayyan, 263
Dhū Mikhbar, *220, 235, 254, 301*
Dhū al-Qariyāt, *156, 157, 160, 182, 185, 198*
Dhū al-Qarnayn, 315, 318
Dhū al-Suwayqatan, 414–16
Dhukhayra, 279
Dīnār b. Dīnār, *151, 207, 215*

Eagle's Pass, 276, 278
earthquake(s), 120, 144, 159, 344, 378–87, 396
Edessa, 165
Egypt, xiii, 53, 96, 105, 113, 126, 137, 142, 144, 147, 169, 176, 253, 272–3, 290, 299n, 439, 444
attacks upon, 260, 287–8, 315–19, 414, 433
banners in, 139, 145, 158, 160, 189
people of, 12, 138, 157, 293, 309, 438
Epiphanius the Monk, 347n
Ethiopians, 51, 70, 220, 288, 388
attacking Egypt, 415–19
attacking Mecca/Medina, 414, 415
Euphrates River, 106, 114, 115, 159, 189–90, 216, 217, 239, 262, 326–7, 330, 371, 380, 383–5, 389, 405, 419–20, 422, 423, 435, 439
Eusebius, 288, 417
Eve, 260, 443

Fāmiya, Lake, 144, 145
Al-Faraj b. Yaḥmad, *311*
Fāthūr Ibrāhīm, 203
Fāṭima, descendants of, 110, 155, 195, 200, 211, 213–14
Al-Fazārī, 22
Fihr *see* Quraysh
Filasṭīn, 116, 127, 133–4, 143, 144, 145, 148, 157, 160, 216, 253, 260, 299, 433
Fitna (tribulation), xv
Franks, 442
Fusṭāṭ, 288, 297, 416, 445
Bridge of, 149, 160

Gabriel, 185, 247, 267, 339, 396, 399, 404, 435
Galilee, Sea of, xvi, 165, 207, 362, 363, 366, 368
Ghassān (tribe), 216, 368
Gog and Magog, 362–73, 407
  description of, 361–2
  listing of, 367, 369, 372
  Sea-dragon and, 364–5
Gold, red, 28n
Gospel, 204, 286
Ghūṭa, of Damascus, 135, 278

Ḥabīb b. Ṣāliḥ, *140*
Ḥaḍramawt, 313
Ḥafṣa, *185*
Ḥajjāj b. Yūsuf al-Thaqafī, 57–8, 79, 87, 146, 299
Al-Ḥakam, 156, 157
Al-Ḥakam b. `Utayba, *28*, *419*
Hamdān (tribe), 312, 324
Ḥammād b. Salama, *412*
Hammam, *45*
Ḥamrā' (non-Arab foreigners), 222, 224, 249, 265–6
Ḥamza b. `Abd al-Muṭṭalib, 259, 285
Ḥanash b. al-Ḥārith, *403*
Ḥarastā, 111, 120, 144, 173n, 176
Al-Ḥārith b. `Abdallāh, *133*, *152*, *338*, *360*, *374*
Al-Ḥārith b. Ḥarmal, *297*
Al-Ḥārith b. Mālik, known as Barsā', *418*
Ḥarīz b. `Uthmān, *240*; 239
Ḥarmala, *72*
Ḥarra, Battle of, 183
Ḥarrān, 164, 165, 166, 439–41
Harshā, 391
Hārūn al-Rāshid (caliph), 112
AL-Ḥaṣ, 162, 163, 166, 167
Al-Ḥasan b. `Alī, *30*, *31*, *32*, *49*, *56*, *68*, *79*, *94*, *130*, *175*, *176*, *214*, *328*, *350*, *384*, *395*, *424*; 48, 78, 82, 87, 90, 108, 159, 214
Al-Ḥasan b. `Alī b. Muḥammad, *109*
Hāshimite (title), 179, 180, 200, 298, 387
Hashemites, 101, 108, 111, 112, 144, 153, 158, 174, 177, 179, 211, 305
  Caliph of, 182, 221, 230
  Mecca/Medina, 184, 196, 434
  women of, 171
Ḥassān b. `Aṭiyya, *145*, *253*, *308*, *334*, *362*, *370*, *385*
Ḥāṭib b. Abī Balta`a, 415
Al-Ḥaw`āb, 33
Ḥarārīn, 399
Ḥawāzin (tribe), 442
Ḥawshab, *219*
Al-Haytham b. al-Aswad, *328*, *427*
Al-Haytham b. Mālik al-Ṭā'ī, *333*
Ḥazn b. `Abd `Amr, *14*
Hebron, 132–3
Heraclius (emperor), 124, 285, 287, 303, 305–6, 308, 312
Ḥijāz, 126, 132, 151, 162, 168, 181, 186, 202, 259, 422
Hilal b. Yasāf, *49*, *53*, *60*
Ḥimṣ (Emesa), 98, 99–100, 108, 125, 133, 134, 142, 145, 147, 149, 150, 163, 164, 168, 177, 309, 434
  Byzantines attacking, 245, 253, 263, 265, 268–9, 276–7, 278, 305
  description of, 263–4, 270, 273–4, 275, 284, 312, 399
  tribal violence in, 238–41, 314
Ḥimyar (tribal grouping), xxix, 51, 216, 220, 231, 238–40, 241, 266, 289, 300, 307, 311
Hind "Liver-Eating Woman," 163n, 167, 177
Al-Hind daughter of al-Muhallab, *94*
Ḥīra, 108n, 419
Hishām (caliph), 57, 59, 60, 97, 154, 321n, 425
Hishām b. `Āmir, *320*
Hishām b. `Urwa, *343*
Hiyam, 226
Hour, Portents of, 395–405
Ḥudaybiyya, Day of, 35, 285
Ḥudhayfa b. al-Yamān, *2*, *4*, *5*, *6*, *9*, *10*, *11*, *12*, *15*, *17*, *20*, *21*, *22*, *24*, *25*, *26*, *28*, *29*, *34*, *36*, *41*, *42*, *45*, *58*, *62*, *63*, *65*, *68*, *70*, *83*, *87*, *102*,

109, 115, 122, 131, 138, 142, 143, 158, 172, 235, 236, 250, 280, 312, 323, 329, 332, 341, 346, 352, 373, 374, 377, 405, 413, 414, 422, 424, 425, 429, 437, 444; 25, 69, 105, 223
Qur'ānic exegesis of, 172–3
Ḥumayd b. Hilāl, *77*
Ḥunayn, Battle of, 285
Hurmuzān, 7
Ḥusayn b. `Alī, *343*; 48, 78, 159, 212, 433
Hussein, Saddam, xxxiv

Ibn `Abbās *see* `Abdallāh b. `Abbās
Ibn Abī Ḥudhayfa, 444
Ibn Abī al-Hudhayl, *403*
Ibn al-`Afar, 112 (Hārūn al-Rāshid)
Ibn al-Asha`th, 64
Ibn Athāl, 108
Ibn Dhū al-Kalā`, *423*
Ibn Fātik al-Asadī, *124*
Ibn Khuthaym, *93, 137*; 39
Ibn Lahī`a, *417*; 189, 292
Ibn Mas`ūd *see* `Abdallāh b. Mas`ūd
Ibn Maurice, 296
Ibn Muḥayrīz, *292, 324*
Ibn Qaṭan, 341
Ibn Ṣayyād (Jewish Dajjāl), 342–3
Ibn Sās`id, 328
Ibn Shawdhab, *58, 177*
Ibn Shihāb *see* al-Zuhrī
Ibn Wahb *see* `Abdallāh b. Wahb
Ibn al-Zubayr *see* `Abdallāh b. al-Zubayr
Ibn Zuhayr, probably Qasāma b. Zuhayr, *157*
Ibn Zurayr al-Ghāfiqī, *213*
Ibrāhīm b. `Abdallāh b. al-Ḥasan, *428*
Ibrāhīm b. Abī `Abla, *26, 325*
Ibrāhīm b. Maysara, *206*
Ifrīqiyā, 176, 287, 438
Ihab Path, 390
`Ikrima, *54, 377, 391*
`Imrān b. Ḥaṣīn, *16*
`Imrān b. Sulaym al-Kalā`ī, *268*
India, raid on, 231–2, 237–8, 438
Iram (Damascus), 111, 136, 155, 157, 203
Iraq, 17, 88, 116, 158, 324, 333
people/army of, 166, 168, 170, 262, 309, 422, 434
`Irbāḍ b. al-Sāriyya, *95*
Isaac, 266
Iṣfahān, 341
Ishmael, 41
Islam, becomes a stranger, 222, 233, 374
`Isma b. Qays al-Sulamī, *140, 141*
Ismā`īl b. al-`Alā' b. Muḥammad al-Kalbī, *139*
Ismā`īl b. Muḥammad b. `Amr b Sa`d, *227*
Israelites, 124, 244, 298, 406, 430
Isrāfīl, 248
Iṣṭakhr, 178, 179
`Itrīs b. `Urqūb, 75
`Iyāḍ b. `Uqba, *295*

Jābir (title), 48, 218, 224, 232
Jābir al-Sadafī, *231, 321, 386*
Jābir b. Azdād, 364–5
Jābir b. `Abdallāh, *48, 81, 208, 395, 397, 398*
Jābir b. Samura, *40*
Jābir b. Zayd al-Azdī, *71*
Al-Jābiya, 148, 165
Gate, 229
Jadīs (tribe), 216, 224, 234, 266, 336
Ja`far b. Sayyār al-Shāmī, *204*
Ja`far al-Ṭayyār, 171n
Jaffa, 260, 269, 282, 283, 312
Jāhiliyya (ignorance), 6, 50, 59, 62, 76, 83, 97, 103, 110, 150, 159, 208, 219, 375
Jamājim, Battle of, 38, 64
Jammā'wayn, 186
Jarm (tribe), 201
Jawmṭīs, Field of, 443
Jayḥūn/Jayḥān River (Amu Darya), 112, 389
Jayrūn Gate, 203

Al-Jazīra, 17, 60, 96, 103, 114, 115, 116, 127, 168, 279, 290, 379, 419–20, 423
Ass of the, 104, 430; *see also* Marwān II
Christians of, 243, 294
Jericho, 170, 368
Gate, 284
Jerusalem, 20, 45, 181, 198, 208, 219, 225, 228, 237, 280, 323, 347, 368
as bayt al-maqdis, 13, 174, 180, 199, 202, 207, 210, 218, 220, 223, 224–5, 232, 250, 253, 259, 262, 272, 278, 283, 284, 286, 297, 308, 309–10, 337, 339, 346, 348, 350, 355, 359, 367, 372, 378, 387, 390, 393
as *iliyā*, 109, 151, 176, 197, 209, 222, 225, 291, 297, 348, 352
Caliph in, 201, 221, 227, 230, 309
Jesus, 17, 29, 132, 221, 232, 237–8, 258, 396, 411
Dajjal and, 330, 333, 346–8, 350, 354, 357
family of, 190, 192, 360, 373
Gog and Magog and, 366–7
Mahdi and, 206, 212, 213–14, 231
return of, 241, 249, 280, 321, 323, 338, 345, 351–2, 353–4, 355, 356, 359, 426
rule of, 351, 358–61, 372
Jew, a, 51, 263, 357
Jews, 205, 206, 332, 334, 351–2, 399
Dajjāl and, 332, 334–6, 341–3, 350, 353–4, 359
Gate, 270, 313
Jifār, 442–3
Jinn, 336, 336–7, 390, 397, 435
John the Baptist, 117
Jordan River (Valley), 310, 337, 400, 442
Joseph, 376
Jubayr b. Nufayr, *139, 152, 232, 306, 328, 334, 368, 399, 428, 429*
Judhām (tribe), 224–5, 234, 255, 282, 283, 360, 368
Juhayna (tribe), 433
Jūkhā River, 422
Jumay`, *33*
Junāda b. `Īsā al-Azdī, *372*
Junayd b. al-Sawdā', *36*
Jundub b. `Abdallāh al-Bajalī, *64, 67, 82, 88, 92*
Jurhum (tribe), 220
Justinian II (emperor), 287, 296

Ka`b al-Aḥbār, *11, 19, 20, 25, 27, 34, 41, 42, 44, 50, 51, 52, 56, 65, 71, 89, 91, 97, 104, 106, 108, 109, 111, 112, 114, 115, 117, 121, 124, 125, 126, 127, 128, 131, 135, 139, 141, 144, 145, 146, 151, 150, 153, 156, 159, 160, 161, 162, 163, 167, 173, 176, 177, 182, 186, 188, 190, 199, 201, 203, 204, 205, 209, 213, 214, 215, 217, 218, 219, 220, 221, 223, 224, 225, 227, 228, 230, 231, 232, 236, 237, 238, 239, 240, 241, 242, 249, 253, 255, 256, 258, 262, 264, 269, 271, 274, 275, 278, 279, 280, 281, 282, 283, 289, 291, 292, 293, 298, 299, 300, 304, 305, 307, 308, 309, 312, 313, 319, 322, 323, 324, 326, 327, 328, 329, 331, 334, 335, 337, 346, 347, 348, 351, 353, 355, 359, 360, 361, 362, 364, 365, 368, 370, 373, 375, 378, 380, 388, 389, 392, 405, 415, 416, 418, 419, 422, 423, 425, 426, 429, 430, 435*; 7, 10, 42, 43–4, 50, 60, 98, 129, 273, 369, 381
manic behavior of, 313–14
Ka`b b. Murra, *86*
Ka`ba, 146, 193–4, 354, 392, 403
destroyed by Ethiopians, 414, 415–16
Khābūr River, 165
Kalb (tribe), 187, 198, 199, 200, 201, 202–3, 250, 314
Kalbite woman, son of, 151, 162
Kathīr b. Murra, *24, 97, 119, 122, 123, 131, 134, 135, 323, 334, 397, 405, 406*
Khālid b. Kaysān, 283
Khālid b. Ma`dān, *119, 123, 153, 163, 311, 380*; 300
Khālid b. Sumayr, *74*

Khālid b. `Urfūṭa, 72
Khālid b. al-Wālid, 11, 152
Khālid b. al-Walīd b. `Uqba, 78
Khālid b. Yazīd b. Mu`āwiya, *123*; 15, 151, 154, 156, 433
Khālid b. Zuhayr al-Kalbī, 143
Khalīfa b. al-Ḥasan, *91*
Khāqān (Turkish title), 121
Khārija, *160*
Kharijites, 286
Kharqadūna, 440
Khazars, 116, 421
Khiḍr, 340, 344
Khubāb b. al-Arat, *84*; 94n
Al-Khumayrā', 279
Khurāsān, 57, 100, 101, 106, 109, 117, 127, 150, 164, 175, 179
  Dajjāl and, 328–9
  people of, 169, 173, 418, 420, 422
Khuthaym al-Ziyādī, *292*, *297*
Khūz, 421
Kināna, 202
Kinda, 145, 158, 160, 188
Kirmān, 301, 421
Kūfa, 53, 78, 149, 157, 158, 162, 166, 167, 168, 169, 170, 177, 186, 196, 202, 204, 329
  Byzantines and Syrians attack, 262, 275
  destruction of, 173, 174, 401, 422, 432, 434
Kūfat al-Anbār, 163
Kulthūm al-Khuzā`ī, *89*
Kurayb, 230
Kurds, 424
Kurz b. `Alqama al-Khuzā`ī, *2*, *92*
Kuswa River, 335
Kūthā, 328

Lakhm (tribe), 216, 224–5, 234, 282
Laydīn, 434
Layth, *154*, *417*
Lebanon, 428
Leo the Isaurian (emperor), 285
Levi son of Jacob, tribe of, 325
Libya, 287–88, 318, 417
Lydda, Gate of, 346–7

Madā'in (Ctesiphon), 85, 179, 275
Madhḥij (tribe), 187, 216, 312, 324
Maghrib (Muslim west), 104, 105, 113, 138, 141, 142, 164, 188, 326
  People of, 161, 162, 175, 189, 290–1
Mahdi (title), 41, 49–50, 431
Mahdi (messianic figure), 110, 169, 218, 258
  appearance of, 111, 149, 174–5, 177, 178, 180, 187, 188, 189, 191, 192, 193, 210, 426
  conquests of, 115, 203, 208
  description of, 209–10, 211, 212–14
  justice, 205–6
  reluctance of, 194, 195–6, 201
  rule of, 150, 198, 204–5, 207, 225, 227–8, 314
  Sufyānī and, 196–7, 199, 202–3
Majma` b. Jāriya, *347*
Makḥūl, *8*, *57*, *101*, *115*, *116*, *118*, *253*, *308*, *400*, *420*, *423*, *424*
Mālik al-Ashtar, 67
Mālik b. Dīnār, *88*
Ma`mar, 39
Ma`mar b. Ṭāwūs, *93*, *137*, *340*, *344*
Manbij, Bridge of, 391
Al-Ma'mūn (caliph), 111n, 169
Māndarūn, 151, 162
Al-Manṣūr al-Yamānī (title), 41, 48, 49–50, 156, 159, 174, 219, 231, 258, 431–2
  ruler, 226, 442
Marḥūm b. Qaṭṭār, *77*
Marīs, 293. 297
Marj `Adhrā', 442
Marj Ḥimār, 420
Marj al-Ṣufar, 161, 440
Marj al-Thaniyya, 162
Marwā, Hill of, 414
Marwān b. al-Ḥakam (Caliph), 15, 54, 55, 56, 68, 71, 79, 95, 96
Marwān II (caliph), 59, 97, 103, 104, 106, 107, 430
  Siege of Ḥimṣ, 99–100
Marwanids, 156, 243, 429
Marw (Marv) al-Rūdh, xiii, 181, 186, 328, 427

Maryūṭ, 287
Masḥal Monastery, 107, 263, 269, 270, 274
Mashraf, 128
Maṣīṣa, 284
Maslama b. `Abd al-Malik, *242*; 141, 247n
Maslama b. Makhrama, *444*
Maslama b. Mukhallad al-Anṣārī, 12, 416
Masrūq, *32, 86, 89, 376*; 11
Maṭar al-Warrāq, *188, 204, 205*
Mawālī (clients), 109, 131, 159, 179, 217, 224, 230, 243, 250, 427
  fighting qualities of, 246, 252, 259, 266, 277, 288–9, 307, 443
Mawjib, 309
Māzin, Market of, 160
Mecca, 10, 16, 19, 45, 74, 75, 121, 149, 151, 181–3, 200, 220, 389
  Beast appears in, 409–10, 413
  Dajjāl and, 339, 348–9, 383
  Mahdi taking refuge in, 193–4, 195, 196, 201
  splitting the moon at, 376–7
  swallowing up by the earth, 184, 185–6
Medina, 16, 19, 45, 65, 78, 88, 132, 151, 161, 173–4, 181–3, 220, 251, 256, 386, 389–90
  appearance of the Mahdi in, 196–7
  fighting between Medina and Mecca, 182, 184–5
  people taken from, 389–90, 392–3, 394
  rRefuge from the Dajjāl, 344, 348–9, 383
Memphis, 416–17
Mercy, Gate of, 199
Messianic age, 351, 353–4, 355–6, 357–61, 367, 373
Michael, 204, 247, 267
Minā (place), 119, 193, 376–7
Minā, *56*
Miqdām b. Ma`dīkarib, *135, 334*
Moses, 5, 40, 47n, 204, 360
  Rod of, 286, 297
Mt. Abū Qays, 10
Mt. Carmel, 226
Mt. Ḥaṣā, 149
Mt. Jūdī, 8, 332, 398
Mt. Khunāsīra, 166
Mt. Lebanon, 253, 273, 293, 297, 310, 398, 399, 442
Mt. Mu`taq, 133, 245
Mt. of Olives, 284, 336
Mt. Qāsyūn, 446
Mt. Sal`, 256
Mt. Sanīr (Hermon), 399, 442
Mt. Sinai, 134, 362–3, 368, 370, 371, 398
Mt. Tabor, 332, 398
Mt. Thawr, 336
Mu`ādh b. Jabal, *9, 28, 324, 383, 392, 393, 394*
Al-Mu`allī b. Rāshid al-Nabbāl, *445*
Mu`āwiya b. Abī Sufyān, *9, 96, 114, 134, 377, 421, 422*; 19, 48, 49, 52–3, 54, 55, 59, 95, 101, 108, 269n, 278, 303, 328, 393, 402, 425, 426, 430
  Church of, 269n
Mu`āwiya b. Qurra, *124*
Muḍar (tribal confederation), 217–18, 223, 225, 229, 236
Al-Mufarrij (title), 224, 232
Al-Mughīra b. `Abd al-Raḥmān al-Makhzūmī, *191* and n
Al-Mughīra b. Abī Shu`ba, *345*
Al-Mughīra b. al-Akhnas, 71
Mughīth al-Awzā`ī, *44, 52*
Muhājir b. Ḥabīb, *285, 306, 308*
Muhājir b. Nabbāl, *123*
Muḥammad (prophet), 75, 98, 325, 361, 369
  Community of (Muslims), 106, 195, 255, 406, 425, 430
  family of, 109, 116, 169, 170, 174, 177, 190, 192, 212–13, 445
  Ibn Ṣayyād and, 342–3
Muḥammad (unidentified), *90*
Muḥammad b. `Abd al-Raḥmān b. Abī Dhi'b, *10*
Muḥammad b. Abī Bakr, 32
Muḥammad b. `Alī, *104, 152, 156, 185, 197*
Muḥammad b. al-Asha`th, *130*

Muḥammad b. al-Ḥanafiyya, *83, 100, 110, 111, 144, 150, 155, 160, 174, 230, 426*; 212
Muḥammad b. Ḥāṭib, *33*
Muḥammad b. Ja`far b. `Alī, *151*
Muḥammad b. Ka`b al-Quraẓī, *140*
Muḥammad b. Maslama, *71*; 72
Muḥammad b. Muḥammad b. `Alī al-Ṣayrafī al-Anṣārī, 446
Muḥammad b. Sa`īd, 289
Muḥammad b. Sīrīn, *54, 80, 85, 109, 127, 188, 204, 205*
Muḥammad b. Yazīd, 43
Muḥārib (tribe), 223, 235
Mujāhid, *3, 64, 89, 93, 401, 418*; 10, 414
Al-Mukhtār b. Abī `Ubayd al-Thaqafī, 58n, 60, 74
Al-Mundhir b. al-Zubayr, 75
Murra b. Rabī`a, *229*
Mūsā b. Nuṣayr, *295*
Mūsā b. Sulaymān, 240
Mūsā b. Ṭalḥa, 74
Musallima (new Arab Muslims), 131, 247
Musaylima, 56, 321, 343
Muslim b. Yassār, 64
Muslims, 108
Al-Mustawrid al-Qurashī, *293, 425*
Muzayna (tribe), 392–3, 394
Muzdalifa, 413

Nabīsha al-Khyar, 445
Al-Nabk, 279
Naḍīr (tribe), 391
Al-Naḍr b. Shumayṭ, *426*
Nāfi`, 58
Najda, 16, 87, 214
Al-Nājib b. Sarī, *132, 146, 147, 150, 168, 437*
Najrān, 348
Nāṣir-i Khusraw, 347n
Nāth, 437
Nawf al-Bikālī, *126, 204*; 106, 347 and n, 393–4, 401, 427
Al-Nazzāl b. Sabra, *55*
Nicea, 292
Nikiu, 316
Nile River, 133, 146, 400, 435
Nisībīn, 179, 440
Nizār (tribal confederation), 222, 228, 441
Noah, 126, 322, 437
Al-Nu`mān b. Muqarrin, *29*
Nu`aym, *218*; xii–xiv, 190, 256

Orontes River, 245, 283

People of the Book, 72, 330
People of the House, 175, 195, 199, 211, 214
People of the Trench, 348
Persia, 245, 292, 307, 311
Persians, 51, 108, 220, 236
Pharaoh, 117, 416–17
  Believer of the family of, 285
Psalms, 306
"Pure Soul," 94, 178n, 182, 183, 186, 191, 209n
Pyramids, 287

Qabīṣa b. Barā', *383*
Qabīṣa b. Dhu'ayb, *379*
Qādisiyya, Battle of, 403
Qaḥṭān, 48, 222, 228, 442
Qaḥṭāni (title), 50, 218–19, 231, 235
Qamar/Nimr b. `Ibād, 168, 434
Qamūliya, 259, 443
Qarīn, 136
Qasāma b. Zuhayr, *395 see* Ibn Zuhayr
Al-Qāsim Abū `Abd al-Raḥmān, *90, 222, 257, 387*
Al-Qāsim b. Abī Bazza, *375*
Qatāda, *186, 195, 197, 206, 211, 214, 363*
Qawṣ/Basrā, 328
Qays (tribal confederation), 116, 170, 185, 217, 223, 225, 235–6, 266, 282, 307, 389–90
  `Aylān, 420
Qays b. Abī Ḥāzim, *5, 390*
Qays b. `Ubbād, *31 34, 38*
Qedar, 282, 305
Qinnasrīn, 116, 246, 265, 271, 279, 312, 324

Qirqīsiyā (Carchemish), 114, 149, 155, 162, 163, 169, 170, 173, 432
Quḍā`a (tribal confederation), 142, 143, 161, 216, 238–40, 250
Qulzum, 398
Qūmas, 178
Quraysh (tribe), 36, 40–1, 49–50, 51, 74, 103, 129, 143, 144, 157, 166, 195, 208, 210–11, 214, 440
  destruction of, 216, 218–19, 220–1, 223–4, 225, 228–9, 235–6, 354, 376, 434, 445
  ruler of, 227–8, 232–44, 315
  women of, 171
Qūs, 335
Al-Quṭayfa, 279

Rabdha, 65, 72
Rabī`a (tribe), 30, 225
Rabī`a b. al-Fārisī, *297*
Rāḥiṭ, Battle of the Field of, 365
Rajā' b. Abī Salama, 100
Rajā' b. Ḥaywa, *404*
Ramla, 144, 147, 442
  of Ifrīqiyā, 289
Al-Raqqa, 164, 167–8
Rāshid b. Dā'ūd al-Ṣanā`ānī, *108*
Rāshid b. Sa`d, *54, 180, 307, 376*
Rastan, 312
  Gate/Market, 239, 269
Rawḥ b. Zinbā`, 136
Rawḥa, Mountain road of, 357
Rayy, 175
  Dawlāb al-Rayy, 178
Rhodes, 298
Ribāḥ b. al-Ḥārith, *85*
Rock Face, 299
Rome, 230, 234, 245, 249, 255, 264, 286–7, 289, 291–2, 295–6, 299, 308, 438
Romania, 299
Ruqayya River (Black River), 246

Ṣabbāḥ, *45, 207, 215, 426*
Sa`d b. Abī Waqqāṣ, *9, 376, 381, 399, 427*; 77
Sa`d b. Ibrāhīm, *75*
Sa`d b. Mālik, *73*
Sa`d b. Zur`a, *106*
Ṣafiyya, *386*
Sa`īd b. `Abd al-`Azīz, *56*
Sa`īd b. Jābir, *303*
Sa`īd b. Jubayr, *298, 437*
Sa`īd b. Khālid, 57
Sa`īd b. Marthad Abū al-`Āliyya, *108*
Sa`īd b. Masrūq, *400*
Sa`īd b. Muhājir al-Wiṣābī, *132, 141*
Sa`īd b. al-Musayyib, *44, 46, 57, 89, 102, 118, 129, 140, 177, 190, 191, 193, 380*
Ṣāf *see* Ibn Ṣayyād
Ṣafā, hill of, 412–13, 414
Al-Saffāḥ (title), 41 and n, 48, 49–50, 156, 208, 231, 258, 431–2
Safīna, *45, 46, 425*
Ṣafwān b. `Abdallāh, *125, 147, 283, 381*
Sahl b. Ḥunayf, *35, 39*
Sahl b. Sa`d, *403*
Sakāsik (tribe), 95, 121
Al-Sakhrī, 148–9, 202–3; *see also* al-Sufyānī
Sakūn (tribe), 238
Salām (title), 48, 49, 231
Salama b. Nufayl, *8, 381*
Salamiyya, 167, 434
Salīḥ (tribe), 247
Ṣāliḥ b. `Abdallāh b. Qays b. Yassār, 259, 292, 443
Sālim, *214, 322, 328, 342, 347, 357, 391*
Salmān al-Fārisī, 43–4, 346
Salmān b. Sumayr al-Alhānī, *169, 170*
Samosata, 133
Ṣamṣama, 243, 294, 310
Samura b. Jundab, *8*
Ṣana`ā', 159, 294, 321
Al-Saqr b. Rustum, *141, 143, 210, 215*
Sarbal, 279
Ṣārifiyya, 262
Sarj al-Yarmūkī, *41*
Sarsinā, 296
Satan, 141, 190–1, 192, 240–1, 430
Sawas River, 442
Sayḥān River, 389
Sayyār b. Salāma, *84*

Shabab, 151
Shahr b. Ḥawshab, *118, 123, 191, 193, 393, 394, 401*
Shajar, 151
Shaqīq, 11, 35
Sharīk, *112, 121*
Sheba, 282, 304–5
Shu`ayb, 360
Shu`ayb b. Ṣāliḥ, 150, 174, 175, 177, 179–80, 195
Shu`ba, 372
Shufay b. `Ubayd al-Aṣbaḥī, *113, 315, 316*; 15
Shuraḥbīl b. Dhī Ḥimaya, 108
Shuraḥbīl b. Muslim al-Khawlānī, *137*
Shurayḥ b. `Ubayd (`Abd), *180, 320, 370, 381, 384*
Ṣiffīn, Battle of, 8, 19, 20, 21n, 35, 64
Sijistān, 420, 422
Ṣila b. Zufar, 60, 374
Slavs, 285, 423
Solomon son of David, 230, 334
Solomon's Pass, 270
Sufyān al-Kalbī, *96, 118, 176, 209*
Sufyān b. `Awf al-Ghāmidī, 311
Sufyān b. al-Layl, *78*
Sufyān b. `Uyayna, 63, 369, 387
Sufyānī, 16, 40, 111, 115, 118, 119, 123, 147, 427, 431
- career of, 116, 143, 148–9, 155, 156, 159, 170, 178, 180, 433–4
- cruelty of, 154, 156–7, 158, 162–4, 168, 171, 173, 181–3, 434
- description of, 152, 247
- Mahdi and, 188, 192, 198, 199, 200, 202–3
- supporters of, 153, 161, 175
- swallowing up his army, 184–5, 186–7, 195, 200

Suhayl b. Dhakwān, *58*
Sulaymān b. `Abd al-Raḥmān b. Sunna, *257*
Sulaymān b. `Aṭā' b. Yazīd al-Laythī, *146*
Sulaymān b. Ḥāṭib al-Ḥimyarī, *125*
Sulaymān b. `Īsā, *151, 207, 225, 326, 347, 360, 367*
Sulaymān b. Ṣurad, *31, 37*
Sulaymān (caliph), 56, 60
Al-Ṣunābiḥī, *77, 225*
Al-Surāt, 136
Sūsiya, 270
Suwayd b. Ghafala, *70*
Syria, 11, 12n, 16, 17, 45, 53, 57, 68, 73, 74, 96, 97, 121, 122, 123, 127, 176, 182, 197, 204, 222, 293, 298, 326, 422, 431, 433, 438
- banners in, 110, 113, 143, 145, 148, 155, 158, 180, 189, 198
- Christians of, 243, 274
- Civil War, xxxv
- coastal, 147, 245, 260, 269–73, 290, 299, 307–8
- Dajjāl and, 332–6, 344, 349, 356–7
- description of, xv–xvi, 124–5, 126, 165, 264
- destruction of, 104, 105, 114, 135, 139, 142, 159, 161, 163, 167, 199, 216, 235–6, 251–3, 439–41
- Gathering people to, 389–95, 405
- "Holy Land," 169, 170, 262
- tribulation in, 191, 201, 256, 259, 420, 444

Tadmur, 156, 167
Al-Ṭā'if, 182–3
Takhūm Khurāsān, 179
Takhūm Zaranj, 178
Ṭalḥa b. `Aṭā', *321*
Ṭalḥa b. `Ubaydallāh, 16, 30, 36, 38, 43, 64, 67, 75
Taliban, xxxiv–xxxv
Tall Samā, 159
Tamīm (tribe), 174, 175, 177, 179–80
Tamīm al-Dārī, xvi
Tangiers, 287
Tanūkh (tribe), 247, 250
Ṭawāna, 14
Ṭāwūs, *21, 34, 39, 65, 80, 122, 205, 206, 207, 208, 213, 328, 357, 358, 379, 445*
Taymā', 98, 426
Ṭayyī' (tribe), 247
Ṭayyiba (Medina), 252
Ṭayyiba (opponent of the Dajjāl), 322

Thaqīf (tribe), 58, 60
Thawbān, *103, 161, 166, 175, 235*
Ṭibāq, 151
Tiberias, 154, 165, 398, 445
  Lake of, 368; *see also* Galilee, Sea of
Tiberius, 293, 296, 306, 312, 315, 317
  false, 242–3
Tigris River, 115, 171, 216, 371–2, 419–20
Tihāma, 412
Torah, 41, 50, 203–4, 205, 361, 430
Tortosa, 269, 274
Tripoli, Sea of, 441
Tubay` b. `Āmir, *50, 56. 95, 96, 98, 126, 141, 154, 175, 181, 185, 225, 239, 254, 298, 317, 324, 360, 361, 363, 426, 444*; 268
Tubba`, 224–5
Turks, 113, 114, 115, 116–17, 155, 173, 208, 285, 290, 301, 341, 414
  attacks of, 419–25
Tustar, 7
Tyre, 136, 229, 314, 443
  curse of, 304

`Ubāda b. al-Ṣāmit, *321*
`Ubayd b. Rafī`, *415*
`Ubayd b. `Umayr al-Laythī, *340, 341*
`Ubaydallāh b. Abī Ja`far, *5*
Ubayy b. Ka`b, *384*; 172, 343
Ubulla, 418, 422
Uhbān al-Ghifārī, daughter of, *38, 64*
Uḥud, Battle of, 285
`Ulayy b. Ribāḥ, *302*
`Umar b. `Abd al-`Azīz, *51, 85, 387*; 44, 49, 57, 58, 205, 206, 213
`Umar b. al-Khaṭṭāb, *42, 51, 54, 58, 127, 146, 218, 397, 412, 415, 417, 423*; 7, 11, 19, 33, 41, 43–4, 45, 47, 49, 52–3, 57, 70, 111, 172, 173, 204–5, 208, 342, 381, 386, 388, 403, 430
`Umar b. Sa`d, *73*
`Umayr b. Hāni', *17, 21, 87, 133, 325*
`Umayr b. Isḥāq, *28*
`Umayr b. Mālik, *295*
Umayyads, 16, 41, 55, 58, 93, 94, 95, 97, 101, 105, 109, 160, 178, 189, 290, 296, 426, 429
  "Sons of the Blue-Eyed Woman," 45, 54
Umm al-`Arab, 144
Umm al-Dardā', *96*
Umm Ḥabība, 161
Umm Salama, *68*; 57
Umm Sharīk, 350
`Umrān b. Sulaym al-Kalā`ī, *235*
Al-`Uqaylī, *52, 53*
`Uqba b. Abī Zaynab, *100*
`Uqba b. `Āmir, *66, 131, 136, 147*
Al-Uqḥawāna, 165
Al-Urdunn, 133–4, 143, 148, 149, 160, 308, 331, 336, 442
`Urwā b. Qays, *11, 296*
`Urwa b. Ruaym, *379, 397*
`Uryān b. Haytham, *400, 402, 430, 436*
Usāma b. Zayd, *5*; 72, 75, 79
Usayyid b. al-Mutashammis, *3, 92*
`Utba b. Ghazwān al-Sulamī, *45, 46*
`Utba b. Tamīm al-Tanūkhī, *139*
`Uthmān b. `Affān, 5, 14, 19, 31, 33, 34–5, 40n, 41, 47, 49, 52–3, 58, 61, 65, 70, 71, 73, 78, 80, 81, 82, 84, 89, 90, 444

Wabr/Wabīr, 187
Wādī `Ar`ar, 129
Wādī `Araj, 129
Wādī al-Shajar, 129
Wādī al-`Unṣul, 148
Wādī al-Yābis, 152, 433
Al-Waḍīn b. `Aṭā', *132, 164*
Wahb b. Jābir al-Khaywānī, *408*
Wahb b. Munabbih, *321, 371, 373, 398, 399, 406, 410*
Wāhib b. Abī Mughīth, *75*
Al-Walīd I (caliph), 56–7
Al-Walīd II (caliph), 56–7, 96, 98n, 113, 140
Al-Walīd b. `Ayyāsh, 16
Al-Walīd b. Hishām, *51, 166*
Al-Walīd b. Muslim, *113, 120, 121, 140, 156, 158, 161, 164, 180, 199, 206, 227, 426*; 143, 176, 209, 256, 303

Al-Walīd b. `Uqba, *75*
Wardān, *416*
Wasīm, 415, 416, 417
Weeks, Apocalypse of, 165, 326, 437–44
Willibald, 241n

Al-Yadayn, 168
Yaḥyā b. Jābir, *129*
Yaḥyā b. Abī Kathīr, *341*
Al-Yamānī (title), 170
Ya`qūb b. Isḥāq, *167*
Yarmūk, Battle of, 49, 256, 305
Yashū`, 41, 52, 98, 430–3
Yathrib (Medina), 259, 443
Yazīd I (caliph), 48, 49, 57, 59, 393, 400
Yazīd II (caliph), 97, 98n,103
Yazīd b. Abī `Amr al-Saybānī, *42, 45, 274, 284, 345, 346*
Yazīd b. Abī Ḥabīb, *16, 33, 57, 427*
Yazīd b. Khālid b. Yazīd, 57
Yazīd b. Khumayr, *334*
Yazīd b. al-Muhallab, 77
Yazīd b. Sharīk, *55*
Yazīd b. Shurayḥ, *334, 397, 406*
Yazīd b. Ziyād al-Aslamī, *296*
Yemen (region), xxix, 16, 122, 204, 223, 251, 256, 293, 393–4, 409, 434, 442
(tribal confederation), 143, 214, 216, 217, 222–3, 224, 226, 227, 229, 234, 238–41, 282, 299–300, 304, 307, 309, 312, 392
Yūnis b. Sayf al-Khawlānī, *301*
Yusayr b. `Amr, *286*
Yūsuf b. `Abdallāh b. Salām, *106, 361*

Ẓafar, 50–1, 220, 236
Zayd b. Arqam, *70*
Zayd b. Aslam, *362, 401*
Zayd b. Thābit, 85
Zaynab daughter of Jaḥsh, *369, 387*
Zion, Gate of, 260, 443
Zirr b. Ḥubaysh, *9, 214*
Ziyād b. Abihi, 55, 82, 87
Zīzā', 223
Al-Zubayr b. `Awwām, *34*; 16, 30, 36, 43, 49
Zughar, Spring of, xvi
Zuhayr b. Sālim, *381*
Al-Zuhrī, *36, 79, 97, 100, 101, 104, 112, 118, 119, 139, 143, 144, 147, 160, 161, 181, 183, 186, 188, 190, 192, 194, 195, 198, 201, 214, 215, 216, 229, 255, 383, 394*; 2, 57, 59–60
Zurāra, *84*

EU representative:
Easy Access System Europe
Mustamäe tee 50, 10621 Tallinn, Estonia
Gpsr.requests@easproject.com

www.ingramcontent.com/pod-product-compliance
Lightning Source LLC
Chambersburg PA
CBHW052053300426
44117CB00013B/2101
* 9 7 8 1 4 7 4 4 4 4 0 8 8 *